State Crime
Volume I

The International Library of Criminology, Criminal Justice and Penology
Series Editors: Gerald Mars and David Nelken

Titles in the Series:

State Crime
Volume I
Defining, Delineating and Explaining State Crime

Edited by

David O. Friedrichs

Department of Sociology/Criminal Justice, University of Scranton

Ashgate

DARTMOUTH

Aldershot • Brookfield USA • Singapore • Sydney

Published by
Dartmouth Publishing Company Limited
Ashgate Publishing Limited
Gower House
Croft Road
Aldershot
Hants GU11 3HR
England

Ashgate Publishing Company
Old Post Road
Brookfield
Vermont 05036
USA

British Library Cataloguing in Publication Data
State crime
  1. Political crimes and offenses – Great Britain
  I. Friedrichs, David O.
  345.4′1′023

Library of Congress Cataloging-in-Publication Data
State crime / edited by David O. Friedrichs.
       p.   cm.
   Includes bibliographical references.
   Contents: v. 1. Defining, delineating, and explaining state crime
 — v. 2. Exposing, sanctioning, and preventing state crime.
   ISBN 1–85521–964–6 (set : hb)
   1. Political atrocities.   2. Political persecution.   3. Genocide.
  4. State-sponsored terrorism.   I. Friedrichs, David O.
  HV6322.S73   1998
  364.1′3—dc21
                                                                    98–3787
                                                                    CIP

Printed by Galliards, Great Yarmouth

ISBN 1 85521 964 6

Contents

PART V EXPLAINING STATE CRIME

Acknowledgements

The editor and publishers wish to thank the following for permission to use copyright material.

American Society of Criminology for the essay: William J. Chambliss (1989), 'State-organized Crime – The American Society of Criminology, 1988 Presidential Address', *Criminology*, **27**, pp. 183–208.

Association for Humanist Sociology for the essays: David Kauzlarich, Ronald C. Kramer and Brian Smith (1992), 'Toward the Study of Governmental Crime: Nuclear Weapons, Foreign Intervention, and International Law', *Humanity and Society*, **16**, pp. 543–63; David Kauzlarich (1995), 'A Criminology of the Nuclear State', *Humanity and Society*, **19**, pp. 37–57; David Norman Smith (1995), 'The Genesis of Genocide in Rwanda: The Fatal Dialectic of Class and Ethnicity', *Humanity and Society*, **19**, 57–73.

Blackwell Publishers for the essay: David Nelken and Michael Levi (1996), 'The Corruption of Politics and the Politics of Corruption: An Overview', *Journal of Law and Society*, **23**, pp. 1–17. Copyright © 1996 Blackwell Publishers Ltd.

Butterworths for the essay: Stanley Cohen (1993), 'Human Rights and Crimes of the State: The Culture of Denial', *Australian and New Zealand Journal of Criminology*, **26**, pp. 97–115, by permission of Arie Frieberg, the President of the Australian and New Zealand Society of Criminology.

Global Options for the essay: Harry Brill (1992), 'Government Breaks the Law: The Sabotaging of the Occupational Safety and Health Act', *Social Justice*, **19**, pp. 63–81.

Guilford Publications, Inc. for the essay: Israel W. Charney (1986), 'Genocide and Mass Destruction: Doing Harm to Others as a Missing Dimension of Psychopathology', *Psychiatry*, **49**, pp. 144–57. Copyright © 1986 by the Washington School of Psychiatry.

Richard Harding (1983), 'Nuclear Energy and the Destiny of Mankind – Some Criminological Perspective', *Australian and New Zealand Journal of Criminology*, **16**, pp. 81–92. Copyright © 1983 Richard Harding.

Interdisciplinary Research Programme on Root Causes of Human Rights Violations for the essay: Barbara Harff and Ted Gurr (1996), 'Victims of the State: Genocides, Politicides and Group Repression from 1945 to 1995', in Albert J. Jongman (ed.), *Contemporary Genocides: Causes, Cases, Consequences*, Leiden: PIOOM, pp. 33–58.

Series Preface

The International Library of Criminology, Criminal Justice and Penology, represents an important publishing initiative designed to bring together the most significant journal essays in contemporary criminology, criminal justice and penology. The series makes available to researchers, teachers and students an extensive range of essays which are indispensable for obtaining an overview of the latest theories and findings in this fast changing subject.

This series consists of volumes dealing with criminological schools and theories as well as with approaches to particular areas of crime, criminal justice and penology. Each volume is edited by a recognised authority who has selected twenty or so of the best journal articles in the field of their special competence and provided an informative introduction giving a summary of the field and the relevance of the articles chosen. The original pagination is retained for ease of reference.

The difficulties of keeping on top of the steadily growing literature in criminology are complicated by the many disciplines from which its theories and findings are drawn (sociology, law, sociology of law, psychology, psychiatry, philosophy and economics are the most obvious). The development of new specialisms with their own journals (policing, victimology, mediation) as well as the debates between rival schools of thought (feminist criminology, left realism, critical criminology, abolitionism etc.) make necessary overviews that offer syntheses of the state of the art. These problems are addressed by the INTERNATIONAL LIBRARY in making available for research and teaching the key essays from specialist journals.

GERALD MARS
Professor in Applied Anthropology, University of Bradford
School of Management

DAVID NELKEN
Distinguished Research Professor, Cardiff Law School,
University of Wales, Cardiff

Introduction

This volume on state crime has been published at the very end of the twentieth century. Some of the nineteenth-century utopian social philosophers harboured the hope that a future without war, violence and crime might be realized. Obviously this hope did not come to pass in the twentieth century. On the contrary, the twentieth century has been characterized by extraordinarily high levels of war, violence and crimes of all types, by any criteria. And states (or those acting in some fashion on behalf of states) have been complicit in a disproportionate share of such destructive activity. Indeed, serious students of the twentieth century would surely agree that far more violence has been carried out in the name of states – and far more property has been destroyed – than can be attributed to conventional offenders.

From some ideological perspectives, state crime has always been regarded as the most significant form of crime and an inevitable result of power being concentrated in the hands of the few. At least some of those on both the far right and the far left of the ideological spectrum have embraced this view. Furthermore, from an anarchist perspective, the very existence of states can be regarded as a crime against humanity (see, for example, Krimerman and Perry, 1966; Shatz, 1971). From mainstream and conventional vantage points, however, the notion of state crime has tended to be resisted.

A number of general observations can be made about state crime, and its somewhat paradoxical character or status. First, insofar as the state is the primary source of both the laws that define crime and the institutions of enforcement and adjudication, the concept of state crime is especially problematic and open to challenge. Second, for many of those who accept the claim that crimes in a meaningful sense are carried out on behalf of states or through the use of state resources, it is particularly disorienting to acknowledge this fundamental contradiction with the state's professed claim to advance and protect the general welfare. Third, if it is obviously true that conventional crime (interpersonal homicide, rape, robbery and so on) has been the primary focus of public fear of crime, it is surely disturbing to realize that the largest scale of criminal harm has been a consequence of state crime. Fourth, the field of criminology has historically concerned itself primarily with the study of conventional crime and conventional offenders, and it is dismaying to confront the general neglect of the topic of state crime in the criminological literature.

State crime as a major focus of criminological attention has yet to be realized. Nevertheless, it may be worth reminding ourselves that some other significant specialities within criminology have experienced an unusually long gestation period. Edwin H. Sutherland (1940) made his celebrated call for more attention to white-collar crime in 1939. Apart from his 1949 book on this topic there were only a small number of substantive responses to Sutherland's call over a period of several decades. The substantial growth of a white-collar criminological literature occurred primarily in the final two decades of the twentieth century; certainly, by the mid-1990s there was quite a volume of literature (see, for example, Friedrichs, 1996a; Nelken, 1994a). The explicit – or implicit – call for more criminological attention to state crime is, for the most part, quite recent (see Harding, Chapter 10 in this volume; Chambliss, 1989, Chapter 13 in this volume; Cohen, Chapter 5 in this volume), but the call for such attention is not entirely new (see Proall, Chapter 1 in this volume). A number of criminologists – for example, Schafer (1974), Roebuck and Weeber (1978), Ingraham (1979), Tunnell (1993) and Hagan (1997) – have produced books on political crime, which have adopted a fairly inclusive concept which includes both state-directed and anti-state activities. Of course, attempts have been made by various authors – representing disciplines other than criminology – to make sense of state wrongdoing or repressiveness generally (for example, Comfort, 1950; Wolfe, 1973). There is a fairly large literature on various forms of wrongdoing by governmental officials, produced by historians, political scientists, sociologists, law professors and criminologists, among others, with some special emphasis on corruption (for example, Becker and Murray, 1971; Blackstock, 1966; Chambliss, 1988; Douglas and Johnson, 1977; Lieberman, 1972; Miller, 1976, 1992; Noonan, 1984; and Wise, 1976). At least some texts on crime generally (for example, Michalowski, 1985; Beirne and Messerschmidt, 1995), and on white-collar crime, occupational crime or elite deviance (for example, Friedrichs, 1996a; Green, 1997; Simon, 1996) have devoted space to state crime, governmental crime, state authority occupational crime or political (elite) deviance. In *Crimes of the Criminal Justice System* Henderson and Simon (1994) have focused on wrongdoing within one component of the state. Gregg Barak (1991), with his edited volume *Crimes by the Capitalist State*, and Jeffrey Ian Ross (1995), with his edited volume *Controlling State Crime*, have produced books with a very specific focus on state crime. Others who have addressed this topic, or have put together anthologies, are not necessarily self-identified criminologists, but rather are, for example, political scientists (Lopez and Stohl, 1983; Stohl and Lopez, 1984, 1986; Bushnell *et al.*, 1991). Some of the relevant literature on state crime has been produced by (or on behalf of) international human right organizations (for example, Amnesty International, 1983; Brown, 1985; Human Rights Watch, 1972; Stunton, Fenn and Amnesty International 1991; and World Watch, 1992). Of course, there is a very large literature – produced by academics affiliated with a range of disciplines, as well as by journalists – that deals with specific forms of state crime, such as genocide and corruption, and specific cases of criminal states or of state crimes, such as Nazi Germany and the Iran/Contra arms case (some relevant works are cited further on). Both within criminology and within other related disciplines, however, attention to state crime at the century's end can still be characterized as a marginal enterprise.

The question of why there has been such a dearth of attention to state crime within criminology (or political science) has been a common point of departure for the relatively few anthologies on the topic. One can begin by noting the difficulty of achieving consensus on the matter of properly defining state crime, and especially whether admittedly harmful or destructive activities carried out on behalf of states are best defined as crimes. Altogether, the general public as a whole has been socialized to think of crime in conventional terms, and is typically resistant to the notion of 'state crime'. And such indifference, discomfort, or outright hostility has tended to characterize those who pursue the study of crime and criminal justice professionally, as well. State crime has not traditionally been regarded as an important (or appropriate) focus for graduate education in criminology and criminal justice, and few academics and researchers are likely to have received any significant exposure to the topic or encouragement to pursue it. In a parallel vein a focus on state terrorism has been denounced by some political scientists and historians as 'skewed', 'biased', 'ideological', 'not in the mainstream of the literature', and 'out of touch with real political events' (Stohl and Lopez, 1984: 3). To date, at least, a focus on state crime cannot be recommended as a particularly efficient approach to academic and professional success. Furthermore, it is hardly surprising that it has typically been more difficult to obtain research funding for state crime from state entities (in some cases, raising the prospect of biting the hand that you hope will feed you). And for those who surmount the various hurdles just described, the challenges of obtaining access to research venues and credible data tend to exceed those facing the researcher of more conventional criminological and criminal justice topics.

If, at the century's end, state crime still has a somewhat marginal status in criminology as well as in other disciplines, a guiding premise for these two volumes is that scholarly attention to state crime both should and can increase exponentially in the new century. The premise for the assertion that attention to state crime should increase is this: the greatest threat to the well-being and survival of human beings, through the twenty-first century, comes from state crime. In stating such a premise it does not follow that one is underrating the scope of the threat posed by other forms of crime, including conventional predatory crime, organized crime, white-collar crime and anti-state terrorism. But the state continues to have the largest measure of resources, the most potent capacity to mobilize, and control over the most formidable coercive or destructive forces and weapons relative to any other entity. Arguably, the single greatest threat to the survival of humanity, as the twenty-first century begins, is the threat of nuclear war. Of course, the state is also complicit in other large-scale threats, including ecocide, overpopulation and the spread of infectious disease. Natural disasters such as earthquakes and floods obviously have a large destructive potential. But, in terms of intensity, magnitude and severity, the deliberate actions of state officials seem to represent the largest threat of all.

If the potential harm of state crime overshadows other forms of crime, the challenge to criminologists and criminal justicians should be quite clear. It is a further premise of these volumes that it is necessary to carefully and quite systematically delineate the ways in which state crime and its control differs from other forms of crime and their control. Even if it is conceded that many important dimensions of state crime (and its control) require analysis from disciplinary vantage points such as international relations and political science generally, it remains true that a criminological/criminal justice approach should have something to contribute. The recasting of issues surrounding state crime in specifically criminological terms has the potential to not only enhance understanding of such crime (and its control), but can also provide a useful comparative vantage point for analysing issues pertaining to more traditional criminological concerns.

Those who have edited other volumes in the International Library of Criminology, Criminal Justice and Penology have surely had to contend, in many cases, with an embarrassment of riches. The literature on criminal careers, policing and juvenile delinquency, for example, is very large. In the case of state crime the editor faces the following dilemma: on the one hand there is indeed a massive literature on activities that could be classified as manifestations of state crime. On the Nazi state and the Holocaust alone, for example, the volume of published work is quite overwhelming. On the other hand, very little of this literature takes a distinctly criminological approach to the topic. Indeed, many would presumably argue that such matters as war-making, violations of international law, human rights abuses, genocide, nuclearism and the like are not properly defined as criminological topics, but are more appropriately addressed as issues in international relations or comparative politics (as examples).

The present volumes have as fundamental objectives the bringing together of some of the best (and most neglected) contributions to the understanding of state crime and its control. This mission encountered some obstacles. First, it is the editor's impression that a disproportionately high percentage of the published work pertinent to state crime has been published in book form, not in the form of articles. Second, some of the best or most directly relevant recent work on state crime has been published as chapters in yearbooks or in edited books, such as the aforementioned volumes edited by Barak (1991), Tunnell (1993), and Ross (1996). Third, journal articles that do pertain to state crime (in at least some sense) are to be found in an exceptionally broad range of journals, cutting across many different disciplines. Accordingly, the frameworks of analysis, underlying assumptions, definitions of concepts and stylistic formats are also exceptionally disparate.

Due to the unusually high degree of dissensus about the very nature and character of state crime it must be conceded that selections included here are likely to be somewhat controversial as well. At this relatively early stage in the emergence of a criminology of state crime, however, such controversy is both inevitable and ideally constructive. The overriding hope here is that these volumes will contribute to the recognition that the topic of state crime merits more attention from criminologists; that they will serve as a useful point of departure for those interested in exploring specific dimensions of state crime; and that they will contribute to an ongoing dialogue on the appropriate parameters of the phenomenon of state crime as well as the most fruitful approaches to understanding it.

Conceptual, Definitional and Methodological Issues

It is quite commonly conceded that the conceptual, definitional and methodological issues in the realm of state crime are especially daunting, and that any systematic treatment of state crime must grapple with these issues (for example, Barak, 1991; Ross, 1995). State crime, political crime, human rights issues and 'legitimate' military, diplomatic and domestic initiatives of sovereign states are entangled in complex ways, and accordingly must be disentangled (see, for example, Hess, 1977; Howard and Donnelly, 1986; Schwelb, 1946; Sjoberg *et al.*, 1995). The problem of bias is especially intense in the inherently ideological realm of state crime. For example, in the broader area of international relations, some commentators hold that a Western perspective dominates, and Non-Western perspectives tend to be disregarded or disparaged (Puchala, 1997). More narrowly, Stanley Cohen (1996: 6) has suggested that 'early attempts to define the concept of state crime and link it to human rights violations failed because they were too wooly and polemical'. In his view, the concept of 'human rights violations' is more promising than the traditional criminal law model in terms of offering 'clearer criteria for regarding genocide, mass political killing, torture and extra-judicial executions as criminal', although he concedes that this concept also encompasses non-state actions (Cohen, 1996: 6). Incidentally, Cohen (1996: 14) notes the paradox that those calling for criminalization of state acts often represent progressive political forces historically associated with calls for decriminalization.

My own attempt at a resolution of the definitional or conceptual dilemma can be briefly summarized (Friedrichs, 1995; 1996a, 1996b). First, I suggest that it is necessary to recognize that the familiar term 'political crime' has been the source of a particularly large measure of confusion, especially insofar as it has been applied to both crimes of the state and anti-state crimes (such as assassination, espionage and terroristic activities of dissident political groups).

Ideally, in my view, this confusion could be somewhat minimized if the term 'political crime' were reserved for anti-state activity, although this is probably neither a practical nor realistic objective. The term 'political crime' has especially limited use as an operational concept; rather, it is likely to survive as a term with a broad, heuristic application. My own preference would be to adopt the term 'governmental crime' to encompass harmful acts carried out on behalf of the state as well as harmful (or illegal) acts carried out by state officials for their own benefit (or the benefit of their party). The term 'state crime' is best applied, then, to harmful acts carried out by state officials on behalf of the state. Genocide represents one especially momentous form of state crime. In this context, it is necessary to recognize the differences between acts deemed to be in violation of international law, acts deemed to be in violation of state law and acts deemed to be harmful by some other criterion (for example, by the standards of some international human rights organization, such as Amnesty International). The term 'criminal state' has been invoked, although it is somewhat controversial. In the twentieth century it was probably most widely applied to Nazi Germany, although many other states – for instance, the Stalinist Soviet Union and the Iraq of Saddam Hussein (Conquest, 1986, 1990; Al-Khalil, 1989; Sciolino, 1991) – have been characterized as criminal states. I have provisionally suggested that the terms 'repressive state', 'corrupt state', and 'negligent state' could be applied to certain states to capture the essential focus of their criminality, although I certainly recognize that such terms are vulnerable to criticism on a number of grounds.

The term 'political white-collar crime' seems to be especially appropriate for harmful acts carried out by state officials for their own benefit, or that of their political party. Corruption, or the acceptance of illegal bribes, represents one particularly familiar form of such political white-collar crime, although this familiar term also raises formidable definitional challenges (see, for example, Gardiner, 1993; Johnston, 1996). However, in view of the generally wider acceptance of, and familiarity with, the term 'state crime' (compared with 'governmental crime') that term has been adopted for the present volumes. Political white-collar crime, then, has been classified as a hybrid form of state crime, in the sense that it involves state officials misusing their office, but doing so with motivations and a *modus operandi* quite parallel to that of private sector white-collar crime.

In this section a variety of attempts to contend with the challenge of defining, conceptualizing and studying state crime are made.

Louis Proall was a French Court of Appeal Judge at Aix. It seems appropriate to commemorate the one hundredth anniversary of the publication in English of his *Political Crime* – a pioneering effort at focusing criminological attention on the crimes of statesmen and politicians – by opening the present volume with the concluding chapter of Proall's book. In the preface of his book Proall observed that 'There are no greater malefactors than the political malefactors who foment divisions and hatreds by their ambition, cupidity, and rivalries'. (p. xxv). In his concluding chapter Proall condemns the corruption of politics by 'Machiavelism' (*sic*). In modern, democratic societies, he declares, it is no longer either necessary or defensible for states to be governed by such principles. He believes that, in an age where political leaders can expect to be held accountable by public opinion, they will be more circumspect about adopting criminal expedients to achieve their objectives. Proall calls for a return to higher principles in political life and the reintegration of morality in the conduct of the political leadership. He also calls for a policy privileging international equilibrium over conquest and arbitration over warfare. He concludes that 'Politics without morality are the ruin of society' (p. 18). Proall's prescription may seem somewhat utopian, but the whole history of the twentieth century has demonstrated the tragic consequences of disregarding his noble advice, and also the inestimably high price we have paid for state crime.

Irving Louis Horowitz is Hannah Arendt Distinguished Professor of Sociology and Political Science at Rutgers, the State University of New Jersey (USA), and a longstanding student of many issues pertinent to political crime and state crime. His book *Taking Lives: Genocide and State Power*, was published in a fourth edition in 1997. In 'Counting Bodies: The Dismal Science of Authorized Terror', based on a lecture delivered to the Institute of Jewish Affairs on 9 March 1989, in London and presented as Chapter 2, Horowitz begins with some estimations of the staggering cost – in terms of lives – of state crimes, and then proceeds to make some crucial conceptual distinctions between deaths from natural causes (such as plagues) and social causes: the Holocaust and genocides generally; genocides and warfare; state-sponsored murder and all other forms of state-sponsored violence and misanthropy; actual and symbolic genocides; and collective and individual killing.

Gregg Barak is Professor of Sociology and Criminal Justice at Eastern Michigan University (USA) and a leading advocate for more attention to state crime. He edited *Crimes by the Capitalist State – An Introduction to State Criminality* (1991). In Chapter 3, 'Crime, Criminology and Human Rights: Towards an Understanding of State Criminality', Barak provides some basic rationales for studying state crime and reviews some of the issues involved in its study. He discusses factors making the study of state crime difficult and the interrelationship of state crime with other forms of crime. He also reviews the development of state crime in the United States and explores the connections between the study of state crime and human rights violations. In his concluding observations he reiterates the importance of studying state crime.

David Kauzlarich is Assistant Professor of Sociology at Southern Illinois University-Edwardville, Ronald C. Kramer is Professor of Sociology at Western Michigan University, and Brian Smith is a Ph.d candidate in sociology at Western Michigan University (USA). They have been active students of state crime for some years; Kauzlarich, in particular, has been an energetic organizer of panels focusing on state crime at sociological and criminological conferences. In Chapter 4, 'Toward the Study of Governmental Crime: Nuclear Weapons, Foreign Intervention, and International Law', they specifically call for viewing state crime in the context of a broader understanding of law and crime. They address some of the relevant definitional issues, favouring a criterion of 'socially injurious' acts to define crime. In particular, they stress the importance of the threat of organized violence by the government, and in this context review the use of nuclear weapons by the United States. The legality of nuclear weapons, and their threatened use, is challenged by international law. The United States is found to have been in violation of international law, with its intervention in Nicaragua characterized as a form of organized criminal violence. These authors conclude with a call for more criminological attention to state crime.

Stanley Cohen is presently Martin White Professor of Sociology at the London School of Economics and Political Science (UK), after many years on the faculty of the Institute of Criminology at Hebrew University. He is the author of a number of influential books on a range of criminological topics, but in recent years his interests have shifted to human rights issues. His essay, 'Human Rights and Crimes of the State: The Culture of Denial' (Chapter 5) was originally presented as the John Barry Memorial Lecture at the University of Melbourne on 30 September 1992. Cohen begins his lecture by specifically invoking Sutherland's celebrated call for more attention to white-collar crime; in a parallel vein he calls for more criminological attention to crimes of the state. While acknowledging some growth of such attention, Cohen asserts that the connection with human rights has been largely overlooked, despite the growth of an international human rights movement. He considers and responds to some of the objections to the notion of state crime. He then highlights the role of 'denial', in various forms, in the manifestation of state crime. Cohen closes with some cautionary observations about the complicity of at least some dimensions of postmodernist analysis in the denial of state crime.

The Varieties of State Crime

State crime takes many forms. In view of the definitional and conceptual controversies dealt with in the previous section it goes without saying that there exists no full consensus on the activities properly included under the heading of state crime. On the one hand, genocide and terroristic acts directed toward citizens would tend to be included on a list of state crimes formulated by most, if not all, serious students of state crime. On the other hand, war-making and 'nuclearism' are considerably more problematic (as would be true, as well, of imperialism and the sabotaging of a legislative act). The latter activities are much more likely to be regarded as matters of international relations and political strategy than as crimes in any conventional sense. More specifically, while the notion of war crimes is quite widely accepted, the notion of war as crime is far more contentious; an unprovoked initiation of nuclear war would be widely regarded as a crime on a monstrous scale, but the strategic development of a nuclear arsenal (to say nothing of nuclear energy) is perceived quite differently by many members of society. Nevertheless, in light of the immense harm involved, the inclusion of war and nuclearism in the context of a survey of the varieties of state crime would seem to be warranted.

On war generally as a form of crime, Charles Tilly (1985: 169) has argued: 'If protection rackets represent organized crime at its smoothest, then war making and state making – quintessential protection rackets with the advantage of legitimacy – qualify as our largest examples of organized crime.' For Tilly, states have been created by war-making, and states ultimately became the largest-scale, most efficient users of violence. Accordingly, 'Banditry, piracy, gangland rivalry, policing and war-making all belong on the same continuum.' (Tilly 1985: 170) This bluntly stated linkage between war-making and other forms of criminal activity, by an eminent student of history and sociology, deserves to be more widely acknowledged and adopted. Any serious consideration of warfare as a form of crime might begin with some general studies of war (for example, O'Connell, 1989; Preston and Wise, 1979). On a philosophical plane there is the enduring issue of just and unjust wars (see, for example, Walzer, 1977; Regan, 1996; Welch, 1993). In the modern context the use of chemical and biological weapons, to say nothing of nuclear weapons, has generated new issues concerning the criminality of war (Harris and Paxman, 1982; Huppauf, 1997; Markusen and Kopf, 1995). Other 'weapons' of warfare of long standing – for example, rape – have increasingly been condemned as criminal in the modern context (Allen, 1996). And then certain specific wars, or actions carried out in conjunction with those wars – for example, the Vietnam War (Shawcross, 1979; Taylor, 1970; Young, 1991) – have been particularly vulnerable to claims of criminality.

Surely the threat of nuclear war, or nuclear terrorism, is one of the most frightening prospects for the new century, if not the single most potentially destructive form of human activity (see

Schell, 1982). Ronald C. Kramer and Sam Marullo (1985: 283) have asserted that 'We believe that the prevention of nuclear war is the foremost political, social and moral issue of our time'. Again, despite the existence of a very large literature on nuclearism, and issues pertaining to nuclear arms and nuclear war, sociologists (and criminologists) have demonstrated relatively little interest in war generally and nuclear war in particular (Kramer and Marullo, 1985; Garnett, 1988; Beckman, 1992; Kurtz, 1992). Furthermore, there is controversy on the appropriateness of drawing parallels between the threat of nuclear war and genocides such as the Holocaust – as Robert J. Lifton and Eric Markusen (1990) do in *The Genocidal Mentality*, and Eric Markusen and David Kopf (1990) do in *The Holocaust and Strategic Bombing* – or in applying a criminological framework to the nuclear issues (Minear, 1995; Levene, 1996). More than a half century after the dropping of atomic bombs on Hiroshima and Nagasaki the character of the decision involved – that is, as a legitimate act of expediency in the context of war or as a morally indefensible act of genocide – continued to be debated (see, for example, Gerson, 1995). Many criminologists have analysed the massive proliferation of conventional firearms; the Cold War arms race and the proliferation of 'indefensible weapons' in the form of nuclear arms raises parallel concerns (Lifton and Falk, 1982; Thompson, 1985; Kurtz, 1989). With all due respect for the endless complexity of the issues involved, given what is at stake here, a consideration of a criminological analysis would seem to be more than warranted – as I argued some years ago (Friedrichs, 1985). Very late in the twentieth century the International Court of Justice condemned as illegal the use or threatened use of nuclear weapons (Kramer and Kauzlarich, 1997). Although it remains to be seen whether the nuclear nations of the world will in time fully support this proclamation, it does provide one more substantial point of departure for a criminological approach to nuclear issues.

Genocide, as noted, could be characterized as the paradigmatic case of state crime, if the notion of state crime is recognized at all. Raphael Lemkin (1944: 79) is credited with having introduced the term 'genocide', towards the end of the Second World War, to describe 'a coordinated plan of different actions aiming at the destruction of essential foundations of the life of national groups, with the aim of annihilating the groups themselves'. Since that time there have been many attempts to define the term, create typologies of genocide and distinguish between related forms of state-sanctioned killing (see, for example, Beres, 1985; Chalk, 1989; Dadrian, 1975; Fein, 1990, 1993; Freeman, 1986; Harff and Gurr, 1990; Lane, 1970). A large number of books and anthologies on genocide have been produced (Andreopolous, 1994; Chalk and Jonassohn, 1990; Charny, 1982, 1994; Chorover, 1979; Dobkowski and Walliman, 1992; Horowitz, 1997; Kressel, 1996; Kuper, 1981; Manvell and Fraenkel, 1967; Porter, 1982; Rummel, 1990, 1991, 1992, 1994a; Walliman and Dobkowski, 1987). Surely the Holocaust – the systematic extermination of Jews (and others) by the Nazis – is the most thoroughly documented and studied case of large-scale genocide, with a vast literature (see, for example, Bauer, 1982; Dawidowicz, 1975; Fein, 1979; Gilbert, 1985; Goldhagen, 1996; Hilberg, 1961; Hirschfeld, 1986; Levin, 1973; Reitlinger, 1961; Yahil, 1990). A considerable literature has been produced on other cases of genocide: for example, the Armenians early in the twentieth century (Boyajian, 1972; Dadrian, 1986; Gurun, 1989; Hovannisian, 1986; and Melson, 1992), and more recently in Cambodia (Barron and Paul, 1977; Chandler, 1991, 1992; Criddle and Mam, 1987; Etcheson, 1984; Jackson, 1989; Kiernan, 1986, 1996; Stuart-Fox and Ung, 1985; Szymusiak, 1987) and East Timor (Budiardjo and Liong, 1984; Dunn, 1983; Kohen and Taylor, 1979; Taylor, 1991). The foregoing are, of course, highly selective examples, with the list of potential cases seemingly endless, including the mass 'collectivization' or 'cultural revolution' cases of the Soviet Union and the People's Republic of China, and the late twentieth-century cases of Bosnia and Rwanda. Somewhat more controversially, the 'conquest of paradise' – that is, the European conquest of the Americas – has been characterized by some as a massive form of genocide (see, for example, Sale, 1990; Churchill, 1992, 1994; Stannard, 1992; Wolff, 1961). In sum, the specific parameters of genocide, the unique and parallel dimensions of the Holocaust and other cases of genocide, and the application of new terms such as 'politicide' and 'democide' to particular forms of state-organized mass killing, are all significant issues in this context.

State-sponsored crime takes many forms, with lines of demarcation not always sharp and clear. State repression of citizens can be taken to refer to a fundamental denial of human rights to citizens (with the denial of the right to life simply the most extreme manifestation of repressive policies) (Hoefnagels, 1977). Virtually by definition, dictatorships encompass repressive policies, although the notion of repression has also been applied to self-proclaimed democracies such as the United States (see, for example, Chirot, 1994; Goldstein, 1978, 1983; Rubin, 1987; Wolfe, 1973). Apartheid South Africa – prior to democratization late in the twentieth century – can be cited as one classic case of a repressive state, insofar as the thrust of state policies was not genocidal, but was rather directed toward denying the majority of citizens fundamental human rights (Sparks, 1990). However, many other states have been characterized as repressive, including the Peoples Republic of China (Brook, 1992) and various Latin American countries such as Argentina and El Salvador (Duff and McCamant, 1976; Fish and Sganga, 1988; Guest, 1990). Again, the claim of state repression is inevitably particularly vulnerable to the charge that it reflects a particular ideological agenda rather than an autonomous characterization of criminal acts on behalf of states.

Within this context, the claim may be put forward that states are engaged in, or sponsoring, terrorism. As we move into the twenty-first century, terrorism – while hardly a new phenomenon – has become a growing preoccupation of both states and citizens. Indeed, terrorism is the focus of a volume in the International Library of Criminology series. As Conor Gearty (1996: xi) notes in his introduction to this volume, the subject of terrorism is 'shrouded in terminological confusion'. States and governments have historically emphasized the dimension of terrorism that involves subversive or anti-state activities, and surely the public at large has been influenced by this view. But Professor Paul Wilkinson (1984), identified in the *Terrorism* volume as Britain's leading terrorism expert, has estimated that states are involved in approximately 25 per cent of the incidents of international terrorism. Furthermore, states directly sponsor or implement actions that constitute what has been called a 'wholesale' form of terrorism, either against some of their own citizens or citizens of other countries (Chomsky, 1988; Chomsky and Herman, 1979; Falk, 1988; Frappier, 1984; George, 1991; Herman, 1982; Klare and Arnson, 1981; Perdue, 1989). The specific scope and dimensions of state-sponsored terrorism has been a matter of some controversy, and has been characterized in various ways (Berman and Clark, 1992; Chapman, 1981; Crenshaw, 1990; Horowitz, 1973; Marks, 1992; Shank, 1991; Wardlaw, 1984–85; Wilkinson, 1974, 1981). But it is clear that terrorism, in at least some of its manifestations, is one significant form of state crime.

A certain proportion of state crime is carried out in the highest levels of government, within the executive branch. In the United States the Pentagon Papers case, the Watergate case, and the Iran/Contra arms case are illustrative examples (Gravel, 1971; White, 1975; Draper, 1991; Ledeen, 1988; Marshall *et al.*, 1987). Also, state agencies have been principal players in state crime, whether or not it is characterized as a form of terrorism. They have, for example, carried out political killings for the state (Amnesty International, 1983), torture (Kadish, 1989; Moore, 1989; Peters, 1985), violence in connection with the war on drugs (Mellem, 1994), the use of *agents provocateurs* (Marx, 1974), as well as other crimes, including frauds and forgeries (Blackstock, 1966). Some specific state agencies – for example, in the United States, the CIA and the FBI, and other police agencies – have been accused of carrying out various illegal activities, especially against dissident groups (Blackstock, 1976; Churchill and Vander Wall, 1988; Garrow, 1981; Glick, 1989; Halperin *et al.*, 1976; Marx, 1990; Poveda, 1982; Weyler, 1992; Wise, 1976; Wise and Ross, 1964; Woodward, 1987). Criminal justice agencies at all levels have been accused of abuses of power, taking the form of crimes against citizens, with particular attention directed toward police misuse of force (Barker and Carter, 1991; Fyfe and Skolnick, 1993; Henderson and Simon, 1994). Altogether, the study of state crime has to attend to the specific operation of state agencies.

Crime is most typically conceived of as an action. In some instances, however, the failure to act may be defined as criminal. Within conventional criminological terms the failure to file an income tax return is often given as a classic example of an omission that may result in criminal charges. Within the context of state crime, we may refer to 'crimes of state omission' or the negligent state (Barak, 1991; Friedrichs, 1996a). As one example, 'ecocide' has been defined as 'states ... causing or permitting harm to the natural environment on a massive scale ... [constituting] ... a breach or duty of care to humanity in general ...' (Gray, 1996, p.216). Obviously, specific actions of states and many other entities (for example, corporations) or individuals are responsible for ecocide, but the recognition of state complicity for environmental victimization by inaction is growing; the scale of harm from environmental damage, and its immense potential for devastating harm as we move through the new century, makes ecocide a major form of state crime (Penz, 1996; Williams, 1996). Other serious manifestations of state crimes of omission could include infancy mortality and AIDS-related deaths preventable by governmental action (Friedrichs, 1996a). Within the framework of state crime Gregg Barak and Robert M. Bohm (1989) have argued that we should be more concerned with the crime of homelessness – that is, the failure of an affluent state and society to provide for the fundamental needs of all citizens – than with the crimes of the homeless. Bohm (1993), following up on this, identifies some 'social relationships that arguably should be criminal', including: the grossly inequitable distribution of wealth in the United States, poverty, hunger, institutionalized racism, institutionalized sexism and the like. Needless to say, any such extensions of the concept of state crime or criminality are highly controversial. With that caveat in mind, one should at least be open to considering the criminological implications of certain forms of governmental inaction.

War-making

Ted Robert Gurr is Distinguished University Professor, Center for International Development at the University of Maryland (USA) and a leading student of large-scale forms of violence over a period of several decades. War is an enduring form of human activity that has been characterized in many ways, from glorious and necessary to evil and criminal. The destructive force of war surely qualifies it as crime in terms of measurable harm perpetrated on humans. In Chapter 6, 'War, Revolution and the Growth of the Coercive State', Gurr begins his analysis by noting that late twentieth-century states are extraordinarily powerful and resilient agencies, with an immense capacity to mobilize resources to advance their ends. Modern states have used force and the threat of force (by warfare) to consolidate (or extend) their rule. He identifies the attributes of different types of state, and their affinity with the use of force and violence, paying particular attention to 'garrison states'. Gurr concludes his analysis by de-veloping some generalized propositions about the consequences of state's uses of extreme coercion in domestic and international disputes.

Genocide

Ward Churchill is a Professor and Director of the Educational Development Program at the University of Colorado, Boulder (USA), who has been active with the American Indian move-ment and has published extensively on various aspects of state crime. In 'Genocide: Toward a Functional Definition' (Chapter 7) Churchill addresses both the complex definitional issues surrounding this familiar term and what he takes to be some common misunderstandings involved in its application, especially due to the politicization of the term. He also reviews the historical evolution of the term 'genocide' and some of the theoretical initiatives surrounding it. A typology recognizing different gradations of genocide is developed, with an emphasis on the somewhat controversial notion of cultural genocide. Although Churchill's attempt to broaden the definition of genocide will certainly be resisted by some, he does provide a provocative framework for further debate on this issue.

Barbara Harff is a Professor at the US Naval Academy, Annapolis; her co-author, Ted Robert Gurr, has been identified earlier in connection with another contribution to this volume. In 'Victims of the State: Genocides, Politicides and Group Repression from 1945 to 1995' (Chapter 8) Harff and Gurr's chapter is part of an on-going research program identifying cases of collective victimization of ethnic, religious, national and political groups by the state, from 1945 on. They examine a large number of such cases (drawing upon two sets of data) with the objective of identifying groups especially vulnerable to massive violence. Ideally this effort contributes to monitoring situations of vulnerability to genocide and fosters further research.

Albert Breton is a Professor of Economics at the University of Toronto and Ronald Wintrobe is a Professor of Economics at the University of Western Ontario (CAN). In 'The Bureaucracy of Murder Revisited' (Chapter 9) Breton and Wintrobe review the familiar Nuremberg defence, that the accused were cogs in a bureaucratic structure, as endorsed by Hannah Arendt in her celebrated *Eichmann in Jerusalem* (1963). The authors re-examine the record in the case of Adolf Eichmann and propose an alternative view of Eichmann as a competitive entrepreneurial bureaucrat. This analysis is valuable, therefore, in that it provides an understanding of large-scale state genocide that reconciles institutional structures and pressures with individual choices and actions.

Nuclearism

Richard Harding is a Professor of Law at the University of Western Australia. Chapter 10, 'Nuclear Energy and the Destiny of Mankind – Some Criminological Perspectives' was his Presidential Address to the Criminology Section of the Australian and New Zealand Association for the Advancement of Science in May 1982. He begins his Address by noting that even the most ideologically opposed students of crime share the aim of a continuing existence for mankind, but notes that much criminological energy is devoted to relatively trivial and narrowly conceived issues when compared with the fundamental threat to the continuation of human activity posed by nuclear weapons and nuclear energy. In this essay, Harding makes a pioneering contribution to the review of developments pertaining to the diffusion of nuclear weapons and the inevitable mishaps associated with nuclear energy from the specific perspective of their relevance to criminologists. He calls for criminologists to move away from 'mini-criminology' and to focus their attention on the nuclear threat to human survival.

David Kauzlarich (a co-author of Chapter 4) is one of the very few criminologists to have responded to Richard Harding's appeal. In 'A Criminology of the Nuclear State' (Chapter 11) Kauzlarich develops a specific framework for studying and understanding the threatened and actual use of nuclear weapons as a form of governmental crime. He reviews the history of the legal debate on nuclear weapons and identifies some bases for regarding the threatened use of nuclear weapons as illegal and criminal. He believes that the relative success of a historically recent extension of the legalistic response to white-collar and corporate crime provides a precedent for such a response to the nuclear threat.

State-sponsored Terrorism and Crimes Against Citizens

Philip Jenkins is a Professor of History and Religious Studies at Pennsylvania State University (USA) with a longstanding interest in criminological issues. In Chapter 12, 'Whose Terrorists? Libya and State Criminality', Jenkins focuses on the characterization, by many Western nations, of a relatively small state, Libya, as a criminal or terrorist state. The difficulties involved with the term 'state criminality' are examined in this essay. Jenkins does not dispute that the Libyan government of Muammar Qaddafi supported guerilla movements involved in terrorism, but he goes on to explore the many forms of complicity by British and American intelligence entities. He raises the provocative question of whether stigmatization as a criminal state is a function of objective facts or of the relative political weakness of the stigmatized state.

J.D. Van der Vyver is Professor of Law at the University of the Witwatersrand (South Africa). In 'State Sponsored Terror Violence' (Chapter 13), written as the apartheid regime was coming to an end, Van der Vyver reviews the means – fundamentally at odds with the constituent elements of a just system of law – used by the South African authorities to maintain power. A discussion of the definitions of terrorism provides a point of departure for characterizing state-sponsored terror. The links of state-sponsored terror violence with the lack of legitimacy of the apartheid regime, and some of the pernicious consequences of state terrorism, are explored.

Harry Brill is on the faculty of the Sociology Department at the University of Massachusetts-Boston (USA). Ordinarily, governmental crime is conceived in terms of egregious actions undertaken by state actors on behalf of the state. In Chapter 14, 'Government Breaks the Law: The Sabotaging of the Occupational Safety and Health Act', Brill directs attention to the obverse problem – namely, the formidable harm that results from a governmental failure to act or to fully implement laws intended to protect citizen constituencies from harm. The Occupational Safety and Health Administration (OHSA) has been one of the most controversial of American governmental regulatory agencies, recurrently attacked as overzealous in its enforcement of economically counterproductive regulations. In this essay, however, Brill identifies and discusses various failures of OSHA to implement protective regulations, thereby increasing the chances of American workers being injured or made sick by work-related conditions.

Hybrid Forms of State Crime

Much harmful and illegal activity does not fit neatly into one of the standard categories of criminal activity. In the case of state crime, in particular, it is often interrelated or interconnected with other forms of criminal conduct. Ultimately, one cannot adequately discuss and analyse state crime without taking these interconnections into account. In Part III such interconnections are considered. First, there is the relationship to organized crime – a relationship with a long and enduring history. The term 'organized crime' is itself rather problematic, as it is defined in various ways; and 'state-organized' crime can refer to both crime directed by state officials and cooperative criminal enterprises involving both state entities and syndicated crime groups. Rather than attempt here to tackle some of the complex conceptual issues, interested readers are referred to the Nikos Passas Introduction to *Organized Crime* (1995) in the International Library of Criminology series, which also notes connections between state agencies and organized crime.

Second, there is the relationship to corporate crime – one that assumes increasing significance in a world characterized by the growth and expansion of large-scale corporations, especially multinationals. Corporate crime itself is one major manifestation of white-collar crime. Again, the reader is referred to the Introduction to David Nelken's (1994b) *White-Collar Crime* in the International Library of Criminology series as well as to my own text *Trusted Criminals* (Friedrichs, 1996a). The term 'state–corporate' crime was introduced by Kramer and Michalowski (1990) to refer to cooperative criminal enterprises involving the state and corporate enterprises. The involvement of some major German corporations, such as I.G. Farben, with the Nazi regime in the use of slave labour, the development of concentration camps and the extermination process itself are classic illustrations of state–corporate crime (see Borkin, 1978).

Third, there is the relationship (or parallelism) with the occupational form of white-collar crime, with the corruption of state officials defined as a public sector equivalent to the fraudulent activities of private sector professionals, entrepreneurs and employees. Various attempts have been made to delineate the different dimensions of corruption (see, for example, Heidesheimer, 1996; Meny, 1996); and corruption has been shown to be an entrenched or institutionalized feature of the polity in many countries, including the United States, the People's Republic of China and the Philippines (Meier and Holbrook, 1992; White, 1996; Carbonell-Catilo, 1986). Many books have been published that explore some of the conceptual and general dimensions of corruption (for example, Alatas, 1990; DeLeon, 1993; Rose-Ackerman, 1978), its inter-connections with other forms of criminal activity (for example, Chambliss, 1988), its history in a particular society (for example, Miller, 1976, 1992), or a particular type of corruption, such as bribery (for example, Noonan, 1984). As was noted earlier, political corruption can be classified as a form of political white-collar crime. Insofar as personal benefit and enrichment rather than a state interest is most typically involved – and, indeed, the state may be considered a victim of political white-collar crime – at least for a certain proportion of corruption it becomes difficult to disentangle purely personal and political objectives, and the state (or state agency) becomes a direct instrument of corruption.

State-organized Crime

William Chambliss is Professor of Sociology at George Washington University (USA) and a leading figure in conflict/radical/critical criminology over a period of several decades. 'State-organized Crime' (Chapter 13) was his 1988 Presidential Address to the American Society of Criminology. In a series of works Chambliss has concentrated on the network of relations between governmental officials, criminal justice agencies, legitimate businesses and organized crime entities. State-organized crime is illegal activity engaged in by state officials on behalf of the state. Chambliss reviews the historical complicity of the state in such activities as piracy, smuggling, assassinations, criminal conspiracies and spying on citizens, distinguishing such activity from illegal or unethical official actions carried out for personal gain, or at odds with institutional policy objectives. He provides an interpretation of these activities within the framework of his well known dialectical theory which highlights contradictions between state objectives (and different entities) that cannot be fully resolved by legal actions, hence leading to criminal activity.

State–Corporate Crime

David Kauzlarich and Ronald C. Kramer are the co-authors of Chapter 16, 'State–Corporate Crime in the US Nuclear Weapons Production Complex'. In this essay, they adopt as a point of departure the concept of state–corporate crime (originally introduced by Kramer and Raymond Michalowski) as 'organizational misconduct that occurs at the interstices of corporations and governments' (p. 328). The authors then explore environmental crimes committed in conjunction with the production of nuclear weapons – a cooperative enterprise between the state and private corporations. Kauzlarich and Kramer apply a number of different, and integrated, theoretical perspectives to the understanding of this type of crime and demonstrate the mutual complicity of the state and private enterprise.

Political White-Collar Crime

David Nelken is Distinguished Research Professor of Law, Cardiff Law School (Wales) and Professor of Sociology, Macerata University (Italy); Michael Levi is Professor of Criminology at the University of Wales (UK). In 'The Corruption of Politics and the Politics of Corruption: An Overview' (Chapter 17) Nelken and Levi provide, as the essay title suggests, a contemporary, critical overview of corruption. Although they note that corruption has historically been viewed as a problem of underdeveloped nations it has also been a formidable problem in Western democracies. Nelken and Levi review the complex of links between political financing, fraud and money-laundering, in relation to both corruption itself and the complex cycles of corruption and reform. They note that, as the case of China seems to demonstrate, a movement towards a market economy may expand opportunities for corruption but, in general, democratization should produce a reduction of tolerance of corruption. Finally, the authors review the various possible solutions to the problem of corruption, while fully acknowledging the paradoxes implicit in these solutions.

Comparative Dimensions of State Crime

The notion of a 'comparative criminology' – formally introduced by Hermann Mannheim (1964) in a book of that name – is most typically taken to focus on the systematic comparison of crime (and criminal justice systems) in different countries (Beirne and Hill, 1991; Fields and Moore, 1996). Barton Ingraham (1979) has studied political crime in Europe comparatively, as one relevant example. Interest in comparative criminology in this sense has grown significantly, although it has also been criticized as overdescriptive and insufficiently theoretical in orientation (Evans *et al.*, 1996). Furthermore, the notion of a 'comparative criminology' can be defined more broadly than in cross-cultural terms alone. According to Paul Friday (1996: 229):

> [Comparative criminology] is a *perspective* that relies on a macro analysis to place crime in a broader social context. The comparative perspective seeks to identify both commonalities and differences within and between cultural, legal, political, economic, and certainly historical contexts.

Moreover, David Bayley (1996) notes that, since all science is comparative, the term 'comparative criminology' should not be conflated with 'international'. In this section, therefore, the term applies not only to cross-cultural dimensions of a comparative criminology, but also provides a comparative context for understanding state crime, and the exercise of state power, relative to other forms of crime. Some theoretical works, and studies of particular forms of state crime, adopt a comparative perspective in one of these senses (for example, Baumeister, 1997; Chalk and Jonassohn, 1990; Falk, 1988; Horowitz, 1997; Lifton and Markusen, 1990; Markusen and Kopf, 1995; Medard, 1986; Melson, 1992; Patterson, 1982; Payne, 1973; Shawcross, 1985; Uekert, 1995; Walliman and Dobkowski, 1987). Jennifer Turpin and Lester R. Kurtz (1996: 2) in *The Web of Violence*, promote the view that there are significant interconnections between macro-level and micro-level violence and they note that 'Social scientists have done surprisingly little research that explores the links between interpersonal, collective, national, and global levels of violence'. Mark Cooney (1997), in 'From Warre to Tyranny: Lethal Conflict and the State', systematically explores the impact of the state (in terms of the character of state authority) on various forms of lethal conflict (that is, war, rebellion, homicide and execution). This analysis exemplifies a broadly comparative criminology, insofar as it incorporates a theoretical perspective, a cross-cultural dimension and a comparison of quite different manifestations of extreme violence. The essays in this section, therefore, were selected with the concept of a comparative criminology, such as Cooney's approach suggests, in mind.

In 'State Violence and Violent Crime' (Chapter 18), Ronald Kramer argues that state violence must be understood both in its own terms and in connection with more conventional forms of violence. Structural violence (especially in Third World countries) is a form of state crime and is state terrorism. But institutional violence generally must also be evaluated in relation to interpersonal violence.

Henry Huttenbach is Professor of History at The City College of the City University of New York. In 'Locating the Holocaust on the Genocide Spectrum: Towards A Methodology of Definition and Categorization' (Chapter 19) Huttenbach reviews some of the principal positions on whether or not the Holocaust, arguably the single best known large-scale state crime of the twentieth century, was unique and what its relationship is to other cases of genocide. He scrupulously sorts through some of the complex definitional issues and the terminology involved in this issue. A guiding premise of this essay is that a resolution of the relationship of the Holocaust to other genocides provides a basic starting point for comparative studies of state crime. Huttenbach calls for a reasonably simple definition of genocide but, above all, aspires to promote discussion and debate.

Peter Harris is Professor of Political Science at the University of Hong Kong. In Chapter 20, 'Socialist Graft: The Soviet Union and the People's Republic of China – A Preliminary Survey', Harris tackles the paradox of corruption in socialist systems, insofar as it has historically been associated with capitalist societies. In this context, he reviews the Marxist vision of a society without graft and examines the character of graft in the former Soviet Union and in China. Harris identifies some dimensions of socialist states that promote corruption and characterizes socialism and corruption as mutually reinforcing.

Stephen Riley is Professor in the Department of International Relations and Politics, North Staffordshire (Stoke on Trent, UK). In 'Political Scandal: A Western Luxury?' (Chapter 21) he notes the ubiquity of such scandals. The Bhopal affair represents one form of scandal illustrative of the management of scandal by a Third World government. In the case of Mobutu Sese Seko's regime in the (former) Zaire, characterized by massive corruption and abuse of human rights, we witness a significant complicity of Western states. Such complicity also exists in the case of illicit drug traffic through Central America and the Caribbean. Altogether, although political scandals are not necessarily a 'Western luxury', Riley concludes that Western interests are often implicated in such scandals in Third World countries.

Explaining State Crime

Generations of criminologists have contended with the formidable challenge of attempting to explain crime and, as all students of criminology know, the outcome has been a somewhat bewildering range of theories, from biogenetic to structural. In the case of state crime specifically, one approach has been to link it with a broad understanding of the phenomenon of evil (see, for example, Baumeister, 1997; Coser, 1969; Sanford *et al.*, 1971; Staub, 1989). Of course, many other approaches have adopted a narrower focus, ranging from the role of ethnicity and nationalism to the social psychology of obedience and conformity (Alexander, 1948–49; Gamson, 1995; Hamilton, 1986; Kelman, 1973, 1976; Kelman and Hamilton, 1989; Milgram, 1963, 1974; Peattie, 1984; Scheff, 1994; Van den Berghe, 1990). In between the metaphysical and the individual or group level, such crime is explained on a structural or an organizational level (Ermann and Lundman, 1978; Ostergaard, 1986; Nash, 1980). In view of the complexity of state crime, and the fact that it operates on quite different levels virtually by definition, the challenge of generating explanatory schemes or theories is especially daunting. In the case of genocide, for example, the range of explanations has been particularly broad. More than a half century after the single most intensively studied case of genocide – the Holocaust perpetrated by Nazi Germany – historians continue to engage in heated debate on its causes. For example, Daniel Goldhagen's (1996) *Hitler's Willing Executioners* – with its emphasis upon an 'eliminationist antisemitism' as a primary factor in the Holocaust – has generated considerable controversy. In the case of state repression it has been explained in terms of local cultures and elite decision-making, as well as by the international political and economic context. However, on the basis of empirical study, various factors are found to be interrelated with state repression (Duff *et al.*, 1976; Gartner and Regan, 1997; Henderson, 1991; Lopez and Stohl, 1989; Mitchell and McCormick, 1988; Park, 1987; Poe and Tate, 1994; Regan, 1995). State crime, by its very nature, in fact requires attention to the interaction of macro-level and micro-level factors. Furthermore, the diversity of manifestations of state crime precludes the development of any general theory of such crime. The essays reprinted in Part V, therefore, reflect some of the quite different approaches to explaining and understanding state crime.

Randall Collins is Professor of Sociology at the University of Pennsylvania. His 'Three Faces of Cruelty: Towards a Comparative Sociology of Evil' (Chapter 22) is an erudite disquisition on the manifestation of human cruelty. He considers the relationship of violence to social structure, paying particular attention to seminal social theorists and specifically exploring the perspectives of such theorists on ferociousness, callousness and asceticism. Although these human propensities are not all directly related to state crime they do have some connection with it. Collins contends that, in contemporary society, ferocious cruelty has diminished and is no longer structurally induced, but the dangers of callousness have increased (ascetic cruelty has had its ups and downs). Altogether, he provides us with an opportunity to appreciate some connections between our principal social theories and some forms of state crime.

Israel Charny is Executive Director of the Institute of the International Conference on the Holocaust and Genocide in Jerusalem and Associate Professor of Social Work at Tel Aviv University. In 'Genocide and Mass Destruction: Doing Harm to Others as a Missing Dimension of Psychopathology' (Chapter 23) Charny calls for an expansion to standard classification systems in psychopathology to include abuses and destruction of other people. He focuses on the need to understand how 'normal' people come to be involved in committing atrocities. Such an endeavour raises some questions of value systems in relation to scientific work and the dangers of politicizing psychiatry, as Charny notes, but he offers one approach to understanding how state crimes come to be carried out.

David Norman Smith is Professor of Sociology at the University of Kansas. In Chapter 24, 'The Genesis of Genocide in Rwanda: The Fatal Dialectic of Class and Ethnicity', he argues that the global dynamic of accumulation of capital is illustrated, at least in part, by the genocide in Rwanda. The transformation from a comparatively stable kingdom into a culture of genocide is linked with the colonial legacy and the complicity of economic pressures emanating from capitalist institutions such as the International Monetary Fund and the World Bank. Smith repudiates an explanation for the genocide based simply on tribal rivalry; rather, he believes that the Rwandan genocide is best understood in terms of the intersection of ethnicity and ethnocentrism.

R.J. Rummel is Professor of Political Science at the University of Hawaii at Manoa (USA) and an especially prolific author on state-generated violence in all its many forms. 'Democracy, Power, Genocide and Mass Murder' (Chapter 25) begins with an estimation of the scope of state-initiated killings in this century and introduces the term 'democide' to describe some forms of state killing (for example, deliberately creating a famine) not encompassed by the term 'genocide'. Rummel poses a theoretical hypothesis that the more democratic freedom a nation has the less likely its government will commit democide and supports this with an examination of 218 twentieth-century regimes. If he is correct that democracy tends to deter governmental violence it is surely no absolute deterrent. Although this thesis is widely embraced in some form in Western democratic states, it also devalues the complicity of such states in all manner of state crimes, as documented elsewhere in these volumes.

Concluding Remarks

All of the essays brought together in this volume (as well as in Volume II) offer some insights on dimensions of state crime and its control. Although most of this work has not been produced by self-identified criminologists, the relevance of their work for criminological concerns is a guiding premise of this volume. To date, as noted earlier, only a handful of criminologists have focused their attention on state crime. Ideally, a growing number of criminologists will recognize its significance and the contribution criminology can make to its understanding and prevention. Much more work is needed in the form of a systematic comparative analysis of state crime and conventional forms of crimes, their parallels and differences. In this vein we can ask exactly how far theories (and empirical findings) pertaining to conventional forms of crime take us in a mission directed toward understanding state crime.

Ideally the present volume, which inevitably includes only a highly selective sample of essays and bibliographic references, can contribute to the development of a fully realized criminological framework for the study of state crime and can also provide a significant springboard for further work.

Acknowledgements

First, I would like to thank David Nelken, a general editor of the International Library of Criminology, Criminal Justice and Penology, for inviting me to put together this volume and for his advice and encouragement. It was a pleasure, as well, to work with the very capable editorial staff of Ashgate/Dartmouth. I received assistance from librarians at the University of Scranton, and appreciated the opportunity to use libraries at Cornell University, New York University, Rutgers University and Georgetown University. I consulted the following in-dividuals for advice, and I appreciate their suggestions and their encouragement: Gregg Barak; Stanley Cohen; Frank Hagan; David Kauzlarich; Jeffrey Ian Ross, Martin D. Schwartz; and Kenneth Tunnell. I also found it helpful to discuss some of my ideas in connection with this project with two students, Victoria Wysocki and Jenny Pane. I am also grateful for a University of Scranton Faculty research grant that was essential for funding visits to some major research libraries and for copying costs. As always, the loving support of my wife Jeanne and my children, Jessica and Bryan, has made it possible for me to engage in professional projects such as this.

Finally, I would like to dedicate these volumes to the memory of my parents – refugees from a criminal state (Nazi Germany). I also hope they serve as still another memorial to the countless millions of victims of state crimes.

References

Alatas, Syed Hussein (1990), *Corruption: Its Nature, Causes and Functions*, Aldershot: Avebury.
Alexander, Leo (1948–49), 'War Crimes and their Motivations', *Journal of Criminal Law and Criminology*, **39**, pp. 298–326; 553–64; **40**, pp. 3–27.
Al-Khalil, Samir (1989), *Republic of Fear – The Inside Story of Saddam's Iraq*, New York: Pantheon Books.

Allen, Beverly (1996), *Rape Warfare: The Hidden Genocide in Bosnia-Herzegovina and Croatia*, Minneapolis, MN: University of Minneapolis Press.

Amnesty International (1983), *Political Killings by Government*, London: Amnesty International.

Andreopoulous, G.J. (ed.) (1994), *Genocide*, Philadelphia: University of Pennsylvania Press.

Arendt, Hannah (1963), *Eichmann in Jerusalem: A Report on the Banality of Evil*, New York: The Viking Press.

Barak, Gregg (ed.) (1991), *Crimes by the Capitalist State*, Albany, NY: State University of New York Press.

Barak, Gregg (1993), 'Crime, Criminology and Human Rights: Toward an Understanding of State Criminality', in Kenneth D. Tunnell (ed.), *Political Crime in Contemporary America – A Critical Approach*, New York: Garland, pp. 207–30.

Barak, Gregg and Bohm, Robert M. (1989), 'The Crimes of the Homeless or the Crime of Homelessness? On the Dialectics of Criminalization, Decriminalization, and Victimization', *Contemporary Crises*, **13**, pp. 275–88.

Barker, Thomas and Carter, David L. (eds) (1991), *Police Deviance* (2nd edn), Cincinnati, OH: Anderson.

Barron, John and Paul, Anthony (1977), *Peace with Horror: The Untold Story of Communist Genocide in Cambodia*, London: Hodder and Stoughton.

Bauer, Yehuda (1982), *A History of the Holocaust*, New York: Franklin Watts.

Baumeister, Roy F. (1997), *Evil: Inside Human Cruelty and Violence*, New York: W.H. Freeman and Company.

Bayley, David H. (1996), 'Policing: The World Stage', *Journal of Criminal Justice Education*, **7**, pp. 241–51.

Becker, Theodore L. and Murray, Vernon G. (eds) (1971), *Government Lawlessness in America*, New York: Oxford University Press.

Beckman, Peter (1992), 'Sociology and Nuclear Weapons: A View From Outside', *Sociological Forum*, **7**, pp. 7–28.

Beirne, Piers and Hill, J. (1991), *Comparative Criminology: An Annotated Bibliography*, New York: Greenwood.

Beirne, Piers and Messerschmidt, James (1995), *Criminology*, Fort Worth, TX: Harcourt Brace.

Beres, Louis Rene (1985), 'Genocide', *Policy Studies Review*, **4**, pp. 397–406.

Berman, Maureen and Clark, Roger S. (1992), 'State Terrorism: Disappearances', *Rutgers Law Journals*, **13**, pp. 531–77.

Blackstock, Nelson (1976), *Cointelpro: The FBI's Secret War on Political Freedom*, New York: Random House.

Blackstock, Paul W. (1966), *Agents of Deceit: Frauds, Forgeries and Political Intrigue Among Nations*, Chicago: Quadrangle.

Bohm, Robert M. (1993), 'Social Relationships That Arguably Should Be Criminal Although They Are Not: On the Political Economy of Crime', in Kenneth D. Tunnell (ed.), *Political Crime in Contemporary America – A Critical Approach*, New York: Garland, pp. 3–30.

Borkin, Joseph (1978), *The Crime and Punishment of I.G. Farben*, New York: Free Press.

Boyajian, Dickran H. (1972), *Armenia: The Case for a Forgotten Genocide*, Westwood, NJ: Educational Book Crafters.

Brook, Timothy (1992), *Quelling the People: The Military Suppression of the Beijing Democracy Movement*, New York: Oxford University Press.

Brown, Cynthia (1985), *With Friends Like These: The America Watch Report on Human Rights and U.S. Policy in Latin America*, New York: Pantheon Books.

Budiardjo, Carmel and Liem Soei Liong (1984), *The War against East Timor*, London: Zed Books.

Bushnell, P. Timothy, Shlapentokh, Vladimir, Vanderpool, Christopher K. and Sundram, Jeyaratnam (1991), *State Organized Terror: The Case of Violent Internal Repression*, Boulder, CO: Westview Press.

Carbonell-Catilo, Aurora (1986), 'The Philippines: The Politics of Plunder', *Corruption and Reform*, **1**, pp. 235–43.

Chalk, Frank (1989), 'Definitions of Genocide and Their Implications for Prediction and Prevention', *Holocaust and Genocide Studies*, **4**, pp. 149–60.

Chalk, Frank and Jonassohn, Kurt (1990), *The History and Sociology of Genocide: Analysis and Case Studies*, New Haven, CT: Yale University Press.

Chambliss, William (1988), *On the Take: From Petty Crooks to Presidents* (2nd edn), Bloomington, IN: Indiana University Press.

Chandler, David P. (1991), *The Tragedy of Cambodian History: War, Politics and Revolution Since 1945*, New Haven, CT: Yale University Press.

Chandler, David P. (1992), *Brother Number One: A Political Biography of Pol Pot*, Boulder, CO: Westview Press.

Chapman, Robert D. (1981), 'State Terrorism', *Conflict*, **3**, pp. 283–98.

Charny, Israel W. (1982), *How Can We Commit the Unthinkable? Genocide: The Human Cancer*, Boulder, CO: Westview Press.

Charny, Israel W. (1994), *The Widening Circle of Genocide*, New Brunswick, NJ: Transaction.

Chirot, Daniel (1994), *Modern Tyrants: The Power and Prevalence of Evil in Our Age*, Princeton, NJ: Princeton University Press.

Chomsky, Noam (1988), *The Culture of Terrorism*, Boston: South End Press.

Chomsky, Noam and Herman, Edward (1979), *The Washington Connection and Third World Facism*, Nottingham: Spokesman.

Chorover, Stephan (1979), *From Genesis to Genocide*, Cambridge, MA: MIT Press.

Churchill, Ward (1992), 'Deconstructing the Columbus Myth: Was the "Great Discoverer" Italian or Spanish, Nazi or Jew?', *Social Justice*, **19**, pp. 39–55.

Churchill, Ward (1994), *Indians 'R' Us? Culture and Genocide in Native North America*, Monroe, ME: Common Courage Press.

Churchill, Ward and Vander Wall, Jim (1988), *Agents of Repression: The FBI's Secret Wars Against the Black Panther Party and The American Indian Movement*, Boston, MA: South End Press.

Cohen, Stanley (1996), 'Crime and Politics: Spot the Difference', *British Journal of Sociology*, **47**, pp. 1–21.

Comfort, Alex (1950), *Authority and Delinquency in the Modern State*, London: Routledge and Kegan Paul.

Conquest, Robert (1986), *The Harvest of Sorrow: Soviet Collectivization and the Terror-Famine*, New York: Oxford University Press.

Conquest, Robert (1990), *The Great Terror: A Reassessment*, New York: Oxford University Press.

Cooney, Mark (1997), 'From Warre to Tyranny: Lethal Conflict and the State', *American Sociological Review*, **62**, pp. 316–38.

Coser, Lewis (1969), 'The Visibility of Evil', *Journal of Social Issues*, **25**, pp. 101–9.

Creighton, Colin and Shaw, Martin (eds) (1987), *The Sociology of War and Peace*, Dobbs Ferry: Sheridan House.

Crenshaw, Martha (1990), 'Is International Terrorism Primarily State-Sponsored?', in Charles W. Kegley jr, *International Terrorism – Characteristics, Causes, Controls*, New York: St Martin's Press, pp. 163–69.

Criddle, Joan D. and Mam, Teeda Butt (1987), *To Destroy You is No Loss: The Odyssey of a Cambodian Family*, New York: Atlantic Monthly Press.

Dadrian, Vahakn N. (1975), 'A Typology of Genocide', *International Review of Modern Sociology*, **15**, pp. 204–15.

Dadrian, Vahakn N. (1986), 'The Naim-Andonian Documents on the World War I Destruction of the Ottoman-Armenians: The Anatomy of Genocide', *International Journal of Middle East Studies*, **18**, pp. 311–70.

Dawidowicz, Lucy S. (1975), *The War Against the Jews 1933–1945*, New York: Holt, Rinehart and Winston.

DeLeon, Peter (1993), *Thinking About Political Corruption*, New York: M.E. Sharpe.

Dobkowski, Michael and Wallimann, Isidor (eds) (1992), *Genocide in Our Time*, Ann Arbor, MI: Pierian Press.

Douglas, Jack D. and Johnson, John M. (eds) (1977), *Official Deviance: Readings in Malfeasance, Misfeasance, and Other Forms of Corruption*, Philadelphia: Lippincott.

Draper, Theodore (1991), *A Very Thin Line: The Iran-Contra Affair*, New York: Hill and Wang.

Duff, Ernest A. and McCamant, John F. (1976), *Violence and Repression in Latin America*, New York: Free Press.

Dunn, James (1983), *Timor: A People Betrayed*, Brisbane: Jacaranda Press.

Etcheson, Craig (1984), *The Rise and Demise of Democratic Kampuchea*, Boulder, CO: Westview Press.

Ermann, M. David and Lundman, Richard J. (1978), 'Deviant Acts by Complex Organizations: Deviance and Social Control at the Organizational Level of Analysis', *Sociological Inquiry*, **19**, pp. 55–67.

Evans, T. David, LaGrange, Randy L. and Willis, Cecil L. (1996), 'Theoretical Development of Comparative Criminology: Rekindling an Interest', *International Journal of Comparative and Applied Criminal Justice*, **20**, pp. 15–29.

Falk, Richard A. (1988), *Revolutionaries and Functionaries: The Dual Face of Terrorism*, New York: E.P. Dutton.

Fein, Helen (1979), *Accounting for Genocide: National Response and Jewish Victimization During the Holocaust*, New York: Free Press.

Fein, Helen (1990), 'Genocide: A Sociological Perspective', *Current Sociology*, **38**, pp. 1–126.

Fein, Helen (1993), 'Discriminating Genocide from War Crimes: Vietnam and Afghanistan Reexamined', *Denver Journal of International Law and Policy*, **22**, pp. 29–63.

Fields, C.B. and Moore, R.H. jr (eds) (1996), *Comparative Criminal Justice*, Prospect Heights, IL: Waveland.

Fish, Joe and Sganga, Cristina (1988), *El Salvador: Testament of Terror*, New York: Olive Branch Press.

Frappier, J. (1984), 'Above the Law: Violations of International Law by the U.S. Government from Truman to Reagan', *Crime and Social Justice*, **21–22**, pp. 1–36.

Freeman, Michael (1986), 'Genocide and Social Science', *Patterns of Prejudice*, **20**, pp. 3–15.

Friday, Paul C. (1996), 'The Need to Integrate Comparative and International Criminal Justice into a Traditional Curriculum', *Journal of Criminal Justice Education*, **7**, pp. 227–39.

Friedrichs, David O. (1985), 'The Nuclear Arms Issue and the Field of Criminal Justice', *The Justice Professional*, **1**, pp. 5–9.

Friedrichs, David O. (1995), 'State Crime or Governmental Crime: Making Sense of the Conceptual Confusion', in Jeffrey Ian Ross (ed.), *Controlling State Crime: An Introduction*, New York: Garland, pp. 53–79.

Friedrichs, David O. (1996a), *Trusted Criminals: White Collar Crime in Contemporary Society*, Belmont, CA: ITP/Wadsworth.

Friedrichs, David O. (1996b), 'Governmental Crime, Hitler and White Collar Crime: A Problematic Relationship', *Caribbean Journal of Criminology and Social Psychology*, **2**, pp. 44–63.

Fyfe, James J. and Skolnick, Jerome H. (1993), *Above the Law: Police and the Excessive Use of Force*, New York: The Free Press.

Gamson, William A. (1995), 'Hiroshima, the Holocaust, and the Politics of Exclusion', *American Sociological Review*, **60**, pp. 1–20.

Gardiner, John A. (1993). 'Defining Corruption', *Corruption and Reform*, **7**, pp. 111–24.

Garnett, Richard A. (1988), 'The Study of War in American Sociology: An Analysis of Selected Journals, 1936 to 1984', *The American Sociologist*, Fall, pp. 270–82.

Garrow, David (1981), *The FBI and Martin Luther King*, New York: W.W. Norton.

Gartner, Scott S. and Regan, Patrick M. (1997), 'Threat and Repression: The Non-Linear Relationship Between Government and Opposition Violence', *Journal of Peace Research*, **33**, pp. 273–87.

Gearty, Conor (ed.) (1996), *Terrorism*, Aldershot: Dartmouth.

George, Alexander (ed.) (1991), *Western State Terrorism*, New York: Routledge.

Gerson, Joseph (1995), *With Hiroshima Eyes: Atomic War, Nuclear Extortion, and Moral Imagination*, Philadelphia: New Society Publishers.

Gilbert, Martin (1985), *The Holocaust: A History of the Jews of Europe During the Second World War*, New York: Holt, Rinehart and Winston.

Glick, Brian (1989), *War at Home: Covert Action Against U.S. Activists and What We Can Do About It*, Boston: South End Press.

Goldhagen, Daniel Jonah (1996), *Hitler's Willing Executioners – Ordinary Germans and the Holocaust*, New York: A.A. Knopf.

Goldstein, Robert Justin (1978), *Political Repression in Modern America: From 1870 to the Present*, Cambridge, MA: Schenkman Publishing.

Goldstein, Robert Justin (1983), *Political Repression in 19th Century Europe*, Totawa, NJ: Barnes and Noble.

Gravel, Mike (ed.) (1971), *The Pentagon Papers*, 4 Vols, Boston: Beacon Press.

Gray, Mark Allan (1996), 'The International Crime of Ecocide', *California Western International Law Journal*, **26**, pp. 215–17.

Green, Gary (1997), *Occupational Crime*, (2nd edn), Chicago: Nelson-Hall Publishers.

Guest, Iain (1990), *Behind the Disappearances: Argentina's Dirty War Against Human Rights and the United Nations*, Philadelphia: University of Pennsylvania Press.

Gurun, Kamuran (1989), *The Armenian File: The Myth of Innocence Exposed*, London: K. Rustem & Bro. and Weidenfeld & Nicolson Ltd.

Hagan, Frank E. (1997), *Political Crime: Ideology and Criminality*, Boston, MA: Allyn & Bacon.

Halperin, Morton H. *et. al.* (1976), *The Lawless State: The Crimes of the U.S. Intelligence Agencies*, New York: Penguin.

Hamilton, V.L. (1986), 'Chains of Command: Responsibility Attribution in Hierarchies', *Journal of Applied Social Psychology*, **16**, pp. 118–38.

Harff, Barbara and Gurr, Ted Robert (1990), 'Victims of the State: Genocides, Politicides and Group Repression Since 1945', *International Review of Victimology*, **1**, pp. 1–19.

Harris, Robert and Paxman, Jeremy (1982), *A Higher Form of Killing: The Secret Story of Chemical and Biological Warfare*, New York: Hill and Wang.

Heidesheimer, Arnold J. (1996), 'The Topography of Corruption: Explorations in a Comparative Perspective', *International Social Science Journal*, **149**, pp. 337–48.

Henderson, Conway (1991), 'Conditions Affecting the Use of Political Repression', *Journal of Conflict Resolution*, **35**, pp. 120–42.

Henderson, Joel H. and Simon, David R. (1994), *Crimes of the Criminal Justice System*, Cincinnati, OH: Anderson.

Herman, Edward S. (1982), *The Real Terror Network – Terrorism in Fact and Propaganda*, Boston, MA: South End Press.

Hess, Henner (1977), 'Repressive Crime and Criminal Typologies: Some Neglected Types', *Contemporary Crises*, **1**, pp. 91–108.

Hilberg, Raul (1961), *The Destruction of the European Jews*, New York: Harper & Row.

Hirschfeld, Gerhard (ed.) (1986), *The Policies of Genocide: Jews and Soviet Prisoners of War in Nazi Germany*, London: Allen & Unwin.

Hoefnagels, Marjo (1977), *Repression and Repressive Violence*, New Brunswick, NJ: Transaction.

Horowitz, Irving Louis (1973), 'Political Terrorism and State Powers', *Journal of Political and Military Sociology*, **1**, pp. 147–57.

Horowitz, Irving Louis (1997), *Taking Lives – Genocide and State Power*, (4th edn), Brunswick, NJ: Transaction Publishing.

Hovannisian, Richard G. (ed.) (1986), *The Armenian Genocide in Perspective*, New Brunswick, NJ: Transaction Books.

Howard, Rhoda E. and Donnelly, Jack (1986), 'Human Dignity, Human Rights, and Political Regimes', *American Political Science Review*, **80**, pp. 801–17.

Human Rights Watch (1992), *Human Rights Watch World Report, 1993*, New York: Human Rights Watch.

Huppauf, Bernd (ed.) (1997), *War, Violence and the Modern Condition*, Berlin: W. De Gruyter.

Ingraham, Barton L. (1979), *Political Crime in Europe – A Comparative Study of France, Germany and England*, Berkeley, CA: University of California Press.

Jackson, Karl (ed.) (1989), *Cambodia 1975–1978: Rendezvous with Death*, Princeton, NJ: Princeton University Press.

Johnston, Michael (1996), 'The Search for Definitions: The Vitality of Politics and the Issue of Corruption', *International Social Science Journal*, **149**, pp. 321–37.

Kadish, Sanford H. (1989), 'Torture, the State, and the Individual', *Israel Law Review*, **23**, pp. 345–56.

Kelman, H.C. (1973), 'Violence without Moral Restraint: Reflections on the Dehumanization of Victims and Victimizers', *Journal of Social Issues*, **29**, pp. 25–61.

Kelman, H.C. (1976), 'Some Reflections on Authority, Corruption, and Punishment: The Social Psychological Context of Watergate', *Psychiatry*, **39**, pp. 303–17.

Kelman, Herbert C. and Hamilton, V. Lee (1989), *Crimes of Obedience*, New Haven, CT: Yale University Press.

Kiernan, Ben (1986), *Cambodia: Eastern Zone Massacres*, New York: Columbia University.

Kiernan, Ben (1996), *The Pol Pot Regime – Race, Power, and Genocide in Cambodia under the Khmer Rouge, 1975–1979*, New Haven, CT: Yale University Press.

Klare, Michael and Arnson, Cynthia (1981), *Supplying Repression: U.S. Support for Authoritarian Regimes Abroad*, Washington, DC: Institute for Policy Studies.

Kohen, Arnold and Taylor, John (1979), *An Act of Genocide: Indonesia's Invasion of East Timor*, London: TAPOL.

Kramer, Ronald C. and Marullo, Sam (1985), 'Toward a Sociology of Nuclear Weapons', *The Sociological Quarterly*, **26**, pp. 277–92.

Kramer, Ronald C. and Michalowski, Raymond J. (1990), 'State-Corporate Crime', a paper presented at the Annual Meeting of the American Society of Criminology (Baltimore), 7–12 November.

Kramer, Ronald C. and Kauzlarich, David (1997), 'The International Court of Justice Opinion on the Illegality of the Threat or Use of Nuclear Weapons: Implications for Criminology', a paper presented at the Annual Meeting of the American Society of Criminology (San Diego), 16–21 November.

Kressel, Neil J. (1996), *Mass Hate: The Global Rise of Genocide and Terror*, New York: Plenum Press.

Krimerman, Leonard I. and Perry, Lewis (eds) (1966), *Patterns of Anarchy*, New York: Doubleday.

Kuper, Leo (1981), *Genocide: Its Political Use in the Twentieth Century*, New York: Penguin Books.

Kurtz, Lester R. (1989), *The Nuclear Cage: A Sociology of the Arms Race*, Englewood Cliffs, NJ: Prentice Hall.

Kurtz, Lester R. (1992), 'War and Peace on the Sociological Agenda', in Terence C. Halliday and Morris Janowitz (eds), *Sociology and its Publics*, Chicago: The University of Chicago Press, pp. 61–98.

Lane, Eric (1970), 'Mass Killing by Governments: Lawful in the World Legal Order', *International Law and Politics*, **12**, pp. 239–80.

Ledeen, Michael (1988), *Perilous Statecraft: An Insider's Account of the Iran-Contra Affair*, New York: Charles Scribner's Sons.

Lemkin, Raphael (1944), *Axis Rule in Occupied Europe*, New York: Howard Fertig.

Levin, Nora (1973), *The Holocaust: The Destruction of European Jewry, 1933–1945*, New York: Schocken Books.

Levene, Mark (1996), 'Ways of Seeing Killing', *Patterns of Prejudice*, **30**, pp. 65–71.

Lieberman, Jethro K. (1972), *How the Government Breaks the Law*, Baltimore, MD: Penguin Books, Inc.

Lifton, Robert Jay and Falk, Richard (1982), *Indefensible Weapons: The Political and Psychological Case Against Nuclearism*, New York: Basic Books.

Lifton, Robert J. and Markusen, Eric (1990), *The Genocidal Mentality – Nazi Holocaust and Nuclear Threat*, New York: Basic Books.

Lopez, George A. and Stohl, Michael (eds) (1989), *Dependence, Development, and State Repression*, Westport, CT: Greenwood Press.

Mannheim, Hermann (1964), *Comparative Criminology*, New York: Houghton Mifflin.

Manvell, Roger and Fraenkel, Heinrich (1967), *Incomparable Crime: Mass Extermination in the 20th Century: The Legacy of Guilt*, London: Heinemann.

Marks, Thomas (1992), 'Terror versus Terrorism: The Case of the Philippines', *Low Intensity Conflict and Law Enforcement*, **1**, pp. 215–36.

Markusen, Eric and Kopf, David (1995), *The Holocaust and Strategic Bombing – Genocide and Total War in the Twentieth Century*, Boulder, CO: Westview Press.

Marshall, Jonathan, Scott, Peter Dale and Hunter, Jane (1987), *The Iran-Contra Connection: Secret Teams and Covert Operations in the Reagan Era*, Boston: South End Press.

Marx, Gary (1974), 'Thoughts on a Neglected Category of Social Movement Participant: The Agent Provocateur and the Informant', *American Journal of Sociology*, **80**, pp. 402–42.

Marx, Gary (1990), *Undercover: Police Surveillance in America*, Berkeley, CA: University of California Press.

Medard, J-F. (1986), 'Public Corruption in Africa: A Comparative Perspective', *Corruption and Reform*, **1**, pp. 115–31.

Meier, Kenneth J. and Holbrook, Thomas M. (1992), ' "I Seen My Opportunities and I Took 'Em": Political Corruption in the American States', *The Journal of Politics*, **54**, pp. 135–54.

Mellem, Roger D. (1994), 'Governmental Violence in the War Against Drugs', *International Journal of Comparative and Applied Criminal Justice*, **18**, pp. 39–51.

Melson, Robert F. (1992), *Revolution and Genocide: On the Origins of the Armenian Genocide and the Holocaust*, Chicago: University of Chicago Press.

Meny, Yves (1996), ' "Fin de siècle" Corruption: Change, Crisis and Shifting Values', *International Social Science Journal*, **149**, pp. 309–20.

Michalowski, Raymond J. (1985), *Order, Law and Crime*, New York: Random House.

Milgram, Stanley (1963), 'Behavioral Study of Obedience', *Journal of Abnormal and Social Psychology*, **67**, pp. 371–8.

Milgram, Stanley (1974), *Obedience to Authority*, New York: Harper and Row.

Miller, Nathan (1976), *The Founding Finaglers*, New York: David McKay.

Miller, Nathan (1992), *Stealing From America*, New York: Paragon House.

Minear, Richard H. (1995), 'Atomic Holocaust, Nazi Holocaust: Some Reflections', *Diplomatic History*, **19**, pp. 347–65.

Mitchell, Neil J. and McCormick, James M. (1988), 'Economic and Political Explanations of Human Rights Violations', *World Politics*, **40**, pp. 476–98.

Moore, Michael S. (1989), 'Torture and the Balance of Evils', *Israel Law Review*, **23**, pp. 280–344.

Nash, Henry J. (1980), 'The Bureaucratization of Homicide', *Bulletin of Atomic Scientists*, **36**, pp. 22–7.

Nelken, David (1994a), 'White-Collar Crime', in Mike Maguire, Rod Morgan and Robert Reiner (eds), *The Oxford Handbook of Criminology*, Oxford: Clarendon Press, pp. 355–92.

Nelken, David (ed.) (1994b), *White-Collar Crime*, Aldershot: Dartmouth.

Noonan, John T. (1984), *Bribes*, Berkeley, CA: University of California Press.

O'Connell, Robert L. (1989), *Of Arms and Men: A History of War, Weapons, and Aggression*, New York and Oxford: Oxford University Press.

Ostergaard, Clemens Stubbe (1986), 'Explaining China's Recent Political Corruption', *Corruption and Reform*, **1**, pp. 209–33.

Park, Han S. (1987), 'Correlates of Human Rights: Global Tendencies', *Human Rights Quarterly*, **9**, pp. 405–13.

Passas, Nikos (ed.) (1995), *Organized Crime*, Aldershot: Dartmouth.

Patterson, Orlando (1982), *Slavery and Social Death: A Comparative Study*, Cambridge, MA: Harvard University Press.

Payne, Robert (1973), *Massacre, the Tragedy of Bangladesh and the Phenomenon of Mass Slaughter Throughout History*, New York: Macmillan.

Peattie, Lisa (1984), 'Normalizing the Unthinkable', *Bulletin of Atomic Scientists*, **40**, pp. 32–6.

Penz, Peter (1996), 'Environmental Victims and State Sovereignty: A Normative Analysis', *Social Justice*, **23**, pp. 41–61.

Perdue, William D. (1989), *Terrorism and the State: A Critique of Domination Through Fear*, New York: Praeger.

Peters, Edward (1985), *Torture*, Philadelphia: University of Pennsylvania Press.

Poe, Steven C. and Tate, C. Neal (1994), 'Repression of Human Rights to Personal Integrity in the 1980s: A Global Analysis', *American Political Science Review*, **88**, pp. 853–72.

Porter, Jack Nusan (1982), *Genocide and Human Rights: A Global Anthology*, Washington DC: University Press of America.

Poveda, Tony G. (1982), 'The Rise and Fall of FBI Domestic Intelligence Operations', *Contemporary Crises*, **6**, pp. 103–18.

Preston, Richard, and Wise, Sydney (1979), *Men in Arms: A History of Warfare and its Interrelationships with Western Society*, (4th edn), New York: Holt, Rinehart and Winston.

Puchala, Donald J. (1997), 'Some Non-Western Perspectives on International Relations', *Journal of Peace Research*, **34**, pp. 129–34.

Regan, Patrick M. (1995), 'The Systematic Study of the Causes of Political Repression: A Retrospective Survey with Suggestions for Further Research', *Australian Journal of Political Science*, **30**, pp. 137–45.

Regan, Richard T. (1996), *The Just War*, Washington DC: Catholic University Press.

Reitlinger, Gerald (1961), *The Final Solution: The Attempt to Exterminate the Jews of Europe 1939–1945*, New York: A.S. Barnes.

Roebuck, Julian and Weeber, S.C. (1978), *Political Crime in the United States*, New York: Praeger.

Rose-Ackerman, Susan (1978), *Corruption – A Study in Political Economy*, New York: Academic Press.

Rose-Ackerman, Susan (1996), 'Democracy and "Grand" Corruption', *International Social Science Journal*, **149**, pp. 365–80.

Ross, Jeffrey Ian (ed.) (1995), *Controlling State Crime*, NY: Garland Publishing Co.

Rubin, Barry (1987), *Modern Dictators – Third World Coup Makers, Strongmen, and Populist Tyrants*, New York: McGraw-Hill.

Rummel, R.J. (1990), *Lethal Politics: Soviet Genocide and Mass Murder Since 1917*, New Brunswick, NJ: Transaction Publishers.

Rummel, R.J. (1991), *China's Bloody Century: Genocide and Mass Murder*, New Brunswick, NJ: Transaction Publishers.

Rummel, R.J. (1992), *Democide: Nazi Genocide and Mass Murder*, New Brunswick, NJ: Transaction Publishers.

Rummel, R.J. (1994a), *Death By Government*, New Brunswick, NJ: Transaction Press.

Rummel, R.J. (1994b), 'Power, Genocide and Mass Murder', *Journal of Peace Resolution*, **31**, pp. 1–10.

Sale, Kirkpatrick (1990), *The Conquest of Paradise*, New York: Knopf.

Sanford, Nevitt, Craig Comstock and Associates (1971), *Sanctions for Evil*, Boston: Beacon Press.

Schafer, Stephen (1974), *The Political Criminal: The Problems of Morality and Crime*, New York: The Free Press.

Scheff, Thomas J. (1994), *Bloody Revenge: Emotion, Nationalism, and War*, Boulder, CO: Westview Press.

Schell, Jonathan (1982), *The Fate of the Earth*, New York: Avon.

Schwelb, Egon (1946), 'Crimes against Humanity', *The British Yearbook of International Law*, **23**, pp. 178–226.

Sciolino, Elaine (1991), *The Outlaw State – Saddam Hussein's Quest for Power and the Gulf Crisis*, New York: John Wiley.

Shank, Gregory (1991), 'Contragate and Counterterrorism: An Overview', *Crime and Social Justice*, **27–28**, pp. i–xxvii.

Shatz, Marshall (ed.) (1971), *The Essential Works of Anarchism*, New York: Bantam.

Shawcross, William (1979), *Sideshow: Kissinger, Nixon and the Destruction of Cambodia*, London: Deutsch.

Shawcross, William (1985), *The Quality of Mercy: Cambodia, Holocaust and Modern Conscience, With a Report from Ethiopia*, New York: Simon & Schuster.

Simon, David R. (1996), *Elite Deviance*, (5th edn), Boston, MA: Allyn & Bacon.

Sjoberg, Gideon, Gill, Elizabeth, Williams, Norma and Kuhn, Kathryn E. (1995), 'Ethics, Human Rights and Sociological Inquiry: Genocide, Politicide and Other Issues of Organizational Power', *The American Sociologist*, Spring, pp. 8–19.

Sparks, Allister (1990), *The Mind of South Africa*, New York: Knopf.

Stannard, David E. (1992), *American Holocaust: Columbus and the Conquest of the New World*, New York: Oxford University Press.

Staub, Ervin (1989), *The Roots of Evil: The Origins of Genocide and Other Group Violence*, Cambridge, England: Cambridge University Press.

Stohl, Michael and Lopez, George A. (eds) (1984), *The State as Terrorist: The Dynamics of Governmental Violence and Repression*, Westport, CT: Greenwood Press.

Stohl, Michael and Lopez, George (eds) (1986), *Governmental Violence and Repression: An Agenda for Research*, Westport, CT: Greenwood Press.

Stuart-Fox, Martin with Ung, Bunheang (1985), *The Murderous Revolution: Life and Death in Pol Pot's Kampuchea*, Chippendale, NSW Australia: Alternative Publishing Cooperative Ltd.

Stunton, Marie, Fenn, Sally and Amnesty International (1991), *The Amnesty International Handbook*, Claremont, CA: Hunter House.

Sutherland, Edwin H. (1940), 'White-collar Criminality', *American Sociological Review*, **5**, pp. 1–12.

Sutherland, Edwin H. (1949), *White Collar Crime*, New York: Holt, Rinehart & Winston.

Szymusiak, Molyda (1987), *The Stones Cry Out: A Cambodian Childhood, 1975–1980*, London: Jonathan Cape.

Taylor, John G. (1991), *Indonesia's Forgotten War: The Hidden History of East Timor*, London: Zed Books.

Taylor, Telford (1970), *Nuremberg and Vietnam: An American Tragedy*, New York: Bantam.

Thompson, E.P. (1985), *The Heavy Dancers*, New York: Pantheon.

Tilly, Charles (1985), 'War-Making and State-Making as Organized Crime', in Peter B. Evans, Dietrich Rueschemeyer and Theda Skocpol (eds), *Bringing the State Back in*, Cambridge, MA: Cambridge University Press, pp. 169–91.

Tunnell, Kenneth D. (ed.) (1993), *Political Crime in Contemporary America*, New York: Garland Publishing Co.

Turpin, Jennifer and Kurtz, Lester R. (1996), *The Web of Violence – From Interpersonal to Global*, Urbana: University of Illinois Press.

Uekert, Brenda K. (1995), *Rivers of Blood: A Comparative Study of Government Massacres*, New York: Praeger.

Van den Berghe, Pierre (ed.) (1990), *State Violence and Ethnicity*, Boulder, CO: University Press of Colorado.

Walliman, Isidor and Dobkowski, Michael N. (ed.) (1987), *Genocide and the Modern Age: Etiology and Case Studies of Mass Death*, New York: Greenwood Press.

Walzer, Michael (1977), *Just and Unjust Wars*, New York: Basic Books.

Wardlaw, Grant (1984–85), 'Terrorism: State Involvement Adds a New Dimension', *Pacific Defense Reporter*, **11**, pp. 59–60.

Welch, David A. (1993), *Justice and the Genesis of War*, Cambridge: Cambridge University Press.

Weyler, Rex (1992), *Blood of the Land – The Government and Corporate War Against First Nations*, Philadelphia, PA: New Society Publishers.

White, Gordon (1996), 'Corruption and the Transition from Socialism in China', *Journal of Law and Society*, **23**, pp. 149–69.

White, Ralph (ed.) (1986), *Psychology and the Prevention of Nuclear War*, New York: New York University Press.

White, Theodore H. (1975), *Breach of Faith – The Fall of Richard Nixon*, New York: Dell.

Wilkinson, Paul (1974), *Political Terrorism*, New York: John Wiley & Sons.

Wilkinson, Paul (1981), 'Can a State Be a Terrorist?', *International Affairs*, **57**, pp. 467–72.

Wilkinson, Paul (1984), 'State-Sponsored International Terrorism: The Problem of Response', *World Today*, **40**, pp. 292–98.

Williams, Christopher (1996), 'An Environmental Victimology', *Social Justice*, **23**, pp. 16–40.

Wise, David (1976), *The American Police State – The Government Against the People*, New York: Random House.

Wise, David and Ross, Thomas B. (1964), *The Invisible Government – The CIA and U.S. Intelligence*, New York: Random House.

Wolfe, Alan (1973), *Repression: The Seamy Side of Democracy*, New York: McKay and Company.

Wolff, Leon (1961), *Little Brown Brother: America's Forgotten Bid for Empire which Cost 250,000 Lives*, New York: Longmans, Green and Co.

Woodward, Bob (1987), *Veil: The Secret War of the CIA: 1981–1987*, New York: Simon and Schuster.

World Watch (1992), *Human Rights Watch World Report 1993*, New York: Human Rights Watch.

Yahil, Leni (1990), *The Holocaust: The Fate of European Jewry, 1932–1945*, New York: Oxford University Press.

Young, Marilyn (1991), *The Vietnam Wars: 1945–1990*, New York: HarperPerennial.

Part I
Conceptual, Definitional and Methodological Issues

[1]

CONCLUSION.

Politics are not above the moral law—Machiavelli's doctrines are immoral rather than profound—An immoral policy is unworthy of modern society—The moral standard of politicians is determined by public opinion—Moral beliefs are the only remedy for political corruption—Modern society is suffering from moral disease—The principles of international politics—The true field of international rivalry—International arbitration—Politics without morality mean the ruin of society.

Politics have become discredited by the employment of culpable expedients and the adoption of immoral maxims; for their reputation to be retrieved they must be brought into accord with morality. After having resorted for so long to cunning and falsehood, to intrigue and violence, politics, were it only for the novelty of the thing, should try the effect of fair dealing, tolerance, and justice. To-day, more than at any period, novelty is liked. And what greater novelty could there be than politics conducted on moral lines ? It is possible that people will end by recognising that in public as in private life honesty is the most effective and the most skilful policy. Not only should Machiavelism be loathed by honourable people, but it should be regarded as fatal to the true interests of nations. A great policy cannot be immoral. Craft and violence may

340

CONCLUSION.   341

score ephemeral successes, but they do not assure the greatness and prosperity of a country. The successes achieved by an immoral policy are not lasting; sooner or later nations, like individuals, politicians, just as private persons, are punished for the evil or rewarded for the good they do. Political crimes are punished more often than is supposed. Those who put their adversaries to death by poison or upon the scaffold often undergo a like fate; those who send others into exile are exiled in their turn.

There is more immorality than profoundness in Machiavelism. It was not a shifty and violent policy that was pursued by Saint Louis, L'Hopital, Henry IV., Sully, Turgot, Franklin, or Washington. Their example shows that it is possible to be a great King, a great Minister, a great citizen, and at the same time an honest man. On the other hand, mighty geniuses have been the ruin of the peoples they have governed, because they despised justice and pursued a Machiavelian policy. Napoleon I., who was solely guided by reasons of State, lost his senses in the end and embarked upon the war in Spain and the Russian campaign. Danton and Robespierre, who did not lack talent, brought the Republic to ruin through trying to save it by the Terror. Liberty is not to be imposed by the guillotine; fraternity is not established by the extermination of its adversaries; the reign of justice and equality is not founded by popular or judicial massacres.

The disciples of Machiavelli declare that politicians should resort to violence and even to crime, if to do so be necessary for the safety of the people, but what they call the safety of the people is often nothing more than the safety of their rule. The authors of the 18th Fructidor, who carried out that *coup d'état* under pretext of saving the Republic, violated the law solely with a view to escaping a personal danger; and far from saving the Republic, by demanding the intervention of a general they created a precedent for the 18th Brumaire. The public safety is an excuse for all violence and every iniquity. Moreover, when a political crime is really committed to assure the safety of the people, there is no proof that the crime is necessary, or that the people might not have been saved by other means. The safety of the people lies rather in respect for legality than in its violation. A people that does its duty can await the future with confidence; if it suffers for the moment in the cause of justice it is rare that the day of reparation does not dawn, for in the case of nations, as in that of individuals, it is virtues that elevate them and vices that debase them.

A Machiavelian policy is not a great policy; to practise it a great genius is not necessary. It is easier to govern by expedients than by principles. What is more, there has ceased to be any necessity for a policy of this sort in modern societies. It is comprehensible that Machiavelli's prince, that is to say, an absolute sovereign,

CONCLUSION.   343

should find it to his interest to sow division among his subjects in order to rule them; on the other hand, the maxim, "Promote division in order to reign," is out of place in a free Government that is supported by opinion and whose interest it is to unite and not to divide the community. Terror may be an instrument of government for a popular or military dictator, but it becomes inapplicable under a government of opinion. This being the case, instead of saying, as under the old system of politics, "Cunning, still cunning, and always cunning; audacity, again audacity, and always audacity," the watchword ought to be under the modern system of politics, "Straightforwardness, still straightforwardness, and always straightforwardness; justice, still justice, and always justice."

Diplomatic dissimulation becomes more difficult with the publication of parliamentary debates. This publicity, which has its inconveniences, offers the advantage that it is profitable to morality. It is impossible for a Minister to confess in a public discussion that he harbours unjust projects. Moreover, as public opinion becomes more enlightened, and acquires greater weight, its sound common sense takes the place of the finessing of the diplomatists. A crafty policy is not always the most skilful. Henry IV. did not have recourse to craft.[1] A diplomatist who is in

---

[1] When he was still merely the King of Navarre, he declared with justifiable pride in a proclamation: "Who can reproach the King of Navarre with having ever broken his word?"

344   *POLITICAL CRIME.*

the habit of resorting to falsehood ceases to inspire confidence and at once loses the greater part of his authority.

A policy based upon immorality is antiquated and unworthy of modern society; it pre-supposes contempt for humanity, and an antagonism that ought not to exist between those who govern and those who are governed. The policy of free peoples ought not to resemble the policy of absolute sovereigns; it is founded upon the respect of legality.

Whatever the sceptics may say, craft and violence are not necessities of politics. As society becomes more enlightened, politics may attain to greater perfection. Corruption is not an indispensable method of government; liberty can exist without license. It is allowable to hope for a state of things in which the administration will be impartial, the legislation equitable, the elections sincere, and in which industry and merit will be rewarded. The European Governments show better faith in respect to their financial engagements at the present day than in the past; they are conscious that it is to their interest not to tamper with their coinage, and not to go bankrupt, and for the reason that public confidence in their credit is their principal force. Why should they not arrive at understanding that they ought to have the same respect for liberty and human life as for the public debt?

The progress of public reasonableness is most of all to be counted upon to render politics more

CONCLUSION.   345

straightforward and more in accordance with
equity. Politicians, assemblies, and sovereigns,
knowing that they will be called upon to give an
exact account of their conduct before the tribunal
of public opinion, will become more circumspect
in the employment of expedients of a kind to
arouse public indignation. Politics should serve
an educational purpose as well as maintain
order and protect material interests. Men are
governed by ideas and sentiments as well as by
appeals to their interests and to force. A lofty
sentiment does not spoil politics. The great
advances made in the sphere of politics have
been advances of a philosophical order and have
been due to an application of Christian philosophy.
Unprincipled politics are Pagan politics, and their
result is not the progress of society. The true
policy consists in an application of reason to the
affairs of the State.

Scepticism has brought into existence at the
present day a generation of politicians who set
more store upon palpable realities than upon
principles. A policy of expedients and of vulgar
satisfactions is the outcome of scepticism. The
change that has taken place in our political
morals has deep and remote causes. A people
that used to be chivalrous, that despised money,
that was fired with ardour for noble causes, now
for political liberty, now for military glory, does
not become positively sceptical, indifferent to
principles, and attached to material interests in
a day. This change of character is the result of

the numerous deceptions it has experienced, of the frequent revolutions it has undergone, but also of the weakening of spiritual beliefs.

"When a republic is corrupt," says Montesquieu, "none of the evils that crop up can be remedied, except by removing the corruption and reinstating principles; any other corrective is useless or a fresh evil."[1] The suppression of the parliamentary régime would not be a remedy, the establishment of a dictatorship would be a fresh evil and a worse evil. The true remedy consists in a return to principles. Politics, like human life, need to be spiritualised unless they are to fall into the mire and to remain there. To change the persons composing the political world would be insufficient, unless a moral reform be effected at the same time. Clearly if the new politicians were as devoid of principles as the old, all that would have been done would have been to exchange fat for lean kine, who in turn would wish to wax fat. Between fatted sceptics and lean sceptics the difference is but slight, or if there be any difference it is rather in favour of the former. Obviously satiated sceptics are less dangerous than sceptics whose appetites are keen, because it may be hoped that, having looked after their own interests, they will at last look after those of the country. This, according to Saint Simon, was the cynical remark made by Maison when the direction of the finances was taken from him. "They are making a mistake,"

---

[1] "Esprit des Lois," Bk. VIII., ch. xii.

CONCLUSION.   347

he exclaimed, "for I had looked after my own interests and was going to look after theirs."

A return to principles and moral beliefs and the substitution of ideas for appetites are, in consequence, the true remedies for that hideous malady political corruption. It is only in the power of great passions to drive petty passions from the field. As long as noble sentiments, love of country and of liberty and purifying beliefs, are not revived in a country the parliamentary atmosphere will remain vitiated.

Doubtless to exercise authority it is not sufficient to be above reproach; a clear intellect, tact, and experience are necessary. Talent, however, without morality is insufficient, and mere intelligence is no preservative against moral backslidings. Nobody would entrust his daughters or his fortune to the care of a clever but dissolute and extravagant man. Why then confide the country and the public fortune to the care of men of pleasure, who easily develop into men whose sole concern is money? When a money- and pleasure-loving man declares himself a friend of the people, who can believe in his sincerity? Affection is not proved by words, but by acts. The true sentiments of politicians are not to be judged by their professions of faith or their humanitarian speeches, but by their character and their habitual conduct. The probity expected of the head of a Government involves not only his own personal integrity, but the choice on his part of men of integrity for his Ministers. "If we

348 *POLITICAL CRIME.*

would pass for men of integrity," says Cicero, "we should not only display probity ourselves, but exact it of those about us."[1]

Statesmen would avoid many political errors if they were more respectful of justice; their political errors are often moral errors; their good sense and their skilfulness suffer in proportion as they swerve from the dictates of equity; they abandon themselves to passions that cloud their intelligence. Just ideas and wise resolutions are inspired by an upright conscience, whose qualities influence the intelligence. To be a man of good sense it is sufficient to be an honest man.

By again becoming moral, politics would be brought back into unison with common-sense, and would be cured of two serious diseases called the Socialist madness and the Anarchist madness that are the result of the sophisms by which we are inundated, and of the letting loose of evil passions. We lack reasonableness at the present day; our brains are disordered; our good sense, a quality that used to be particularly distinctive of the French, has been affected by innumerable philosophical, economical, and political sophisms that reach us from Germany, Italy, England, the East, and even from India. Good sense has ceased to guide our thoughts and actions since we have adopted German pessimism and socialism, English evolutionism, Italian scepticism, Russian Nihilism, and Asiatic Buddhism. Let us become Frenchmen again and Christians,

[1] " Second Speech against Verres," Bk. II., § 10.

CONCLUSION.   349

let us return to the school of good sense and morality.

The malady from which contemporary society suffers is a moral disease rather than a political or economical disease. It is doubtless useful to improve institutions and to reform abuses, but how much more necessary it is to reform morals and to give tone to men's minds by healthy ideas and moral beliefs. If society is to be saved from the corruption by which it is invaded, and from the revolutionary barbarism by which it is threatened, spiritualist teachings must be restored to the place they formerly occupied in men's minds and in politics; this is the only way to save them from the clutches of envy and hatred.

The sentiment of duty and of personal responsibility must be re-established in the public mind and in the education of the young. It is necessary to fight against the sophisms which lead to the absorption of the individual by the State, and to the conversion of every citizen into a part of a colossal machine that produces wealth and distributes it according to each man's needs. The true remedy for the crises we are traversing is a return to the old morality, which teaches that working-men in common with their employers are intended to do their duty, and to labour, and have their responsibilities. What other doctrine will teach the rich the spirit of sacrifice, and the voluntary renunciation of what is superfluous, and the poor the obligation of personal effort, the merit of patience, and respect for legality?

350   *POLITICAL CRIME.*

It is not by encouraging atheism and materialism that a Government effects an improvement
in morals, that it stills passions and relieves
wretchedness. Hostility to religion is contrary to
sound politics. Merely from the utilitarian point
of view the blindness and perversity are incomparable of those incredulous fanatics who would
rob their fellows of the beliefs in which they find
consolation. Who can deny that the religious
sentiment conduces to morality? The more
religious citizens there are in a State, the fewer
are the restless spirits, the Socialists and the
Anarchists. In a period of scepticism, materialism, positivism, evolutionism, and nihilism, who
can dream of denying the immense services rendered by Christianity in inculcating the dignity of
human nature and the obligatory character of
duty, and in opposing the worship of an ideal to
the worship of the golden calf? In a society in
which there is talk of nothing else but of the
struggle for life, of the rights conferred by might,
of the elimination of the weak, of the disgrace of
poverty, of the all-powerfulness of wealth, religion
teaches self-sacrifice, respect, and love for the
poor, and responsibility before God and before the
conscience. At a period in which Socialism,
grown more and more threatening, demands that
the State should be omnipotent, Christianity again
performs a useful work in standing out for the
rights of the human being and the rights of the
conscience, and in setting limits to the action of
the State. If spiritual beliefs were not regaining

their hold over men's minds one would be forced
to tremble for the future of society, for "there
comes a day when truths that have been scorned
announce themselves by thunder-claps."[1]

Nations, too, in their mutual relations, have
every interest not to separate politics from morality. A sound policy, no less than morality, dictates to them justice and charitableness, which
are alone capable of preserving peace and with it
the benefits it carries in its train. The policy
that teaches nations that they should envy, hate,
and injure each other, that their conduct should
be solely guided by their interests, and that the
difficulties that crop up between them should be
settled by force alone, such a policy is criminal
and mistaken. The statesmen who counsel this
narrow and egoistical, this envious and malevolent policy, are shortsighted, they are merely alive
to the interests of the moment that are a source
of division, but they are blind to the interests
which the peoples have in common, and above all
to the disastrous consequences of antagonism
and war; they do not keep in view the benefits
of peace and the horrors of war.

How far preferable to an envious and ambitious
policy that divides nations would be a just,
friendly, and moderate policy that would bring
them together! How far happier the nations
would be if they would cease to lend themselves
to a revengeful and high-handed policy! What a
pitch of prosperity Europe would have reached if,

[1] E. Augier, "La Contagion," Act IV., scene iv.

realising the project of Henry IV., it had applied
to politics the rules of good sense and Christian
morality. The aspect of the world would be
changed if the nations, considering themselves
members of the same family, would banish violence and craft from their councils. The policy
of Christian peoples is still Pagan: it must become
Christian if the world is to enjoy peace.

Carried away by his somewhat excessive
enthusiasm for military glory, M. Thiers has
remarked: "What purpose would the strength of
nations serve if it were not expended in attempts
to gain the mastery over each other?" It seems
to me, however, that the strength of nations
might be more usefully employed than in realising
dreams of conquest, which are so dearly paid for
in money and blood, and which end in disasters
and catastrophes. Every time that a nation has
sought to conquer other nations, it has caused
torrents of blood to flow without profit to itself.
All those who have entertained dreams of conquest have met with failure. To establish their
supremacy Charles V. and Napoleon I. caused
millions of men to perish, and they were unable to
attain their goal: the former died in a convent,
the latter on the rocks of Saint Helena; Spain
and France were ruined by their ambitious policy.
To how many conquerors may not these words of
the Bible be applied: "The hammer that shattered
the nations of the universe has itself been broken
in pieces."

A policy that aims at international equilibrium

CONCLUSION. 353

is better than a policy of conquest.[1] Empires that are too vast cannot last; they succumb, sooner or later, to a coalition between the other nations. That one nation should rule over another is always a danger to the common liberty, for a nation that is too powerful, like a too powerful sovereign, has a difficulty in keeping within the limits of a wise moderation. If the desire for domination be of value as a motive force in politics, why should not moral domination achieved through science, literature, and institutions be made the object of the activity of nations?

Sceptics are disposed to smile when they hear moralists express the hope that international wars will cease, and that arbitration will take the place of recourse to force. Lord Salisbury, however, who at one time considered this hope a dream, is now of opinion that it is realisable. "Civilisation," he has said, "has substituted law court decisions for duels between private persons and conflicts between the great. International wars are destined in the same way to give place to the courts of arbitration of a more advanced civilisation."[2] In 1883 Switzerland and the

[1] "I have persistently shown myself to be hostile to conquest; I was not even willing, at the time of our greatest military prosperity, that we should make the Rhine the limit of our territory." ("Exposé de la Conduite Politique de M. Carnot," p. 50.)

[2] Speech delivered at Hastings, May 18, 1892. I borrow this quotation from a very interesting paper by M. Arthur Desjardins ("Académie des Sciences Morales et Politiques," July, 1892). Henry IV., who was in no way a dreamer, had considered possible the substitution of arbitration for the employment of force, and the constitution of a European confederation.

354 *POLITICAL CRIME.*

United States pledged themselves to submit to a court of arbitration all difficulties arising between them during a period of thirty years. In 1888 France contracted a similar engagement with the Equatorial Republic. In 1890 the plenipotentiaries of seventeen American Republics, assembled at Washington, admitted the principle of permanent arbitration.

It may be hoped, in consequence, that war will become rarer and rarer in proportion to the progress of civilisation and of the moral and economical solidarity existing between different nations. The new engines of war, the destructive force of which augments every day, also contribute to the maintenance of peace, because peoples and sovereigns recoil in terror from the frightful consequences of a war waged with such formidable engines of destruction. The tendency of public opinion is more and more to compel Governments to maintain peace. It may be hoped in consequence that war, which is already more civilised, will become of rarer occurrence.

Sully, whom this idea had caused to smile in the first instance, ended by esteeming it possible. "I remember," he says, "that the first time I heard the King discuss a political system by which all Europe might be divided and governed like a family, I scarcely listened to the Prince. Thinking that he only spoke in this way to amuse himself, or perhaps to have the honour of having profounder and more acute opinions upon politics than ordinary men, my answer assumed partly a jesting tone, partly a tone of compliment. . . . I was convinced at the finish that, however disproportioned the means might seem to the end, a series of years during which every act, whether in connection with negotiations, finances, or the remaining necessary matters, should constantly be made to bear upon the object in view, would smooth away many difficulties."

CONCLUSION.   **355**

Still, as peoples and sovereigns have a tendency to become intoxicated by success, historians and moralists ought to unite their efforts to combat their unruly impulses. Historians, who habitually admire success, too often forget, when narrating wars, to inquire into their morality and utility; they almost always exalt the conquerors, and in this way corrupt public opinion, by accustoming it to allow itself to be dazzled by success. They should keep a little of the admiration they lavish upon conquerors for the upright men who have given evidence of their love of humanity and of their respect for human life.

As to the moralists, it is necessary that they should unceasingly combat the sophisms of immoral politics by declaring that reasons of State are the negation of reason; that the object of government is not to divide but to unite; that the lesser morality does not destroy the higher morality, because there are not two moralities; that public safety lies in justice alone; that the end does not justify the means; that illegitimate means result in the end being unattained; that right is superior to might; that justice is the supreme law; that the maxim that right is on the side of the strongest is a maxim good enough for wolves but not for men.

Science without conscience, Rabelais has said, is the ruin of the soul. Politics without morality are the ruin of society.

THE END.

[2]

Counting Bodies: the Dismal Science of Authorized Terror

In the bitter, so-called scientific study of state-sponsored terror or the mass destruction of human beings, few factors have been as telling, or as contentious, as raw numbers. The evidence for the presence of genocide rests, after all, on the body counts of untold victims whose remains attest to the tragedy in which they participated – usually unwillingly and often unknowingly. I call the study of genocide an excercise in *counting bodies*; the assessment which follows also constitutes a footnote to my earlier work.[1]

In raw numerical terms, the source of the killing in this century tells the story: governments have been directly responsible for the deaths of roughly 120 million people, while war (both international and civil) accounts for thirty-five million deaths. In other words, in this century, really in the last forty-five years, over three-and-a-half times more people have been killed by their own governments than by opposing states.[2]

A further breakdown reveals that of the 120 million killed by their own governments, over 95 milllion have been in communist states, and another 20 million in non-communist, authoritarian states. What we are dealing with is not some side-show in this century, but increasingly the main event – perhaps the only event, given the increasingly high risk of conventional warfare in this post-nuclear environment.

The importance of body counts is at least as well recognized by perpetrators of systematic acts of destruction as by those victims seeking moral restitution and historical recognition. Thus, in every major genocide, government authorities responsible for genocide have contested the numbers of victims involved. Whilst there may be something grisly about determining the qualitative worth of a genocide by the quantitative figures involved, the need to convert such data into a meaningful theoretical construct that helps us appreciate the grim potentials of state-sponsored murder is manifest.

I should like to examine the current theoretical interest in state-sponsored mayhem, and indicate how known information on the number of

PATTERNS OF PREJUDICE, vol. 23, no. 2, 1989

Reproduced with permission from Irving Louis Horowitz , 'Counting Bodies: The Dismal Science of Authorized Terror', © (1989), by permission of Sage Publications Ltd. Originally appeared in *Patterns of Prejudice* in a volume edited by David O. Friedrichs on *State Crime*.

people killed can affect such larger considerations.[3] I shall restrict myself to
the following paired concepts: (1) natural forms of catastrophe as distinct
from socially sanctioned murder; (2) systematic slaughter versus accidental
or random killing; (3) genocide as distinct from warfare; (4) state-sanctioned
murder in contrast to extra-legal terror; and (5) actual body counts as
distinct from symbolic or cultural assaults. I am not engaging in
Manicheism, or in contrasting good and evil. Rather, my purpose here is to
explore significant distinctions in the authority of states ranging from pale
grey to pitch black.

These five constructs by no means exhaust ways of looking at genocidal
data; but taken as a cluster they do provide general theoretical guidelines for
addressing, and ultimately resolving, long-standing concerns in the evolution of social research. This may appear to be a rather meagre recompense
for the punishment absorbed by millions. But insofar as social research can
provide a basis for early warning signals, and help prevent future mayhem
and murder, this is at least a useful starting place.[4]

There remain serious obstacles to incorporating the study of genocide as
part of the core rather than periphery of research in political sociology.
Qualitative problems cannot readily be ignored. For example, how does one
distinguish between state-sponsored terror, quasi-sponsored terror through
private armies, like the Ton Ton Macoutes in Haiti, and anti-state forms of
terrorist activities such as that practised by Bader-Meinhoff in Germany, or
the Red Brigades of Italy and Japan, and countless other groups and individuals. Literally thousands of groups currently operate outside the law
and in accordance with moral codes that seek nothing less than the radical
transformation of civilization; and failing that goal, its destruction.[5]

Terrorism is a technique available to all and seemingly used by all.
There are Armenian groups in opposition to Turkish groups; anti-
communist alliances against communist-dominated guerrillas; Afghan collectives and Jewish brigades; pro-Chinese versus pro-Albanian factions
within communist groups; religious and secular revolutionary groups within
the Arab world. Unlike genocidal conditions, terrorism often involves a
strange balance of extra-governmental forces — a balance that prevents 'final
solutions'.

In this century, terrorism has become a basic norm, no less than a form
of political combat using military and extra-legal means. Having
acknowledged this, the very plurality of terrorist clusters ensures a strange
democracy of the smoking gun. At the very least, this pluralism of the extremes makes improbable the easy triumph of any single group, and denies
any one individual the possibility of mobilizing a state for genocidal destruction. This distinguishes the present epoch from the earlier pre-Second World
War period in which there was a concentration of weapons, as well as conspiracies, in comparatively few hands.[6]

On the other hand, terrorism is sometimes justified as a defence of the

6 Counting Bodies: the Dismal Science of Authorized Terror

present, of the state as such. Emissaries of Turkey, for example, constantly adduce this argument when they reject the claim that the Armenians were simply dangerous secessionists. Another caveat is that lumping together all people numerically fails to distinguish between those truly subject to genocidal massacre and those being killed as an adjunct of a wartime effort, as is the case with the official Nigerian position on the civil wars (with Biafra) of the 1960s; or for that matter, the war in Afghanistan in the 1980s.

Simply providing raw quantitative data does not resolve outstanding qualitative problems. However, the statistical study of genocide does make possible the resolution of some long-standing issues in the distinction between democracy and dictatorship, issues that have long awaited an objective indicator so that this distinction can become a useful heuristic device in the research and policy communities.

Perhaps it is wise to think differently about this newest entry into the dismal science of society. Genocide may best be viewed in terms of paired opposites, or at least contrasting nuances. This may be the best way to incorporate the horrors of the twentieth century into the common vernacular of social science, and hence transform the study of mass murder by state power into an early warning system against just such disastrous events.

Distinguishing the natural from the social

The first and perhaps all too obvious point to make in the study of genocide is that it differs in kind and nature from the study of plagues. The spread of the bubonic or black plague in the fourteenth and fifteenth centuries of Europe was catastrophic by any standard of measurement. Between 1346-1350 it is believed that the disease put an end to the population rise that had characterized later medieval society. Within this four-year period, Europe lost roughly twenty million lives because of the 'Great Dying' or 'The Pestilence' which, apparently, was carried through bites from fleas on rodents throughout Europe and Asia.

Even though the causes of the plague remained virtually unknown until nearly the beginning of the twentieth century, various pathological explanations were offered. These focused on punishment for sins and transgressions, but the natural or pathogenic sources of the plague had a binding effect on the population, through a realization that larger, mysterious forces were allied against the human race as a whole, and hence had to be dealt with in some sort of uniform manner. Travellers were quarantined, strangers ostracized and passengers diverted to other shores. But the natural or supernatural basis of the plague did not generate struggles between peoples.

In the case of genocide — and again, at the risk of labouring the obvious — the source of mass death is known to be social, that is, the liquidation of human beings by other humans. As a result, the divisive consequence of genocide contrasts markedly with the unifying character of the bubonic plagues. In the concentration camps, who shall perish was diabolically jux-

taposed against who shall live. Genocide was selective and systematic, not individual and random. The human objects selected for perdition were chosen
'anthropologically', as the Nazis liked to say: on the basis of religion, ethnicity, race, or other ascribed features. This is a radically different and quite
twentieth century invention, in contrast to plagues which were not so much
an invention as a series of unplanned catastrophes.

Before leaving the theme of the distinction between the natural and the
social, it is important to remind ourselves of the continuities of life. This
theme, so brilliantly and beautifully articulated by the late Loren Eiseley,[7]
has sometimes degenerated into a mystic pantheism that is self-defeating.
But in its purest form, it is an awareness that all life has a common basis and
common origins, and hence is worthy of our respect. Earlier arguments
about the levels of life and their worth, or whether the human species is the
fulfilment of other forms of life, as Darwin held, have now shifted. In this
sense, the emergence of sociobiology is a powerful instrument for sensitizing
the human race about its continuities with the natural environment. But this
remains only a caveat. Discontinuities of the biological and the sociological
remain the bedrock for distinguishing between natural plagues and artificial, that is humanly willed, genocides.

Distinguishing the Holocaust from genocides

One of the most nettlesome and contentious issues involves claimants for
Holocaust status.[8] Why should this be an issue to begin with? Perhaps the
answer lies in the awareness that, even within categories of genocide, there
are gradations of horror. Each victimized group wishes to claim the ultimate
honour for itself. A review of the situation of Poland under German occupation should shed some light on the distinction between genocide and the
Holocaust.

Between 1939 and 1945, some three million non-Jewish Poles, about 10
per cent of the population, were murdered by the Nazis. During this same
period three million Jews living in Poland were also annihilated, about 90-95
per cent of the Jewish population in this nation. The fact that, in both cases,
each group lost three million people disguises the fact that the Polish nation,
and 90 per cent of Poles, survived the war. The Jewish community of Poland
was eradicated. And the small number of Jews that did survive Nazism did
not survive the subsequent waves of communist repression in that country.

Lucy Dawidowicz[9] has commented on this unique example of a
Holocaust and a genocide taking place at the same time within one land. She
put the issues squarely:

However much the Poles suffered under the German occupation — and they suffered
gravely — their situation was not comparable to that of the Jews. The Jews were a national minority of three million; the Poles the majority of over 30 million. The Jews,
before they were murdered, were locked inside ghettos, deprived of their freedom of
movement; the Poles were allowed a minimum of local self-government and mobility
within their places of residence. The Jews were being systematically starved; the Poles

8 Counting Bodies: the Dismal Science of Authorized Terror

were undernourished. The Jews were altogether denied medical care and medicines. The Jews had no military supplies; the underground Polish Home Army had considerable reserves of material.

In short, the Germans doomed the Poles to bondage and slavery; they condemned the Jews to annihilation.[10]

In the Nazi Holocaust we had the definite presence of racist, annihilating behaviour which was directed specifically against the Jews. This pariah status was absent even in such diabolical and widespread genocides as those launched against the Armenian people. Even Armenian analysts have drawn a distinction between an effort to exterminate, as conducted against the Jews, with a 'pronounced effort to mingle Armenian blood with the gene-pool of the new homogenized Turkish nation'.[11] Such Turkish actions, and the later Nazi effort to integrate the Aryan-looking Poles into the Greater German hegemony, indicate traditional dominant class efforts to convert the infidels and the heathens, and the use of selective killing as a mode of intimidation and persuasion.

In both the Armenian and Polish cases, we are dealing with terrible tragedies. But the fact that there was little racism in the ideology that authorized and legitimized the liquidation of large portions of both peoples, raises anew the need for an analysis that would permit us to condemn all forms of torture and torment while carefully distinguishing the Holocaust from genocide, and even widespread pogroms and selective assaults upon a minority group by a majority system, from the collective destruction of a whole people, otherwise known as genocide.

We have a paired set of continuums: history does not proceed in a straight line from genocide to civility, from state-sponsored murder to limits on the state by its citizens. Instead, we have circumstances, in even the most highly developed nations, when the distinction must be made between the collective and total murder of a population, and a selective and partial murder of a subject population. And grim though this distinction may be, the failure to make it would result in a reprehensible misrepresentation of history no less than a profound error in the social analysis of the sources of genocide.

Distinguishing genocide from warfare
Increasingly, a consensus is developing that genocide is to suicide what warfare is to murder: that is to say, genocide is a self-inflicted wound by the state upon its own subjects; whereas warfare is the defence of the state against external incursions, or when offensive, the attempt to eliminate external enemies or to seize an advantage by their defeat.

Another way of formulating this issue is to see genocide as an advanced form of state terrorism, a premeditated use by elites within a society to maintain or extend their power over a target group within the same state which is perceived as a threat. Those states with long histories of internal repression tend to be the same ones that have exhibited patterns of genocide in modern times. Czarist Russian traditions were continued and refined rather than terminated under Stalinist rule in the Soviet Union; the same can be said, to a lesser degree, of the changeover, otherwise structurally deep, from the Ottoman Empire to the Turkish Republic.

It is important to note that wars are made by people upon other people. Democratic and libertarian states, no less than repressive or totalitarian states, make war as an instrument of foreign policy. Indeed, wars have been fought between democratic and authoritarian states throughout the twentieth century. And while this is by no means a simple struggle between good and evil, the fact does remain that wars are common to all sorts of social systems. Genocide, on the other hand, defines a particular social system — the totalitarian system.

Civil conflicts often create moral ambiguities for outsiders. Struggles endemic to a single nation sometimes take on such extraordinary proportions that charges and claims of genocide are raised. Here we may confine ourselves to the Nigerian Civil War, in which the internal struggle between the Hausa and Ibo peoples spilled over into genocidal patterns. Some have estimated that three million people died in this struggle, and have blamed the indifference of the advanced nations and the hypocrisy of the United Nations.[12] But the fact remains that a civil war was transformed into a systematic effort to destroy a people. One might place the autogenocide which took place in Cambodia under Khmer Rouge domination in a similar category of national horror that acted in the name of national liberation.

Soon after the fall of Biafra in 1970, a modest relief effort began. What the relief workers found represents the outer limits of warfare and the initial stages of a genocide: of an estimated 5.8 million Ibos, 970,000 suffered from oedema, marasmus or kwashiorkor. Nearly one third of Biafra's children showed signs of severe malnutrition, and these were the lucky ones. It was too late for the estimated one million Ibos who had died — in part as a result of the Nigerian government's blockade of humanitarian relief during the war.

The rules of war in advanced nations become muddled when war is conducted without rules in the less developed nations. Indeed the level of social and economic development of a nation extends to how it conducts conflicts: when a society has firm and clear rules of combat, then the civilian-military distinctions are much sharper than in areas of the world where such standards for conflict do not obtain.

Distinguishing state-sponsored murder from all other forms of state-sponsored violence and misanthropy

Perhaps the most troublesome category confronting the analyst of genocide is those forms of state-sponsored mayhem that fall short of collective murder, but not by much. Deportation is such an instance. A claim frequently made

10 Counting Bodies: the Dismal Science of Authorized Terror

by students of the Armenian genocide is that the Turkish mass deportation of Armenians from their cultural and geographical roots constituted a protracted form of genocide, since Armenians, so dislodged, could not recreate their society or culture in a generationally meaningful way.[13] The difficulty with this argument is that however nasty, brutish and difficult such a life became, there was no explicit physical dismemberment. This absence is critical: the Turkish beys, like the Czarist counts, were cruel and malevolent beyond words, but the Armenians survived as a people, as did the Jews of pre-Communist Russia.

A more dramatic example is the recent experience of the Kurds, a people whom Turkey, Iran, Iraq and Syria have all tried to assimilate – but to no avail. In the current decade, the Iraqis have probably been the most savage: some 300,000 Kurds have been forcibly deported from their mountainous regions, and resettled in the deserts of the South.[14] This Arabization policy extended to the division of contiguous Kurdish lands and finally to the outright destruction of Kurdish villages. When this failed to disperse the Kurds as a people, 3,500 out of 5,000 Kurdish villages were destroyed, and chemical weapons were used against the people. It is estimated that 100,000 Kurds have perished, while 500,000 have been relocated.

The level of atrocity against Kurds is systematic and brutal, involving the loss of a great many lives, the forceful assimilation of people into new regions, and just about every horror that can be adduced. In the face of such overwhelming tragedy and evidence of destruction, the United Nations failed even to pass a resolution on the illegitimacy of chemical warfare. And yet, without passing moral judgment on who suffers more, the living or the dead, the fact remains that the Kurdish people have survived as a people. The question of 'amnesty' for the Kurds may be vile and hypocritical on the part of Iraq, but the fact that it has been offered shows the absence of a genocidal programme to annihilate totally a thriving people.

One scholar of African genocide has recently introduced the notion of 'selective genocide', looking specifically at the treatment of the Hutus by the Tutsi people in Burundi.[15] In 1972, it was estimated that 100,000 Hutus were killed in retribution for their effort to seize power from the Tutsi-dominated government. And again in 1988, when a local struggle between Tutsi and Hutu villagers erupted into a broad-ranging struggle to oust a mayor, the Burundi army moved in, shooting every Hutu in sight. Estimates of the number of Hutus killed range from 5,000 to 20,000 victims, plus another 40,000 who fled to neighbouring Rwanda – again to the colossal silence of world bodies of law and order.

But calling this assault on the Hutu people a genocide is as problematic as is using the term genocide with respect to the massacre of the Kurdish people. Despite the brutality and the savagery involved, the Hutu people survive, and the dominant regime denies any systematic effort at total destruction of a whole people. In this sense, the use of such terms as selective

genocide, like the notion of cultural genocide, is essentially an emotive effort
to lay claim to the special character of mass murder, perhaps to heighten the
sense of the horrors these oft-neglected peoples have experienced.

It may seem terribly harsh to make such surgical distinctions between
varieties of death and varieties of cruelty. But that is precisely the challenge
that social research must confront in the study of genocide. Such careful
distinctions are made not for the purpose of choosing between forms of evil,
but in order to evaluate what consequences these evils bring about. As
Goethe said, in the real world, the choices that one makes are not so much
between good and evil, as between forms of evil. And the study of such forms
shows what separates death, the ultimate punishment allowing no retribution or correction, from all other forms of victimization where, in theory at
least, recovery if not retribution is possible.

There will be honest differences of opinion and continuing debate on
such concepts as gradations of genocide as well as the distinction of genocide
from other forms of statist assault on human dignity and tranquillity. But
out of the ashes of such debates and discussions an honest social science can
emerge, one with the power of quantitative analysis on one hand, and the
force of moral judgement on the other. This, at any rate, is the promise of
the widespread study of genocide now underway in many lands and many
contexts.[16] One can take only small comfort in the fact that social theory is
developing such concepts as the measurement of deaths *vis-à-vis* forms of
mayhem. But this does not negate the responsibility of the social sciences to
join forces in order to combine the best of the value-free traditions of study
with the value-linked approaches to policy on genocide.

Distinguishing between actual and symbolic genocide

For those who would instruct others on the meaning of the Holocaust and
genocide in general, there is a need to avoid cheapening this whole tragic
theme by spreading its meaning to include cultural deprivation or the
punishment of select individuals, even if they symbolically represent whole
populations. The lynching of blacks in the Reconstruction period was terrible. But at its worst epidemic proportions just prior to the First World War it
could be measured in hundreds per annum. The bulk of the black population was suppressed and discriminated against, but it was not summarily liquidated. In this very fact there is an essential distinction to be made between a democratic United States and a totalitarian Nazi Germany.

Likewise, one must distinguish between such things as exile and death.
The Mariel boat lift sent 125,000 Cubans to American shores. This was a
tragic episode in the life of Cuba, but it was not a disastrous episode in the
lives of Cubans. That distinction is significant for its post-exilic consequences. Likewise, it may be true that the Koreans were used as slave labour
and systematically deprived of their culture throughout the Japanese occupation of 1910-1945. But this too was a reversible process, and ultimately,

12 Counting Bodies: the Dismal Science of Authorized Terror

a failed policy. And here we must make sharp distinctions within less than democratic regimes, no less than between systems of political rule.

The point is hard to accept in emotional terms, but all the more significant in empirical terms: actual genocides involve real deaths. These deaths are not reversible by posthumous rehabilitation, party edict, or collective assumptions of guilt. They are finite events that are final as well as finite. So-called symbolic or cultural genocide, whether experienced by the Irish, the blacks or the Koreans, is reversible. However, the very attention which the issue of genocide inspires aims precisely to reverse trends of neglect or cultural suppression.

That said, it would be dangerous and a disservice to the sobriety of this topic to melt the specific notion of genocide into a general discourse on human failings. To do so is to convert into pestilence and decimation all the tragic injuries human beings heap on each other. In short, it is to trivialize and sentimentalize the subject of genocide. Most forms of exploitation and decimation are tragic but also finite; subject over time to correction. It is the irreversibility of state murder that gives the subject of genocide its unique and awesome dimension. And the study of genocide gives to the social sciences a tool for the analysis of whole societies, one that puts the social sciences back in touch with common sense, not to mention with the common people they so often claim to serve.

Distinguishing the collective from the individual

A key distinct quality of genocide is its collective nature. This is a source of anguish when it comes to attributing responsibility. Unlike criminal behaviour and punishment of criminals, genocide does not involve individuals acting on their own initiative, who may be punished. For genocide carries the force of law no less than the power of the state. The valiant efforts of the Nuremberg trials notwithstanding, confusion and ambiguity on the subject of genocide remain because human liquidation is done in the name of state authority, and with legal sanction. Hence the executioners are in part relieved of any feeling of transgression or guilt by the official character and collective nature of genocide.[17] Punishment is carried out by impersonal forces, extending from special militia to engineering corps.

The very inability to identify specific individuals who carry out such crimes, and who are punishable for such crimes, is a basic characteristic of genocidal environments. An additional problem is the often-encountered failure to identify individual victims which makes escape from punishment as well as from moral judgement possible. In democratic societies, collective guilt is not a concept readily admitted. Indeed, individual punishment for specific crimes is the very essence of liberal environments. The complex legal issues which genocide raises make it clear that punishment of war criminals is not the same as attributing responsibility for mass murder. The difference between national leaders, middle echelon bureaucrats, technicians carrying out instructions and general populations which are compliant, all point to the need for an area of law that has yet to come into its own nearly half a century after the Holocaust.

In Raul Hilberg's study of how the German railway system was mobilized to transport Jews to their deaths, it is apparent that the entire technical apparatus of railroad workers, office managers, and individual civilians riding the trains, had to be aware of the human cargo involved.[18] How does one go about punishing all those involved in the transport of human cargo to their ultimate deaths? The massive character of this operation and the millions of victims involved, make the issue of numbers of transgressors a central concern, but one without resolution.

Western law is based upon individual punishment for specific deeds. Western morals are equally built upon individually internalized codes of conduct. It may be an over-simplification, but one of the most interesting aspects (if one may dare use such a phrase) of the study of genocide is to discover how it is that some people can transgress the law and escape not only punishment, but even feelings of guilt for what they have done. How individual behaviour translates into collective behaviour, into the administration no less than the execution of sanctioned murder, is the focus for the advanced social and psychological study of genocide in this century.

In this essential unity of human behaviour, I am reminded of Jane Goodall's reflections on the historic treatment of the chimpanzee – that primate more like the human in genetic terms than any other in the animal kingdom. In discussing the human beings who are responsible for chimps used in experimental settings, she wrote:

> They are victims of a system that was set up long before the cognitive abilities and emotional needs of chimpanzees were understood. Newly-employed staff members, equipped with a normal measure of compassion, may well be sickened by what they see. And in fact, many of them do quit their jobs, unable to endure the suffering they see inflicted on the animals, and feeling powerless to help. But others stay on and gradually come to accept the cruelty, believing that it is an inevitable part of the struggle to reduce human suffering.[19]

Similarly, acts of genocide can be undertaken in the belief that to do so, to remove enemies of the state, is to purify the society. The engineering of death is a continuum, just as life itself. Perpetrators of death do not see themselves as engaged in personal evil, but in collective good. That is the final irony left by the Nazi doctors working on their Jewish victims. Even when personal doubts do arise, they are readily rationalized by the belief that their actions bestow benefits upon those who still live.

We do not need to enter a debate over vivisection to understand the linkage of all living creatures. The disjunction between means and ends, between the utilization of cruelty, torture, mayhem and murder for supposedly noble ends of a supposedly good society is at the root of the arbitrary taking of human life. The branches, or means, are many, some of which have been herein discussed. But I now firmly believe that the root, the end, is singular.

14 Counting Bodies: the Dismal Science of Authorized Terror

If this is the case, then we may be within sight of a fundamental understanding of human behaviour that has been the goal of social research since its inceptiom. That we have had to endure a century of genocide to locate the wellsprings of an integrated, general theory is a tragic and admittedly terrible price to pay for knowledge. But perhaps that is also the lesson of social life: the struggle for knowledge takes place in the crucible of savage acts. The struggle for the preservation and extension of life teaches us that the good is not always the pleasant. The study of genocide is a painful confirmation of such an axiom. Out of the ashes of despair may come the hope of a better social science — and perhaps a better society as well.

Notes

This article is an edited version of a lecture, 'Taking Lives and Measuring Death: Social Science and the Holocaust', chaired by Dr Elisabeth Maxwell and delivered to the Institute of Jewish Affairs, on 9 March 1989, in London.

1 In my earlier work, *Taking Lives: Genocide and State Power* (New Brunswick and London). I sought to develop a typology of state systems: ranging from the libertarian at one end to the genocidal at the other — with a range of negotiated order that includes as essential social psychological characteristics, guilt, shame, toleration and so forth. In this paper, my aim is more precisely located on developing a typology of repressive state systems — systems which permit the taking of lives, ranging from highly selective circumstances, as with capital punishment, to highly inclusive categories, as with genocide. It is also an effort to appreciate that even within the idea of genocide, some profound differences in approaches to the issue of state terror need examination.

2 R. J. Rummel, 'Deadlier than war', *Institute of Public Affairs Review*, vol. 41, no. 2, spring 1985, 24-30.

3 While there has been a substantial body of writings on the Holocaust and genocide in general from the social science community, comparatively little has been written on how the structure of social scientific work changes as a result of such fundamental processes of genocidal systems in the technological structures of industrial societies. See Zygmunt Bauman, 'Sociology after the Holocaust', *British Journal of Sociology*, vol. 39, no. 4, December 1988, 469-97.

4 Robert J. Lifton, *The Nazi Doctors: Medical Killing and the Psychology of Genocide* (New York 1986).

5 Edward F. Mickolus, Todd Sandler and Jean M. Murdock, *International Terrorism in the 1980s: A Chronology of Events. Vol. 1: 1980-83* (Ames 1989).

6 Irving Louis Horowitz, 'The texture of terrorism: socialization, routinization and integration', in Roberta Sigal (ed.), *Political Learning in Adulthood: Sourcebook of Theory and Research* (Chicago 1989), 286-314.

7 'Silent bones and fallen kingdoms', in Kenneth Heuer (ed.), *The Lost Notebooks of Loren Eiseley* (Boston 1987), 20-3.

8 One widely held view about the Holocaust is that 'it was part and parcel of a syncretistic ideology combining key tenets of conservatism, reaction and fascism'. While such a view, most ably propounded by Arno Mayer in *Why Did the Heavens not Darken: The 'Final Solution' in History* (New York 1988), 449, has a prima facie attractiveness, it tends to wash out some critical elements: the specific role of the Jews in history long before there was a final solution; the uses of antisemitism and racism by communist no less than fascist regimes; and finally, the existence of fascist regimes that did not engage in the final solution — these themes are all dealt with in *Taking Lives*.

9 Lucy S. Dawidowicz, *The War Against the Jews: 1933-1945* (New York 1975), 150-66.

10 Iwona Irwin Zarecka, *Neutralizing Memory: The Jew in Contemporary Poland* (New Brunswick and Oxford 1988).

11 Vahaku N. Dadrian, 'The role of Turkish physicians in the World War I genocide of Arme-

nians', *Holocaust and Genocide Studies*, vol. 1, no. 2, 1986, 169-92.
12 Dan Jacobs, *The Brutality of Nations* (New York 1987).
13 Vahaku N. Dadrian, 'The Naim-Andonian documents on the World War I destruction of Ottoman Armenians: the anatomy of a genocide'. *International Journal of Middle East Studies*, vol. 18, no. 3, 311-59.
14 Vera B. Seedopour, 'Iraq attacks to destroy the Kurds'. *The Institute for the Study of Genocide Newsletter*, vol. 1, no. 2, autumn 1988, 2-11.
15 Rene Lemarchand, *Selective Genocide in Burundi* (London 1974).
16 Barbara Harff and Ted Robert Gurr, 'Genocides and politicides since 1945: evidence and anticipation', *Internet on the Holocaust and Genocide*. no. 13, December 1987.
17 Ted Robert Gurr, 'Persisting patterns of repression and rebellion: foundations for a general theory of political coercion' in Margaret P. Karns (ed.), *Persistent Patterns and Emergent Structures in a Waning Century* (New York 1988), 149-68.
18 Raul Hilberg, 'German railroads/Jewish souls', *Society*, vol. 14, no. 2, November-December 1976, 60-74.
19 Jane Goodall, 'A plea for chimps', *New York Times Magazine*, 17 May 1987, 108-20. See also her *The Chimpanzees of Gombe* (Cambridge. Mass. 1986).

IRVING LOUIS HOROWITZ is Hannah Arendt Distinguished Professor of Sociology and Political Science at Rutgers University, New Brunswick, and president of the Transaction Society. Among his works are *Israeli Ecstasies/ Jewish Agonies, Taking Lives: Genocide and State Power* and *Foundations of Political Science*.

[3]

Crime, Criminology and Human Rights:
Towards An Understanding of State Criminality[1]

Gregg Barak, Alabama State University

This paper explores issues related to the analysis of a type of criminality frequently ignored in criminological literature: crimes of the state. It explores the potential of critical criminology to deal with state criminality via investigation of such issues as state interventions, overlapping activities of criminal versus non-criminal organizations and the distinction between individual and state actors. The paper specifically examines state criminality via analysis of the activities of the CIA and FBI in the United States. These activities include methods of surveillance, wiretapping, mail tampering, and the use of agents provocateurs. It also examines issues related to relativity in the definition of terrorism and the use of terrorism by the state. It is argued that, unless criminologists begin to address these issues, criminologists may find themselves in the awkward position of aiding the criminalization of non-criminal peoples around the world.

State criminality or the harm illegally or legally organized and inflicted upon people by their own governments or the governments of others have skimpily but increasingly been documented by social scientists/criminologists (Schwendinger and Schwendinger, 1970; Block and Chambliss, 1981; Falk, 1988a; Block, 1989; Chambliss, 1989; Luyt, 1989; Scott, 1989; Zwerman, 1989; and Barak, 1990). Nevertheless, it is still safe to argue that after some twenty years of recognizing state criminality as a concept, little progress has been made in either precisely specifying what the various forms of 'state criminality' are, or, in analyzing such 'case studies' as those which present themselves, for example, before the United Nations Human Rights Commission. In other words, despite the many mass mediated discussions of these 'crimes against humanity' as found in publications like *Newsweek, Time,* and *The Wall Street Journal,* or in those more critically-oriented discussions as found in such publications as *Mother Jones, The Nation,* and *In These Times,* one still observes a scarcity of scholarship by criminologists on this topic. Until such time as this scarcity is removed, or until such time as there is serious development in the study of state criminality, there will remain significant gaps in the study of crime and in the study of the state and social control.

More specifically, the relationship between state criminality and social control requires recognition by criminologists that we, too, play a role in not only defining the boundaries of the discipline, but in helping to create what constitutes 'crime' in the real world. It is important, therefore, that as critical criminologists, we develop ways of communicating progressive perspectives on crime and social justice to popular audiences (Barak, 1988). It is my further contention that the study of state criminality must become central to the study of crime and social control,

11

The Journal of Human Justice, Vol. 2, No. 1, Autumn, 1990

if we are to develop a left realist critical criminology that is capable of intersecting with the common-sense social reality of crime and violence. Efforts at developing an understanding of these relationships have been occurring for the past couple of decades. Beginning in the late sixties and early seventies, revisionist historians and critical sociologists alike were starting to focus attention on the interrelationships between the modern state and the various systems of social control (Cohen and Scull, 1985).

Out of this work there has re-emerged the 'macro' or classical 19th century socio-historical interest in the importance of the connections between questions of order, authority, power, legitimization, hegemony, organization, and change. These questions of social control have gone well beyond the 'micro' or predominant 20th century questions which merely created various typologies of the means and processes involved in the socialization of conformity. The abandonment of a social-psychological perspective on a social control divorced from the history and the politics of individual, group, and class struggles, and the preference for a social control grounded in the interplay of cultural production, ideological construction, and political economy, has served to resurrect the role of the state as central to each of these areas of social control.

It was precisely these 'macro' political and economic relations, ignored by traditional or positivist criminology during most of the 20th century, that has historically limited the scope of the field to the study of the criminal behavior of the powerless. Gradually, however, over the past fifty years there has been an expansion over the 'acceptable' boundaries of criminological focus to include the criminal behavior of the powerful, beginning with the professional, white-collar, organized, and most recently, corporate criminals. During this shifting in criminological paradigms, the establishment of a critical criminology reunited the study of the state with the study of crime which had previously been separated by positivist criminology. Although progress has been made in describing the integral connections between class, race, gender, crime, social control, and the state, very little light has been shed upon understanding the role and the development of state organized criminality in the reproduction of both the crimes of the powerful and the powerless. Before such an understanding can come about there must first be a development of state criminality and its legitimation within the field of criminology.

TOWARDS AN UNDERSTANDING OF STATE CRIMINALITY

Is it not an ultimate contradiction that the state has been both a crime-regulating and crime-generating institution? That is to say, the state through its formal and informal policies not only engages in crime control, but it also engages in the development of crime, its own and others. As a criminogenic institution, the state not only violates the rights of individuals, but it contributes to the production of other forms of criminality as well. From the

Gregg Barak

perspective of critical criminology, these injuries or harms ('crimes') may or may not violate law *per se*.

The criminological journey toward the development of a criminology of state criminality will not be accomplished without resistance from both inside and outside the boundaries of academic criminology. Simply put, there are a number of disciplinary biases and political obstacles to overcome. To begin with, the study of state criminality is problematic because the very concept itself is controversial. This is due, in part, to the debate over whether or not one should define 'crime' in terms other than the law codes of individual nations.

Traditional criminology has always ascribed to the legalistic state definition of crime, investigation and analysis confined to legally proscribed behavior and its control (Schwendinger and Schwendinger, 1970; Platt, 1974; Michalowski, 1985). Outside of the conventional confines of criminology have been those acts such as imperialism, exploitation, racism, and sexism or those acts not typically prosecuted such as tax-evasion, consumer fraud, government corruption, and state violence. Critical criminology, accordingly, has not confined itself to studying legally defined crime. Utilizing other definitions such as crimes against humanity or politically defined crime, critical criminology has studied harmful and injurious behavior which may or may not be sanctioned by particular nation-states' definitions of illegality, but which are recognized in the 'higher' criteria established in various international treaties, covenants, or laws. Therefore, for the purposes of this discussion, crimes by and of the state, like those crimes against the state, may be viewed similarly as involving exploits of both a violent and non-violent nature. They may, in fact, involve violations of the same established legal relations or prohibitions, including but not limited to such behaviors as: murder, rape, espionage, cover-up, burglary, illegal wiretapping, illegal break-in, disinformation, kidnapping, theft, assassination, terrorism, secrecy, unaccountability, corruption, exporting arms and importing drugs illegally, obstruction of justice, perjury, deception, fraud, and conspiracy. In addition, state criminality may include the more general transgression of both domestic and international laws, not to mention the more subtle institutional relations or behaviors which cause social injury such as the bankrupting and the destroying of whole economies or the violation of universally shared notions of fundamental human rights.

Now then, these critical definitions of crime which have opened up the scope of 'criminality' have certainly not as yet been adopted by conventional criminologists nor even considered by the general public. In fact, both leftists and rightists, inside and outside of criminology, have found such conceptualizations of crime to be unreal, unnatural, idealistic, impractical, or irrelevant. The point, however, is that for those critical criminologists who think otherwise, the time is long past due for the serious development of the substantive areas of state criminality. Through this type of critical

13

The Journal of Human Justice, Vol. 2, No. 1, Autumn, 1990

development within criminology there stands the possibility of transforming the very nature of the study of criminality from the individual to the political.

In order to carry out such a criminological agenda, investigators cannot be deterred in their study of state criminality by the lack or failure of the state to adjudicate itself or its agents as criminals. After all, just because it has been the case that states have chosen to ignore, dismiss, or down play their own criminality, it does not follow that we criminologists should do the same. Similarly, criminologists should extricate themselves from the trap of viewing state crimes within the old political double standard: treating the phenomena as though it involves the behavior of certain designated 'bad guy' states and not the behavior of so-called 'good guy' states.

For example, the case of terrorism presents much theoretical, strategic, and ideological work to be done. Scholarly interest in this area, especially as conducted by students of criminology and criminal justice, has been highly focused or selected on some but not all terrorist acts. This selectivity refers not only to countries emphasized and neglected, but to the various forms of terrorism committed. By most legally-defined or state-based notions of terrorism, the typically incorporated crimes include those 'retail' terrorist acts committed by groups or individuals against agents or symbolic representatives of a real or imaginary enemy state. Typically omitted from most discussions are those 'wholesale' acts of terrorism waged by state-supported networks against various independence or national revolutionary movements (Chomsky and Herman, 1979; Herman, 1982).

Or what about the role of covert and overt aid in the domestic affairs of developing nations, especially in trying to effect the outcomes of elections? It used to be in the glory days of the American empire, that neither the President, the Congress, nor the people considered whether we had a right to intervene in the domestic affairs of another nation. U.S. aid in those days, mostly covert, "was routine, and so pervasive as to be immune to political criticism" (Weinstein, 1989: 14). But with respect to the practicalities, if not the underlying principles, U.S. foreign policies are now beginning to be publicly questioned. At the same time, however, for example, the Bush administration during its first year in office, attempted to redefine the term assassination in an effort to circumvent President Ford's 1975 executive order formally banning U.S. assassinations of foreign officials. According to a recent 'memorandum of law,' the original order has not been changed, only watered down to exclude the possibility of assassination without premeditation (Wright, 1989: 1C). Whatever the state finally decides about these 'murders,' elections, and other forms of covert and overt intervention, criminologists should not be precluded from exploring and examining these actions as state crimes against humanity.

Like the study of corporate crime the study of state crime is problematic because it involves examining behaviors engaged in by agents and

Gregg Barak

organizations which are both socially and politically acceptable (Clinard and Yeager, 1980; Ermann and Lundman, 1982). Access to studying the politically powerful, especially with respect to deviant behavior, has always been difficult. While both corporate and state criminality have the potential for undermining the very stability of the system that the corporate-state strives to protect, it is the latter crimes by the state which pose the greater threat to the political legitimation of the system as a whole. State criminality, in other words, provides the type of inherent contradictions which simultaneously challenge the prevailing political ideology yet accommodate the same behavior in the name of greater common interests or national security. The political repression or governmental crimes committed against the Chinese demonstrators in 1989 was an excellent example of this point. To label and to study such behavior as criminal was to participate in a de-legitimation of the Chinese state; one can well imagine the consequences for any Chinese criminologist who would have attempted to examine this form of state criminality.

Analysis of state criminality is further complicated because it involves not only the overlapping activities of 'criminal' and 'non-criminal' organizations, but also because it involves the study of state-supported corruption and violence which never can be totally separated from individual acts of criminality and terrorism as each is somehow related to the inequitable distribution of economic wealth and legal-juridical privileges. Concerning the former set of relationships, Block summarized the situation nicely when he argued that traditionally organized crime and state organized crime are inseparable in many cases because:

> organized crime has been and continues to be inextricably linked to transnational political movements and to that segment of the American political establishment known as the espionage community or more aptly, the transnational police force" (1986: 59).

He further concluded that this kind of interplay between organized and state criminality results in the situation where:

> it may very well be the case that certain political assassinations or other intelligence moves may be done not in the interests of foreign policy carried out by hired goons and thugs, but rather in the interest of drug smugglers and international gamblers carried out by their clients in the intelligence services (1986:76).

As for the connections between individual criminality and state criminality, Dieterich has argued, for example, that the material debasement of the "majority of the Latin American peoples is an inevitable consequence of the current capitalist accumulation model" (1986: 50) and the physical and psychological submission of these peoples "into a state of apathy and fear is a functional prerequisite for that accumulation model." On the U.S. domestic front, Henry (1990) has already demonstrated the relationship between a 'free market' economy and street criminality as both are tied to policies of omission and marginality and to the viability of informal economic activity as an alternative response to legitimate work. Therefore, the ability of

15

The Journal of Human Justice, Vol. 2, No. 1, Autumn, 1990

criminology to recognize not only the criminal content and the criminogenic nature of various forms of state intervention into the affairs of other countries, but also the criminality and the crime-producing influences of domestic policies of non-interventionist omission, becomes a necessary prerequisite for the development of the serious study of state crimes.

In sum, the development of a criminology of state criminality requires that criminologists move way beyond the rather one-dimensional media portrayals and political discourse associated with the selectively chosen crimes by the state. In order to establish a criminology of the structural and etiological reasons ('causes') of state criminality, criminologists and other legal and political scientists must first present the kinds of conceptual frameworks which not only incorporate the full array of state crimes, but which can aid us in understanding the relative harm and injury inflicted by the behaviors and policies of nation-states.

STATE CRIMINALITY AND THE U.S. EXPERIENCE

It should be pointed out that state criminality is not indigenous or symptomatic of any particular socio-economic formation, including pre-capitalist, capitalist, or socialist. As far back as the fifth century A.D., for example, state criminality had been acknowledged in the course of realizing that the actions of pirate bands were essentially the same as those actions of states and empires. That is to say, both pirates and empires had the capacity to seize property by force or violence. The only real difference between the two was the scale of their endeavors, and the success of pre-states or empires to impose a justifying rhetoric or ideology for their theft of land, property, and people (Jenkins, 1988; Chambliss, 1989). In the contemporary world, of course, regardless of the particular socio-economic and state formation, crimes by and of the state can be found globally. In other words, historically it has been the case that both democratic and undemocratic regimes have engaged in state criminality. It may very well be the case, that political repression and state crime have less to do with the democratic nature of the government *per se*, and more to do with the power of a particular state regime such as the U.S. or the U.S.S.R.

A glance at the 'democratic' history of the United States reveals the patterned actions of state criminality. Whether we are discussing the 19th century crimes of the U.S. government which were in violation of the fundamental rights of Native and African American peoples, or we are examining those state crimes which have violated the legal and civil rights of workers, minorities, and dissidents over the past century, the evidence clearly demonstrates that these crimes were not accidental or due to some kind of negligence. On the contrary, those state actions engaged in and/or the consequences of the policies of a developing political economy were the outcome of premeditated and intentional decisions. In fact, some of these

Gregg Barak

'crimes against humanity,' such as slavery, were in full compliance with the supreme laws of the land.

In light of these historical realities, the student in 20th century state criminality of the U.S., for example, when studying the role of the Federal Bureau of Investigation as a formal institution of social control, should strive for an integration of the dual-sided nature of state 'crime-fighting' and 'political-policing.' The Palmer Raids and the Red Scare of 1919, the McCarthyism of the early 1950s, and the counter-insurgency campaigns of the late 1960s and early 1970s used against those citizens protesting the involvement of the U.S. in Southeast Asia, reveal a domestic history of extraordinary political repression or state criminality against those who have seriously challenged or posed any kind of a threat to the status quo (Glick, 1989). Such activities, covert and overt, have not been limited to domestic enemies alone, but have included foreign political enemies as well. Since it was established in the late 1940s, The Central Intelligence Agency has had a rather consistent history of supporting repressive dictators in such countries as Cuba, Iran, the Philippines, Nicaragua, Brazil, South Korea, and Argentina, and of overthrowing or destabilizing democratically elected governments in Guatemala, Chile, Jamaica, and Nicaragua — to name only a few (Bodenheimer and Gould, 1989). Here again, as with the domestic state crimes, these international state crimes, would appear to select their victims in response to the needs of laissez-faire or the free market economy, consistent with the real or the perceived needs of capitalist accumulation.

What these domestic and international examples of state crime have shared in common has been their ongoing series of legal and illegal clandestine operations used against those politically-labelled deviants. Within the United States, the FBI's Cointelpro, or counter-intelligence programs, of the 1960s and 1970s used against the Black Panther Party for Self-Defense, the anti-war movement, and the American Indian Movement, included a variety of illegal and unconstitutional techniques to de-legitimate or to otherwise criminalize lawful organizations (Churchill and Wall, 1988). These state crimes have involved such everyday illegal activities as surveilling, burglarizing, and tampering with the mail. In addition, there have been the more exotic forms of state criminality such as employing propaganda to smear progressive organizations, or sending out disruptive *agents provocateurs* (Wolfe, 1973; U.S. Congress, 1976; Caute, 1978; and Churchill and Wall, 1988).

The study of state criminality, more so than the study of any other form of criminality, is by definition a highly politicized undertaking. In other words, the study of state crimes cannot be separated from the emotionally-charged landscape of a changing political economy, which involves among other things, the study of law, power, and ideology as well as the study of public policy, foreign and domestic. A case in point is the study of terrorism where one person's 'terrorist' has been another person's 'freedom fighter.' For

The Journal of Human Justice, Vol. 2, No. 1, Autumn, 1990

example, with respect to U.S. supported state terrorism, it should be recognized that such forms of state criminality as the involvement in systemic counter-revolutionary warfare, pro-insurgency, or interventionism, are responsible for all kinds of human casualties. The tens of thousands of lost lives and an even larger number of permanently injured citizens of Latin American countries, over the past few decades, reveals just some of the harm done by international state criminality. I refer specifically to the illegal detentions and the mass torturing, murdering, and kidnapping by U.S. trained secret police and militia in such countries as Guatemala and El Salvador (Nelson-Pallmeyer, 1989).

This kind of U.S. state-engaged criminality or what has otherwise euphemistically been referred to by the military, the U.S. State Department, and the mass media as 'low-intensity' conflict or warfare, has been virtually ignored by students of governmental or organizational crime. Such state policies have been designed "not only to defend the U.S. empire against the rising challenges from the poor but also to conceal from U.S. citizens the unpleasant consequences of empire" (Nelson-Pallmeyer, 1989: 2). These low-intensity activities have involved an unprecedented degree of coordination among the White House, the National Security Council, the Central Intelligence Agency, the State Department, the Agency for International Development, conservative private aid groups, and a semi-private network of drug-runners, arms merchants, and assassins (Nelson-Pallmeyer, 1989). The 'secret' crimes of low-intensity conflict have strived to integrate the more traditional military, political, economic, and psychological aspects of warfare with the more modern, technological aspects of mass communications, private consumption, and social control. Such interventionism, for example, into the affairs of Nicaragua eventually wore the people down and contributed to the defeat of the Sandinistas in the elections of 1990.

The study of U.S. state criminality should not only include those 'proactive' crimes of the state, at home or abroad, such as the Iran-Contra Affair and the subsequent behaviors of the Contras and Sandinistas or the recent invasion of Panama, but they should also include the crimes by state 'omission' such as the denial of the fundamental right to work for an adequate income or the right to be permanently free of homelessness in a society as rich as the United States. With respect to the former crimes by the state, the syndicated columnist, David Broder, has drawn out the important parallels between Oliver North and Manuel Noriega. In response to an editorial which appeared in *The Wall Street Journal* shortly after General Noriega and his people stole the results of the May 1989 election in Panama, Broder maintained that the correct lesson to learn was the one concerning U.S. hypocracy in relationship to Noriega in particular and to the crimes against the people of Nicaragua in general. He wrote:

18

Gregg Barak

> When the executive branch of the U.S. government evades laws passed by Congress, when it brushes aside the verdict of the World Court on its illegal mining of Nicaraguan harbors, then it cannot be surprised when the head (Noriega) of a client government decides to ignore the election returns (Broder, 1989: 2B).

With respect to the crimes of omission, it is precisely those state domestic and economic policies of non-interventionism and de-regulation which have combined not only to deny people of their basic human needs, but which have also helped to contribute to the production of the more traditional forms of criminality (Henry, 1990; Barak, 1991).

In the context of global human rights for the people of both developed and developing countries, therefore, it is my contention that the study of state criminality should be connected to those struggles which have historically attempted to expand the notions of fundamental justice for all. In the next section, I will attempt to show the linkages between crime, criminology, and human rights and the worldwide effort of the United Nations Human Rights Commission to challenge some of the more commonly experienced state crimes against humanity.

THE POLITICS OF HUMAN RIGHTS VIOLATIONS

The politics of struggling for worldwide social justice and the politics of condemning the human rights abuses of nation-states by such organizations as Amnesty International or the United Nations Human Rights Commission (UNHRC) will not put an end to the global spectacle of human rights violations and to the suffering of millions of people any time in the near future. More likely, the politics of condemning human rights violations will continue to 'heat up' as the strength of the various geographical blocs continue to increase. Most recently, for example, regional blocs involving nations from Latin America, Africa, and the Middle East have begun to 'rival' the blocs of the two superpowers and the older European nations. For example, at the 1990 UNHRC meetings in Geneva, resolutions were passed against the human rights abuses of the Israeli re-settlement of Soviet Jews in the Occupied Territories and the U.S. invasion of Panama. At the same time, the Commission rejected a loosening of the sanctions on South Africa. China, however, despite the massacre at Tiananmen Square, managed to escape an official sanction from UNHRC. Also escaping sanction were the 1989 human rights abuses which occurred in such other countries as Guatemala, Iraq, Sri Lanka, Cambodia and the Philippines. What effects the current democratic revolutions in Eastern Europe and the Soviet Union will have on the centuries-old struggle for social justice is still too early to discern.

The problem in studying the politics of human rights violations cannot be separated from the problem of studying state criminality because they are both related to the basic issue of confronting the fundamental and irreconcilable differences between empire and social justice. Countries which have lived under the 'sphere of influence' of the U.S.S.R. or the U.S.

19

The Journal of Human Justice, Vol. 2, No. 1, Autumn, 1990

have experienced various forms of exploitation and domination. Neither superpower has been very likely to admit to its own crimes against humanity. In fact, both countries have gone to great lengths to rationalize and justify their politically necessary behavior. Through propaganda and disinformation efforts, each of the superpowers have attempted to suppress or to put a noble label around their seamy and contradictory behavior as these have been in conflict with the professed ideals of each country.

The principles for addressing human rights abuses globally have been evolving at least since the French and American revolutions. Today the means for addressing these violations include the shaping of world opinion and the holding of nation-states accountable to edicts of international law, to global treaties and declarations, and to universal concepts of human rights, in short, supporting those worldwide efforts aimed at achieving self-determination and independent development for all peoples of the earth. The role of the United States in the domestic and international affairs of developing nations serves as an example. Since 1945, U.S dominated foreign intervention in places like Africa and Asia have certainly served more as a deterrent than as a facilitator of the materialization of human rights for Third World people. And for the past two decades, of all governments in the West, it has been the U.S. that has most consistently opposed the realization of the right of self-determinism by the peoples of developing nations. As Falk (1989) has argued, it comes as no surprise, therefore, that the United States has been the nation consistently portrayed as an implacable foe of the rights of people. This hegemonic resistance by the U.S. places both ideological and physical obstacles in the way of maximizing human rights worldwide.

When it has come to the ratification of the major multi-lateral human rights agreements or instruments, the USA has one of the very worst records among Western liberal democracies. By refusing to sign and recognize these various documents, the U.S. has, at least indirectly, contributed to the world-wide abuse of human rights. For example, it was not until 1988 that the United States finally ratified the Prevention and Punishment of the Crime of Genocide which was opened for signature in 1948. As of 1989 the U.S. had still failed to ratify such human rights documents as the Convention on the Reduction of Statelessness (1961), the International Convention on the Elimination of All Forms of Racial Discrimination (1965), the American Convention on Human Rights (1965), the International Covenant on Economic, Social and Cultural Rights (1966), the International Covenant on Civil and Political Rights (1966), the International Convention on the Suppression and Punishment of the Crime of Apartheid (1973), and the Convention on the Elimination of All Forms of Discrimination Against Women (1979).

Naturally, signing and enforcing any of the documents that have identified and attempted to de-legitimate those public and private policies, domestic and foreign, which have helped to reproduce crimes against humanity, have often

Gregg Barak

been correctly viewed as impediments to capital accumulation. This is true whether we are discussing developed or developing nations. With regard to the post-1945 construction of a USA foreign policy based on isolationism and interventionism, the international recognition of 'human rights' as legally binding, would certainly help to alter the philosophy of a leadership that has never truly "trusted law or morality or international institutions as the basis for maintaining international security" (Falk, 1988b: 4). Grounded in the failures of Wilsonian idealism and the inter-war diplomacy, U.S. post World War II diplomacy, policy, and ideology has always been based on the belief that the way to peace (and 'democracy') was through superior military power and the contradictory preparation for war as the only basis for peace. Perhaps, in light of the current thawing of the Cold War, and in response to the liberalization and democratization in Eastern Europe and the Soviet Union, the U.S. may be 'forced' to rethink its policies, for example, on low intensity conflict.

The mere rejection of low intensity conflict as business as usual or its recognition as a form of state criminality *vis-à-vis* the internationalization of human rights law, would, in effect, outlaw such behaviors as counter-revolutionary terrorism and structural violence that afflict the poor and underdeveloped peoples of the world. Accordingly, Falk has stressed that:

> the rights of peoples can be undertook at its deepest level as a counter-terrorist code of rights and duties, especially directed against state terrorism of the sort associated with foreign policies of leading imperial governments (1989: 68).

More generally, resisting all forms of state criminality is no simple enterprise as it calls for challenging the prevailing ideologies of militarism, nationalism, and regionalism. The struggle for world peace, social justice and the reduction in the crimes of and by the state also necessitates, on the one side, a decreasing role of the national police apparatuses and, on the other side, an increasing role of multi-lateral cooperation among nations. To put it simply, this utopian world vision requires that peoples of the global community understand that "no problem we face, not the nuclear one, not the ecological one, not the economic one, can possibly be handled, even addressed, on a unilateral national basis" (Ellsberg, 1988: 18).

Nevertheless, some people have argued that it is simply naive to believe that these kinds of agreements are going to eliminate the state criminality of human rights abuses. After all, as they say, these agreements have no teeth. Others, however, have argued that it is just as naive to dismiss these efforts simply because of the politicalization of the process itself. In other words, since the end of WWII the struggle for social justice in general and the work of the UNHRC in particular has minimally functioned to successfully:

> establish norms and goals for the international community. The growing consensus on an expanded definition of fundamental human rights can be linked to the existence of U.N. covenants and the efforts of the Commission (Allen, 1990: 12).

21

The Journal of Human Justice, Vol. 2, No. 1, Autumn, 1990

Karel Vasak, former UNESCO legal advisor, has called on nation-states worldwide to sign on to what has been termed the 'third generation of rights.' The third generation of rights goes further in its attempts than the 'first' and 'second' generation of rights did in their attempts to maximize the realization of human rights for all the people of the world. Each generation of politically evolved human rights violations have been the product of different historical struggles waged by people without rights to obtain them. With each passing historical period, there has been the expansion of both the notions associated with fundamental rights and with respect to whom those rights pertained.

The first generation of rights have been referred to as 'negative rights' in that they have called for restraint from the state. These rights were derived from the American and French revolutions and the struggle to gain liberty from arbitrary state action. These rights can be found in the Civil and Political Rights of the International Bill of Rights. The second generation of rights have been referred to as 'positive rights' in that they have required affirmative action on the part of the state. These rights can be found in the Economic, Social, and Cultural Rights of the International Bill of Rights. They emerged from the experiences of the Soviet Union and they also resonate in the welfare state policies of the West.

Finally, the third generation of rights has called for international cooperation. These rights are currently evolving out of the condition of global inter-dependence confronting the earth today. For example, in 1990, UNHRC members introduced a resolution that "encouraged an expanding role for the world body in defining the relationship among technology, development and the ecological integrity of the planet" (Adler, 1990: 13). The UNHRC resolution, while not recommending any action at this time, has gone on record to say:

> that the preservation of life-sustaining ecosystems under conditions of rapid scientific and technological development is of vital importance to the protection of the human species and the promotion of human rights (Quoted in Allen, 1990: 13).

Such a resolution, of course, recognizes that human rights obligations can no longer be satisfied within the boundaries of individual nations. Therefore, the rights of people independent of states, are required not only for a reduction in state organized violence and the maintenance of world peace, but for the protection of the environment and for a massive scale of global development (Crawford, 1988).

Putting human rights into practice by all types of universal agreements reached by both state and non-state representatives, is certainly one of the prerequisites for a reduction in all forms of state criminality, especially the more blatant forms often ignored by even the most 'democratic' of nations like the United States. The argument here is that a recognition of these critical relationships by criminology and the adoption of basic human rights obligations as part and parcel of a progressive criminological practice, are

Gregg Barak

absolutely essential for the establishment of a criminology of state criminality. Moreover, without the legitimation of the study of state criminality both inside and outside of our academic discipline, criminology will remain captive of the prevailing social and moral contexts of legally defined state crime.

CONCLUSION

This essay has implicitly argued that state criminality is ubiquitous. It has also been explicitly argued that state criminality is victim-producing and criminogenic. Consequently, crimes by and of the state are responsible for much of the global crime, injury, harm, violence, and injustice. Historically, it has been suggested that we are in the emerging period of the third generation of rights as evidenced by various declarations and the expanding movement or struggle on behalf of universal human rights. Accordingly, I have contended that the time has come for criminologists to actually devote serious time to the study of state organized crime.

If such work is finally emerging,[2] then the lag in time between the introduction of the concept 'state' to the field of criminology and the actual practice of studying state criminality, may be roughly parallel to the time lag between the introduction of white collar/corporate crime as a concept and the actual practice of studying this form of criminality. That is to say, it took some two decades after Sutherland first introduced 'white collar crime' before criminologists were seriously engaged in studying the crimes of the 'privately' powerful. It now appears that it may have also taken about two decades between the time, when radical criminologists of the late sixties first introduced the concept of state criminality to the discipline, and the time when criminologists finally began to seriously examine the crimes of the 'publicly' powerful.

To reiterate, whether the study of state criminality involves the detailed investigation of agents or organizations violating the rights of its own citizens, or whether it involves the examination of inter-state terrorism, or whether it involves exploring the patterned interaction between the two, analysis requires that criminologists and others appreciate the two-sided and often hypocritical nature of this form of political deviance. A case in point would demand the unraveling of the connections between the U.S. savings and loan (S L) 'scandal' and the involvement of known CIA agents and members of organized crime. Of course, with respect to these S L state-organized thefts, what laid the foundation or ground work was the federal deregulation of the S L industry passed into law by a bi-partisan Congress during Ronald Reagan's first term as President. Without this change in the legal structure and in the policies controlling the operations of the individual savings and loans, there would not have been the institutionalized opportunity for the biggest theft in U.S. history. A theft which is currently being estimated, at a cost to the American taxpayers, of something on the order of $500 billion to one trillion dollars (Reeves, 1990).

The Journal of Human Justice, Vol. 2, No. 1, Autumn, 1990

Moreover, with respect to the study of state criminality and crime in general, both the S L thefts and the S L bail-outs as well as the de-regulation itself, cannot be divorced from the underlying changes in the political economy which were creating economic dilemmas that de-regulation sought to obviate. Failure to develop such macro-level analyses and criminological constructs of the crimes of the powerful, typically results in very unsatisfying and highly reductionist analyses about individual greed and organizational survival divorced from the political economy itself. Such contradictory analyses, which are perhaps better than no analyses at all, may help explain to some degree why it has often been the case that these allegedly unacceptable behaviors can be so easily swept under the political and criminological carpets.

In *Revolutionaries and Functionaries: The Dual Face of Terrorism,* Falk (1988a) has underscored this point with respect to state terrorism in particular. He has argued persuasively that unless there is the development of both objective and neutral scholarship and action, then the chances are strong that the study and transformation of political violence and state criminality will fall victim to the often employed double standard of justice. This kind of victimization can come about by the unscientific and uncritical acceptance of the language and discourse used to describe politically deviant global behavior. As criminologists, therefore, not only should we be involved in the process of demystifying political deviance, but we should also be on the look-out for all forms of state criminality brought about by anti-democratic and repressive forces, whether they operate at home or abroad.

I know that there are skeptical criminologists out there, consisting of both the sympathetic left and the adversarial right, who question not only the value of a criminology of state criminality, but of an expanded definition of 'criminality' in the first place. These criminologists and others have asked me, for instance, what kinds of contributions can criminologists make to the study of crimes by and of the state that the other social scientists and even journalists could not make? Let me briefly respond to each of these concerns.

Regarding the appropriateness of a criminology of state criminality and the expanded definition of crime: First, I believe that both are consistent with the more critical trends in criminology as represented traditionally by arguments advanced by Sellin and Sutherland in the 1930s and 1940s, and more recently by the radical arguments advanced by Chambliss, Quinney, Platt, and others beginning in 1970 with the Schwendingers' classic statement: "Defenders of Order or Guardians of Human Rights." Second, as I have argued throughout this essay and elsewhere, the serious study of the systems of exploitation, including the state and its policies as a crime producing institution, have yet to be considered, especially as these are related to the processes of both victimization and criminalization.

Gregg Barak

As for the critical contributions that I believe could be made by the scientific study of state criminality as opposed to the traditionally 'non-criminological' study of crime by other social scientists, or by those treatments of the mass mediated or even the alternatively mediated discussions of crime by journalists, they appear to me to be self-evident. As students of the convergence of crime, law, justice, control, politics, and change, criminologists are in the unique position of having a focus on the interaction of the dynamics of these properties as they have shaped the development of crime, criminology, and social control. Bringing this kind of 'special' knowledge to the study of state criminality presupposes having undergone the type of demystification of crime and justice not typically experienced by either social scientists in general or journalists in particular. And, I would argue that while this will vary by degree, it is still equally true of bourgeois or critical social scientists and of mainstream or alternative journalists.

In the end, if criminology does not become engaged in the serious study of crimes by and of the state, then this omission will not only have stood in the way of criminology providing the complete picture of crime, but it will have been partially responsible for the reproduction of the ongoing criminalization and victimization of people around the globe. Stated differently, the lines of inquiry pertaining to the theoretical questions posed by the crimes of the powerful and by the relationships between social control and social justice, requires that the examination of state criminality be central to this whole area of investigation. Finally, to confront state criminality as a legitimate enemy of civil society is to join the struggle for universal human rights and social justice.

The Journal of Human Justice, Vol. 2, No. 1, Autumn, 1990

ENDNOTES

1. An earlier version of this manuscript was presented at the annual meetings of the American Society of Criminology in Reno, Nevada (November 1989) and to the Department of Criminology at the University of Ottawa (January 1990). With respect to this substantially revised version, the author wishes to acknowledge the feedback and discussion generated by the persons in attendance in Ottawa. He would also like to thank the anonymous reviewers of the earlier draft for their criticisms and suggestions.

2. See, for example, my forthcoming edited anthology of original essays on state criminality, *Crimes by the Capitalist State: An Introduction to State Criminality*.

REFERENCES

Allen, Terry, "The Politics of Human Rights" *In These Times*, April 25-May 1, 1990:12-13.

Barak, Gregg, *The Violence of Homelessness in America*, New York, 1991.

Barak, Gregg, (ed). *Crimes by the Capitalist State: An Introduction to State Criminality*, Albany, N.Y.: State University of New York Press, 1990.

Barak, Gregg "Newsmaking Criminology: Reflections on the Media, Intellectuals, and Crime." *Justice Quarterly* 5, 4, 1988:565-587.

Block, Alan, "Violence, Corruption, and Clientelism: The Assassination of Jesus de Galindez, 1956" *Social Justice* 16, 2, 1989:64-88.

Block, Alan "A Modern Marriage of Convenience: A Collaboration Between Organized Crime and U.S. Intelligence" Robert J. Kelley, (ed.), *Organized Crime: A Global Perspective*, Totowa, N.J.: Rowman and Littlefield, 1986.

Block, Alan and William Chambliss *Organizing Crime*, New York: Elsevier, 1981.

Bodenheimer, Thomas and Robert Gould *Rollback! Right-wing Power in U.S. Foreign Policy*, Boston: South End Press, 1989.

Broder, David "Lawlessness At Home Invites Defiance" *The Montgomery Advertiser and The Alabama Journal*, Sunday, May 14, 1989.

Caute, David *The Great Fear: The Anti-Communist Purge Under Truman and Eisenhower*, New York: Simon and Schuster, 1978.

Chambliss, William "State-Organized Crime" *Criminology* 27, 2, 1989:183-208.

Chomsky, Noam and Edward S. Herman *The Washington Connection and Third World Fascism*, Boston: South End Press, 1979.

Churchill, Ward and Jim Vander Hall *Agents of Repression: The FBI's Secret Wars Against The Black Panther Party and The American Indian Movement*, Boston: South End Press, 1988.

Clinard, Marshall and Peter Yeager *Corporate Crime*, New York: The Free Press, 1980.

Cohen, Stanley and Andrew Scull (eds) *Social Control and the State*, Oxford: Basil Blackwell, 1985.

Crawford, James *The Rights of Peoples*, Oxford: Oxford University Press, 1988.

Gregg Barak

Dieterich, Heinz "Enforced Disappearances and Corruption in Latin America" *Crime and Social Justice*, No. 25, 1986.

Ellsberg, Daniel Remarks presented at the session, "The Growth of the National Security State," at the conference on *Anti-Communism and The U.S..:History and Consequences,* sponsored by the Institute for Media Analysis, Inc., Harvard University, Nov. 11-13, 1988.

Ermann, David and Richard Lundman *Corporate and Governmental Deviance: Problems of Organizational Behavior in Contemporary Society,* New York: Oxford University Press, 1982.

Falk, Richard "United States Foreign Policy as an Obstacle to the Rights of People." *Social Justice*, 16, 1, 1989:57-70.

Falk, Richard *Revolutionaries and Functionaries: The Dual Face of Terrorism,* New York: E.P. Hutton, 1988a.

Falk, Richard Remarks presented at the session, "The Growth of the National Security State," at the conference on *Anti-Communism and The U.S.:History and Consequences,* sponsored by the Institute for Media Analysis, Inc., Harvard University, Nov. 11-13, 1988b.

Glick, Brian *War At Home: Covert Action Against U.S. Activists and What We Can Do About It,* Boston: South End Press, 1989.

Henry, Stuart "The Informal Economy: A Crime of Omission by the State?" G. Barak (ed.), *Crimes by the Capitalist State: An Introduction to State Criminality* Albany, N.Y.: SUNY Press, 1990.

Herman, Edward *The Real Terror Network: Terrorism in Fact and Propaganda,* Boston: South End Press, 1982.

Jenkins, Philip "Whose Terrorists? Libya and State Criminality" *Contemporary Crises,* 12 (2) 1988:1-11.

Luyt, Clifford "The Killing Fields: South Africa's Human Rights Record in Southern Africa' *Social Justice* 16 (2) 1989:89-115.

Michalowski, Raymond *Order, Law, and Crime: An Introduction to Criminology,* New York: Random House, 1985.

Nelson-Pallmeyer, Jack *War Against the Poor: Low-Intensity Conflict and Christian Faith,* Maryknoll, N.Y.: Orbis Books, 1989.

Platt, Tony "Prospects for a Radical Criminology in the United States" *Crime and Social Justice* (Spring-Summer) 1974:2-10.

Schwendinger, Herman and Julia Schwendinger "Defenders of Order or Guardians of Human Rights?" *Issues in Criminology*, 5, (2) (Summer), 1970:123-157.

Scott, Peter [Northwards Without North: Bush, Counterterrorism, and the Continuation of Secret Power" *Social Justice*, 16 (2) 1989:1-30.

U.S. Congress Senate Select Committee to Study Governmental Operations with Respect to Intelligence Activities, vol. 6, *Intelligence Activities: Senate Resolution 21,* Washington, D.C.: Government Printing Office, 1976.

Weinstein, James "Now That It's Out in The Open, The Underlying Principles Should Be Debated" *In These Times*, October 11-17, 1989.

The Journal of Human Justice, Vol. 2, No. 1, Autumn, 1990

Wolfe, Alan *Repression: The Seamy Side of Democracy*, New York: McKay and Company, 1973.

Wright, Robin "U.S. redefining ban on assassinations" *The Montgomery Advertiser and Alabama Review Journal*, October 15, 1989.

Zwerman, Gilda "Domestic Counterterrorism: U.S. Government Response to Political Violence on the Left in the Reagan Era" *Social Justice* 16 (2,)1989:31-63.

[4]

Toward The Study of Governmental Crime: Nuclear Weapons, Foreign Intervention, and International Law*

David Kauzlarich
Ronald C. Kramer
Brian Smith
Western Michigan University

Reflexive Statement

As peace activists and professional criminologists, we believe that there is much to be gained if state violence were to be viewed in the context of law and crime. As active participants in various forms of the peace movement, we have long been concerned with the question of how to advance people's understanding of the actual consequences and threat of state violence. To see such violence as "crime" and a violation of law may aid in that struggle. As humanistic criminologists we have long been discontent with the restrictive parameters of traditional criminological study. We believe that a criminology concerned about its integrity and relevance should make the violence of nation-states a central concern of the field.

Introduction

> If protection rackets represent organized crime at its smoothest, then war making and state making-- quintessential protection rackets with the advantage of legitimacy--qualify as our largest examples of organized crime (Tilly 1985, p. 169).

> The most fundamental problem facing us today is the seemingly implacable expansion of the means of violence in the hands of nation-states. There is no

---

*We would like to thank Ray Michalowski for his helpful comments on an earlier draft of this paper.

544 Humanity & Society

> matter that presses more heavily upon the
> contemporary world than the actuality of international
> violence and the looming threat of nuclear war (Giddens
> 1987a, p. 182).

The organized violence perpetrated by the governmental agencies of nation states is one of the most important problems facing the world today. In this paper we will argue that most of the violent acts of governments can and should be included as a core criminological concern in the future through the epistemological framework of international law.

From White Collar to State-Organized Crime

It has been over fifty years now since Sutherland (1940) invented the concept of white collar crime. His pioneering work significantly altered the discipline of criminology by directing attention to the crimes of the powerful in addition to the traditional focus on the street crimes committed by lower class individuals and gangs. Sutherland's work on white collar crime eventually gave rise to the study of organizational crime, illegal acts committed by collectivities (Cohen 1990; Gross 1978; Schrager & Short 1978). The study of organizational crime has grown tremendously over the past two decades. Most of the attention has been concentrated on two types of organizations: (1) private business corporations and (2) government or state agencies.

While the study of corporate crime has become well established (Clinard & Yeager 1980; Cullen, Maakestad & Cavender 1987; Hochstedler 1984), the study of the criminality of state agencies has not. The role of the state has expanded greatly in this century and the state has become a major focus of political and historical sociology in recent years (Block 1987; Evans, Rueschemeyer & Skocpol 1985; Held 1989; Thomas & Meyer 1984). But research on the crimes of the state has lagged behind and is widely scattered. While Chambliss (1988a, 1988b, 1989) has done a considerable amount of research in this area, and a few other criminologists have directed attention to this topic (Simon & Eitzen 1990; Ermann & Lundman 1987; Roebuck & Weeber 1978; Grabosky 1989; Barak 1991), much of the work on state or government crime has been done outside the boundaries of criminology.[1]

Thus, in large part, criminologists have seriously neglected the important problem of organized violence committed by governmental agencies. While there are a number of reasons for this neglect, we will focus on one major reason: the traditional definition of

Toward The Study of Governmental Crime 545

crime as a violation of state criminal law. After discussing the limitations of state definitions of crime, we will propose that standards derived from international law serve as an epistemological framework for the study of government crime.

From State Definitions to International Law

> . . .it is not the social harms punishable by law which cause the greatest misery in the world. It is the lawful harms, those unpunishable crimes justified and protected by law, the state, the ruling elites that fill the earth with misery, want, strife, conflict, slaughter and destruction (Tifft & Sullivan 1980, p. 9).

The organized violence committed by the state has not been a central concern of criminologists primarily because of the acceptance of state definitions of crime as the only legitimate criteria for the inclusion of behavior within the boundaries of criminological study. As Cohen (1990) states: "Governments and their agencies do not commit crimes, but only because the criminal law does not take cognizance of them as criminal actors" (p. 104). He goes on to note that, "they do, however, produce lots of noncriminal deviance..." (p. 104).

We believe that this distinction between criminal and noncriminal deviance, however useful it is in the study of law and the social construction of crime, is not helpful in drawing the boundaries around the behavioral realities of crime. As critical criminologists, we argue that the classification of behavior as criminal for the purposes of scholarly research should not be limited only to state definitions, but can and should include other standards as well. Specifically, we contend that the principles and substantive content of international law can and should be employed as standards by which the violence of nation-states can be examined as a criminological question.

We start with the premise that no behavior is inherently criminal. There is no act that is in and of itself criminal. Criminality is not a quality that resides within behavior or persons. If one accepts this presupposition, then it follows that, in any arena we can identify (political or scholarly for example), some definitional process is a necessary condition for the existence of "crime". Since criminal behavior is not pre-given, there must be some procedure that can be used to identify acts which are criminal and acts which are not. Every political jurisdiction, for example, must develop some legal process to classify acts as criminal. Some legal mechanism must be used to select

546 *Humanity & Society*

out certain behaviors and define them as criminal (leaving other behaviors as non-criminal). The state establishes legislative bodies to pass criminal laws (and therefore create crime), police agencies to enforce these laws, prosecutorial units to bring charges based on these laws, and courts to convict and punish individuals who have violated the laws (thereby creating criminals). These laws and their supporting institutions are rooted in the moral values and concrete interests of those who create them, or of their political supporters.

Just as political authorities follow a value and interest laden process to classify behavior as criminal for the purposes of formal social control, so too must criminologists follow a value and interest laden process to classify behavior as criminal for the purposes of scientific study. In the case of criminologists, however, there is no formal mechanism to create these definitions as there is within the state. Criminologists, therefore, are faced with a dilemma: how do we identify behavior as criminal for the purpose of study? The easiest way, and the traditional way of course, is to simply borrow the set of legal standards created by the state. Thus, crime is conventionally defined as the violation of state criminal law. Indeed, as we have noted, many criminologists regard these legal standards as the only permissible set of standards that can be used to define crime within the discipline of criminology.

By choosing this definition of crime, criminologists decide to use the moral values and legal norms encoded in the criminal law as the set of standards by which to classify behavior as criminal for the purpose of scientific study. This choice, however, requires a value judgement on the part of the criminologist that it is more appropriate for political authorities to select the behavior that criminologists will study than to allow criminologists to set up their own independent criteria. As Sellin (1938) pointed out, this clearly results in a loss of scientific autonomy for the criminologist. Furthermore, this choice of a legal definition has important moral and political implications. As critical criminologists have pointed out, such a definition restricts criminologists to the study of those acts which are legally defined as criminal by the state, thus excluding other types of socially harmful and morally insensitive behavior, especially those perpetrated by the state, ruling elites and corporate organizations. As Tifft and Sullivan (1980) note: "By assuming definitions of crime within the framework of law, by insisting on legal assumptions as sacred, criminologists comply in the concealment and distortion of the reality of social harms inflicted by persons with power" (p. 6).

On scientific, moral and political grounds, critical criminologists argue that we must not be limited to state definitions of crime in the

Toward The Study of Governmental Crime 547

study of criminal behavior. Critical criminology must reformulate the definition of its subject matter so that all of the acts that violate the emancipatory values we champion are brought within the boundaries of the discipline. Such a definition will force us to openly confront the moral and political choices involved in defining any act as criminal. The major problem facing this effort is the difficulty of translating rather abstract emancipatory values such as freedom, social justice, equality, democracy and solidarity into a specific set of standards that can be used to classify behavior as criminal for theoretical and research purposes. How can we create a definition of crime that will bring organizational and institutional harms within the boundaries of criminology? Those who would advocate expanding the definition of crime beyond the categories of criminal law must confront the vital task of delineating a moral and scientific basis for correctly applying the category of crime to socially injurious acts engaged in by the state (Schwendingers 1977).

Over the years a number of attempts have been made to expand the definition of crime beyond the traditional criminal law approach (see Kramer 1982). Many of these attempts have been related to the issue of white collar crime. For example, Sutherland (1940, 1949) argued that civil and regulatory law can be used to classify white collar crime as "real crime." This expanded legal definition drew sharp criticism from some (Tappan 1947), but it has become widely accepted by those who study white collar and corporate crime today.

Critical criminologists, however, insist the definition of crime must be expanded beyond state definitions entirely. They have proposed a variety of "social" definitions of crime. The concepts of human rights and peoples' rights have figured prominently in these efforts (McCaughan 1989). The Schwendingers (1970) were the first to propose a social definition of crime based on the notion of fundamental, historically determined, human rights. Others have followed the Schwendingers lead in using the notion of human rights as the basis for the definition of crime (Galliher 1989).

One other fruitful avenue to consider in the search for an effective way to translate emancipatory values into a set of specific standards to classify behavior as criminal for scientific purposes is in the area of international law. Many emancipatory values, peoples' rights and human rights have received legal expression through various international treaties and agreements (Akehurst 1987; Ferencz 1980; McCaughan 1989). Michalowski and Kramer (1987) have suggested that to bring the transgressions of transnational corporations within the purview of criminological work we utilize the standards contained in the United Nations Draft Codes of Conduct on Transnational Corporations. As they note (1987):

> The general principles outlined in the U. N. codes, as well as the specific provisions under each, provide a conceptual framework which allows us to expand the scope of inquiry without the epistemological hazards of definitions derived from personal conceptions of human rights. The U. N. codes represent the current stage of political struggle to refine the concept of human rights, and rights of national sovereignty, vis-a-vis large, transnational, corporate institutions. As such they are the appropriate reference point for understanding what constitutes transgressions by these institutions. (p. 47)

In the same way, we propose that the general principles and substantive content of various forms of international law constitute the specific standards that we use to classify the socially injurious actions of states and government agencies as crime for the purposes of criminological study. As Held (1989) points out: "Rights and duties are recognized in international law which transcend the claims of nation-states and which, whilst they may lack coercive powers of enforcement, have far reaching consequences" (p. 202).

In the two case studies that follow, we present two examples of organized violence on the part of the United States government and discuss the relevant portions of international law which allow us to make the judgment that these acts constitute criminal behavior worthy of criminological study.

The United States and Nuclear Weapons

> . . .the almost total absence of attention to the nuclear arms issue by criminal justicians, in their professional capacity, may well represent both a lack of scholarly imagination as well as gross form of professional irresponsibility (Friedrichs 1985, p. 5).

In 1942, under a racquet court at the University of Chicago, the first self-sustaining nuclear reaction took place. The top-secret Manhattan Project was soon established to design, test, and manufacture atomic weapons. Less than three years later, the product of these series of experiments, the atomic bomb, was dropped on

Toward The Study of Governmental Crime 549

Japan, destroying the cities of Hiroshima and Nagasaki. Thus, the United States became the first country to use nuclear weapons against an adversary.

Not only was the United States the first, and to this point, the only country to have actually used nuclear weapons, but it soon became U. S. government policy to threaten to use these weapons of mass destruction to ensure "peace." Shortly after the atomic bombs were dropped on Japan, President Truman said, "I shall give further consideration. . .as to how atomic power can become a powerful and forceful influence towards the maintenance of peace" (quoted in Williams & Cantlelon 1984, p. 77). Hence, the birth of the doctrine of nuclear deterrence.

This doctrine, based on the idea that the possession and threatened use of nuclear weapons will deter enemy aggression, has retained its popularity with every administration since Truman's. In 1982, President Reagan asserted that, ". . .it still takes weapons to prevent war" (quoted in Williams & Cantelon 1984, p. 212). Although the concept of nuclear deterrence has been given different interpretations over the years, ". . .it still remains the military theology of our times" (Williams & Cantelon 1984, p. 234).

The importance of the doctrine of deterrence cannot be over-estimated. Due to this doctrine, the United States government has stockpiled well over 23,000 nuclear weapons (Cochran, Arkin, Norris, & Sands, 1989). Nuclear deterrence became a kind of strange addiction wherein more weapons and more powerful warheads were needed to provide an illusion of "security." But it would have taken only 1,000 warheads to completely destroy the former Soviet Union as a functioning society (LaRocque 1988).

It is commonly thought that the United States has not actively considered using nuclear weapons since 1945. However, Ellsburg (1981) has documented twelve separate occasions since World War II in which the U. S. has considered and/or threatened to use nuclear weapons. He writes, "In most of (these cases). . .the aim was to coerce in urgent circum- stances a much weaker opponent that possessed no nuclear weapons at all. In the remaining cases, the object. . .was to intimidate the Soviet Union" (p. vii).

The irrational and dangerous stockpiling of nuclear warheads, the bureaucratic planning to employ these weapons, the policy of first use of nuclear devices to respond to conventional attack in Europe, and the documented threats to use nuclear weapons in order to coerce an opponent in times of crisis, all reflect a "genocidal mentality" on the part of the United States government and its representatives (Lifton & Markusen 1990). We argue that these actions and policies of the United

States government constitute organized criminal activity that can be brought within the parameters of criminology through the use of international law.

The primary function of international law is "the elimination of the arbitrary use of force and violence in international relations" (Meyrowitz 1981, p. 77). The most basic principle of international law holds that "the aim of war should be to conquer the enemy, not destroy him" (Lawyers' Committee on Nuclear Policy 1990, p. 6). Embedded within international law are the Laws of Armed Conflict: principles and rules regulating the conduct of armed hostilities between states (Builder & Graubard 1982). These laws derive from three sources: "(1) basic principles, such as humanity and military necessity, (2) the custom or conduct of nations in conflict, and (3) international agreements, such as treaties and resolutions" (Builder & Graubard 1982, p. 4).

Nuclear weapons are not generally prohibited by international law except for a few treaties which outlaw their existence in specific areas: The Treaty of Tlatelol of 1967 prohibits the use, manufacture, production, or acquisition of nuclear weapons in Latin America; The 1960 Antarctic Treaty denuclearized Antarctica; The 1966 Treaty on Principles Governing the Activities in Exploration and Use of Outer Space outlaws nuclear weapons in outer space; and the Treaty Banning Nuclear Weapons from the Sea-Bed and Ocean Floor (1970) prohibits the installation or testing of nuclear weapons in oceans (Meyrowitz 1981). Except for these four treaties, nuclear weapons are not specifically prohibited in a general context, i.e., there are no treaties which explicitly prohibit "nuclear weapons." However, as Weston (1983) points out, "While the lack of an explicit ban may mean that nuclear weapons are not illegal per se, the fact is that the restraints of the conduct of war have never been limited to explicit treaty prohibitions alone" (p. 228). Thus, to address the issue of the legality of nuclear weapons, the conglomeration of principles generically referred to as the Laws of Armed Conflict must serve as the primary basis of such examination.

The legality of nuclear weapons is most often challenged through the interpretation of five basic decisions or conventions which comprise the vast majority of principles in the Laws of Armed Conflict: (1) The Declaration of St. Petersburg (1868), (2) The Hague Convention and Regulations of 1907, (3) The Geneva Gas Protocol of 1925, (4) The Geneva Convention (1949), and (5) the Additional Protocol of the 1949 Geneva Convention (1977). Several legal scholars have derived six principles from these sources of international law to challenge the legality of nuclear weapons (Lawyers' Committee on

Toward The Study of Governmental Crime 551

Nuclear Policy 1984, 1990; Meyrowitz 1981, 1990; Vickman 1988; Weston 1983). These principles are:

1. It is prohibited to use weapons or tactics that cause unnecessary or aggravated destruction and/or suffering;[2]

2. It is prohibited to use weapons or tactics that cause indiscriminate harm as between combatants and noncombatants, military and civilian personnel;[3]

3. It is prohibited to effect reprisals that are disproportionate to their antecedent provocation or to legitimate military objectives, or disrespectful of persons, institutions, and/or resources otherwise prohibited by the laws of war;[4]

4. It is prohibited to use weapons or tactics that cause widespread, long-term, and severe damage to the natural environment;[5]

5. It is prohibited to use weapons or tactics that violate the neutral jurisdiction of non-participating states;[6]

6. It is prohibited to use asphyxiating, poisonous, or other gas, and all analogous materials or devices including bacteriological methods of warfare.[7]

These six principles are generally accepted and considered binding by the vast majority of countries (Lawyers' Committee on Nuclear Policy 1990). Clearly, each of these principles seems relevant to the nuclear weapons challenge. Because the effects of a nuclear attack are unpredictable (principles 3 and 5), indiscriminate (principle 2), and capable of mass annihilation (principles 1, 4, and 6), it seems clear that the principles and standard of international law would be violated by the execution of a nuclear attack, regardless of the intensity.

The actual use of nuclear weapons would be a violation of the United Nations Charter. On several occasions, the U. N. has condemned the use of nuclear weapons as an "international crime." On November 24, 1961, the General Assembly declared in Resolution 1653 (XVI) that "any state using nuclear or thermonuclear weapons is to be considered as violating the Charter of the United Nations, as acting contrary to the law of humanity, and as committing a crime against mankind and civilization" (Lawyers' Committee on Nuclear Policy 1990, p. 16). The principles laid down by the Genocide Convention of 1948 and the Nuremburg Charter also indicate that the use of nuclear weapons would be illegal. As Mohr (1988) points out, "There is only one conclusion: as a matter of principle and substance, international humanitarian law or the laws of armed conflict are fully relevant to the nuclear challenge" (p. 16).

The threat to use nuclear weapons is also prohibited by international law. In a lawsuit filed on behalf of the "People of the World", Judge Francis A. Boyle (quoted in Vickman 1988) declared:

> The threat to use nuclear weapons (i.e., nuclear deterrence/terrorism) constitutes ongoing international criminal activity. Namely, planning, preparation, solicitation, and conspiracy to commit crimes against peace, crimes against humanity, war crimes, genocide as well as grave breaches of the Four Geneva Conventions of 1949, the Additional Protocol I of 1977, the Hague Regulations of 1907, and the Genocide Convention of 1948. (p. 4)

Just as we outlaw the manufacture, possession, and ownership of certain weapons and drugs because of their consequences, so too under international law have the manufacture, possession, and ownership of nuclear weapons been prohibited. The same arguments outlined above concerning the use of nuclear weapons, provide a sound legal basis for criminalizing their manufacture and possession. As the Lawyers' Committee on Nuclear Policy (1984) observes:

> If a course of action is illegal, then the planning and preparation for such an action are, by legal and moral logic, also forbidden. Moreover, the attack on the legality of manufacturing and possessing nuclear weapons is all the more necessary given the increasing prospects for the "accidental" use of nuclear weapons arising out of today's dangerous first-strike strategies. (p. 151)

In conclusion, the actual use of nuclear weapons, as well as the manufacture, possession, and threat to use nuclear weapons are all prohibited by international law.[8] The United States has executed a nuclear attack, manufactured nuclear weapons for 45 years, and has threatened to use these weapons on several occasions. The conclusion is clear: The United States government stands in direct violation of international law, the Laws of Armed Conflict, and the Charter of the United Nations. Thus, U.S. nuclear weapons policy constitutes organized criminal violence which can and should be brought within the boundaries of criminological study.

United States Intervention in Nicaragua

The history of Twentieth Century Nicaragua is a case study of different techniques of foreign intervention. From direct military intervention and occupation, the creation and maintenance of a surrogate police/army force, to the inaccurately labeled "low-intensity warfare," the United States has sought politically and economically to control Nicaragua. In the following case study we will demonstrate that U. S. actions in Nicaragua have consistently violated the standards and philosophy of international law. Thus, as with U.S. weapons policy, U.S. intervention in Nicaragua can be addressed as an important criminological concern.

We will examine the two most recent cases of intervention in Nicaragua. First we will look at U. S. support for the Somoza family dynasty and the National Guard police/army force it controlled from 1933 to 1979; second, we will describe U. S. efforts to overthrow the Sandinista government which resulted from the popular revolution against Somoza.

The United States first intervened militarily in Nicaragua in the 1850s. From 1911 to 1933 U. S. Marines occupied Nicaragua, during the last seven years undertaking "the region's first counterinsurgency war" (Barry & Preusch 1986, p. 272). Domestic pressure in the States and lack of military success in Nicaragua forced the Marines to end the occupation. To take their place, the Marines created a surrogate security force of Nicaraguans called the National Guard.

Until the success of the Sandinista revolution, the National Guard enabled the Somoza family dynasty to control Nicaragua. While the Somoza family amassed much of Nicaragua's wealth and "ruled the country as a private fiefdom" (LaFeber 1984, p. 69), the Guard protected against popular uprisings.

Human rights in Nicaragua were subject to the whims of Somoza and the Guard, and were, therefore, largely non-existent. By the mid-1970s, after Somoza declared a state of siege, the human rights violations increased. Amnesty International's 1975-76 report states (1976) that "torture, arbitrary detention and 'disappearance' appear increasingly characteristic of the human rights situation in Nicaragua..." (pp. 105-106). A 1976 Amnesty mission to Nicaragua reported the occurrence of:

> Wholesale killing of peasant farmers (campesinos) and
> their disappearance after detention. . .rural camps used
> for large-scale detentions of campesinos. . .burning of

crops, homes and farm buildings. . .severe and
prolonged torture. (pp. 25-32)

Describing the National Guard's role in Nicaragua's human rights
violations, Amnesty (1976) stated:

This broad range of human rights violations under the
state of siege can be largely attributed to the unchecked
action of the combined army-police force, the Guardia
Nacional. (p. 106)

Despite its horrible human rights record, the Somoza regime,
"enjoyed total support from Washington" (LaFeber 1984, p. 226). The
United States not only created the Guard, but also maintained it by
providing training, equipment and financial support. From 1950 to
1979, 5,673 Guardsmen were trained under U. S. programs. Among
the courses taught at the U. S. operated Army School of the Americas
were "Counter- insurgency Operations, Urban Counterinsurgency,
Military Intelligence Interrogator. . ." (Klare & Arnson 1981, p. 49).
Even after training for such forces as the Guard was Congressionally
outlawed in late 1974, the Guard "continued to receive funding and
training" (Klare & Arnson 1981, pp. 50-52) through various loopholes.

From 1950 to 1979, Nicaragua received $40.4 million in military
aid, and was allowed to purchase $9.6 million in arms from the U. S.
government and U. S. private firms. Included in the arms sales were
rifles, pistols, revolvers, submachine guns, gas grenades and
projectiles, gas masks and bayonets, weapons "intended for internal
use, to control strikes and disorders and to suppress dissent," rather
than to defend the country from external attack (Klare & Arnson 1981,
p. 4).

The U. S. also bolstered the Somoza regime economically, even
helping the Guard to cloak its counterinsurgency efforts as economic
development programs. "U. S. assistance formed the backbone of the
dictatorship of Anastasio Somoza," writes Barry and Preusch, (1988, p.
194).

Barry and Preusch, (1988) detail how U. S. Agency for International Development economic programs were administered by the
Guard in areas where anti-Somoza sentiment was strong. Such
programs, he states, were not designed to significantly improve
peasants' living standards, but "to improve the public image" of the
Guard (p. 96).

Although the Carter Administration ended military aid during
Somoza's final struggle against the Nicaraguan people, economic aid

Toward The Study of Governmental Crime 555

continued. "Despite frequent revelations about government corruption and human rights abuses, economic assistance continued to flow to Nicaragua until the last days of the Somoza regime" (Barry & Preusch 1988, p. 195).

In July of 1979, the Nicaraguan people, led by the Sandinista Front for the Liberation of Nicaragua (FSLN), overthrew the Somoza regime. Even before the revolution's final military victory, the United States was intervening to gain control of post-Somoza Nicaragua. To influence segments of the broad-based revolution, "Carter authorized covert CIA support for labor unions, the press, and other elements within Nicaragua that could be controlled by the United States" (Barry 1988, pp. 199-200). Carter Administration goals centered around keeping the National Guard intact and preventing changes in Nicaraguan economic policy (Sklar 1988).

Two months after Carter left office, President Reagan signed a finding which "authorized a $19.5 million aid program of expanded CIA activity (in Central America). . .including assistance to Sandinista opponents inside Nicaragua" (Sklar 1988, p. 72). Armed Nicaraguan exiles, many of them former National Guard members, were organized by the CIA into the Nicaraguan Democratic Front (FDN), the Contras.

Illustrating the ties between Somoza's Guard and the Contras, Barry and Preusch (1986) observe that:

> A 1985 study entitled Who Are The Contras? by the Arms Control and Foreign Policy Caucus of the U. S. Senate revealed the degree to which the FDN was a reincarnation of Somoza's National Guard. The study found that 46 of the FDN's 48 military leaders had been members of the Guardia. (p. 277)

Given the horrendous human rights record of the Guard, it was not surprising that the Contras also used tactics that consistently violated international law and human rights standards. The Contras targeted hospitals, schools, and bridges for destruction. Workers on Nicaragua's campaign against illiteracy were murdered. Sklar (1988) noted that the human rights group Americas Watch found in a March 1985 study that:

> The Contra forces have systematically violated the applicable laws of war throughout the conflict. They have attacked civilians indiscriminately; they have tortured and mutilated prisoners. . .(they) practice terror as a deliberate policy. (p. 187)

U. S. responsibility for Contra human rights violations went far beyond funding the counterrevolutionary group. The discovery of a manual prepared under the direction of the head of the CIA's Latin American division revealed more direct U. S. involvement. Titled Psychological Operations in Guerilla Warfare, the manual "advocated a mix of political propaganda and terror to dominate the population" (Sklar 1988, p. 178). A second CIA manual, titled Freedom Fighter's Manual was also found. Tactics it suggested ranged "from petty acts to life-threatening violence. . ." (Sklar 1988, p. 183).

After growing impatient with the Contras' lack of military effectiveness, the CIA began to take more direct actions to overthrow the Nicaragua government. The CIA, according to LaFeber (1984):

> Directed the mining of Nicaraguan harbors and blew holes into a dozen foreign ships. . .directed air and sea attacks on Nicaraguan port facilities and oil refineries. . .conducted bombing raids over Nicaragua from air fields in Honduras and Costa Rica. (p. 315)

U. S. intervention in Sandinista Nicaragua also involved political and economic measures designed to complement the military actions. Opposition groups received U. S. funding: 1984 FDN Presidential candidate Arturo Cruz received CIA funds; anti-Sandinista newspaper La Prensa received U. S. National Endowment for Democracy funds; a Nicaraguan labor union received AIFLD funds. Former Contra spokesman Edgar Chamorro stated (quoted in Sklar 1988) that:

> Approximately 15 Honduran journalists and broadcasters were on the C.I.A.'s payroll, and our influence was thereby extended to every major Honduran newspaper and radio and television station. (p. 132)

In 1983, President Reagan "slashed Nicaragua's sugar quota by 90%. . .a clear breach of international trade laws. . ." (Barry 1988, p. 212). The Reagan Administration also opposed all loans to Nicaragua from international lending institutions. Along with mining Nicaragua's harbors, the CIA instructed the Contras "to destroy export crops (especially coffee and tobacco), and to attack farms and cooperatives" (Sklar 1988, p. 134). U. S. Agency for International Development programs, used in Nicaragua during the 1960s and 1970s to benefit the National Guard, were during the 1980s "used to shore-up the anti-

Toward The Study of Governmental Crime 557

Sandinista private sector and to build an internal counterrevolutionary force" (Barry 1988, p. 205).

Through the framework of international law, the actions we have described can be conceptualized as organized criminal violence. Article 5 of the Universal Declaration of Human Rights states that "No one shall be subjected to torture or to cruel, inhuman, or degrading treatment or punishment." Article 9 states that "No one shall be subjected to arbitrary arrest." Article 20(1) states that "everyone has the right to freedom of peaceful assembly and association" (Blaustein, Clark, & Sigler 1987). Somoza's Nicaragua consistently violated these and many other articles of the Declaration. The first article of the International Covenants on Economic, Social and Cultural Rights, and of Civil and Political Rights, states that "all peoples have the right of self-determination." Central to Somoza's Nicaragua was the suppression of political and economic self-determination.

United States support of the National Guard was a clear violation of international law and human rights standards and thus can be considered criminal. Support of the Guard denied Nicaraguans even the most basic human rights, as well as rights to economic and political freedom. While Somoza owned roughly 20% of Nicaragua's wealth, "two out of three children were undernourished and two out of three peasant farmers were completely landless or had plots too small for subsistence" (Sklar 1988, p. 9).

As Klare and Arnson (1981) argue, "logic suggests that any government which assists another in the abuse of human rights. . .is an accessory to such offenses and should be condemned accordingly" (p. 7). By maintaining the National Guard, even after knowledge of their human rights violations was widespread, and by sustaining the puppet Somoza regime, the United States was a very active accessory to the violations of international law of pre-Sandinista Nicaragua.

U. S. support for the Contras also consistently violated international law and human rights, including Article 2(4) of the United Nations Charter, which prohibits the use of force against another state. In June of 1986, the World Court, the principal judicial organ of the United Nations, ruled that the Charters of the U. N. and Organization of American States were violated by U. S. support for the Contras. In its ruling, (quoted in Briggs 1987) the Court:

> Decides that the United States of America, by training, arming, equipping, financing, and supplying the Contra forces or otherwise encouraging, supporting, and aiding military and paramilitary activities in and against Nicaragua, has acted, against the Republic of Nicaragua,

in breach of its obligation under customary international law not to intervene in the affairs of another state. (p. 79)

On the question of whether U. S. political intervention in Nicaragua constitutes a violation of international law, Damrosch (1989) argues that "a state violates the nonintervention norm when its nonforcible political activities prevent the people of another state from exercising the political rights and freedoms that form part of the evolving body on international human rights law" (p. 6).

On the question of economic intervention, Farer (1985) argues that it "is aggression when, and only when, the objective of the coercion is to liquidate an existing state or to reduce that state to the position of a satellite" (p. 413). The World Court found that "it strains belief to suppose that a body formed in armed opposition to the Government of Nicaragua, and calling itself the 'Nicaraguan Democratic Force' intended only to check Nicaraguan interference in El Salvador and did not intend to achieve violent change of government in Nicaragua" (quoted in Highet 1987, p. 34). Given this finding, it strains belief that U.S. political and economic intervention designed to complement the Contras military intervention did not also violate customary international law.

Conclusion

While space limitations have precluded a full discussion of the two cases and the standards and philosophy of international law, we believe that we have demonstrated that standards derived from international law can serve as an epistemological framework for the future study of governmental crime. Organized criminal violence by states and governmental agencies are among the most destructive and costly crimes that can be committed. We hope that in the future, more and more criminologists turn their attention to the study of these criminal acts.

A focus on governmental crime through the epistemological framework of international law also opens up other important criminological topics for study. For example, how can international law be more effectively enforced? What sanctions can be applied to outlaw nation-states through an international court system? How can governmental crime be deterred? What is the process through which international law is created? Clearly, criminologists have much to contribute in these areas. We hope they will seize the opportunity to

Toward The Study of Governmental Crime 559

make such contributions to our understanding of governmental crime and international law.

NOTES

1. Sociologists like Giddens (1987a; 1987b) and Tilly (1985) have done important work on nation-states and the use of organized violence, and Kelman and Hamilton (1989) have written an impressive book on what they call "crimes of obedience," many of which are performed in response to orders from governmental authorities. Non-sociologists have also analyzed "how the government breaks the law" (Lieberman 1972), from the crimes of the U. S. intelligence agencies (Halperin, Berman, Borosage, & Marwick 1976) to state violations of international human rights around the world (Chomsky 1987, 1988; Frankel 1989; Herman 1982; Laqueur & Rubin 1989).
2. Derived from: Article 23 of the Hague Regulations, Article 25 of the 1949 Geneva Convention, and the Declaration of St. Petersburg.
3. Derived from: Article 48 of the Additional Protocol of 1977, the Geneva Convention IV "Convention on the Protection of Civilian Persons in Time of War," and the Declaration of St. Petersburg.
4. Derived from: Articles 20, 51, 53, and 55 of the 1977 Geneva Additional Protocol.
5. Derived from: Article 35 (3) of the 1977 Geneva Protocol Additional.
6. Derived from: the Hague Convention of 1907.
7. Derived from: the Geneva Gas Protocol of 1925.
8. This conclusion has also been drawn by the Michigan Nuremberg Campaign, a project of Michigan Faith and Resistance, a statewide organizing and education movement. The Michigan Nuremberg Campaign has filed a citizens' petition to state and local authorities requesting the investigation/prosecution of officers and directors of Williams International Corporation (which designs and tests cruise missile engines) and the Commanders of Wurtsmith Air Force Base. The legal brief filed in support of this petition by lawyers Anabel Dwyer and Deborah Choly draws heavily on various forms of international law.

560 Humanity & Society

REFERENCES

Akehurst, M. 1987. *A Modern Introduction to International Law*. London: Allen and Unwin.

Amnesty International. 1976. *The Amnesty International 1975-76 Report*. London: Amnesty International Publications.

Amnesty International. 1977. *The Republic of Nicaragua: An Amnesty International Report Including The Findings of a Mission to Nicaragua, 10-15 May 1976*. London: Amnesty International Publications.

Barak, G. (Ed.) 1991. *Crimes by the Capitalist State*. Albany: State University of New York Press.

Barry, T. & Preusch, D. 1986. *The Central American Fact Book*. New York: Grove Press.

Barry, T. & Preusch, D. 1988. *The Soft War: The Uses and Abuses of Economic Aid in Central America*. New York: Grove Press.

Blaustein, A. P., Clark, R. S., & Sigler, J. A. 1987. *Human Rights Sourcebook*. New York: Paragon House Publishers.

Block, F. 1987. *Revising State Theory: Essays in Politics and Postindustrialism*. Philadelphia: Temple University Press.

Briggs, H. 1987. "The International Court of Justice Lives up to its Name." *American Journal of International Law* 81: 78-86.

Builder, C. H. & Graubard, M. H. 1982. *The International Law of Armed Conflict: Implications for the Concept of Assured Destruction*. Santa Monica, CA: The Rand Corporation.

Chambliss, W. 1988a. *On the Take: From Petty Crooks to Presidents* (rev. ed.). Bloomington: Indiana University Press.

Chambliss, W. 1988b. *Exploring Criminology*. New York: Macmillan.

Chambliss, W. 1989. "State-organized Crime." *Criminology* 27: 183-208.

Chomsky, N. 1987. *On Power and Ideology*. Boston: South End Press.

Chomsky, N. 1988. *The Culture of Terrorism*. Boston: South End Press.

Clinard, M. B. & Yeager, P. C. 1980. *Corporate Crime*. New York: The Free Press.

Cochran, T. B., Arkin, W. M., Norris, R.S., & Sands J. I. 1989. *Nuclear Weapons Databook: Soviet Nuclear Weapons, Vol. 4*. New York: Harper & Row.

Cohen, A. K. 1990. "Criminal Actors: Natural Persons and Collectivities." Pp. 101-25 in *New Directions in the Study of Justice, Law, and Social Control*, by Arizona State University School of Justice Studies. New York: Plenum Press.

Cullen, F. T., Maakestad, W. J., & Cavender, G. 1987. *Corporate Crime Under Attack: The Ford Pinto Case and Beyond*. Cincinnati: Anderson Publishing.

Damrosch, L. F. 1989. "Politics Across Borders: Nonintervention and Nonforcible Influence Over Domestic Affairs." *American Journal of International Law* 83(1): 1-50.

Toward The Study of Governmental Crime 561

Ellsburg, D. 1981. "Call to Mutiny." Pp. i-xxviii in *Protest and Survive,* edited by E. P. Thompson & D. Smith. New York: Monthly Review Press.

Ermann, M. D., & Lundman. R. J. 1987. *Corporate and Governmental Deviance: Problems of Organizational Behavior in Contemporary Society* (3rd ed.). New York: Oxford University Press.

Evans, P., Rueschemeyer, D. & Skocpol, T. 1985. *Bringing the State Back In.* Cambridge: Cambridge University Press.

Farer, T. J. 1985. "Political and Economic Coercion in Contemporary International Law." *American Journal of International Law* 79(2): 405-413.

Ferencz, B. B. 1980. *An International Criminal Court--A Step Toward World Peace: A Documentary History and Analysis.* (Vols. 1-2). New York: Oceana Publications.

Frankel, M. 1989. *Out of the Shadows of Night: The Struggle for International Human Rights.* New York: Delacorte Press.

Friedrichs, D. 1985. "The Nuclear Arms Issue and the Field of Criminal Justice." *The Justice Professional* I: 5-9.

Galliher, J. F. 1989. *Criminology: Human Rights, Criminal Law, and Crime.* Englewood Cliffs, NJ: Prentice Hall.

Giddens, A. 1987a. "Nation-states and Violence." *Social Theory and Modern Sociology,* (pp. 166-182). Stanford: Stanford University Press.

Giddens, A. 1987b. *The Nation-State and Violence.* Berkeley: University of California Press.

Grabosky, P. N. 1989. *Wayward Governance.* Australian Institute of Criminology.

Gross, E. 1978. "Organizational Crime: A Theoretical Perspective." Pp. 55-85 in *Studies in Symbolic Interaction,* edited by N. K. Denzin Greenwich, CN: JAI Press.

Halperin, M. H., Berman, J. L., Borosage, R. L., & Marwick, C. M. 1976. *The Lawless State: The Crimes of the U.S. Intelligence Agencies.* New York: Penguin Books.

Held, D. 1989. *Political Theory and the Modern State.* Stanford: Stanford University Press.

Herman, E. S. 1982. *The Real Terror Network: Terrorism in Fact and Propaganda.* Boston: South End Press.

Highet, K. 1987. "Evidence, the Court, and the Nicaragua Case." *American Journal of International Law* 81(1): 1-56.

Hochstedler, E. 1984. *Corporations as Criminals.* Beverly Hills: Sage Publications.

Kelman, H. C., & Hamilton, V. L. 1989. *Crimes of Obedience.* New Haven: Yale University Press.

Klare, M. T., & Arnson, C. 1981. *Supplying Repression: U. S. Support for Authoritarian Regimes Abroad.* Washington: Institute for Policy Studies.

562   Humanity & Society

Kramer, R. C.   1982.   "The Debate Over the Definition of Crime: Paradigms, Value Judgments, and Criminological Work."   Pp. 33-58 in *Ethics, Public Policy, and Criminal Justice,* edited by F. Elliston & N. Bowie. Cambridge, MA: Oelgeschlager, Gunn & Hain.

LaFeber, W.   1984.   *Inevitable Revolutions: The United States in Central America.* New York: W. W. Norton & Company.

Laqueur, W., & Rubin, B.   1989.   *The Human Rights Reader* (rev. ed.). New York: Meridian.

LaRocque, G.   1988.   "What Should we defend? A New Military Strategy for the United States."   *The Defense Monitor XVII* 4: 1-8.

Lawyers Committee on Nuclear Policy.   1984.   *Statement on the Illegality of Nuclear Weapons.* New York: Lawyers' Committee on Nuclear Policy, Inc.

Lawyers Committee on Nuclear Policy.   1990.   *Statement on the Illegality of Nuclear Weapons.* New York: Lawyers' Committee on Nuclear Policy, Inc.

Lieberman, J. K.   1972.   *How the Government Breaks the Law.*   Briar Cliff Manor, NY: Stein and Day.

Lifton, R. J., & Markusen, E.   1990.   *The Genocidal Mentality: Nazi Holocaust and Nuclear Threat.* New York: Basic Books.

McCaughan, E.   1989.   "Human Rights and Peoples' Rights: An Introduction."   *Social Justice* 16: 1-7.

Meyrowitz, E. L.   1981.   "The Status of Nuclear Weapons Under International Law."   *The Guild Practitioner* 38: 65-82.

Meyrowitz, E. L.   1990.   *Prohibition of Nuclear Weapons: The Relevance of International Law.* Dobbs Ferry, NY: Transnational Publishers.

Michalowski, R. J. & Kramer, R. C.   1987.   "The Space Between Laws: The Problem of Corporate Crime in a Transnational Context."   *Social Problems* 34: 34-53.

Mohr, M.   1988.   "International Humanitarian Law and the Law of Armed Conflict: Its Relevance to the Nuclear Challenge."   Pp. 83-90 in *Lawyers and the Nuclear Debate,* edited by M. Cohen & M. E. Govin. Ottawa, Canada: University of Ottawa Press.

Roebuck, J., & Weeber, S.   1978.   *Political Crime in the United States.*   New York: Praeger.

Schrager, L. S., & Short, J. F. Jr.   1978.   "Toward a Sociology of Organizational Crime."   *Social Problems* 25: 407-419.

Schwendinger, H. and Schwendinger, J.   1970.   "Defenders of Order or Guardians of Human Rights?"   *Issues in Criminology* 5: 123-157.

Schwendinger, H. and Schwendinger, J.   1977.   "Social Class and the Definition of Crime."   *Crime and Social Justice* 7: 4-13.

Sellin, T.   1938.   *Culture, Conflict and Crime.* New York: Social Science Research Council.

Simon, D. R., & Eitzen, D. S.   1990.   *Elite Deviance* (3rd ed.).   Boston: Allyn and Bacon.

Toward The Study of Governmental Crime *563*

Sklar, H. 1988. *Washington's War on Nicaragua*. Boston: South End
    Press.
Sutherland, E. H. 1940. "White Collar Criminality." *American Sociological
    Review* 5: 1-12.
Sutherland, E. H. 1949. *White Collar Crime*. New York: Dryden. (Re-issued
    by Holt, Rinehart, & Winston, New York, 1961).
Tappan, P. 1947. "Who is the Criminal? " *American Sociological Review*
    12: 96-102.
Thomas, G. M. & Meyer, J. W. 1984. "The Expansion of the State." *Annual
    Review of Sociology* 10: 461-482.
Tifft, L. & Sullivan, D. 1980. *The Struggle to be Human: Crime,
    Criminology, and Anarchism*. Sanday, Orkney, U.K.: Cienfuegos Press.
Tilly, C. 1985. "War Making and State Making as Organized Crime." Pp.
    169-91 in *Bringing The State Back In*, edited by P. Evans, D.
    Rueschemeyer & T. Skocpol. Cambridge: Cambridge University Press.
Vickman, L. 1988. *Why Nuclear Weapons are Illegal*. Santa Barbara, CA:
    Nuclear Age Peace Foundation.
Weston, B. H. 1983. "Nuclear Weapons and International Law:
    Prolegomenon to General Illegality." *New York Law School Journal
    of International and Comparative Law* 4: 227-256.
Williams, R. C., & Cantelon, P. L. 1984. *The American Atom: A
    Documentary History of Nuclear Policies From the Discovery of
    Fission to the Present*. Philadelphia: University of Pennsylvania
    Press.

[5]

AUST & NZ JOURNAL OF CRIMINOLOGY (July 1993) 26 (97-115)   97

HUMAN RIGHTS AND CRIMES OF THE STATE:
THE CULTURE OF DENIAL*

Stanley Cohen†

Introduction

For personal and political reasons that I won't impose on you, I have gradually moved during the last decade from "doing" criminology to "doing" human rights. Living these years in Israel and faced by the mass violation of Palestinian rights in the Israeli Occupied Territories, my academic pre-occupations have made way for more activist work in the human rights field.

This has meant dealing with different subjects from those of traditional criminology or even the broader discourse of the sociology of law and social control. It has also meant getting used to a different style of work; the rhythms of human rights organisations (deadline, press conference, organising, casework) are not those of the leisurely university life; the genre of a human rights report (as I painfully discovered) is not the same as a paper for an academic journal. This is altogether a different intellectual subculture, with its own people, preoccupations, values and references.

Of course, these different worlds do meet. Some subjects appear to be pretty much the same (law, police, prisons, courts, violence, victims, justice . . .); there are the familiar debates between practitioners and theorists; research methods are not very different from regular social science work (a shoddy human rights report is bad for the same reasons as a shoddy research paper).

The research project on which I have just started working, though, stems more consciously from my human rights involvement than my academic criminology. So, when I was invited to give this lecture, my first thought was that I had nothing much to say to a criminological audience. On second thoughts, it seemed to me that the ways these fields have diverged despite their common grounds seemed worthy of attention. To frame my human rights topic for a criminological audience might be a worthwhile exercise.

My lecture has two aims. The first is to note some substantive lines of enquiry about my subject, the sociology of denial. The second is to suggest that the criminological agenda should take into account the subject of crimes of the state and its even wider referent, that is, human rights violations. Pretentiously — others before me have tried and failed — this second task is comparable to what Sutherland set himself in placing white collar crime on the criminological agenda.

Which of these two tasks is more important? Frankly, the first — the substance of my question. But in deference to the occasion — the John Barry Memorial Lecture at the conference of the Australian and New Zealand Society of Criminology — I'll start with my second task, looking for the criminological connection.

Criminology and Crimes of the State

It would be ludicrous to claim that Western criminology over the past decades has completely ignored the subject of state crime or the broader discourse of human

---

* John Barry Memorial Lecture, University of Melbourne, 30 September, 1992. The research referred to in this lecture is funded by a grant from the Ford Foundation International Human Rights Programme.
† Institute of Criminology, Faculty of Law, Hebrew University, Jerusalem 91905, ISRAEL

98   STANLEY COHEN   (1993) 26 ANZJ Crim

rights. My case does not need the standard PhD opening: everyone has ignored the subject except me. What I am saying, is that the subject has often been raised and then its implications conveniently repressed. This is a process strangely reminiscent of my substantive interest in the sociology of denial: how information is known but its implications are not acknowledged.

The first significant confrontation with the subject came in the early phase of radical criminology in the late sixties. That favourite debate of the times — "who are the *real* criminals?" — naturally turned attention from street crime to white collar/corporate crime and then to the wider notion of "crimes of the powerful". The particular context of the Vietnam War, pushed our slogans ("Hey, hey LBJ! How many kids have you killed today?") explicitly in the direction of "crimes of the state".

In criminology, this sentiment was expressed in the much cited paper by the Schwendingers (1970) entitled "Defenders of Order or Guardians of Human Rights?" Looking back at this text, it appears a missed opportunity to deal with the core issues of state crime.

Quite rightly, the Schwendingers saw themselves going in the same direction, but a step further than Sutherland by invoking the criterion of *social injury* to define crime. In the case of white collar crime, this mandated us to go beyond criminal law into the areas of civil and administrative law. The Schwendingers then noted that if Sutherland had consistently followed what they rightly call his "ethical" rather than legal categorisation, he should also have arrived at those other socially injurious actions which are not defined as either criminal or civil law violations. So far, so good. But their argument then goes awry.

Firstly, they cite as examples of other socially injurious action (their only examples) "genocide and economic exploitation". Now, besides the fact that these are hardly morally equivalent categories, genocide is crucially different from economic exploitation. It is recognised in current political discourse as crime by the state; it is clearly illegal by internal state laws; and since the Nuremberg Judgements and the 1948 UN Convention Against Genocide, it is a "crime" according to international law. Genocide belongs to the same conceptual universe as "war crimes" and "crimes against humanity". By any known criteria, genocide is more self evidently criminal than economic exploitation.

The Schwendingers make no such distinctions nor try to establish the criminality of human rights violations. Instead they launch into a moral crusade against imperialistic war, racism, sexism and economic exploitation. We might agree with their ideology and we might even use the term "crime" rhetorically to describe racism, sexism and economic exploitation. This type of sixties rhetoric indeed anticipates the current third and fourth generation "social rights". A more restricted and literal use of the concept "state crime" however, is both more defensible and useful. If we come from the discourse of human rights, this covers what is known in the jargon (for once, not euphemistic) as "gross" violations of human rights — genocide, mass political killings, state terrorism, torture, disappearances. If we come from the discourse of criminology, we are talking about clear criminal offences — murder, rape, espionage, kidnapping, assault.

I don't want to get into definitional quibbles. Enough to say that the extension of criminology into the terrain of state crimes, can be justified without our object of study becoming simply everything we might not like at the time. Let us see what happened after that mid-sixties to mid-seventies phase when questions about state crimes and human rights were placed on the criminological agenda by the radicals.

What mostly happened was that the human rights connection became lost. In the discourse of critical criminology, the putative connection between crime and politics took two different directions, both quite removed from the idea of state crime.

The first was the short-lived notion of the criminal as proto-revolutionary actor and the extension of this to all forms of deviance. This whole enterprise — referred to as the "politicisation of deviance" — was soon abandoned and eventually denounced as naive, romantic and sentimental.[1] The second connection — which turned out the more productive — was the focus on the criminalising power of the state. This led to the whole revisionist discourse on the sociology of law, social control and punishment that has remained so salient and powerful.

But neither direction leads anywhere near towards talking about state crimes. The subject simply faded away from criminological view in the mid-seventies to mid-eighties. By the time left realist criminology appeared, we move entirely from "crimes of the state" back to the "state of crime." Today, the subject has re-appeared from two contexts, one *external* to the discipline, the other *internal*.

The *external* context is the incremental growth of the international human rights movement itself. Emerging from the United Nations Charter and the great declarations and conventions of the next decade, from international governmental organisations such as UNESCO and the Council of Europe, from fledgling pressure groups such as Amnesty International to the vast current list of national and international non-governmental organisations, the human rights movement has become a major institutional force. Pushed by the rhetorical use of "human rights" by the Carter Adminstration about Latin America and its critique of the Soviet Union, the ideal of human rights took on a powerful life of its own. It has become a secular religion.

This discourse, of course, is very dense, complex and contradictory (*Social Justice*, 1989). "Human Rights" has become a slogan raised from most extraordinary different directions. Progressive forces and organisations like Amnesty can enlist famous rock stars to perform in defence of international human rights. Right wing pressure groups in the USA can unseat politicians and defeat Supreme Court nominations by invoking the human rights of the unborn foetus. Civil liberties groups defend pornography on the grounds of freedom of speech and the women's movement attack this freedom as an assault on the human rights of women. Nations with the most appalling record of state violence and terror can self-righteously join together in the UN to condemn other nations for their human rights violations. Some human rights activists are awarded the Nobel Peace Prize, others are jailed, tortured, have disappeared or been assassinated. The human rights of one group are held sacred, the rights of another totally ignored . . . and so on.

But whatever the concept of human rights means, it has become a dominant narrative. Arguably, with the so-called death of the old meta-narratives of marxism, liberalism and the cold war, human rights will become *the* normative political language of the future. I have no time to go into its conceptual ambiguities — the difference between civil and human rights, the relationship between political and human rights work, the tension between universalism and cultural relativism. Nor can I raise the numerous policy issues of policing, enforcement and international law. One of the most salient issues for criminologists, raised dramatically by the current horrors in the former Yugoslavia, is the long-proposed establishment of an international criminal tribunal.

So this is one way — from the outside — that criminologists as citizens who read the news, must have become aware of the subject of human rights violations and crimes of the state. Not that you know about this awareness if you just read

100   STANLEY COHEN   (1993) 26 ANZJ Crim

criminological texts. There is, however, one *internal* way in which the subject has been registered in criminology. This is through the growth of victimology.

There are many obvious echoes of human rights issues in victimological literature — whether in the feminist debate about female victims of male sexualised violence; in talking about children and children's rights; in the concern about victims of corporate crime, ecological abuse, etc. Some students (Karmen, 1990) find these echoes only in "radical" rather than "conservative" or "liberal" victiminology. The conservative tendency is concerned with victims of street crime, making offenders accountable, encouraging self reliance and advocating retributive justice. The liberal tendency includes white collar crime, is concerned with making the victim "whole" and advocates restitution and reconciliation. Only the radical tendency extends to all forms of human suffering and sees law and the criminal justice system as implicated in this suffering.

This distinction, though, between conservative, liberal and radical tendencies is not always clear. And in the context of one crucial subject — what happens to state criminals such as torturers after democratisation or a change in regime — the distinction breaks down altogether. Here, it is the "radicals" who call for punishment and retributive justice, while it is the "conservatives" who invoke ideals such as reconciliation to call for impunity.[2]

In any event, these external and internal inputs are slowly making their way into criminology. In the mainstream, this can be seen in recent standard textbooks which explicity deal with the subject of state crime, and others which consider the human rights definition of crime.

In the radical stream, there is Barak's recent (1991) volume *Crime By the Capitalist State*. The editor makes a strong case for including state criminality in the field of criminology — both on the grounds that the consequences of state crimes are more widespread and destructive than traditional crime and because this would be a logical extension of the already accepted move into the field of white collar crime. The overall tone of the volume, though, is too redolent of the sixties' debates: general ideas about discrimination and abuse of political and economic power, the focus only on capitalism and the disproportionate attention on worldwide low intensity warfare by the USA (CIA, counter-insurgency etc).

Despite this recent interest, major gaps in the criminological discourse remain:

(a) First, there is little understanding that a major source of criminalisation at national and international levels draws on the rhetoric of human rights. Significant waves of moral enterprise and criminalisation over the last decade are derived not from the old middle-class morality, the Protestant ethic nor the interests of corporate capitalism, but from the feminist, ecological and human rights movements. A major part of criminology is supposed to be the study of law making — criminalisation — but we pay little attention to the driving force behind so many new laws: the demand for protection from "abuses of power". The radical slogans of the sixties have become the common place of any government and inter-government forum. Alongside our standard research on domestic legislatures and ministries of justice, we should see what our foreign ministries are doing — at the Council of Europe, the United Nations, etc.

(b) Another important defect in recent literature is its American focus. It is pre-occupied with "exposures" — of the CIA (eg, drug running in Vietnam), FBI surveillance methods, the global drug wars, international arms dealing, etc. This results in a certain ethnocentrism, but also allows the derivative subjects (political economy, globalisation, state propaganda, illegal clandestine operations, counter intelligence) to be denied as being "normal politics" (like the white collar crime

HUMAN RIGHTS AND CRIMES OF THE STATE: THE CULTURE OF DENIAL   101

issue allowed the denial of "normal business"). For my purposes here, I want to stress not the politicality of the subject but its criminality. For this, we don't need theories of the state, we need merely to pick up the latest Amnesty Annual Report.

(c) If we have missed something about law making, we have ignored even more the facts of victimisation. Again, there is a ritualistic acknowledgement of the damage, harm and violence that are the obvious consequences of state crime – and then we return to easier topics. It is as if we don't want to face these facts; as if – to anticipate the substance of the second part of my lecture – we have denied their implications. I am aware that phrases such as "crimes of the twentieth century" sound bombastic – but for vast populations of the world, this is a fair characterisation of those "gross violations of human rights": genocide, mass political killings, disappearances, torture, rape by agents of state.[3]

This terrible record is known but (as I will show) simultaneously not known. Take genocides and mass political killings only: the Turkish genocide of at least a million Armenians; the Holocaust against six million Jews and the hundreds of thousands of political opponents, gypsies and others; the millions killed under Stalin's regime; the tribal and religious massacres in Burundi, Bengal and Paraguay; the mass political killings in East Timor and Uganda; the "autogenocide" in Cambodia; the "ethnic cleansing" in Bosnia; the death squads and disappearance in Argentina, Guatamala, El Salvador. Or take torture – a practise supposedly eradicated from Europe by the beginning of the 19th century and now routinely used in two thirds of the world.

To add up the deaths, injuries and destruction from all these sources and then compare this to the cumulative results of homicide, assault, property crime and sexual crime in even the highest crime countries of the world, is too tendentious an exercise, too insulting to the intelligence. One cannot calibrate human suffering in this way.

But criminologists do, after all talk about offence "seriousness". The standard literature in this area – and allied debates on culpability, harm, responsibility and the "just desserts" model – already compares street crime with white collar crime. A current important contribution (von Hirsch and Jareborg, 1991) tries to gauge criminal harm by using a "living standard analysis". Von Hirsch and his colleague have argued ingeniously that criminal acts can be ranked by a complicated scale of "degrees of intrusion" on different kinds of legally protected interests: physical integrity; material support and amenity; freedom from humiliation; privacy and autonomy.

What von Hirsch calls "interests" are strikingly close to what are also called "human rights". His examples, however, come only from the standard criminological terrain of citizen against citizen. Including corporate crime would extend the list to (business) organisations against citizen. This is certainly an interesting and worthwhile exercise. It allows, for example, the ranking of forcible rape by a stranger as very grave because this is so demeaning and gross an attack against the "freedom from humiliation" interest; therefore rape at gun point becomes more serious than armed robbery; date rape comes lower on the cumulative scale on grounds that threat to bodily safety is eliminated, and so on.

But neither crimes of state nor the wider category of "political crime" are mentioned. There is no logical reason why the identity of the offender should be assumed to be fixed as citizen against citizen, rather than state agent against citizen when talking about, say, murder, assault or rape. In fact, there are good **moral** reasons why any grading of seriousness should take this into account – in particular, the fact that the very agent responsible for upholding law, is actually responsible for the crime. And there is a good *empirical* reason: that for large parts of the world's

102   STANLEY COHEN   (1993) 26 ANZJ Crim

population, state agents (or para military groups, vigilantes or terrorists) are the normal violators of your "legally protected interests"

I don't want to oversimplify the many conceptual objections and obstacles that criminologists will legitimately raise to my glib appeal to include state crime in our frame of reference. Most such objections fall under two categories:

First, there are the equivalent arguments to those used in the field of corporate crime — that the state is not an actor and that individual criminal responsibility cannot be identified. For corporate crime, this objection has been disposed of often enough, most recently (and to my mind convincingly) by Braithwate and Fisse (1990). The corporation engages in rational goal seeking behaviour; it can act; it can have intentions; it can commit crimes. This is just as (though more complicatedly) true for the state.

The second objection (again paralleled from Sutherland onwards in the case of corporate crime) is that the resultant action is not "really" crime. Here, the counter-arguments are complicated and come from a number of different directions: (i) an appeal to international law and conventions on such concepts as "war crimes" or "crimes against humanity"; (ii) a demonstration that these acts are illegal by domestic criminal law and fit all criteria of "crime"; (iii) and even if the acts in question are legal by internal state jurisdiction, then the question arises of how this legal legitimation occurs. We have to remember (perhaps by inscribing this on our consciousness each morning) that state crimes are not just the unlicenced terror of totalitarian or fascist regimes, police states, dictatorships or military juntas. And in even the most extreme of these regimes, such as Nazi Germany, the discourse of legality is used (Muller, 1991).

One of the clearest and most eloquent texts for understanding these symbiotic issues of responsiblity and criminality, is the 1985 trial in Argentina of the former military junta members responsible for the mass killings, atrocities, disappearances of the "dirty war". Reports of this trial (eg, by Amnesty International) should be on all criminology reading lists.

The reasons why we don't make these connections are less logical than epistemological. The political discourse of the atrocity is, as I will soon show, designed to hide its presence from awareness. This is not a matter of secrecy, in the sense of lack of access to information, but an unwillingness to confront anomalous or disturbing information. Take the example of torture. Democratic-type societies — the French in Algeria (Maran, 1989); the British in Northern Ireland; the Israelis in the Occupied Territories (Cohen, 1991) — could all proclaim their adherence to international conventions and domestic laws against torture. This called for a complex discourse of denial that what they were doing constituted torture. No, it was something else, "special procedures" or "moderate physical pressure". So something happened — but it was not illegal. In more totalitarian societies (with no accountability, no free press, no independent judiciary) denial is simpler — you do it, but say you do not. Nothing happened.

The standard vocabulary of official (government) denial weaves its way — at times simulaneously, at times sequentially — through a complete spiral of denial. First you try "it didn't happen". There was no massacre, no one was tortured. But then the media, human rights organisations and victims show that it does happen: here are the graves; we have the photos; look at the autopsy reports. So you have to say that what happened was not what it looks to be but really something else: a "transfer of population", "collateral damage", "self defence". And then — the crucial subtext — what happened anyway was completely justified — protecting national security, part of the war against terrorism. So:

HUMAN RIGHTS AND CRIMES OF THE STATE: THE CULTURE OF DENIAL 103

- It doesn't happen here
- If it does, "it" is something else
- Even if it is what you say it is, it is justified

Faced with this spiral of denial, criminologists may not be expected to respond very differently from ordinary citizens. But the debate is only a little more complex and dramatic than debates about whether white collar crime is really crime. I say more "dramatic" because we are forced back not just to questions about what is normal business, but what is the normal state. Take, for example, the question of jurisdiction and punishment. Precisely because we expect so little from domestic and international law as sanctions against gross state crimes (against our own or other citizens), we seldom frame human rights violations in criminal terms. Talking about the limitations in the 1948 UN Convention Against Genocide and in the UN Charter itself, the anthropologist, Leo Kuper, remarks with characteristic irony that an unstated assumption of the international discourse is that:

> ... the sovereign territorial state claims, as an integral part of its sovereignty, the right to commit genocide or engage in genocidal massacres against people under its rule, and that the United Nations for all practical purposes, defends this right (Kuper, 1981, p 161).

Obviously, this is very complex territory — more complex than I can even hint at here — and it is understandable why mainstream criminology is reluctant to become too immersed in these debates. Their absence in "left realist" criminology is stranger to explain. After all, the ontological base here is a realist philosophy which starts with harm, victimisation, seriousness, suffering and supposed indifference to all this by the adolescent left idealism of the sixties.

I will return to some possible explanations for this blindsight. On one level, this is nothing more sinister than a Western ethnocentrism preoccupied with its own national concerns and secure in the great achievement of liberal capitalism; the separation of crime from the state. On another more interesting level, this stems from the universal tendency to see only what is convenient to see.

The Culture of Denial

Let me now turn to my substantive topic — denial. How did I get to this subject?

During the decade in which I have lived in Israel, but especially the past five years of the *intifada* (the uprising of Palestinians in the Occupied Territories), I have been puzzled by the apparent lack of overt reaction (dissent, criticism, protest) in just those sectors of Israeli society where one would expect to be reacting more. In the face of clear information about what's going on — escalating levels of violence and repression, beatings, torture, daily humiliations, collective punishment (curfews, house demolition, deportations), death-squad-type killings by army undercover units — the level of shame, outrage and protest, is not psychologically or morally appropriate.

Of course there are no objective scales of psychological or moral "appropriateness". But many observers, inside and outside the country, have sensed that this part of the public should find something more disturbing and be prepared to act accordingly.

Remember that I am talking not about that clear majority of the population who support these measures and would not object to even more severe repression. My object of study is the minority: the enlightened, educated middle class, responsive to messages of peace and co-existence, first to condemn human rights violations everywhere else in the world.

104   STANLEY COHEN   (1993) 26 ANZJ Crim

Note that unlike most societies where gross human rights violations occur, the facts are both private and public knowledge. Nearly everyone has direct personal knowledge, especially from army service. These are not conscripts or mercenary soldiers drawn from the underclass; everybody serves (including the middle class liberals) or has a husband, son, cousin or neighbour in reserve duty. There is a relatively open press, liberal in tone, which regularly and clearly exposes what is happening in the Occupied Territories. No one — least of all the group which interests me — can say those terrible (though, as I will show, complicated) words "I didn't know."

It is way beyond my scope to discuss the special reasons in Israel for denial, passivity or indifference. These are part of a complex political history — of being Jewish, of Zionism, of fear and insecurity. I mention this case only because it led me to comparisons, to looking for similarities and differences in other societies. I went back to my experience of growing up in apartheid South Africa. More fatefully, I turned to the emblematic events of this century: the Holocaust "texts" about the good Germans who knew what was happening; the lawyers and doctors who colluded; the ordinary people who passed by the concentration camps everyday and claimed not to know what was happening; the politicians in Europe and America who did not believe what they were told. Then from this one historical event, I went to the contemporary horrors reported every day in the mass media and documented by human rights reports — about Bosnia, Peru, Guatamala, Burma, Uganda . . .

All this — and the relevant social scientific literature — led me back to versions of the same universal question. This is not Milgram's famous question of how ordinary people will behave in terrible ways, but rather how ordinary, even good people, will not react appropriately to knowledge of the terrible. Why, when faced by knowledge of others' suffering and pain — particularly the suffering and pain resulting from what are called "human rights violations" — does "reaction" so often take the form of denial, avoidance, passivity, indifference, rationalisation or collusion?

I have mentioned the official state discourse: the pure denials (it didn't happen, they are lying, the media are biased, the world community is just picking on us) and the pure justifications (deterrence, self defence, national security, ideology, information gathering). But my concern is not the actor but rather (back, in a curious way, to labelling theory!) the audience. In the triangle of human suffering so familiar to criminologists — the victim, to whom things are done; the perpetrator, who is actively causing the suffering; the observer who sees and knows — my interest lies in this third corner: the audience, the observers, the bystanders.

For my purposes here, I want to consider a specific group of observers — not those whose avoidance derives from (crudely speaking) their *support* for the action. If they see nothing morally wrong or emotionally disturbing in what is happening, why should they do anything? In this sense, their denial or passivity is "easy" to explain. My interest is more in the subgroup who are ideologically predisposed to be against what is happening, to be disturbed by what they know. How do they react to their knowledge of the terrible?

Before presenting some lines of enquiry into this subject, let me note an important distinction which I won't have time to follow through. In talking about the denial of atrocities or human rights violations, there is a world of difference between reacting to your own government's actions as distinct from what might be happening in a distant country. My response, say, as an Australian, to newspaper revelations about the treatment of Aborigines in custody, follows different lines from my response to sitting in Melbourne and reading a human rights report about death squads in El Salvador.

HUMAN RIGHTS AND CRIMES OF THE STATE: THE CULTURE OF DENIAL   105

I have only just started work on this subject and can present you with not much more than my original research proposal. First, I will list some of the more useful bodies of literature which deal — directly, but more often obliquely — with the general phenomenon of denial. Then I will give a preliminary classification of the major forms of denial. Finally, I will note a few questions from my fieldwork on human rights organisations. Through interviews, analysis of publications, educational material advertisements and campaign evaluations, I am trying to understand how human rights messages are disseminated and received.

This last part of the work is a study in communication. The *sender* is the international human rights community (directly or through the mass media). The *audience* is our real and metaphorical bystanders. The *message* is something like this (to quote from an actual Amnesty International advert in Britain in 1991):

> *Brazil has solved the Problem of how to keep kids off the street. Kill Them.*

What bodies of literature might be of relevance?

(1) The Psychology of Denial

Orthodox psychoanalysis sees denial as an unconscious defence mechanism for coping with guilt and other disturbing psychic realities. Freud originally distinguished between "repression" which applies to defences against internal instinctual demands and "denial" (or what he called "disavowal") which applies to defences against the claims of external reality.

With a few exceptions, pure psychoanalytic theory has paid much less attention to denial in this sense than repression (but see Edelstein, 1989). We have to look in the more applied fields of psychoanalysis (or its derivatives) for studies about the denial of external information. This yields a mass of useful material. There is the rich literature on the denial of knowledge about fatal disease (especially cancer and more recently, AIDS) affecting self or loved ones. More familiar to criminologists, there is the literature on family violence and pathology: spouse abuse, child abuse, incest etc. The concept of denial is standard to describe a mother's reaction on "discovering" that her husband had been sexually abusing their daughter for many years: "I didn't notice anything". In this case, the concept implies that in fact the mother did "know" — how could she not have? — but that this knowledge was too unbearable to confront.

The subject of denial has also been dealt with by cognitive psychology and information theory. Of particular interest is the "denial paradox": in order to use the term "denial" to describe a person's statement "I didn't know", you have to assume that he or she knew or knows about what it is he or she claims not to know (otherwise the term "denial" is inappropriate).

Cognitive psychologists have used the language of information processing, selective perception, filtering, attention span etc, to understand the phenomenon of how we notice and simultaneously do not notice (Goleman, 1985). Some have even argued that the neurological phenomenon of "blindsight" suggests a startling possibility: that one part of the mind may know just what it is doing, while the part that supposedly knows, remains oblivious of this.

We are all familiar, from basic social psychology, with the notion of cognitive bias: the selection of information to fit existing perceptual frames. At the extreme, information which is too threatening to absorb is shut out altogether. The mind somehow grasps what is going on, but rushes a protective filter into place, steering information away from what threatens. Information slips into a kind of "black hole of the mind" — a blind zone of blocked attention and self deception. Attention is

106   STANLEY COHEN   (1993) 26 ANZJ Crim

thus diverted from facts or their meaning. Thus, the "vital lies" sustained by family members about violence, incest, sexual abuse, infidelity, unhappiness. Lies continue unrevealed, covered up by the family's silence, collusion, alibis and conspiracies (Goleman, 1985).

Similar processes have been well documented outside both the social psychology laboratory and intimate settings like the family. The litany by observers of atrocities is all too familiar: "we didn't see anything", "no one told us", "it looked different at the time".[4]

In addition to psychoanalytical and cognitive theory, there is also the tradition in philosophical psychology concerned with questions of self knowledge and self deception. The Sartrean notion of "bad faith" is of particular interest in implying — contrary to psychoanalytical theory — that the denial is indeed conscious.

(2) Bystanders and Rescuers

Another body of literature more obviously relevant (and more familiar to criminologists) derives from the victimological focus on the bystander. The classic "bystander effect" has become a cliche: how witnesses to a crime will somehow disassociate themselves from what is happening and not help the victim. The prototype is the famous Kitty Genovese case. (One night in New York in 1964, a young woman, Kitty Genovese, was savagely assaulted in the street just before reaching her apartment. Her assailant attacked her over a period of forty minutes while she struggled, battered and screaming, to reach her apartment. Her screams and calls for help were heard by at least 38 neighbours who, from their own windows saw or heard her struggle. No one intervened directly or by calling the police. Eventually a patrol car arrived — too late to save her life.)

Studies of the bystander effect (Sheleff, 1978) suggest that intervention is less likely to occur under three conditions: —

(i) *Diffusion of responsibility* — so many others are watching, why should I be the one to intervene? Besides, it's none of my business.

(ii) *Inability to identify with the victim* — even if I see someone as a victim, I won't act if I cannot sympathise or empathise with their suffering. We help our family, friends, nation, in-group — not those excluded from our moral universe. (*Journal of Social Issues*, 1990). In fact, those who are outside our moral universe may be blamed for their predicament (the common experience of women victims of sexual violence). If full responsibility is laid on the political out-group (they provoked us, they had it coming), this releases you from your obligation to respond.

(iii) *Inability to conceive of effective intervention* — even if you do not erect barriers of denial, even if you feel genuine moral or psychological unease ("I feel so awful about what's going on in Bosnia", "I just can't get those pictures from Somalia out of my mind"), this will not necessarily result in intervention. Observers will not act if they do not know what to do, if they feel powerless and helpless themselves, if they don't see any reward in helping, or if they fear punishment if they help.

These processes are of obvious relevance to my work on human rights violations. There are immediate and literal "bystanders": all massacres, disappearances and atrocities have their witnesses. And there are also metaphorical bystanders; remember the reader looking at the Amnesty adverts about street kids being killed in Brazil or dissidents being tortured in Turkey: Is this really my problem? Can I identify with these victims? What can I do about it anyway?

The obverse of the bystander effect has generated its own special discourse. Just as interesting as the social bases of indifference, are the conditions under which people are aroused to intervene — often at great personal cost and risk. There is a vast ranging literature here: experimental studies on the social psychology of altruism and pro-social behaviour; the sociology of charity and philanthropy; philosophical and economic discussions of altruism (notably attempts to reconcile the phenomenon to rational choice theory); historical studies of helping, rescuing, altruism, the Good Samaritan. The best known of this work deals with rescuers of Jews in Nazi Europe (Oliner and Oliner, 1988).

(3) Neutralisation Theory

More familiar ground to criminologists, is the body of literature known as "motivational accounts" or "vocabulary of motives" theory. The application of this theory in Sykes and Matza's (1957) "techniques of neutralisation" paper is a criminological classic; there is no need to explain the idea to this audience.

The theory assumes that motivational accounts which actors (offenders) give of their (deviant) behaviour must be acceptable to their audience (or audiences). Moreover, accounts are not just *post facto* improvisations, but are drawn upon in advance from the cultural pool of motivational vocabularies available to actors and observers (and honoured by systems of legality and morality). Remember Sykes and Matza's original list; each technique of neutralisation is a way of denying the moral bind of the law and the blame attached to the offence: denial of injury ("no one got hurt"); denial of victim ("they started it"; "it's all their fault",); denial of responsibility ("I didn't mean to do it", "they made me do it"); condemnation of the condemners ("they are just as bad") and appeal to higher loyalties (friends, gang, family, neighbourhood).

Something very strange happens if we apply this list not to the techniques for denying or neutralising conventional delinquency but to human rights violations and state crimes. For Sykes and Matza's point was precisely that delinquents are *not* "political" in the sense implied by subcultural theory; that is, they are not committed to an alternative value system nor do they withdraw legitimacy from conventional values. The necessity for verbal neutralisation shows precisely the continuing bind of conventional values.

But exactly the same techniques appear in the manifestly political discourse of human rights violations — whether in collective political trials (note, for example, the Nuremberg trials or the Argentinian junta trial) or official government responses to human rights reports (a genre which I am studying) or media debates about war crimes and human rights abuses. I will return soon to "literal denial", that first twist of the denial spiral which I identified earlier (it didn't happen, it can't happen here, they are all liars). Neutralisation comes into play when you acknowledge (admit) that something happened — but either refuse to accept the category of acts to which it is assigned ("crime" or "massacre") or present it as morally justified. Here are the original neutralisation techniques, with corresponding examples from the realm of human rights violations:

- *denial of injury* — they exaggerate, they don't feel it, they are used to violence, see what they do to each other.
- *denial of victim* — they started it, look what they've done to us; they are the terrorists, we are just defending ourselves, we are the real victims.
- *denial of responsibility* — here, instead of the criminal versions of psychological incapacity or diminished responsibility (I didn't know what I was doing, I blacked out, etc) we find a denial of individual moral responsiblity on the grounds of obedience: I was following orders, only

doing my duty, just a cog in the machine. (For individual offenders like the ordinary soldier, this is the most pervasive and powerful of all denial systems).

• *condemnation of the condemners* — here, the politics are obviously more explicit than in the original delinquency context. Instead of condemning the police for being corrupt and biased or teachers for being hypocrites, we have the vast discourse of official denial used by the modern state to protect its public image: the whole world is picking on us; they are using double standards to judge us; it's worse elsewhere (Syria, Iraq, Guatamala or wherever is convenient to name); they are condemning us only because of their anti-semitism (the Israeli version), their hostility to Islam (the Arab version), their racism and cultural imperialism in imposing Western values (all Third World tyrannies).

• *appeal to higher loyalty* — the original subdued "ideology" is now total and self-righteous justification. The appeal to the army, the nation, the *volk*, the sacred mission, the higher cause — whether the revolution, "history", the purity of Islam, Zionism, the defence of the free world or state security. As the tragic events of the last few years show, despite the end of the cold war, the end of history and the decline of meta narratives, there is no shortage of "higher loyalties", old and new.

Let us remember the implications of accounts theory for our subject. Built into the offender's action, is the knowledge that certain accounts will be accepted. Soldiers on trial for, say, killing a peaceful demonstrator, can offer the account of "obeying orders" because this will be honoured by the legal system and the wider public. This honouring is, of course, not a simple matter: Were the orders clear? Did the soldier suspect that the order was illegal? Where in the chain of command did the order originate from? These, and other ambiguities, make up the stuff of legal, moral and political discourses of denial.

I have no time here to apply each of these theoretical frameworks — psychoanalysis, cognitive psychology, bystander theory, motivational accounts etc — to my case study of reactions to knowledge of human rights violations and state crimes. (There are obviously also many other relevant fields: political socialisation and mobilisation, mass media analysis, collective memory). For illustration only, let me list some elementary forms of denial which these theories might illuminate.

I will distinguish three forms of denial, each of which operates at (i) the individual or psychic level and (ii) at the organised, political, collective or official level.

(1) Denial of the Past

At the individual level, there are the complex psychic mechanisms which allow us to "forget" unpleasant, threatening or terrible information. Memories of what we have done or seen or known are selected out and filtered.

At the collective level, there are the organised attempts to cover up the record of past atrocities. The most dramatic and successful example in the modern era is the eighty years of organised denial by successive Turkish governments of the 1915-17 genocide against the Armenians — in which some one and half million people lost their lives (Hovanissian, 1986). This denial has been sustained by deliberate propaganda, lying and cover-ups, forging of documents, suppression of archives and bribing of scholars. The West, especially the USA, has colluded by not referring to the massacres in the UN, ignoring memorial ceremonies and by surrendering to Turkish pressure in NATO and other arenas of strategic cooperation.

The less successful example, of course, is the so called "revisionist" history of holocaust of European Jews, dismissed as a "hoax" or a "myth".

At both levels, we can approach the process of denial through its opposite: the attempt to recover or uncover the past. At the individual level, the entire psychoanalytic procedure itself is a massive onslaught on individual denial and self-deception. At the political level, there is the opening of collective memory, the painful coming to terms with the past, the literal and metaphorical digging up of graves when regimes change and try to exorcise their history.

(2) *Literal Denial*

Here we enter the grey area sketched out by psychoanalysis and cognitive theory. In what senses can we be said to "know" about something we profess not to know about? If we do shut something out of knowledge, is this unconscious or conscious? Under what conditions (for example, information overload or desensitisation) is such denial likely to take place?

There are many different versions of literal denial, some of which appear to be wholly individual, others which are clearly structured by the massive resources of the state. We didn't know, we didn't see anything, it couldn't have happened without us knowing (or it could have happened without us knowing). Or: things like this can't happen here, people like us don't do things like this. Or: you can't believe the source of your knowledge: — victims, sympathisers, human rights monitors, journalists are biased, partial or ignorant.

The psychological ambiguities of "literal denial" and their political implications are nicely illustrated by the psychoanalyst John Steiner's re-interpretation of the Oedipus drama (Steiner, 1985 and 1990).

The standard version of the legend is a tragedy in which Oedipus is a victim of fate who bravely pursues the truth. At the beginning he does not know the truth (that he has killed his father, that he had sexual relations with his mother); at the end he does. This is taken as a paradigm for the therapeutic process itself: the patient in analysis to whom, gradually and painfully, the secrets of the unconscious are revealed. But alongside this version, Steiner shows, Sophocles also conveys a quite different message in the original drama: the message is that the main characters in the play must have been aware of the identity of Oedipus and realised that he had committed patricide and incest. There is a deliberate ambiguity throughout the text about the nature of this awareness — just how much did each character know? Each of the participants (including Oedipus himself) and especially the various court officials, had (good) different reasons for denying their knowledge, for staging a cover up. The Oedipus story is not at all about the discovery of truth, but the denial of truth — a cover up like Watergate, Iran Contra. Thus the question: how much did Nixon or Bush "know"?

The ambiguity about how conscious or unconscious our knowledge is, how much we are aware of what we say we are unaware, is nicely captured in Steiner's title "Turning a Blind Eye". This suggests the possibility of *simultaneously* knowing and not knowing. We are not talking about the simple lie or fraud where facts are accessible but lead to a conclusion which is knowingly evaded. This, of course is standard in the organised government cover up: bodies are burnt, evidence is concealed, officials are given detailed instructions on how to lie. Rather, we are talking about the more common situation where "we are vaguely aware that we choose not to look at the facts without being conscious of what it is we are evading". (Steiner, 1985, p 61)

110   STANLEY COHEN   (1993) 26 ANZJ Crim

(3) Implicatory Denial

The forms of denial that we conceptualise as excuses, justifications, rationalisations or neutralisations, do not assert that the event did not happen. They seek to negotiate or impose a different construction of the event from what might appear the case. At the individual level, you know and admit to what you have done, seen or heard about. At the organised level, the event is also registered but is subjected to cultural reconstruction (for example, through euphemistic, technical or legalistic terminology). The point is to deny the implications — psychological and moral — of what is known. The common linguistic structure is "yes, but". Yes, detainees are being tortured but there is no other way to obtain information. Yes, Bosnian women are being raped, but what can a mere individual thousands of miles away do about it?

"Denial of Responsiblity", as I noted earlier, is one of the most common forms of implicatory denial. The sociology of "crimes of obedience" has received sustained attention, notably by Kelman and Hamilton (1989). The anatomy of obedience and conformity — the frightening degree to which ordinary people are willing to inflict great psychological and physical harm to others — was originally revealed by Milgram's famous experiment. Kelman and Hamilton begin from history rather than a university laboratory: the famous case of Lieuenant Calley and the My Lai massacre during the Vietnam War in May 1968 when a platoon of American soldiers massacred some 400 civilians. From this case and other "guilt free" or "sanctioned" massacres, they extract a rather stable set of conditions under which crimes of obedience will occur:

(i) *Authorisation*: when acts are ordered, encouraged, or tacitly approved by those in authority, then normal moral principles are replaced by the duty to obey;

(ii) *Routinisation*: the first step is often difficult, but when you pass the initial moral and psychological barrier, then the pressure to continue is powerful. You become involved without considering the implications; it's all in a day's work. This tendency is re-inforced by special vocabularies and euphemisms ("surgical strike") or a simple sense of routine. (Asked about what he thought he was doing, Calley replied in one of the most chilling sentences of all times: "It was no big deal");

(iii) *Dehumanisation*: when the qualities of being human are deprived from the other, then the usual principles of morality do not apply. The enemy is described as animals, monsters, gooks, sub-humans. A whole language excludes them from your shared moral universe.

The conditions under which perpetrators behave can be translated into the very bystander rationalisations which allow the action in the first place and then deny its implications afterwards. As Kelman and Hamilton show in their analysis of successive public opinion surveys (in which people were asked both to imagine how they would react to a My Lai situation themselves and to judge the actual perpetrators), obedience and authorisation are powerful justifications. And observers as well as offenders are subject to desensitisation (the bombardment by horror stories from the media to a point that you cannot absorb them any more and they are no longer "news") and dehumanisation.

My research on human rights organisations (national and international) deals with their attempts to overcome these barriers of denial. What is the difference between working in your own country and trying to arouse an international audience in distant and different places? What messages work best in mobilising public action (whether going to a demonstration, donating money or joining an organisation like Amnesty International)? Does focusing on a country work better than raising an issue (such as torture or the death penalty)? And which countries or which issues? Are some techniques of confronting denial — for example, inducing guilt or representing the horrors more vividly — counter-productive? Is there competition for the human rights message within the same audiences (for example, from the environmental movement)? . . .

Conclusion

It is difficult to find a conclusion for one lecture of this type, even harder for two. My first lecture was an attempt to nudge criminologists to be interested in state crimes and human rights violations. My second lecture was a sketch for a sociology of denial. In both cases, all I have done is to place familiar issues in different packages.

Instead of a conclusion, let me instead end with two footnotes. One raises — dare I say — some meta-theoretical issues; the other introduces a little optimism into an otherwise bleak story.

(1) Meta Theory

I mentioned the strange neglect of these issues by new realist criminologists and suggested that what is at stake is their sense of reality. But "reality" is not a word used too easily these days — or if used, only politically correct in inverted commas. This is the legacy of post structuralism, deconstructionism and post modernism. There are a number of trends in post modernist theory which — usually unwittingly — impinge on the human rights discourse. Let me mention a few such meta issues:

First, there is the question of moral relativism. This is the familiar claim — now supposedly finally vindicated — that if there is no universal, foundational base for morality (the death of meta-narratives), then it is impossible to stake out universal values (such as those enshrined in human rights standards). Then comes the derivative claim that such values and standards are Western, ethnocentric, individualistic, alien and imposed.

Now, whatever the historical record, this claim has some strange political implications. The standard and age-old government denials of the applicability of international human rights norms — we are different, we face special problems, the world doesn't understand us — now acquire a new philosophical dignity. And further, the condemners are condemned for being ethnocentric and imperialist.

A similar problem comes from the assertion that local struggles for human rights lose their meaning because they are informed by the very universal foundations and master narratives now so thoroughly discredited or tarnished. This is again a complex debate; I side with those who argue that no amount of deconstructive scepticism should deny the force with which we defend these values. It is surely a bizarre sight for Western progressives to be telling human rights activists from the Third World or Eastern Europe that their struggle is, after all, not worth the candle.

A second problem is posed by the proclaimed end of history. This is the current round of the old "end of ideology" game: the collapse of international socialism finally proving the triumph of Western democratic capitalism. Besides the poverty of the case itself, it can make little sense for those still living between death squads, famine, disease and violence. For them, history is not over. But even if one meta narrative has won and there is nothing left for "history" in the industrialised world, then how does this world react to what is happening elsewhere? Why — if not because of racism, selfishness, greed, and the type of denial I've talked about — do the victors not devote more resources to achieve these values elsewhere?

A third post modernist theme is even more directly relevant to my subject here — and potentially even more destructive. This is the attack on all modes of rational

112 STANLEY COHEN (1993) 26 ANZJ Crim

enquiry which work with positivist categories of reality. The human rights movement can live without absolute, foundational values. But it cannot live with a theory which denies any way of knowing what has really happened.[5] All of us who carried the anti-positivist banners of the sixties are responsible for the emergent epistemological circus.

Its apotheosis was reached a year ago. On 29 March 1991, shortly after the cessation of hostilities in the Gulf War — just as thousands were lying dead and maimed in Iraq, the country's infra-structure deliberately destroyed by savage bombing, the Kurds abandoned to their fate — the high priest of post-modernism, Jean Baudrillard, published an article entitled "The Gulf War Has Not Taken Place" (Baudrillard, 1991 b). The "true belligerents" he argued, are those who thrive on the ideology of the truth of this war.

He was only being consistent with an article he wrote a few days before the war (Baudrillard, 1991 a) in which he predicted that it would never happen. The war existed only as a figment of media simulation, of imaginary scenarios that exceeded all limits of real world facticity. The war, Baudillard had solemnly declared, was strictly unthinkable except as an exchange of threats so exorbitant that it would guarantee that the event would not take place. The "thing" would happen only in the minds of its audience, as an extension of the video games imagery which had filled our screens during the long build up. Dependent as we all were — prime time viewers as well as generals — on these computer generated images, we might as well drop all self-deluding distinctions between screen events and "reality".

Given this "prediction", it was unlikely that Baudrillard would be proved wrong if the war really did break out. So indeed the "war" — a free floating signifier, devoid of referential bearing — did not happen. To complain that he was caught out by events only shows our theoretical naivete, our nostalgia for the old truth-telling discourses.

What does one make of all this? I take my cue from Christopher Norris (1992) who has devoted a splendid polemical book to attacking Baudrillard's theses on the Gulf War. Norris is by no means a philistine critic or an unregenerated "positivist". He is the author of altogether sympathetic studies of Derrida and deconstructionism. And he concedes that Baudrillard makes some shrewd observations about how the war was presented by its managers and the media: the meaningless statistical data to create an illusory sense of factual reporting, the absurd claims about "precision targeting", and "clever bombs" to convince us that the mass destruction of civilian lives were either not happening (literal denial) or were accidental (denial of responsibility).

But Norris is now appalled by the precious nonsense to which the fashionable tracks of post modernism have led. What disturbs him is how seriously these ideas were taken, ". . . to the point where Baudrillard can deliver his ludicrous theses on the Gulf War without fear of subsequent exposure as a charlatan or of finding these theses resoundingly disconfirmed by the course of real-world events". (Norris, p 17)

It is beyond my scope and competence to consider Norris's explanation for how these ideas emerged and just where they lost their plausibility. He places particular importance on the curious ascendancy of literary theory as a paradigm for other areas of study. There is the bland assumption that because every text involves some kind of narrative interest, therefore there is no way to distinguish factual, historical or documentary material on the one hand from fictive, imaginary or simulated material on the other. With no possible access to truth or historical record, we are asked, Norris shows, to inhabit a realm of unanchored persuasive utterances where rhetoric goes all the way down and where nothing could count as an argument against what the media or governments would have us currently believe.

This re-definition of history finds strange echoes, as Norris notes, among the right wing revisionist historians of the holocaust, ". . . those for whom it clearly comes as good news that past event can only be interpreted according to present consensus values, or ideas of what currently and contingently counts as 'good in the way of belief'" (Norris, p 21). In the case of current events, like the Gulf War, we are left with no resources to deal with the obvious contradictions between official propaganda and personal witness (for example, about the bombing of the Amiriyah civilian air raid shelter). The cult following of these ideas by some intellectuals reflects, as Norris suggests, their lack of desire to make any political judgement, their cynical acquiescence in the war. If the war was so unreal, so completely beyond our competence to judge as informed observers, then we can say nothing to challenge the official (media sponsored) version of events.

My point in raising this example is simple. If the Turkish government can deny that the Armenian genocide happened; if revisionist historians and neo-Nazis deny that the Holocaust took place; if powerful states all around the world today can systematically deny the systematic violations of human rights they are carrying out — then we know that we're in bad shape. But we're in even worse shape when the intellectual *avant garde* invent a form of denial so profound, that serious people — including progressives — will have to debate whether the Gulf War actually took place or not.

(2) Acknowledgement

I promised a more optimistic second footnote. This is not to cheer you up, but just to be honest. Denial has it opposites. What has to be understood are the conditions under which denial does not occur, in which the truth (even if this concept is disappearing down the post modern black hole) is acknowledged, not just its existence but its moral implications.

After all, in the Milgram experiment, somewhere around 30% of the subjects (depending on the conditions) did not push the button. In Kelman and Hamilton's public opinion surveys, again another 30% would not obey orders to shoot innocent women and children. In the middle of even the most grotesque of state crimes, such as genocide, there are extraordinary tales of courage, rescuing and resistance. Acts of altruism, compassion and pro-social behaviour are woven into the social fabric. Above all, there is the whole human rights movement itself, which over the last three decades has mobilised an extraordinary number of people into wholly selfless behaviour to alleviate the suffering of others — whether by giving money, writing to a prisoner of conscience or joining a campaign.

In my initial interviews with human rights organisations, I was surprised to hear a sense of optimism. Yes, there are some people (referred to in the trade as the "ostriches") who do not want to know. But most organisations were certain that their potential pool has not been reached. I mentioned to one of my interviewees the cynical notion of "compassion fatigue" — that people are just too tired to respond, they can't bear seeing any more pictures of the homeless in the streets, victims of AIDS, children starving in Somalia, refugees in Bosnia. Her response was that the concept was a journalistic invention; what there is, is media fatigue.

This is where we return to the state of hyper-reality which post modernist theories have so well exposed. The question is right open: Will the type of manipulation and simulation seen in the Gulf War dominate, creating indeed a culture of denial? Or can we conceive of a flow of information which will allow people to acknowledge reality and act accordingly?

This might seem a pretentious question for us humble criminologists to consider, but I hope that you will allow me to get away with it.

NOTES

1 I have examined elsewhere the move in alternative criminology from "idealism" to "realism", see Cohen (1988; 1990).

2 On the issues in bringing torturers to justice after the regime changes in Brazil and Uruguay, see Weschler (1990).

3 On rape and sexual abuse in custody, see Amnesty International reports in 1992, especially on India, Turkey, Philippines, Guatamala and Uganda.

4 For a nuanced historical reconstruction of the perceptions of villagers living next to the Mauthausen concentration camp complex, see Horwitz, 1992.

5 My minor personal involvement in this debate — as the object of a radical post-modern critique for foolishly using objective standards of knowledge (in a report on torture in Israel) — is recorded in Cohen (1991).

REFERENCES

Barak, Gregg, (ed) (1991) *Crimes By the Capitalist State: An Introduction to State Criminality*, State University of New York Press, Albany.

Baudrillard, Jean (1991, a) "The Reality Gulf" *The Guardian*, 11 January.

— (1991,b) "La guerre du Golfe n'a pas eu lieu" *Liberation*, 29 March.

Braithwaite, John and Fisse, Brent (1990) "On the Plausibility of Corporate Crime Theory", in W. Laufer and F. Adler (eds) *Advances in Criminological Theory*, Vol II, Transaction, New Brunswick.

Cohen, Stanley (1988) *Against Criminology*, Transaction, New Brunswick.

— (1990) "Intellectual Scepticism and Political Commitment: The Case of Radical Criminology", Bonger Memorial Lecture, University of Amsterdam.

— (1991) "Talking About Torture in Israel" *Tikkun*, Vol 6, No 6 pp 23-30, 89-90.

Edelstein, E L et al (eds) (1989) *Denial: A Clarification of Concepts and Research*, Plenum Press, New York.

Goleman, Daniel (1985) *Vital Lies, Simple Truths: On the Psychology of Self Deception*, Simon and Schuster, New York.

Horwitz, Gordon (1992) *In the Shadow of Death: Living Outside the Gates of Mauthausen*, Free Press, New York.

Hovanissian, Richard G (ed) (1986) *The Armenian Genocide in Perspective*, Transaction, New Brunswick.

Journal of Social Issues (1990) Special Issue on "Moral Exclusion", Vol 46.

Karmen, A (1990) *Crime Victims: An Introduction to Victimology*, Brooks Cole, California.

Kelman, Herbert C and Hamilton, V Lee (1989) *Crimes of Obedience*, Yale University Press, New Haven.

Kuper, Leo (1981) *Genocide*, Penguin Books, London,

Maran, Rita (1989) *Torture: The Role of Ideology in the French-Algerian War*, Praeger, New York.

Muller, Ingo (1991) *Hitler's Justice: The Courts of the Third Reich*, Harvard University Press, Cambridge.

Norris, Christopher (1992) *Uncritical Theory: Postmodernism, Intellectuals and the Gulf War*, Lawrence and Wishart, London.

Oliner, Samuel and Oliner, Pearl (1988) *The Altruistic Personality: Rescuers of Jews in Nazi Europe*, Free Press, New York.

Schwendinger, Herman and Schwendinger, Julia (1970) "Defenders of Order or Guardians of Human Rights" *Issues in Criminology*, Vol 7, pp 72-81.

Sheleff, Leon (1978) *The Bystander*, Lexington.

Social Justice (1989) Issue on "Human Rights and People's Rights", Vol 16.

Steiner, John (1985) "Turning a Blind Eye: The Cover Up for Oedipus" *International Review of Psycho-Analysis*, Vol 12, pp 161-72.

— (1990) "The Retreat from Truth to Omnipotence in Sophocles" *Oedipus at Colonus, International Review of Psycho-Analysis*, Vol 17, pp 227-37.

Sykes, Gresham and Matza, David (1957) "Techniques of Neutralization: A Theory of Delinquency" *American Sociological Review*, Vol 22, pp 664-70.

Von Hirsch, Andrew and Jareborg, Nils (1991) "Gauging Criminal Harm: A Living-Standard Analysis", *Oxford Journal of Legal Studies*, Vol II No 1 pp 1-38.

Weschler, Lawrence (1990) *A Miracle, a Universe: Settling Accounts with Torturers*, Penguin Books, New York.

Part II
The Varieties of State Crime

War-making

[6]

Modern states are powerful, resilient institutions, the most durable of which have established and consolidated their rule through conquest, revolution, and war. Successful involvement in violent conflict leads to the development of militarized and police states and reinforces elite political cultures that favor the use of coercion in future disputes. If warfare has unfavorable outcomes, elites will prefer noncoercive strategies in the future. From these and other propositions are derived models of the processes by which garrison states emerge and persist in autocracies and democracies. States with high material capabilities are more likely to become garrison states than weaker states, which tend to avoid international conflict and to rely on accommodation in internal conflicts. States with low political capabilities are susceptible to revolutionary overthrow and the establishment of revolutionary garrison states. The role of diversion of domestic conflicts to the external environment also is considered. One general conclusion is that only homogeneous democracies with low power capabilities and limited alliance obligations are unlikely to develop the institutions and political culture of militarized and police states.

WAR, REVOLUTION, AND THE GROWTH OF THE COERCIVE STATE

TED ROBERT GURR
University of Colorado, Boulder

THE BASES OF STATE POWER

The late twentieth-century state, James Rosenau to the contrary, is an extraordinarily powerful and resilient set of institutions. The largest members of this political species, which populate most of the northern part of the globe, are the most powerful human agencies ever devised. I use *power* in a precise sense: These states, typified by the regimes of the United States, France, the Soviet Union, and China, command more resources, absolutely and in proportion to the capabilities of their societies, and have greater capacities to organize and deploy human and material resources in the service of state policies, than any historical

COMPARATIVE POLITICAL STUDIES, Vol. 21 No. 1, April 1988 45-65
© 1988 Sage Publications, Inc.

State Crime I

political systems, including the largest of empires. The point can be substantiated by reference to data on the proportional size of the public sector, which in Western democracies has grown to approximately half of total national productivity, and the size and technical proficiency of military establishments.[2]

The material bases of the modern state's power have been conceptualized, and measured, in terms of the national territory's raw materials, population, energy and steel production, and military establishment. The analysis of the changing distribution of capabilities among states has been of primary concern in realist analyses of the balance of power and equally central to the empirical study of the causes of war.[3] The state's growing capacity to raise manpower and money is a recurring issue in the comparative study of national development (see the contributions to Tilly, 1975). The political bases of state power are equally or more important, but less readily indexed. The logic I follow is that capabilities, as conceptualized by Singer et al. (1972), represent the potential for, or "necessary conditions" of, state power. The three political bases of state power identified below are, by extension, conditions that determine the extent to which the state apparatus and rulers are able to recruit, extract, and organize human and material resources, then use them coherently (efficiently over time) in the service of the state's interests.[4] (1) Internal divisions along lines of communal and class cleavage almost always are a source of resistance to state efforts to mobilize human and material resources. The reduction and management of those divisions, by whatever combination of coercion and compromise, is a necessary political condition for optimum mobilization of national resources. (2) A second political basis of state power is the extent of the state's *legitimacy*: I use the term to denote people's acceptance of rulers' right to make binding decisions. Legitimacy determines the extent of voluntary compliance with state policies aimed at mobilizing and using resources. (3) The third basis is the capacity of the state apparatus to reach prompt and relevant decisions under both routine and crisis conditions. Decisional efficacy, as Eckstein denotes this property (1971), is essential for coherent use of mobilized resources in the pursuit of the state's objectives, whatever they may be.[5]

International bases of state power also bear mentioning. To a variable but usually limited extent, states can enhance their capabilities by drawing on external resources from other states: money, human skills, military aid. Considerably more important is the operation of the international capitalist system, which over time has contributed enormously to the material resources available to states at the core.[6] Whereas the world capitalist system has been of greatest benefit to states at the core, weaker states (not all of which are on the economic periphery) have gained some political benefits from the infrastructure of the modern international system. By *infrastructure,* I mean the organization of states into regional groups, blocs, and alliances. During historical periods of unrestrained international competition, weak states were often absorbed by powerful neighbors; since World War II, small states facing internal or external threats usually are propped up by the military, diplomatic, and material support of neighboring states and bloc leaders (on the persistence of weak African states, see Jackson and Rosberg, 1982).

COERCION AND THE
GROWTH OF STATE POWER

The assertions of the above three paragraphs may be debatable but are not at issue in this article. They are treated as assumptions that provide the foundation for a closer theoretical examination of the sources of states' coercive capacities. The first premise of the specific argument is that the means of state coercion and the disposition of rulers to use them are grounded in the historical experience of each successful state. Recurring deadly conflicts have accompanied the establishment and expansion of powers of most contemporary states. The states that dominate the modern global system and set the standards to which emerging nationalist elites aspire are those that have most effectively organized and deployed the means of coercion in the face of internal and external challenges. This is not to assert that the modern state rules necessarily or exclusively by force. Internal political consensus and acceptance of a state's claims to legitimacy are vitally important mechanisms of rule: Consent freely given is cheaper and more reliable than consent given under duress. A similar principle operates in the international arena: Negotiation, compromise, and respect for international standards of conduct are preferred, because they are usually less costly and more predictable, as alternatives to warfare.

The fact remains that force—the threat and use of deadly violence—is and always has been the *ultima ratio regnum.* All the durable states of the modern world established and consolidated rule over their national territories by the successful use of force: by revolution; by suppressing rebellions and secessions; by forcibly subordinating and integrating, in diverse combinations and sequences, neighboring peoples, reluctant aborigines, ethnic minorities, lords and merchants, peasants and laborers, kulaks and capitalists. Most of the durable states also have aggressively projected and defended their interests vis-à-vis bordering states in wars and lesser militarized disputes. Those with few wars, notably in Latin America, have benefited from the policing role of larger powers. The fact that some durable states, like those of Sweden and Switzerland, rarely make use of coercion in contemporary domestic or international disputes does not contradict the general assertion: Historically, these states relied on force to establish their internal authority and international legitimacy, and each maintains a substantial military establishment to give credibility to contemporary policies of neutrality.

One specific consequence of recurring involvement in war, internal or external, is the development of specialized organizations ready to fight future wars. A fateful threshold was passed when the states of early modern Europe began to establish standing armies and navies to replace the feudal levies, mercenaries, volunteers, and privateers upon whom earlier monarchs had relied. A permanent military establishment was not enough to guarantee a state's survival in the international competition that reduced the number of European polities from approximately 500 proto-states in 1500 to about 20 national states and empires in 1900 (Tilly, 1975: 17-46), but it most certainly helped, especially for the states that took the lead in the development of new military tactics and weaponry (see McNeil, 1982). In the exemplary case of Prussia, the quality of arms and armies was instrumental in transforming a small, resource-poor, peripheral state into the organizing force of Germanic Europe. Revolution also has been a powerful stimulus to the development of new model armies, which then are deployed against counterrevolutionaries and foreign enemies. Adelman (1985) demonstrates convincingly that England, France, Russia, and China emerged from revolutionary conflicts with vastly strengthened armies.

There have been parallel though less widely recognized processes in the development of agencies of internal security. European states began to establish specialized police forces in the late eighteenth and early nineteenth centuries: rural forces in response to rebellions, for example, by the British in Ireland; urban ones in response to the growing disorder of expanding cities (see Bayley, 1975; Gurr, 1976: 118-123). The last century has witnessed the development of new and more specialized agencies aimed at controlling political opposition, including paramilitary units, security services, and secret police. The circumstances of their establishment and their size and scope are telling indicators of a state's concern about and capacity for maintaining internal order. A systematic comparative history of such agencies remains to be written.

Secret police are a particularly notorious species of internal security agencies, notorious because they have been widely used by authoritarian states as the instruments of massive political repression and murder.

Typically, secret police have been established during episodes of intense political conflict and have continued to operate afterward under the direct control of the central organs of the state. The *Schutzstaffeln* (SS) is an example of such an agency: It was formed in 1925 as an instrument of Hitler's struggle for political power and, after the Nazi victory, was employed to consolidate and extend it. From 1932 on, Himmler and the leaders of the SS sections helped both to define and to execute the coercive policies of the Nazi state: suppressing Communist and Socialist opposition, eliminating potential opponents in occupied areas, forceable resettlement of "slave" people, reprisals, and implementation of the Final Solution (Koehl, 1983). The secret police of Czarist Russia was founded in 1881, during a period of revolutionary activity. Later known as the *Okhrana*, it used surveillance, agents provocateur, and systematic campaigns of arrest, exile, and execution against revolutionaries and other political dissidents. It was also the inspiration for and direct ancestor of the Soviet secret police agencies: In December 1917, six weeks after the Bolshevik revolution, the *Cheka,* later known as OGPU, was established to deal with counterrevolutionaries. The Okhrana's extensive files on dissidents, revolutionaries, and collaborators continued to be used by the Cheka under the direction of the same official, one Zheeben (Ivianski, 1980: 59). The Cheka practiced revolutionary counterterror during the Civil War; OGPU provided the armed force and executioners for Stalin's forced collectivization of the peasantry in 1930-32 (Conquest, 1986); and its successor, the NKVD, carried out the 1936-1938 purges in which more than half a million political activists died (Gouldner, 1977-78).

War and revolutionary conflicts leave legacies other than armies and secret police. The general principle is that elites who have secured state power and maintained their positions by violent means are disposed to respond violently to future challenges. The rational basis of their calculations is easily specified: Successful use of coercion enhances leaders' assessment of its future utility. Probably of equal importance is a normative factor that gets less attention in the literature: Elites who are successful in the violent pursuit and defense of power become habituated to the political uses of violence, and their acceptance of coercive violence becomes part of the elite political culture, or "myth," of their cadre and successors.

There is a great deal of scattered evidence, some direct and some inferential, about the circumstances in which rulers and functionaries have become habituated to political murder. Studies of the bureaucrats, physicians, guards, and others who implemented the Nazis' Final Solution are particularly detailed and instructive.[7] We can infer that the recurring episodes of mass murder in Stalin's Russia were a reflection of Stalin's own disregard for the lives of any who stood in the way of his policies, imprinted on the operating code of security agencies and the political belief structures of a generation of Soviet leaders. From a different century and a different continent, we have testimony that the traditional rulers of Baganda and the Zulu (under the paramount chief, Shaka) repeatedly committed large-scale, ritualistic political murders— in Walter's interpretation (1969), for the purpose of demonstrating their absolute power. Part of the explanation may lie in the fact that these rulers also were leaders in their people's recurring wars with neighbors and thus were habituated to violence. This is another subject that awaits comparative social research: the circumstances in which elite and mass political cultures accept and celebrate what an American historian has called "patriotic gore." Luckham (1984) argues, with suggestive evidence, that a pervasive "armament culture" has been nurtured in contemporary Western societies that habituates people to weaponry and rationalizes its past and potential uses.

The general arguments developed above can be stated in these propositions:

Proposition 1: States involved in recurring episodes of violent conflict tend (a) to develop and maintain institutions specialized in the exercise of coercion; and (b) to develop elite political cultures that sanction the use of coercion in response to challenges and perceived threats.

Proposition 2: To the extent that coercive strategies lead to conflict outcomes favorable for the political elite, their preference for those strategies in future conflict situations is reinforced. To the extent that coercive strategies have unfavorable outcomes, political elites will prefer noncoercive strategies in future conflicts.

These propositions are general ones, applicable to both domestic and international conflict. The next section derives some implications of the propositions for different types of states from different conflict situations.

THE EMERGENCE OF
MILITARIZED AND POLICE STATES

National population, resources, and productivity provide the foundations of state power, whereas effective national power depends on the state's capacity to mobilize, organize, and deploy those resources efficiently in the service of its objectives. Under what circumstances have ruling elites chosen to concentrate national and political resources in the means of coercion? The broad outline of the answer follows from the preceding propositions: States that have repeatedly faced and success-fully responded to domestic and international conflicts are most likely to have developed the characteristics of "garrison states." Lasswell (1962) defined the garrison state as one dominated by specialists in the management of violence. He anticipated that democracies as well as autocracies, armed with the instruments of modern science and technology, could become predominantly concerned with—one might say fixated on—the expectation of violent challenges and the need to contain and respond to them (pp. 51-54).

I intend the garrison state concept to designate states that maintain large-scale military and/or internal security establishments, and whose elite political culture sanctions the use of extreme coercion. Such states are not necessarily dominated by Lasswell's specialists in violence. In democratic garrison states, as he recognizes, the specialists in violence may be subordinate to elected officials who have broader interests. Or, in Fitch's (1985) interpretation of the garrison state concept, "effective power would be concentrated in the hands of a loosely knit elite of civilianized military officers and militarized civilians, with increasing integration of corollary skill elites" (p. 32). In my conceptualization, the distinction between civilian and military elites is not consequential: The garrison state is characterized by a high concentration of coercive power and a disposition, by those at the center of the state apparatus, to use it.

Lasswell (1962: 53) also distinguishes military and police states, but does not elaborate on the distinction. It is crucial to my conception of the origins and character of garrison state. The *militarized state,* the term used here, maintains a large military establishment and is ruled by an elite whose policy agenda is dominated by preparations for war and national defense. The *police state* maintains a large internal security establishment and is ruled by an elite that relies primarily on coercion to control domestic opposition and implement state policies. Clearly the extent of militarization and reliance on coercion to maintain internal order are variables that can be treated as such in empirical analysis. This article is concerned with the conditions of the more extreme manifesta-tions of the phenomena: The emergence of a persisting pattern of garrison state institutions and attitudes. Therefore my propositions refer to the categorical types, though most of them can also be rephrased in continuous terms.

Another qualification: Some contemporary states have both sets of traits, but that does not justify treating all garrison states as similar. Whereas the United States and the USSR are both militarized states, the former has no semblance of the Soviet Union's internal security apparatus nor the elite preoccupation with suppressing dissent. The Third World affords many examples of police states whose elites, armies, and security establishments are almost entirely fixated on internal order: Chile under Pinochet and Zaire under Mobutu are archetypical.

The historical dynamics by which militarized and police states have evolved also differ. Propositions 3 and 4 are probabilistic statements that follow from general propositions 1 and 2: *Proposition 3:* Frequent involvement in violent international conflicts, and relative success in those conflicts, leads to the development of militarized states. *Proposition 4*: Frequent success in the use of state-organized violence for national consolidation and the suppression of internal challenges leads to the development of police states.

These propositions implicitly raise the question of what happens to states that are unsuccessful in the use of coercion against opponents. The historical answer is that many of them did not survive. Losers in international war were absorbed into empires, suffered territorial and material losses, or were forced into a subordinate relationship with the winner. Contemporary political elites are well aware of these historical possibilities and tend to respond to challenges in keeping with their capabilities. With regard to war, weak states—those with limited power capabilities—tend to avoid involvement except when acting in consort with powerful allies (see Bueno de Mesquita, 1981). A proposition and corollary follow from the arguments: *Proposition 5*: States with limited power capabilities tend to avoid involvement in war. *Corollary 5a*: States with limited power capabilities tend not to become militarized states.

Israel and Vietnam are apparent exceptions to the corollary but in fact support it. Both Israel and the revolutionary government of North Vietnam faced tremendous international pressures during their formative years as states. Both had the political capacities for maximum mobilization of their limited resources to confront external challenges, and succeeded.[8] In each case, the legacy of winning was the creation of a potent though very expensive military establishment and a strong disposition among the political elite (and in Israel, the general public) to employ force in future international disputes. In both respects, these two states are anomalies among the small states of the global system. One also can speculate that they will retain the characteristics of military states only in the face of external challenges: The costs and risks of chronic belligerence for small states are too great to be sustained over the longer run.

The consequences of failure to suppress internal challenges are more diverse. States that have failed to win civil wars have disintegrated into several still weaker states. States that have been too weak to counteract revolutionary challengers generally come under new management. Typically, their new revolutionary elites are committed to strengthening the state apparatus. In three social revolutions studied by Skocpol (1979), she attributes the state-strengthening impulse to international competition. In four "revolutions from above" examined by Trimberger (1978), the new military-bureaucratic elites were concerned to establish stable and powerful nation-states based on autonomous industrial development. The arguments developed above suggest that another dynamic also is at work, surely a more immediate one: New revolutionary elites are preoccupied first and foremost with securing their power against counterrevolutionaries and would-be separatists. They cannot be expected to have any inhibitions about using violence for that purpose. And the means for doing so are readily available: The revolutionary fighters and zealots become the cadre of new or trans-formed agencies of state security. In Conquest's account (1986) of the forced collectivization of the Soviet peasantry, for example, one finds many references to revolutionary veterans, a dozen years after 1917, serving as OGPU and militia officers.

Thus, in the aftermath of revolutionary seizures of power, the apparatus of control and internal security is customarily the first part of the state to be built up, and postrevolutionary states are highly likely to take on the characteristics of police states. Most of the successful revolutionary struggles of this century, right or left, have spawned police states whose security agencies inherited the personnel, mission, and means of the revolution: the Soviet Union, Fascist Italy, Nazi Germany, Falangist Spain, Communist China, Castro's Cuba, Vietnam, Kampuchea under the Khmer Rouge, revolutionary Iran. Among the handful of apparent exceptions are wars of revolutionary independence, as in Indonesia and Algeria. The lack of counterrevolutionary resistance after independence may explain why institutionalized police states did not emerge in these countries. The argument can be summarized in another proposition: *Proposition 6*: Postrevolutionary states that face internal resistance in the immediate aftermath of revolution tend to become police states.

Postrevolutionary states also are highly likely to become institutionalized autocracies. The term is not a synonym for "police state." The institutions and practices of a police state are inconsistent with plural democracy and consistent with autocracy, but not all autocracies base their political authority primarily on coercion. The contemporary regimes of Singapore, Burma, Malawi, Saudi Arabia, Tunisia, and Hungary—among others—sharply restrict political participation and opposition but have enough popular support that police-state tactics are ordinarily unnecessary.

DEMOCRACIES AND THE USES OF COERCION

In the face of widespread and persistent opposition, autocracies can and do develop into police states. Leftist opposition in Argentina during the 1960s provided the *causus belli* for the police state tactics exemplified by the "dirty war" in which at least 9,000 civilians were murdered by death squads and military executioners between 1976 and 1980. Plural democracies also sometimes employ police state tactics against extreme opposition,[9] but do not become full-fledged police states unless and until they undergo a shift to autocratic rule. Such transitions occurred in Uruguay and Chile in 1973. In Uruguay, democratic rule was suspended so that security forces could have a free hand to deal with the Tupamaro revolutionaries. In Chile, a long-lived democratic regime was overthrown by the military, which quickly developed a full-fledged security apparatus to suppress the leftists who had supported the democratically elected Allende regime (see Duff and McCamant 1976: 183-200).

In general, plural democracies make little use of police state tactics because historically they have been relatively successful in using noncoercive means to defuse and deflect challenges. The argument derives from my observations about the historical sequences of conflict and political reform in Western societies, and from evidence about contemporary responses to protest by democratic and autocratic regimes. Regimes, like protesters and rebels, develop repertoires of action for use in conflict situations and a set of normative beliefs about which kinds of actions are most appropriate in which circumstances. The elites of democratic states have developed and employ a complex repertoire of noncoercive responses to challenges: increased channels of political participation, redistribution, symbolic and substantive shifts in public policy, cooptation of opposition leaders, diversion of affect and attention onto external targets. Also included in the repertoire are coercive means, but the popular and elite political cultures of durable democracies emphasize norms of compromise and responsiveness. Officials who use or condone violence against domestic opposition risk the loss of legitimacy and office as a consequence. Practical as well as normative considerations play a part. Both European and Third World democracies like India have track records of using reforms, concessions, and diversion to defuse opposition, which gives their elites confidence about their successful use in future conflicts.[10]

This proposition and corollary are the counterpart to propositions about reliance on coercion by the elites of garrison states: *Proposition 7*: Frequent success in the use of reforms, concessions, and displacement to manage internal challenges leads to the development of the institutions and norms of democratic rule. *Corollary 7a*: Democratic states are unlikely to rely mainly on coercion in response to internal challenges.

MODELS AND LINKAGES

The foregoing arguments are summarized and extended in the accompanying figures. They show the predominant sequences by which militarized and police states emerge and are reinforced in three types of political systems, given different levels of national capability. Let me comment briefly on the models, with particular attention to what they imply about the enduring question of the linkages between domestic and external conflict.

WAR AND THE MILITARIZED STATE

The paths to the development of militarized states in autocracies (Figure 1) and democracies (Figure 2) are identical. For states with high power capabilities—population, resources, productivity—war and lesser international disputes are likely to have favorable outcomes, which enhances the bellicose state's effective power and reinforces its militariza- tion. Powerful states also are more likely than weak states to use their power actively in the pursuit of state objectives, which in turn increases the likelihood that they will face future challenges from other states whose interests are threatened. A series of positive feedback effects thus enhance the war-proneness of most global and regional powers, whether autocratic or democratic in their political organization. Weak states, by contrast, are less likely to be successful in international conflicts, therefore tend to avoid it, and are less likely to develop the traits of militarized states.

INTERNAL CONFLICT AND REVOLUTION

Institutionalized autocracies and democracies have evolved distinct modes of response to violent internal challenges: The former rely more

56   COMPARATIVE POLITICAL STUDIES / April 1988

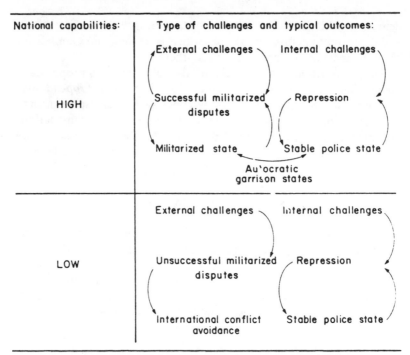

National capabilities:

Type of challenges and typical outcomes:

Figure 1: The Emergence and Persistence of Garrison States in Institutionalized Autocracies

on systematic coercion (the police state models in Figure 1), the latter on conflict-management techniques denoted "compromise" in Figure 2. Both of these tend to be stable, conflict-dampening systems. The most numerous exceptions to these patterns are found in states with limited political capacities for control, organization, and mobilization. Such states are characterized in various ways in the literature: They do not "penetrate" or effectively control their societies, political competition in them is uninstitutionalized or "anocratic," the style of governance is "personalist" or "Praetorian." By any label, they have limited political capabilities either to wage war or to control internal challenges. They rely mainly on coercion in response to internal challenges, as shown in Figure 3, but coercion so sporadically and inconsistently applied that it often stimulates still greater challenges. Such states have chronically unstable coercive rule, characterized by positive feedback loops between repression and challenges.

These politically weak states are particularly susceptible to revolutionary takeovers by successful challenges. When revolutionary victory is won after a protracted war that hardens the attitudes and military

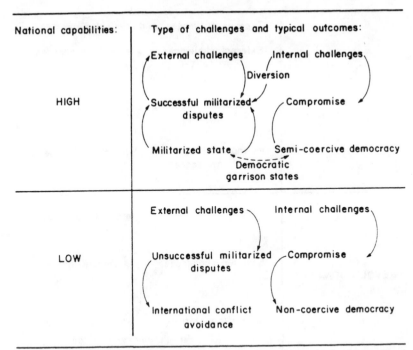

Figure 2: The Emergence and Persistence of Garrison States in Institutionalized Democracies

capabilities of the new leaders, very different patterns of conflict behavior emerge in them. Domestically they rapidly develop the traits of stable police states, though often at horrific cost to people who have opposed the revolution.[11] Successful revolutions also breed external challenges, by revolutionaries who seek to export their revolution and foreign opponents seeking to overthrow or preempt them. With the exception of Zambia, every successful mass revolution since 1970 has precipitated new militarized international conflicts: Kampuchea, Vietnam, Nicaragua, Iran.[12] Thus postrevolutionary regimes rapidly acquire both facets of the garrison state. Their leaders continue to rely on the coercive strategies that brought them to power, using revolutionary fighters as the backbone of new armies to oppose foreign enemies and new agencies of internal control. These regimes become, in other words, revolutionary garrison states.

LINKAGES

The postrevolutionary states exhibit in striking degree the reinforcing connections between internal and external coercion. The disposition of

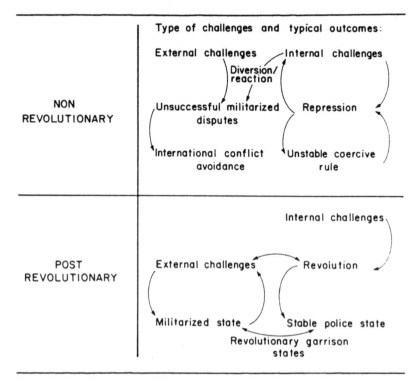

Figure 3: The Emergence and Persistence of Garrison States in Regimes with Low
         Political Capabilities

revolutionary elites to rely on force readily generalizes from the revolutionary to the postrevolutionary situation and from internal to external conflict: Violence is justified against all enemies of the revolution. The organizational consequences are parallel, in fact often overlapping: The personnel and agencies of warfare and internal security are interchangeable, though functional specialization between them develops more or less quickly.

The question is whether there is similar but more subtle generalization in other kinds of political systems. I suggest that there are strong linkages of this sort in the militarized autocracies and somewhat weaker ones in militarized democracies. Such linkages are not a consequence of institutional interchangeability because these kinds of states have sharply differentiated institutions of warfare and internal control. Rather, the linkage is to be found primarily in the dispositions and decisional calculus of rulers and leaders. In powerful autocracies, the normative disposition to rely on coercion, and estimates of its utility, are reinforced by both domestic and international experience.

In powerful democracies, I postulate a weaker tendency whereby elites who become convinced of the efficacy of force in the international arena also place considerable value on it in some kinds of domestic disputes. I would expect this disposition to be activated in several kinds of circumstances. First, the elites of democratic garrison states will be particularly sensitive to internal challenges that threaten to weaken the country's international position. Therefore internal support for a country's foreign opponents and opposition to militarization are particularly likely to trigger coercive elite responses, not solely or necessarily because of the objective extent of threat but because coercion is assumed, by bellicose elites, to be an appropriate response to any threat to the state's international position. Second, elites of democratic garrison states are more likely to employ coercion against domestic opponents in the aftermath of successful wars than at other times because they are "heady with victory." To be more precise, the successful use of international coercion increases confidence in its domestic utility and decreases, at least temporarily, normative restraints on the domestic uses of coercion. Both tendencies are checked by the operating norms of democracy: State elites themselves and the public generally prefer compromise over coercion. It is this countervailing tendency, inherent in the democratic ethos and the operation of competitive politics, that makes the linkage between international and domestic coercion weaker in democracies than in autocracies. Evidence that may be relevant to this hypothesis are findings by Stohl (1976) and Rasler (1986) that the twentieth-century wars fought by the United States were usually followed by periods and episodes of repression. Stohl attributes the pattern to the reaction of political and economic elites to the upward mobility of subordinate groups during wartime; Rasler thinks that nonaccommodating administrations are responsible. My argument suggests the complementary interpretation that American elites gained confidence through successful war in the efficacy of coercion. The implication is that postwar repression in democracies is a pattern that should be most pronounced following successful wars in powerful democratic garrison states.

DIVERSION

Diversion, a term used by Hazelwood (1975), is the deliberate projection or extension of internal conflicts onto the external environment.[13] It has often been evoked in the literature as a common, even primary connection between domestic and international conflict. Until recently, cross-national statistical studies concluded that diversion is not a strong force (see Stohl, 1980) despite suggestive case- and country-study evidence of its occurrence. A major recent contribution is Russett's study (1988) of major powers' participation in international disputes since 1853. The results show, among other things, a recurring connection in democratic countries, but not others, between short-term economic decline, increasing protest and repression, and participation in international disputes. In the United States, there is a pronounced association between low economic growth, electoral pressure (an impending national election), and American involvement in international conflict. Russett's conclusion from his extensive evidence is that in democracies, "participation in international conflict becomes an alternative state policy for dealing with protest especially if repression fails."

In the context of the propositions developed here, my hypothesis is that diversion of internal conflict is common only in states (a) in which rulers are directly threatened by popular discontent and (b) in which the international costs of diversion are likely to be less than the internal gains. There are two kinds of political systems in which these conditions commonly coincide: in weak regimes with low political capabilities, and in militarized democracies. In weak regimes, which are chronically subject to potentially revolutionary challenges, diversion of public attention and disaffection by a carefully chosen foreign adventure is potentially less costly than revolution. This is nonetheless risky business because foreign disputes may escalate in unpredictable ways, as they have for Libya under Colonel Gadhafi. If unsuccessful, they add to pressures for revolutionary change. Diversion for these regimes is likely to be chosen only because its potential gains—displacing threatening discontents, mobilizing popular support—outweigh, in the short run, its potential costs. This argument is represented graphically in the "diversion/reaction" linkage shown in Figure 3. Postrevolutionary regimes may also benefit from the internal solidarity that comes from foreign conflict, but they seldom need to provoke fights for that purpose. Their external enemies usually are quite real and threatening.

The calculus of elites in powerful militarized democracies will be rather different: Diversion is likely to appear to be high in potential gains, both domestically and internationally, and low in potential costs. These states are confident of their military capacity and of the likelihood of winning a limited dispute, and well aware of the electoral advantages of uniting public opinion behind a winning team. Institutionalized autocracies have less to gain politically from diversion because their rulers do not need electoral validation and rely mainly on coercion to minimize internal challenges. The weak democracies are far less likely to choose diversion because their elites have little to gain domestically or internationally from them. Thus a diversion linkage is shown for powerful democracies in Figure 2, but not for autocracies or weak democracies.

No type of regime is likely to risk a major international conflict as a diversion mechanism because full-scale war has high potential costs, even for powerful states. Thus evidence of diversion is likely only with regard to limited international disputes. This is in fact what Hazelwood (1975) found using crude aggregate data: Domestic conflict (across all countries) predicted less intense conflict better than more intense conflict.

CONCLUSIONS

I have developed some general propositions about the consequences of states' uses of extreme coercion in domestic and international disputes. Some of the propositions refer to generic processes about what political elites learn about the utilities of violence. Others refer to the conditioning effects of their countries' power capabilities and types of political system. The arguments appear to be internally consistent and not wildly at odds with comparative evidence on the emergence of variants of the garrison state. Throughout I have been more concerned about the logical consistency of the theory and models than the evidence, in the expectation that the argument will provoke the kinds of empirical research needed to validate and qualify it.

The general propositions and models have other important implications that have not yet been developed. It can be demonstrated, for example, that given these assumptions there are tendencies in the international system that lead to the continued expansion of garrison state phenomena. Only homogeneous democracies with low power capabilities and limited alliance obligations are insulated from the development of the institutions and political culture of militarized and police states. The argument also implies that chronic international conflict undermines the maintenance of noncoercive means of managing internal conflict, both in specific countries and in the international system as a whole. There may be "idealistic" paths to a national and global future with diminished reliance on violence for the management of conflict, but they are sharply constrained by the realistic propositions and models advanced here.

NOTES

1. The essential ideas of this article were presented at a Roundtable on "The Garrison State as Amplifier of International Conflict," American Political Science Meetings, Washington, DC, August 1986. My ideas on the sources of international conflict have been substantially influenced by a seminar on conflict behavior that I have taught jointly with Manus Midlarsky at the University of Colorado. James Caporaso offered useful comments on an earlier version. Hayward Alker (1988) has urged me to break away from pessimistic realist assumptions.

2. In four Western European countries for which time-series data are available, budgeted central government expenditures as a percent of GNP increased from an average of 6.4% in 1875 to 11.2% in 1925 and 44.1% in 1982 (from Gurr and King 1987: 26). In research thus far unpublished, I have documented a tenfold growth in the size of armies relative to total population in France and England from 1066 to World War II. A detailed historical account of the growth of military capabilities among European states since the medieval epoch is McNeil (1982).

3. See Waltz (1979) and Gilpin (1981). The seminal empirical study on capabilities and war is Singer et al. (1972). Zinnes (1980) reviews the empirical evidence to 1979. Major recent studies that have used this operational approach to capabilities in studies of the onset of war are Organski and Kugler (1980) and Bueno de Mesquita (1981).

4. This kind of political or functional approach to assessing state power has been developed, inter alia, by Organski and Kugler (1980: 33-38, 66-103), Snider (1986), and Gurr (1988). Most would regard it as complementary to, rather than as an alternative to, the material capabilities approach.

5. Most of the new literature on the autonomous state attributes a single objective or interest to the state. Buchanan (1975) from a conservative perspective and Levi (1981) from a radical one impute to officials a desire to maximize resources. Nordlinger (1986) argues that the common denominator of state interest is the enhancement of state autonomy. Skocpol (1985: 9-15) briefly acknowledges that autonomous states pursue diverse purposes. For a more elaborate specification of types and hierarchies of state interests, see Gurr and King (1987: chap. 1), who distinguish among short-term and long-term, and primary and expedient, interests of elected and administrative officials.

6. To sketch an argument very briefly, my assumption here is neomercantilist rather than Wallerstinian: Successful states at the center of expanding networks of trade and industrial production have generally promoted that expansion and have benefited as a consequence from growing tax revenues and cheaper and more abundant commodities and manufactured goods—commodities and goods that have public as well as private uses.

7. See, for example, Sereny's (1974) portrait of the commandant of the Treblinka Extermination Camp, Lifton's (1986) study of Nazi physicians who murdered in the name of science, and analyses by Charny (1982) and Kelman (1973) of the psychological processes by which ordinary people can become guiltless agents of mass murder.

8. On the relative capabilities of these two states and their opponents, see Organski and Kugler (1980: 74-103, passim). In the late 1970s, both devoted more than 20% of their GNP to military purposes, compared with 12.2% for the USSR and 5.1% for the United States, and a median international value of 3.0% (Taylor and Jodice 1983: 24-26).

9. Examples are the tactics used by American police agencies against armed black militants in the 1968-72 period and the West German responses to the Baader-Meinhof revolutionary terrorists and their successors.

10. This argument deserves more detailed development than I can give it here. Some evidence and interpretations that support it are summarized in several of my recent essays (Gurr 1979, 1980, 1986).

11. In a comparative study of genocides and politicides since 1945, we find that 12 of 41 were carried out by new elites in the immediate aftermath of revolutionary seizures of power (Harff and Gurr, 1988). The mass political murders in Pol Pot's Kampuchea are an extreme example of a common phenomenon.

12. Zeev Maoz (1987) reports evidence that this kind of phenomena has been pervasive in the international system since 1816. He finds that "revolutionary states (whether new entrants into the club of nations or existing states that have undergone revolutionary regime change) tend to be involved in a relatively large number of international disputes in the initial period following independence or the regime change" by comparison with other states, including those which have undergone evolutionary change (personal communication, March 30,(1987).

13. The term is used in preference to *displacement* because the latter implies an unconscious psychological process. I regard diversion, when it happens, as a deliberate policy choice of national elites.

REFERENCES

ADELMAN, J. R. (1985) Revolution, Armies, and War: A Political History. Boulder, CO: Lynn Rienner.

ALKER, H. R., Jr. (1988) "Emancipatory empiricism: Towards the renewal of empirical peace research," in P. Wallensteen (ed.) Peace Research. Boulder, CO: Westview.

BAYLEY, J. D. (1975) "The police and political development in Europe," pp. 328-379 in C. Tilly (ed.) The Formation of National States in Western Europe. Princeton, NJ: Princeton Univ. Press.

BUCHANAN, J. M. (1975) The Limits of Liberty: Between Anarchy and Leviathan. Chicago: Univ. of Chicago Press.

BUENO DE MESQUITA, B. (1981) The War Trap. New Haven, CT: Yale Univ. Press.

CHARNY, I. W. (1982) How Can We Commit the Unthinkable? Genocide: The Human Cancer. Boulder, CO: Westview.

CONQUEST, R. (1986) The Harvest of Sorrow: Soviet Collectivization and the Terror-Famine. New York: Oxford Univ. Press.

DUFF, E. A. and J. F. McCAMANT (1976) Violence and Repression in Latin America: A Quantitative and Historical Analysis. New York: Free Press.

ECKSTEIN, H. (1971) The Evaluation of Political Performance: Problems and Dimensions. Beverly Hills, CA: Sage Professional Papers in Comparative Politics 01-017.

FITCH, J. S. (1985) "The garrison state in America: a content analysis of trends in the expectation of violence." J. of Peace Research 22: 32-45.

GILPIN, R. (1981) War and Change in World Politics. Cambridge: Cambridge Univ. Press.

GOULDNER, A. W. (1977-78) "Stalinism: a study of internal colonialism." Telos 34 (Winter): 5-48.

GURR, T. R. (1976) Rogues, Rebels and Reformers: A Political History of Urban Crime and Conflict. Beverly Hills, CA: Sage.

GURR, T. R. (1979) "Alternatives to violence in a democratic society," pp. 491-506 in H. D. Graham and T. R. Gurr (eds.) Violence in America: Historical and Comparative Perspectives. Beverly Hills, CA: Sage.

GURR, T. R. (1980) "On the outcomes of violent conflict," pp. 238-294 in T. R. Gurr (ed.) Handbook of Political Conflict: Theory and Research. New York: Free Press.

GURR, T. R. (1986) "The political origins of state violence and terror: a theoretical analysis," pp. 45-71 in M. Stohl and G. A. Lopez (eds.) Government Violence and Repression: An Agenda for Research. New York: Greenwood.

GURR, T. R. (1988) "The political dimension of national capabilities: concepts and measurement." Int. Interactions 14: 133-139.

GURR, T. R. and D. S. KING (1987) The State and the City. London: Macmillan; Chicago: Univ. of Chicago Press.

HARFF, B. and T. R. GURR (1988) "Toward empirical theory of genocides and politicides: identification and measurement of cases since 1945." Int. Studies Q. 32(3).

HAZELWOOD, L. A. (1975) "Diversion mechanisms and encapsulation processes: the domestic conflict-foreign conflict hypothesis reconsidered," in P. J. McGowan (ed.) Sage International Yearbook of Foreign Policy Studies, Vol. 3. Beverly Hills, CA: Sage.

IVIANSKI, Z. (1980) "Provocation at the center: a study in the history of counter-terror." Terrorism: An Int. J. 4: 53-88.

JACKSON, R. H. and C. G. ROSBERG (1982) "Why Africa's weak states persist: the empirical and the juridical in statehood." World Politics 35: 1-24.

KELMAN, H. (1973) "Violence without moral restraint." J. of Social Issues 29 (4): 26-61.

KOEHL, R. L. (1983) The Black Corps: The Structure and Power Struggles of the Nazi SS. Madison: Univ. of Wisconsin Press.

LASSWELL, H. D. (1962) "The garrison-state hypothesis today," pp. 51-70 in S. Huntington (ed.) Changing Patterns of Military Politics. New York: Free Press.

LEVI, M. (1981) "The predatory theory of rule." Politics and Society 10: 431-465.

LIFTON, R. J. (1986) The Nazi Doctor: Medical Killing and the Psychology of Genocide. New York: Basic Books.

LUCKHAM, R. (1984) "Of arms and culture." Current Research on Peace and Violence 7 (1): 1-64.

MAOZ, Z. (1987) "Joining the club of nations: political development and international conflict, 1816-1976." Presented to the International Studies Association Annual Meeting, Washington, DC, April 15.

McNEIL, W. H. (1982) The Pursuit of Power: Technology, Armed Force, and Society since A.D. 1000. Chicago: Univ. of Chicago Press.

NORDLINGER, E. (1986) "Taking the state seriously," in M. Weiner and S. P. Huntington (eds.) Understanding Political Development. Boston: Little, Brown.

ORGANSKI, A.F.K. and J. KUGLER (1980) The War Ledger. Chicago: Univ. of Chicago Press.

RASLER, K. (1986) "War, accommodation, and violence in the United States, 1890-1970." Amer. Pol. Sci. Rev. 80: 921-945.

RUSSETT, B. M. (1988) "Economic decline, electoral pressure, and the initiation of international conflict," in C. Gochman and A. N. Sabronsky (eds.) Prisoners of War.

SERENY, G. (1974) Into that Darkness: An Examination of Conscience. New York: McGraw-Hill.

SINGER, J. D., S. BREMER, and J. STUCKEY (1972) "Capability distribution, uncertainty, and major power war, 1820-1965," pp. 19-48 in B. M. Russett (ed.) Peace, War, and Numbers. Beverly Hills, CA: Sage.

SKOCPOL, T. (1979) States and Social Revolutions: A Comparative Analysis of France, Russia, and China. Cambridge: Cambridge Univ. Press.

SKOCPOL, T. (1985) "Bringing the state back in: strategies of analysis in current research," pp. 3-37 in P. B. Evans et al. (eds.) Bringing the State Back In. Cambridge: Cambridge Univ. Press.

SNIDER, L. W. (1986) "Identifying the elements of state power: where do we begin?" Claremont Graduate School. (unpublished)

STOHL, M. (1976) War and Domestic Political Violence: The American Capacity for Repression and Reaction. Beverly Hills, CA: Sage.

STOHL, M. (1980) "The nexus of civil and international conflict," pp. 297-330 in T. R. Gurr (ed.) Handbook of Political Conflict: Theory and Research. New York: Free Press.

TAYLOR, C. L. and D. A. JODICE (1983) World Handbook of Political and Social Indicators (3rd ed.), Vol. 1: Cross-National Attributes and Rates of Change. New Haven, CT: Yale Univ. Press.

TILLY, C. [ed.] (1975) The Formation of National States in Western Europe. Princeton, NJ: Princeton Univ. Press.

TRIMBERGER, K. E. (1978) Revolution from Above. New Brunswick, NJ: Transaction.

WALTER, E. V. (1969) Terror and Resistance: A Study of Political Violence. New York: Oxford Univ. Press.

WALTZ, K. E. (1979) Theory of International Politics. Reading, MA: Addison-Wesley.

ZINNES, D. A. (1980) "Why war? Evidence on the outbreak of international conflict," pp. 331-360 in T. R. Gurr (ed.) Handbook of Political Conflict: Theory and Research. New York: Free Press.

Ted Robert Gurr is Professor of Political Science and Director of the Center for Comparative Politics at the University of Colorado, Boulder. He also is a Distinguished Visiting Fellow at the Center for International Development and Conflict Management at the University of Maryland. He has written more than a dozen books and monographs on political conflict, criminal justice, and other public policy issues, including Why Men Rebel *(winner of the Woodrow Wilson Prize as best book in political science of 1970);* Rogues, Rebels, and Reformers: A Political History of Urban Crime and Conflict *(1976); and* The State and the City *(with Desmond S. King, 1987). A new edition of his* Violence in America: Historical and Comparative Perspectives *(1969, with Hugh Davis Graham) is in preparation. One of his current research projects is a global analysis of communal groups in conflict; another is the historical analysis of the relations between war, revolution, and the growth of coercive states in Western societies.*

Genocide

[7]

Alternatives XI (1986), 403–430

Genocide: Toward a Functional Definition

WARD CHURCHILL*

> Genocide is always and everywhere an essentially political decision.
>
> *Irving Louis Horowitz†*

One of the more perplexing problems confronting contemporary socio-political theorists concerns the persistence of genocide, both as an overt instrument of state policy and as an almost incidental by-product of the functioning of advanced industrial society. While it can be said with virtual certainty that genocide today exists on a widespread and possibly growing basis, it cannot be correspondingly contended that the phenomenon is understood.

At the most fundamental level, it may be asserted that we presently lack even a coherent and viable description of the processes and circumstances implied by the term "genocide". A host of theses attempt to offer sociological definitions, variously holding that the essence of the genocidal process may be discerned in the physical liquidation of individual members of targeted groups, that meaning should be associated with the scale of annihilation or the specific nature of the state apparatus established to effect the lethal process. Among the more juridically minded, definitional questions seem to center upon the literal intent of the perpetrators of specific mass murders and the locus of conceptual lines differentiating genocide from the related crimes of war and crimes against humanity. The aggregate result, however, provides not so much for clarity and understanding of the subject discussed, but for a confusing and highly volatile welter of definitional contradictions.

In such a context, it is clear that effective analytical endeavors and resultant bodies of law and policy cannot emerge. To be sure, without the latter we cannot hope to stop the cancer of genocide, a disease that everyone seems to agree must be expunged. Indeed, as things now stand, we cannot even rationally hope to bring its consumptive proliferation under control.

The purpose of this essay, then, is to make some small contribution to a better understanding of genocidal occurrences, at least to the extent that it may be readily understood and agreed when a genocide is taking place. To

* Director, Educational Development Program, University of Colorado, Boulder, CO 80309, USA; and United Nations Delegate, International Indian Treaty Council.
† From Dr. Horowitz's *Genocide: State Power and Mass Murder* (New Brunswick, NJ: Transaction

this end a number of the prevailing notions of the phenomenon, both legal and sociological, will be discussed in passing as a means to arrive at a single typology. Such a synthesis should yield a greater utility for judicial, political and scholarly work on genocide than is currently possible. The reader is cautioned that no single study of this sort can lay claim to being either an exhaustive or definitive examination of the subject matter. Rather, it is intended to spark further consideration of the topic at hand and, hopefully, to bring about a refocusing of research.

An elemental confusion

All too often, otherwise sensitive and thoughtful individuals are reduced to defensive simplisms and mechanistic formulations when the word "genocide" is discussed. Many, of whom *Likud*-oriented Zionists are perhaps the most pronounced examples, are wont to restrict definition to the narrow (and perhaps marginal) arena of the Hitlerian slaughter mills. While the political reasons for this Zionist posture may be somewhat nebulous, the emotional reasons are not. As Robert Davis and Mark Zannis, Canadian researchers into the question of genocide, have noted: "The argument is sometimes made that to define genocide in terms other than mass homicide is to cheapen its currency and make a mockery of the memory of the millions who died in Hitler's holocaust."[1] However, as the authors go on to observe, the situation is really rather more complex.

> No one would deny the unspeakable horror of the Nazi mass murder. [But] the quality that made these deeds truly monstrous is the realization that ... man has attained the capacity to systematically wipe out an entire race ... *To destroy a people and their shared life is the crime,* and it can be accomplished as efficiently by means other than mass homicide (emphasis added).[2]

Such a view is in accord with the expressed opinions of Adolph Hitler himself, as when he stated that "[t]here are many ways, systematical and comparatively painless, or at any rate bloodless, of causing undesirable races to die out."[3] Elsewhere, in discussing the planned destruction of Europe's Jews, Gypsies, Slavs and Poles, he explained that "I don't necessarily mean destroy; I will simply take systematic measures to dam their great fertility."[4] Of course, actual circumstances forced the compression of Hitler's agenda for the elimination of "undesirables," with results that are far too well known to bear recounting here. What is important to recall is that until the so-called "Wannsee Conference" of January 20, 1942, Nazi policy was formally committed to relocation/deportation as the "solution of the race question," and that this earlier phase held precisely the same goal as "the final solution" (i.e., eradication of the targeted groups in Europe).[5]

Among the most common ideologically motivated misinterpretations of the meaning (real or potential) of genocide are those evident in the posturings of subscribers on one side or the other of the Cold War. Among orthodox Marxists it is commonly held that the phenomenon is specifically linked to machinations of "late capitalism," a matter to be overcome through appropriate application of socialist principles. While there is undoubtedly a certain merit to the Marxian analysis, it is an obviously skewed perspective, opting as it does to ignore numerous situations—and their causes—within the socialist world itself.

Instances which bring up the question of genocide abound in China, Vietnam and other socialist states. However, the example of the USSR, as the first and ostensibly most developed socialist country, seems particularly instructive. Here, Nikolai K. Deker and Andrei Lebed have compiled a survey of what they believe would be traditionally posited as cases of Soviet genocide. The list includes the complete destruction of such peoples as the Crimean Turks, Kalmyks, various nationalities of the north Caucasus and the Volga Germans. Also at issue for Deker and Lebed is the partial destruction of other peoples such as the Armenians, Azerbaidzhanis, Belorussians, Georgians, Jews, (Great) Russians, Turkestanis and Ukrainians, as well as the complete or partial destruction of religious groups including Moslems, Buddhists, Catholics and Autocephelics.[6]

For what may be politically obvious reasons, Marxist polemicists on the subject of genocide tend to remain silent on such matters, regardless of the clear theoretical significance involved. The Marxian analysis of genocide (either as to its meaning or its causes) cannot therefore be said to be particularly more helpful than that of Zionism in contributing substantially to the evolution of a coherent definition or causal theory of the phenomenon.[7]

Similarly, proponents of anti-communist "Free World" ideology, whether in its corporate-liberal or conservative variants, tend to focus exclusively on examples drawn from the socialist bloc, ignoring even the most obvious circumstances and practices of countries comprising their "sphere of influence." A salient example of this is represented by a *Time* magazine article by David Aikman published on July 31, 1978, and entitled "Cambodia: An Experiment in Genocide." According to Aikman, the Khmer Rouge regime in Kampuchea (revolutionary Cambodia) had by the time of his writing exterminated more than a million people from its total population of 7 million. He went on to note that "somehow the enormity of the Cambodian tragedy—even leaving aside the grim question of how many or how few actually died in the [Khmer Rouge] experiment in genocide—has failed to evoke an appropriate response of outrage in the West." Yet as Noam Chomsky and Edward S. Herman observed, "Figures apart, what is striking about this claim is that nowhere in the article is there reference to any US responsibility, no indication that deaths from starvation or disease may be something other than a 'bloodbath' by the Khmer Rouge."[8] After all, the extent and effects of long term US saturation bombing of Kampuchea's major food producing areas—a factor which could hardly have avoided engendering massive starvation and accompanying disease—was well known.[9]

With the postulations on genocide extended by anti-communists as tainted in those of their Marxist opponents, and for quite identical reasons (albeit, in mirror image), it follows that so-called free world analyses will yield no more utility in arriving at adequate definitions of either the fact or function of genocide than do Marxist or Zionist models. No matter in which direction we turn for guidance at present, conventional perceptions of genocide are so politicized and circumscribed as to be useless or worse. Rather than fostering clarity and understanding of the phenomenon so as to lead to an effective means of combating it, they induce an elemental confusion that forestalls remedy. To unravel and move beyond this current impasse, it is necessary to trace the historical contours of the evolution of genocide.

The evolution of a concept

The period following World War I saw a good deal of concern and debate in international circles about the level of casualties inflicted through the application of Karl von Clausewitz's famous formulation that "war is politics pursued by other means." Perhaps the major impetus leading to such considerations was the scale and sheer barbarity evident in the conduct of the First World War itself. Nonetheless, special attention was focused on the policies of the Turkish Ottoman Empire toward its Armenian minority population, from 1915 onward. As Vahakn N. Dadrian summarized the situation:

> In 1915, the leaders of the Turkish Empire put into action a plan to remove and exterminate its Armenian population of approximately 1,800,000 persons. The Turks were not particular about the methods they employed to this end: of at least a million and a half Armenians forced to leave their homes, supposedly to be deported, from 600,000 to 800,000 were murdered before ever reaching their destinations. Descriptions of this massacre clearly indicate an attempt to deliberately, systematically exterminate all or most of this group.[10]

Attempts to come to grips with the ramifications of the Turkish horror fell somewhat naturally upon the League of Nations. The League, not unlike the academic organizations from which it drew expertise and guidance, lacked any sort of formal conceptualization that could accommodate what had transpired. Casting about for a basis in extant law from which to develop a legalistic proscription of conduct such as that visited on the Armenians, the League's scholars were forced to make do with Article 22 of the 1907 (Fourth) Hague Convention: "The right of belligerents to adopt means of injuring the enemy is not unlimited . . ." Consequently, intellectualization of the destruction of the Armenians was made to run in channels describing the Turks as being on one side of the war (aligned with Germany), while the Armenians, being of "Russian" descent, were consigned to being on the other (allied) side.

If the description thus tendered failed to match the circumstances that occurred, neither did the corrective legislation produced at the 1929 Geneva Convention on the Rules of War. Although an entire battery of international law was created to protect civilians in time of war, its provisions were designed essentially to accommodate the civilian population of one country when invaded by another, or the civilians of one nation trapped by a sudden declaration of war within the territory of another (hostile) power. Not much was said concerning the possibility that a given country might unleash its armed power upon its *own* citizenry, or that civilians might well be liquidated en masse by military or other means during periods not typically understood as constituting "times of war."

The Geneva Convention was, of course, following an honorable tradition dating back at least to the third century AD, with the famous pronouncement of St. Augustine of Hippo that war might be divided into two types: just and unjust. While it was the duty of moral men to pursue just warfare, it was equally their duty to refuse participation in unjust wars, and to punish those who nonetheless chose to pursue them. The intent of the Convention, at least in part, was to define actions such as those undertaken by the Turks as clearly constituting "unjust war," and therefore to be illegal. Nevertheless, it was apparent almost from the outset that the supposed remedy was a failure.

The rise and consolidation of Hitlerian Germany ultimately crystallized what was bothersome and lacking in the League's appreciation of what had occurred in Turkey. By 1944, Professor Raphael Lemkin had coined a new word to describe the phenomenon and had provided a remarkably lucid and sensitive definition (for a first effort):

> Generally speaking, genocide does not necessarily mean the immediate destruction of a nation, except when accomplished by mass killings of all members of a nation. It is rather intended to signify a coordinated plan of different actions aimed at the essential foundations of the life of national groups, with the aim of annihilating the groups themselves. The objectives of such a plan would be the disintegration of the political and social institutions of culture, language, national groups, and the destruction of the personal security, liberty, health, dignity and even the lives of the individuals belonging to such groups. Genocide is directed against individuals, not in their individual capacity, but as members of the national group.[11]

Elsewhere in his seminal treatise, Lemkin noted that "Genocide has two phases: one, destruction of the national pattern of the oppressed group; the other, the imposition of the national pattern of the oppressor."[12] He also called for the establishment of "[p]rocedural machinery for the extradition of [war] criminals . . . [and] an adequate machinery for the international protection of national and ethnic groups."[13]

In light of the dimensions of the Holocaust accompanying the Second World War, Lemkin's pioneering analysis and suggestions began to bear fruit within two years. On December 11, 1946, the newly founded United Nations General Assembly passed Resolution 96(I), which stated in part:

> Genocide is a denial of the right of existence of entire human groups as homicide is the denial of the right to life of individual human beings; such a denial of the right of existence shocks the conscience of mankind, results in great losses to humanity in the form of cultural and other contributions represented by these human groups, and is contrary to moral law and to the spirit and aim of the United Nations.

And lest anyone misunderstand that the General Assembly was concerned only with the particular form(s) of genocide visited upon Europe's "untermenschen" by the Nazis, the Resolution continued:

> *Many* instances of such crimes of genocide have occurred when racial, religious, political and other groups have been destroyed, entirely or in part (emphasis added).

Finally, the Resolution concluded that "[t]he punishment of genocide is a matter of international concern." This language was endorsed by every nation participating in the formation of the UN, and no exception has been entered by any nation joining since.

To be sure, the preoccupation of the international community during this period was with the punishment of the perpetrators of genocidal criminality inside the vanquished Third Reich. Accordingly, the first—and, to date, only—precedent of the desired international punishment for the crime of genocide was a series of trials, executions and imprisonments of the Nazi hierarchy at Nuremburg, Germany.

Ultimately, the "Nuremburg Doctrine" under which Nazi and other World War II defendants were prosecuted encompassed three discrete areas of criminality:

> *Crimes Against the Peace* encompassed a range of acts broadly construed as indicating the planning or otherwise preparing for an unprovoked war (such as a war of conquest; generally termed "aggressive war").
>
> *War Crimes* included the actual waging of an aggressive war as well as violation of specific tenets of codified international law such as focusing military attacks upon civilian targets, utilizing proscribed weapons, mistreating prisoners of war and so forth.
>
> *Crimes Against Humanity* was taken to include actions directed against noncombatant populations for other than strictly military reasons. These included imposing conditions of slave labor, massive forced relocation, deprivation of fundamental human rights and the like.

As Telford Taylor, US Chief Counsel at Nuremburg tells us, the third category was created specifically to get at the notion of genocide.[14]

Twenty-three nations adhered to the formal treaty instrument under which the Nuremburg trials were conducted, a process which opened with Chief Justice Robert H. Jackson stating that "if it is to serve any useful purpose it must condemn aggression by any other nations, including those who now sit here in judgment." Upon completion of the trials, the UN General Assembly affirmed "the principles of international law" embodied in their administration.[15] When the Nuremburg criminal proceedings ended in 1950, Taylor estimated conservatively that some 10,000 persons, two-thirds of them in Europe, had been tried.[16]

Even as the Nuremburg trials proceeded, the UN was energetically considering measures to provide a fuller and more precise codification of the crime of genocide under international law than that provided by the aforementioned Crimes Against Humanity which was felt to overlap too much with war crimes and to deal inadequately with group *destruction* rather than group abuse as a crime. On March 28, 1947, the UN Economic and Social Council passed Resolution 47 (IV), calling upon the Secretary General to draw up a draft convention on genocide. The secretariat's draft document (UN Document A/362) was duly generated, pushed through the organization's various review and revision processes and, in 1948, became the *United Nations Convention for the Prevention and Punishment of the Crime of Genocide.*

Although the Convention was severely weakened in its passage from draft to final form by the political necessity of accommodating an array of objections to various provisions from a number of nations (most notably the United States),[17] it still offered sufficient latitude for thoughtful interpreters to begin to systematically recognize genocide when it occurred, at least in particular major contours. Genocide was specified to be those actions that affect an identifiable racial, ethnic or religious group, whether in whole or in part, in the following ways:

(a)   Killing members of the group.
(b)   Causing serious bodily and mental harm to members of the group.
(c)   Deliberately inflicting on the group conditions of life calculated to bring about its physical destruction in whole or in part.
(d)   Imposing measures intended to prevent births within the group.
(e)   Forcibly transferring children of the group to another group.

In addition, not only was the actual execution of these actions considered criminal within the meaning of the Convention, conspiracy to commit such acts and incitement of others to commit such acts were also held to be crimes.

The Convention provides that "Any contracting party may call upon the competent organs of the United Nations to take such action under the Charter of the United Nations as they consider appropriate for the prevention and suppression of acts of genocide." It also binds the contracting parties to "pledge themselves in such cases to grant extradition in accordance with their laws and treaties in force." Further:

> Persons charged with genocide or any other acts enumerated [in the Convention] shall be tried by competent tribunal of the State in the territory of which the act was committed, or by such international tribunal as may have jurisdiction with respect to those Contracting Parties which shall have accepted its jurisdiction.

With overwhelming international ratification of the Convention essentially committing most of the world to abide by its content on pain of criminal prosecution, and with the precedent of a full-fledged international tribunal similar to that posited in the Convention having just convened in Nuremburg,[18] the UN then proceeded *not* to follow up with hammering out the precise jurisdictional mechanism(s) through which all this might be facilitated. Perhaps the most compelling reason for this sudden loss of momentum was the flat refusal of the United States to ratify the Convention (the only major nation to refuse) on the grounds that it would "interfere with exercise of its national sovereignty."[19] The Convention has since languished, an ineffectual and rhetorical gesture, little more. The UN forum, a vehicle which should have yielded a significant broadening, deepening and maturity of the general understanding of genocide over the past four decades, has proved itself barren. To date, there has been no further formal development of the conceptualization of genocide within the UN; needless to say, there has been no genocide-related sanction applied, never mind indictment or prosecution of perpetrators of genocide under UN auspices since the Convention went into effect.

In retrospect, the minimal progress in dealing with genocide is perhaps not surprising. The same United States that had played a major role in emasculating the secretariat's draft convention before scuttling it altogether was soon busily obtaining the early release from prison of many Nazi criminals that the international tribunal it had been so instrumental in forming had convicted and sentenced.[20] As Ladislas Farago summed up the situation:

> In the early fifties, the Allies magnanimously amnestied thousands of Nazi criminals, the exact circumstances of which represent a festering but carefully concealed scandal. As the Cold War was heating up, in a process begun in 1946 by Secretary of State James F. Byrnes and inspired by Dean Acheson, the United States shifted its traditional alignment in Europe from Britain and France to the renascent Germany of Konrad Adenauer. The great pied piper of Bonn (whose own chief aide was a former Nazi official who had drafted the lethal anti-Jewish laws) promoted the idea, at first subtly, then vigorously, that the wholesale prosecution of Nazis was putting "a heavy psychological burden on the rearmament problem" in the course of West Germany's rehabilitation for its role in the "defense of Western Europe."[21]

Theoretical forays

With legalistic channels at least temporarily denuded of potential, consideration of genocide in any meaningful sense became the domain of academics. Much of this work was sterile, consisting of a seemingly endless recapitulation of the horrors of Auschwitz and Babi Yar, perpetual dissections of this and that aspect of the Nazi death-delivery mechanisms, and a constant righteous belaboring of the obvious: the form of genocide peculiar to Nazi Germany could never be allowed to happen again.

Of course, there were flashes of brilliance within the gloom, as when Hannah Arendt remarked upon "the banality of evil" in her study of Adolf Eichmann, a major player in the Nazi genocide. Her point was that, rather than being some sort of "outlaw aberration," nazidom and the individuals who by-and-large composed it were dull, ordinary and well within a conventional "business as usual" status quo:

> [W]e are forced to conclude that Eichmann acted fully within the kind of judgement required of him: he acted in accordance with the rule, examined the order given to him for its "manifest" legality,

namely regularity; he did not fall back upon his "conscience," since he was not one of those who was unfamiliar with the laws of his country.[22]

From this, it might be argued that the primary basis for the popular perception of the Nazis' unique culpability lay, not with their patent deviation from the norms of civilized behavior, but with their advancement of certain forms of it "to excess." To this extent, genocide would be a much more widely practiced activity than most people (or governments) would be comfortable in admitting. Such an analysis would conform well to Adolf Hitler's own impression that he was basing his racial policies upon earlier models, notably those of Britain in handling the Boers and the United States' treatment of American Indians during the nineteenth century.[23]

Having opened the intellectual door slightly toward examining genocide as a phenomenon possessing at least a potentially broad range of forms and permutations that extend across a wide array of societies, and having been rather thoroughly chastised by a number of scholars within her own Jewish community for her efforts, Arendt abruptly abandoned the field. Scarcely a year after her Eichmann foray, she was at work negating the import of her own glimpse at the face of genocidal reality and reinforcing the conventional wisdom that insisted on the link between genocide and "totalitarianism" being absolute:

> At this point the fundamental difference between the totalitarian and all other concepts of law comes to light. Totalitarian policy does not replace one set of laws with another, does not establish its own *consensus juris*, does not create, by one revolution, a new form of legality. Its defiance of all, even its own positive laws implies that it believes it can do without any *consensus juris* whatever . . . It can do without the *consensus juris* because it promises to release the fulfillment of law from all action and will of man.[24]

In other words, Arendt's final explanation of Eichmann and genocide lay precisely in the very "outlaw" social characteristics she herself had so clearly and firmly rejected by previously describing him as being so commonplace as to be banal. Perhaps such a gross contradiction in Arendt's otherwise acute perceptions can be accounted for in what must have been the utterly terrifying realization that, if Eichmann could truly be said to symbolize "everyman," then genocide must be an integral aspect even of the society in which she found herself. Unable to countenance the possibility of genocide as a norm rather than an aberration, she beat a hasty if not altogether tenable intellectual retreat.

Others, however, did pick up Arendt's initial theme. Irving Louis Horowitz, for example, announced in the introduction to his monograph on the subject (dedicated to Arendt) that "Genocide is not simply a sporadic or random event such as the Katyn Forest Massacre in which 15,000 Polish troops were presumed to have been destroyed by the Red Army during World War II. In addition to its systematic character, genocide must be conducted with the approval of, if not direct intervention by, the state apparatus."[25]

Having thus allowed for a possible proliferation of genocidal activities well
beyond the definitional constraints typically applied, Horowitz proceeded to
utilize illustrative examples of what he held to be genocides as diverse as the
violencia in Colombia, the United States' handling of its "Indian question,"
and Idi Amin's performance in Uganda, in addition to such standard fare as
the 1915 Turkish slaughter of Armenians, the Holocaust and the Stalinist
policy of reducing nationalities.

Horowitz also attempted to go beyond the definitional characteristics of the
UN Convention, rendering a description of genocide which would be more
functional in terms of perceiving and understanding when genocide occurred,
if not to prevent or punish it:

> In addition to the legal definition of genocide, it is necessary to add a
> sociological dimension. Two points must be subsumed under such a
> heading: first, genocide represents a systematic effort over time to
> liquidate a national population, usually a minority; second, it
> functions as a fundamental political policy to assure participation by
> the citizenry.[26]

He goes on to note that, "There are exceptions to each point. Sometimes, as it
is in the apartheid policy of South Africa, it is the minority that practices
forms of genocide on the majority. Also, there are many cases in which overt
statements of a government only vaguely reflect its covert actions, for
instance, the case of Soviet policy toward its national minorities."[27]
Additionally, "A formal distinction between genocide and assassination is
also required. Genocide is . . . *a structural and systematic destruction of innocent
people by a state bureaucratic apparatus* (emphasis in the original)."[28]

In the third, expanded, edition of his book, Horowitz added much that was
of a purely polemical nature—that is, subscribing to the "Free World"
posture inherent to the cold warrior, thereby ignoring much and elsewhere
insisting upon driving round pegs into square holes—hence diluting the
sharpness of its initial impact upon the mythology of genocide.[29] Nonetheless,
he did include another essay that represented a significant contribution
toward clarifying the meaning of the term. Entitled "Genocide and
Holocaust: On the Exclusivity of Collective Death," this short piece virtually
demolished the major tenets advanced by Emil Fackenheim, perhaps *the*
leading proponent of the Zionist "exclusivity of the Jewish experience" idea.[30]
Again, the door to a broader understanding of genocide has been wedged
open, if only slightly.

Horowitz had called for the incorporation of genocide as a central issue of
the social sciences and pointed to "the possibility of defining the state not in
terms of communism, liberalism, or conservatism, but to what degree it
permits the official and arbitrary termination of the lives of its citizens."[31] But
it may be safely asserted that precious few scholars have followed this lead,
including Horowitz himself (it is instructive that he deleted this phrase from
later versions of his own material).[32] Consequently, the prevailing
definition(s) of genocide remain lacking.

Definitional problems

A central difficulty inherent to present conceptualizations of genocide goes to a contradiction embedded in the juridical logic applied to the initial formulation(s) of the term. Having likened genocide to murder (albeit of a group rather than of an individual) in its description, the United Nations promptly dropped this illuminating parallel, stating that, "In the present Convention, genocide means any of the following acts committed *with intent* to destroy, in whole or in part, a national, ethnical, racial, or religious group (emphasis added)."

Following the original analogy with the crime of murder, what was ultimately described in the Convention as constituting the crime of genocide parallels *only* murder in the first degree (i.e., murder committed with intent and premeditation, the worst and most severely punished type). The question that must be posed now is whether the UN was attempting to proscribe and penalize the actual destruction of groups, or the intentions of the perpetrators. Since all accounts (and UN records) bear out that the UN desired to achieve the former rather than the latter result, using the word "intent" becomes extremely problematic.

In developed statutory codes such as that of the United States, it is clearly acknowledged that murder can be and is often accomplished in a range of degrees. Only first degree murder requires intent, a subjective and exceedingly difficult factor to prove in most cases. Thus, there is a second degree of murder covering actions where the death of the victim is not necessarily sought or desired by the perpetrator, but where death occurs while the perpetrator is engaged in some other form of suspect or illegal behavior. There is also a third degree of murder, often called "negligent homicide," where the death of the victim is not directly intended but resulted from the irresponsible or insensitive conduct of the perpetrator.[33]

Finally, there is a non-murder category covering inflicted deaths, usually called "manslaughter," in which it is held that the perpetrator definitely did *not* seek or desire the death of the victim, but that the victim was killed through the poor judgment of the perpetrator. In general, all actions resulting in the death of another are construed as culpable (and punishable) in common law unless there is clear evidence that the killer acted in self-defense, forestalling a potentially lethal threat forthcoming from the victim. "Justifiable homicide" is then held to pertain.

This formulation of the criminal code is quite consistent with the eleventh century strictures on universal mayhem advanced by St. Thomas Aquinas in his *Summa Theologiae*: "It is to them that it belongs to bear the sword in combats for the defense of the State against external enemies . . . those attacked must, to a fault, deserve to be attacked . . . [and] those who wage wars justly have peace as the object of their intention." It also accords with slightly less archaic principles such as Francisco Suarez's observation that defensive war is always just because "the right of self-defense is a natural and necessary one."[34]

Further, the multifaceted structure of the code concerning homicide allows for the cognitive apprehension of victimization in a variety of forms rather than locking the analyst/observer into entirely subjective—or even conjectural—estimations of the intentions of the victimizer(s). That this more sensitive and rational approach to defining genocide was avoided by the UN is in many ways inexplicable. The confusion and arcane debate (How many angels *can* dance on the head of a pin?) engendered by its flawed formulation, on the other hand, seems beyond any doubt.[35]

In pursuit of the proof of intent to establish genocide as required by the UN, quite serious analysts of the question have become obsessed with locating systemic instruments designed to *directly* and efficiently obtain genocidal results. Horowitz, to name a prime example, uses the word "systematic" no less than 54 times in one 31-page effort to explain what is required to make "genocidal society."[36] All of this leads, sometimes inadvertently or even reluctantly, back to the flimsy premise that genocide must be identified by its structural correspondence to the forms exhibited in the Third Reich. It omits altogether the possibility (indeed, probability) that such specifically focused evidence may *or may not* be present in a given instance of genocide.

No less, it evades the fact that governments, the same as murderers, are quite capable of masking and/or lying about both the nature of their actions and the intentions underpinning them. One can hardly expect that every incidence of genocide will be accompanied by the clear record of intentions offered by Nazi Germany. Even in that case, as Davis and Zannis have pointed out:

> If the genocide convention had been in force in Hitler's time, he almost certainly could be expected to have replied to charges of genocide in the following manner: "Quite the contrary, I abhor genocide and worked in a singular effort to punish and prevent dangerous elements in the Jewish community who were engaged in a sinister plot to wipe out the entire Aryan race. No one has worked harder than I to uphold the genocide convention and I wholeheartedly subscribe to it."[37]

Such a contentious and restrictive environment concerning what can and cannot rightly be viewed as truly genocidal activity has engendered considerable trepidation on the part of many individuals concerned with the issue. Lord Bertrand Russell, who was well aware of the semantic and definitional pitfalls involved in deploying genocide as a charge under international law, to give but one prominent example, chose to empanel his 1967 tribunal investigating US conduct in Vietnam as a body to inquire into possible war crimes rather than genocide per se. This led to a lengthy examination of American bombing patterns, deployment of certain types of ordnance and the like, as well as to an attempt to assemble a battery of charges on the waging of aggressive war and crimes against the peace, similar in their particulars to those brought at Nuremburg.[38]

Insofar as the Russell Tribunal was taken seriously—and it was, as is evidenced by the wide range of US intellectual debate it sparked (or which at least cited it extensively), a matter that became of more than passing interest to the US government—it was immediately drawn into a quagmire of protocol and stipulations within the relatively highly evolved Laws of War. This led Telford Taylor, an expert on the subject and rather sympathetic to the tribunal's aims, to conclude on a point-by-point basis that the legal logic imbedded in the charges was faulty or impossible under existing treaties and conventions. Although he never quite brought himself to employ the word genocide, Taylor did observe that Crimes Against Humanity seemed a more fruitful avenue of pursuit, and that the Russell Tribunal was missing the mark in hammering at the notion of war crimes.[39]

It was left to Jean-Paul Sartre, the tribunal's executive president, to essentially concur with Taylor's assessment and to go beyond it. Altering the apparent thrust of the tribunal's findings, Sartre branded the nature of the US actions in Southeast Asia as genocide, without equivocation or mitigation. In its essence, Sartre's thesis was as radical as it was simple. The proof of genocide, he asserted, lies in the results of policy, not in the intentions by which it may be undertaken. The fact of Vietnamese decimation in itself established that genocide was occurring in Indo-China, regardless of the US government's oft stated rationale that its intent was to liberate the Vietnamese and safeguard their freedom. Negative intentions need not be proven, Sartre held, in order to observe that negative results attended given policies; and it is the results—not the intentions—which are at issue.[40]

Moreover, he continued, intent itself seemed sufficiently established by the fact that the United States was determined to fight a counter-insurgency war in Vietnam. It is axiomatic within military doctrine that suppression of a bonafide popular insurgency entails eliminating "the sea" in which the insurgents swim; that is, the conduct of warfare on the populations rather than military formations per se. This, Sartre points out, is an *inherently* genocidal proposition accepted willingly by the Americans from the moment General William Westmoreland undertook his "strategy of massive attrition." The United States was clearly perpetrating genocide in Southeast Asia; whether this was/is a crime prosecutable under existing international law was/is another question.[41]

Following Sartre's breakthrough, reference to American genocidal practices in Indo-China became quite common,[42] as did reference to related categories (some of them virtually coined for the occasion), such as "ecocide."[43] At the level of international law, not much was done other than the entering of a pair of resolutions, one on November 29, 1972; and the other on December 9, 1974, that might be viewed as attempts to curtail under the Laws of War certain military practices upon which the United States relied heavily in Indo-China. The first of these, Resolution 2932 A (XXVII) deplores the use of napalm and other incendiary weapons in all conflicts. The second, Resolution 3255 B (XXIX) condemns the use of these weapons in circumstances which affect human beings or may cause damage to the environment and/or natural resources; all states are urged to refrain from production, stockpiling, proliferation and use of such weapons.[44]

In essence, the definitional problems associated with the concept of genocide that led to such intellectual convolutions as sketched above could be reasonably easily resolved by simply following the prescriptions established through the statutory codes on murder, the crime to which genocide has been compared all along. We will then be able to confront the specter of group destruction without becoming inevitably mired in considerations of government intentions, whether they matter (other than to establish the degree of criminality involved), whether given actions would be more appropriately or fruitfully termed war crimes than genocide, and so forth.

A typology of genocide

With certain modifications, the existing UN Convention could be utilized for purposes of offering a more adequate definition. Perhaps the simplest to realize in this connection would be the elimination of the emphasis on demonstrating intent. More difficult (though possibly not, as the United States—apparently the major obstruction in this regard—only ratified the Convention in February 1986, and may therefore be in less of a position to object than was the case in 1947) would be the reinsertion of the two major deletions from the original secretariat's draft convention:

(1) The two aspects of cultural genocide originally broken out in their own right would becomes points *f* and *g* of the acts of genocide enumerated under Article III of the Convention and,
(2) Article III would conclude with the observation that genocidal processes might be considered in a two-fold light rather than being restricted to overt destruction only.[45]

Finally, it seems likely that an entirely new article will need to be written and inserted into the Convention before it can assume true functional utility, either definitionally or juridically. This would be designed to articulate the varying types or degrees of genocide possible, and should probably echo the gradient statutory code pertaining to individuated murder:

> *Genocide in the First Degree* would encompass instances where clear intent to commit genocide was evident, could be documented/ proven, and where the systematic/efficient focus of policy and resources toward accomplishment of genocide has occurred. Historical examples of this degree of genocide, which may serve to orient us to it, might be that undertaken by Nazi Germany, the USSR under Stalin and much of US conduct towards its aboriginal population during the 19th century.
> *Genocide in the Second Degree* would encompass instances where intent to commit genocide *per se* is unclear, but where genocide occurred while its perpetrator was engaged in otherwise criminal activities such as the waging of aggressive war, territorial expropriation, etc. Historical examples of this degree of genocide would include the US "effort" in Southeast Asia, the Turkish reduction of Armenians, the military strategy directed toward its Algerian colony by France during the late 1950s, and Japanese policies in occupied China before and during the Second World War.[46]
> *Genocide in the Third Degree* would encompass instances where

genocidally specific intent is probably lacking, and where the perpetrator is not otherwise engaging in activities judged to be illegal, but—through recklessness, insensitivity, or some combination—the perpetrator allows genocide to occur as an "inevitable by-product" of its national activities (water diversion, mineral extraction and other forms of majority group "development" come immediately to mind as the possible generative processes in this regard). Historical examples of this sort of genocide are aspects of forced collectivization in China, some elements of the Khmer Rouge "autogenocide" in Kampuchea, much of 20th century US and Canadian policy towards their Indian populations, 20th century Australian and New Zealand policies toward their aboriginal populations and Vietnamese practice regarding the so-called "Montagnard" population of the Annamese Cordillera.

Genocide in the Fourth Degree, which should be viewed as corresponding to manslaughter rather than murder, would accommodate instances where intent, other forms of criminality and reckless insensitivity are all unclear or lacking, but where genocide nonetheless occurs. Such cases, where poor (or arrogant) judgement is at issue rather than overt maliciousness, might seem fewer than in the other three categories, but include US assimilation and termination programs directed at American Indians ("for their own good") in the 20th century, certain Arab "development" efforts extended at the South Sahara Bedouins, aspects of the Soviet collectivization experience and so on.[47]

While such a multilayered gradient of criminality would do much to release the concept of genocide from its present straight-jacket of definition, it would in itself do little to resolve the jurisdictional problems associated with enforcement of the convention, as with other elements of international law. This seems all the more true in a period when the president of the United States, for example, has suggested that World Court authority extends no further than the arbitration of trade matters between nation-states,[48] and that ratification of the Genocide Convention itself may now be undertaken without fear of its ultimate enforcement.

It is all well and good to argue, as Richard Falk has, that "[t]he President is bound to act in accordance with governing law, including international law. The customary and treaty norms of international law enjoy the status of 'the laws of the land' and the President has no discretion to violate these norms in the course of pursuing objectives of foreign policy."[49] The suggestion that violations of international standards are, or should be, accommodated within the domestic laws of each nation is of course accurate, and would go far toward solving the dilemma of jurisdiction. If accepted on its merits, it would also lead undoubtedly toward the consolidation of a viable World Court system in the future.

We are, however, confronted with the sad fact that Nuremburg remains the sole instance of the effective prosecution of national *policymakers* (as opposed to occasional enlisted marines or low ranking officers) for engaging in the sort of illegality really at issue. It is also self-evident that we cannot rely on the absolute military defeat of any government guilty of genocide as an expedient to seeing justice done and the crime deterred. In a formal sense, then, the jurisdictional question may be so problematic as to seem to thwart the purpose of improving upon present understanding of genocide (or crimes against humanity, war crimes, etc.).

A possible way out of this apparent impasse is pointed out by Falk when he notes that a strictly formal application of legalism, which he terms "the indictment model," is hardly the only means of bringing the law to bear. To the contrary, he rightly contends that "a conception of crime based on a community's obligation to repudiate certain forms of governmental behavior and the consequent responsibility of individuals and groups to resist policies involving this behavior" is often more effective, especially as regards application of international law.[50]

Indeed, while the formal prosecution of government, military and corporate leaders for all manner of violations of international law has languished since 1950, Falk's "responsibility model." has seen considerable active service. One need only examine the outcome of the political careers of Lyndon B. Johnson and Richard M. Nixon in the United States to acquire a glimpse of the potential afforded by Falk's thesis. More sharply, the assignment of individual responsibility to Indira Gandhi for her policies vis-à-vis India's Sikh religious community is also instructive.

Viewed in this light, an improved codification of genocide, allowing for a more sensitive and flexible interpretation of the phenomenon as well as a far broader range of culpability than is presently the case in international law, would be an extremely hopeful sign. Augmented as it surely would be by elaboration from disciplines such as sociology and political science, a typological recodification of the Genocide Convention would go far toward providing an adequate conceptual basis for an effective global *consensus juris* vis-à-vis genocide in all its ugly manifestations. Surely such a development cannot be other than a positive step towards the humane world order system called for so eloquently by Falk and others.[51]

Additional difficulties

Establishment of the sort of flexible and graduated schema of culpability in the perpetration of genocide proposed in the preceding section can achieve something of its full utility only when two further conceptual barriers are overcome. These can be viewed as associated with ideas of genocide being an act or process of some specific magnitude (vast numbers of bodies must be generated by a genocide) and employing a specific methodology (killing people outright). Each assumption will be examined in turn so that they might respond and be useful to those who would challenge the "appropriateness" of certain of the illustrations accompanying the typology.

The question of scale

Although there is nothing in present legal language or in serious theoretical studies concerning genocide that posits scale of destruction as a criterion, popular conception seems to hold that without vast numbers of bodies whatever has occurred cannot appropriately be considered as constituting that particular crime. No doubt this situation derives from an understandable (and perhaps subconscious) association of the term itself specifically with the Holocaust. Nonetheless, as was noted earlier, however understandable such associations may be, they tend to muddle rather than clarify the issue.

If an effective model of community responsibility is ever to emerge, the circumstances involved in the genocidal context must be understood as that an identifiable *group* of people *as such* is being or has been destroyed, regardless of the size of that group. The literal number of individual people slaughtered in a given process is not in itself indicative of genocide; there is no magical "body count" below which genocide cannot rightly be said to exist. While the scale of destruction will necessarily run into millions when a large group such as the Khmers or Jews is targeted, the numbers of victims involved in the genocide of smaller peoples such as culturally distinct indigenous tribal peoples around the world may amount to only a few thousand or, in some cases, even a few hundred.

Thus it does not make sense to argue that the destruction of approximately one-third of the total Jewish population in the 1940s is somehow a "greater crime" or "worse" than the destruction of perhaps 80 per cent of the total Cheyenne population during the 1860s and 1870s. Granted, in the former case, upwards of 6 million individuals were killed while in the latter instance the figure may well be less than 3,000. But in terms of *group* destruction, the subsequent ability of the Jewish people to recover and sustain itself *as a group* was obviously much greater than that of the Cheyennes. This is not a calculation to be taken lightly if genocide is to be comprehended in its rightful sense as group destruction, rather than as merely a fancy-labeled version of the rather clearer-cut crime of mass murder.

From this perspective, historical examples of genocide begin to proliferate. Horowitz mentions the British destruction of the Zulus during the nineteenth century, as well as Belgian policies toward the tribal peoples of present day Zaire which were implemented during the same period.[52] The holocaust perpetrated by the Spanish in the Caribbean, in which the Arawaks for example were entirely obliterated, also comes to mind. Similarly, there is the utter and complete Spanish destruction of Aztec and other tribal societies flourishing in sixteenth century Mexico, as well as the British demolition of native Hawaiian culture, the "conquest" of the Maoris of New Zealand and the "settlement" of Australia's aborginal interior. US history is also quite replete with instances other than the example of the Cheyenne: the "removal" of the so-called Five Civilized Tribes from the southeast during the 1830s is a salient example, as are the Round Valley Wars in California and the Kit Carson Campaign against the Navajo later in the century. Clearly, the list could go on and on.[53]

It is important to bear in mind when engaging in such considerations that we are by no means restricted to the arena of historical inquiry. Entirely similar processes are at work in the contemporary setting. Norman Lewis has this example of Brazil during the 1970s:

> The huge losses sustained by the Indian tribes in this tragic decade were catalogued. Of 19,000 Munducurus believed to have existed in the thirties, only 1,200 were left. The strength of the Guaranis had been reduced from 5,000 to 300. There were 400 Carajas left out of 4,000. Of the Cintas Largas, who had been attacked from the air and driven into the mountains, possibly 500 survived out of 10,000. The proud and noble nation of the Kadiweus—the Indian Cavaliers— had shrunk to a pitiful scrounging band of about 200. A few hundred only remained of the formidable Chavantes, who prowled in the background of Peter Fleming's Brazilian journey, but they had been reduced to mission fodder—the same melancholy fate which had overtaken the Bororos, who had helped change Levi Strauss's views on the nature of human evolution. Many tribes were now represented by a single family, a few by one or two individuals. Some, like the Tapiunas—in this case from a gift of sugar laced with arsenic—had disappeared altogether. It is estimated that between 50,000 and 100,000 Indians survive today. Brazil's leading social historian believes that not a single one will be alive by 1980.[54]

The Brazilian social historian referred to by Lewis was somewhat off on his timetable, though not in the spirit of his projection, as is evidenced by the fact that the Brazilian government is still quite busy killing Indians today.[55] Nor is Brazil alone in its lethal policies towards Indians—*as* Indians—in the topical context. Richard Arens has compiled a volume detailing the slaughter of the Ache people of Paraguay in which a contributor notes that:

> I can state that at least 343 persons have been killed ouright or enslaved and induced to die between September 1968 and June 1973 . . . Turning from these minimum figures . . . one must note that at least three Northern Ache tribes have disappeared between 1968 and 1972, either through killing or kidnapping, by private or official hunts . . . In my judgment, it is reasonable to say that approximately 50 percent of Northern Ache men, women and children have been wiped out by disease, despair and murder between 1962 and 1972. All these figures refer exclusively to the Northern Ache. I have no exact data about the Ache living further to the south. It seems highly probable, however, that they too have been the victims of massacre and enslavement.[56]

Elsewhere in the same volume, Elie Wiesel, one of the great students of the Holocaust, having first acknowledged that he had always resisted any sort of comparison to the genocide of European Jewry, professed that the record in Paraguay was sufficient to alter his assessment and that "our society prefers not to know anything about all that. Silence everywhere. Hardly a few words in the press. Nothing is discussed at the UN, or among the politicized intellectuals or the moralists. The great conscience kept quiet."[57] Well intentioned though he undoubtedly was, Wiesel dramatically underestimated the legacy of confusion concerning the meaning of genocide created by 30-odd years of insistence upon "the uniqueness of the Jewish experience" he himself had done so much to create. "The great consciences," by and large, preferred to debate whether the Ache example was significant enough, or monumental enough even to warrant "proper" identification as a genocide.

The situation is hardly unique. Noam Chomsky, to name but one example, has consistently encountered such semantical polemics, beginning with his efforts to expose the decimation of h'Mong tribesmen in Laos during the mid-1960s.[58] This has continued up through his attempts to alert people to the impact of the Indonesian invasion and occupation of East Timor during the late 1970s.[59] Even the Public Broadcasting System has been accused of "terminological overkill" when, in a 1984 documentary film, it described the wanton destruction of Guatemalan Indians as being "a hidden holocaust."

The Americas, of course, are not the only—or even necessarily the primary—locale in which "small scale" exterminations have occurred, are occurring, or will occur in the future. There is every indication that similarly horrible events occur in virtually every corner of the planet. This is all the more reason why it should be unequivocally asserted that, simply because a group may be small and "marginal," its physical eradication is no less genocidal than on the rare occasions when larger groups are targeted for extinction.

Cultural genocide

Not only must juridical appreciations of genocide be steered clear of confinement to the concept of specific intent, popular conceptions of the phenomenon itself must also be guided away from butchery per se regardless of scale. Here, a formulation offered by Richard Arens seems especially helpful:

> Genocide can take the form of what anthropologists have called deculturation, and it can involve the disintegration of some or all of the following: political and social institutions, culture, language, national feelings, religion, economic stability, personal security, liberty, health and dignity. It does not take much imagination to see death in the destruction of a population's health or economic stability. We need not, however, depend on imagination and empathy alone. Deculturation has been studied for decades, and its lethal effects have been demonstrated beyond reasonable doubt.[60]

What Arens is describing is sometimes disparagingly referred to as "cultural genocide" by those who insist on seeing extermination factories and crematoria as "proof" that genocide is actually taking place. As Davis and Zannis have observed in this regard:

> One should not speak lightly of "cultural genocide" as if it were a fanciful invention ... The cultural mode of extermination is genocide, a crime. Nor should "cultural genocide" be used in the

game: "Which is more horrible, to kill and torture; or, to remove the reason and will to live?" Both are horrible.[61]

Actually this case was well presented in 1948 by the Lebanese representative to the ad hoc committee revising the UN draft genocide convention. Commenting on the "actual and intentional destruction of a human group as such," he concluded that it was necessary to acknowledge that each human group, definable as such, has a right to be considered as "an absolute entity which it would be criminal to attack." He also noted that world conscience was revolted by—or *should* be revolted by—"the thought of the destruction of a group, *even though the individual members survived* (emphasis added)."[62]

The key to the problem lies in the use of the term "destruction." All too often this has been interpreted in the narrowest possible sense (i.e., in the more-or-less immediate physical death of group members) although this is quite illogical even under existing descriptive language. The first point of the 1948 Convention that enumerated genocidal activities concerns the killing of group members; it would of course be redundant to proscribe it a second time, never mind five times over. Yet something other than sheer physical death has always been implied within the notion of group destruction. Davis and Zannis pose these questions:

> What constitutes the "death" of a group, which may disintegrate while the lives of its individual members may proceed more or less intact? Under what conditions may a group be "killed" or "destroyed"? Is there a "group existence," separate from the lives of its members, which may follow a separate course unparalleled by the rights of its members? If so, can a "group" be defined in such a way as to spell out the conditions under which it can be "killed" or "destroyed"?[63]

The authors answer each question in the affirmative, citing the original UN Secretariat's draft convention which covered such "slow death measures," now termed "cultural genocide," as forced transfer of children to another human group, forced and systematic exile of individuals representing the culture targeted, the prohibition on the use of a national language, systematic destruction of books printed in a national language, systematic destruction of historical or religious monuments (or their diversion to alien uses), suppression of new publications concerning a definable group, destruction or dispersion of documents or objects pertaining to the historical, artistic and religious heritage of a targeted group and the like. They then conclude that:

> A culture's destruction is not a trifling matter . . . If people suddenly lose their "prime symbol," the basis of their culture, their lives lose meaning . . . A social disorganization often follows such loss, they are often unable to insure their own survival . . . The loss and human suffering of those whose culture has been healthy and is suddenly attacked and disintegrated is incalculable.[64]

As it was the United States, followed closely by Canada, which led the effort to delete such considerations from the Genocide Convention during the 1947–48 draft revision process, we would do well to pay particular attention to possible motives for such obstructionism. Upon even superficial examination, it is readily observable that both nations consistently engaged in what has been openly termed as "assimilationist policies" directed at indigenous populations within their borders. Aspects of these policies have and in many instances still include the legal suppression of indigenous religions and languages, the unilateral supplanting of indigenous governmental forms, the compulsory "education" of indigenous youth (often entailing their forced transfer to "boarding schools") in accordance with cultural and religious mores antithetical to their own, the unilateral imposition of definitions of group membership based upon "blood quantum" (eugenics) formulas rather than nationality, and the unilateral extention of "trust responsibility" (under the transparently neocolonial concept of plenary power) over the entire range of their affairs. Such policies make perfect sense when it is understood that the stated objective of forced assimilation is to bring about the complete dissolution of the targeted groups *as such*, causing their disappearance ("death") as individual members are absorbed into "mainstream society," they are but clinical descriptions of the process of cultural genocide.[65]

Occasionally, such policies jell into a more blatantly physical form, as when the Canadian government drowns the homeland of the James Bay Cree in the world's largest hydroelectric project, the US government announces plans to forcibly relocate and disperse some 13,500 traditional Navajos from their homeland in Arizona in order to mine coal there, or when either government announces the "termination" (the ending of legal existence of) an identified indigenous people.[66] Again, cultural if not physical genocide is implicit in the United States having done 80 percent of its uranium mining and 100 percent of its uranium production on Indian land since 1960, thereby rendering the landbase itself uninhabitable in many areas and ultimately forcing the dispersal of tribal groups.[67]

More often, however, procedures of cultural genocide pioneered in North America seem to have become an item of export to countries sympathetic to such ideas of organization and development, bearing out Arendt's thesis on the commonality, even banality, of genocidal evil to a degree and in ways she never envisioned. This is certainly the case in South Africa, as George M. Fredrickson has demonstrated compellingly.[68] And virtually all of the Americas south of the Rio Grande have, to one extent or another, adopted North American assimilationist postures as a means of furthering the "development" of their indigenous populations, a situation clearly echoed in Australia, New Zealand, portions of Indonesia and at various other points in the Pacific Basin.[69]

Throughout the continent of Africa even the most progressive governments seem to have determined that "tribalism" is the greatest problem confronting the consolidation of the new nation-states. Often their boundaries were, ironically enough, demarcated across "problematic" tribal territories not by progressive Africans, but by their European colonizers in years gone by. Hence, "detribalization" (another word for assimilation) seems to have become something of a continental priority, completing at an accelerated pace the process of emulsifying traditional African societies *as such* that was initially introduced by Europeans during the sixteenth century.[70]

As Richard Sklar put it, "tribalism is widely supposed to be the most formidable barrier to national unity in Africa . . . [and] nearly every African state has at least one serious problem of ethnic or regional separation."[71] One need only look to the writings of Ghana's Kwame Nkrumah, in expositions intended not only to explain the policies of his own government but to chart a course for all of progressive Africa, to find Sklar's perception validated.[72] More concretely, there is Julius Nyerere's plan of village collectivization advanced under the Arusha Declaration. Initiated in Tanzania in 1967 as a means of "unifying and developing" tribal economies, *ujamaa* in 1974–75 became a mass forced relocation program designed to eradicate "recalcitrant" tribal societies.[73]

The basic thrust of the Tanzanian process of group destruction should be understood in the context of Nyerere's outspoken admiration for the Marxist-Leninist Mengista regime in Ethiopia at the onset of its virulent policy of forcibly incorporating Eritrean tribal peoples "into the revolution."[74] And it should not be divorced from the rather less doctrinaire and dramatic example of Kenya, summed up by Colin Leys:

> Analytically speaking, the peasantry [tribal peoples] in African may be best seen as a transitional class, in between the period of primitive cultivators living in independent communities and that of capitalist development in which peasants are restratified into capitalists and proletarians; but under the conditions of growth of neocolonialism it seems clear that in Kenya at least the stage during which the peasantry itself goes through the process of development [is occurring].[75]

In a single collection of essays concerning revolutionary Africa, John S. Saul identifies similar thinking and processes of compulsory tribal group dissolution as occurring in Mozambique, Zimbabwe, Angola, Uganda and elsewhere.[76]

In South and Southeast Asia, the same principles apply as the virulence of India's policies suppressing ethnic and religious minorities are rivaled only by those of Bangladesh and Thailand. Likewise, the Burmese attempt to force incorporation of the Kachin into their "developing state," the Vietnamese pursue the same course with respect to the Rhade and other Montagnard peoples of the highlands region, and the Manila government proceeds in the same direction against the Moros of the southern Philippines. Nor, on their part, do the Kurds of Persia, the Sammis of northern Scandinavia or the Innuits of the Arctic circumpolar region fare better.[77]

As was previously noted, the compulsory homogenization of various "national minorities" within the so-called "socialist bloc" of nations has been endemic since the 1920s. Left or right, regardless of geographical location or variations of practice and intent, the problem—which is so pervasive as to have entered social science terminology as the principle of "cultural leveling"—remains essentially the same. This is true whether it assumes the form of Israeli treatment of Palestinian Arabs or the present Sandanista effort to compel the effective absorption of Miskito, Sumu and Rama Indians into the overall structure of Nicaragua's "revolutionary state."

The point at issue is that whole cultures, whole peoples are being forced to cease to exist *as such*. The result is genocide whether such elimination is accomplished in the name of racial/cultural superiority on the one hand, or on the basis of technological/economic development on the other. Until the principle is accepted that the essence of genocide is to be discovered in the coercive elimination of human groups per se, by *whatever* means and under *any* rubric, the term will likely not only remain ill-defined, but largely devoid of any practical meaning at all.

Conclusion

If this essay has accomplished anything, it is hoped that it has compellingly demonstrated the inadequacy of current definitional criteria describing genocide, and pointed out that viable conceptual alternatives to the present muddle exist. This is in conformity with the objective, stated in the introduction, of (re)opening fundamental questions rather than sealing them off.

The process of tracing the evolution of the concept of genocide as a criminal phenomenon distinct from any other, a process which contained clearly critical elements of analysis, was not intended to condemn the groups and individuals cited. Rather, it was utilized as a way of clarifying the kinds of ideological, political and emotional factors which have served to theoretically constrain understanding of the phenomenon itself. Criticism is thus offered in the spirit that only in the cognizance of the nature of conceptual inadequacy can it be transcended, offset or corrected, and more appropriate or functional understanding allowed to emerge.

In arguing toward a broadening of the definition of genocide to include not only large and small group annihilation, but externally imposed group destruction per se, I have sought to come to grips with the central element of genocide as a contemporary and historical fact, accurately detected by Raphael Lemkin and others but somehow lost within the polemics of codification and application. Hopefully, this "return to basics" will prove useful in establishing a more generalized understanding of when and where genocide has occurred and is occurring, in fact if not codified in law.

The posited "typology of genocide," on the other hand, represents a suggestion as to how law might seek to follow sound appreciations of genocide as a socio-political reality, rather than attempting to restrict understanding to some narrower theoretical paradigm. In extending the analogy of genocide to murder in what I take to be its logical dimensions, the typology should be viewed not as a "plan," but as a model through which—if it were appropriately developed—juridical apprehensions of genocide might be made to conform more closely to the nature of the phenomenon. Such a development in law could hardly help but benefit the emergence of a more just and humane world order.

While attempting to articulate the basis for a more functional definition of genocide, one which takes into account the full range of gradients and nuances marking the phenomenon, I have sought to avoid the pitfalls of ideological posturing, drawing examples from both communist and non-communist nations, as well as from both contemporary and historical events. I will, however, confess to the exercise of a certain "bias"—no doubt already noticed by the discerning reader—believing as I do that traditional indigenous cultures and societies possess every right to their continued existence as do their industrialized, "developing" or at any rate "modern" counterparts.

This "indigenist" notion that genocide permeates transideological scientism's obliteration of indigenous peoples in the name of technology and order is one that I hope to see considered and discussed in many quarters. And I will readily admit a firm desire to see "progress" tempered, both socially and legally, by formal acknowledgment of the *absolute* right of *all* peoples to the conditions necessary to the perpetuation of themselves *as peoples*.

Notes and references

1. Robert Davis and Mark Zannis, *The Genocide Machine in Canada: The Pacification of the North* (Montreal, Canada: Black Rose Books, 1973), p. 179.
2. Ibid.
3. Quoted in Herman Raushning, *The Voice of Destruction* (New York: Putnam & Sons, 1940, p. 138.
4. Ibid.
5. Concerning the Wannsee Conference, see Williams L. Shirer, *The Rise and Fall of the Third Reich: A History of Nazi Germany* (New York: Simon & Schuster, 1960), p. 965. On Nazi policy concerning the Jewish question in the period prior to the conference, see Heinz Hohne, *The Order of the Death's Head: The Story of Hitler's SS*, trans. Richard Barry (New York: Coward-McCann, Inc., 1969), pp. 196–258.
6. Nikolai K. Deker and Andrei Lebed, *Genocide in the USSR: Studies in Group Destruction* (New York: The Scarecrow Press, 1958).
7. An excellent example of the Marxist deployment of the term "genocide" is to be found on pp. 440–1 of *The Large Soviet Encyclopedia (Bolshaya sovetskaya enstisklopedia)* (Moscow: State Publishing House, 1952), therein, genocide is defined as "an offshoot of decaying imperialism."
8. Noam Chomsky and Edward S. Herman, *After the Cataclysm: Postwar Indochina and the Reconstruction of Imperial Ideology (The Political Economy of Human Rights, Vol. II)* (Boston: South End Press, 1979), p. 164.
9. A comprehensive analysis of the US impact upon Kampuchea (Cambodia), including detailed maps of the "overlapping box" method of US saturation bombing before 1975, is found in William Shawcross, *Sideshow: Nixon, Kissinger and the Bombing of Cambodia* (New York: Simon & Schuster, 1979). Of particular interest is Shawcross's citation, on p. 375, of an April 1975 US Aid report which noted that, "Slave labor and starvation rations for half [of Kampuchea's] people . . . will be a cruel necessity for this year, and general deprivation and suffering will stretch over the next two or three years [as a result of the American bombing]. Such information became increasingly and conveniently "lost" in the Western examination of Pol Pot's "autogenocide."
10. Vahakn N. Dadrian, "Factors of Anger and Aggression in Genocide," *The Journal of Human Relations,* vol 19, no 3, 1971, p. 384.
11. Dr. Raphael Lemkin, *Axis Rule in Occupied Europe* (Concord, NH: Rumford Press/Carnegie Endowment for International Peace, 1944), p. 79. It is noteworthy that Lemkin's book was acquired by the McGill Law Library in 1945, but despite its obvious importance as a groundbreaking text in an important aspect of international law, it was checked out only twice in the subsequent 28 years.

12. Ibid.
13. Ibid.
14. Telford Taylor, *Nuremburg and Vietnam: An American Tragedy* (New York: Quadrangle Books, 1970), p. 96.
15. Ibid, p. 14.
16. Ibid, p. 28.
17. Among the more important provisions of the secretariat's draft convention scrapped largely at the insistence of the United States were the inclusion of two categories of genocidal activity: (1) Planned disintegration of the political, social or economic structure of a group or nation, and (2) Systematic moral debasement of a group, people, or nation. Additionally, the draft convention contained an important nuance deleted from the final version, again largely at the insistence of the United States. This concerns defining genocidal acts in a two-fold way: (1) The destruction of a group (in whole or in part) and, (2) Preventing the preservation and development of the group. Ultimately, only the first of these two was retained. ·
18. An interesting point in reference to the International Military Tribunal which tried many of the Nuremburg defendants is made by Ladislas Farago in his *Aftermath: Martin Bormann and the Fourth Reich* (New York: Simon & Schuster, 1974). This is that there was nothing in the Charter, subscribed to by the participating nations, which set a concluding date for the tribunal's activities. Hence, its mandate might be correctly viewed as still being in effect and the tribunal might be properly and legally reconvened at any time. It could serve not only to continue to try Nazi criminals (as Farago suggests), but, at least in principle, could serve as the instrument of justice for those guilty of comparable crimes in subsequent years; the covenants employed at Nuremburg, after all, covered categories of criminality rather than membership in given nationalities or political parties per se. A legitimate means to solve at least a portion of the jurisdictional problems/questions associated with the 1948 Genocide Convention therefore exists in a technical sense. But there has never been an effort to use this means in any way.
19. Davis and Zannis (Note 1), p. 21. Since their analysis the United States Senate has finally ratified the convention; it was signed into law by Ronald Reagan in February 1986.
20. Perhaps the most notorious example of this sort of thing was the release of Alfred Krupp von Bohlen und Hallbach on February 3, 1951. Krupp had served barely three years of a prison sentence passed on him for crimes including the massive use of slave labor in keeping his sprawling armaments empire humming on behalf of the Third Reich. Krupp's release was effected by John J. McCloy, acting on behalf of the US government, which felt Krupp's managerial genius would be a significant tool in bolstering a revived German industry in following an anti-Communist Cold War course. This is well detailed in William Manchester's, *The Arms of Krupp, 1857–1968* (New York: Bantam Books, 1968), pp. 754–770.
21. Farago (Note 18), p. 19. Throughout his book, Farago illustrates his point with a number of case studies including, for example, that of Alfred Franz Six (recounted on pp. 326–327). Six (NSDAP No. 245,670/1930; SS No. 107,840/1935) was a Brigadeführer (major general) in the SS by the end of the war. Apparently a former university professor, he had attained his high rank via the expedient of excellent performance with the Einsatzgruppen (murder squads) butchering Jews in the USSR. He was sentenced on April 10, 1949, by an American military tribunal, to serve 20 years imprisonment for his crimes. By early 1951, US General Thomas Handy had reduced his sentence by half. Shortly thereafter, he was amnestied and released on orders from US High Commissioner in Germany, John J. McCloy. He immediately entered an executive position with Porsche-Diesel, within which he rose to become publicity and advertising manager by 1965. All the while he served as a "consultant" with the Gehlen Organization—a reconstitution of the Nazi Abwehr intelligence apparatus—assisting US intelligence in conducting propaganda operations against the Soviet Bloc.
22. Hannah Arendt, *Eichmann in Jerusalem: A Report on the Banality of Evil* (revised and enlarged edition) (New York: Penguin Books, 1965). Arendt has the good grace to note, on p. 294, that Israeli troops were being subjected to similar sorts of pressures, as was Eichmann, in Israel's prosecution of its war against the Palestinian population (but she chooses not to

428   *Genocide: Toward a Functional Definition*

develop the implications of this). She also observes on p. 40 that Eichmann believed, with apparent sincerity, that he himself was an ardent Zionist (again, she fails to speculate upon the implications of this).

23. Hitler's candid views on such matters are brought out in the memoirs of his confidant, Heinrich Hoffmann, *Hitler Was My Friend* (London: Burke Publishers, 1955) and elsewhere. They are noted by John Toland in his definitive two volume biography of the Nazi dictator, *Adolf Hitler* (New York: Doubleday, 1976).

24. Hannah Arendt, *The Origins of Totalitarianism* (New York: Harcourt, Brace & World, 1976).

25. Irving Louis Horowitz, *Genocide: State Power and Mass Murder* (New Brunswick, NJ: Transaction Books, 1976), pp. 1–6.

26. Ibid., p. 18.

27. Ibid.

28. Ibid.

29. Irving Louis Horowitz, *Taking Lives: Genocide and State Power* (New Brunswick, NJ: Transaction Books, 1982).

30. Ibid., pp. 193–212.

31. Horowitz (Note 25), p. 31.

32. Horowitz (Note 29), p. 23.

33. An interesting argument is offered by Hugo Adam Bedau, in an essay entitled "Genocide in Vietnam?" (Virginia Held, et al., editors), *Philosophy, Morality, and International Affairs* (London: Oxford University Press, 1974), pp. 5–46, that yet another category of murder might be used to parallel genocide. Commonly termed "felony murder," this category is one in which death is not inflicted directly by the perpetrator in any way at all, but in which death nonetheless ensues to the victom as a by-product of the perpetrator's commission of other criminal (felonious) acts. It is probable that any comprehensive typology of genocide will ultimately include a clear analogy to this category.

34. Francisco Suarez (1548–1617), as quoted in Taylor (Note 14), p. 63.

35. Bedau (Note 33), provides an excellent illustration of the sorts of convoluted reasoning which occur under the rigid application of the intent criteria as the only possible definition under which conceptions of genocide may be lodged.

36. Horowitz (Note 25).

37. Davis and Zannis (Note 1), p. 18.

38. John Duffett (editor), *Against the Crime of Silence: Proceedings of the Russell War Crimes Tribunal* (New York/London: O'Hare Books/Bertrand Russell Peace Foundation, 1968).

39. Taylor (Note 14). Taylor actually went further than suggesting another focus, stating in his conclusion on p. 207 that, "Somehow we failed ourselves to learn the lessons we undertook to teach at Nuremburg and that failure is today's American tragedy." (One assumes it was also something of a tragedy for the Vietnamese, Kampucheans and the Laotians victimized by America's failure to learn its own lessons.) By my conservative count, Taylor's is one of not less than 40 widely read volumes referenced closely to the Russell Tribunal proceedings which emerged in the US during the period. Government participants such as Robert McNamara and Clark Clifford have acknowledged that the growing degree and quality of accusations of US criminality made them increasingly uncomfortable in pursuing Johnson's policies in Southeast Asia.

40. Jean-Paul Sartre, *On Genocide* (Boston: Beacon Press, 1968), pp. 57–85

41. All this was, of course, before Daniel Ellsberg "leaked" the so called "Pentagon Papers" in which "confidential" US goals, objectives and assessments of methodologies were spelled out. This thoroughly eliminated the contrived murk surrounding the question of American intentions in Southeast Asia, but nonetheless resulted in no charges being brought. See *The Pentagon Papers: The Defense Department History of the United States Decisionmaking on Vietnam* (Gravel Edition) 4 volumes (Boston: Beacon Press, 1971).

42. See, for example, *The Dellums Committee Hearings on War Crimes in Vietnam* (New York: Vintage Books, 1972); Noam Chomsky, *For Reasons of State* (New York: Vintage Books, 1973); and all the testimony collected in the Winter Soldier Archive in Berkeley, CA (very little of which has been published).

43. Barry Weisberg, *Ecocide in Indochina: The Ecology of War* (San Francisco: Canfield Press, 1970).

44. While the United States was a signatory to both of these Resolutions, it by no means has

refrained from the production (including the development of new forms, such as pyophoric incendiaries based on depleted uraniun), stockpiling or proliferation. See Frank Barnaby (editor), *Incendiary Weapons* (Cambridge, MA: MIT Press, 1975), pp. 101–109. In terms of use of incendiaries, this has only been indirect: a notable example was the Israeli army's massive use of American-supplied white phosphorous ordnance, with full US diplomatic support, against Beirut in 1982. See Noam Chomsky, *The Fateful Triangle: The United States, Israel and the Palestinians* (Boston: South End Press, 1983).

45. Even without the latter pair of insertions, the elimination of words such as "knowingly" and "with intent" from the Convention, coupled to the latitude of interpretation arguably possible under Article III (d), should provide flexibility of analysis and response heretofore impossible under the Convention, a situation which might well cover the ground implied by the insertions themselves.

46. For purposes of this paper, Bedau's analogy to Felony Murder should be considered as encompassed under Genocide in the Second Degree.

47. In the event that this last category seems unfair, it should be noted that under common law, "good intentions" do not necessarily mitigate results. US courts have, for example, undertaken the successful manslaughter prosecution of "holy roller" parents who, with the best intentions (the salvation of their children's immortal souls, in their view), have denied medical treatment to their offspring. When the children die, the parents are held accountable; why should governments be less so, in principle?

48. The Reagan administration response was sparked by the Sandinista government of Nicaragua bringing a dispute before the World Court in The Hague, Netherlands during 1984. The Sandinistas argued that the US action of mining its harbors was a violation of international law. The Court agreed and called for removal of the mines. Interestingly, the mines were removed even while the US was preparing a response challenging the Court's authority to reach a finding in the matter.

49. Richard Falk, "International Law and the United States' Role in the Vietnam War," in Jay W. Baird, (editor), *From Nuremburg to My Lai* (Toronto: D.C. Heath & Co., 1972), p. 189. All Professor Falk had to do in order to discern the practical fallacy of this argument was to review the history of relations extant between the US government and American Indian; of 371 formal treaty agreements entered into by the US with various Indian sovereignties since 1789, *all* were systematically violated, and remain so to this day. It seems likely that the process of treaty violation was designed as an integral aspect of American expansion in precisely the same fashion as became evident in Hitlerian *realpolitik*.

50. Richard Falk, "Ecocide, Genocide, and the Nuremburg Tradition of Individual Responsibility," in Held, et al. (Note 33), p. 126.

51. See, for example, Richard Falk, *The End of World Order: Essays on Normative International Relations* (New York: Holmes & Meier, 1983), especially "Part Five: Normative Horizons," pp. 277–336.

52. Horowitz (Note 25), pp. 56–57.

53. A sample of literature addressing the examples provided include Lynwood Carranco and Estele Bear, *Genocide and Vendetta: The Round Valley Wars of California* (Norman, OK: University of Oklahoma Press, 1983), Maurice Collins, *Cortez and Montezuma* (New York: Avon Books, 1944); Jennings C. Wise, *The Red Man in the New World Drama* (New York: Macmillan Publishing Co., 1971); Gloria Jahoda, *The Trail of Tears: The Story of the American Indian Removals, 1813–1855* (New York: Holt, Reinhart & Winston, 1975).

54. Norman Lewis, "Genocide," in: *A Documentary Report on the Conditions of the Indian People of Brazil* (Berkeley, CA: American Friends of Brazil/*Indigena*, 1974), pp. 9–10.

55. *The Yanomami Indian Park: A Call For Action* (Boston, MA: Anthropology Resource Center, 1981).

56. Mark Munzel, "Manhunt," in: *Genocide in Paraguay*, Richard Arens (editor), (Philadelphia, PA: Temple University Press, 1976), pp. 37–38.

57. Elie Weisel, "Now We Know," in Arens (Note 56), p. 167.

58. Noam Chomsky, *American Power and the New Mandarins* (New York: Pantheon Books, 1967), pp. 168–190.

59. Noam Chomsky and Edward S. Herman, *The Washington Connection and the Third World Fascism (The Political Economy of Human Rights, Vol. I)* (Boston, MA: South End Press, 1979), pp. 129–204.

60. Arens (Note 56), p. 137.
61. Davis and Zannis (Note 1), p. 18.
62. *U.N. Doc. E/A.C. 25/S.R. 1-28.*
63. Davis and Zannis (Note 1), p. 18.
64. Ibid., p. 20.
65. A sampling of available literature taking up this theme includes, of course Davis and Zannis (Note 1). Also see Estelle Fuchs and Robert J. Havighurst, *To Live on This Earth: American Indian Education* (New York: Anchor Books, 1973); Vine Deloria Jr. and Clifford M. Lytle, *The Nations Within: The Past and Future of American Indian Sovereignty* (New York: Pantheon Books, 1984); Vine Deloria Jr. and Clifford M. Lytle, *American Indians, American Justice* (Austin: University of Texas Press, 1983).
66. Concerning James Bay, see Davis and Zannis (Note 1). On the planned forced relocation of Navajos from the Big Mountain area of Arizona, see Jerry Kammer, *The Second Long Walk: The Navajo-Hopi Land Dispute* (Albuquerque, NM: University of New Mexico Press, 1978) or Ward Churchill, "Navajos: No Home on the Range," *The Other Side*, vol 21, no 1, January-February 1985, pp. 22–27. Concerning termination, see Sarah M. Sneed, "Termination: The Indian Trust Responsibility During the Eisenhower Administration," unpublished honors paper submitted to Professor George Pilcher, University of Colorado/Boulder, April 5, 1982.
67. For an overview of the uranium contamination problem in the United States, see Ward Churchill and Winona LaDule, "Radioactive Colonization and the American Indian," *Socialist Review*, vol 15, no 3, Berkeley, CA, May-June 1985. This particular problem also applies to Namibia and Australia.
68. On this possibly odd-sounding point, see George Frederickson, *White Supremacy: A Comparative Study in American and South African History* (New York: Oxford University Press, 1981).
69. Although it is an imperfect document, the most comprehensive recounting of the conditions referred to here are to be found in Jose R. Martinez Cobo, *Study of the Problem of Discrimination Against Indigenous Populations*, United Nations Document E/CN.4/Sub.2/1983/Add. 8., September 30, 1983.
70. As Kenneth L. Adelman describes in his *African Realities* (New York: Crane, Russak & Co., 1980), p. 5, "Meeting in Berlin in 1884, the European Powers carved up Africa without taking into account geographic and demographic conditions in that distant continent. Their legacy—borders making little if any political, ethnic, economic or strategic sense—set the stage for decades of squabbles, if not all out wars, by the fiercely nationalistic new states . . . Since ethnic groups straddle borders, conditions are ripe for irredentism . . . Even Africa's sacrosanct principle of 'territorial integrity' does not help much with states that never, in fact, accepted the old boundaries (such as Somalia) or with those plagued with secessionist movements (such as Eritrea and Biafra). After all, Biafra was recognized as 'independent' by Tanzania, Zambia, Gabon and the Ivory Coast."
71. Richard Sklar, "Political Science and National Integration—A Radical Approach," *The Journal of Modern African Studies*, vol 9, no 2, 1971, pp. 137–138.
72. Kwame Nkrumah, *I Speak For Freedom: A Statement of African Ideology* (New York: Praeger Paperbacks, 1961), e.g., p. 167, ". . . [we] are opposed to imperialism, colonialism, racial, tribal and religious chauvinism." Again, on the following page, he states: '. . . until we purge from our minds this tribal chauvinism and prejudice of one against the other, we shall not be able to cultivate the wider spirit of brotherhood which our objective Pan Africanism calls for. We are all Africans and peoples of African descent . . ." In other words, the distinct identities and continuing existence of tribal peoples *as such* is something to be eliminated from the progressive scenario.
73. Adleman (Note 70), pp. 126–127.
74. Ibid., pp. 130–131.
75. Colin Leys, "Politics in Kenya: The Development of Peasant Society," *The British Journal of Political Science*, no 1, 1970, p. 326.
76. John S. Saul, *The State and Revolution in Eastern Africa* (New York: Monthly Review Press, 1979). It should be noted that Saul does not offer his recounting of group emulsification as a criticism of the states in question.
77. Cobo (Note 69).

[8]

Victims of the State: Genocides, Politicides and Group Repression from 1945 to 1995

Barbara Harff, Ted Robert Gurr

This chapter is concerned with the collective victimisation of ethnic, religious, national and political groups by the state. In ongoing research the first author has identified more than 70 communal and political groups which have been victimised in 48 episodes of genocides and politicides between 1945 and the mid-1990s. The second author's world survey of minorities at risk identifies 88 communal and regional groups that in the mid-1990s were subject to deliberate political, economic, or cultural discrimination and another 22 groups in conflicts that could have genocidal outcomes. A comparative analysis of these two sets of information enables us to identify groups, including survivors of previous genocides and politicides, which could become tomorrow's victims of massive violence.[1] From a perspective of prevention these high-risk groups should be the focus of careful monitoring and early warning assessments by the international community.

Why States victimise Groups

Discrimination against communal and political groups has many historical origins. Some are residues of historical conflicts among groups, others are the result of immigration by alien minorities, some are incidental consequences of the political expansion of a nation-state's authority over previously autonomous groups. Our particular concern is with the circumstances in which the powers of the modern state are deliberately used to suppress or systematically eliminate members of distinct ethnic, religious, national or political groups.

What is it about the state, and the victims, that makes some kinds of groups targets of the most severe kinds of repression and violence? In some instances an inactive communal group is singled out for attack and dispersal because it stands in the way of national expansion. Historical episodes include the treatment of many native peoples of the Americas and the aborigines of Tasmania. In other instances governments respond tit for tat with violent tactics in an attempt to quell politically organised groups that actively seek to alter power relations within an internationally recognised state, as is the case in Kurdistan. When state repression is met with further resistance, leaders may be provoked to return violence disproportionately. This is the strategy of politicide, in which governing authorities choose to respond to challenges by killing as many members of the group as is necessary to shatter their capacity to persist and act as a collectivity. In some such cases many individual members of the group survive.

The worst of all possibilities is that in which a state systematically seeks to destroy, as a matter of policy, all members of a communal group irrespective of their actions. 'Guilt' is established not by action or association, but is assigned to all those who share the defining ascriptive characteristics. This was the Nazis' intent with respect to Jews and Roma (gypsies).

The state's involvement in genocides and politicides may be more or less direct. Not all are carried out by uniformed agents of the government. In others, leaders assist or knowingly acquiesce in the killing of undesirable groups by vigilantes, 'deathsquads', or private militias. And in some instances governments simply neglect their obligations to protect vulnerable minorities who are attacked by murderous mobs or profiteers. The Tasmanian aborigines were exterminated when settlers hunted them down like rabbits, with the acquiescence of colonial authorities. Contemporary episodes are found in the treatment of the Aché Indians in Paraguay and some of the tribes of the Brazilian Amazon.

The essential quality of all these episodes is that the state or dominant social groups make a concerted, persistent attempt to destroy a communal or political group, in whole or in part. More precisely, geno/politicide is defined as *the promotion, execution and/or implied consent of sustained policies by governing elites or their agents - or in the case of civil war either of the contending authorities - that result in the deaths of a substantial portion of a communal, political, or politicised communal group.* We distinguish between two types of episodes. In genocides the victimised groups are defined primarily in terms of their communal characteristics. In politicides, by contrast, groups are defined primarily in terms of their political opposition to the regime and dominant groups.

Our definition of genocide parallels the United Nation's Genocide Convention, which prohibits 'killing members of a group' and 'deliberately inflicting on the group conditions of life calculated to bring about its physical destruction in whole or part.' We differ by excluding that part of the Convention which prohibits actions 'causing serious bodily or mental harm to members of the group,' because this would extend the definition to innumerable instances of groups which have lost their cohesion and identity, but not their lives, as a result of processes of socio-economic change. The Convention does not include groups of victims defined by their political position or actions. Our concept of politicide is used to encompass such politically-defined victims.[2]

Table 1 identifies the victims in 48 episodes of genocides and politicides since World War II. The emphasis on post-World War II cases helps focus attention on the frequency of such episodes since the world community became aware of the atrocities committed during the Holocaust.

Operational Guidelines

Three operational guidelines were used to identify victims of geno/politicides. First, the state's complicity in mass murder had to be established. Any persistent, coherent pattern of action by the state and its agents, or by a dominant social group, that brought about the destruction of a people's existence, in whole or in part, was considered *prima facie* evidence of state responsibility.[3] Unfortunately in many cases of geno/politicides the existence of a coherent pattern of destruction can only be clearly identified after many people are killed. In the following section we develop the argument that groups whose human rights are systematically violated are potentially targets of more extreme forms of victimisation. Inequality, discrimination, even state terror are not, of themselves, evidence of geno/politicide. But they are early-warning indicators that the victimised groups are at risk of more extreme threats to their existence.

A second operational issue concerns the duration of a group's victimisation. The physical destruction of a people requires time to accomplish: it implies a persistent, coherent pattern of action. Thus, Table 1 includes only episodes that lasted at least six months. Brief episodes of killings such as the massacres of Palestinians at the Chatilla and Sabra camps in Beirut in 1982 are not found on our list, though some observers have called them a genocide. Like many other massacres, they do not meet our criteria for geno/politicide. They were spontaneous eruptions of mob anger or one-time acts by armed bands or out-of-control soldiers, not part of a sustained campaign carried out by or with the acquiescence of authorities. At the other end of the time spectrum are attacks on a group that recur episodically and reflect the objectives of different regimes within a single state. An example is the series of Iraqi campaigns against Kurds from 1960 to 1975; we treat them as a single episode of victimisation. The Iraqi Kurds were targeted again in 1988-1994, long enough after the previous killings ended that it is treated as a new episode.

Third, in principle 'body counts' do not enter into the definition of what constitutes an episode of victimisation. A 'few hundred' killed constitutes as much a genocide or politicide as the death of thousands if the victim group is small in number to begin with. This is especially important in cases where the destruction of small groups goes without note, for example when it occurs in the context of larger episodes of massive state repression. Our list of victimised groups probably omits some such small groups.

Some episodes not included in the table may also meet the criteria. We have identified other possible cases, such as the reprisal killings of southerners in Chad 1985-86 by a newly empowered regime dominated by northerners, and killings of civilians during the Russian invasion of Chechenia in 1994-95. Lack of information is a recurring problem. Often the difficulty lies in detecting malicious intent in practices which lead to a group's destruction. Sometimes what starts as a brief violent encounter between military forces and citizen groups may lead to a coherent policy of repression ending in geno/politicide. In other circumstances no prior provocation takes place, yet the state relentlessly pursues and abuses victim groups without ever passing the threshold between sporadic killings and geno/politicide. This threshold is equivalent to the difference between terror and extermination. In case of state terror, authorities arrest, persecute or execute a few members of a group in ways designed to terrorise the majority of the group into passivity or acquiescence. In the case of geno/politicide authorities physically exterminate enough (not necessarily all) members of a target group so that it can no longer pose any conceivable threat to their rule or purposes.

Genocides and Politicides: The Victims

Of the 48 episodes in Table 1 seven are considered pure genocides, i.e., the victims are defined primarily in terms of their communal characteristics. We distinguish between two types of genocide, hegemonical genocide and xenophobic genocide. In the former the primary motive of the ruling group is to subordinate a communal group by killing enough of its members that the survivors have no will or capacity to resist, whereas in the latter, elite ideology calls for the elimination of the 'offending' communal group.

Three xenophobic episodes occurred in the less-developed world, their victims numbering indigenous tribes such as the Aché Indians in Paraguay, a prosperous immigrant minority (the Ibos in Northern Nigeria), and members of a religious minority (the Arakanese Muslims of Burma). In these xenophobic cases there was no deliberate sustained policy of extermination dictated and organised by ruling groups. Rather, rulers tacitly encouraged or acquiesced in genocidal actions initiated out of private animosities. This was quite different for the hegemonical genocides. Stalin's policies against Meshketians, Crimean Tatars, Chechens, Ingushi, Karachai and Balkars were part of a sustained policy to subordinate these groups by killing or dispersing virtually all of their members.

In seven episodes, coded GP in Table 1, there were multiple victims, some of them defined communally and others politically. In Kampuchea, for example, the Khmer Rouge sought to eliminate not only the urban people but also the rural Muslim Cham minority.

In 32 episodes of politicide, coded P or PG in Table 1, the victims were distinguished primarily by their political orientation, not by their communal identities. There are four variants of this type of mass murder. A common variant is repressive politicide, in which ruling groups retaliate against adherents of political parties, factions or movements because of their support for oppositional activities. Common tactics are secret operations in which Communist sympathisers are executed or murdered, for example in Argentina, El Salvador, Indonesia and India. Other cases have taken place in African states in which newly-empowered leaders use extreme and deadly repression against any and all groups suspected of opposition, tactics followed by Macias in Equatorial Guinea and, on some occasions, by Mobutu in Zaire.

Repressive/hegemonical politicides are similar except that the political opposition often coincides with the victimised group's communal identity. However, evidence suggests that regime repression ends when acts of resistance end, implying that the political rather than communal characteristics of the group determines their victimisation. In 1947, the mainland Chinese nationalists, who had taken over control of Taiwan from the Japanese, killed at least 10,000 Taiwanese political activists, not because they were Taiwanese but because they had supported nationalist resistance to mainland control. The eleven such episodes in Table 1 are coded PG.

Revolutionary mass murder is another common type of politicide. Here new regimes committed to bringing about fundamental social, economic and political change, kill those perceived as standing in the way to achieve such ends. The victims sometimes include cadres lacking revolutionary zeal, rich peasants, landowners, supporters of old regimes and former officials. Marxist-Leninist regimes which came to power through protracted armed struggles provide most of the post-1945 examples. The Nazis' treatment of political opponents after 1932 and the Iranian revolutionaries' persecution of Baha'is and Mujahedeen between 1981 and c. 1989 suggest that politicide is a common consequence of revolutions irrespective of their ideological foundations.[4]

The least common type of politicides is retributive mass murder. In these cases subordinate or oppositional groups seize power and kill their former masters/ oppressors in an act of vengeance. Examples are the Hutu rulers killing their former Tutsi masters in Rwanda (1963-64) and the Pinochet regime retaliating against leftist supporters of Allende. The latter is an example of counter-revolutionary politicide, carried out by conservative forces in retaliation against the quasi-revolutionary policies of their predecessors.

Fatalities in most episodes of geno/politicide are rarely known with precision. Estimates vary widely, as is evident from Table 1, and in some instances are not available at all. At least nine million people have died in these human disasters, perhaps as many as twenty million. Even the low estimate exceeds the number of battle-related fatalities in international and civil wars since 1945.[5]

Some general observations can be offered about the victims of these episodes. Genocidal victims are most often minorities whose cultures are sharply distinct from the dominant group. The victims of politicide typically have either long-standing aspirations of independent nationhood or are members of groups actively opposing existing regimes.

It is sometimes argued that communal membership is the underlying reason for oppositional activity. Certainly this was not the case of the Jews and Gypsies prior to the Holocaust, but it was the reason for the persecution of the Kurds in Iraq and Iran. It is difficult to ascertain whether or not persecution leads to national consciousness and the desire to break away from the dominant group or vice versa.

Jewish national consciousness prior to the Holocaust was barely an issue in Western Europe; Zionism had gained little support among Western European Jews. The Nazis did not persecute Jews because of their political activities, but because Nazi ideology excluded them as undesirables from the dominant group. This is different from the Kurdish case. Kurds have battled for independence ever since the disintegration of the Ottoman Empire, and in Iraq ever since the early 1930s. They are a people with a distinct history and language and live in a geographically contiguous area now part of four different states. In the turbulent years after World War I, which saw the formation of many Middle Eastern states, the Kurds had neither the backing nor the good luck to become an independent state. Kurdish nationalism was and is well developed. The relentless pursuit of their national aspirations accounts for much of their present status as a persecuted minority. In principal, Kurds have had the option to work within the political establishments of Turkey, Iraq, and Iran.[6]

Obviously this categorisation of episodes poses a question which lies at the center of this chapter: which groups are the likely targets of discriminatory policies and under which circumstances do states engage in the deadly destruction of a people? Our analysis of the phenomena should be considered preliminary, awaiting further operationalisation and analyses of the data summarised here and in the following section.

Minorities at Risk: Definitions and Data on Group Discrimination in 1995

Genocides and politicides are extreme but far from inevitable consequences of long-term conflicts between dominant and subordinate groups. One tell-tale manifestation of conflicts with genocidal potential is discriminatory treatment of ethnic, religious, national, and regional minorities by dominant groups. By discriminatory treatment we mean that such groups are systematically denied economic or political opportunities, valued cultural practices, or the enjoyment of group autonomy, that are available to other groups in their society. Such differential treatment may occur either as a result of widespread social practice or of deliberate government policy, or - most commonly - of both. We characterise such groups as 'minorities at risk': they are already victimised by invidious treatment and, potentially, are victims of more extreme policies.

Our approach to identifying minorities at risk differs from that taken in the human rights literature. Whereas human rights analyses specify universal rights and identifies categories of peoples and countries which do not enjoy some or all of those rights,[7] we use an internal standard of comparison. Minorities at risk are subject to invidious treatment by comparison to the treatment of, or rights enjoyed by, other groups in their society. It may be true, as apologists for the Israeli government have argued, that Arab citizens of Israel have more rights and opportunities than the citizens of most Arab states. Arab-Israelis are nonetheless 'at risk' because they are systematically denied some rights enjoyed by Jewish Israelis.

In ongoing research we have identified and gathered basic information on communal groups in the contemporary world that at risk by the two general criteria described below. Reports on successive phases of the project are Gurr and Scarritt 1989, Gurr 1993, and Gurr 1995. Note that the *Minorities at Risk* study does not include potentially victimised groups that are defined solely in class or political terms, like the *kulaks* in Stalin's Russia and the Mujahedeen in revolutionary Iran. Only groups that are defined at least in part by communal markers - ethnicity, language, religious belief, regional or historical origin - are included. Contemporary Islamic movements illustrate the threshold between what groups are included and excluded. If Islamic activists are distinguished from their opponents by some other kind of persisting, ascriptive division, they are included: examples are the Moros in the Philippines (Muslims in a predominantly Christian society) and the Shi'ite minority in Saudi Arabia (a 1200-year old communal division), but not militant Islamicists in Egypt or Algeria. The latter are contemporary political movements that recruit adherents by appeals to faith; they do not yet have the enduring, ascriptive qualities of communal groups.

These are the criteria used to identify 'minorities at risk' of conflict and victimisation.

1.   The group collectively suffers, or benefits from, systematic discriminatory treatment vis-à-vis other groups in a state. Discrimination may limit a group's political participation and rights, economic opportunities, or the expression of its culture: use of its own language, observance of its religious beliefs, practice of customary ways of life. The most serious kinds of discriminatory treatment are those that are the result of deliberate public policy or widespread social practice or both. Groups also may suffer from the burdens of past discrimination: the malign consequences of segregation in the US and restrictions on the rights of indigenous peoples throughout the Americas have persisted long after governments outlawed them. The *Minorities at Risk* project, from which this information is taken, includes groups subject to past as well as present discrimination. The total number of groups in the study as of September 1995 is 271 of whom 227 are disadvantaged because of past or contemporary discrimination. The groups most seriously at risk are the 88 peoples who are subject to discrimination as a matter of government policy.[8]

2.   The group is the focus of political mobilisation and action in defense or promotion of its self-defined interests. Most groups targeted by discrimination have taken some kind of action to assert their collective interests in the political arena. Other groups take political action because of historical grievances such as a tradition of autonomy lost, or memories and myths of victimisation by other communal groups. When communal groups mobilise for political action, they are at risk of retaliation from the state and other groups. Rebellious groups are especially subject to attack and new or intensified discriminatory policies. About three-quarters of the 271 groups in the *Minorities at Risk* study have initiated some kind of political action in the last decade. The mobilised groups most seriously at risk are those involved in civil and communal warfare. In 1994-95 there were 22 peoples engaged in serious conflicts who were not then targets of deliberate discrimination. Depending on the course and outcomes of conflicts, they may become either victims or victimisers.

The two general criteria, discrimination and mobilisation, are supplemented by these operational rules. (1) Include only communal groups at risk in countries with a 1990 population greater than one million. (2) Include only groups that number 100,000 or, if fewer, that exceed 1 % of a country's population. (3) Analyse groups separately in each country in which they meet the other criteria, e.g., Roma (gypsies) are coded in each of 11 European countries. (4) Analyse groups at the highest politically-meaningful level analysis. For example, native peoples in the US are analysed as a single group because many share a sense of pan-tribal identity and because they share a common status vis a vis the US government. In Mexico, by contrast, two native peoples - the Mayans and Zapotecs - have won distinct political statuses and thus are analysed separately from other groups.

Risk Assessments for Historically-Victimised Groups

In Table 2 we juxtapose information about 37 communal victims of genocides and politicides since 1945 with independent assessments about their current status from the *Minorities at Risk* project. The victimised groups can be ordered into six categories.

• Three of the 37 groups are passive victims of repressive state policies that have assumed genocidal proportions in the past. (1) The Rohingya Muslims of Myanmar's Arakan province have twice been the targets of deadly military and civilian attacks, in 1978 and 1991-92, aimed at pushing survivors into neighboring Bangladesh. (2) The Baha'is are persecuted as heretics in Iran. There have no changes in basic policies aimed at eliminating these groups, only in tactics. (3) The situation of Burundi's Hutu is somewhat different. After a generation of discrimination and victimisation by Tutsi rulers they have won legal protections and a share of power. But Tutsi militants do not accept power-sharing and continue to carry out deadly reprisals against them. The long-run risks of victimisation are very high in all three cases.

• Four historically-victimised groups have established their own states: the Bengalis of Bangladesh, the Malagasy of Madagascar, the Kurds of northern Iraq, and the Issaq of Somaliland. The latter two are de facto states, their sovereignty not recognised by the international community, and the people of both are at great risk of future attacks if and when governments in Baghdad and Mogadishu are able to reassert their power.

• Eight groups continue to be victimised and are at high risk because of their thus-far unsuccessful attempts to establish their own states. The Bosnian Muslims are the

only ones likely to succeed. Chechen ethnonationalists are doomed to the same fate as the southern Sudanese, the people of East Timor, Kurds in Iran, Tibetans, and Ibo (Igbo) in Nigeria: all have suffered devastating human and material losses as a result of failed rebellions, all but two are still subject to discriminatory policies of repressive control. In southern Sudan, East Timor, and Iranian Kurdistan the conflicts and killings continue. Weakening of central government control or resolve are likely to prompt intensified conflict in these three situations as well as in Tibet.
• A third kind of outcome of ethnonational rebellions is illustrated by the Baluchi in Pakistan, the Hmong in Laos, and the Ibo(Igbo) in Nigeria. Their rebellions prompted massive and indiscriminate government violence, but after resistance ended, governments followed policies of accommodation. (1) The Baluchi tribesmen regained some autonomy from the Karachi government in 1980, though they remain marginalised in national politics. (2) The Ibo(Igbo) of eastern Nigeria fought a separatist civil war in 1967-70, prompted by genocidal attacks on emigre Ibo(Igbo) communities in the North. Following their military defeat, and deaths from mass starvation that some claimed were genocidal, the Nigerian government followed policies of reconciliation that left the Ibo(Igbo) in a somewhat disadvantaged position, but at no great risk of future victimisation or rebellion. (3) During the Vietnam war many Hmong were encouraged by US support to rebel against the Pathet Lao government. They suffered grievous losses and forced resettlement but, since the 1980s, the government has sought to incorporate them in Laotian government and society.
• Fifteen historically-victimised groups in Table 2 live in states with new regimes that follow substantially different policies toward ethnopolitical minorities. Most of these groups are no longer subject to discriminatory policies and are at low risk of future victimisation. (1) The Cham of Cambodia and the Aché in Paraguay benefit from regime policies that are intended to compensate for past wrongs. (2) Five of the groups victimised by Stalin's wartime policies of forcible relocation have been reincorporated in Russian and Ukrainian life, though at some disadvantage. (3) In Uganda General Musaveni's regime follows relatively even-handed policies toward five groups that were victimised by the old regimes of Idi Amin and Milton Obote. Only the Baganda have attracted political restrictions, due to their pursuit of greater autonomy than is consistent with the new regime's policies. (4) The Kongo in Angola and Bubi in Equatorial Guinea both are represented in the ruling coalitions of successor regimes, and thus shielded from serious victimisation. (5) The only potentially high-risk group in this category are the new Tutsi rulers of Rwanda. They are threatened by vengeful Hutu militants, now in exile, who may mount a new invasion to regain the power they lost in 1994. If they do, genocide against Tutsi and Hutu moderates can be expected to resume again.
• The final category consists of three groups that have been victimised because of their role in revolutionary conflicts. (1) The Chinese in Indonesia were slaughtered in 1965-66 because they were thought to support a failed Communist takeover. Continued discrimination against them is a legacy of suspicions about their loyalties.

Economically they are useful to the Indonesian elite, thus increased victimisation is unlikely. (2) The 1992 Shi'ite rebellion in Iraq is much more recent and justifies policies of repressive control. They are too numerous and international constraints on the Iraqi regime too great for any short-term increase in victimisation - unless they organise a new rebellion. (3) Some native Guatemalans have supported leftist insurgents since the late 1960s, prompting widespread massacres and death squad killings that ebbed after democratic elections in the late 1980s, but still recur sporadically. Thus, the episode is ongoing, but victimisation is only likely to increase if hard-line elements of the military seize power again.

Communal Groups Subject to Discriminatory Policies in 1994-95

Another 97 communal groups at risk in the mid-1990s are identified in Table 3. Fifty-eight of them are included because they are targets of discriminatory policies, 18 because they are engaged in civil wars and rebellions, 21 because they meet both criteria. These groups have much the same kinds of status and are involved in the same kinds of conflicts as the high-risk groups in Table 2 (included in Table 3 for purposes of comparison) except that most have not experienced massive and deadly state repression in recent decades.

Three different kinds of discriminatory policies are identified in the table. (1) Political discrimination (P) refers to policies (or in some instances pervasive social practices) that restrict group members' rights to organisation and participate political-ly, and to representation in the political elite and the military establishment. (2) Economic discrimination (E) refers to policies (or in some cases pervasive social practices) that contribute to material inequalities: restrictions on employment and access to higher education, and denial of access to or control of land and other resources. (3) Cultural discrimination (C) refers to policies and practices that limit or prohibit a group from use of its language, practice of its religion, or observance of customary lifeways.

Political discrimination affects 74 of the groups at risk and is the most threatening because it means that groups so affected are less able than others to defend or promote their collective interests by conventional political means. Economic dis-crimination affects 46 groups in Table 3, cultural restrictions are imposed on 44 groups. Other things being equal, the likelihood that discriminated communal groups will resist politically tends to be greatest when political discrimination is combined with one or both the other two kinds of restrictions. This likely means a wider and deeper set of grievances within the group, and therefore greater chances that they can be mobilised in support of protest movements, rebellion, and civil war.

Risk Assessments of Future Victimisation of Communal Groups

Information from our studies of geno/politicide and minority status can be used to assess the risks that each of the groups in Table 3 are likely to be (further) victimised in the future, based on the following arguments and assumptions. First, groups which are now politically mobilised and engaged in rebellion are more likely to encounter massive state violence than quiescent groups. Escalating sequences of challenge and response can be observed in many conflicts between dominant groups and their challengers. They certainly have characterised relations between Hutu and Tutsi, northern and southern Sudanese, and Kurdish vs. Arab (and Turkish and Iranian) nationalists.

Second, we assume that minorities at risk in democratic states are less likely to encounter murderous repression than minorities in autocratic states. The rights and status of minorities in Western multi-party states enjoy greater protection for numerous reasons. Minorities can and do build coalitions of support to protect their position. Governments dependent upon electoral support have evolved a variety of non-violent and reformist strategies for dealing with minority issues.[9] Moreover, as an empirical observation, democratic societies are less susceptible than authoritarian ones to elite ideologies of racial hatred and extermination. Four of the six groups in advanced industrial democracies listed in Table 3 have more or less equal economic opportunities but are denied full political rights because of their immigrant status. In France, Germany, and Northern Ireland they are mainly at risk from attacks by communal rivals and xenophobic right-wingers, not government policy. This is not to claim that blacks and Hispanics in the US, or North Africans in France, or Turkish workers in West Germany are wholly free from repression or discriminatory treatment. Our argument is that no ethnic minority in any late-twentieth century Western democracy has more than the most remote chance of being murdered en masse.

The third assumption on which we base risk assessments is that the use of protracted repression against a minority is likely to be self-reinforcing, irrespective of the type of political system. There are two rationales. Firstly, elites who rely on repression become habituated to its use. Secondly, any shift to more conciliatory policies after repression risks the intensification of resistance.[10] Such deadly cycles of repression and resistance are not likely to be broken unless the victimised group is annihilated or a new regime comes to power with a commitment to alternative policies.

Risk assessments of victims of past geno/politicide are summarised above. Of the additional 97 groups at risk in Table 3, we assign high or very high risk of future victimisation to 42, based on the three general criteria specified above. The regional distribution of these groups is as follows:

- Asia: 13 high-risk groups, 8 of them involved in ongoing civil wars and rebellion;
- Post-communist Europe: 11 high-risk groups, 4 of them in ongoing civil wars and rebellion;

- Africa south of the Sahara: 9 high-risk groups, 4 of them in ongoing civil wars and rebellion;
- North Africa and the Middle East: 7 high-risk groups, 4 of them in ongoing civil wars and rebellion;
- Latin America: 2 high-risk groups, neither in open conflict.

Rebellious Groups at Highest Risk of Victimisation: In summary, 30 of the high-risk groups from Table 3 (including those previously victimised) are in serious conflicts and thus susceptible to new or recurring political genocides of the kinds labelled PG in Table 1 (politicides against politically-active communal groups). Such outcomes are particularly likely for these 24 groups:
- Serbs in Croatia (a nominally-democratic regime that has consistently rejected the obligation to protect minority rights);
- Muslims in Indian Kashmir (where Indian forces operate with virtually no restraints against suspected rebels and their supporters);
- Hazaris, Tajiks, and Uzbeks in Afghanistan (depending on the composition of the coalition that eventually wins effective control of the Afghan state);
- Kachin, Karen, and Shan in Myanmar (depending on whether their leaders chose to accept their cooptation by the military regime or to continue resistance);
- East Timorese in Indonesia;
- Sindhis and Mohajirs in Pakistan (if their communal conflict and rebellions continue, and if the military again takes power);
- Baluchi and Kurds in Iran (if their rebellions intensify);
- Kurds in Iraq and Turkey;
- Ovimbundu in Angola and Tuareg in Mali and Niger (if they persist in violent opposition to regimes that appear ready for accommodation);
- Issaq in Somaliland/Somalia and the Dinka, Nuba, and Shilluk in Sudan (rebels in countries where no accommodation appears possible);
- Hutu in Burundi and Rwanda (depending on actions by Hutu militants now in exile, and on the capacity of regimes in both countries to exercise restraint in response to attacks).

High-Risk Groups Victimised by Discrimination: It can be argued that the potential or ongoing victimisation of the groups listed above is a more or less 'obvious' outcome of protracted communal conflict. They are the groups most likely to generate new or freshened flows of refugees and to provide media images of brutalised and starving victims. It may be more important to call attention to the following list of high-risk groups that are not now in open resistance. They are somewhat less visible than the groups identified above. Some already are, all should be the objects of close international monitoring and remedial efforts. They are:
- In post-Communist Europe: the Roma, Russians in the Baltic states, and non-Slavs in the rump state of Yugoslavia;

- In Asia: the Lhotshampas (Nepalese) in Bhutan; the Rohingya Muslims in Myanmar; the Tibetans; the Turkmen (Uighers, Kazakhs, and others) in the People's Republic of China; and the Montagnards in Vietnam;
- In North Africa and the Middle East: Berbers in Algeria; Copts in Egypt; Baha'is in Iran; and Shi'ites in Iraq;
- In Africa south of the Sahara: the Kikuyu, Luo, and Luhya in Kenya; the Ogoni in Nigeria; and the Banyarwandans in Zaire;
- In Latin America: the indigenous people of the Brazilian rainforest; and the Haitians in the Dominican Republic.

The fact of discriminatory treatment is not debatable for most of these groups, all are to some degree victims of invidious treatment by the societies and states in which they live. Assessments of their future fate are necessarily speculative and require more evidence and better theory, an issue which we address briefly in the conclusion.

Conclusions: Factors leading to Genocides and Politicides

We assume that the state's arbitrary killing of members of a group is a crime. Genocides and politicides are not primarily consequences of the victims' behavior, rather they are first and foremost consequences of the policies of states and their political leaders. Political leaders have alternatives, victims rarely do. Moreover, the contemporary state's capacity for committing such crimes is most often far superior to that of other social units.

The generic state has no inherent qualities which over time induce it to engage in genocides or politicides. Rather elites can respond to a variety of imperatives. In democratic theory the ideal state is a manager of conflicting interests, striving to serve all its citizens in an impartial role. At worst, state power is held by a rapacious elite which engages in predatory behavior and widespread killings of all who might oppose it. In fact contemporary states do not exist in a vacuum. Rather they are to a significant degree dependent on a public willing to support their various roles and actions. Most are also subject to international constraints on the unbridled exercise of state coercion.

Some specific internal factors which lead toward genocide and politicide can be identified, based on our own observations and others' comparative research.[11] Plural (multi-ethnic) societies, especially those in which one communal group has dominated others, are especially prone to political mass murder. The violent history of a state, i.e., its recurrent abusive treatment of opponents and minorities, also figures prominently in the genesis of future geno/politicides. A violent history helps establish, and is reinforced by, a cultural disposition to accept violence as a means to maintain power and to settle disputes between peoples. This is fertile ground for the emergence of exclusionary, racist doctrines of national protection or social purification. Such doctrines help justify the destruction of victim groups by blaming and dehumanising them.

These historical and cultural factors are activated in particular political circumstances, especially during and after struggles for power among contending groups. In plural societies power struggles sometimes give rise to unholy alliances in which the price of political support is the state's persecution of the old enemies of its new allies. Newly-empowered elites, and threatened old ones, are particularly likely to increase terror tactics to maintain or consolidate their power. A violent past helps justify their present resort to violence while an exclusionary ideology defines the target group and provides a warrant for their murder. In societies which become polarised in this way, threatened elites often get substantial support from key publics for policies of unrestrained violence. Inflammatory public speeches and rhetoric along with widely publicised 'tough' actions against the target groups are part of the process which elicits this support.

During the Cold War international restraints on genocidal and political policies followed from the loose bipolar structure of the international system. States which were part of the sphere of influence of the superpowers were likely to have their internal behavior scrutinised by the dominant power. Unfortunately, strategic interests sometimes outweighed humanitarian concerns, but rarely to the degree that geno/politicides were condoned by the dominant partner. States which were relatively unimportant to superpower interests were more likely to get away with massive internal repression without undue interference, though in such cases lesser regional powers may intervene, as India did in East Pakistan in 1971, and Tanzania in Uganda in 1979. International restraints worked, and continue to work, on the assumption that policy makers in potentially genocidal states are aware of their relative position vis-à-vis major powers and the likelihood of international intervention. We further assume that external powers will actively sponsor some kind of intervention or intervene directly if a partner's action becomes an embarrassment to the professed goals of the dominant partner, or if internal repression interrupts the free flow of transactions or information. We also can report one important recent research finding, based on analysis of events during the 12 months preceding the occurrence of genocidal and near-genocidal activities in Bosnia (1992), Burundi (1993), and Rwanda (1994), and in Abkhazia (a non-case, in 1992). Analysis of these four cases strongly suggests that well-intentioned international meddling in potentially-genocidal situations that is not backed up by credible tactics and strategies is potentially deadly to a targeted group.[12]

Two complementary kinds of research should be done by scholars concerned with the state's victimisation of communal and political groups. One is to further develop and test theories about the causes and processes which lead states to commit geno/politicides. The comparative analysis of information on the historical episodes in Table 1 is a means to that end. The second approach is applied research in which the status of high-risk minorities is monitored and interpreted in terms of these emerging theoretical models. The comparative analysis of the two datasets summarised in this chapter thus provides one of the bases for a systematic system of early warning.[13] Real-time monitoring of interactions between governments and high-risk minorities should provide the information needed by activists and public and private international organisations to anticipate humanitarian crises to bring world attention to bear on abusive governments.

References

Dyadkin, I.G., *Unnatural Deaths in the USSR, 1928-1954.* (Tania Deruguine, trans.) New Brunswick, NJ: Transaction Books, 1983.

Gurr, T.R., Peoples against States: Ethnopolitical Conflict and the changing World System. *International Studies Quarterly* 38 (September 1994), pp. 347-377.

Gurr, T.R., Communal Conflicts and Global Security. *Current History* 94 (May 1995), pp 212-217

Gurr, T.R. and Scarritt, J.R., Minorities' Rights at Risk: A Global Survey. *Human Rights Quarterly*, 11, (August 1989), pp. 375-405.

Neckrich, A.M., *The Punished People: The Deportation and Fate of Soviet Minorities at the End of the Second World War.* (G. Saunder, trans.) New York: W.W. Norton, 1978.

Vickery, M., *Cambodia 1975-1982.* Boston: South End Press, 1984.

Notes

1. Comparative information on genocides and politicides is being gathered in an ongoing project directed by the first author, supported in part by grants from the US Naval Research Council, the United States Institute of Peace, and the National Science Foundation. Each of 48 episodes has been documented and coded based on the analysis of case studies (such as Vickery's 1984 study of the Kampuchean politicide) and journalistic material. An earlier version of the dataset is described in detail in Harff 1992. Michael Dravis at the University of Maryland's Center for International Development and Conflict Management provided extensive assistance in updating the dataset.

    Comparative information on the status of communal groups has been coded by the second author in the *Minorities at Risk* project and has been analysed in a series of publications (Gurr and Scarritt 1989, Gurr 1993, Gurr 1994, and Gurr 1995). The research has been supported by the National Science Foundation, the United States Institute of Peace, the Korea Foundation, the Academic Support Program of the US Department of Defense, and the University of Maryland's General Research Board. Research assistants who contributed substantially to the collection and analysis of the data reported in this chapter include Shin-wha Lee, Mizan Khan, Michael Haxton, Pamela Burke, Kelly Collier, Michael Dravis, Jonathan Fox, and Anne Pitsch. The project is based at the Center for International Development and Conflict Management, University of Maryland, College Park, MD 20742.

    The views and conclusions expressed here are those of the authors and have not been subject to prior approval by any agency of the United States government or other sponsoring institutions.

    The juxtaposition and joint analysis of these two datasets was first prompted by comments from participants at an invitational seminar of the International Conference on the Holocaust and Genocide organized by Israel W. Charny in Jerusalem in June 1987. The initial analysis was published in *International Review of Victimology*, Vol. 1, 1989, pp. 23-41. The updated analysis for this chapter was prepared at the invitation of Alex Schmid and Albert Jongman of the PIOOM Foundation at the University of Leiden, the Netherlands.

2. For a more detailed discussion see Harff, B. 'Recognizing Genocides and Politicides.' In: Fein, H. (Ed.) *Genocide Watch*. New Haven: Yale University Press, 1992, pp. 27-41.

3. See Gurr, T.R. 'The Political Origins of State Violence and Terror: A Theoretical Analysis.' In: Stohl, M., Lopez, G.A. *Government Violence and Repression. An Agenda for Research*. New York, Greenwood Press, 1986, pp. 46-48.

4. See Gurr, T.R. 'War, Revolution, and the Growth of the Coercive State.' *Comparative Political Studies, 21* (April 1988), pp. 45-65 and Harff, B. 'Genocide as State Terrorism.' In Stohl, M., Lopez, G.A. (Eds.) *Government Violence and Repression: An Agenda for Research*. Westport, CN: Greenwood Press, 1986, pp. 165-187.

5. See Harff, 1988.

6. See Gurr, T.R., and Harff, B. *Ethnic Conflict in World Politics*. Boulder, CO: Westview Press, 1994, chapters 4 and 6.

7. For example Dominguez, J.I. 'Assessing Human Rights Conditions.' In: Dominguez, J.I. et al. (Eds.) *Enhancing Global Human Rights*. New York: McGraw-Hill, 1979, pp. 19-116 and Falk, R. (1981). *Human Rights and State Sovereignty*. New York: Holmes and Meier, 1981, pp. 332-337.

8. Advantaged minorities - those that benefit from discrimination against other groups - are included in the study but not discussed here. They are 'at risk' because they potential targets of retaliatory discrimination and persecution by empowered majorities. The 1994 genocide against Tutsi in Rwanda was rationalised by playing on fears that they sought to reestablish their historic status as a dominant minority.

9. See Gurr, T.R. *Minorities at Risk: A Global View of Ethnopolitical Conflict*. Washington, DC: United States Institute of Peace Press, 1993, chapter 10.

10. For a general theory of state coercion see Gurr, T.R. 'War, Revolution, and the Growth of the Coercive State.' *Comparative Political Studies*, 21, April 1988, pp. 45-65.

11. Harff, B. 'The Etiology of Genocide.' In: I. Wallimann and M. Dobkowski, (Eds.) *Genocide and the Modern Age: Etiology and other Case Studies of Mass Death*. Westport CN: Greenwood Press, 1987, pp. 41-59, Harff, B. (1987b). *The State as Mass Murderer: A Theory of Genocides and Politicides*. Unpublished paper. Harff, B. (forthcoming) 'Early Warning of Potential Genocide: The Cases of Rwanda, Burundi, Bosnia, and Abkhazia.' Chapter 3 in Gurr, T.R. and Harff, B. *Early Warning of Communal Conflicts and Humanitarian Crises*. Tokyo: United Nations University Press, forthcoming. Fein, H. 'Accounting for Genocide after 1945: Theories and some Findings.' *International Journal of Group Rights* 1, 1993a, pp. 79-106. Fein, H. *Genocide: A Sociological Perspective*. London: Sage for the International Sociological Association, 1993b. Kuper, L. *Genocide: Its Political Use in the Twentieth Century*. New Haven: Yale University Press, 1984. Wallimann, I., and Dobkowski, M.N. (Eds.) *Genocide and the Modern Age: Etiology and Case Studies of Mass Death*. Westport, CN: Greenwood Press, 1987.

12. See Harff, B. (forthcoming) 'Early Warning of Potential Genocide: The Cases of Rwanda, Burundi, Bosnia, and Abkhazia.' Chapter 3 in Gurr, T.R. and Harff, B. *Early Warning of Communal Conflicts and Humanitarian Crises*. Tokyo: United Nations University Press, forthcoming.

13. Charny, I.E. *How Can We Commit the Unthinkable? Genocide: The Human Cancer*. Boulder, CO: Westview Press, 1982. Gurr, T.R. and Harff, B. *Early Warning of Communal Conflicts and Humanitarian Crises*. Tokyo: United Nations University Press, forthcoming.

Table 1: Genocides and Politicides since World War II[1]

Country	Type	Dates of Episode[2]	Communal Victims	Mixed Communal and Political Victims	Political Victims	Number of Victims[3]
USSR[4]	P	1943-1947			Repatriated Soviet nationals	500,000-1,100,000
USSR[4]	G	11/1943-1/1957	Chechens, Ingushi, Karachai, Balkars			230,000
USSR[4]	G	5/1944-1968	Meshketians, Crimean Tatars			57,000-175,000
China	PG	2/12/1947		Taiwanese nationalists		10,000-40,000
USSR[4]	P	10/1947-1950		Ukrainian nationalists		200,000-300,000
Madagascar	P	4/1947-12/1948		Malagasy nationalists		10,000-80,000
PR China	P	1950-1951			Kuomintang cadre, landlords, rich peasants	800,000-3,000,000
North Vietnam	P	1953-1954			Catholic landlords, rich and middle peasants	15,000
Sudan[5]	P	1956-1972		Non-muslim African Southerners		100,000-500,000
PR China	GP	1959		Tibetan Buddhists, landowners, nationalists		65,000
Iraq[5]	PG	1960-1975		Kurdish nationalists		10,000-100,000
Angola	P	5/1961-1962	Kongo tribe		Assimilados	40,000
Algeria	P	7/12/1962			Harkis (French-Muslim troops), OAS supporters	12,000-60,000
Paraguay	G	1962-1972	Aché Indians			900
Rwanda	PG	1963-1964		Tutsi ruling class		5,000-14,000
Zaire[6]	P	2/1964-1/1965	Europeans, missionaries		Educated Congolese	1,000-10,000
Burundi[5]	PG	1965-1973		Hutu leaders, peasants		103,000-205,000
Indonesia	PG	10/1965-1966	Ethnic Chinese		Communist cadre	500,000-1,000,000
South Vietnam	P	1965-1972			Civilians in NLF areas	475,000
China	P	5/1966-1975			Cultural Revolution victims	400,000-850,000
Guatemala	PG	1966-1984	Indians		Leftist	30,000-60,000

50

Country	Type	Dates of Episode[2]	Communal Victims	Mixed Communal and Political Victims	Political Victims	Number of Victims[3]
Nigeria	G	5-10/1966	Ibo living in the North			9,000-30,000
India	P	1968-1982			Naxalites	1,000-3,000
Equatorial Guinea	GP	3/1969-1979		Bubi tribe, political opponents of Macias		1,000-50,000
Pakistan	PG	3-12/1971		Bengali nationalists		1,250,000-3,000,000
Uganda	GP	2/1971-1979	Karamojong, Acholi, Lango; catholic clergy		Political opponents of Idi Amin	100,000-500,000
Chile	P	9/1973-1976			Leftists	2,000-30,000
Pakistan	PG	1973-1977	Baluchi tribesmen			5,000-10,000
Ethiopia	P	1974-1979			Political opposition	30,000
Angola (possible)	P	1975-1995			Civilians	250,000-500,000
Cambodia (Kampuchea)	GP	1975-1979	Muslim Cham		Old regime supporters, urban people, disloyal cadre	800,000-3,000,000
Indonesia	PG	12/1975-Cont.		East Timorese nationalists		60,000-200,000
Argentina	P	1976-1980			Leftists	9,000-30,000
Zaire[5]	P	1977-1983		Tribal and political opponents of Mobutu		3,000-4,000
Afghanistan	P	1978-1989			Supporters of old regime, rural supporters of rebels	1,000,000
Burma	G	1978	Muslims in border region			under 10,000
Uganda	GP	1979-1/1986	Karamojong, Nilotic tribes, Bagandans		Supporters of Amin regime	50,000-100,000
El Salvador	P	1980-1992			Suspected leftists	20,000-70,000
Mozambique	P	1980-1992			Civilians	500,000(?)
Iran	GP	1981-1989	Kurds, Baha'is		Mujahedeen	10,000-20,000
Syria	P	4/1981-2/1982			Muslim Brotherhood	25,000-45,000

Country	Type	Dates of Episode[2]	Communal Victims	Mixed Communal and Political Victims	Political Victims	Number of Victims[3]
Sudan	GP	1983-Cont.		Dinka, Shilluk, Nuba and others		500,000-1,500,000
Ethiopia	PG	1984-late 1980s		Civilians in North, Tigreans		?
Burundi (possible)	G	1988	Hutu civilians			50,000-100,000(?)
Iraq	PG	1988-1994		Kurds, Marsh Arabs, politically active Shi'ites		?
Somalia	PG	5/1988-1989	Issaq clan			?
Bosnia	G	5/1992-1994	Bosnian Muslims			200,000
Rwanda	GP	1994		Tutsis, moderate Hutus		500,000

Notes to Table 1:
1. Geno/politicide is the promotion, execution and/or implied consent of sustained policies by governing elites or their agents - or in the case of civil war either of the contending authorities - that result in the deaths of a substantial portion of a communal and/or politicised communal group.
2. Type codes are defined as:
   G = genocide, victims defined communally
   P = politicide, victims defined politically
   PG = politicide against politically-active communal groups
   GP = episodes with mixed communal and political victims
3. The victims include all civilians reported to have died as a direct consequence of regime action, including victims of starvation, disease and exposure as well as those executed, massacred, bombed, shelled, or otherwise murdered. Numbers of victims are seldom known with any exactitude, and sometimes no estimates of any kind are available. The numbers shown here represent the ranges in which the 'best estimates' or guesses fall.
4. The first three Soviet episodes all begin during and as a consequence of World War II but continued well past the war's end; hence they are regarded as postwar episodes. The second, third, and fourth Soviet episodes all involved the rapid, forced deportation of national groups to remote areas under conditions in which many died of malnourishment, disease, and exposure. Few of these victims were deliberately murdered. The terminal dates for the second and third cases represent the dates on which rights of citizenship were restored to the survivors. Estimates of deaths vary widely, as in most other episodes. Our coding of deaths is based on the more direct and detailed analysis of A.M. Nekrich, *The Punished People: The Deportation and Fate of Soviet Minorities at the End of the Second World War.* New York: W.W. Norton, 1978, rather than the demographic projections of J.G. Dyadkin, *Unnatural Deaths in the U.S.S.R., 1928-1954.* New Brunswick, N.J.: Transaction Books, 1983.
5. These episodes are discontinuous, including two or more distinct periods of mass murder, typically initiated in response to renewed resistance by the victim group.
6. Killings by the short-lived Congolese People's Republic between February 1964 and the recapture of its Stanleyville capital in January 1965.

Table 2: Status in 1995 of Communal Victims of Post-World War II Genocides and Politicides

Post-Communist Europe

Region and Country	Group(s)	Status in 1995[1]	Chances of future victimization[2]
Russia	Chechens	Policy disc (P) Active separatism	High
Russia	Ingush, Karachai, Balkars	Social disc (P,E) Active separatism	Medium
Russia	Meshketians	Residual disc (P,E)	Low
Ukraine	Crimean Tatars	Residual disc (P,E,C)	Medium
Bosnia	Muslims	Policy disc in Serb-held areas (P,E,C)	Ongoing

South, Southeast, and Pacific Asia

Region and Country	Group(s)	Status in 1995	Chances of future victimization
Burma	Rohingya Muslims	Policy disc (P,E,C)	Very high
China (PRC)	Tibetans	Policy disc (P,E,C)	Very high
Indonesia	Chinese	Policy disc (P,E)	Low
Indonesia	Timorese	Policy disc (P,E,C)	Ongoing
Cambodia	Cham	New regime[3] Remedial policies	Very low
Laos	Hmong (Meo)	Residual disc (P,E)	Medium
Pakistan	Baluchi	Policy disc (P,E)	Medium
Pakistan	Bengalis	Own state	Nil

Middle East and North Africa

Region and Country	Group(s)	Status in 1995	Chances of future victimization
Iraq	Kurds	Policy (P,E) Active separatism	Very high
Iraq	Shi'ites	Policy disc (P)	High
Iran	Kurds	Policy disc (P,E)	Ongoing
Iran	Baha'is	Policy disc (P,E,C)	Very high

Africa South of the Sahara

Region and Country	Group(s)	Status in 1995	Chances of future victimization
Angola	Kongo	Policy disc (P)	Low
Burundi	Hutu	Social disc (P,E)	Very high
Equatorial Guinea	Bubi	New regime[3]	Conditional[4]
Madagascar	Malagasy	New regime[3]	Nil
Nigeria	Ibo	Social disc (P)	Low
Rwanda	Tutsi	New regime[3]	Conditional[4]
Somalia	Issaq	De facto independence	Conditional[4]
Sudan	Dinka, Nuba, Shilluk	Policy disc (P,E,C) Active seaparatism	Ongoing
Uganda	Bagandans	Policy disc (P)	Medium
Uganda	Acholi, Lango, Karamojong, Kakwa	New regime[3] No discrimination reported	Conditional[4]
Zaire	Europeans	Most have left Zaire	Low

Latin America

Region and Country	Group(s)	Status in 1995	Chances of future victimization
Guatemala	Mayans	Policy disc (P,E,C)	Ongoing
Paraguay	Aché	Remedial policies	Low

Notes to table 2:

1. *Social discrimination* = groups coded 'substantial political underrepresentation (P) or poverty (E) due to prevailing social practice by dominant groups. Formal public policies toward the group are neutral or, if positive, inadequate to offset active and widespread practices of discrimination.'

    Policy discrimination = groups coded 'public policies (formal exclusion or recurring repression or both) substantially restrict to group's political participation (P) or economic opportunities (E) in comparison with other groups.'

    Groups coded C are subject to active *cultural discrimination* (discriminatory restrictions affecting 3 or more types of cultural activity).

    Residual discrimination refers to lower levels of discrimination of the above types.
2. The likelihood that discrimination and repression will increase in the 1995-2000 period. Based on the group's current status, the political characteristics of the state in which they reside, and the extent and character of any ongoing conflict. See text for elaboration.
3. New regimes have come to power that follow fundamentally different policies toward previously victimized groups.
4. Risks of victimization are low to nil if present regime remains in power; if new regime dominated by opposing groups comes to power, risks of renewed victimization are high to very high.

Table 3: A Watch List of Potential Victims: Rebels and Targets of Systematic Policies of Discrimination in 1994-1995[1]

Advanced Industrial Democracies

Region and Country	Groups and Conflicts[2]	1995 Numbers (000)[3]	Status in 1995	Chances of future victimization[5]
Northern Ireland	*Catholics*	565[6]	Social disc (E)	Low
France	Afro-Arabs	1,952	Policy disc (P,C)	Medium
Germany	Turks	1,619	Policy disc (P)	Low[7]
Greece	Roma	140	Policy disc (P)	Low
Japan	Koreans	710	Policy disc (P,C)	Very Low
Switzerland	Foreign workers	1,300	Policy disc (P)	Very low

Post-Communist Europe

Region and Country	Groups and Conflicts[2]	1995 Numbers (000)[3]	Status in 1995	Chances of future victimization
Albania	Greeks	150	Policy disc (P,C)	High
Azerbaijan	*Armenians*	90	Policy disc (P,C)	High
Bosnia	Muslims	1,757[8]	Civil war	Ongoing
Bosnia	*Serbs*	1,318[8]	Civil war	High
Bosnia	*Croats*	679[8]	Civil war	Medium
Bulgaria	Roma	500	Policy disc (P)	Medium[7]
Croatia	*Serbs*	315[9]	Policy disc (P,E)	Very high
Croatia	Roma	240	Policy disc (P,E)	Medium[7]
Czech Republic	Roma	200	Policy disc (P)	Medium[7]
Estonia	Russians	450	Policy disc (P)	High
Georgia	*Abkhaz*	95	Policy disc (P)	Medium
Georgia	*Ossetians*	160	Policy disc (P)	Medium
Latvia	Russians	850	Policy disc (P, E)	High
Macedonia	Albanians	460	Cultural disc (C)	Medium
Moldova	*Transdnistr Slavs*	1,200	Residual disc (C)	Low
Romania	Magyars	1,710	Cultural disc (C)	Medium
Romania	Roma	1,470	Policy disc (P,E)	High[7]
Russia	*Chechens*	958[11]	Policy disc (P)	High
Russia	Tatars	5,500[11]	Policy disc (E)	Low
Slovakia	Magyars	578	Cultural disc (C)	Medium
Yugoslavia	Albanians	1,750	Policy disc (P,E,C)	Very high
Yugoslavia	Magyars	360	Policy disc (P,E,C)	High
Yugoslavia	Sandzak	186	Policy disc (P,E,C)	High

South, Southeast, and Pacific Asia

Region and Country	Groups and Conflicts[2]	1995 Numbers (000)[3]	Status in 1995	Chances of future victimization
Afghanistan	*Hazaris*	3,700	Civil war	High[7]
Afghanistan	*Tajiks*	7,254	Civil war	High
Afghanistan	*Uzbeks*	4,407	Civil war	High
Bangladesh	*Chittagong Hill Tr.*	750[12]	Residual disc (P,E)	Medium
Bhutan	*Lhotshampas*	480	Policy disc (P,E,C)	High
Myanmar	Rohingya Muslims	7,450	Policy disc (P,E,C)	High
Myanmar[13]	Zomis/China	1,070	Policy disc (E)	Medium
Myanmar[13]	*Kachin*	530	Policy disc (P,E)	High
Myanmar[13]	*Karen*	4,480	Policy disc (P)	High
Myanmar[13]	*Mon*	1,100	Policy disc (P,E)	Medium
Myanmar[13]	*Shan*	3,520	Policy disc (P,E)	High
PR China	**Tibetans**	5,380	Policy disc (P,E,C)	Very high
PR China	Turkmen	8,500	Cultural disc (C)	High
India	*Kashmiris*[14]	8,340	Policy disc (P,C)	Very high
India	Muslims	108,000	Cultural disc (C)	Medium[7]
India	*Nagas*[14]	1,050	Social disc (P)	Medium
India	*Sikhs*[14]	18,600	Policy disc (P,E)	Low
India	*Tripuras*[14]	750	Social disc (P,E)	Medium
India	*Bodos*[14]	4,234	Cultural disc (C)	Medium
Indonesia	**Chinese**	5,440	Policy disc (P)	Low
Indonesia	**Timorese**	800	Policy disc (P,E,C)	Ongoing
Indonesia	**Papuans**	1,250	Policy disc (P,E)	Medium
Cambodia	Vietnamese	320	Policy disc (P,E,C)	medium[7]
Papua New Guinea	*Bougainville*	140	Social disc (E)	Medium
Pakistan	**Baluchi**	5,530	Policy disc (P)	Medium
Pakistan	Ahmadis	4,700	Policy disc (E,C)	Medium
Pakistan	Hindus	2,200	Policy disc (P,E,C)	High[7]
Pakistan	*Sindhis*	13,700	Communal conflict	High[7]
Pakistan	*Mohajirs*	10,800	Communal conflict	High[7]
Philippines	*Moros*[14]	4,650	Social disc (E)	Medium
Sri Lanka	*SR Tamils*	2,215	Residual disc (P,E)	Medium
Vietnam	Montagnards	1,270	Policy disc (P,E)	High

North Africa and the Middle East

Region and Country	Groups and Conflicts[2]	1995 Numbers (000)[3]	Status in 1995	Chances of future victimization
Algeria	Berbers	7,145	Cultural disc (C)	High[7]
Egypt	Copts	4,974	Policy disc (P,C)	High[7]
Iran	Baha'is	574	Policy disc (P,E,C)	High
Iran	*Baluchi*	1,134	Social disc (P)	High
Iran	*Kurds*	6,038	Policy disc (P)	High
Iran	Turkmens	967	Policy disc (P,C)	Low
Iran	Christians	300	Policy disc (P,C)	Medium
Iraq	Kurds	4,880	Policy disc (P,E)	Very high
Iraq	Shi'ites	10,600	Policy disc (P)	High
Israel	Arabs	1,060	Policy disc (P,E)	Low
Israel (Occ.Terr.)	*Palestinians*	2,700	Policy disc (P,E)	High
Jordan	Palestinians	2,380	Policy disc (P)	Low
Lebanon	Palestinians	230	Policy disc (P)	Medium
Morocco	Saharawis	200	Policy disc (P,E)	Medium
Saudi Arabia	*Shi'ites*	530	Policy disc (P,C)	Medium
Turkey	*Kurds*	11,100	Policy disc (P,C)	High

Africa South of the Sahara

Region and Country	Groups and Conflicts[2]	1995 Numbers (000)[3]	Status in 1995	Chances of future victimization
Angola	Kongo	1,540	Policy disc (P)	Low
Angola	*Ovimbundu*	4,100	Social disc (P)	Very high
Angola	*Cabinda*	175	Social disc (P,E)	Medium
Burundi	Hutu	5,390	Social disc (P,E)	Very high[7]
Djibouti	*Afar*	119	Social disc (P,E)	Medium
Kenya	Kikuyu	6,100	Policy disc (P,E)	High
Kenya	Luo	4,100	Policy disc (P,E)	High
Kenya	Luhya	3,800	Policy disc (P,E)	High
Mali	*Tuareg*	540	Policy disc (P,E.C)	Very high
Mauritania	Black Moors	816	Policy disc (E)	Medium
Niger	*Tuareg*	1,270	Policy disc (P,E,C)	High
Nigeria	Yoruba	25,000	Policy disc (P)	Medium
Nigeria	Ogoni	550	Policy disc (P,E)	High
Rwanda	*Hutu*	6,750[15]	New regime	High[7]
Sierra Leone	Mende	1,570	Policy disc (P)	Low
Somalia	Issaq	3,550	Self-procl.Indep.	High
Sudan	Dinka,Nuba, Shilluk	7,200	Policy disc (P,E,C)	Ongoing
Zaire	Luba-Kasai	2,628	Policy disc (P,E)	Medium
Zaire	Banyarwanda	2,000	Policy disc (P)	High

Latin America and the Caribbean[16]

Region and Country	Groups and Conflicts[2]	1995 Numbers (000)[3]	Status in 1995	Chances of future victimization
Bolivia	H Indigenous	4,440	Cultural disc (C)	Low
Bolivia	L Indigenous	200	Cultural disc (C)	Low
Brazil	L Indigenous	323	Cultural disc (C)	High[7]
Chile	Indigenous	589	Cultural disc (C)	Low
Dominican Rep.	Haitians	600	Policy disc (P,E)	High
Ecuador	L Indigenous	120	Cultural disc (C)	Low
Ecuador	H Indigenous	4,608	Cultural disc (C)	Low
Guatemala	Mayans	3,216	Policy disc (P,E,C)	Ongoing
Mexico	*Mayans*	2,682	Cultural disc (C)	Medium
Mexico	Zapotecs	751	Cultural disc (C)	Medium
Mexico	O Indigenous	7,296	Cultural disc (C)	Low
Paraguay	Indigenous	90	Cultural disc (C)	Low
Peru	H Indigenous	9,065	Cultural disc (C)	Medium
Peru	L Indigenous	477	Cultural disc (C)	Low

Notes to Table 3:

1. This table is based on 1994-95 information and includes all ethnopolitical groups that are coded for the highest current levels of political, economic, and/or cultural discrimination in Phase III of the *Minorities at Risk* project, plus groups in civil wars and rebellion, irrespective of current levels of discrimination. Victims of past geno/politicides from table 2 are included here, **in bold face**, if they are subject to high levels of discrimination or are ongoing targets of victimisation.

2. Groups listed in *italics* were involved in 1994-95 in intense conflicts (rebellion, mass protest, or communal warfare).

3. Projections derived by applying precentage estimates of group size in the 1980s to estimates of country population in 1995. Few countries other than the advanced industrial societies report census data on minority group members, therefore many such estimates have wide error margins and some are little more than conjectures.

4. *Social discrimination* = groups coded 'substantial political underrepresentation (P) or poverty (E) due to prevailing social practice by dominant groups. Formal public policies toward the group are neutral or, if positive, inadequate to offset active and widespread practices of discrimination.' Note that groups experiencing social discrimination are included in this table only if they are engaged in ongoing rebellion in 1994-95.
   Policy discrimination = groups coded 'public policies (formal exclusion or recurring repression or both) substantially restrict the group's political participation (P) or economic opportunities (E) in comparison with other groups.'
   Cultural discrimination = discriminatory restrictions, due to public policy or social practice, affecting 3 or more domains of groups' cultural activities (C).

5. The likelihood that discrimination and repression will increase in the 1995-2000 period. Based on the group's current status, the political characteristics of the state in which they reside, and the extent and character of any ongoing conflict. See text for more detail.

6. 1990 estimate.

7. These groups are most at risk from escalating attacks from other communal groups, including members of the dominant group acting privately.

8. 1992 data, prior to the outbreak of civil war and ethnic cleansing.

9. Excluding an estimated 200,000 Serbs who fled from the Krajina area in August 1995.

10. Most national minorities in Russia have not yet been coded; others, especially from the Caucasus, are likely to be added.
11. 1989 census data.
12. 1992 estimate.
13. The Myanmar government has reached accommodations with representatives of some factions of these groups. Regional rebellions reached a low ebb in 1994-95 but some resistance continues, especially by elements of the Karen and Shan.
14. Only some factions of these groups support open rebellion against the government, e.g., Muslims in Kashmir, the Khalistan Liberation Force and several similar Sikh militant groups in Punjab, and the United Liberation Front in Assam.
15. Prior to massive refugee flight in 1994. As of 9/95 relatively few have returned but militants among the refugees are reportedly preparing to lead an invasion.
16. 'Indigenous' refers to indigenous peoples. The prefix H refers to indigenous highland peoples, L to lowland peoples. In Mexico specific groups are distinguished; the prefix O refers to 'other' indigenous people. 'Africans' refers to people of African descent, who often have distinctive local names, e.g., Afro-Brazilians (in Brazil), Black Caribs (In Honduras).

[9]

The Bureaucracy of Murder Revisited

Albert Breton

University of Toronto

Ronald Wintrobe

University of Western Ontario

The paper reexamines the question of the guilt of subordinates in large organizations, a question posed with special force by Hannah Arendt in her book on Adolf Eichmann. He consistently claimed innocence on the ground that he was only following orders. Arendt accepted this picture of the regime but nevertheless indicted him for "crimes against humanity." The paper suggests that this model of the Nazi bureaucracy is false: in the Nazi bureaucracy of murder, as in other large bureaucracies, subordinates competed with each other to advance the goals of superiors they trusted. In this context, their guilt is easily established.

I. Introduction

Should Adolf Eichmann have been found guilty of the crimes for which he was charged and condemned in 1962 by the court in Jerusalem? Were the 18 Nazi leaders condemned by the International Military Tribunal in Nuremberg similarly guilty? Were the three de-

The order of the authors' names, though alphabetical, was obtained by random selection as a contribution to reducing the lexicographic bias of citation indexes. An earlier version of this paper was presented at a joint session of the Public Choice Society and Arizona State University Centennial celebration and at Carleton University. We would like to thank participants in those seminars as well as Stanley Winer and Bob Young for comments and suggestions. We are also grateful to Robert Breton, who collected papers and books for us and abstracted a large literature.

[*Journal of Political Economy*, 1986, vol. 94, no. 5]

fendants—Fritzche, von Papen, and Schacht—who were acquitted by that tribunal innocent? Seventeen minor subordinates from Auschwitz were pronounced guilty at the Frankfurt trial, while others were acquitted. On what logical or legal principle were those and other verdicts based?

This question persists because in every case the accused made and continue to make what appears to be a perfectly sound defense: They are not guilty because they were merely subordinates in large organizations (bureaucracies)—"cogs in a machine"—obeying "superior orders." In all the trials noted above the defendants repeatedly made this point.

Perhaps even more interesting, the bureaucratic status of the defendants has often been acknowledged by the judges presiding over the trials, by the prosecuting and defense lawyers, by the jurors (when they were used), as well as by the scholars and reporters writing on the trials.[1] All these people struggled with the problem they thought was posed by that subordinate status. They did so because they all more or less explicitly based their reasoning on a common "theory" of bureaucracy. That theory states that, in large organizations, orders typically emanate from the top and are implemented through a chain of command by subordinates at lower echelons of the organization. In such a context, even though the crimes perpetrated by the organization itself may be enormous, it is deemed difficult to assign individual responsibility for the crimes to anyone except the one or the few at the very top. Everyone else, it is assumed, simply obeyed orders.

The classic and perhaps the most provocative analysis of this issue is that presented by Hannah Arendt in her famous book on Adolf Eichmann's trial and on the Nazi bureaucracy, *Eichmann in Jerusalem.* In it, she so forcefully addressed the question of guilt within the framework of the commonly accepted theory of bureaucracy that the book can be used as the basic reference point on the subject.

As we know from Arendt and from others, for a good part of his career, Eichmann occupied desk IV-B-4 in the SS (*Schutzstaffel,* or guard detachment): he was Chief of Jewish Affairs. From 1933 to 1939, he organized the expulsion of Jews from Germany and Austria. After that, he had the administrative responsibility for organizing their deportation to the concentration camps. He was the transport

---

[1] A prime case is Arendt (1976). To illustrate, in a 1964 postscript to the *New Yorker* articles reprinted as *Eichmann in Jerusalem,* she writes: "Of course it is important to the political and social sciences that the essence of totalitarian government, and perhaps the nature of every bureaucracy, is to make functionaries and mere cogs in the administrative machinery out of men, and thus to dehumanize them. And one can debate long and profitably on the rule of Nobody, which is what the political form known as bureaucracy truly is" (p. 289). See also Shirer (1960) and Bracher (1970).

"coordinator" of the Final Solution to the Jewish question. Arendt portrayed him as "the perfect bureaucrat," and indeed he presented himself that way at his trial. His basic defense was that he only acted under superior orders. At one point, in what, according to Harold Rosenberg (1961, p. 380 n.*), was one of the climactic moments of the trial, he "stepped out of his glass cage to defend himself with—an organization chart"! He would say things like "officialese is my only language"; he argued that he could not be responsible for the deaths of the Jews because his office did not deliver the Zyklon B cyanide gas to the camps. He said that he was not an anti-Semite and that he would send his own father to death if ordered to do so.

The prosecution tried to paint him as an archfiend—a sadistic and vicious Jew hater who enjoyed sending millions to their deaths. The problem, at least as Arendt saw it, was that he simply did not appear that way—neither at the trial, nor at his interrogations, nor in the historical record. He appeared to be "normal" and was pronounced normal by six psychiatrists (as one of them put it: "he is more normal than I am after examining him"). Arendt coined the phrase "the banality of evil" to describe a system in which normal people could be induced to perform hideous acts under orders. This idea was subsequently taken up by the social psychologist Stanley Milgram (1974) in his famous "obedience" experiments. These offered compelling scientific evidence that a high percentage of normal people would in fact become agents in a destructive process, even when the consequences of their actions were entirely apparent, and when they had nothing to gain by doing so.

Was Eichmann guilty? Arendt argued that he was. She argued that it was true, broadly speaking, that he only followed orders, that he was, indeed, a mere "cog in a wheel," but that a cog in a machine that is perpetrating monstrous acts is responsible for those acts. In her view, it was essentially the monstrosity of the acts that produced the responsibility.

A not dissimilar argument was developed by the judges at Nuremberg, although the criterion of guilt in their case was derived from a "knowledge test." This can be appreciated, to some extent, by reference to a fragment of the final verdict read to the International Tribunal by judge Francis Biddle:[2] "Hitler could not make aggressive war by himself. He had to have the cooperation of statesmen, military leaders, diplomats, and businessmen. When they, *with knowledge of his aims,* gave him their cooperation, they made themselves party to the

---

[2] The statement is in respect of the first indictment formulated in the charter for the tribunal and pertains to crimes against peace, including the launching of an aggressive war, but it can easily be applied to the other indictments.

plan he had initiated. They are not to be deemed innocent because Hitler made use of them *if they knew what they were doing*" (Conot 1983, p. 493; emphasis added).

It is not much of a surprise, therefore, that all the defendants, in addition to claiming that they were obeying superior orders, asserted that they were ignorant of anything going on in Germany and in the East, in their bureaucratic organizations, or even in their own bureaus.[3] They obeyed orders "blindly," as the saying goes.

Ignorance, in turn, tends to be accepted by all who are involved in these matters (judges, lawyers, writers, etc.) to be a natural outcome of the formal hierarchical character of bureaucracies in which a subordinate's behavior and activity are formally defined only within the confines of his or her department or bureau. This is succinctly encapsulated in the archetypal exchange between Avner Less (a captain in the Israeli police appointed to conduct the pretrial interrogation) and Eichmann:

> LESS: Very well, but in all your statements you keep hiding behind "it wasn't in my department," "it wasn't in my province," "the regulations" . . . .
> EICHMANN: Yes, Herr Hauptmann [Mr. Captain], I have to do that, because as head of Bureau IV B 4 I was really not answerable for everything, but only for my rather narrowly circumscribed department. [von Lang 1983, p. 105]

A profound difficulty with either of these lines of reasoning—that of Arendt and that of the Nuremberg judges—is that they cannot draw a line between the perpetrators of the crime and their victims. As is well known and was pointed out by Arendt, in every country they occupied, the Germans set up Jewish councils. These councils, *under orders backed by threats*, actively participated in rounding up and selecting Jews for deportation; moreover, in the camps, some of the actual killing was done by Jews. Although Arendt absolved the Jews of any guilt in their own destruction, noting the extreme threats to which they were subjected and claiming that "no non-Jewish group or people had [ever] behaved differently" (1976, p. 11), the problem remains that, given her conception of how the Nazi regime functioned, there simply is no obvious criterion on which to distinguish the behavior of Eichmann and of other criminals from that of their victims. *Both acted "under orders."*

---

[3] Even "Mulka and others" from Auschwitz pleaded ignorance (see Naumann 1966). Naumann points out that Mulka—though he was an SS *Obersturmfuhrer* (first lieutenant) and the adjutant to the commandant of Auschwitz—claimed that "he had seen nothing and had not issued any orders. Moreover, he was careful not to question the legality of the killing of prisoners, of which he had heard rumors, for that would have meant signing his own death warrant: 'I had a responsibility toward myself' " (p. 20).

At this point, the reader should note that this dilemma arises only because the Nazi bureaucracy is modeled as an authoritarian or command system. So the question must be asked: Does the authoritarian model provide a good explanation for the behavior of the SS? Is this conception of Nazi Germany useful? And, by extension, are such intellectual constructions as Orwell's *Nineteen Eighty Four* or "Japan Inc." helpful in understanding how these and other societies actually operate? In the command model, superiors are assumed to give all orders and to direct (coordinate) all operations, while subordinates are assumed to obey. Furthermore, because the model does not meaningfully distinguish between bureaus and bureaucracies, competition is automatically, if inadvertently, ruled out: all bureaus (bureaucracies) are taken to be monopolies.[4] We hope to show, on the basis of evidence presented by Arendt herself in *Eichmann in Jerusalem* and evidence from standard historical sources, that the Nazi regime— the Nazi "bureaucracy of murder" in Arendt's words (1976, p. 172)— cannot be understood by using such a model of bureaucracy.

An alternative model is needed.[5] Such an alternative can begin with the notion that superiors and subordinates, in effect, trade with each other. Superiors seek to buy "informal services"—that is, services that cannot be codified in formal documents and that are the result of the initiative and enterprise of subordinates—to advance their own ends; in exchange they are willing to make "informal payments," which can include more rapid promotions, better offices, travel and signing privileges, use of company car, and so on, all quid pro quos that are not part of formal contracts. If people exchange, they must be assumed to be searching for the best terms to consummate these exchanges, and therefore they must be assumed to compete. But we must be careful not to restrict the notion of competition in bureaucracies to price competition. Indeed, the competition between bureaus and that between networks for resources, as well as the competition between bureaucrats for jobs, is just as likely to take the form of coming up with new ideas, new initiatives, new policies, or projects leading to what is now often called Schumpeterian competition or entrepreneurship.

---

[4] The sway that the monopoly-bureau assumption has on even the more important economic analysts of bureaucracy can be gauged by observing that, in his review of our book on bureaucratic conduct (Breton and Wintrobe 1982), Niskanen (1983) does not even mention our analysis of interbureau competition, even though that analysis occupies over 25 percent of the book, is central to many of its results, and runs in direct opposition to Niskanen's own (1971) model. It is true that the idea that bureaucracies are not monolithic structures is commonplace in the sociological, psychological, and political science literature. However, competition is typically seen as retarding rather than promoting the achievement of organizational goals in that literature.

[5] For a more complete description of the model briefly outlined in the following paragraphs, see Breton and Wintrobe (1982).

But there is a problem. Because of the nature of the services provided and because of the properties of the resources used in these superior-subordinate exchanges, the largest fraction of them will not be spot transactions, but sometimes the payment and at other times the services rendered will come first, with varying lags between the two. If a subordinate performs a service for a superior, how can he or she be sure that a payment will be forthcoming? Since nothing is formalized, contractual enforcement is surely out of the question. Does that mean that, contrary to what we assume, exchange cannot take place?

Exchanges that are based not on contractual enforcements but on the prospects of future trades have been analyzed by Telser (1980), Klein and Leffler (1981), and Shapiro (1983). In the analysis of bureaucracies, we (Breton and Wintrobe 1982) have suggested that it is trust (or loyalty) that permits informal exchanges to take place between superiors and subordinates. In other words, it is when subordinates trust their superiors to pay for informal services, and when superiors trust their subordinates to deliver the services promised, that exchanges can be consummated.

Trust, however, will not be restricted to relationships between superiors and subordinates; it will also govern relationships between subordinates. Therefore, we need another assumption to complete this brief description of our model. That assumption involves distinguishing between two kinds of trust networks: one pertaining to trust relationships between superiors and subordinates, which we call vertical networks based on vertical trust, and another one based on trust between subordinates, which we call horizontal networks that rest on horizontal trust. Our assumption is that superior-subordinate or vertical trades are primarily efficient trades (they advance the goals of superiors), while subordinate-subordinate or horizontal trades are primarily inefficient trades (they retard or impede the superiors' achievement of their objectives).

Objections to this assumption can be made. It could, for example, be argued that the cooperation of subordinates is useful to a shirking or embezzling boss or that horizontal cooperation can *raise* productivity, as in Alchian and Demsetz's (1972) analysis of production. However, a necessary (but not sufficient) condition for horizontal cooperation to raise productivity is that the number of subordinates be small. In an assembly line, for example, cooperation among subordinates can be used only to slow the line down. To speed it up, cooperation among everyone working on the line is required, and it is extremely unlikely that the required multilateral trades that would make this possible could take place. So, at a minimum, one can rationalize our assumption concerning horizontal trades as applying to the typical large bureaucratic organization.

Our assumption that vertical trades are predominantly efficiency enhancing can be rationalized on the grounds that the number of trades required to effect vertical cooperation is always relatively small, except in the very largest organizations. This is one way of explaining why classical "diseconomies of large-scale management" seem to make their appearance only in very large organizations.

The foregoing discussion points to the structure of the paper. In the next section, we seek to show that the Nazi bureaucracy was, indeed, a very competitive one, and in Section III, we argue that, at least until the last days of the Nazi regime, there was extensive vertical trust between superiors and subordinates. Neither of us is a historian. However, the evidence needed to support these arguments is available in standard historical sources. It is because the theoretical "lens" through which the facts are viewed is different from that of Arendt and others that the portrait of Eichmann and the other SS that emerges is so strikingly different and, we believe, more accurate. Section IV addresses the issue of the guilt or responsibility in "criminal" bureaucratic regimes and points to possible extensions of the analysis. Section V concludes the paper.

II. Competition in the Nazi State

> It must be remembered that all these organs, wielding enormous power, were in fierce competition with one another—which was no help to their victims, since their ambition was always the same: to kill as many Jews as possible. This competitive spirit . . . inspired in each man a great loyalty to his own outfit. [Arendt 1976, p. 71]

How did the bureaucracy of murder work? It is true that Eichmann carried the formal responsibility for Jewish affairs, as his title implied, but that did not mean that his desk had a monopoly in the area. In fact, there was fierce competition on the part of many to deal with the Jewish question. The reason is simple: It was widely appreciated throughout the Nazi bureaucracy that, in the eyes of the political leadership, "solving" the Jewish question had a priority that was second only to the war, and possibly not even second to that. Otherwise, it is difficult to explain that as late as 1942–43, when trains were desperately needed to transport materials to the various fronts, the Final Solution, rather than being scaled down, was speeded up (Dawidowicz 1975, pp. 191–96). One reason why it was so well known that the Jewish question was a priority of the leaders is that abundant resources were put at the disposal of those who chose to take initiative and to show enterprise in the pursuit of the Final Solution—in particular at the disposal of the SS.

That the political demand on the part of the top echelons in the hierarchy was strong and that a number of agencies competed for a larger role in the Nazi solution to the Jewish question is explicitly recognized by Arendt herself:

> [Eichmann's] chief competitors were the Higher S.S. and Police Leaders, who were under the direct command of Himmler, had easy access to him, and always outranked Eichmann. There was also the Foreign Office, which, under its new Undersecretary of State, Dr. Martin Luther, a protégé of Ribbentrop, had become very active in Jewish affairs. . . . It occasionally issued deportation orders to be carried out by its representatives abroad, who for reasons of prestige preferred to work through the Higher S.S. and Police Leaders. There were, furthermore, the Army commanders in the Eastern occupied territories, who liked to solve problems "on the spot," which meant shooting; the military men in Western countries were, on the other hand, always reluctant to cooperate and to lend their troops for the rounding up and seizure of Jews. Finally, there were the Gauleiters, the regional leaders, each of whom wanted to be the first to declare his territory *judenrein*, and who occasionally started deportation proceedings on their own. [Arendt 1976, pp. 151–52]

The competition among the many agencies and bureaus reflected the general operation of the Nazi bureaucracy. Schemes were constantly being put forward by rival power centers or rival entrepreneurs, and Hitler would choose among them. Some were "successful," others not. Among the latter we note: Gottfried Feder (the economics ideologue), who was given a post as undersecretary in the Ministry of Economics but was rapidly ejected by the more orthodox Schacht (Shirer 1960, p. 261); Alfred Rosenberg (commissioner for the central control of questions connected with the East-European region), who was given the responsibility for the East but found himself unable to compete with Himmler's SS and other agencies in the area and was eventually ridiculed by Hitler (Holborn 1969, p. 809; Bracher 1970, p. 411; Dawidowicz 1975, p. 19); and Hans Frank (reich commissar for the coordination of justice in the states and for the renewal of jurisprudence), who was not successful in persuading Hitler to draw up a new legal code (Broszat 1981). These "failures," and many others like them, are one measure of the existence and strength of competition.

Organizational charts are unable to tell us much, at least at first blush, about the networks of trust in bureaucracies. As a rule, they are not capable either of telling much about the extent of competition between bureaus and bureaucrats because, by their very nature, they are designed to show the "orderly" lines of authority. But in the case of the Nazi bureaucracy of murder, the overlapping lines of command, the confusion of jurisdictions, and the duplication of responsibilities are, to some extent, apparent in formal organizational charts, which, we must insist, were not produced by the Nazi authorities but by historians and analysts.[6] If the reader consults such a chart (e.g., in Conot 1983, p. 223), the overlapping jurisdiction of Himmler, Goering, Heydrich, and (after his assassination) Kaltenbrunner and Muller will be readily apparent.

Even those who, like Eugen Kogon, appear to place considerable importance on the formal structure of the bureaucracy—which he would most surely have called the bureaucracy of hell—acknowledge that "the many diversified branches of [the whole machine] enjoyed considerable degrees of independence" (1980, p. 7). The independence of the various bureaus and bureaucrats is also recognized by Broszat (1981). Conot remarks that "Himmler was free to undertake whatever tasks he saw fit" and that, even though Heydrich was accountable to both Himmler and Goering, "neither took an active interest in his operations [so that], he could play them off against each other when necessary, and in practice act virtually independently" (1980, p. 131).

The lines of command were so imprecise that contradictory testimony as to who was responsible for what could easily be given. For example, one of the witnesses at Nuremberg declared that "even in Heydrich's lifetime, Eichmann occupied a dominant, not to say absolute, position, which increased steadily in scope. At Reich Security he handled the whole Jewish sector independently. From Heydrich's death to the end, he was directly responsible to Himmler. This was generally known at Reich Security" (von Lang 1983, p. 120). Eichmann, who was not at Nuremberg, vehemently protested this description, arguing that it was surely self-serving on the part of the witness because, by placing the responsibility for crimes on an absentee, it was hoped that the person present could be exonerated.

The overlapping competitive structure of the Nazi state is well described by Shirer (1960, pp. 275–76):

> Old party comrades such as Goering, Goebbels, Himmler, Ley and Schirach were given free rein to carve out their own empires of power—and usually profit. Schacht was given a

---

[6] "For the judges and other participants in the Nuremberg trial, the comprehension of the Nazi's governmental structure proved a major challenge; and Lawrence [the British judge], to a certain extent, remained puzzled by the snarls, overlapping, and confusion until the end" (Conot 1983, p. 131).

free hand at first to raise the money for expanding government expenditures by whatever sleight of hand he could
think up. Whenever these men clashed over the division of
power or spoils, Hitler intervened. He did not mind these
quarrels. . . . Thus he seemed to take delight at the spectacle
of three men competing with each other in foreign affairs:
Neurath, the Foreign Minister, Rosenberg, the head of the
party's Foreign Affairs Department, and Ribbentrop, who
had his own "Ribbentrop Bureau" which dabbled in foreign
policy.

That description of foreign policy formulation and implementation
could be repeated for many other areas of policy, including that involving the Final Solution to the Jewish question.

In addition to the loose formal organizational lines of command,
about which more evidence could easily be cited if space permitted,[7]
another indicator of competition among bureaus in the Nazi state is
the imprecision of the orders emanating from the top. When orders
do not have specific content and when they are not directed at anyone
in particular, they will elicit a large response from diverse quarters. In
other words, they will lead to competitive behavior.

At his trial in Jerusalem, Eichmann explained how things were
done in the Third Reich. He stated: "Whenever Hitler made a speech
in which he was particularly violent about the Jews, we knew something would come from Himmler" (von Lang 1983, p. 98). Or also:
"No sooner had Hitler made a speech—and he invariably touched on
the Jewish question—than every party or government department
felt that it was up to them to do something" (p. 59).

We suggest that the imprecision in the orders is one of the reasons
why, as time went on, the number of bureaus that wanted and sought
to participate in the Final Solution grew almost without bound.
Arendt writes descriptively that "the inexhaustible source of trouble,
as he [Eichmann] saw it, was that he and his men were never left
alone, that all these other State and Party offices wanted their share in
the 'solution,' with the result that a veritable army of 'Jewish experts'
had cropped up everywhere and were falling over themselves in their
efforts to be first in a field of which they knew nothing" (1976, pp.
72–73). Eichmann himself declared to Avner Less: "You can't imagine the difficulties I ran into, the tedious, tooth-and-nail negotiations,
the thousands of objections raised by the various agencies. They all
felt it was their business" (von Lang 1983, p. 67). The duplication and

---

[7] See, e.g., the discussion in Bracher (1970, pp. 277–78).

overlap of responsibility characteristic of Nazi policy in this area are well summarized in Gordon (1984, pp. 144–45):

> How did Hitler delegate authority over racial issues? He did not authorize one central agency to handle the "Jewish Question." Instead, he encouraged a multitude of agencies in both party and state to dabble in racial politics. This structural fragmentation created anarchy among competing agencies and resulted in contradictory policies. Hitler chose from among these contradictory policies; his choices depended on his estimate of domestic opinion, party unity, and foreign affairs. He then allowed his many agencies to compete in implementing the approved policy. This resulted in further power struggles, after which Hitler acknowledged the emerging victor as the "primary authority" in racial matters. Between 1933 and 1938 party agencies were "primary authorities"; between 1938 and 1939 the SS and party contested for power; and after 1939 the SS was the "primary authority." Agencies that lost out in these struggles for power were not eliminated, however; they were allowed to meddle in their role as second- and third-rate powers.

Another indicator of competition is provided by historical evidence of entrepreneurship within the bureaucracy on the racial issue. Suggestions for a final solution to the Jewish question were often voiced in the bureaucracy. For example, a top civilian official (Friedrich Ubelhor) in the district of Lodz in 1939 suggested that the ghetto being planned there should be only a temporary measure toward a more "permanent" solution. Governor Hans Frank also put this same idea forward a year later in 1940. In July 1941, another official by the name of Hoppner sent Eichmann the official minutes of a discussion on the Jewish question in the Wartheland that proposed extermination. Hoppner asked Eichmann for his comments, adding "these things sound to some extent fantastic, but in my view absolutely practicable" (Dawidowicz 1975, p. 218).

Eichmann himself had, for a time, played a fairly prominent role in the bureaucracy, especially with respect to the deportation of Jews from Germany and from the Western occupied countries. He obtained that position, not because he was good at following orders, but through entrepreneurship. He accumulated more power into his hands in the same way that a competitive firm accumulates more customers: by being better than his competitors. In the very early years of his career, Eichmann was in charge of the Jewish desk in the SS office in Munich, but there was another desk for Jewish affairs in the Berlin Gestapo (Dawidowicz 1975, p. 107). Eichmann learned a little Hebrew and read books by Zionist leaders; he was commended for this. In 1938, the authorities decided on the policy of forced emigration for the Jews; Eichmann was sent to Vienna to organize their expulsion from Austria. Many of the Jews there were eager to leave (most of the prominent ones had already been put in prison), but a bottleneck was created by the number of papers every emigrant had to assemble to get out. Eichmann invented an assembly line system that integrated all the offices concerned: the Ministry of Finance, the income tax people, the police, and the Jewish leaders—all housed under one roof. He also sent Jewish functionaries abroad to solicit foreign exchange from Jewish organizations so that the Jews could buy the visas needed for emigration.

As Arendt (1976, pp. 44–45) put it, in the end it was like an automatic factory: "At one end you put in a Jew who still has some property, a factory, or a shop, or a bank account, and he goes through the building from counter to counter, from office to office, and comes out at the other end without any money, without any rights, with only a passport on which it says: 'You must leave the country within a fortnight. Otherwise you will go to a concentration camp.' " As a result of the assembly line system, in 8 months 45,000 Jews left Austria, whereas no more than 16,000 left Germany. Eichmann was promoted to the rank of *Obersturmbannfuhrer* (lieutenant colonel).

Later, when the war broke out, forced emigration was no longer possible, and it looked to Eichmann as if he might be out of a job. He hatched or resurrected a number of schemes, including the establishment of separate Jewish states in Madagascar and in German-occupied Poland, where he went on his own initiative to reconnoiter the territory. Despite this impressive entrepreneurship, events moved too fast for him, and in 1941 Hitler ordered the Final Solution in which Eichmann was to act only as a transportation man.

While this was a big assignment, it was not as important as Eichmann had hoped for. A different bureau than Eichmann's was put in charge; the Final Solution was officially given, not to Heydrich's Office for Reich Security (the RSHA), which included Eichmann's Jewish Affairs desk, but to a rival agency within the SS, the Economics and Administration Affairs Office (the WVHA) under Oswald Pohl. Eichmann was never to rise as high in the hierarchy as he felt he deserved. But as discussed in the next section, he continued to behave as an energetic bureaucratic entrepreneur.

III. The Efficiency of Competition in the Bureaucracy of Murder

> On the other hand he [Hitler] remained loyal to his old comrades from the fighting days of the party. To be

> sure, whoever opposed him could be certain of the dictator's ruthless vengeance. But if a man merely proved ineffective in his job, Hitler was unlikely to remove him. In general, Hitler cherished faith more than expertness. [Holborn 1969, p. 750]

Earlier we suggested that, from the point of view of superiors, competition between bureaus and bureaucrats is efficient—furthers and promotes their interests and objectives—if loyalty or trust between superiors and subordinates is such that subordinates feel that they can supply informal services—noncodified, noncontractual, or informal services—and expect to be rewarded for them. In the absence of loyalty, subordinates would presumably perform the tasks they are formally required to but would—especially if there exists considerable trust between them—engage in actions that, even if they were not outright sabotage, would be geared to the direct interests of subordinates and not to those of superiors. From the point of view of the latter, then, competition would be inefficient; that is, the initiative and enterprise instigated by competition would be counterproductive.

In the foregoing section, we sought to demonstrate that the Nazi state was intensely competitive. We argued that what, to many, appeared to be confusion, duplication, overlap, and even disorder was the outward manifestation of an extremely competitive social structure. In this section we will endeavor to marshal some evidence to show that the rank and file of the bureaucracy of murder was very loyal to the Nazi leadership; that, in other words, the SS slogan "My honor is my loyalty" (Kogon 1980, p. 199) was not an empty one, but at least to some extent a reflection of a true state of affairs.

We must insist at the outset that it is not easy to document the existence of loyalty or trust from standard historical sources. A reason for this is surely the fascination of students of the regime for the formal relationship between members of the organization. It is true that one sometimes encounters affirmations as the following: "This *close confidant* of Goering" (Rudolf Diels); or "his [Himmler's] *closest intimate*, Reinhard Heydrich" (Kogon 1980, p. 9); or "He [Ribbentrop] . . . quickly proved his *devotion* to him [Hitler]" (Holborn 1969, p. 773); or "His [Hess's] career was that of a follower . . . with well-nigh religious *faith* in the Fuhrer" (Bracher 1970, p. 280); or again "Wilhelm Frick, the Minister of the Interior and one of Hitler's most *faithful* followers" (Shirer 1960, p. 219; all emphasis added); and many others such as the quotation at the beginning of this section, all of which suggest the existence of loyalty. But reasonable knowledge of the full network of trust relationships in the National Socialist regime does not, to our knowledge, exist.

Because of this state of affairs one is left with the necessity of inferring the existence of trust networks indirectly from particular behavior and activities.

In our book (Breton and Wintrobe 1982) we showed that organizations in a democratic society (firms and governments) can provide an incentive to subordinates to accumulate more vertical and less horizontal trust by (1) providing opportunities for rapid advancement within the organizations and by (2) monitoring or policing or otherwise (e.g., by transfers or reorganization) discouraging horizontal associations (collusion) among subordinates. We would expect political dictatorships also to use these instruments.

Political dictatorships also possess a larger variety of sanctions to deal with horizontal associations and are of course much less restricted in their capacity to use them. In addition, the destruction of alternative opportunities for advancement in competing organizations is a powerful weapon to encourage subordinates to further their careers by investing in loyalty to the regime. Consequently, we believe that it may not be necessary to introduce such concepts as brainwashing, the manipulation of human personality, and others like them that are so often employed to deal with human behavior in totalitarian societies: the unusual amount of loyalty that appears to exist in such regimes could be an entirely rational response to the unusual structure of incentives facing people.

In the case of Hitler's Germany, it is widely known that the building of trust assumed enormous importance. Indeed, according to Arendt herself, the central characteristic of "totalitarian" movements, "compared with all other parties and movements . . . is their demand for total, unrestricted, unconditional, and unalterable loyalty of the individual member" (1973, p. 323). She also describes one organizational device by which the movement created loyalty: its carefully graduated and fluctuating hierarchy of militancy. Thus the masses who were part of the movement were divided into two categories, sympathizers and members. Moreover, Hitler "was the first to devise a conscious policy of constantly enlarging the ranks of sympathizers while at the same time keeping the number of party members strictly limited" (p. 366). And "this relationship . . . is repeated on different levels within the movement itself. As party members are related to and separated from the fellow-travelers, so are the elite formations of the movement related to and separated from the ordinary members" (p. 367). This pattern is analyzed with particular reference to the SS:

> Another advantage of the totalitarian pattern is that it can be repeated indefinitely and keeps the organization in a state of fluidity which permits it constantly to insert new layers and define new degrees of militancy. The whole history of

> the Nazi party can be told in terms of new formations within
> the Nazi movement. The SA, the stormtroopers (founded in
> 1922), were the first Nazi formation which was supposed to
> be more militant than the party itself; in 1926, the SS was
> founded as the elite formation of the SA; after three years,
> the SS was separated from the SA and put under Himmler's
> command; it took Himmler only a few more years to repeat
> the same game within the SS. One after the other, and each
> more militant than its predecessor, there now came into be-
> ing, first, the Shock Troops, then the Death Head units (the
> "guard units for the concentration camps"), which later were
> merged to form the Armed SS (*Waffen-SS*), finally the Secu-
> rity Service (the "ideological intelligence service of the
> Party," and its executive arm for the "negative population
> policy") and the Office for Questions of Race and Resettle-
> ment (*Rasse- und Siedlungswesen*), whose tasks were of a "posi-
> tive kind"—all of them developing out of the General SS,
> whose members, except for the higher Fuehrer Corps, re-
> mained in their civilian occupations. To all these new forma-
> tions the member of the General SS now stood in the same
> relationship as the SA-man to the SS-man, or the party mem-
> ber to the SA-man, or the member of a front organization to
> a party member. [P: 368]

The incentives that this system gives to accumulate vertical loyalty
(and to prevent the accumulation of horizontal trust) are obvious.
Unlike a conventional hierarchy, the possibilities of advancement in
this system are almost never ending, and a paramount criterion for
advancement is loyalty: "the fluctuating hierarchy, similar to that of
secret services, makes it possible, even without actual power, to de-
grade any rank or group that wavers or shows signs of decreasing
radicalism by the mere insertion of a new more radical layer, hence
driving the older group automatically in the direction of the front
organization and away from the center of the movement" (p. 369).

How much more sophisticated is this analysis from *The Origins of
Totalitarianism* compared with the simple-minded command image of
the Nazi hierarchy to be found in *Eichmann in Jerusalem*. Indeed,
in the first book, Arendt explicitly disavows the command model:
"[in] the organization of an army and the military dictatorship established after its model . . . absolute power of command from the top
down and absolute obedience from the bottom up correspond to the
situation of extreme danger in combat, *which is precisely why they are not
totalitarian*. . . . Every hierarchy, no matter how authoritarian in its
direction, and every chain of command, no matter how arbitrary or

920   JOURNAL OF POLITICAL ECONOMY

dictatorial the content of orders, tends to stabilize and would have restricted the total power of the leader of a totalitarian movement" (pp. 364–65; emphasis added).

The leader's power in the totalitarian movement is analyzed in terms of his capacity to keep his subordinates from trusting each other: "His position within this intimate circle depends upon his ability to spin intrigues among its members and upon his skill in constantly changing its personnel. He owes his rise to leadership to an extreme ability to handle inner-party struggles for power" (p. 373).

The other major device used by the Nazis to encourage loyalty to the regime was the systematic neutralization or destruction of alternative centers of power (competing organizations): the *lander* (regional governments), the unions, other "horizontal" associations, and of course the other political parties. The facts are well known (see, e.g., Broszat 1981, chaps. 3–5); it would serve no purpose to recount them anew here. Of particular interest, however, was the policy of the Nazis toward the civil service.

After Hitler's accession to power in 1933, he had to govern in addition to holding on to power. He could have governed through the existing bureaucratic machinery of the German state inherited from the Weimar Republic. Indeed, if the conventional theory of bureaucracy, which assumes that subordinates in large organizations are neutral individuals obeying orders from above, is correct, then Hitler would simply have had to take that bureaucracy over, issue orders, and observe them being carried out.

But the evidence goes in the opposite direction. Indeed, it shows that, in many bureaus and more particularly in the bureaus that were the most important for the implementation of Nazi objectives, Hitler and the National Socialist leadership proceeded to displace the established civil service (see Broszat 1981). The general drift is well described in a sad letter to Hitler from Wilhelm Frick around 1940:

> I have, my Führer, always seen it as my duty as your civil service Minister since 1933 [he was then Reich Minister of the Interior], to make available to you for the great tasks of state policy a highly qualified professional civil service and to develop in it the old Prussian conception of duty as well as the National Socialist character, as is the case with the German armed forces. The course of the last years makes me doubt, however, whether my efforts can in any way be regarded as successful. To an ever growing degree, according to the agreed observations of my department *and all other departments*, bitter feelings are spreading in the professional civil service about the lack of appreciation of their abilities

and services as well as of unjustified neglect. The feeling of being left defenceless is beginning to cripple the best creative forces. . . . There can no longer be any talk whatever of the professional civil service being preferred as a body *enjoying the special trust of the state leadership.* . . . The civil service is also suffering badly from the fact that new tasks are not being entrusted to it, but to the Party organizations, although this often concerns genuine administrative duties. [Quoted in Broszat 1981, pp. 257–58; emphasis added]

What seems to have been the case throughout the bureaucracy was particularly marked in respect of the War Ministry, the conduct of diplomacy and foreign affairs, the police, and, of course, the extermination of the Jews for which there was, obviously, no pre-Hitler bureaucratic organization.

A final measure still of the extent of the trust between the Nazi leadership and subordinates in the organization is provided by what happened when it became obvious that the Third Reich was collapsing. This episode provides a good illustration of one of our basic contentions about trust: that, however extreme (large) it might be, it is not necessarily "blind" and it is never "total, unrestricted, unconditional, and unalterable," as Arendt (1973, p. 323) suggests the regime demanded and sometimes implies that its members supplied. Instead, we suggest, loyalty rises or falls, depending on a number of things, especially the anticipated future prospects of the regime. What happened was that competition within the bureaucracy continued, but now it was inefficient in that it was not geared to the objectives of superiors.

As early as 1944, Himmler had come to the view that the war was lost and, in defiance of Hitler's wishes, asked Eichmann to stop killing Jews. He assumed that the Allies, in their gratitude for this act, would make him prime minister of postwar Germany! According to Arendt, Eichmann sabotaged his orders as much as he felt he could. When there were no trains available for transporting Jews from Hungary in 1944, Eichmann organized foot marches, and when Himmler ordered him to desist, he threatened to obtain a decision from Hitler himself. As a result, in January 1945, Eichmann's old enemy Kurt Becker (who was cooperating with Himmler's plan to sell Jews) was promoted to colonel and Eichmann was transferred out of his Desk on Jewish Affairs to the insignificant one dealing with the fight against churches.

Later, Himmler directly "deserted the sinking ship of state. The Reuter dispatch told of his secret negotiations with Count Bernadotte and his offer to surrender the German armies in the West to

Eisenhower. To Hitler, who had never doubted Himmler's absolute loyalty, this was the heaviest blow of all" (Shirer 1960, p. 1122).

When Goering, in April 1945, sought to reactivate the 1941 decree that made him deputy führer by sending a telegram to Hitler that was signed "Your loyal, Hermann Goering," Hitler reacted by saying that "Goering has betrayed and deserted both me and his Fatherland" and adding "no allegiances are kept, no honor lived up to, no disappointments that I have not had, no betrayals that I have not experienced" (Shirer 1960, p. 1119).

In addition to the Himmler and Goering actions, there were others such as Ribbentrop, who was negotiating in Sweden, and Speer, who was "urging commanders such as Manteuffel to disobey orders to destroy bridges, dams and factories rather than leave them to the enemy" (Toland 1976, p. 1174). Borman was right to declare "treachery seems to have replaced loyalty" (Shirer 1960, p. 1121). And Hitler was also right to say "I am lied on all sides" and to add "those arrogant, tedious, indecisive SS are no good to me any more" (Toland 1976, pp. 1172, 1198).

IV. Bureaucratic Responsibility[8]

In a bureaucracy characterized by rigorous and unflagging competition between its personnel and agencies and in which, at least until the

---

[8] A related issue of bureaucratic responsibility, but one that is not addressed in this paper, is that of the liability of superiors for the criminal actions of subordinates. This issue does not, to our knowledge, arise in the Nazi regime, in which the senior principals were obviously guilty, but it is a common issue in cases of corporate malfeasance. For example, in the well-known electrical conspiracy cases of 1960–61, one of the protagonists, General Electric, apparently engaged in 19 price-fixing cartels for a period of 10 years. The practices, according to at least one observer, were "an open secret to the rest of the industry" (Smith 1963, p. 123). Judge Ganey, who heard the case, stated that "I am not naive enough to believe General Electric didn't know about it and that it didn't meet with their hearty approbation" (p. 114). Nevertheless, although a number of junior executives were successfully prosecuted, senior management was not because attorneys for the government felt that they did not have sufficient evidence to claim that any of them "had knowledge of the conspiracy . . . nor that any of these men personally authorized or ordered commission of any of the acts charged" (p. 134). Similarly, in the recent E. F. Hutton scandal, in which Hutton pleaded guilty to 2,000 counts of defrauding banks through deliberate overdrafting of company funds, a report commissioned for Hutton by former Attorney General Griffin Bell exonerates the president from responsibility "because the corporate structure did not assign [President] Ball the task of controlling cash management or supervising audit controls" (Wallace and Crock 1985, p. 34). Again the implicit theoretical model of an organization is the command model. In the absence of evidence of formal directives to commit criminal acts, it is held that senior management cannot be held liable for them, despite evidence in both cases that the actions were commonly practiced among subordinates, that the results were highly profitable to the companies involved, and that, at a minimum, it would not have been unreasonable for senior management to suspect that criminal activities were responsible for those profits. This liability standard is misdi-

closing days of the war, that competition furthered the interests of the rulers because trust between these rulers and their subordinates was strong, what can be said about the responsibilities of the subordinates for the actions of the regime? More specifically, what is the responsibility of an individual SS officer like Eichmann for the crimes perpetrated by the regime and by the agency he was heading?

To answer these questions, consider two hypothetical situations. Suppose first that Eichmann, rather than being employed by the SS, had been self-employed—he had owned a transportation company— and rather than a rank, a salary, and a prospect for promotions, he had had the opportunity to bid against other companies for a contract that involved transporting millions of people to their deaths. If he had been the lowest bidder or the one who promised to move the maximum number of persons to their deaths for a fixed sum, he would have been given the contract. If he had lost out in the bidding, he might have received other contracts or nothing at all. Nothing else would have happened to him.

In such a circumstance, we suggest that no one would have any difficulty in assigning responsibility and that all would convict Eichmann of guilt. Indeed, on canonical principles of responsibility, whether as principal or as accessory, no new issue is raised by that case. We suggest that the incentives facing Eichmann—and other subordinates like him—were no different from those assumed in our hypothetical situation. Eichmann did not obey *orders* any more than a self-employed entrepreneur does when he or she responds to the *demands* of the marketplace in order to make money. His rewards took the form of promotions, perquisites, and power rather than negotiated contractual sums, but that makes no difference to the question of his guilt or innocence.

Furthermore, as successful entrepreneurs in a competitive environment, Eichmann and all others like him must be assumed to have had knowledge of existing opportunities as well as of the possibilities of new opportunities. Aggressive entrepreneurs are always on the lookout for ways of improving their position. Guilt and responsibility derive from entrepreneurship in a criminal venture, not from a claimed bureaucratic ignorance of the facts.

---

rected as well as weak. It is easy to imagine that superiors, operating on the basis of vertical trust with their subordinates, could encourage illegal practices among subordinates without ever giving direct orders to perform them. Indeed, they could cultivate such practices even while giving direct orders not to engage in them. Developing an appropriate standard for the liability of superiors for the actions of subordinates is no easy task, but an appropriate standard would take into account the actual incentives that superiors create for subordinates and would note that the mere existence of orders or rules prohibiting illegal acts does not absolve superiors of responsibility.

Turning to the second hypothetical situation, suppose instead that a gun had been held to Eichmann's head and that he had been told to carry out orders or face execution for disobedience. In that case, it would appear to be hard to hold him responsible for carrying out the orders received. There is considerable evidence (Robinson 1965; Dawidowicz 1975, 1981) that these were in fact the incentives facing members of the *Judenrate* (the Jewish councils) and the Jewish commandos in the concentration camps. The argument of Arendt that "it was undeniable that he [Eichmann] had always acted upon 'superior orders' " (1976, p. 294) but that "all the cogs in the machinery, no matter how insignificant, are in court forthwith transformed back into perpetrators, that is to say, into human beings" (p. 289) is logically invalid and raises a false issue. It is invalid because, if Eichmann did merely follow orders that were backed by possible sanctions, he could not be found guilty for reasons already indicated. It is a false issue because Eichmann did not merely follow orders and, furthermore, would in all likelihood not even have been sanctioned, let alone executed, if he had pursued the Nazi solution to the Jewish question with less zeal. He would simply have participated less in the informal rewards that would then have gone to the more ardent entrepreneurs.

Eichmann—like innumerable other Nazi subordinates—was a competitive entrepreneurial bureaucrat in a very competitive bureaucracy. It was this combined with his loyalty that explains his efficiency. And it is the fact that there were thousands of Eichmanns, all entrepreneurial and competitive and all fiercely loyal to their superiors, that explains the terrible efficiency of the Nazi bureaucracy of murder. We suggest that there is little to be feared from the standard picture of a totalitarian society in which "cogs," watched by Big Brother or his equivalent, carry out orders emanating from the top. Such a society would collapse in inefficiency. What is infinitely more fearsome is the capacity of a dictatorship to use the principle of competition to organize terror and murder.

V. Conclusion

The question addressed in this paper is not a new one, but it is one that was posed with particular force by the events that took place in Nazi Germany: Should subordinates in large organizations be held responsible for criminal acts that they do not deny having committed but claim to have perpetrated under orders? A number of answers have been provided to this question, but all, to our knowledge, accept the question as reflecting reality in an exact way.

The reason why everyone accepts the question as asked is simply that the image or theory of bureaucracy that is almost universally held is one that is developed from the hypothesis that in large organizations subordinates are given orders from above and, if they are to remain subordinates, have no choice but to obey. Saddled with such a theory, serious people, convinced of the guilt of the subordinates, have sought rationales for their conviction in different directions. We have outlined Hannah Arendt's and the Nuremberg judges' rationales earlier. They do not strike us as being very robust.

We reject the question as asked. We do not accept that subordinates in large organizations obey orders. Instead, we argue, they are placed in a competitive framework in which they are rewarded for entrepreneurial initiatives that promote the interests and objectives of their superiors. The more useful they are to their superiors, the larger the rewards. We have sought to show that the bureaucratic structure of Nazi Germany was extremely competitive, that the bureaucrats—SS officers, heads of concentration camps, and so forth—active in the bureaucracy were energetic, entrepreneurial, and competitive and that, except at the end, subordinates were intensely loyal to their superiors.

If that model of bureaucracy, based on competition and exchange, describes well the Nazi regime, the question asked above, once reformulated to eliminate the element of compulsion, is easily answered, and that answer must be affirmative.

References

Alchian, Armen A., and Demsetz, Harold. "Production, Information Costs, and Economic Organization." *A.E.R.* 62 (December 1972): 777–95.

Arendt, Hannah. *The Origins of Totalitarianism.* 2d ed. New York: Harcourt Brace Jovanovich, 1973.

————. *Eichmann in Jerusalem: A Report on the Banality of Evil.* Rev. ed. New York: Penguin, 1976.

Bracher, Karl D. *German Dictatorship: The Origins, Structure, and Effects of National Socialism.* New York: Praeger, 1970.

Breton, Albert, and Wintrobe, Ronald. *The Logic of Bureaucratic Conduct: An Economic Analysis of Competition, Exchange, and Efficiency in Private and Public Organizations.* New York: Cambridge Univ. Press, 1982.

Broszat, Martin. *The Hitler State: The Foundation and Development of the Internal Structure of the Third Reich.* London: Longmans, 1981.

Conot, Robert E. *Justice at Nuremberg.* New York: Harper and Row, 1983.

Dawidowicz, Lucy S. *The War against the Jews, 1933–1945.* New York: Bantam, 1975.

————. *The Holocaust and the Historians.* Cambridge, Mass.: Harvard Univ. Press, 1981.

Gordon, Sarah A. *Hitler, Germans, and the "Jewish Question."* Princeton, N.J.: Princeton Univ Press, 1984.

Holborn, Hajo. *A History of Modern Germany.* Vol. 3. *1840–1945.* New York: Knopf, 1969.

Klein, Benjamin, and Leffler, Keith B. "The Role of Market Forces in Assuring Contractual Performance." *J.P.E.* 89 (August 1981): 615–41.

Kogon, Eugen. *The Theory and Practice of Hell: The German Concentration Camps and the System behind Them.* New York: Berkley, 1980.

von Lang, Jochen (ed.). *Eichmann Interrogated: Transcripts from the Archives of the Israeli Police.* Toronto: Lester and Orpen Denny, 1983.

Milgram, Stanley. *Obedience to Authority: An Experimental View.* New York: Harper and Row, 1974.

Naumann, Bernd. *Auschwitz: A Report on the Proceedings against Robert Karl Ludwig Mulka and Others before the Court at Frankfurt.* New York: Praeger, 1966.

Niskanen, William A., Jr. *Bureaucracy and Representative Government.* Chicago: Aldine-Atherton, 1971.

———. Review of *The Logic of Bureaucratic Conduct* by Albert Breton and Ronald Wintrobe. *J. Econ. Literature* 21 (December 1983): 1494–95.

Robinson, Jacob. *And the Crooked Shall Be Made Straight: The Eichmann Trial, the Jewish Catastrophe, and Hannah Arendt's Narrative.* London: Macmillan, 1965.

Rosenberg, Harold. "The Trial and Eichmann." *Commentary* 32 (November 1961): 369–81.

Shapiro, Carl. "Premiums for High Quality Products as Returns to Reputations." *Q.J.E.* 98 (November 1983): 659–79.

Shirer, William L. *The Rise and Fall of the Third Reich: A History of Nazi Germany.* New York: Simon and Schuster, 1960.

Smith, Richard A. *Corporations in Crisis.* New York: Doubleday, 1963.

Telser, Lester G. "A Theory of Self-enforcing Agreements." *J. Bus.* 53 (January 1980): 27–44.

Toland, John. *Adolf Hitler.* New York: Ballantine, 1976.

Wallace, David G., and Crock, Stan. "The Hutton Investigation: Speaking Softly and Carrying No Stick." *Bus. Week* (September 23, 1985), p. 34.

Nuclearism

[10]

AUST & NZ JOURNAL OF CRIMINOLOGY (June 1983) 16 (81-92)

NUCLEAR ENERGY AND THE DESTINY OF MANKIND— SOME CRIMINOLOGICAL PERSPECTIVES*

Richard Harding†

Introduction

The criminology to which we are accustomed takes as its fundamental given value the existence of mankind and the continuation of human activity and social organization. Seen from this perspective, such diametrically opposed theorists as Hans Eysenck and Frank Pearce have more uniting them than dividing them. So too did such noted practitioners as J Edgar Hoover and Andreas Baader. Likewise, Ayatollah Khomeini has more in common with the late Shah of Iran than with Allah.

All political conflicts, however apparently radical, are thus in truth marginal, for their premise has been the continuation of the human race and the preservation of all that which epitomizes homo sapiens. The protagonists of the status quo and the disciples of reform or revolution are each seeking to occupy the same ground.

Criminology has given us some wonderfully perspicacious insights into how this process occurs or can be undermined or made to commence with the dice loaded. It has identified false arguments, and described the techniques by which a supposedly neutral criminal law becomes an instrument of political repression or control. It has developed methodologies and approaches for demonstrating the true nature of social phenomena. Arguably, the single most important of these approaches is the inadequacy of concentrating concern upon *deviants* alone; we must study also *deviance* as being endemic to human existence. "The fault, dear Brutus, is not in our stars" — though it may be for some of us. Nor is it merely in our environment; though it is for many. "It is in ourselves", also — a view which brings the whole range of human conduct within the potential scope of criminology.

Yet for all that, criminology is, I believe, in danger of running into a dead end. It is overburdening itself with trivia, falling into the self-indulgence of internecine squabbles, telling us what we already know, looking for short-term gratification. If I am correct in this diagnosis, why is it so, how has this come about? Part of the answer lies, I believe, in the fact that too many criminologists have fought shy of grappling with the new technologies; as a consequence criminological agenda are still set by reference to the sorts of issues that existed and could in principle have been perceived in the 1930s. Certainly, researchers now bring to their studies the sophistication and argumentative style of the 80s; but they are not asking questions for this decade, much less questions for the twenty-first century.

In the 1980s there is, in fact, only one important set of questions to ask: what can criminology and criminologists do to decrease the chances of the extinction of mankind and the destruction of the planet? The principal question within such a set of questions obviously relates to nuclear weapons and nuclear energy. It is a question

---

* An amended version of the Presidential Address to the Criminology Section of ANZAAS, May 1982.
† Professor of Law, University of Western Australia.

82   R HARDING   (1983) 16 ANZJ Crim

which should be a major pre-occupation of every discipline. As far as criminology is concerned, however, a survey of the major English language journals — including *Contemporary Crises* and the *British Journal of Criminology* — revealed only one published article on any aspect of nuclear energy in the last 10 years.[1] Whilst it will not be argued that criminological attention should be confined to the nuclear debate, this hiatus in the literature is nevertheless a remarkable one.

Nuclear Power and Nuclear Weapons

The accident at Three Mile Island nuclear power plant in March 1979 provides a case study of what criminology could contribute to the nuclear debate. I shall analyse it quite fully, therefore. Before doing so, it is necessary to lay some quite extensive groundwork; after doing so, the value and relevance of analysing Australia's nuclear position from a criminological perspective should become apparent.

The first point to stress is this: that the nuclear fuel cycle is a *total system*. Participation in any part of it is participation in every part of it. If this truism needs documentation, the calm analysis of the Fox Report supplies it.[2] More recently, Pringle and Spigelman have put it as follows:

> Nations without nuclear weapons will always want them if others have them, and *the easiest way to acquire them will be through nuclear power programmes*[3]. Thus the core of the proliferation problem is the expansion of nuclear-generated electricity: more nuclear power plants mean more fissile material available for diversion into bomb projects. There is no way of preventing this at present: the nuclear materials market is far too large and too diverse to be controlled through export sanctions, and the current early warning system of a diversion of nuclear material, known as safeguards, is inherently defective.[4]

The second point is this: that there can be no such thing as a "limited" nuclear war nor is such a war "winnable". This should not need saying, but in the present political climate — particularly in Washington — it does. There is a desperate deficiency of imagination in high places[5], a deficiency which is leading to the abandonment of the concept of Mutual Assured Destruction (MAD) and its replacement by a scenario of graduated nuclear warfare in which *military* targets will be progressively vaporised until such time as the Baddies, recognizing the superior virtue of the Goodies, desist.[6]

Part of the explanation for this twisted self-delusion undoubtedly arises from the fact that the world's only model for the use of nuclear weapons followed exactly this pattern. The Baddies *did* desist. But of course they did not themselves possess nuclear weapons. However, even at this point the seductive and comforting model of Hiroshima and Nagasaki persists. For all the devastation of those bombs, at least the survivors could seek refuge elsewhere; an infrastructure of support and aid continued to exist. Japan itself not only survived but has risen again. Too many citizens and far, far too many politicians seem to regard nuclear warfare as a sort of chronic version of Hiroshima — appalling, yes, but producing human drama and heroism; catharsis paving the way for resurrection. This illusion is fostered by the very language of analysis — "yellow*cake*", "*enrichment* of uranium", "military *hardware*", "*Cruise* missiles", "*baby* nukes", "members of the ICBM *family*", etcetera[7] — and by the abstraction of horrendous facts into harmless sounding small numbers — a *one* megaton or even a *ten* megaton device.

Yet what is the reality? In an immensely courageous series of articles, Jonathan Schell has sought to awaken paralysed imaginations[8]. Without hysteria or melodrama but permitting his readers no retreat into abstractions, he has described the horrifying destructive effects of a single bomb — initial nuclear radiation, electro-magnetic pulse, thermal pulse, blast-wave and local fallout. "Naturally, when many of these bombs are exploded the scope of these effects is increased accordingly. But, in addition, these primary effects produce innumerable secondary effects on societies and natural environments, some of which may be even more harmful than the primary ones."[9] Schell goes on to describe them. I shall not do so myself; there is a limit to how much we can all take at one reading. Suffice to say that what happened at Hiroshima was less than one-millionth a part of the holocaust at present levels of world nuclear armament.

There is one further point which we cannot and must not finesse, however. It is the destruction of the Earth's ozone layer. In a holocaust in which ten thousand megatons were detonated in the Northern Hemisphere, the reduction of ozone would be 70% in that hemisphere and 40% in our own hemisphere. (The USSR is thought to possess some 11,000 megatons of nuclear weapons, and the USA about 4000 megatons.) The ozone layer would probably never return to normal, and at best would take at least 30 years to do so. Its existence is, of course, crucial to life on earth. For Schell, therefore, "the primary question is not how many people would be irradiated, burned or crushed to death by the immediate effect of the bombs, but how well the ecosphere, regarded a single living entity, on which all forms of life depend for their continued existence, would hold up. The issue is the habitability of the earth . . . Death cuts off life; extinction cuts off birth".[10]

There is, then, no comfort for any of us. When I come later to what Australia should do, and thus what criminologists can do to influence Australia's conduct, it will not be from the point of view of finding a hole for us to hide in whilst the rest of the world is blasted to perdition. The whole world is trapped in the "theoretically sophisticated but often humanly deficient world of nuclear strategic theory . . . . The outbreak of nuclear hostilities in itself assumes the collapse of every usual restraint of reason and humanity. Once the mass killing of a nuclear holocaust had begun, . . . it is hard to imagine what force could be counted on to hold the world back from all-out destruction."[11] Schell concludes: "Once we learn that a holocaust *might* lead to extinction, we have no right to gamble because if we lose the game will be over, and neither we nor anyone else will ever get another chance. Therefore, although scientifically speaking, there is all the difference in the world between a mere possibility that a holocaust will bring about extinction and the certainty of it, morally they are the same, and we have no choice but to address the issue of nuclear weapons as though we knew for a certainty that their use would put an end to our species."[12]

This brings us full circle to the fact that the nuclear fuel cycle is a total system. Participation in it is, morally and practically, participation in the construction of nuclear weapons. This is a point to which I shall return when looking at Australia's position and the impact which Australian citizens and criminologists may be able to make upon it.

For now, however, let us examine the question of nuclear reactors, why they go wrong and what insights criminologists can offer to the developing debate about nuclear energy.

Three Mile Island

The worst nuclear accident in the world's history occurred in 1958 at Kyshtym in the USSR, when a radioactive waste dump exploded. Little detail is known about it. However, it seems that hundreds of square kilometres around the area still resemble a moonscape, and that the carcinogenic and mutagenetic effects are still becoming manifest[13]. The accident at Three Mile Island came within a whisker of relegating Kyshtym to the position of second-worst nuclear accident in the history of the world.

The events in question began at 4.01 am on 28 March 1979. A maintenance crew working to clear the sludge from a small pipe known as a polisher inadvertently choked off the main feedwater system to Generating Unit 2, then operating at 97% capacity. The unit automatically shut down, and within seconds the three emergency feedwater pumps went into action. So far so good. However, so violent had been the response of the reactor to its sudden shutdown that the pressure of the coolant water had increased to the point of forcing open a relief valve. As the new source of water took over, the valve should have closed down. The monitoring light in the control room in fact indicated that this had occurred. But in reality the valve had jammed open, allowing the coolant to escape from the reactor. To make matters worse, only *one* of the emergency pumps was feeding water into the reactor, for in the course of routine maintenance a few days earlier someone had closed the valves of the other two and failed to re-open them. To compound matters, three pumps which were part of a high-pressure water injection system were shut down by an operator who was under the impression from his analysis of the control-room information that the first-stage emergency pumps were working and that the pressure-relief valve was now shut. Another operator interpreted the control room readings to mean that there was too much water, not too little, in the reactor, and opened a drain line, thus effectively doubling the severity of the coolant loss.

This catalogue of errors — or to use the jargon "common-mode failure" — continued, with instrument problems, equipment malfunctions, computer system breakdowns and operator confusion. As a consequence, all the uranium fuel rods overheated, with about one-third of the core being reduced to rubble. Radioactive hydrogen gas escaped into the atmosphere; millions of gallons of radioactive water were released into the auxiliary containment buildings. It took 16 hours of crisis for officials to diagnose the problem correctly, and begin to take the actions which pulled the situation back from the ,brink. A further month's delicate manoeuvring was needed to stabilize the reactor. Now the whole power station remains shut down — a monument to the immense problem of how safely to de-commission defunct nuclear facilities.

The whole incident has attracted a flood of literature, none of it so far as I am aware published in criminological journals or written by persons who would describe themselves as criminologists. Let me try to capture the tone of some of it, beginning with the contribution of a nuclear scientist, Daniel Ford.[14] Recognizing that the causation of the particular accident was brought about by a combination of human and mechanical failure, Ford argues as follows:

> The preferable approach to the problem of human error is for plant designers to provide positive physical safeguards aimed at protecting all critical equipment in the plant from inadvertent or inappropriate human tampering. Such measures could be compared to some of the steps that many parents take in an effort to childproof a house — capping electrical outlets, installing special locks on windows, putting gates on staircases . . . . Comprehensive automation is obviously the most far-reaching counter-measure that can be taken at a nuclear power plant to reduce the opportunity for human error[15].

Ford also points out that "specific safety-related instructions, careful training and repeated exhortations would be of considerable value"[16]. But he is in no doubt as to the superiority of further technological refinements.

NUCLEAR ENERGY & THE DESTINY OF MANKIND 85

A social scientist, Larry Hirschorn, is more optimistic about the value of training[17]. He castigates present practices: "One suspects that the workers in general are still treated as electrical power workers and are expected to contribute little to and have little impact on plant operation."[18] The training he urges is not merely in skills but what he calls "meta-skills", a skill for acquiring skills.

The Three Mile Island case leads to new definitions of the workers and the machine. The machine must be viewed in terms of its failure mode on the one side (taking due account of the nesting of machine systems in larger human ones) and in terms of the interface between the operator and the machine on the other. The worker must be viewed as one who acquires a meta-skill or a skill for acquiring skills. This becomes the basis for his conceptual flexibility, for his ability to solve novel problems not anticipated by the machine designers. Only in this way, only with these new conceptions, can we develop safe, effective and productive automatic machine systems.[19]

He is sanguine about the prospects of doing so, confident in talking about a "new concept of the worker".[20] He even manages to draw a nine-box chart in which he correlates possible problems with the organizational level at which they must be framed, mapped and solved.[21]

The Kemmeny Commission, set up by President Carter to inquire into the accident, focussed on the supervisory system which would be appropriate for nuclear reactors. The Nuclear Regulatory Commission, in 1979, had still not rid itself of the hangover of self-regulation with which the nuclear industry had started out. Its personnel largely comprised the also-rans of nuclear engineering; its powers were ambiguous; and its will to use the powers it did possess was doubtful. (When a call was made to the NRC's Philadelphia Office at 7.24 am on 28 March 1979 to notify a "general emergency", no one had yet come on duty and a message had to be left with the answering service.[22]) Accordingly, the Kemmeny Report specified 42 particular reforms by which the performance of the NRC should be improved; some of these related to increased powers, others to the internal administration of the Commission.

By way of final illustration, let me refer to the work of Mr Charles Ehret, a pioneer of a science calling itself chrono-biology.[23] Ehret and others found the most striking aspect of Three Mile Island the fact that it occurred during the "grave-yard shift", 11.00 pm to 7.00 am. To such researchers, the chances of human errors of diagnosis and action would have been reduced, perhaps eliminated, if the workers had been in a good state of "chrono-hygiene" — which could have been brought about by a more appropriate diet, less use of rotating shifts, and a working environment better designed to cue the body's circadian rhythm.

So there we have it. The joint wisdom of these analysts would lead us to suppose that Three Mile Island would not have occurred — and no future such accident will occur — if the reactor had been automated in a man-proof way, operated by workers trained in meta-skills and possessing a desirable degree of chrono-hygiene, and watched over by a vigilant and fearless Regulatory Commission. What can our criminological knowledge tell us about all this, what can criminologists contribute to this particular debate?

As regards Ford's analysis, what he is seeking is an escape-proof prison or a robbery-proof bank. Criminologists could tell him — and this insight has been promoted in popular perception to the level of a law, Murphy's Law — that there can never be an escape-proof prison, let alone hundreds or thousands of them. And they can tell him too that, for all the alarm systems and bullet proof glass and automatic screens, the only kind of robbery-proof bank is one without staff or customers or, finally, money.

As for Hirschorn, he is locked into Durkheimian anomie theory. For him, sub-standard worker performance is remediable by greater job-involvement and more decision-making at the workface. Part of that process involves problem identification and solving; training is a pre-requisite for responsibility, and responsibility requires better training. This is fine if one is talking of a car-assembly plant or a post-office or an abattoir. Productivity will be increased and mistakes will be reduced in number. But they will not be eliminated. The disingenuity of Hirschorn's gung-ho faith is harmless enough at the level of a defective automobile or a dead letter or mutton dressed up as lamb. But it is dangerous nonsense with nuclear reactors, which are different in kind not merely degree from any other industrial operation. Moreover, he seems to be totally unaware of the problem of industrial sabotage — a matter upon which criminologists could offer him important insights.

The Kemmeny Commission is scarcely less naive than Ford and Hirschorn. The model it urges is, in essence, that of external policing of police misconduct. Who cops the coppers? Preferably not the cops themselves, but specialized investigators or an Ombudsman or even citizen review boards. Within Australia, this is a debate to which I have made some contribution. But in doing so, I have not imagined for one moment that *any* system one could dream up and implement would eliminate police corruption or wrongdoing, merely that it might improve the detection rate and thereby indirectly reduce a little the deviance rate. The external review model pre-supposes and accepts the inevitability of the continuance of deviance, and criminologists know that it can be founded on no other premise. In the nuclear power industry, we must find a model that eliminates deviance altogether.

Finally, I come to Ehret. His views are the quaintest of them all. His approach is equivalent to the criminology of bumps-on-the-head and hormonal disturbance and XYY chromosomes. Does he need to be told that people with splendid round skulls and balanced hormones and XY chromosomes, and even people in an ideal state of chrono-hygienic health, still fall short from time to time of desirable standards of behaviour?

So what do we have left over from all this? We have four perspectives, each of which contains some element of truth but all of which are fatally flawed. Even if all these modes of analysis were adopted and faithfully implemented, we would still have a defective system. In identifying *deviant* parts of the system, parts that did not work the way they were meant to if order was to be preserved, all these analysts lose sight of the inevitability of *deviance* in human affairs.

Criminologists understand and accept that there is a point at which one is powerless to affect or even to comprehend deviance. In our normal daily concerns, it does not matter a great deal; the resultant problems remain, broadly speaking, manageable. They are part of the frame of life. But nuclear energy is different in kind. All the analyses I have referred to point in one direction only — a direction that criminologists can see vividly even if thinkers from other disciplines cannot. It is this: that the lesson of Three Mile Island is that no nuclear reactor system is safe or can ever be made safe. Nuclear energy is an unacceptable facet of society and must at all costs be eliminated totally from society.

Australia and the Nuclear Fuel Cycle

Let me now summarize what I believe to be Australia's current involvement with the use of nuclear energy and the potential use of nuclear weapons. My political argument will be that, as a nation, we are uniquely well placed to renounce every aspect of the nuclear fuel cycle and that, in doing so, we would gain immense moral authority to influence the fate of the world. Australia can begin to nudge the nuclear debate back from the arid and inevitably fatal level of strategic considerations to the realm of morality. I say "inevitably fatal", because as criminologists we *know* that the ultimate deviance will occur if it can occur. It may happen because of the actions of a deviant person — for example, an unstable President if one may refer to Dr Kissinger's memoirs,[24] or a deranged general or a Kamikaze terrorist from a group which comes to possess such weapons.[25] It may occur because of unanticipated computer failures — as has almost happened several times in the last few years. But happen it will, despite all the subtleties of the Permissive Action Link and all the instant communication of the hotline and all the prayers of popes and prelates, for deviance is endemic to human affairs. People simply do not behave as, ideally, they should — whether from envy, vengefulness, incompetence, pride or thoughtlessness.

A strategy for nuclear disarmament must be found. Renunciation by a previously-committed stakeholder such as Australia could provide the moral stimulus to shift the nuclear debate into a different conceptual framework. As criminologists we should be asking ourselves — what experience and intellectual insights can we contribute to the argument for Australian renunciation of every part of the nuclear fuel cycle? In that context, let me now summarize what I believe to be Australia's involvement.

(a) *Mining*

Production continues at three uranium mines — Mary Kathleen, Ranger and Nabarlek. Proven deposits have been identified in numerous other parts of Australia. Development of these reserves has been delayed by world over-supply. Nevertheless, exploration for other economically recoverable deposits is continuing. At present Australia commands some 10% of the world uranium supply market.

(b) *Milling*

Uranium ore is treated chemically to turn it into uranium oxide or yellowcake. This process produces tailings — radioactive waste — which must be stored near the milling site.

(b) *Stockpiling*

Over-supply leads to excessive stockpiling, both of uranium ore and of yellowcake. For example, ore is stockpiled at the Ben Lomond Site (50% owned by Total Oil of France) and yellowcake at Mary Kathleen.

(d) *Conversion and enrichment*

Yellowcake must be converted into uranium hexafluoride before it can be enriched. Enrichment means boosting the proportion of fissile uranium-235 so that it is suitable for fissile reaction. A conversion plant could, in principle, be established without a twin enrichment plant. The notion of doing so — at Port Pirie in South Australia — has recently been under discussion[26]. However, the value added to the uranium by conversion is relatively insignificant, whilst the problems of safe transportation would be increased. Possibly on this account the South Australian Premier has invited a Japanese consortium to carry out a feasibility study with regard to establishing an enrichment plant also in that State[27]. He is hopeful that the completion of this study by mid-1982 will be followed by the establishment of such a plant by 1990.

(e) *Nuclear power plants*

The Western Australian Government has for many years toyed with the possibility of building a nuclear power plant. The New South Wales Opposition leader has recently committed himself to the view that nuclear power *must* be developed in that State by the year 2000[28]. There have been distinct hints that the State Electricity Commission of Victoria has been thinking in the same way[29]. The Australian Atomic Energy Commission is on record as anticipating that there will be at least 900 megawatts of nuclear power installed in Australia by the year 2000[30]. In a speech in New York in July 1981 the Prime Minister stated his Government's commitment to the development of nuclear power[31].

It can thus be seen that Australia, as well as facilitating the completion of the nuclear power cycle by others, is also intent on completing it within its own shores.

(f) *Production safety standards*

All of the foregoing processes possess tangible dangers over and above the fact that they are integral parts of the nuclear fuel cycle. Poisoning by radon gas, high incidence of leukemia, seepage of radioactive tailings into the water supply, genetic defects and so on are now well-documented phenomena associated with various stages of the nuclear fuel cycle.

To the extent that nuclear materials *can* be handled safely, regulation and supervision are less likely to be ineffective if carried out by a relatively disinterested party. Yet in the Razor Gang Report of April 1981 the Federal Government announced that it would be withdrawing from this area and leaving it to the States and the Northern Territory[32]. As in every other area of industrial safety, the temptation to cut corners is likely to be irresistible, particularly in a context of world over-supply where those Governments will be in competition with each other.

(g) *Safeguards*

This word describes the international system of treaties designed to ensure that nuclear material supplied for non-military purposes is not diverted to explosive uses. An integral part of this system is inspection by the International Atomic Energy Agency. In authorizing uranium exports in 1977, the Federal Government made much of its adherence to this system. Yet one can hardly quarrel with Pringle and Spigelman's view that it is "inherently defective"; the most cursory knowledge of, for example, the world arms trade or of the diversion of pharmaceutical drugs to unauthorized outlets makes this apparent enough. The Federal Government has evidently come to share this view. The logic and morality of such an insight is to cease exporting uranium altogether. But for the Government the only lesson to be learnt is a commercial one — to water down safeguards so that uranium sales may be maintained even to countries such as the Societ Union which refuse to accept IAEA inspection. Thus it is that, at this very moment, a shipment of Australian uranium is en route to Riga[33].

(h) *Hospitality for vessels and aircraft carrying nuclear arms*

Port and base facilities are now available in Australia for US vessels and aircraft carrying nuclear arms. The most notable of these are Cockburn Sound, in Western Australia, and Darwin.

(i) *Communications facilities for nuclear delivery systems*

None of us needs to be reminded of the significance of Pine Gap and North West Cape. If nuclear war comes, Australia will have been an accessory.

(j) *Tolerance for nuclear testing in the Pacific*

The 1979 South Pacific Forum toned down significantly a motion from Papua-New Guinea about the de-colonization of French Polynesia. The significance of this, in terms of the nuclear debate, is that it is likely that an independent Polynesia would be far less tolerant of French nuclear testing in the Pacific. Australia condoned the' watering-down of this motion[34].

The Dynamics of Renunciation

The foregoing summary is by no means exhaustive. It is sufficient, however, to demonstrate that Australia's present stake in nuclear affairs is very substantial. It is this very fact which would make renunciation so cogent from a moral point of view. Moreover, within the Southern Hemisphere the immediate political impact would be considerable[35]. It is just conceivable that Australia could influence in a unique way the slowly-awakening world debate about the likely extinction of mankind.

What chance is there of Australia taking such a stand? Obviously, none at all if we do not discuss the issues. But at least they are now being discussed, in all sorts of ways and from all sorts of perspective. For example, nuclear energy is under attack because of its enormous costs in the face of falling demand, rising fixed costs and massive, unanticipated de-commissioning costs[36]. The "energy-gap" prognostications which provided the launching-pad for the initial growth of nuclear energy are being assailed and shown to be false. The possibilities of "soft" energy technology are being explored[37]. The question of a Regional anti-Proliferation Treaty is being discussed, albeit from the point of view that continuing Australian participation in the nuclear fuel cycle is the appropriate starting-point[38]. All around the world, citizens are forming mass movements to express their desperate concern. What can criminologists — hitherto so silent — add to this debate, what can we do to enhance the climate for renunciation?

Everyone will, I hope, have his own insights and opinions. Let me tentatively offer two or three of my own, starting with the role of workers. Last year, when the ACTU decided to let the export of Mary Kathleen yellowcake proceed, the public was regaled with "Don't blame us; we have to get what work we can at times like these; we can't be expected to carry the can for everyone else" protestations. The worker as victim of the capitalist system — a variant of the soldier or the bureaucrat as the powerless recipient of superior orders. It didn't do for Adolf Eichmann, and it won't do I suggest for Australian workers involved in the uranium industry. They are exercising free will, and criminologists can help bring about a recognition of this.[39]

With regard to mine-owners, criminologists can mount a two-pronged attack. They can invoke and explain the significance of the massive literature about the activities of multi-national corporations so as to raise consciousness within the community of the fundamental conflict between multi-national and national interests and, by extension, between multi-national and universal interests. In addition, they can pursue vigorously the ever-present definitional debate — by what criteria does one judge whether conduct is deviant? Familiar arguments about the cultural and chronological relativity of deviance take on a special force in the context of the nuclear fuel cycle.

As for the US alliance, we all know that the last Australian Government which contemplated modifying the Pine Gap arrangements was ousted, probably after being destabilized by the CIA. Perhaps the present ALP leadership is mindful of this as it expresses support in principle for the full nuclear panoply of the US alliance with only minor reservations in the form of an Australian involvement in the passing of messages of military import[40]. Yet from a criminologists's point of view what stands out about the events of 1975 is surely that Mr Whitlam had failed to utilize effectively the power of office to define the debate which should have occurred. At no stage did he take the Australian public into his confidence about the US communications facilities in Australia; instead of labelling the American presence for what it is he allowed the battle to be fought within existing definitions. To compound matters, the ALP indulged in some quite unnecessary deviance of its own (the Khemlani affair), thus permitting the Whitlam Government to be effectively labelled as deviant by others. Of course, in one sense Whitlam was "more sinned against than sinning". But in the context of the nuclear debate the greatest sin of all is to botch an opportunity. Criminologists can help set the framework of the nuclear debate so that renunciation becomes not just politically feasible but also morally imperative. To quote Schell one last time: "As long as politics fails to take up the nuclear issue in a determined way, it lives closer than any other activity to the lie that we have all come to live — the pretence that life lived on top of a nuclear stockpile can last".[41]

Criminology in the Eighties

I started by saying that criminology is in danger of running into a dead end. Its non-contribution to the most important issue facing civilization is shocking. Does this mean that the only worthwhile criminologist is, in my view, a nuclear disarmer and the only responsible field of research the nuclear fuel cycle? The answer to this question is, of course, No. There are other matters of primary criminological concern — matters of almost equal importance if less urgency. They include: genetic engineering, environmental despoliation and over-population. Their common denominator is the fundamental threat they pose to the frame of human life.

Criminological attention should also be devoted to any subject-matter whose understanding is instrumental to these primary concerns. An unjust or repressive world, a world in which means come to dominate ends and form to overwhelm substance is a world less likely to survive for future generations. Thus racism, sexism, computerization, communications, monetary policy, work organisation and, generally, the relationship of the State to individuals are all proper concerns of instrumental criminology. So too is any aspect of social organization or conduct which tends to disable mankind from utilizing to the full his intellect and maturity in seeking to control fundamental threats to survival. However, the more these concerns manifest themselves at the micro-level, the more tenuous their instrumental value will be. Surely, sentencing patterns in magistrates' courts at Wagga Wagga, or recidivism rates amongst female juvenile offenders convicted of car-stealing in Whyalla, or police perceptions of porn-shop users at Wollongong, or unreported domestic violence in Woolloomooloo are simply not worth bothering about in the 1980s. We know already that the circle is round and the square has four sides. To

NUCLEAR ENERGY & THE DESTINY OF MANKIND   91

prove the criminological equivalent of this over and over again is a waste of time and talent. What might, perhaps, have been good stuff in the 40s and 50s is irresponsible self-indulgence in the 80s. There is no time left for mini-criminology.

Australian criminologists have the ability to set an agenda for the 80s, one whose principal item is to save mankind from extinction and to preserve the frame of life. This terrible challenge is before us; it is our responsibility to accept it.

ACKNOWLEDGMENT

The author wishes to thank Mrs Sally Williams for her assistance in research and Mr Bill Ford for his general advice and support.

NOTES

1 Other journals surveyed were the *Journal of Research in Crime and Delinquency*, the *Journal of Criminal Law and Criminology* and the *Australia and New Zealand* Journal of Criminology. The only article found on any aspect of nuclear energy was by Woods, GD (1975) "The Possible Criminal Misuse of Atomic or Biochemical Materials" 8 *ANZJ Crim* 113.
2 *The Ranger Uranium Environmental Inquiry, First Report* (1976), in particular chapters 12-16, Australian Government Publishing Service, Canberra.
3 My emphasis.
4 Pringle, P and Spigelman, J (1982). *The Nuclear Barons* pp 445-6. London, Michael Joseph.
5 This could hardly be better illustrated than by the following statement made by a high Reagan administration official, Mr T K Jones (Under Secretary of Defense for Strategic Theater Nuclear Forces): "Dig a hole, cover it with a couple of doors, and then throw three feet of dirt on top. Everyone's going to make it if there are enough shovels to go around". *Time Magazine*, 29 March 1982, p 13.
6 This view has recently been expressed by T Pipes, US National Security Council senior adviser on the Soviet Union and Eastern Europe, *Washington Post*, 5 April 1982. It seems symptomatic of the approach currently being taken in Washington.
7 See Nash, H T (1980). "The Bureaucratization of Homicide" in *Protest and Survive* (Eds E P Thompson and D Smith). London, Penguin.
8 *The New Yorker*, February 1, 8 and 15, 1982. These articles have subsequently been published as a book, *The Fate of the Earth*. New York, Knopf.
9 *The New Yorker*, 1 February 1982, p 56.
10 Ibid, p 61; 8 February 1982, p 60.
11 Ibid, 1 February 1982, p 71.
12 Ibid, p 113.
13 Pringle and Spigelman, pp 231-6.
14 *The New Yorker*, April 6 and 13, 1981.
15 April 6 1981, p 66.
16 Id.
17 Hirschorn, L (1980) "Work and Workers in Post-Industrial Settings: The Case of Nuclear Reactors" (Paper presented to the Meeting of the American Association for the Advancement of Science, San Francisco.)
18 Ibid, p 12.
19 Id.
20 Ibid, p 9.
21 Ibid, p 14.
22 Ford, April 6 1982, p 54.
23 *The West Australian*, 27 April 1982, quoting from the Chicago *Sun-Times*. See also *The Age*, 15 April 1982 p 7.
24 Kissinger (1982). *Years of Upheaval*. London, Weidenfeld & Nicholson.
25 See Woods, GD (1975) "The Possible Criminal Misuse of Atomic or Biochemical Materials" 8 *ANZJ Crim* 113.
26 Australian Atomic Energy Commission Report for 1981, pp 56-7.
27 Statement of 14 April 1982, made in Tokyo.
28 *The Australian*, 22 April 1982.
29 See Hansard (H or R) 11 March 1981, p 690.

30 Atomic Energy in Australia (July 1980), cited by Mr W Hayden in Hansard (H of R) 19 August 1981, p 523.
31 *Melbourne Age*, 9 July 1981.
32 Ministerial Statement, Review of Commonwealth Functions, 30 April 1981, p 26.
33 Milliken, *National Times*, 7-13 February 1982, pp 24-5.
34 Dalton, J (1981). *France in the South Pacific*, pp 6-7. Melbourne, Dyason House Papers, vol 8, No 1. No 1.
35 Antarctica is already a nuclear-free zone. Such a move would leave only Argentina and South Africa with a stake in the nuclear fuel cycle.
36 See, eg Falk, J (1981). "The Political Economy of the Nuclear Industry" *Journal of Australian Political Economy* 10: 47.
37 See, eg Nicholls, J and Bell, M (1977) "A Nuclear-Free World" in *Ground for Concern* (Ed M Elliott). Melbourne, Penguin.
38 Weltman, J J (1979) "Toward A Regional Anti-Proliferation Policy for Australia" Australian Outlook 33: 281.
39 See *The Australian*, 12 August 1981. The ALP leadership is thought to favour softening the anti-uranium platform of the party because it is feared its continuance might cost the party four seats at the next federal election: see Kitney, *National Times*, 13 December 1981, p 3. See also the *Australian Financial Review*, 11 December 1981, p 3 and the *Australian Financial Review*, 28 April 1982, p 2.
40 See the statement of Mr Lionel Bowen, *The Australian*, 27 April 1982. He considered Australia's interests in US utilization of North West Cape would be sufficiently protected if an Australian representative in Washington had access to American strategic policy relevant to the use of the Cape. Mr Hayden has hitherto considered that an Australian veto on the transmission of military messages through the Cape's facilities would be a requisite safeguard. Neither policy represents renunciation; one is condonation, the other a futile formality.
41 Schell J, *The New Yorker*, 8 February 1982, p 94.

[11]

A Criminology of the Nuclear State

David Kauzlarich,
St. Joseph's University

REFLEXIVE STATEMENT

The collapse of the Soviet Union and its satellites has not meant the end of the nuclear threat. Nuclear weapons and their corresponding policies continue to represent the greatest danger to the survival of the globe. As many activists against, and scholars of, state violence have suggested, one possible avenue toward the eradication of some injurious state policies is through the use of international law. While it is naive to believe that international law *per se* can provide the necessary coercive power to seriously reduce harmful state actions, there is evidence to suggest that these laws can help further the identification of some state practices as officially "criminal" thereby increasing the possibility that they might be subject to formal juridical attention and control. From a humanist perspective, it seems remiss not to consider the utility of international laws when considering state actions and policies in general, and a very serious error not to examine the vast amount of international law which holds direct relevance to the nuclear weapons challenge. This article reflects my concern with conjoining humanism and criminology, and is principally written to introduce the neglected association between international humanitarian laws and the weapons which most threaten human existence.

INTRODUCTION

> Investigators cannot be deterred in their study of state criminality by the lack or failure of the state to adjudicate itself or its agents as criminal. After all, just because it has been the case that states have chosen to ignore, dismiss, or down play their own criminality, it does not follow that we criminologists should do the same (Barak 1993, p. 211).

The criminological study of the state or of governments (see Friedrichs (1995); Henry (1991) for distinctions) has blossomed in recent years. With the publication of Gregg Barak's (1991) *Crimes by the Capitalist State*, Ken Tunnell's (1993) *Political Crime in Contemporary America*, and Jeffrey Ian Ross' (1995) *Controlling State Crime*, the *modern* framework for the study of crimes by institutions occupied by governmental elites has been clearly

My thanks to Ron Kramer, Ray Michalowski, Susan Caringella-MacDonald, and Helenan Robin for their helpful comments on earlier drafts of this paper.

38 *Humanity & Society, Volume 19, Number 3, August, 1995*

established, at least for the critical criminological community. This is not to say that governmental malfeasance was ignored prior to the 1990's, or that criminologists as a whole believe the state can be studied as a criminal agent. It is to say, however, that the recent surge of scholarship in this area is quite encouraging, and that it has become more difficult than ever for criminologists to be nescient of its disciplinary significance.

Scholars of governmental crime have begun exploring the value of international law in the incrimination of harmful, or potentially harmful, actions of the state (e.g. Barak 1990, 1991; Boyle 1989, 1984; Dieterich 1986; Falk 1989; Frappier 1984; Galliher 1989; Hazlehurst 1991; Kauzlarich, Kramer and Smith 1992; Molina 1995; Ross 1995; Yarnold 1995; Zilinskas 1995). While there is no definitional consensus, those working in the area recognize that these various international conventions, rulings, and covenants have real substance and relevance to the criminological study of the state. Indeed, employing both international law and the notion that governments can act as criminal agents expands conceptions of the epidemiology of crime in the sense that some behaviors commonly not considered criminal may in fact be legally prohibited.

As the conceptual frameworks march on, there is also a noticeable surge in research into the behavioral and phenomenological nature of governmental crime. However, one type of injurious state policy which has been largely ignored by criminologists is the threat of nuclear war. Common sense tells us that if anything should be considered criminal, it is the conspiracy to use and the actual use of weapons which can literally annihilate every living thing several hundred times over. What is not common sense, though, is that there are several international laws which clearly outlaw the threat to use and actual use of these weapons of mass destruction.

It is the purpose of this paper to continue the discourse on governmental crime by offering a legal framework for the incrimination of United States nuclear weapons policy. In doing so, it draws attention to the vast amount of scholarly work in the legal community on the nuclear weapons issue, as well as the utility of what are commonly known in the political and military science communities as the laws of war, international principles which have received less criminological recognition than transnational human and civil rights law. Given that many criminologists are probably unfamiliar with these laws, and that the criminological community has not adequately addressed the use and actual use of nuclear weapons, this paper focuses on the international legal *prohibitions and frameworks* which are particularly relevant to placing nuclear weapons and their corresponding policies within a criminological context. Therefore, the important questions of enforcement, adjudication, and the etiology of actions which violate these laws are not explored. It is of course recognized that the construction, violation, and control of nuclear crimes in particular, and governmental crime in general, are extremely important to visit if empirical and theoretical work on the crimes of the state is to advance. But in order to move to questions of control and the etiology of nuclear crimes, a definitional and epistemological framework for the incrimination of nuclear weapons must first be established. To this end, the paper begins with a brief discussion of definitional and typological questions related to governmental criminality. The remaining sections are devoted to specifying the international legal prohibitions and outright criminality of many of the United States' nuclear weapons policies.

A DEFINITION AND TYPOLOGY OF GOVERNMENTAL CRIME

Threats to use and the actual use of nuclear weapons are examples of governmental crime, envisioned here as *an illegal or socially injurious act of omission or commission by an individual or group of individuals in an institution of legitimate governance which is executed for the consummation of the operational goals of that institution of governance.* This definition, like that of Barak (1991), Henry (1991) and Clinard and Quinney's (1973) notion of corporate crime, requires that governmental crime be viewed in institutional or structural terms, rather than on an individual level of analysis. Instead of seeing governmental crime's origins in personal desires for self-gratification or profit, the phenomenon is conceptualized here as a product of organizational pressures for the achievement of some governmental goal. This position is taken because even a cursory glance at the behavioral qualities of the instances in which nuclear weapons have been threatened leads one to the conclusion that to reduce these actions to individual inclinations is to ignore many of the historical, structural, and social antecedents which undoubtedly play roles in the genesis of the behaviors.

The definition also requires that for any (in)action to be labeled governmental crime, there must be an identifiable, be it direct or indirect, injury to human beings or the natural environment. Acts which are legally defined as criminal and which are contrary to the right of self-determination and the realization of peaceful existence, along with other humanist conceptions of human and peoples' rights (McCaughan 1989), are therefore appropriate subjects of study under this conceptualization. Employing only a legalistic definition of crime has definite limitations, as discussed repeatedly in criminological debates over the appropriate definition of crime (Bohm 1993; Kramer 1982; Schwendingers 1970; Sutherland 1945; Tifft and Sullivan 1980). And as Barak (1991) and others have pointed out, these limitations become especially noticeable and particularly acute when one desires to study the criminality of a state, the institution which creates and enforces law. While space limitations preclude a thorough examination of these important definitional questions, it is quite true that when state definitions of crime are accepted uncritically, criminologists lose a degree of autonomy, perhaps become indirect or ancillary agents of the state, and overlook the political nature of law (Caulfield and Wonders 1993; Quinney 1977; Schwendingers 1970; Sellin 1938). But, of course, this does not mean that criminologists, critical or otherwise, should prohibit themselves from employing law, be it international or domestic. Indeed, an important point here, as outlined by the Schwendingers (1977) and others, is that criminologists acknowledge the *limitations* of these legal definitions, and not hastily, to be

40   *Humanity & Society, Volume 19, Number 3, August, 1995*

pedestrian, "throw the baby out with the bath-water". All law is political, just as conservative, quasi-legalistic, and radical interpretations of the proper subject of the criminological enterprise. If we were to eschew things because they are political, we would keep nothing, including alternative definitions of crime.

There is a practical consideration behind using law whenever possible in the definition and study of governmental crime – the prospect for legitimacy. Of the many reasons social harms definitions of crime have been rejected by traditional criminologists, the most prominent has been the perceived subjectivity and politicality of the approach. But a definitional framework which includes actual law, (political definitions with the added power of legitimacy), holds substantially more affinity with the traditional etiological concern of criminology – transgressions of law (Kauzlarich 1994). Thus, the method of incriminating the harmful actions of governments through international law not only advances a humanist perspective on crime and criminality, as outlined later, but is also more likely to gain acceptance in wider audiences, as evidenced by the World Health Organization's (WHO) recent request to the International Court of Justice (ICJ) to make an advisory judgment on the legal status of nuclear weapons. As Kuhn (1962) brilliantly discovered, a paradigmatic change may have less to do with the intrinsic validity of a theoretical movement than the political legitimacy of the theory. It is therefore reasonable to in part justify a more legalistic approach on the hypothesis that there is a substantially larger opportunity for this conceptualization to become assimilated into the major currents of the discipline of criminology. Additionally, the use of law in labeling an action criminal is likely to be perceived by the general public as having more legitimacy than social harms approaches. This may become important if we are interested in beginning to construct possible avenues toward *newsmaking criminology*, as outlined by Barak (1994). While it is quite clear that the organized conspiracy to use and to threaten to use omnicidal weapons can be analyzed from a social harms or human rights definition of crime, there are also *many* legal frameworks which provide courses of incrimination. These international prohibitions, generically known as the laws of war, have been overlooked by many criminologists, and appear to provide fruitful avenues for advancing a peacemaking criminology of nuclear weapons (Pepinsky and Quinney 1991).

The definition proposed here necessarily involves at least four general kinds of governmental criminality. While there have been several attempts to provide substantive typologies of white collar crime (e.g. Beirne and Messerschmidt 1995; Coleman 1994; Friedrichs 1992, 1992a, 1995; Geis and Meier 1977; Green 1990; Michalowski 1985; Quinney 1977), it might be useful to classify governmental transgressions of law spatially.

Domestic-International Governmental Crime (DIGC)

Criminal acts by governments that occur within the state's geographic jurisdiction which run contrary to the state's obligation under international law.

Examples of such actions would be transgressions of the International Covenant on Civil and Political Rights, of the International Convention on the Elimination of All Forms of Racial Discrimination, and of the Convention on the Political Rights of Women.

International-International Governmental Crime (IIGC)

Criminal acts by governments which occur outside the state's geographic jurisdiction in violation of international law. Examples include violations of the Genocide Convention, the Geneva Conventions, and the Nuclear Non-Proliferation Treaty.

Domestic-Domestic Governmental Crime (DDGC)

Criminal acts which occur within the state's geographical jurisdiction in violation of the criminal or regulatory code of that state. Examples include police violations of procedural and civil law and violations of a state's constitution.

International-Domestic Governmental Crime (IDGC)

Criminal conduct by a government abroad in violation of its own criminal or regulatory code. Most illustrative of this phenomenon is the United States Iran-Contra incident.

This typology, while admittedly elementary, has value because it allows us to think more freely about, and to borrow less sparingly from, the varied international and domestic laws which could be legitimately employed as an epistemological framework for criminology. The most suitable mechanisms for the scholarly classification of illegal governmental actions under international law (types DIGC and IIGC), are (a) those laws which a government has accepted through ratification, the standard used by traditional scholars of international law, and (b) customary international law, which although sometimes uncodified, serves as a legal standard for state behavior (Bledsoe and Boczek 1987; Builder and Graubard 1982). While this manner of defining crime has limitations in its applicability to many harmful activities of governments, it is intended as an *alternative* or complimentary conceptualization, rather than as a substitution for sociological, traditional-legal, or critical definitions of crime. However, as we will see below, relatively few limitations are engendered by using international law to place nuclear weapons policies within a defensible criminological framework.

THE ILLEGALITY OF NUCLEAR WEAPONS

The overwhelming normative consensus now operative in international society would legally condemn all contemplated roles for nuclear weapons ... not even a retaliatory use of nuclear weapons could be easily reconciled with most interpretations of the laws of war (Falk 1983, p. 527).

42   *Humanity & Society, Volume 19, Number 3, August, 1995*

Contrary to popular conceptions, every U. S. presidential administration from Truman to Clinton has in one form or another threatened an enemy state with atomic or nuclear weapons (Blechman and Kaplan 1978; Ellsburg 1981; Lifton and Falk 1991). Some of these threats were tacit (Truman's against Iran in 1946; Eisenhower's 1954 offer to the French in order to maintain control of Indochina; Kennedy's against the Soviet Union at numerous points in his administration), while others have been quite conspicuous, especially Eisenhower's 1953 threat against North Korea and China, and Nixon's 1969 threats against North Vietnam and China. And as recently as December, 1994, the popular press (NBC News, 1994) reported that high-level U.S. Department of Defense officials remarked that an Iraqi use of biological weapons against its enemies in the Middle East would result in a U.S. nuclear response. Whether U.S. officials were sincere in threatening a nuclear rejoinder, one must conclude that these weapons continue to be an important component of international-military policy, and furthermore, that the nuclear threat is very much alive, even with the end of the Cold War.

History of the Legal Debate

The status of nuclear weapons under international law has received substantially more attention in the scholarly legal community than in criminology. Most legal scholars interested in the issue have approached the question by reference to the laws of war, which are considered legally binding principles governments are obliged to conform to both in times of war and in their general military planning. These laws are essentially a conglomeration of principles based on the general postulate that humanity and proportionality are keys to protecting nonbelligerents in times of international conflict. They are also "generally aimed at protecting individuals and objects in armed conflicts against the effects and horrors of war" (Mohr 1988, p. 83). There are five fundamental principles of the laws of war:

(1) That in any armed conflict the right of the parties to choose methods of warfare is not unlimited;
(2) That only as much force may be used as is required to overpower the enemy;
(3) That superfluous injury and unnecessary suffering must be avoided;
(4) That a certain amount of chivalry, fairness, and respect should prevail even in the relations between hostile parties; and
(5) That the use of weapons or tactics that cause indiscriminate harm as between combatants and noncombatants is prohibited (Bledsoe and Boczek 1987; Lawyers Committee on Nuclear Policy 1990).

The laws of war are found in international agreements, treaties, and various customary laws. They are neither changed nor destroyed on any of the following bases:

(1) That the law is alleged to be vague or uncertain;

(2) That military necessity makes it impossible to comply with the law;

(3) That the opposing state is guilty of the same or other violations of the law; and

(4) That the law has been so widely violated that it is no longer binding (Miller 1975).

Arguments on both sides of the legal status of nuclear weapons hinge on interpretations of the laws of war. Let us first discuss the claim that use and threat to use nuclear weapons are legal under international law. It must be remembered, however, that most legal scholars agree that most uses and threats to use nuclear weapons do indeed violate many international laws. Nevertheless, it is important to review the arguments to the contrary, most of which were published between 1945 and 1960. The three main theses of such a position are: (1) There is insufficient scientific evidence on the effects of nuclear weapons, (2) The laws of war have become impotent with the emergence of nuclear weapons, and (3) There is no express prohibition of nuclear weapons.

The first argument, that insufficient scientific evidence exists to reasonably calculate the effects of an nuclear bombing, is of course archaic. When Lauterpacht (1952), Stone (1954), Tucker (1950) offered this contention, there indeed may have been limited information, especially to the general public, on the effects of nuclear weapons. The only available evidence at the time these scholars wrote was the United States bombings of Hiroshima and Nagasaki, and this information was not readily attainable in the 1950's. Given that the primitive atomic bombs dropped on the country of Japan did not result in wholesale deaths of the entire Japanese citizenry, and that some individuals indeed survived these bombings, these scholars determined that the laws of war are not necessarily broken by the use of nuclear weapons.

This argument is no longer employed because in the contemporary period it makes little sense to suggest that we have no scientific understanding of the effects of nuclear weapons. Many studies have established the general contours of the destruction which would be caused by even a moderate use of nuclear weapons (see Office of Technology Assessment 1979; McNaught 1984; Perdue 1989; United Nations 1980, 1990; World Health Organization 1987). Although it seems unnecessary to examine all the documented evidence on the power of these weapons, Perdue (1989, p. 73), after reviewing the scientific evidence, concluded the following:

In the event of a major exchange, estimates of quick death range from several hundred million people to the World Health Organization's figure of 1.1 billion people. The number of critically injured who would require available health care would perhaps approach another 1 billion persons. Given such an event, the basic services and organizations of society would collapse. Medical care, water, electricity, fuel transportation, communication, food supplies, sanitation, and civil services would all be devastated.

44   *Humanity & Society, Volume 19, Number 3, August, 1995*

The bombings of Hiroshima resulted in 130,000 Japanese deaths within three minutes of the detonation of the bomb; 70,000 died later as a result of exposure to radiation (Weiner 1990). Today, the total stockpile of nuclear weapons exceeds the explosive power of the Hiroshima bombing by over 3 million. Given these disturbing facts, most find it difficult to accept the argument that the use of and threat to use nuclear weapons would be lawful because of an inadequate understanding of the results of a nuclear exchange.

The second defense of the legality of nuclear weapons is that the laws of war have become obsolete in the nuclear age. Claimed by such scholars as Stowell (1945), Thomas (1946), Borchard (1946), and Baxter (1953), the idea here is that many of the laws of war were written prior to the genesis of the atomic weapon, and thus are not subject to the laws regulating contemporary governmental military planning. While it is undoubtedly true that some of the principles of the laws of war were penned prior to the nuclear age, these laws have been consistently interpreted by both scholars and the courts as attempts to control any weapon or any method of warfare. In like manner one need only note that while the U.S. Constitution's framers were not cognizant of all the potential behaviors to consider when creating the Bill of Rights, the basic principles of the Constitution are continually used to judge the lawfulness of actions (Meyrowitz 1990). Additionally, since international laws not concerning the laws of war have been interpreted as binding on new technological and political developments, so too do the laws of war hold jurisdiction over nuclear weapons (Meyrowitz 1990). One must also consider that a significant number of the conventional laws of war have been developed in the age of the nuclear weapon, such as the Genocide Convention and the Geneva Conventions.

The third most common position in defense of the legality of nuclear weapons is that there exists no express prohibition of nuclear weapons in the body of international law. Scholars such as O'Brien (1961) and Schwartzenberger (1958) contend that since there is no treaty, convention, or other international agreement which specifically prohibits the threat to use and actual use of nuclear weapons, one must conclude that these weapons and corresponding policies are lawful. Although at first thought this argument seems reasonable, it becomes less valid when one considers that the entire history of domestic, municipal, and international law is based on precedent setting in which new behaviors are constantly being weighed against existing principles of law. International courts, as we will see in the next section, have consistently allowed the interpretation of behaviors not explicitly prohibited by law to be subject to existing law.

By analogy, imagine how a court or jury would respond to a claim by a defendant that s/he cannot be accused of murder because they killed someone with a weapon not specifically prohibited by law. Thus, anyone who purposefully kills another by using, for example, computer disks to bludgeon, video cassette tape to strangle, or gardening shears to stab, would under this logic be inculpable because the law does not specifically stipulate "computer disks", "video cassette tape", or "gardening shears" as methods of killing. Much more seriously, imagine a Nazi commander defending him or herself on the grounds that the manners of execution employed toward Jews were not specifically prohibited by law, and therefore were legal. The argument that nuclear weapons are legal because they are not specifically mentioned in the laws of war is simply untenable.

The three arguments used to justify the legality of nuclear weapons appear to have little support in the academic legal community. They have been reviewed and briefly critiqued here in order to demonstrate that the legal status of nuclear weapons under international law is neither a new nor an ignored issue in the legal community. The next two sections are devoted to an explication of the specific mechanisms by which U.S. nuclear weapons policies may be classified as criminal under international law.

Conventional International Law

The most unquestionable framework by which to adjudicate the illegality of U.S. nuclear weapons policies is by reference to conventions which have been signed and ratified by the state. By accepting the provisions of a treaty or convention, a state is obligated to comply with both its spirit and specific prohibitions. Three legally binding frameworks have been offered as acceptable frameworks for the incrimination of nuclear weapons and conventional nuclear weapons policy (see Bilder 1984; Boyle 1987; Falk 1983; Feinrider 1982; Fujita 1982; Lawyers Committee on Nuclear Policy 1990; Meyrowitz 1981, 1990; Miller and Feinrider 1984; Mohr 1988; Vickman 1988; Weston 1983, 1983a):

- The 1925 Geneva Protocol for the Prohibition of the Use in War of Asphyxiating, Poisonous, or Other Gases, and of Bacteriological Methods of Warfare (the 1925 Geneva Gas Protocol);
- The 1948 United Nations Convention on the Prevention and Punishment of the Crime of Genocide (the 1948 Genocide Convention) and;
- The 1949 Geneva Conventions (I-IV).

Table 1 documents the year each of these agreements entered into force, the dates on which the United States became legally obligated to comply with these agreements, and the relevant substantive prohibitions found within these agreements. These conventions have been interpreted by many legal scholars as constituting the specific prohibitions which not only outlaw threats and uses of nuclear weapons, but the existence of nuclear weapons per se. (see Lawyers Committee on Nuclear Policy 1990; Meyrowitz 1990; Mohr 1988; Vickman 1988; Weston 1983). Because nuclear weapons are analogous to poisonous gas (the Geneva Gas Protocol), are capable of deleting an entire ethnic or racial group (the Genocide Convention), and would wreak violent death and mutilation (the Geneva Conventions) it is clear that the actual use of these weapons of mass destruction would violate legally binding international laws.

46   *Humanity & Society, Volume 19, Number 3, August, 1995*

Table 1:   **Treaties and Conventions Applicable In Determining the Illegality of
U.S. Nuclear Weapons Policy**

1925	Geneva Gas Protocol
Entered Into Force	February 8, 1928
United States ratified	April 10, 1975
Relevant prohibitions	The use of asphyxiating, poisonous, or other gases, and all analogous liquid materials or devices.
1948	Genocide Convention
Entered Into Force	January 12, 1951
United States ratified	October 14, 1988
Relevant prohibitions	Conspiracy, attempt, complicity, incitement, and actual execution of genocide.
1949	Geneva Conventions (I-IV)
Entered Into Force	October 21, 1950
United States ratified	August 12, 1955
Relevant prohibitions	Violence to life and person, mutilation, cruel treatment and torture of combatants and civilians.

Customary International Law

Despite the importance of international agreements in the contemporary development of the law, any work concerning the laws of war which is limited to international agreements runs the risk of distorting not only the form but also the substance of the law. The codification of rules into particular agreements which began to occur in the second half of the nineteenth century did not displace customary law. (Roberts and Guelff 1982, p. 4)

There are numerous sources of customary international law to draw upon in the incrimination of a state's use of nuclear weapons. The classic statement of the role of customary law is found in the famous Martens Clause of the 1907 Hague Convention IV:

Until a more complete code of the laws of war has been issued, the High Contracting Parties deem it expedient to declare that, in cases not included in the Regulations adopted by them, the inhabitants and belligerents remain under the protection of the rule of the principles of law of nations, as they result from the usages established among civilized peoples, from the laws of humanity, and the dictates of the public conscience. (quoted in Roberts and Guelff 1982, p. 45)

And as stated by the Nuremberg Tribunal in their deliberations over the genocidal practices of the Nazis:

The law of war is to be found not only in treaties, but in the customs and practices of states which gradually obtained universal recognition, and from the general principles of justice applied by jurists and practiced by military courts. The law is not static but by continual adaptation follows the needs of a changing world. (quoted in Roberts and Guelff 1982, p. 41)

Given these guidelines set by jurists in prominent international conclaves, it is clear that for some state action to be considered criminal under international law, no specifically codified law need be broken. State actions can be viewed as lawful or unlawful to the degree that they violate basic codes of behavior as established and practiced by international audiences. Therefore, the argument that the use of nuclear weapons would be lawful given the absence of an express prohibition is sophistical. As Meyrowitz (1990, p. 39) aptly asserts:

> The legality of nuclear weapons cannot simply be judged by the existence or the lack of existence of a treaty rule specifically prohibiting or restricting their use. Traditionally, legal rules, both domestic and international, have been interpreted to encompass matters not specifically mentioned or even contemplated by the drafters of those legal declarations. As a result, the legal status of nuclear weapons must be judged in light of the varied sources of international law ...

Similarly, a Japanese federal court ruled in *Shimoda et al.* v. *the State of Japan* (1963):

> It can naturally be assumed that the use of a new weapon is legal as long as international law does not prohibit it. However, the prohibition in this context is to be understood to include not only the case where there is an express rule of direct prohibition, but also the case where the prohibition can be implied from the interpretation and application by analogy of existing rules of international law (customary and treaties). Further, the prohibition must be understood also to include new cases where, in light of the principles of international law which are at the basis of these rules of international law, the use of new weapons is deemed contrary to these principles, for there is no reason why the interpretation of rules of international law should be limited to literal interpretation, any more than the interpretation of rules of municipal law (quoted in Friedman 1972, p. 1690).

What then are the principles of customary law which hold relevance to the nuclear weapons challenge? The first is that combatants and noncombatants are protected from unnecessary and aggravated suffering. First articulated in the 1907 Hague Conventions, this principle is perhaps the most accepted limitation on states involved in military hostilities (Bailey 1972; Miller 1975; Singh and McWhinney 1989; Weston 1983). The second principle of customary law relevant to the nuclear weapons challenge, also grounded in the Hague Conventions, is that the means of injuring an enemy are not unlimited and that at all times distinction must be made between combatants and civilians. Indicating the profound global support for the relevance of these principles was the unanimously passed December 16, 1965 U.N. General Assembly Resolution 2444 (XXIII) which "underscored the need to apply humanitarian principles to armed conflicts" (Meyrowitz 1990, p. 17).

Additionally, many states have incorporated these principles into their military manuals, a clear indication of acceptance. As one example, the 1956

48   *Humanity & Society, Volume 19, Number 3, August, 1995*

Field Manual published by the U.S. government contains the following provisions (quoted in Singh and McWhinney 1989, p. 55):

2 Purposes of the Law of War: the conduct of armed hostilities on land is regulated by the law of land warfare which is both written and unwritten. It is inspired by the desire to diminish the evils of war by:

a Protecting both combatants and noncombatants from unnecessary suffering.

b Safeguarding certain fundamental rights of persons who fall into the hands of the enemy, particularly prisoners of war, the wounded, the sick, and civilians.

3 Basic Principles

a Prohibitory Effect: The law of war places limits on the exercise of a belligerent's power in the interests mentioned in paragraph 2 and requires that belligerents refrain from employing any kind or degree of violence which is not actually necessary for military purposes and that they conduct hostilities with regard for the principles and purposes of humanity and chivalry.

b Force of Customary Law: The unwritten or customary law of war is binding on all nations.

The U.S. Department of Defense's official field manual also addresses the importance of the laws of armed conflict:

All action of the Department of Defense with respect to the acquisition and procurement of weapons, and their intended use in armed conflict, shall be consistent with the obligations assumed by the United States Government under all applicable treaties, with customary international law, and in particular, with the laws of war (quoted in Falk 1983, p. 526).

Similarly the British Manual of Military Law sets the same limitations on its citizens in recognizing the "principle of humanity which says that all kinds and degrees of violence as are not necessary for the purposes of war are not permitted" (quoted in Singh and McWhinney 1989, p. 56).

Customary law, then, has much influence in prescribing the manner in which states may conduct war. To further buttress the relevance of customary law to the nuclear weapons question, a number of international agreements and United Nations declarations categorically denounce the use and threat of nuclear weapons. The most important of these declarations was the United Nations General Assembly resolution 1653 (XVI) adopted by a vote of 55 to 20 on November 24, 1961. The resolution demonstrates the legal and moral sentiment of the majority of states on nuclear weapons (quoted in Meyrowitz 1990, p. 26):

The use of nuclear and thermonuclear weapons is contrary to the spirit, letter, and aims of the United Nations and, as such, is a direct violation of the Charter.

Any State using nuclear and thermo-nuclear weapons is to be considered as violating the Charter of the United Nations, as acting contrary to the laws of humanity and as committing a crime against mankind and civilization. The use of nuclear and thermo-nuclear weapons would exceed the scope of war and cause indiscriminate suffering and destruction to mankind and civilization ...

Other resolutions of the U.N. General Assembly demonstrate the international community's opposition to nuclear weapons, and thus could be considered a source of customary international law (Meyrowitz 1990; Riggs and Plano 1988). Of particular importance is Resolution 808 (IX) which on November 4, 1954 with a vote of 57 to 1 called for "The total prohibition of the use and manufacture of nuclear weapons and weapons of mass destruction".

While U.N. General Assembly resolutions normally do not have the force of law in a strict sense, they may have legal force "if they are regarded as statements of customary international law or authoritative interpretations of the U.N. Charter" (Riggs and Plano 1988, p. 23). The various U.N. General Assembly resolutions dealing with nuclear weapons outlined above are thus satisfactory frameworks for prohibiting the actual use of nuclear weapons. Because many of these resolutions have been overwhelmingly passed by the international community, have been based on interpretations of customary international law, and have made explicit reference to the laws of humanity and the United Nations Charter, the only reasonable conclusion is that the use of nuclear weapons would transgress international law. Further buttressing this contention is the previously mentioned case of *Shimoda et al.* v. *the State of Japan* (1963), which is the only instance of court action even remotely concerned with legality of the use of nuclear weapons.

In a class action suit, family members and some actual victims of the United States' bombing of Hiroshima and Nagasaki filed a grievance in Japanese federal court seeking damages for injuries sustained from the bombardment. The judges based their analysis on the lawfulness of the bombings, not of nuclear weapons *per se*. Nevertheless the court ruled that the U.S. bombing indeed constituted a violation of international law based on both customary and legally binding treaties:

It is proper to conclude that the aerial bombardment with an atomic bomb of both Hiroshima and Nagasaki was an illegal act of hostilities under international law as it existed at the time, as an indiscriminate bombardment of undefended cities (section 8).

The atomic bombing of both Hiroshima and Nagasaki is believed to be contrary to the principle of international law prohibiting means of injuring

50   *Humanity & Society, Volume 19, Number 3, August, 1995*

the enemy which cause unnecessary suffering or are inhumane (section 11).
(quoted in Friedman 1972, p. 1694):

And in relevance to United States law the court ruled:

> With regard to the United States, it is known that treaties are the supreme
> law of the land in accordance with article 6, paragraph 2, of the
> Constitution of the United States, and that customary international law
> is also part of the law of the land. Such being the case, it would seem
> to be a fair assumption that an act contrary to international law
> constitutes an unlawful act in the municipal law of the United States
> (section 2).

The *Shimoda* case, as a legitimate legal decision, lends strong support to the
contention that the use of nuclear weapons violates several existing international laws.

Illegality of the Threat to Use Nuclear Weapons

Perhaps most germane in determining the legality of the threat to use nuclear
weapons are the principles found in the United Nations Charter. The primary
purpose of the U.N. Charter was to render the use of force between states
unlawful and to end the scourge of war. (Henkin 1991; Swing 1991). According to Henkin (1991, p. 38), the Charter "remains the authoritative statement of
the law on the use of force (and) acts as a principal norm of international law".
The Charter "constitutes basic rules of international conduct that all member
states are ostensibly committed to observe" (Riggs and Plano 1988, p. 24). The
United States has been a member of the U.N. since 1945, the year the
organization was created.

Chapter One, Article One of the U.N. Charter states that the purpose of the
United Nations is:

> To maintain international peace and security, and to that end: to take
> effective collective measures for the prevention and removal of threats to the
> peace ... and to bring about by peaceful means, and in conformity with the
> principles of justice and international law, adjustment or settlement of
> international disputes or situations which might lead to a breach of the peace.
> (quoted in Riggs and Plano 1988, p. 367).

Moreover, Article Two of Chapter One (4) states that

> All members shall refrain from the *threat* or use of force against the
> territorial integrity or political independence of any state, or in any state
> in which the United Nations is taking preventive or enforcement action.
> (quoted in Riggs and Plano 1988, p. 368) (emphasis added.)

The only exception to the prohibition of Article 2(4) on the threat to use force
is found in Article 51 of the Charter:

> Nothing in the present Charter shall impair the inherent right of individual or collective self-defence if an armed attack occurs against a Member of the United Nations, until the Security Council has taken measures necessary to maintain international peace and security. (quoted in Riggs and Plano 1988, p. 370).

The intention of this article is simply to allow a state under attack to defend itself. Importantly, however, the right to defend is limited so that this right is only absolute until the Security Council provides an international plan of action to halt hostilities. Thus, the Security Council ultimately retains the authority to enact responses to an armed invasion.

The specific legal meaning of the Article 51 exception to Article 2(4) has been defined in only one case: *Nicaragua v. The United States* (1986). Here the International Court of Justice (ICJ) ruled that Article 51 applies only when a state has been subjected to an armed attack. The Court ruled:

> States do not have a right of collective armed response to acts which do not constitute an armed attack. If no armed attack occurred, collective self defense is unlawful, even if carried on in strict compliance with the canons of necessity and proportionality (paragraph 237).

The conclusion is unavoidable, then, that when a country threatens or actually uses force against another territory when it itself has not been attacked, an illegal act has occurred (see Boyle 1991; Nuremberg Campaign 1990). Since the occasions in which the United States has threatened to use nuclear weapons have not occurred in response to an armed invasion of the U.S. homeland, the instances in which the U.S. has threatened to use atomic or nuclear must be deemed unlawful. While it may be true that some U.S. treaty obligations treat the invasion of a U.S. ally as an invasion of the U.S. homeland, nuclear weapons threats are still illegal because of their violation of the principles of proportionality and necessity.

Another framework by which to judge the lawfulness of the threat to use nuclear weapons is by reference to the 1945-46 Nuremberg Principles. These principles of international law originated from the Allied prosecution of Nazi war criminals, and are considered legally binding rules of conduct upon all states (Baudot 1977). Table 2 provides a reproduction of the relevant prohibitions created at the Nuremberg Trials.

What is unusual about these prohibitions is the outlawing of not only inhumane behaviors by belligerents at war, but also the significant amount of attention paid to the crimes of conspiracy, planning, and threatening to commit the crimes of murder and other inhumane acts. Moreover, the tribunal convicted many institutions and organizations (not only individuals) such as the German gestapo of conspiracy to violate the principles of humanity and peace (Friedman 1972).

While the magnitude of destruction and murder committed by the Nazis dwarfs the harm that nuclear weapons have been responsible for up to the

Table 2: Substantive Prohibitions Found in the Nuremberg Charter

The following acts, or any of them, are crimes coming within the jurisdiction of the Tribunal for which their shall be individual responsibility.

a   Crimes against Peace: namely, planning, preparation, initiation, or waging of a war of aggression, or a war in violation of international treaties, agreements, or assurances, or participation in a common plan or conspiracy for the accomplishment of any of the foregoing:

b   War Crimes: namely, violations of the laws or customs of war. Such violations shall include, but not be limited to, murder, ill-treatment, or deportation to slave labor or for any other purpose of civilian population of or in occupied territory, murder, or ill-treatment of prisoners of war or persons on seas, killing of hostages, plunder of public or private property, wanton destruction of cities, towns or villages, or devastation not justified by military necessity.

c   Crimes against Humanity: namely, murder, extermination, enslavement, deportation, and other inhumane acts committed against any civilian population, before or during war, or prosecutions on political, racial or religious grounds in execution of or in connection with any crime within the jurisdiction of the Tribunal, whether or not in violation of the domestic law of the country where perpetrated.

SOURCE: Adapted from Roberts and Guelff, 1982.

contemporary period, this does not mean that the basic prohibitions and principles of the Nuremberg Charter are inapplicable to the nuclear question. Since the use of nuclear weapons is a violation of international law (because of their disproportionality and unpredictability), the planning and threat to use these weapons must also be criminal. The legal analogy drawn is this: Much like a Nazi commander's preparation and threat to exterminate Jews and other ethnic groups, the strategies of nuclear deterrence and mutual assured destruction constitute preparation, planning, and threats to use weapons which, if employed in time of war, would clearly violate extant international law. Since the case of the Nazi preparations to commit unquestionably illegal actions is conceptually similar to the planning and threatening of committing unquestionably illegal acts by the governments of the U.S. with nuclear weapons, there seems little question that threatening the use of nuclear weapons is criminal under the legally binding principles of the Nuremberg Charter. As Falk (1983, p. 528) states:

> To the extent existing doctrines and plans rest on a conception of deterrence based on threats to civilian non-combatants and non-military objectives, these (threats) would be illegal under even the narrowest definition of the applicability of international law.

CONCLUSION

The end of the Cold War has not meant the end of the nuclear threat. Despite the clear illegality of the use and threat to use nuclear weapons, these instruments of destruction which are arguably criminal *per se*, continue to enjoy prominence, popularity, and political utility in international relations.

Though a number of treaties have been enacted to control the testing, experimentation, and transfer of military uses of nuclear energy, it is difficult to envision the owners of these weapons discontinuing their organized criminal activity and beginning to comply with applicable international laws. Of course, United States defiance of international legal standards is not limited to the laws of war. Its evasion of criminal labels while tacitly and overtly violating human and civil rights both domestically and abroad further buttresses a point made by many criminologists: Even if it is clear that some governmental behaviors are criminal, the enforcement and application of the law is a highly political process in which those states with the most power will ignore their own or their allies' criminality, and reserve criminal labels for their political and economic enemies. In the case of nuclear weapons policy, this becomes abundantly clear given that the most powerful organ of the United Nations, the Security Council, is largely controlled by those states who possess nuclear weapons.

All of this does not mean that the laws of war are useless. There seem to be at least three levels at which these laws hold criminological utility: (1) Their clear prohibition of the use of nuclear weapons, which adds another framework for the criminological incrimination of the state, (2) A formal legal framework for effecting change in nuclear weapons policy, which may facilitate possible avenues toward a newsmaking or peacemaking criminology, and (3) Their support for the constructionist and political-economy perspectives on the criminalization process. Many more international legal scholars than scholars of crime have understood the legal *and* moral authority held by such laws of war as the Nuremberg Charter, the United Nations Charter, and the Geneva and Genocide Conventions. While these laws are subject to similar political elements which shape the application and enforcement of nation-state criminal law, only a few criminologists have investigated them as an academic path to understanding governmental crime, and as a pragmatic instrument for affecting a more peaceful global environment, the presumed objective of many of these humanitarian laws. Criminologists should not be hasty in rejecting this latter possibility because of the overwhelming political and economic forces operating against the abolition of the nuclear threat. Some of the successes experienced by white collar crime scholars, and to a lesser extent corporate crime scholars, in their use of law as an instrument of incrimination and pragmatic change suggest similar possibilities for legitimizing governmental crime as "real crime". Even though legally defined elite criminality on many occasions goes without the kind of formal adjudication and punishment found in the criminalization procedures of traditional street crime, there at least exists *some* model of formal adjudication which on *some* level aids in decreasing harm caused by the powerful. For the kinds of behaviors discussed in this article, this adjudicatory responsibility rests with the International Court of Justice, which because of the efforts of legal scholars/activists will more than likely hear arguments on the legal status of nuclear weapons this year.

54   *Humanity & Society, Volume 19, Number 3, August, 1995*

REFERENCES

Barak, Gregg. 1994. *Media, Process, and the Social Construction of Crime: Studies in Newsmaking Criminology.* New York: Garland.

— 1993. "Crime, Criminology, and Human Rights: Towards an Understanding of State Criminality." In K. Tunnel (Ed.), *Political Crime in Contemporary America*, pp.207-230. New York: Garland.

— 1991. Crimes by the Capitalist State: *An Introduction to State Criminality.* New York: State University of New York Press.

— 1990. "Crime, Criminology, and Human Rights: Towards an Understanding of State Criminality." *The Journal of Human Justice.* 2 (1): 1-28.

Baudot, Marcel. 1977. *The Historical Encyclopedia of World War II.* New York: Facts on File.

Baxter, Richard Reeve. 1953. "The Role of Law in Modern Warfare." *Proceedings of the American Society of International Law*, 47: 90-98.

Beirne, Piers, and James Messerschmidt. 1995. *Criminology*, (2nd Edition). Fort Worth, Texas: Harcourt Brace College Publishers.

Bialer, Seweryn, and Michael Mandelbaum. 1988. *The Global Rivals.* New York: Alfred A. Knopf.

Bilder, Richard. 1984. "Nuclear Weapons and International Law." In M. Feinrider and A. Miller (Eds.) *Nuclear Weapons and the La*, pp. 131-155. Westport, Connecticut: Greenwood.

Blechman, Barry M., and Stephen S. Kaplan. 1978. *Force Without War: U. S. Armed Forces as a Political Instrument.* Washington, D.C.: The Brookings Institution.

Bledsoe, Robert, and Bloeslaw Boczek. 1987. *The International Law Dictionary.* Santa Barbara, California: ABC-CLIO.

Bohm, Robert M. 1993. "Social Relationships that Arguably Should Be Criminal Although They Are Not: On the Political Economy of Crime." In K. Tunnel (Ed.), *Political Crime in Contemporary America*, pp. 3-30, New York: Garland.

Borchard, Edwin. 1946. "The Atomic Bomb." *The American Journal of International Law*, 40: 161-165.

Boyle, Francis A. 1989. "The Hypocrisy and Racism behind the Formulation of U.S. Human Rights Foreign Policy: In Honor of Clyde Ferguson." *Social Justice*, 16 (1): 71-93.

Boyle, Francis A. 1987. "The Lawlessness of Nuclear Deterrence." *Swords and Plowshares*, 2: 8-9.

— 1985. *World Politics and International Law.* Durham, NC: Duke University Press.

— 1984. "International Lawlessness in the Caribbean Basin." *Crime and Social Justice*, 21-22: 37-57

— 1983. *The Criminality of Nuclear Weapons.* Santa Barbara, California: Nuclear Age Peace Foundation.

Builder, Carl, and M. Graubard. 1982. *The International Law of Armed Conflict: Implications for the Concept of Assured Destruction.* New York: RAND Corporation Publishers.

Caulfield, Susan, and Nancy Wonders. 1993. "Personal AND Political: Violence against Women and the Role of the State." In K. Tunnel (Ed.), *Political Crime in Contemporary America*, pp. 79-100. New York: Garland.

Clinard, Marshall, and Richard Quinney. 1973. *Criminal Behavior Systems: A Typology.* New York: Holt, Rinehart, and Winston.

Coleman, James. 1994. *The Criminal Elite: The Sociology of White-Collar Crime.* Third Edition. New York: St. Martin's.

Dieterich, Heinz. 1986. "Enforced Disappearances and Corruption in Latin America." *Crime and Social Justice*, 25: 40-54.

Ellsburg, Daniel. 1981. "Call to Mutiny." In E.P. Thompson and D. Smith (Eds.), *Protest and Survive*, (i=xxvii). New York: Monthly Review Press.

Falk, Richard. 1989. "United States Foreign Policy as an Obstacle to Realizing the Rights of Peoples." *Social Justice*, 16 (1): 57-69.

David Kauzlarich **55**

— 1983. "Toward a Legal Regime for Nuclear Weapons." *McGill Law Journal, 28*: 519-530.

Feinrider, Martin. 1982. "International Law as the Law of the Land: Another Constitutional Constraint on the Use of Nuclear Weapons." *Nova Law Journal*, 7: 103-128.

Frappier, J. 1984. "Above the Law: Violations of International Law by the US Government from Truman to Reagan." *Crime and Social Justice*, (21-22): 1-36.

Friedman, Leon. 1972. *The Law of War: A Documentary History*. New York: Random House.

Friedrichs, David O. 1995. "State Crime or Governmental Crime: Making Sense of the Conceptual Confusion." In J. Ross (Ed.) *Controlling State Crime*, pp. 53-79. New York: Garland.

— 1992. "Residual White Collar Crime: Cognate Hybrid,and Marginal Forms." Paper presented at the American Society of Criminology Annual Meeting, New Orleans, Lousiana, November.

— 1992a. "White Collar Crime and the Definitional Quagmire: A Provisional Solution." *The Journal of Human Justice, 3* (2): 5-21.

— 1985. "The Nuclear Arms Issue and the Field of Criminal Justice." *The Justice Professional*, 2: 5-9.

Fujita, H. 1982. "First Use of Nuclear Weapons: Nuclear Strategy versus International Law." *Kansai University Review of Law and Politics*, 3: 57-86.

Galliher, John. 1989. *Criminology: Human Rights, Criminal Law, and Crime*. Englewood Cliffs, NJ: Prentice Hall.

Geis, Gilbert, and Robert Meier. 1977. *White Collar Crime*. New York: Free Press.

Green, Gary S. 1990. *Occupational Crime*. Chicago: Nelson-Hall.

Harding, Richard. 1983. "Nuclear Energy and the Destiny of Mankind: Some Criminological Perspectives." *Australian and New Zealand Journal of Criminology*, 16: 81-93.

Hazlehurst, Kayleen M. 1991. "Passion and Policy: Aboriginal Deaths in Custody in Australia." In G. Barak (Ed.) *Crimes by the Capitalist State: An Introduction to State Criminality*, pp. 21-48. New York: State University of New York Press.

Henkin, Louis. 1991. "The Use of Force: "Law and U.S. Policy." In J. T. Swing (Ed.) *Right* v. *Might: International Law and the Use of Force*, pp. 37-70. New York: Council on Foreign Relations Press.

Henry, Stuart. 1991. "The Informal Economy: A Crime of Omission by the State." In G. Barak (Ed.) *Crimes by the Capitalist State: An Introduction to State Criminality*, pp. 253-270, Albany, NY: State University of New York Press.

Herman, Edward. 1982. *The Real Terror Network: Terrorism in Fact and Propoganda*. Boston: South End Press.

Kauzlarich, David. 1994. "Epistemological Barriers to Peacemaking Criminology." *Peace Review*, 6 (2): 165-170.

Kauzlarich, David, Ronald C. Kramer, and Brian Smith. 1992. "Toward the Study of Governmental Crime: Nuclear Weapons, Foreign Intervention, and International Law." *Humanity and Society, 16* (4): 543-563.

Kramer, Ronald C. 1982. "The Debate over the Definition of Crime: Paradigms, Value Judgments, and Criminological Work." In F. Elliston and N. Bowie (Eds.), *Public Policy, and Criminal Justice*, pp. 33-58, Cambridge, MA: Oelgeschlager, Gunn, and Hain.

Kuhn, Thomas. 1962. *The Structure of Scientific Revolutions*. Chicago: University of Chicago Press.

Lauterpacht, Hersch. 1952. "The Revision of the Law of War." *British Yearbook of International Law*, 20: 360-382.

Lawyers Committee on Nuclear Policy. 1993. "Western States Sabotage U. N. Initiative to Test Legality of Nuclear Weapons." *Flash*, 1: 1-2.

— 1990. *Statement on the Illegality of Nuclear Weapons*. New York: Lawyers' Committee on Nuclear Policy, Inc.

Lifton, Robert Jay, and Richard Falk. 1991. *Indefensible Weapons*. (Revised Edition). New York: Basic Books.

Lincoln, W. Bruce. 1968. *Documents in World History: 1945-1967*. San Francisco: Chandler.

McCaughan, Ed. 1989. "Human Rights and Peoples' Rights: An introduction." *Social Justice*, 16 (1): 1-19.

56   *Humanity & Society, Volume 19, Number 3, August, 1995*

McNaught, L.W. 1984. *Nuclear Weapons and Their Effects*. London: Brasseys Press.

Meyrowitz, Elliott. 1981. "The Status of Nuclear Weapons under International Law." *The Guild Practitioner*, 38: 65-81.

— 1990. *Prohibition of Nuclear Weapons: The Relevance of International Law*. Dobbs Ferry, NY: Transnational Publishers.

Michalowski, Raymond. 1985. *Order, Law and Power*. New York: Random House.

Miller, Arthur, and Martin Feinrider. 1984. *Nuclear Weapons and the Law*. Westport, Connecticut: Greenwood Press.

Miller, R.I. 1975. *The Law of War*. Lexington, MA: Lexington Books.

Mohr, Manfred. 1988. "International Humanitarian Law and the Law of Armed Conflict: Its Relevance to the Nuclear Vhallenge." In M. Cohen and M.E. Govin (Eds.), *Lawyers and the Nuclear Debate*, pp. 83-90. Ottawa: University of Ottawa Press.

Molina, Luis F. 1995. "Can States Commit Crimes? The Limits of Formal International Law." In J. Ross (Ed.) *Controlling State Crime*, pp. 349-388. New York: Garland.

Nicaragua v. *United States of America*. 1986 ICP REP. 14

Nixon, Richard M. 1980. *The Memoirs of Richard Nixon*. New York: Grosset and Dunalp.

— 1985. No More Vietnams. New York: Arbor House.

Nuremberg Campaign. 1990. *Violation International Law*. Ocscoda, Michigan: Nuremberg Campaign.

O'Brien, William Vincent. 1961. "Some Problems of the Law of War in Limited Nuclear Warfare." *Military Law Review*, 14: 1-27.

Office of Technology Assessment. 1972. *The Effects of Nuclear War*. Washington, D.C.: U.S. Government Printing Office.

Pepinsky, Harold E., and Richard Quinney. 1991. *Criminology as Peacemaking*. Bloomington: Indiana University Press.

Perdue, William Dan. 1989. *Terrorism and the State: A Critique of Domination Through Fear*. New York: Praeger.

Quinney, Richard. 1979. *Criminology*. (2nd Edition). Boston: Little, Brown.

— 1977. *Class, State, and Crime*. New York: Longman.

Riggs, Robert E., and Jack C. Plano. 1988. *The United Nations: International Organization and World Politics*. Pacific Grove, CA: Brooks/Cole.

Roberts, Adam, and Richard Guelff. 1982. *Documents on the Laws of War*. Oxford: Clarendon Press.

Ross, Jeffery Ian. 1995. *Controlling State Crime*. New York: Garland.

— 1993. "Research on Contemporary Oppositional Political Terrorism in the United States: Merits, Drawbacks, and Suggestions for Improvement." In K. Tunnel (Ed.), *Political Crime in Contemporary America*, pp. 101-120, New York: Garland.

Schwartzenberger, G. 1958. *The Legality of Nuclear Weapons*. London: Stevens and Sons.

Schwendinger, Herman, and Julia Schwendinger. 1977. "Social Class and the Definition of Crime." *Crime and Social Justice*, (7): 4-13.

— 1970. "Defenders of Order or Guardians of Human Rights? *Issues in Criminology*, (5): 123-157.

Sellin, Thorsten. 1938. *Culture, Conflict and Crime*. New York: Social Science Research Council.

Shimoda et al. v. *State of Japan*. 1963. District Court of Tokyo. Reprinted in Japanese Annual of International Law, 1965, 212.

Singh, N., and Edward McWhinney. 1989. *Nuclear Weapons and Contemporary International Law*. Boston: Martinus Nihjoff Publishers.

Stone, Julius. 1945. *Legal Controls of International Conflict: A Treatise on the Dynamics of Disputes and War Law*. London: Stevens and Sons.

Stowell, Ellery C. 1945. "The Laws of War and the Atomic Bomb." *American Journal of Internation Law*, (39): 784-788.

Sutherland, Edwin H. 1945. "Is 'White Collar Crime' Crime?" *American Sociological Revew*, 5 (1): 1-12.

David Kauzlarich **57**

Swing, John Temple. 1991. *Right* v. *Might: International Law and the Use of Force.* New York:" Council on Foreign Relations Press.

Thomas, E. 1946. "Atomic Warfare and International Law." *Proceedings of American Society of International Law* (40): 84-87.

Tifft, Larry, and Dennis Sullivan. 1980. *The Struggle to be Human: Crime, Criminology, and Anarchism.* Sanday, Orkney, U.K.: Cienfuegos Press.

Tucker, Robert W. 1950. *The Law of War and Neutrality at Sea.* Washington, D.C.: U.S. Government Printing Office.

Tunnel, Kenneth. 1993. *Political Crime in Contemporary America.* New York: Garland.

United Nations General Assembly. 1990. *General and Complete Disarmament: Comprehensive Study on Nuclear Weapons.* New York: United Nations Publications

Vickman, Leon. 1988. *Why Nuclear Weapons Are Illegal.* Santa Barbara, CA: Nuclear Age Peace Foundation.

Weiner, T. 1990. *Blank Check: The Pentagon's Black Budget.* New York: Warner Books.

Weston, Burns H. 1983. "Nuclear Weapons and International Law: Prolegomenon to General Illegality." *New York Law School Journal of International and Comparative Law,* 4: 227-256.

Weston, Burns H. 1983a "Nuclear Weapons versus International Law: A Contextual Reassessment." *McGill Law Journal,* 28: 531-549.

World Health Organization. 1987. *Effects of Nuclear War on Health and Health Services.* Geneva: World Health Organization.

Yarnold, Barbara M. 1995. A New Role for the International Court of Justice: Adjudicator of International and State Transnational Crimes." In J. Ross (Ed.) *Controlling State Crime,* pp. 317-348. New York: Garland.

Zilinskas, Raymond A. 1995. "Preventing State Crimes against the Environment During Military Operations: The 1977 Environmental Modification Treaty." In J. Ross (Ed.) *Controlling State Crime,* pp. 235-282. New York: Garland.

State-sponsored Terrorism and Crimes Against Citizens

[12]

Contemporary Crises 12: 5–24 (1988)
© Kluwer Academic Publishers, Dordrecht – Printed in the Netherlands

Whose terrorists?
Libya and state criminality

Philip Jenkins
Pennsylvania State University

In the 1970s and 1980s, Western statesmen and experts often denounced the nation of Libya as a leading culprit in the commission of acts of 'state criminality'. In 1986, this culminated in an attack on that country by US forces, an act of great political and diplomatic significance. However, much less attention has been paid to the criminological significance of this debate, this apparent sequence of crime by and retribution against a nation rather than an individual. If a state can commit a crime, or engage in a pattern of criminality, then it should theoretically be possible to interpret these actions in light of the very substantial body of criminological theory evolved over the last two centuries to explain the behavior of individuals and small groups.

This paper will argue that such an endeavor is not only feasible, but very profitable in explaining the emergence of Libya as a (perceived) 'terrorist state'. Specifically, Libya emerges as a state which has indeed engaged in some of the acts of international criminality alleged against it, though these were by no means as serious or as frequent as those of many other nations, including those most enthusiastic in denouncing Libyan terrorism. Furthermore, Libyan 'criminality' appears to have been most often undertaken on behalf of more powerful nations or interest groups.

In summary, the 'criminalization' of Libya can be seen as fitting very appropriately into the conflict paradigm of criminology. Criminal acts are defined as 'serious' not in terms of any inherent value, but rather through the interests of groups with the power to undertake such definitions – in this case, access to world media. Moreover, we find a phenomenon common from studies of organized crime, namely the use of low-level criminal groups by powerful political or economic interests, even when those powerful interests will find it ideologically useful to denounce and stigmatize their allies. To use a more routine criminological analogy, the Libyan state should thus be seen not as a 'mastermind' of terrorism, but as a 'street' criminal – the sort of offender that attracts law enforcement attention from its visibility rather than from any real menace posed to society at large. (For terrorism generally, see Merkl 1986, Alexander and Myers 1982, Wardlaw 1982.)

But to 'demote' Libya and its notorious leader is not to dismiss the concept

6

of state criminality. Rather than a primary actor, the Libyan state can better be seen as an arena in which other, far more powerful, interests undertake their own actions, which are often criminal. This study thus illustrates the nature and motives of illegal actions by clandestine agencies, an area of criminality that so rarely receives due attention from scholars of criminology.

State criminality

The concept that a state might perform criminal acts is controversial, not least because of the difficulties of defining 'crime' in terms other than the lawcodes of individual nations. If a state obeys its own laws, it can be argued that it should be judged by no higher criteria, whether these are religious, philosophical (a 'Law of Nations') or political (crime as a 'violation of human rights'). However, state criminality is an ancient and powerful notion. In the fifth century A.D., St Augustine was familiar with the idea that pirate bands shared the essential nature of states and empires: both were large groups seizing property by violence. They differed only in the scale of their endeavors, and the success of states in imposing a rhetoric and ideology. This tradition was used by satirists, and finds its highest expression in Henry Fielding's novel of 1743, *Jonathan Wild*. Here, the author draws an extended parallel between the careers of a notorious organized crime group on the one hand, and the early Georgian state on the other.

In the twentieth century, the theory of 'state criminality' found its most sweeping expression in the warcrimes trials held at Nurnberg and (less celebrated) at Tokyo. Here, whole sections of the administrative and military machinery of major states were tried and convicted of criminal acts. In some cases, they were found to have become criminal organizations *ipso facto*, as in the case of the German General Staff. The crimes involved here usually involved novel philosophical definitions of illegal behavior, such as 'levying aggressive war'. However, the Nurnberg precedent was a powerful example for later interpretations of state actions.

In the 1970s, the influential school of radical criminology based in the United States made much use of 'state criminality' theory. Sometimes, the acts so described were what might be termed philosophical, and involved violations of human rights, or persecution on the grounds of race or class. Others, though, described how states engaged in acts which would be described as serious felonies if committed by less powerful groups or individuals. In a scandal like Watergate, certain agencies of government were implicated. In other cases, however the number of agencies so involved was so widespread as to justify the charge that the state itself had become criminal. One of the best examples of this was US intelligence involvement in the south-east Asian narcotics trade in the Vietnam era (McCoy 1972, Block and Chambliss 1981, Chambliss and Mankoff 1976, Turk 1982, Quinney 1975, Box 1983).

More recently, Chambliss has used such incidents to create a systematic theory of 'state organized crime', arguing that states often engage in such 'literal' criminality. Apart from the recent narcotics incidents, his casestudies of such violations include governmental sponsorship of piracy through most of the history of that institution.

In the last two decades, state criminality has become a widely used – if poorly defined – concept. The political values underlying such a discussion have also changed. Chambliss, Quinney, Block and others generally wrote from a radical or liberal perspective. In the present decade especially, the concept has however been 'hijacked' somewhat by conservatives, until crimes by states have become a major target of the rhetoric of the Reagan adminis- tration. Conservatives attack the alleged narcotics trafficking of Bulgaria and Nicaragua; while a keystone of Reagan foreign policy until 1986 was the denunciation of terrorism as a tool of certain Leftist or radical Muslim states. To quote President Reagan:

> So there we have it. Iran, Libya, North Korea, Cuba, Nicaragua – conti- nents away, tens of thousands of miles apart – but the same goals and objectives. I submit to you that the growth in terrorism in recent years results from the increasing involvement of these states in terrorism in every region of the world ... And we are especially not going to tolerate these attacks from outlaw states run by the strangest collection of misfits, looney tunes, and squalid criminals since the advent of the Third Reich (Taheri 1986).

The fact that such a forthright view was largely compromised by the Irangate affair of 1986–87 should not distract attention from the rhetorical importance of state criminality during this decade.

If state criminality had come to be widely accepted, there was as yet no attempt at a 'criminology' of states, though the insights of criminology could in fact be widely applied here. Clearly, individualistic theories of the etiology of crime were less appropriate in explaining the behavior of collective entities such as states, though political conservatives were quick to use polemic imply- ing the literal insanity of leaders such as Qaddafi of Libya or even Khomeini of Iran. In explaining state criminality, a wide variety of explanations is possible, drawn by analogy from accounts of smaller groups. One might, for instance, explore the theory of culture conflict, and suggest that the normal and accept- ed behavior of certain groups or nations might be stigmatized as criminal by other communities with greater power to enforce their definitions. Generally, it will be found that theories of social conflict stand the greatest chance of

8

successful interpretation, success here being measured by intellectual consistency and predictive value.

Initially, many critics of US government policy will note that Western countries are inconsistent in denouncing 'terrorism' by radical countries while sponsoring anti-Communist insurgencies in Nicaragua or Afghanistan. Behavior is thus far more likely to be defined as criminal if it challenges rather than enhances the position of powerful groups in a particular society. However, the significance of power in the definition of serious criminality can be understood more directly if we confine ourselves for the moment to Leftist and radical terrorism. In the Middle Eastern context, there is no question that it is Syria rather than Libya which sponsors radical terrorism with the greatest degree of frequency and success. Apart from controlling the great majority of Palestinian guerrilla groups, Syria directly sponsors numerous ethnic or ideological terror groups – ASALA, the Kurdish Workers' Party, FARL, the Syrian People's Party and others. However, it was Libya rather than Syria which the US chose to attack– both rhetorically and physically – during its 'antiterrorism' campaign of the 1980s.

There were a number of reasons for this: Syria has excellent diplomatic ties to the Soviet Union; it plays a vital role in Middle Eastern politics; and it has good air defenses, all in contrast to Libya (Pienel 1986, Sciolino 1986, Hersh 1987). In the mid-1980s, European writing on Middle Eastern terrorism differed very sharply from American interpretations. Much more emphasis was placed on the role of state sponsorship by Syria and Iran, the latter thought to be extremely active through the Lebanese *Hizbullah.* 'Outsiders' blamed by French authorities for sponsoring terrorism included Iraq, Syria and (with surprising frequency) Israeli *provocateurs.* Libya was scarcely mentioned in events like the Paris bomb campaign in the Fall of 1986. This alternative view goes far towards explaining why European governments were so reluctant to support the US raids on Libya in 1986. However, they were not prepared to denounce them overtly (Marion and Pienel 1986, 1987; Pienel 1986).

In summary, though, we can see many reasons why it is the less powerful and rather marginal state of Libya which receives the brunt of US assaults. In the international community, no less than the national, it is lack of power which exposes one to the likelihood of criminalization and subsequent negative sanctions.

Criminological insights might thus be useful in discussing state illegalities, but with one very significant *caveat.* Sub-national groups may be associated with criminal acts in a variety of ways, laying the foundation for trial, conviction and punishment. In the case of entities as complex as nation-states – even those as small as Libya – there are layers of responsibility to take into account, and one agency might undertake an action without the knowledge or consent of higher authorities. The whole entity might not properly be blamed for such acts.

9

In the Libyan example, completely different problems arise in the firm attribution of blame. Where terrorism and clandestine activities are concerned, we often encounter a 'wilderness of mirrors' in which acts are undertaken on behalf of third parties, often without the perpetrator of an act knowing the true reason or motive. On other occasions, acts are frequently committed as provocations, designed to attract blame to the enemies of those actually responsible. In the 1970s Italy, for example, it was common for groups of the ultra-Right to masquerade as Leftist groups when committing particularly heinous terrorist crimes, chiefly to cast opprobrium on their rivals. 'Libyan terrorism' involves both these problems of interpretation – provocations, and acts committed for a third party. Guilt is therefore very difficult to place in any conventional legal sense, though the Reagan administration rhetoric assumed much more simplistic motives and behavior.

These themes can be illustrated by a casestudy of Libya's involvement with terrorism since 1969. It will be shown that the country was very active in state criminality, but for a very complex array of motives usually far removed from Libyan conditions; and generally arising from the needs of those powers most active in condemning the Qaddafi regime.

Libya and terrorism

Libya is a large North African nation, with perhaps 3.6 million people living in a land area two-and-a-half times that of Texas (some 680,000 square miles). From 1911 to 1942, Libya was a colonial possession of its nearest European neighbor, Italy, a link that would be of considerable significance in later years. The country became formally independent in 1951, and in 1969 a military government led by Muammar el Qaddafi took over by *coup d'etat.*

By this stage, Libya had become enormously important because of its oil wealth, and the fact that oil exports to Europe did not have to go through the Suez Canal (closed after the six-day war of 1967). Libya supplied a quarter of European oil in 1969. At the height of production in 1980, Libya was producing over two million barrels a day, and its oil income was $22 billion. This fell sharply in the next few years. In 1984, Libya exported over ten billion dollars of oil, the chief recipients being Italy ($2.5 billion), West Germany ($2 billion), Spain, France and Turkey (all between $650 and $970 million). Libya needed to import little, and thus ran a steady annual profit of several billions of dollars throughout the 1970s and early 1980s (*New York Times,* 12 January 1986). It thus gained vast amounts of fluid wealth together with substantial political influence (Blundy and Lycett 1987, Wright 1982, Davis 1987, Sherrill 1983. Other works used generally through this article include Abdrabboh 1985, Sono 1984, Harris 1986, Cooley 1982, Pasha 1984, El-Khawas 1986, and Samura 1985).

10

The uses of this wealth were conditioned by Qaddafi's political and religious ideology, a more strongly Muslim version of the pan-Arab nationalism of President Nasser. For Qaddafi, Libya stood at the center of three vital trends – pan-Arabism, pan-Africanism and pan-Islamism. He hoped that he and Libya would unite and lead these three worlds – Arab, African, and Islamic – and consequently began an adventurist and opportunistic foreign policy to this end.

There is no doubt that Libya between 1969 and 1987 attempted to foster and support insurgent or guerrilla movements in many parts of the world, as far afield as the South Pacific and the Caribbean. Examples may be found easily from the literature on terrorism, but the following will indicate the apparently indiscriminate nature of his bounty. In the USA, Libyan money went to the Black Muslim movement of Louis Farrakhan, to the Republic of New Africa, to American Indian activists, and (allegedly) to theEl Rukns street gang in Chicago. In Britain, the profits of Libyan oil flowed to the IRA, to the (Trotskyist) Workers' Revolutionary Party and to the (fascist) National Front (Dobson and Payne 1986: 183–194, Lee and Coogan 1987).

Libyan arms and money were also, apparently, made freely available to terrorist groups, either to undertake their own activities or else to serve as surrogates for the Libyans. Sometimes, the targets were themselves Arabs. At least fourteen Libyan exiles were murdered in different parts of North America and Europe; and a 'Libyan dimension' was seen in acts like the 1975 kidnapping of the OPEC leaders meeting in Vienna. For conservative writer Claire Sterling, Qaddafi in the 1970s was the 'Daddy Warbucks of Terrorism', a primary financier on a world level. According to the same author, Qaddafi in 1976 made a pact with the Algerian government to promote European terrorism. 'Within a year, the rate of terrorist attacks doubled in Ulster, in Spanish Basqueland, in French Brittany, and Corsica' (Sterling 1981: 181–2, 241–254). In the next decade, the US administration claimed to have direct evidence for Libyan participation in a number of Middle East-related terrorist atrocities in Europe, especially those directed against American targets.

Qaddafi as a terrorist sponsor receives far more impressive coverage than he probably deserves. He is certainly credited with the sponsorship of movements in which he plays at best a marginal role. The 'Abu Nidal' group, for example, was a creature of Iraq from 1974 to 1981, and of Syria thereafter; while Libyan attempts to create pro-Qaddafi Palestinian groups have been largely disastrous. In funding mainstream Palestinian groups, Qaddafi has been far more generous with rhetoric than cash, in sharp contrast to the moderate (but generous) Saudis, Kuwaitis, and Algerians (Adams 1986).

Also, there have been *provocateur* attempts to link Qaddafi to bogus terrorist groups. In a 1986 case, a Syrian/Lebanese group known as 'The Call of Jesus Christ' was apprehended in Spain before they could undertake a series of

11

major actions against Spanish and US targets, in which hundreds of civilians would have died. The moderate press in Spain accepted the police view that this was a bogus front group created by French intelligence with a view to smearing Libya, and promoting French interests in their war in Chad (Johnstone 1986, Bearman 1986).

In the United States, the concept of Qaddafi as 'ultimate terrorist' has recently been discussed by Hersh (1987). He places the origins of the theory firmly with CIA director William Casey and some associates in the National Security Council, who allegedly leaked false evidence about Libyan 'terrorism'. The circle responsible for these stories – and the campaign which culminated in the 1986 bombing – was very much the group which earned notoriety in the Iran-Contra affair, which will be discussed later. For Reagan's circle, Libya was a vital enemy – and the new President's first NSC meeting in 1981 focused on Libya as much as Iran.

The conservative views of Libya differ on the issue of Qaddafi's motivation. Sterling and others see him as a Soviet puppet or surrogate in a much broader scheme to destabilize the West. Others view him as an autonomous, though deeply unstable, character – 'mad dog' and 'flaky barbarian' are both terms that have featured in the official vocabulary of the US administration. There is harmony, however, on the wider issues. Qaddafi is seen as a leading financier and practitioner of international terrorism.In turn, 'terrorism' is viewed not as a tactic but a movement, of radical and Muslim foes of 'Judaeo-Christian civilization' (that is, NATO *plus* Israel). In this characterization, there is no implication that political violence might ever be used legitimately against a tyrannical government; or that Rightist movements might ever qualify as 'terrorist' (Netanyahu 1986).

It is possible to accept virtually every particular of the facts outlined above, but still to reject the interpretation of Libyan motives and conduct offered by conservative critics like Sterling, Ledeen, Moss, Henze, Netanyahu and others. That Libya has sponsored criminal and terrorist acts is certain. That it has often been blamed incorrectly for such acts is equally beyond question (for example, the celebrated 'Libyan hit-team' *en route* in 1981 to assassinate President Reagan). Finally, it can also be demonstrated that the terrorist acts in question seem apparently to have a political context wholly different from that originally suggested. In reality, Libya may well be a 'surrogate' terrorist state for many countries instead of, or in addition to, the USSR. Libya, in short, appears to be as much a puppet of Western as of Eastern clandestine agencies (Bearman 1986).

12

Libya and the Communists

For conservative writers like Sterling or Netanyahu, Libya is a close ally of the
Soviets, which deviates only occasionally from the 'Moscow line' (for instance,
on Jewish emigration or the invasion of Afghanistan). The Libyan state
security apparatus makes great use of East German police experts like Karl
Hansch; and in 1976 Libya signed an enormous (multi-billion) arms deal with
the USSR. There are also a number of prominent Libyan leaders or allies said
to have KGB ties, especially Abdul Salem Jalloud, and Palestinian guerrilla
leader Ahmed Jibril (Sterling 1981, Tosches 1985).

   The evidence for Soviet influence on Libya thus stems from the presence of
foreign personnel, and the intelligence connections of certain individuals. The
predilection for Soviet arms can be discounted. Such weapons are popular
worldwide, and the resolutely anti-Communist Contras seem not to have
compromised their integrity by their arms purchases in Poland and China. The
overwhelming impression of the Qaddafi regime is of opportunism. In the
1970s, the country simultaneously obtained arms (or attempted to do so) from
Americans, Soviets, British and Chinese. Western suppliers like the US or
French also tended to impose sudden embargos on arms already paid for,
which the Soviets never did.

   Taking the remaining evidence, it does appear that there is a pro-Soviet
presence in Libya. However, exactly the same sort of 'proofs' can be used to
establish Libya's 'puppet' status for several other countries and most of the
others are firmly members of NATO.

The British context

One of the strongest and most enduring intelligence links of he Qaddafi regime
has been with the United Kingdom. Before taking power, Qaddafi had trained
in England, and spent time in 1966 at a language school at Baconsfield, an
establishment with close SAS and intelligence ies. While here, he received a
British Army psychological evaluation, and may have been viewed as a candidate for recruitment.

   Though his 1969 coup was seen as anti-Western, Qaddafi long acted in a
surprisingly friendly way towards Britain and specifically towards MI6. In 1971
MI6 collaborated closely with Qaddafi in capturing and returning Sudanese
army officers who had attempted a coup in their own country. This cooperation
occurred despite the professed Leftist sentiments of the oup leaders themselves. In the same year, there was apparently joint MI6/Libyan support for
General Amin's successful coup in Uganda. Moreover, there were a number
of occasions in the early 1970s when the British Foreign Office and MI6 vetoed

13

proposed attempts involving British nationals to overthrow or assassinate Qaddafi (Bloch and Fitzgerald 1983, Sampson 1975, Stiff 1986).

There are indications that the Qaddafi regime had strong initial contacts with at least one Western intelligence agency – that of the United Kingdom. More curious is that these contacts seem to continue much later than might seem likely from the superficial hostility of the two nations. Well into the 1980s Qaddafi's bodyguard included SAS and SAS-trained personnel, usually operating through 'old boy' private-security companies; and arms supplies to Libya certainly continued into this decade (*Private Eye* 1984–6 *passim*).

The reasons for this surprising harmony are many, and similar considerations affected the British and subsequent Western operations in Libya. Four main factors can be discerned. First, and most obvious was the central role played by Libya and similar states in the world economic order of the 1970s. Libyan pressure began the spiral of oil prices from 1970 onwards, and it was vital not to see Libyan oil pass to hostile hands. Qaddafi's eccentricities were trivial beside such a consideration. Also, rhetoric and ideology must not interfere with potentially vast sales of arms and consumer goods. In 1982, Britain continued selling military goods (including naval supplies) to Argentina until the very day of the outbreak of the Falkland Islands war.

Second, intelligence agencies needed information on possible terrorism, and friendly relations with Libya might have facilitated the penetration of terrorist groups, whether Palestinian, European or otherwise. This would be a natural and indeed laudable tactic. The other reasons, however, are more questionable, as both involve sponsorship of terrorism by Western intelligence agencies. Through Libya, western agencies like the CIA or MI6 could themselves sponsor terrorism through an ideal and deniable 'cut-out'. Specifically, this would have been very useful in the Europe of the late 1970s, when Communist parties were on the verge of participating in government in France, Spain and Italy. This was a policy deeply feared by the US and Britain as a 'Trojan Horse' towards complete Communist control.

Eurocommunism failed for a variety of reasons, but one factor was the strategy of tension pursued by terrorist groups of the ultra-Right, and of rather mysterious groups claiming extreme Left loyalties. The most celebrated of these was the Red Brigades in Italy, but there were also Breton, Basque and Corsican separatists, and the curious GRAPO movement in Spain. Conservative writers have argued that this new wave of Mediterranean terrorism was a response to Libyan sponsorship. If they are correct, the question still needs to be asked as to whether in turn some other agency, Eastern or Western, was encouraging these acts. Repeatedly, the political alignment of 'Libyan' terrorism appears to lie towards the ultra-Right. Moreover, this was not confined to the 'Eurocommunism' years of 1976–8. In 1986, the Spanish government described a Libyan conspiracy with Francoist military officers to destabilize the Socialist party.

14

The alliance between radical Arabs and European Rightists seems bizarre to an American audience accustomed to hearing political conflicts discussed in terms of east and west, Moscow and Washington. However, it is a natural consequence of events of the 1950s, when European fascist emigrés found sanctuary and common cause with anti-Israeli Arab states like Egypt (Lee and Coogan 1987). Among the most prominent Nazi exiles in Nasser's Egypt was Otto Skorzeny – who in 1974–5 joined Qaddafi in funding a newfascist terrorist network in Europe (Kruger 1980: 210). For many religious Muslims, the atheistic Soviet Union was as hostile as the capitalist USA, and so conventional issues of left and right fell into the background. The consequence, however, was that a 'radical' like Qaddafi was able to share wholeheartedly with the aims of Western covert action in Europe.

Fourthly, and finally, western intelligence agencies may have wished to help Libyan activities explicitly in order to promote unacceptably extreme movements in their own countries. In the United Kingdom, the mid-1970s was a time of deep political conflict when half the officers of the Security Service, MI5, were attempting to destabilize the Labour government. Sponsorship of domestic extremist groups – IRA, Trotskyist or Fascist – permitted the manipulation and possible discredit of perceived enemies, as well as the capability to promote unrest or civil violence in order to create a conservative backlash (De Young 1987).

The 'Libyan Connection', in short, was very useful for Western intelligence agencies, in that it permitted them to pursue a 'strategy of tension', either in their own countries or in targetted allies.

Libya and Italy

Britain was emphatically not the only country dabbling thus in Libyan affairs. Libya was far more crucial to Italy than to any other Western country, and the Italians responded accordingly. Apart from the historic links, there was a sizeable Italian population in Libya, and Italian economic dependence was absolute. Italian oil imports in the late 1970s exceeded $4 billion annually, while Libyan capital had flowed into Italy. The Libyan government even owned 13 percent of the huge corporation FIAT (Spotts and Weiser 1986, Bleakley 1986; in 1986 this investment was sold for $3.15 billion). One of Libya's major representatives in Italy in the 1970s was a Catania lawyer named Michele Papa (Tosches 1986, FBI 1979).

Libyan terrorism was also much more 'sought after' in Italy than elsewhere. The country was undergoing a deep political crisis in which the massive Communist Party was the natural successor to office. In response, there was extensive fascist terrorism, and several coup attempts. Perhaps the most

15

elaborate attempt to forestall leftist victory was the creation of the secret masonic society, P-2, under Licio Gelli. This included over a thousand politicians, business people and administrators, and it was deeply embedded throughout the Italian intelligence community. When the society was exposed and collapsed in 1981, it included the senior staff of all four intelligence agencies, including military intelligence, SISMI (De Lutiis 1985, Lernoux 1984).

P2 was an anti-communist society hat had extensive illegal activities, including the plunder of the Banco Ambrosiano, a billion-dollar crime tha may well be counted among the largest acts of illegality in history. P2 was also active in terrorism. P2 and SISMI agents were apparently responsible for the 1980 bombing of the Bologna rail station, in which 85 people were killed.

This is the vital context of the alleged Libyan role in Italian terrorism. Libya apparently played some role in many terrorist acts in Italy; but in each case, this was an incident where SISMI and P-2 are also leading suspects. The Libyans thus seem to act as allies or surrogates for the Italian ultra-Right, rather than for Soviet-backed or leftist groups.

The pattern can be traced through the decade. Perhaps the best example was the December 1973 terrorist attack at Rome's Fiumicino airport, in which 32 people were murdered by firebombs. This was organized by Ahmed al-Ghafour ('Abu Mahmoud') on behalf of a Libyan-sponsored Palestinian sect, the NAYLP. The mainstream Palestinian groups rejected the act, to the point that they executed Abu Mahmoud the following year. Moreover, the Fiumicino raid seems much more an internal Italian matter than a Middle Eastern one. It occurred at a time of intense *coup*-nervousness (four separate attempts known in 1973–4); and when sections of the ultra-Right deeply feared Communist participation in government. The 'strategy of tension' involved a series of bomb massacres by fascist groups (Brescia, the *Italicus* train); and this may have been one more. In fact, the fascist 'Paladin' network may have participated in the Fiumicino attack itself, and Italian intelligence played a questionable role (De Lutiis 1985: 169–174; Sterling 1981: 247). Yet the direct organization of this attack from Libya seems highly likely, far more so than in many more recent terrorist outrages.

The Fiumicino attack served a clear function in contributing to the destabilization of Italian politics, a shared goal of P2, SISMI and the Libyans. In 1978, similarly, the operation to kidnap former Prime Minister Aldo Moro had clear Libyan connections, but the Red Brigades by this point were thoroughly penetrated by SISMI. Finally, the Bologna bombing was primarily an act of P2 and SISMI; yet Claire Sterling has also indicated the evidence for a Libyan hand in the action. Among those jailed for the Bologna bomb was Claudio Mutti, who had founded the 'Italy-Libya Association' in 1973. He had a long record both as a fascist terrorist, and as a Qaddafi agent and recipient of

16

Libyan money. Mutti belonged to the 'Third Position', an Italian terrorist strand that sought to unite Nazi and Maoist doctrine into a new national revolutionary movement. Judging by Qaddafi's frequent support of such ideas, he seems to find them congenial (Lee and Coogan 1987, Sterling 1981).

During the 1970s, P2 and Libya effectively pursued common goals, even though P2 was a bastion of the ultra-Right, and Libya (supposedly) a Soviet puppet. From the early 1970s, Italian state security led a major operation to arm and train the Libyans, originally establishing *entrée* by exposing an alleged anti-Qaddafi plot. From 1973, Libyan internal security was thoroughly reorganized along the lines of a blueprint proposed by Ambrogio Viviani, a senior intelligence officer and P-2 member (Viviani's 1986 *exposé* of this operation was called 'Qaddafi, My Son). The Italian mission remained powerful throughout the decade, with authorization from Prime Minister Andreotti – himself a P-2 member. The crucial factor was safeguarding the oil concessions of the Italian state oil corporation, ENI (then headed by a P2 member). When criticized by intelligence colleagues for arming Qaddafi, Viviani responded, 'We control the spare parts, the ammunition, the technicians and the military advisers' (Johnstone 1986). By 1977,precisely the same remark could be made by American 'experts'.

Within Italy, Libya funded the neo-fascist movement, MSI, whose leaders in turn advocated Libyan interests in the Italian parliament. And in 1982, the head of Banco Ambrosiano was P-2 member Roberto Calvi, who obtained Libyan support and weapons for the Argentines in their war for the Falkland Islands (Cornwell 1983, Johnstone 1986, Spotts and Weiser 1986).

P2's other financial wizard was Michele Sindona, who had himself dealt closely with Qaddafi in the late 1970s. Sindona is the source for the story that after the US attempted to withdraw economically from Libya, the Italian government came forward in 1984 with a sweeping offer. Italian state corporations would fulfill all the economic and technological functions left by the departing Americans (Tosches 1986: 209–216).

Ironically, it is also Sindona who provided one of the most sweeping accounts of Libya's role as a Soviet puppet:

> Libya today is really only the violent whore of Russia's will – an organizational center through which East Germany, under Soviet command, carries out deeds designed to effect the scattering and withdrawal of American, French, and other NATO forces in the Middle East, and ultimately to destabilize, and disrupt the alliances of Western powers (quoted by Tosches, p. 211).

Even Qaddafi's territorial claims to Mediterranean islands were part of a wider plan, which would ultimately lead to the commando seizure of US missile bases in Sicily.

17

Sindona perfectly presents the Libyan paradox: of a Western-controlled satellite constantly presented as an Eastern mercenary. From the Italian experience, it would be difficult to know either P2 or Libya was the surrogate, and which was the 'puppet-master'. But in any case, there is considerable evidence that they shared common interests, and acted together through clandestine violence and financing.

Libya's American connection

From the mid-1970s, the Americans became the most distinctive Western presence in Libya, rather eclipsing British and Italian predecessors. But these latter provide the essential context for the American 'mission', and no doubt smoothed the path for their NATO allies. Anglo-US intelligence collaboration is an old established pattern, but the Italian role is less familiar. In the late 1970s, Italian contacts with mainstream US intelligence were less than perfect, difficulties culminating in Italy becoming the first NATO country to expel a CIA officer for espionage. But there were very close ties between SISMI, and its P2 controllers, and a hard-Right faction within US politics and intelligence. Together, these two groups appear to have developed the useful ideology that terrorism was a Soviet tool to overthrow the West, the plot being manifested through nations like Libya (Johnstone 1982, 1986; Pazienza 1985).

Perhaps the clearest demonstration of this harmony was the presence of P2 Grand Master Licio Gelli at President Reagan's 1981 inaugural. According to Lernoux, the Italian-American section of the (US) Republican National Committee was chaired by a P2 member, Philip Guarino. According to the same source, another key contact between both P2 and SISMI and the American Right was journalist and scholar Michael Ledeen (Lernoux 1984: 201, 217; Pazienza 1985). Ledeen would later earn celebrity as a prime mover in the Iran-Contra affair (Johnstone 1982, Engleberg 1987, National Security Archive 1987, Tower Commission 1987). Ledeen as a source on terrorism – especially of the 'state-sponsored' variety – is much used by Claire Sterling.

But these contacts are only a small sample of what must have been a flourishing commerce between Italian and US agencies and politicians from the mid-1970s. The ground was clear for US operations in what was one of the greatest diplomatic and intelligence assets available to SISMI – its 'Libyan Connection'. In this context, it seems less remarkable that there should be such strong connections between 'radical' Libya and US intelligence agencies – above all, the CIA (for the diplomatic background, see Haley 1984).

Of course, US involvement in Libya and other 'terrorist states' did not have to wait for British and Italian work to prepare the way for its operations. In 1973, General Vernon Walters of CIA had made a deal with the PLO whereby

18

US targets would not be harmed by Palestinian action – one of a series of pacts negotiated by Western powers at this time. This laid the foundation for US penetration of Palestinian groups. In 1974 the PLO was split by the alleged 'moderation' of Yasser Arafat, and the two factions feuded violently. The moderates took to denouncing their enemies to the CIA, with the consequence that Black September leader Hassan Salameh became in practice a prime American informant. US intelligence therefore had a useful and expanding network within Middle Eastern terrorism by the mid-1970s – a network that apparently flourished until it was crippled by events in Lebanon in 1982–3 (Adams 1986: 91, Frangi 1982).

During the late 1980s, America's Libyan connection was brought to public awareness by the investigations of the 'Irangate' scandal. The Nicaraguan Contra war and subsequent Iranian arms deals had been run by what was effectively a parallel intelligence network and foreign service not subject to Congressional supervision (Tower Commission 1987, National Security Archive 1987). Prominent in this were a group of intelligence and military officers who had in the 1970s been associated with CIA 'renegade', Edwin Wilson. Among this group were Richard Secord, Theodore Shackley, Thomas Clines, Rafael Quintero and others (Maas 1986, 1987).

The core of this group had worked together in Laos in the 1960s, and some of its members were later connected to the Nugan Hand bank in Australia (Schneider 1987, Naureckas and Ryan 1987, Lernoux 1984). Wilson himself was in prison by the time the Contras were created (if not, he later opined, he 'would have headed up this operation'). However, the new scandal prompted a re-examination of the earlier Wilson affair, and its suggestions of clandestine connections between Libya and agencies of US intelligence (Goulden 1984, Maas 1986, 1987; Haley 1984, Bearman 1986).

There is now a substantial literature on Edwin Wilson, but the affair can be seen in clearer terms if the strictly Libyan dimension is brought out more clearly. Wilson was a CIA agent dismissed in 1971, who also worked for the Naval Intelligence unit Task Force 157. He became involved in Middle Eastern arms dealing, but was dismissed for what was apparently a crude attempt to bribe ONI chief Bobby Ray Inman. In early 1976, Wilson proposed to work in Libya, and during that year a group of American intelligence veterans began an operation to train terrorists and saboteurs in Libya. Recruits included CIA veterans, anti-Castro Cubans and Green Berets. The operation continued in full force through 1979 at least, and Wilson was not lured back to the United States for trial until mid-1982. The Wilson team left behind them in Libya a flourishing terrorist-training operation, as well as a munitions stock that included twenty tons of C4 plastic explosive (Maas 1986).

When the Wilson affair became public knowledge, he was denounced as a 'renegade', a cynical 'death merchant' (Goulden 1984). However, the affair is

19

more complex than this would suggest. As Maas (1986) shows, prospective members of the Libyan 'training mission' would often seek clearance and permission for this activity from highly placed officials in government or intelligence. Either Wilson was indeed operating as a real US employee, or else he was working for and with a faction within US intelligencethat was so large and well-placed as to convey the impression that it had wholehearted Administration approval. It is this faction which provided the core of the later Iran/Contra operations of the 1980s. It remains a matter of speculation whether the CIA leadership at the time of the Libyan 'mission' had any awareness of the scheme (in 1976–7, the CIA Director was George Bush) (Ranelagh 1986).

Perhaps the best evidence that Wilson's mission was in some sense official is that what his circle was doing in Libya was very similar to what other NATO countries were accomplishing in exactly these years in other oil-rich states. After the 1973–4 oil crisis, the OPEC states were immensely rich, and spent heavily on internal security. Between 1975 and 1980, it was a BP subsidiary which set up a computerized police surveillance system in Saudi Arabia (Campbell 1979). In Iran, forces like SAVAK and the Imperial Gendarmerie were also expanded from the mid-1970s (Halliday 1979, Rafizadeh 1987). The oil companies took a leading role in finding these services for their invaluable suppliers. In Iran or Saudi Arabia, all this was legal. In Libya, however, such development was unlikely to win either legal or political support if undertaken overtly by US or British agents. Hence, perhaps, the apparently illegal Wilson operation.

But the apparent US friendship to Qaddafi seems less strange in light of the British and Italian experiences already discussed. As early as 1969–70, the State Department was described as friendly to Libyan policies, as Qaddafi's religious commitment was likely to prevent him succumbing to Communism (Sampson 1975). Also at this time, 'the Americans felt that Qaddafi would be fairly easy to control' (Bloch and Fitzgerald 1983: 49). In consequence, US intelligence would repeatedly veto schemes to have Qaddafi assassinated, especially (during 1980 and 1981) when those plots stemmed from the French and Egyptians. Not until the air raids of 1986 was there an apparent US attempt to achieve the same goal (Hersh 1987).

Libya, it seems, was recognized as a useful country for the West; and some of Qaddafi's actions served to split radical elements into hostile factions. In 1978, his government was even responsible for the disappearance and presumed murder of Musa al-Sadr, the greatest Shi'ite leader in Lebanon, and a potential radical figurehead (Ajami 1986; this act in itself also meant that Libya would be excluded from the Iranian-run 'Islamic Jihad' network of the 1980s). According to other sources, the Wilson operation in Libya represented the transplant of a major NATO covert action training facility previously located in Sardinia. The 'new wave' of rightist terrorism in Europe from 1976

20

might therefore be, as Sterling says, a response to Libyan sponsorship. But for whom the Libyans were in turn working remains an open question (De Lutiis 1985, Johnstone 1986).

Most accounts of Wilson in Libya see the US mission moving into effectively a political vacuum, but there is evidence of contact with the existing Western interests there. Wilson and his ally Frank Terpil both had extensive British connections, especially in the Metropolitan Police to whom they sold surveillance equipment. Wilson also shared common cause with P2, for instance, in training and arming Rightist terrorists in Turkey's civil war, the Gray Wolves. It was this organization which produced Papal assailant Mehmet Ali Agca, in an operation in which P2 and SISMI were deeply involved (Herman and Brodhead 1986, Jenkins 1986). Wilson was even alleged to have employed a hitman previously used by P2 financier, Michele Sindona. The Italians in Libya had no reason to resent these newcomers, and every reason to promote their welcome (Hougan 1983, 1984).

It was hypothesized earlier that one motive for allying with such a radical state as Libya might be to provide political ammunition with which one's political opponents could be discredited. In the United States, Libya apparently served this fuction in the late 1970s with the 'Billygate' scandal, when President Carter's brother was implicated in receiving money from Libya (the original contact was made through Michele Papa). In 1980, the scandal was revived with a new story published by conservative journalists Michael Ledeen and Arnauld de Borchgrave (Pazienza 1985, Tosches 1986, FBI 1979). This appeared only weeks before the election, and was particularly damaging to the Carter campaign. It was based in part on material obtained by Ledeen from SISMI, the Italian agency then dominated by P2 members. SISMI gave information derived from Papa which purported to link Billy Carter not only to Qaddafi but to Palestinian terrorists like George Habash. SISMI, naturally, had its own agenda in this by using Libya to promote the conservative cause in the USA and elsewhere.

In the 1980s, it has become apparent that the rhetorical denunciation of a state like Iran as 'terrorist' does not preclude the US government either dealing with that nation, or selling it arms. At the time of writing, there is no evidence that the US has violated arms embargos on Libya in the way that Iranian prohibitions were ignored. However, Libya has received a great deal of US weaponry, and evidence has come to light of attempts to purchase much more. It remains open to question whether a formal governmental role will subsequently become apparent.

The major components of this story include, first, the weapons and explosives obtained through Edwin Wilson. Part of this scheme included some C-130 aircraft purchased by the Libyans, though held up within the US administration. Partly through the work of intermediary Robert Vesco, this release was finally achieved in late 1978. More recently a 1986 federal indictment described a Libyan scheme to purchase similar aircraft and spare parts for $57 million ('Seven accused . . .', 1986).

The suggestion of secret diplomatic dealings with Libya (on the Iranian model) was first made in 1986 in the case of William Wilson, US ambassador to the Vatican. Wilson had created controversy by interceding with the federal government on behalf of Cardinal Marcinkus, who had allegedly been involved in the Ambrosiano scandal with P2 and Roberto Calvi. In 1986, it was reported that Wilson had held talks with Libyan officials, 'apparently without authorization and contrary to Reagan administration policy' (Gelb 1986). By the end of the year, though – in the aftermath of Irangate – it seemed certain that Ambassador Wilson had been negotiating with full Administration backing, conveyed by National Security Advisor Poindexter (Suro 1986).

It is tempting, and inaccurate, to see US or British policies towards Libya (and other radical centers) as chiefly based on hypocrisy. Indeed, there were occasions when one branch of government was denouncing the terrorism and criminality of a particular state, while another was dealing amicably with that same country. In a complex advanced state, government agencies are often so disparate as to be almost balkanized in character. In the United States, there is also a tradition of pursuing unpopular policies through private or quasi-governmental means. Indeed, a British term might well be borrowed here. Non-elective administrative bodies are often known as 'QUANGOS', 'Quasi-autonomous non-governmental organizations' – itself a useful term for the private network in the Iran-Contra affair.

Within a government, there might be a profound conflict of aims, methods and rhetoric between different agencies, of the sort that Libya provoked in the United States. In 1981, for example, there is clear evidence of the emergence of the US government of a hard-line faction headed by William Clark and William Casey who wanted to destroy the Qaddafi regime, by assassination if necessary (Hersh 1987). But it remains unclear whether other groups maintained their easy harmony with Libya despite the rhetoric, and some US corporations remained active there for several years (Hershey 1986, Perlez 1987). Certainly the British intelligence presence continued well into the Thatcher administration, despite the tragic shooting at the Libyan Peoples' Bureau in London in 1984.

By 1985 conflict within the US administration was at its height. At this point, the National Security Council was actively promoting a US/Egyptian scheme to invade Libya, to the horror of the State Department, and with other agencies split (Woodward 1987). Western policies towards 'terrorist states' might not be cynical; but they often appear schizophrenic (Ranelagh 1986: 697–700).

It is difficult to understand the Iran-Contra affair without appreciating that

22

its roots lie in policies towards other 'state terrorists', this time in Libya. Once this is understood, we can appreciate with less surprise why an alleged Libyan 'hit-man' plays so prominent a role in Contra conflicts; and more seriously, that America's Iranian difficulties were far from being either novel or unique. Libya provides the essential prehistory of Irangate.

Conclusion

The government of Muammar Qaddafi has certainly engaged in 'state criminality' in acts of terrorism sponsored by official agencies of the Libyan state. However, these acts are nothing like as frequent or as systematic as has been suggested by Western critics. It is Qaddafi's weakness which leads to his stigmatization, rather than the true seriousness of his nation's crimes.

In the last decade, there has been a dramatic growth of scholarly and journalistic work on terrorism, much of which uses the concept of 'state terrorism'. That such a thing exists is clear. However, each case must be examined very closely before the motives and rationale for such a policy can be understood; and only then can we begin to address questions such as etiology. There could be a 'criminology of states' which would be a valuable addition both to criminology and political science. At present, though, our primary need is to understand that the facts in each case are often far different from the political rhetoric.

Acknowledgements

I am very grateful to Alan Block and Gary Potter for discussions on this topic.

References

Abdrabboh, Bob (ed.) (1985). *Libya in the 1980s*. Washington, DC: International Economic and Research Press.

Adams, James (1986). *The Financing of Terror*. New York: Simon and Schuster.

Ajami, Fouad (1986). *The Vanished Imam*. Ithaca: Cornell University Press.

Alexander, Yonah and Myers, Kenneth A. (1982). *Terrorism in Europe*. New York: St. Martin's.

Bearman, Jonathan (1986). *Qaddafi's Libya*. London: Zed.

Bleakley, Fred R. (1986). 'Fiat's Novel Global Offering', *New York Times*, 26 September.

Bloch, Jonathan and Fitzgerald, Patrick (1983). *British Intelligence and Covert Action*. London: Junction.

Block, Alan and Chambliss, William (1981). *Organizing Crime*. New York: Elsevier.

Blundy, David and Lycett, Andrew (1987). *Qaddafi and the Libyan Revolution*. London: Weidenfeld.

23

Box, Stephen (1983). *Power, Crime and Mystification*. London: Tavistock.

Campbell, Duncan (1979). 'BP Sets Up Saudi Secret Police', *New Statesman*, 23 March.

Chambliss, William and Mankoff, Milton (1976). *Whose Law, What Order?* New York: John Wiley.

Cobban, Helen (1984). *The Palestinian Liberation Organization: People, Power and Politics*. Cambridge University Press.

Cooley, John K. (1982). *Libyan Sandstorm*. New York: Holt, Rinehart and Winston.

Cornwell, Rupert (1983). *God's Banker*. New York: Dodd Mead.

Davis, John (1987). *Libyan Politics: Tribe and Revolution*. London: I.B. Tauris.

De Lutiis, Guiseppe (1985). *Storia dei Servizi Segreti in Italia*. Rome: Riuniti.

De Young, Karen (1987). 'CIA Connection in Plot to Smear Wilson', *Guardian Weekly*, 10 May.

Dobson, Christopher and Payne, Ronald (1986). *War Without End*. London: Harrap.

El-Khawas, Mohammed A. (1986). *Qaddafi*. Brattleboro, UT: Amana Press.

Engelberg, Stephen (1987). 'A Consultant's Role in the Iran Affair', *New York Times*, 2 February.

FBI (1979). Report of interview with Mario Leanza.

Frangi, Abdallah (1982). *The PLO and Palestine*. London: Zed.

Felb, Leslie H. (1986). 'US Diplomat Reportedly Held Talks in Libya', *New York Times*, 23 March.

Gerth, Jeff (1986). 'US Envoy to the Vatican Quits', *New York Times*, 21 May.

Goudel, Joseph (1984). *The Death Merchant*. New York: Simon and Schuster.

Haley, P. Edward (1984). *Qaddafi and the United States Since 1969*. New York: Praeger.

Halliday, Fred (1979). *Iran: Dictatorship and Development*. London: Penguin.

Harris, Lillian Craig (1986). *Libya*. London: Croom Helm.

Henze, Paul (1985). *The Plot to Kill the Pope*. New York Scribners.

Herman, Edward S. (1982). *The Real Terror Network*. Boston: South End.

Herman, Edward S. and Brodhead, Frank (1986). *The Rise and Fall of the Bulgarian Connection*. Sheridan Square Publications.

Hersh, Seymour M. (1981). 'The Qaddafi Connection', *New York Times Magazine*. 2 parts. June.

Hersh, Seymour M. (1987). 'Target Qaddafi', *New York Times Magazine*, 22 February.

Hershey, Robert D. (1986A). 'US Effort on Libya Oil Said to Gain', *New York Times*. 1 July.

Hershey, Robert D. (1986B). 'US Trade With Libya Continues', *ibid*. 9 December.

Hougan, Jim (1983). 'Interview with Frank Terpil', *Penthouse*, December.

Hougan, Jim (1984). *Secret Agenda*. New York: Random House.

Jenkins, Philip (1986). 'The Assassins Revisited', *Intelligence and National Security* 1(3): 459–471.

Johnstone, Diana (1984–7). Numerous articles in *In These Times*.

Johnstone, Diana (1982). 'The Ledeen Connections', *ibid*. 8 September.

Johnstone, Diana (1987). 'Abu Nidal', *ibid*. 15–21 January.

Johnstone, Diana (1986). 'Western Spies Pull the Strings on Terror', *ibid*. 11–24 June.

Kruger, Henrik (1980). *The Great Heroin Coup*. Boston: South End.

Kurz, Anat and Merari, Ariel (1985). *ASALA*. Tel Aviv: *Jerusalem Post* Books.

Lee, Martin and Coogan, Kevin (1987). 'Europe's New Fascists', *Mother Jones*, May.

Lernoux, Penny (1984). *In Banks We Trust*. New York: Doubleday Anchor.

Maas, Peter (1986). *Manhunt*. New York: Random House.

Maas, Peter (1987). 'Oliver North's Strange Recruits', *New York Times Magazine*. January.

Malcolm, Andrew H. (1986). 'Four Gang Members in Chicago are Indicated in Libyan Terror Plot', *New York Times*. 31 October.

McCoy, Alfred (1972). *The Politics of Heroin in South-East Asia*. New York: Harper and Row.

Marion, Georges and Pienel, Edwy (1987A). 'Christians and Muslims in Unholy Terrorist Alliance', *Le Monde*, reprinted in *Guardian Weekly*. May 3.

24

Marion, Georges (1986). 'Portrait of a Terrorist Family', *ibid.* 21 September.

Marion, Georges (1987b). 'Islamic Bombing Campaign Foiled by DST Swoop', *ibid.* 5 April.

Melman, Yossi (1986). *The Master Terrorist: The True Story of Abu Nidal.* New York: Adama.

Merkl, Peter H. (ed.) (1986). *Political Violence and Terror.* University of California Press.

Miller, Judith (1987). 'The Istanbul Synagogue Massacre', *New York Times Magazine*, 4 January.

National Security Archive (1987). *The Chronology.* New York: Warner.

Naureckas, Jim and Ryan, Richard (1987). 'The Lessons of Laos', *In These Times*, 15–21 April.

Netanyahu, Benjamin (ed.) (1986). *Terrorism: How the West Can Win.* New York: Farrar, Straus, Giroux.

Pasha, Aftab Kamal (1984). *Libya and the United States.* New Delhi: Detente.

Pazienza, Francesco (1985). Interview on National Public Radio's, 'All Things Considered', on 29–30 August.

Perlez, Jane (1987). 'Americans Remain in Libya a Year After Ban by US', *New York Times*, 21 April.

Pienel, Edwy (1986). 'Police Narrow Down Syrian Terrorist Connection', *Guardian Weekly*, October.

Pipes, Daniel (1986). 'Syria: The Cuba of the Middle East', *Commentary* 82: 15–22.

Quinney, Richard (1975). *Criminology.* Boston: Little Brown.

Rafizadeh, Mansur (1987). *Witness.* New York: William Morrow.

Ranelagh, John (1986). *The Agency.* New York: Simon and Schuster.

Sampson, Anthony (1975). *The Seven Sisters.* New York: Viking.

Samura, Mohammed O'Bai (1985). *The Libyan Revolution.* Washington, DC: International Institute for Policy and Developmental Studies.

Schneider, Keith (1987). 'North's Aides Linked to Australian Study', *New York Times*, 8 March.

Schumacher, Edward (1986). 'Qaddafi's Troubled Economy', *New York Times*, 2 May.

Sciolino, Elaine (1986). 'Syria Described at Most Effective in Using Terror as Policy Devise', *New York Times*, 25 October.

'Seven Accused in Sale of Planes to Libya', *New York Times*, 24 July.

Sherrill, Robert (1983). *The Oil Follies of 1970–80.* New York: Doubleday.

Sono, Themba (1984). *Libya: The Vilified Revolution.* Langley Park: Progress.

Spotts, Frederic and Weiser, Theodor (1986). *Italy: A Difficult Democracy.* Cambridge University Press.

Sterling, Claire (1981). *The Terror Network.* New York: Berkley.

Stiff, Peter (1985). *See You in November.* London.

Stohl, Michael (1983). *The Politics of Terrorism.* New York: Dekker.

Suro, Roberto (1986). 'Italians Say White House Agreed to Secret US Overtures to Libya', *New York Times*, 19 December.

Taheri, Amir (1986). 'The Fruits of Terror', *New Statesmen*, 28 November.

Tosches, Nick (1986). *Power on Earth.* New York: Arbor House.

Tower Commission (1987). Report of the President's Special Review Board. New York: Bantam.

Turk, Austin (1982). *Political Criminality.* Beverly Hills: Sage.

Wardlaw, Grant (1982). *Political Terrorism.* Cambridge University Press.

Wright, John (1982). *Libya: A Modern History.* London: Croom Helm.

Wright, Robin (1985). *Sacred Rage.* New York: Linden.

Woodward, Bob (1987). 'State Department Acted to Block US-Egyptian Attack on Libya', *Guardian Weekly*, 1 March.

[13]

STATE SPONSORED TERROR VIOLENCE

J D van der Vyver*

Almost all political scientists agree that the destiny of the state is intimately linked to the establishment and maintenance of a public legal order within a certain territory;[1] or, in laymen's language, to maintaining law and order within the limits of its territorial jurisdiction.

To this end the state embodies within its internal structure a particular kind of authority, which might be called 'political power' and which manifests itself as 'power of the sword'.[2] Power of this kind entails the propensity of physical coercion through the agency of the police and ultimately the military forces included in the instruments of government, and its institution and exercise within a defined territory vest exclusively in the respositories of state authority.

Since political power in this sense constitutes a vital instrument of law enforcement, it stands to reason that the state, in order to comply with its leading function of maintaining law and order, must also take precautions to uphold and safeguard its own authority.

However, it is equally important that the subjects be protected against

---

* BCom LLB BA (Hons) (PU vir CHO) LLD (Pret), Professor of Law, University of the Witwatersrand, Johannesburg.

1 H Dooyeweerd *De Strijd om het Souvereiniteitsbegrip in de Moderne Rechts- en Staatsleer* (1950) 54 thus defined the state as: '... een institutaire publiekrechtelijke gemeenschap van overheid en onderdanen op de historische grondslag van een monopolistische organisatie van de zwaardmacht op een territorium'; and see also *Verkenningen in de Wijsbegeerte, de Sociologie en de Rechtsgeschiedenis* (1962) 127; L M du Plessis *Die Juridiese Relevansie van Christelike Geregtigheid* (unpublished LLD thesis PU for CHE 1978) 812: 'Die Staat is 'n menslike instelling binne (of beter: oor) 'n bepaalde grondgebied wat deur 'n juridiese bestemming (die verwesenliking van die ampsgeborgenheid van alle mense binne daardie grondgebied) gekwalifiseer (of "gelei") word'; and also 'Menseregte en Konfliksituasies' 1979 *Koers* 339 at 340: 'Die staat se aard en struktuur word deur die feit dat dit op die handhawing van 'n openbare regsorde binne 'n bepaalde (gewoonlik grond-) gebied bedag is, bepaal'.

2 According to Dooyeweerd, power is vested in the historical aspect of reality in the sense of 'control', 'command', 'mastery' or 'free formative power'. See, for instance, *A New Critique of Theoretical Thought* II (1969) 68-71 and 413; H Dooyeweerd *Roots of Western Culture: Pagan, Secular and Christian Options* (translated by J Kraay) (1979) 66-70. Power in this sense can take on different forms, and one might distinguish between, for instance, the intellectual power that guides an educational institution, the economical power of a business enterprise, the juridical power included in the notion of legal competence, the power of faith which constitutes the focus of an ecclesiastical community, and so on.

the abuse of state authority, because — as everyone knows — power tends
to corrupt....

JURIDICAL POWER RESTRAINTS

For that reason political science is particularly eager to find constitutional
devices for the curtailment of state authority, and over the years it has in
fact produced several feasible strategies that might serve that purpose:
representative government in a democratic dispensation; decentralization
of the instruments of government in a federal structure with autonomous
regional and local bureaucracies; distribution of authority through the
separation of powers; cutting the jurisdiction of political authority down
to size with a view to the state's appropriate sovereign sphere of
competencies as determined by its qualifying function; surveillance of
administrative acts by an ombudsman; subjecting the exercise of political
power to clearly defined legal restraints in accordance with the idea of the
rule of law; and shielding, in a bill of rights régime, a defined enclave of
fundamental freedoms against legislative and administrative encroachment.

The history of western jurisprudence has similarly yielded a set of norms
of procedure and evidence with a view to upholding the basic demands of
fair play in the administration of justice. These so-called procedural
human rights, commonly referred to as the conditions for the due process
of law, have been designed to ensure that the courts could remain impartial
and would function independently of the executive branch of government;
that convictions of the innocent can as far as humanly possible be
prevented; that each person may be presumed innocent; that no one shall
be charged more than once with the same offence; that no one can be
compelled to be a witness against himself; that no decision would be taken
that might adversely affect the interests of any person without that person
having had an opportunity to state his case; that every party in judicial or
quasi-judicial proceedings be afforded the right to legal representation;
that no legislation that might adversely affect the rights or competencies of
a legal subject be introduced with retroactive effect; that no person be
subjected to any form of cruel or inhuman punishment or treatment; and
that no one could arbitrarily be taken into custody or be detained without
the prospect of a fair trial.

These, then, are the rules of the game for the fair, just, and equitable
maintenance of law and order and for safeguarding the authority of the
state within a properly structured political community. Their aim is to
prevent the abuse of political power and to guarantee the dictates of
justice.

It should be noted in passing that none of the above measures to constrain
political power constitutes part of the South African constitutional
system;[3] and in so far as measures for the protection of state security are
concerned, the procedural conditions for the due process of law have also

---

3 See, for instance, J D van der Vyver *Die Grondwet van die Republiek van Suid-Afrika* (1984) 48-83;
   and, with regard to the separation of powers, F J van Zyl & J D van der Vyver *Inleiding tot die
   Regswetenskap* 2 ed (1982) 451-6.

been thrown overboard in this country.[4]
This state of affairs invites disaster!

THE ESCALATION OF RESISTANCE

Gustav Radbruch (1878-1949), member of the neo-Kantian School of Baden,[5] in the post-war phase of his philosophical development,[6] vividly described the course of events that would culminate in such a state of affairs.

The legal idea, said Radbruch, embodies within itself three basic value structures:[7] that of efficacy, legal certainty and justice;[8] that is to say, law that cannot effectively be enforced would be of no consequence; law of which the contents remains unknown is meaningless; and a legal system that has lost track of the people's conception of justice is heading towards catastrophe.

As a relativist, Radbruch acknowledged the possibility of a conflict between these essential substrata of the legal idea. For instance, legal certainty might require adherence to unjust laws in spite of their iniquity; but when legally sanctioned injustices assume such huge proportions that one would begin to doubt the clear meaning of the language used to denote the injustice, the rule would lose its validity and one would then, according to Radbruch, be entitled to appeal to das übergesetzliche Recht[9] — a term

4 See, for instance, the authorities cited in note 3; and also John Dugard *Human Rights and the South African Legal Order* (1978) 250-75; J D van der Vyver 'Kantaantekeninge by die Wet op Binnelandse Veiligheid 74 van 1982' (1982) 45 *THRHR* 294.

5 This particular variety of neo-Kantianism is especially known for its obsession with values and adherence to relativism. In conformity with the first of these two characteristics, Radbruch referred to a contemporary tendency of his time to regard philosophy as a 'science of values, a science of what ought to be' (*Vorschule der Rechtsphilosophie* 2 ed (1959) 19: 'Wissenschaft von den Werten, ... Wissenschaft vom Sollen ...'); and as to the subject-matter of legal philosophy: 'Sie handelt also von den Werten und Zielen des Rechts, von der Idee des Rechts und vom idealen Recht, und findet ihre Fortsetzung in der Rechtspolitik, welche die Verwirklichungsmöglichkeiten des idealen Recht zu ihrem Gegenstand hat' (ibid) ('It deals with the value and purpose of the law, the idea of law and with the ideal law, and is continued in Legal Politics, which has as its subject-matter the practicality of the ideal law'). The aspect of relativism of his legal philosophy was described by Wolfgang Friedmann *Legal Theory* 5 ed (1970) at 192 as follows:
   'This legal relativism is ... concerned with the ultimate meaning of legal systems but does not see its task in suggesting a choice between opposite values. This choice is a matter for personal decisions; a matter not of science but of conscience. Relativism does not evade political decisions, but does not wish to give them a scientific cloak.'

6 Friedmann op cit note 5 at 350-1 pointed out that Radbruch's experience in Nazi Germany led him to abandon many of his earlier ideas and to become a proponent of the doctrine of natural law.

7 These basic value structures would, in the language of the Philosophy of the Cosmonomic Idea of Herman Dooyeweerd, qualify either as (some of the) retrocipatory substrata of the law (efficacy refers back to the historical substratum of the juridical aspect of reality, while legal certainty constitutes a retrocipation of the juridical meaning-kernel to the linguistic aspect of reality), or as an anticipation of the juridical meaning-kernel to the ethical aspect of reality (ie in the case of justice). By regarding juridical efficacy and legal certainty as ingredients of the legal idea, Radbruch in typical neo-Kantian fashion displayed a one-sided ethicized vision of reality.

8 See the chapter on 'Das Idee des Rechts' in *Vorschule der Rechtsphilosophie* op cit note 5 at 24-33.

9 *Vorschule der Rechtsphilosophie* op cit note 5 at 32-3; and see also 37:
   'Die durch das positive Recht gewährleistete Rechtssicherheit eines ungerechten Gesetzes verliert diesen Wert ... wenn die in ihr enthaltene Ungerechtigkeit ein solches Mass annimmt, dass demgegenüber die durch positives Recht gewährleistete Rechtssicherheit nicht ins Gewicht

58   SOUTH AFRICAN JOURNAL ON HUMAN RIGHTS

used by him to denote a system of natural law.[10]

By the same token a discrepancy might arise between the value idea of justice and the law's basic idea of effective implementation: when people are required to obey laws that affront their sense of justice, they would develop a natural tendency to disobey such laws. Those entrusted with the maintenance of law and order would then be compelled to apply with vigour the enforcement mechanisms of the law. However, the coercive implementation of laws perceived by a cross-section of the population as instances of injustice would stimulate rather than counteract resistance — and then more strict means of compulsion would be needed to uphold such laws. In this way the interchange of resistance against the laws in question and increasing austerity in the implementation thereof would escalate to a point where law enforcement can no longer be secured within the confines of the rule of law and the due process of law. Public censure of a body of laws might soon bring the entire system into disrepute, and would almost invariably implicate the very authority of the powers that be. Loss of legitimacy along these lines and in the situation where maintenance of law and order has become a matter of brute force would thus culminate in governmental anarchy; and then, warned Radbruch, the entire régime of state and law would be on the brink of collapse.

I might add that the methods employed by the repositories of political power in attempts to uphold their authority in the final stages of a breakdown in law and order almost invariably include instances of state sponsored terror violence.

TERRORISM DEFINED

Defining terrorism is in itself no easy task.[11] Attempts at scrutinizing the complexities of this concept range from sweeping generalities (terrorism is 'a strategy of the weak'[12]) and commonplace clichés ('one man's terrorist is

---

fällt. Wenn sie also in der Regel der Fälle die Geltung positiven Rechts durch Rechtssicherheit rechtfertigen lässt, so bleibt in gewissen Ausnahme-fällen horrend ungerechter Gesetze die Mögligkeit, solchen Gesetzen ihrer Ungerechtigkeit wegen die Geltung abzusprechen' ('The legal certainty of an unjust law that is guaranteed by positive law, would forfeit this value ... if the injustice embodied in it were to take on such proportions that the legal certainty guaranteed by positive law would no longer be of any consequence. While, therefore, as a general rule the validity of positive law is justified on account of legal certainty, the possibility remains that in certain exceptional cases pertaining to unjust laws, such laws might by virtue of their injustice lose their validity').

See further Radbruch's *Rechtsphilosophie* 7 ed (1970) 353.

10 Op cit note 5 at 113-14.

11 In the early 1970s, when terrorism began to attract world attention, M Cherif Bassiouni & Ved P Nanda *A Treatise on International Criminal Law* (1973) 491 wrote: 'The definition of terrorism is still in the process of being formulated'. See also John Dugard 'International Terrorism: The Problems of Definition' (1974) 50 *International Affairs* 67:

'Basically the problem is to identify those acts of terror designed to bring about political change which disrupt international relations and which the international community considers contrary to desirable international conduct.'

It should be noted that Dugard was here dealing with international terrorism only (see in particular op cit at 74-5). Since then many commendable contributions have seen the light of day that have brought greater clarity to this concept and its manisfestations.

12 Robert H Kupperman & Darrell M Trent *Terrorism: Threat, Reality, Response* (1979) 13.

STATE SPONSORED TERROR VIOLENCE   59

another man's freedom fighter'[13]) to the kind of more detailed precision required for actual ajudication ('the use of violence for political ends [including] any use of violence for the purpose of putting the public or any section of the public in fear'[14]). For the purposes of this survey it will suffice to define terrorism as

'a strategy of violence designed to instill terror in order to achieve a power outcome.'[15]

In broad outline, terrorism thus entails (*a*) acts of aggression[16] (*b*) often aimed at civilian targets[17] (*c*) with a view to promoting a preconceived objective[18] (*d*) by means of intimidating the target of such aggression (which need not be the victims thereof)[19] (*e*) to submit to the demands of the perpetrators[20] (*f*) out of fear emanating from the threat or actual

13 David Carlton 'The Future of Political Substate Violence' in Yonah Alexander, David Carlton & Paul Wilkinson (eds) *Terrorism: Theory and Practice* (1979) 201; and see also David Carlton & Carlo Schaerf (eds) *Contemporary Terror* (1981) 15; Edward S Herman 'U S Sponsorship of International Terrorism: An Overview' (1987) 27-8 *Crime and Social Justice* 1: 'The powerful . . . define terrorism to exclude their own acts and those of their friends and clients.'

14 *Ireland v United Kingdom* (1978) European Court of Human Rights, official text, para 85.

15 Quoted by M Cherif Bassiouni 'Terrorism and Human Rights' (unpublished lectures delivered at the Seventeenth Study Session of the International Institute of Human Rights, Strasbourg, 22-23 July 1986). See also Bassiouni & Nanda op cit note 11 at 491: '. . . terrorism may be defined as acts of international crime committed by means of terror, violence, and intimidation, with a goal of obtaining predetermined goals and purposes'; Saleem Qureshi 'Political Violence in the South Asian Continent' in Yonah Alexander (ed) *International Terrorism: National, Regional and Global Perspectives* (1976) 151: 'Terrorism is the use of violence in order to induce a state of fear and submission in the victim'; T P Thornton 'Terror as a Weapon of Political Agitation' in H Eckstein (ed) *Internal War* (1964) 73, where terrorism is defined as 'a symbolic act designed to influence political behaviour by external means, entailing the use or threat of violence'.

16 In this regard reference might be made to the often quoted strategies of terror in Carlos Marighella's *Minimanual of the Urban Guerilla* (1971) 103: 'Bank assaults, ambushes, desertions and diverting of arms, the rescue of prisoners, executions, kidnapping, sabotage, terrorism, and the war of nerves.' Yonah Alexander 'Terrorism and the Media: Some Considerations' in Alexander, Carlton & Wilkinson op cit note 13 at 159 refers to the terrorist's 'instruments of psychological and physical force — including intimidation, coercion, repression, and, ultimately, destruction of lives and property'.

17 See Mario 'n Mushkat 'The Soviet Concept of Guerrilla Warfare' (1981) 7 *SA Yearbook of International Law* 1 at 4, where civilian targets and 'the suffering of innocent people' are said to be the main targets of a terrorist.

18 Many writers emphasize the political nature of a terrorist's objective. Yonah Alexander op cit note 16 at 159 thus referred to terrorism as 'an expedient tactical and strategic tool of politics in the struggle for power within and among nations . . .'. See also David Carlton op cit note 13 at 201, who includes in the concept of a terrorist 'any perpetrator of substate violence whose motives are broadly of a political character'. However, terrorism need not necessarily be politically motivated and might be resorted to by ordinary criminals or psychopaths (see Grant Wardlaw *Political Terrorism: Theory, Tactics and Counter-Measures* (1982) 8-9). It might furthermore be motivated by either social or political grievances (F C Pedersen 'Comment: Controlling International Terrorism: An Analysis of Unilateral Force and Proposals for Multilateral Co-operation' (1976) 8 *Toledo LR* 209 quoted by T M Kühn 'Terrorism and the Right of Self-Defence' (1980) 6 *SA Yearbook of International Law* 43).

19 Abraham H Miller 'Hostage Negotiations and the Concept of Transference' in Alexander, Carlton & Wilkinson op cit note 13 at 155: 'Terrorism by definition is an act that seeks to influence a population significantly larger than the immediate target'; and see also Wardlaw op cit note 18 at 10.

20 See John Baylis 'Revolutionary Warfare' in John Baylis, Ken Booth, John Garnett & Phil Williams (eds) *Contemporary Strategies: Theory and Policies* (1975) 132 at 137: 'Intimidation and terrorism are used not only to publicize the move, to demoralize the government, and to polarize society but also at times to ensure that people have no alternative but compliance, unless and until the government is able to protect them.'

abhorrence of the act.[21] Perhaps one should exclude from the definition of terrorism the reign of anxiety that attends situations of belligerency,[22] but one should not forget, on the other hand, that terrorism is often not in itself a particular means of aggression but might be only a tool of, for instance, revolution or insurgency.[23]

Depending on one's point of departure, terrorism can be classified into a wide range of categories. Thus, for instance, John Baylis distinguished between *coercive terrorism*, which according to him is designed to demoralize the population and weaken its confidence in the control authorities as well as to make an example of selected victims, and *disruptive terrorism*, which aims at discrediting the government, advertising the movement and provoking the authorities into taking harsh repressive countermeasures.[24] David Carlton refers to qualifications of the term 'terrorism' by the addition of adjectives such as state, national, international or transnational.[25]

With a view to the perpetrators of terror violence, one can similarly distinguish between:

- political dissident groups in a political community seeking to overthrow the government or altering the prevailing governmental policy or constitutional structures;
- opposing groups in a multi-religious, multi-ethnic or multi-racial society;
- occupying military forces attempting to intimidate the conquered population into submission; and
- a governmental authority which, in an endeavour to perpetuate its own position of power or a particular political order, desires to compel its own citizens to conform.[26]

State sponsored terror violence might be confined to 'the extent that governmental authority permits ... intimidatory activity'[27] or could consist of acts of terror against the nationals or governments of other countries (which would mostly consist of the maverick state affording assistance to opposition groups in the form of finance, arms, training and facilities).[28] However, it clearly also includes acts of terror perpetrated by a

21 The distinguishing feature of terrorism, said Wardlaw op cit note 18 at 10, is 'the *design* to create anxiety'. See also Lawrence Freedman 'Terrorism and Strategy' in Lawrence Freedman et al (eds) *Terrorism and International Order* (1986) 56; C J Botha 'Clausewitz's "Kleinkrieg" and Mao's "Fishes in the Water"'; Mushkat in Proper Conceptual Perspective' (1982) 8 *SA Yearbook of International Law* 141 at 147: 'Terrorism is a combination of threats and the actual use of terror to create a psychological effect'; Thornton op cit note 15 at 77, who maintains that terrorism is characterized by 'its high symbolic content'; and see in general Wardlaw op cit note 18 at 8-10.
22 Wardlaw op cit note 18 at 8-9.
23 Cf Baylis op cit note 20 at 137.
24 Op cit note 20 at 150n24.
25 Op cit note 13 at 201.
26 See M Cherif Bassiouni op cit note 15.
27 Cf L C Green 'Legalization of Terrorism' in Alexander, Carlton & Wilkinson op cit note 13 at 176.
28 Lawrence Freedman op cit note 21 at 66-8 seems to confine 'state terrorism' to this kind of activity and mentions as an example United States support for the Contras in Nicaragua. Elsewhere (at 61) he does, however, speak of 'terroristic methods ... adopted by government'. As to the state as sponsor of terrorism in other territories, see Herman op cit note 13 at 8-15. It might be noted that the

STATE SPONSORED TERROR VIOLENCE   61

government against its own citizens. Richard Falk refers to this type of
violent conduct — that is, '[w]hen a government systematically engages in
terror to maintain its political control or intimidate its opposition' — as
'official terrorism'.[29]

Terrorism of the latter kind has received special emphasis in several
instructive expositions of the notion of terror violence. T P Thornton[30]
thus makes a distinction between *agitational terror* — 'terroristic activities
of those who wish to disrupt the existing order and ascend to political
power themselves' — and *enforcement terror* — 'which is used by those in
power who wish to suppress challenges to their authority'. W F May[31]
similarly draws a line between a *siege of terror* — terrorism in the service of
a revolutionary movement — and a *régime of terror* — terrorism in the
service of the established order.

For a proper understanding of state sponsored terror violence as a
particular instance of terrorism in general, the analysis of political
terrorism by P Wilkinson[32] is particularly instructive. He first
differentiates between *political terror*, which consists of isolated acts of
violence but also manifests itself in the form of extreme, indiscriminate and
arbitrary acts of violence, and *political terrorism*, which consists of 'a
sustained policy involving the waging of organized terror either on the part
of the state, a movement or faction, or by a small group of individuals'.[33]
Political terrorism in turn might take on the form of *revolutionary
terrorism*, aimed at bringing about the overthrow of the government or of
the constitutional system,[34] *sub-revolutionary terrorism*, inspired by
political motives other than a revolution or governmental repression,[35] or
repressive terrorism, which he defined as:

'The systematic use of terroristic acts of violence for the purposes of suppressing, putting
down, quelling, or restraining certain groups, individuals or forms of behaviour deemed
to be undesirable.'[36]

Bowyer Bell[37] identified three types of terrorism which are associated
with a government or persons acting on its behalf: *endemic terror*, signified
by a collapse of the state into a condition of barbarism; *authorized terror*,
constituted by the institutionalization of political power for coercive
purposes; and *vigilante terrorism*, that manifests itself through the acts of
private citizens engaged in curbing or eliminating dissent. It should also be

entire volume in which Herman's article appeared, deals with the support rendered by the United
States government to terrorist group in foreign countries.
29 *Human Rights and State Sovereignty* (1981) 162; and as to this category of terrorism, see also
Carlton op cit note 13 at 201-2.
30 Op cit note 15 at 72; and see also Wardlaw op cit note 18 at 10.
31 'Terrorism as Strategy of Ecstasy' (1974) 14 *Social Research* 277; and see also Wardlaw op cit note 18
at 10.
32 *Political Terrorism* (1974); and see also Wardlaw op cit note 18 at 14-5.
33 At 17-18.
34 At 36.
35 At 38.
36 At 40.
37 J Bowyer Bell *Transnational Terror* (1975) 13-15; and see also Juliet Lodge (ed) *Terrorism: A
Challenge to the State* (1981) 4-5.

noted that where a government embarks upon acts of terror against its own citizens, it usually avails itself for this purpose of a massive bureaucracy: police, armed forces, intelligence agencies, a special branch of state officials trained in strategies of terror, immigration personnel, information control agencies and the like. Grant Wardlaw, while highlighting this aspect of institutionalized terrorism, pointed out that an administration of terror directly or indirectly involves large numbers of the population.[38]

THE PROBLEM OF LEGITIMACY

In the history of nations one would find many examples of state sponsored terror violence of this latter kind: the reign of terror by the National Socialist Party of Adolf Hitler in Germany during the era of the Third Reich, 1933-1945; the state of affairs in Greece following the revolution of 1967 when a military junta under Colonel George Papadopoulos took control, suspended the constitutional guarantees against arbitrary arrests and detention, and, prior to the military coup of November 1973 whereby the government of Mr Papadopoulos was overthrown and which preceded the return of Greece to civilian rule in September 1974, brought hundreds of political dissidents to trial without the due process of law;[39] the régime of Idi Amin in Uganda in the period of 1971-1979 when literally tens of thousands of Ugandan citizens lost their lives; the Khmer Rouge régime in Kampuchea during the same period, when thousands of peasants were detained in labour camps and many other dissidents (perhaps as many as three million) were put to death by the authorities; the six years of 'dirty war' in Argentina, which commenced in 1976 when Isabelita Peron was deposed by a military régime and lasted until the Falklands War of 1982, noted particularly for the disappearance of probably as many as 30 000 members of the population,[40] and so on.

And then, of course, there is also the case of South Africa.

These cases of institutional terrorism have one thing in common: a government that seeks to maintain its political power or to preserve a particular constitutional dispensation while it, or the constitutional system in question, lacks legitimacy.

One should in this regard distinguish between the concept of *legality* and that of *legitimacy*. Legality denotes the constitutional lawfulness of a particular régime, constitutional or legal system, or legal rule, while legitimacy belongs to the domain of legal ethics. With a view to the systematics of the Philosophy of the Cosmonomic Idea of Herman Dooyeweerd, the notion of legitimacy might be said to represent a psychical substratum of the law, denoted by the concept of the feeling of

38 Op cit note 18 at 7-8.
39 The violation of human rights in Greece led to several inter-state proceedings before the European Commission of Human Rights. In December 1969, when it had become clear that the Commission's finding would go against Greece, the country withdrew from the Council of Europe. In November 1974 Greece was readmitted to the Council of Europe.
40 See Bassiouni note 15. However, official figures put the number of disappearances during this period at 9 000 and Peter Dale Scott 'Contragate: Reagan, Foreign Money and the *Contra* Deal' (1987) 27-28 *Crime and Social Justice* 110 at 120 puts it at between 6 000 and 15 000.

justice ('regsgevoel') of the community, and which as such embodies within itself an anticipation of the ethical modality.[41] Legitimacy of, for instance, a legal system is governed by the legal community's perception of the law from the perspective of its quality of justice; to possess legitimacy, the legal system requires the support or acceptance of a cross-section of the community on the basis of their sense of justice — a state of affairs that was accurately depicted by F J van Zyl when he (somewhat optimistically) attributed exactly that characteristic to the South African legal system:

> 'Ons regstelsel word naamlik in so 'n mate deur die lede van die samelewing as reg aangevoel en as sodanig aanvaar dat daar, byvoorbeeld, geen twyfel bestaan oor die vraag of 'n hof inderdaad reg spreek of oor die vraag of 'n wet werklik reg bevat nie.'[42]

Legitimacy can, of course, never be calculated with mathematical precision. Its decline, however, is evidenced by that kind and measure of resistance which, for purposes of the maintenance of law and order or of the security of state authority, necessitates abridgments of the rule of law and the due process of law; its manifest erosion sets in when insubordination to such an extent exceeds the normal percentage of a criminal element in society that the administration of justice can no longer take its course within the confines of procedural human rights. Arbitrary powers of law-enforcement agencies within or without a state of emergency, and in particular recourse of the authorities to acts of terror violence, constitute proof a posteriori that the government or the system patently lacks legitimacy.

THE SOUTH AFRICAN PREDICAMENT

I do not share Professor Van Zyl's high regard for the South African legal system — which after all comprises not only Roman-Dutch law but also the statutory sanctioning of racial discrimination and a body of most repressive security legislation and regulations.[43] Nor would I concede that the present government, constitutional arrangement, or legal system enjoys the measure of public acquiescence that would constitute legitimacy.

The Republic of South Africa, on the contrary, finds itself in a fourfold legitimacy crisis:

- The South African government is not a democratically elected or representative authority but owes the mandate of its dominion to a relatively small and racially defined minority group.[44]

---

41 Cf in particular Dooyeweerd *A New Critique of Theoretical Thought* op cit note 2 at 176-80. Dooyeweerd's own analysis here has perhaps been to some extent misguided by the Dutch term 'rechtsgevoel', which does not clearly reflect the fact that one is here concerned with a feeling of *justice* (though that is exactly how the word has been translated in the *New Critique*). He consequently does not expressly mention that the psychical concept upon which the legal concept of 'rechtsgevoel' is based already accommodates an ethical anticipation.

42 Op cit note 3 at 236-7.

43 Van Zyl op cit note 3 at 237 conceded that the South African legislature has had occasion to take precautions for the maintenance of public order which in some instances lack the backing of the sense of justice of a considerable section of the community.

44 The South African political dispensation might from this point of view be characterized as a racially based aristocracy. See Van Zyl & Van der Vyver op cit note 3 at 456-7.

- The South African régime has over the years systematically abused its political trusteeship by pursuing a policy and legislative programme of institutionalized injustices, designed to safeguard the interests of the white minority at the expense of the disfranchised masses.[45]
- The repositories of political power in South Africa have never excelled in the art of lending an ear to the grievances of the disadvantaged sections of the population but, instead, in a consistent pattern of repressive strategies, sought to silence the voices of legitimate protest.[46]
- The official policy of racial discrimination and the unyielding responses of the South African government to sound protests have been condemned in the strongest terms by literally every other member of the international community of states,[47] the promotion and implementation of that policy constitutes a crime in international law,[48] and the sporadic attempts of racial fanatics to find scriptural justification for apartheid has been identified by almost all credible ecumenical institutions in the Western world as an instance of heresy.[49]

The benevolent bonuses that — admittedly — occasionally attended the implementation of government policies could, of course, never outweigh, let alone undo, the concomitant deprivations included in institutionalized discrimination. Injustice simply cannot be absolved by good deeds or incidental generosity. The 'total onslaught' which consequently confronts the authorities in this country has already exceeded the divide where the maintenance of law and order can no longer be orchestrated under the protective guidance of the rule of law and the due process of law.

Included in the techniques of law enforcement and for the protection of state security demanded by this contingency are clearly those that amount to intimidation through the threat and actual perpetration of state imposed terror violence as defined above.

45 For an evaluation of the South African legal dispensation in the light of the dictates of justice, see, for instance, Johan David van der Vyver *Seven Lectures on Human Rights* (1976) 1-20; Dugard op cit note 4 at 53-106; Muriel Horrel *Laws Affecting Race Relations in South Africa (to the end of 1976)* (1978); Sheila T van der Horst & Jane Reid (eds) *Race Discrimination in South Africa: A Review* (1981).

46 The history of security legislation in South Africa (see, for instance, Anthony S Mathews *Freedom State Security and the Rule of Law* ((1986) 33-215) represents the intolerant responses of the South African government to protests against the iniquities of the apartheid system.

47 Robert E Gorelick 'Apartheid and Colonialism' (1986) 19 *Comparative and International Law Journal of South Africa* 70 at 76 reminds us that '[i]t is this racial dimension of apartheid, which reflects the outmoded coloniser-colonised relationship between blacks and whites in Africa, which distinguishes South Africa from other regimes which treat their citizens similarly or even worse'.

48 See, for instance, M Cherif Bassiouni *International Criminal Law: A Draft International Criminal Code* (1980) 76-7; Falk op cit note 29 at 161-2; John Dugard 'The Conflict between International Law and South African Law: Another Divisive Factor in South African Society' (1986) 2 *SAJHR* 1 at 11; and in general the *International Convention on the Suppression and Punishment of the Crime of Apartheid* (GA Res 3068 (XXXIII) 1973), which came into force on 18 July 1976, briefly discussed in Van der Vyver op cit note 45 at 144-6 and (in an extremely negative tone) by H Booysen 'Convention on the Crime of *Apartheid*' (1976) 2 *SA Yearbook of International Law* 56.

49 For instance by the World Alliance of Reformed Churches in a decision of its Ottawa Conference, 25 August 1982. As to the attitude of the Reformed Ecumenical Synod (which denounced apartheid in less drastic terms) see *RES Testimony on Human Rights* (1983) 134-41.

REPRESSION, TOTALITARIANISM, STATE ABSOLUTISM AND TERROR VIOLENCE

The awesome variety of mechanisms used to propagate state sponsored terror violence is seen in the example of South Africa. Such violence requires meticulous preparation: the expansion of state control — including the criminalization — of acts performed by members of the population in the ordinary exercise of their civil rights, such as freedom of association and the right of assembly, freedom of expression and the right to an opinion, and freedom of the press and the right to information (repression); state interference in the sovereign sphere of competencies of social institutions, such as the church, universities, trade unions, and political organizations (totalitarianism); and conferring arbitrary powers on members of the executive branch of government (state absolutism).

Actual terror violence includes:

- intimidation through an assortment of public warnings, directed at (mostly unspecified) 'certain persons or institutions' ['sekere instansies'] and promising state intervention to combat (probably fictitious) instances of putative subversion;
- ostentatious actions at the instance of the security forces or its organized collaborators against a collective or fortuitous victim, such as massive detentions without trial, raids on university campuses, and wreaking havoc in black townships;
- individualized acts of blatant violence, including the wilful damaging or destruction of property, personal humiliation through degrading treatment, bodily assaults, extraction or fabrication of 'admissions' by means of third degree, and physical and mental torture.[50]

The elimination of political dissidents is normally also part of the strategies included in state sponsored terror violence.

LEGITIMACY OF SECURITY LEGISLATION

It should be emphasized that, in the ordinary course of events, security measures constitute an important and essential component of any legal order, namely as an instrument for the protection of the authority of the state against revolutionary forces. The legitimate exercise of such measures, however, ought at all times to remain conditioned by the norms

---

50 As to the occurrence of torture of political detainees, see D Foster, D Davis, D Sandler *Detention and Torture in South Africa: Psychological. Legal and Historical Studies* (1987), to which might be added the widely publicized and reliably attested affidavit of Father Smangaliso Mkhatshwa, Secretary-General of the Catholic Bishops Conference, who was interrogated by security police on 21 August 1986. His affidavit includes the following allegations:

'I was left standing on the same spot for at least 30 hours — a blindfold and handcuffs were always on. My genitals and buttocks were left exposed for at least 29 hours. A watery substance was smeared on my legs and thighs. This, together with the cold air, caused much discomfort. Twice during the interrogation shots were fired from behind and just about the back of my head. I have no idea what instrument was used to fire the shots. A creepy creature or instrument was fed into my backside. From there it would move up and down my legs, thighs and invariably ended up biting my genitals. When I cringed they laughed. The interrogation was punctuated by a string of insults, most of which would be unprintable. One of them threatened to kick me and I was humiliated in various ways.'

66   SOUTH AFRICAN JOURNAL ON HUMAN RIGHTS

of justice embodied in the rule of law and the due process of law.

I am not convinced that arbitrary powers of the executive are or the derogation from procedural human rights is ever warranted, or indeed necessary, for the protection of state authority. The matter has certainly never been investigated in South Africa. It has in fact become evident that the government's policy in relation to state security is founded upon Machiavellian utilitarianism.[51]

Utilitarianism measures the moral tenability of harmful human conduct exclusively in view of its usefulness, efficacy and subservience in relation to a supposedly noble purpose. The more refined manifestations of this approach in the philosophy of, for instance, Jeremy Bentham (1748-1832) requires careful calculations of the 'cost benefits' to be achieved by promoting a particular end at the expense of the interests to be sacrificed, but the less sophisticated varieties of utilitarianism seldom bother to weigh the 'losses' to be suffered against the 'gain' that would accrue from the advancement of a supposedly righteous cause. On the basis of this more rigid form of utilitarianism, Machiavelli (1469-1527) advised persons in authority who wish to remain in power 'to know how to do wrong, and to make use of it or not according to necessity'.[52] Machiavelli's political credo, 'it is much safer to be feared than loved',[53] would endorse the application of any measure of cruelty that might seem expedient for the purpose of safeguarding the station and powers of the incumbents of state authority — including violence, fraud, murder and treason! Machiavelli would have no problems with state sponsored terror violence.

Political expediency was clearly the sole justification tendered by the Commission of Inquiry into Security Legislation (the Rabie Commission) for retaining the dreaded institution of detention for interrogation.[54] The Commission's refusal[55] to inquire into the dubious methods of interrogation which that institution entails,[56] and its reluctance to introduce precautions against improper police conduct,[57] are certainly not

51 See Van der Vyver op cit note 4 at 304-5; J D van der Vyver 'Parliamentary Sovereignty, Fundamental Freedoms and a Bill of Rights' (1982) 99 *SALJ* 557 at 578-9.

52 *Il Principe* (translated by W K Marriott) (1958) 83.

53 Loc cit at 92.

54 See *Die Verslag van die Kommissie van Ondersoek na Veiligheidswetgewing* (RP 90 1981) para 10.78: 'Die getuienis van die polisie . . . is dat die inligting wat hulle deur middel van ondervraging in aanhouding verkry, hulle magtigste en, tot op groot hoogte, hul enigste wapen is om staatsgevaarlike bedrywighede . . . te antisipeer en te bestry . . .' and para 10.79: 'Aanhouding vir die doel van ondervraging is 'n noodsaaklike middel om die polisie in staat te stel om . . .'.

55 Loc cit para 3.29: 'Dit is ons taak om bestaande wetgewing te hersien, en nie om optredes wat in die verlede daarkragtens geskied het, te ondersoek nie' — as though one could thus separate the law from the empirical reality of its implementation.

56 See John Dugard *A Report on the Rabie Report: An Examination of Security Legislation in South Africa* (1982) Centre for Applied Legal Studies 27-30, where, based on 'considerable evidence', he listed as methods of interrogation, physical assault, psychological coercion, degrading and humiliating treatment, standing for long periods of time, long and persistent interrogation, deprivation of sleep, subjection to noise, deprivation of food, and solitary confinement.

57 Following the death in detention of Dr Neil Aggett, the Minister of Law and Order did subsequently issue *Directions regarding the Detention of Persons in terms of Section 29(1) of the Internal Security Act, 1982* Gen N 877 *GG* 8467 of 3 December 1982, amended by Gen N 583 *GG* 10866 of 21 August 1987. My own criticism of the regulations, developed in 'Gedragskode ten aansien van Aanhouding vir Ondervraging' (1983) 1 *Lawyers for Human Rights Bulletin* can be reduced to the following:

indicative of the considered computation of benefits and disadvantages required by the Benthamite variety of utilitarianism. Machiavellianism appeared even more vividly from the parliamentary debate on the provision that finally became s 29 of the Internal Security Act 74 of 1982 — for instance, when the member for Helderkruin and currently Deputy Minister of Information and of Constitutional Planning in the Office of the State President, Dr C J 'Stoffel' van der Merwe, confessed to the preposterous belief that the established principle of criminal procedure, which would rather see nine perpetrators of crime go free than to cause one innocent person to be convicted, does not apply when the security of the state is at stake.[58] Earlier Dr Connie Mulder, at the time Minister of the Interior, bluntly proclaimed that in matters of state security no rules apply. At the National Party congress of Natal held in November 1976, he also said:

> 'If it becomes necessary to choose between the freedom of the state and the freedom of the individual, we will choose the freedom of the state and abandon the freedom of the individual.'[59]

As against these sentiments I wish to reiterate that state sponsored actions that cannot withstand the scrutiny of norms of justice — and particularly those that amount to terror violence — would foment rather than defuse a revolutionary spirit.

SYMBIOSIS OF CONFLICTING TERROR GROUPS

Violence begets violence begets violence begets violence; and there is a strange relationship of mutual symbiosis between adversary terrorist groups. Thus liberation movements that have embarked upon a strategy of terror violence make capital out of acts of state sponsored aggression, and vice versa.[60]

The formative interaction between violence and counter-violence has served the South African government well as an excuse for glossing over its own acts of terror. The current controversy regarding the massive detention of children would illustrate the point.

On 24 April 1987 an affidavit of Major-General F M A Steenkamp, a former head of the security police, was produced in the Cape Provincial Division to oppose an urgent application brought jointly by the

(a) the Code was promulgated under s 29(1) of the Internal Security Act 74 of 1982, which does not authorize such regulations, and is therefore ultra vires; (b) its provisions have been formulated in sweeping language, such as treatment 'in a humane manner', 'the rules of decency', and 'inhuman and degrading treatment', which leaves the police with ample scope to avoid disciplinary action (clause 15); (c) no provision is made for either surveillance of police conduct or for external control measures — it is a case of the police policing the police; and (d) almost every restrictive provision in the Code is subject to wide-ranging conditions and exceptions, which in most cases entirely supersede the rule.

58 *House of Assembly Debates* 17 May 1982 col 7118.
59 Quoted in a leading article in *The Star* 9 November 1976.
60 George Shank 'Counterterrorism and Foreign Policy' (1987) 27-28 *Crime and Social Justice* 33 at 50-3 deals with, and at 60 speaks of, the syndrome of 'self-defence against terrorism' as an excuse for state sponsored terror violence; and in the same volume Noam Chomsky 'International Terrorism: Image and Reality' 172 at 183 reminded us in the same context of the adage: 'The only weapon against terrorism is terrorism.'

Progressive Federal Party (PFP) and Mr Ken Andrew (PFP Member of Parliament for Gardens) to secure the release of juvenile detainees. In his affidavit the Major-General listed 'admissions' of altogether 11 youths relating to violent conduct, including a necklace murder and arson.[61] Particulars of those 'admissions' were tendered to legitimize the detention without trial of children under the age of 18 years.

However, on the date of Major-General Steenkamp's affidavit there were, according to his own testimony, a total of 1 424 children between the ages of 12 and 18 years in detention under the emergency regulations. The alleged criminal conduct of a few was thus relied upon to justify the captivity of hundreds of others; and the few were furthermore never brought to trial so that their 'admissions' could be subjected to judicial scrutiny.

SELF-RIGHTEOUSNESS

The desire of persons engaged in acts of terror to seek justification for their violent conduct is typical of almost every variety of terror violence.

Terrorists, it would seem, are all obsessed with an inflated sense of self-righteousness and a blind faith in the supposed magnanimity of their objective. Like the fanatic in Mr Dooley's telling phrase, they too seem to believe that what they are doing is simply what 'th' Lord wud do if He only knew the facts in th' case'; and such fanaticism, said Arthur Schlesinger Jr,[62] — 'the willingness to sacrifice human beings to abstraction — is a mortal enemy of the human society'.

Institutionalized terrorism in this sense derives impetus from an obsessional conviction that law and order, the rule of a particular interest group, or a certain political dispensation must at all costs and without regard to the means or price be kept intact.

The focus of this controversy in South Africa in itself speaks volumes: the debate has become focussed on law and order *versus* justice rather than law enforcement and internal security *on the basis of* humane fairness and equity; and in this debate spokesmen for 'law and order at all costs' often assiduously abuse the name of John Calvin (1509-1564)[63] — adding vigour to their fascist type preference with reference to their own interpolated versions of Romans 13.[64] The truth is, though, that Calvin himself asserted

---

61 CPD April 1987 Case No 3976/87 postponed sine die. *Die Burger* 25 April 1987. Some of these 'admissions' have been recorded in a booklet by Keith Campbell *Children of the Storm: The Abuse of Children for the Promotion of the Revolution* (1987) 11-19.

62 'The Lessons in History' in H Ober Hess (ed) *The Nature of a Humane Society* (1977) 1 at 33.

63 See, for instance, Republic of South Africa, Constitutional Committee of the President's Council, Second Report on *The Adaptation of Constitutional Structures in South Africa* (PC 4/1982) 9.10.1, where in opposition to the introduction of a bill of rights in South Africa it was said that '... particularly the Afrikaner with his Calvinist background is more inclined to place the emphasis on the state and the maintenance of the state'. This view was echoed by Mr Kobie Coetsee, the Minister of Justice, in H J Coetsee 'Hoekom nie 'n Verklaring van Menseregte nie?' (1984) 9 *J for Juridical Science* 5 at 6. My critical comments are contained in J D van der Vyver 'The Bill-of-Rights Issue' (1985) 10 *J for Juridical Science* 1 at 4-5.

64 See *The Kairos Document: Challenge to the Church. A Theological Comment on the Political Crisis in South Africa* (1986) at 17-20.

STATE SPONSORED TERROR VIOLENCE 69

that justice was an essential ingredient of legitimate government;[65] and he even went so far as to claim that positive law which did not reflect the norms of justice was in reality not law.[66] He also emphatically appealed to the repositories of state authority to care for the well-being of their subjects.[67] An exhaustive analysis of these and other similar utterances of the great reformer led L M du Plessis to conclude:[68]

'Die eie-aard van die staat as 'n geregtigheidsinstelling van God noop die onderdaan tot 'n vrywillige onderwerping aan staatlike owerheidsgesag maar noop terselfdertyd die owerheid tot 'n funksionele begrensing van sy gesag.'

In the saga of self-justification, the perpetrators of non-governmental terrorism rely heavily on claims of legitimacy. Legality would in this instance be out of the question, since the usual strategies of this category of terrorism — murder, abduction, hijacking, mutiny and the like — by definition constitute criminal offences.

Those engaged in state sponsored terror violence, on the other hand, particularly lay claim to legality. Since their acts of terror are in the ordinary course of events prompted by a lack of legitimacy, they never seem to have considerations of justice to go by and therefore have to settle for arguments whereby their violent conduct is being passed off under the label of law and order or national security.

However, state sponsored acts of terror also include criminal conduct and are not necessarily less reprehensible than those orchestrated by non-governmental actors.[69] Their incidence and effect, measured in terms of the number of victims, might in fact be much greater than that of their non-governmental counterparts.[70] Consider in this regard the following:

- Since the inception of detention without trial in the early 1960s more political detainees have died while in custody than the total number of civilians who have lost their lives as a consequence of urban terrorism:[71] some admittedly in consequence of being manhandled (with de facto immunity) by the police (for instance Steve Biko, who died in September 1977), some having been driven to suicide (for instance Dr Neil Aggett, who died in February 1982), and many under extremely suspicious circumstances (for instance trade unionist Andries Raditsela, who died in May 1985).
- In the same period the total number of people detained without trial

65 *Commentarius in Isaiem Prophetam* 32.1.
66 *Institutio* 4.20.
67 *Sermons sur l'Expître aux Ephésiens* 5.21.
68 *Juridiese Relevansie van Christelike Geregtigheid* op cit note 1 at 348.
69 Carlton op cit note 13 at 201.
70 M Cherif Bassiouni 'International Control of Terrorism: Some Policy Proposals' (1981) 37 *International Review of Criminal Policy* (1985) 44 speaks of 'the more brutal and damaging aspects of state-sponsored terror-violence', and referring to the world community's one-sided interest in individual (non-governmental) violence only, he remarked: 'One need only compare the interest generated by the kidnapping and assassination of Italy's Aldo Moro as against that of the estimated three million deaths in Democratic Kampuchea to reach that conclusion.'
71 In its *Fifth Special Report on the State of Emergency* 28 February 1987, para C7, the Detainees' Parents Support Committee reported the sixty-third death in security detention since 1963. Subsequently yet another death in detention has occurred, that of Benedict Mashoke (see (1987) 3 *SAJHR* 268). See also in general Foster et al op cit note 50 at 2.

ran into tens of thousands.[72]

- A recent survey conducted under the auspices of the Institute of Criminology at the University of Cape Town[73] showed that 85 per cent of the sample of detainees included in the inquiry had suffered torture at the hands of the security police, which led to the conclusion that in relation to security detainees '[t]orture, in terms of both physical and psychological abuse, is a relatively standard procedure'.[74]

- Grave suspicion surrounds the unresolved killings of a number of political opponents of the National Party government, such as the Natal University lecturer, Dr Rick Turner, who was shot dead in 1977; civil rights attorney Griffith Mxenge, who was murdered in 1983, and his wife, Victoria, who was assassinated in 1985; United Democratic Front leader Toto Dweba, whose mutilated body was found in a sugar-cane field in Natal in August 1985; four community leaders of Cradock, Matthew Goniwe, Fort Calata, Sparrow Mkhonto and Sicelo Mhlawuli, who were brutally put to death in 1985; a medical doctor and community leader in Mamelodi, Fabian Ribeiro, and his wife, who were killed in 1986; and a director of the Institute for a Democratic Alternative for South Africa, Eric Mntonga, who was murdered in 1987.[75]

- South Africa has also had its share of disappearances, including three leading members of the Port Elizabeth Civic Association, Qaqawuli Godolozi, Sipho Hashe and Campion Galela, who were last seen on 8 May 1985.

- Brutal attrocities by right-wing vigilante groups in various black townships, who seemingly operate either as agents or with the acquiescence of different levels of the establishment, have come to light in a recent report of the Centre for Applied Legal Studies in the University of the Witwatersrand.[76]

Not all instances of murder, disappearance and vigilante outrage can be traced to government agencies, but the total picture that emerges from the state of unrest in South Africa clearly confirms that the country is solidly in

---

72 Statistics submitted by Major-General F M A Steenkamp in April of this year (note 61) indicated that on the date of his statement 4 244 people were being held in custody under the security legislation, compared to 7 790 in June 1986. On this latter date altogether 10 103 people had been taken into custody under security regulations and a further 180 arrests had been made in 1987 (prior to 15 April). In June 1986 a total number of 2 313 of those detained during the current state of emergency had been released without trial and by 15 April 1987 this figure had risen to 14 965. Figures released by the Detainee's Parents Support Committee in June 1987 show that on that date there were 3 450 persons in detention under the emergency regulations (*The Star* 17 June 1987). See also Foster et al op cit note 50 at 216.

73 Foster et al op cit note 50.

74 Foster et al op cit note 50 at 157. See also at 154:
    'The major conclusion to be drawn from the historical review is that detention is unquestionably a political strategy, designed to quell, contain or eradicate democratic political opposition which could threaten the white minority.'

75 The killers of Batandwa Ndondo, co-ordinator of a village health project in Transkei, who was murdered on 24 September 1985, were identified at the inquest into his death as members of the Transkeian Police Force, but no prosecution was instituted.

76 Nicholas Haysom *Mabangalala: The Rise of Right-wing Vigilantes in South Africa* (1986) Centre for Applied Legal Studies.

STATE SPONSORED TERROR VIOLENCE 71

the grip of state sponsored terror violence.

THE PUBLICITY CRISIS

We have established earlier that state sponsored terror violence is almost invariably the result of a lack of legitimacy of a government, constitutional dispensation or legal system, and that the perpetrators of such violence operate under the delusion of their own self-righteousness founded upon their own illusionary evaluation of the expedience, preferableness or excellence of the status quo. In marketing their objective, the government-sponsored terrorists would discover a distinct conflict between the means of their endeavour and the end that is supposed to sanctify those means; and this dichotomy would inevitably render counter-productive their strategy of terror.

Intimidation, after all, can only be effective if the commination of terror is brought to the notice of those whom it was intended to address.[77] Yonah Alexander captured the gist of this truism:[78]

> 'Terrorism, then, like advertising, increases the effectiveness of its message by focussing on spectacular incidents and by keeping particular issues alive through repetition.'

State sponsored terror in the form of assistance to subversive agents in other countries tends to be covert,[79] but terror violence orchestrated by a government or its collaborators for the purpose of intimidating its own nationals into involuntary submission would lose its designed impact if it were to be executed without publicity.

This presents the dilemma referred to above: a government engaged in acts of terror towards its own nationals needs to establish or re-establish its own legitimacy; and acts of terror by virtue of their very nature would inevitably have the opposite effect.

In an attempt to overcome this dilemma, the South African government has exploited the complicated pattern of political loyalties in the country: playing the tyrant in the black community and in respect of carefully selected individuals and institutions known for their particularly vocal opposition to racial discrimination and procedural injustices, while at the same time posing as a citadel of protection as far as the interests of the privileged section of the population are concerned. In doing so it seeks to derive credibility for its own reign of terror by making capital of the violence perpetrated by its more aggressive adversaries — and thereby, as we already know, providing further nourishment for more counter-violence.

In order to maintain the Janus-like disposition of its image, the government has found itself compelled to resort to press censorship and the manipulation of news releases.

Following the promulgation of a state of emergency on 12 June 1986[80] in terms of the Public Safety Act 3 of 1953, the State President issued

---

77 See Freedman et al op cit note 21 at 62-4; Carlton & Schaerf op cit note 13 at 5-7.
78 Op cit note 16 at 160-1.
79 Freedman et al op cit note 21 at 166.
80 Proc R108 *GG* 10279 of 12 June 1986.

72   SOUTH AFRICAN JOURNAL ON HUMAN RIGHTS

regulations[81] which amongst other things imposed severe restrictions on the press in their reporting of unrest-related matters. Some of those regulations were found to be invalid by the Natal Provincial Division of the Supreme Court.[82] Subsequently a new set of security regulations were promulgated[83] whereby, amongst other things, the substantive defects of the earlier regulations were to be remedied. The regulations dealing with 'publications control'[84] prohibit the presence of the mass media at the scene of unrest; the photographing of security action of the police and of a politically inspired attack, rioting and bomb blasts; reporting on actions of the security forces in unrest situations, and so on. These provisions can obviously serve the perpetrators of state sponsored violence to obscure the terroristic nature of their acts.

On 28 August 1987 the existing regulations that curb news reporting and comments were further expanded[85] to make provision for the appointment of a state censor who would give or withhold *prior* approval for the publication of news reports and editorial comments.[86] News reports and comments are to be scrutinized by an anonymous clique of sociologists and psychiatrists (handpicked by the Minister of Home Affairs) who will conduct their inquiry in secret and without affording editors and reporters an opportunity to state their case. The regulations purport to stifle any so-called systematic or repeated effort on the part of 'certain' media to promote a revolutionary spirit, boycott or stayaway actions, civil disobedience or strikes, or to enhance the public image or esteem of unlawful organizations.[87] The point is, though, that a finding of fact in this regard rests with the Minister who acts in consultation with a faceless bunch of government collaborators. A 'finding' by the Minister that a publication *in his opinion* is causing or is calculated to cause a threat to the safety of the public or to the maintenance of public order, or is causing a delay in the termination of the state of emergency (sic), would culminate in a warning and eventually the banning of the publication for a period of not more than three months and/or subjection of the publication in question to state censorship.[88]

This latest assault upon freedom of the press in South Africa, described by the editor of the *Sunday Star* as 'the most insidious move yet against the free flow of information and towards moulding minds',[89] coincided with

81 Proc R109 *GG* 10280 of 12 June 1986 (in particular ss 9-12), amended by Proc R110 *GG* 10293 of 17 June 1986; Proc R121 *GG* 10329 of 27 June 1986; Proc R125 *GG* 10348 of 8 July 1986 (corrected by GN 1610 *GG* 10375 of 25 July 1986); Proc R140 *GG* 10382 of 1 August 1986; and Proc R225 *GG* 10542 of 28 November 1986.
82 *United Democratic Front v State President* 1987 (3) SA 296 (N); *United Democratic Front v State President* 1987 (3) SA 343 (N).
83 Proc R97 *GG* 10772 of 11 June 1987.
84 Section 3.
85 Proc R123 *GG* 10880 of 28 August 1987.
86 Section 7A(3)(a).
87 Cf s 7A(1)(a).
88 Section 7A(1) and (3). In terms of subsec (4) the publisher will be given an opportunity, prior to a warning or any of the further steps contemplated in the section, to submit representations to the Minister.
89 Leader in the *Sunday Star* 6 September 1987.

the creation of the Directorate of Media Relations. The sweeping discretionary powers placed in the hands of the bureaucracy represent the ultimate power base which a repressive government might possibly desire to suppress information, manipulate opinions, and silence opposition through the written word.

THE SENSELESSNESS OF TERROR VIOLENCE

The history of politically inspired violence provides ample proof of the futility of all manifestations of terrorism. It is furthermore as plain as a pikestaff that in the long run an agenda of violence as a means of law enforcement or for the safeguarding of an existing régime or constitutional system would destroy its own objective.

Institutionalized terrorism derives from a lack of legitimacy; and for purposes of regaining public confidence, violence is precisely the wrong medicine: every act of terror violence provokes the implantation of the seed of revolution in the minds of its victims.

There is one proposition concerning terrorism that can probably lay claim to universal accord: although it would be extremely unwise to invite direct confrontation with momentarily superior terrorist forces, one should never give in to violent or intimidatory coercion.

That, in conclusion, is my message to academics and students, who in South Africa are amongst the main target groups of state sponsored terror violence.

For many years now the South African government has joined issue with academicians in consequence of their factual accounts, repudiatory opinions and substantiated protests pertaining to the many injustices engraved in the social condition and political rule of the South African status quo. University autonomy and academic freedom have thus fallen prey to:

- state interference in the admissions policy of educational institutions;[90]
- the banning of important study material;[91]
- withholding information required for academic research or censuring the publication of theses containing particulars of executive mis-management;[92]

---

90 In terms of s 32 of the Extension of University Education Act 45 of 1959 the government took upon itself the competence to regulate, on the basis of race, student admission at universities. This provision has been repealed by the Universities Amendment Act 83 of 1983, but in terms of s 25(2) of the Universities Act 61 of 1955 (added by s 9 of Act 83 of 1983) the payment of subsidies to a university, by ministerial decree, may be made conditional upon implementation by the university of a racially defined quota system pertaining to student admission.

91 Publications may be banned for political reasons under various statutory provisions, including s 47(2)(d) and (e) of the Publications Act 42 of 1974 and s 56(1)(p) of the Internal Security Act 74 of 1982 (prohibiting the production, printing, publication and dissemination of any speech, utterance, writing or statement of certain banned persons). Some years ago Louise Silver in 'The Statistics of Censorship' (1979) 96 *SALJ* 120 established that there had been a rapid increase in the number of items found to be undersirable under s 47(2)(d) and (e) of the Publications Act, and this trend subsequently continued. See Louise Silver 'Trends in Publication Control: A Statistical Analysis' (1983) 100 *SALJ* 520 at 525; André du Toit 'The Rationale of Controlling Political Publications' in *Censorship* (1983) SA Institute of Race Relations 80.

92 A typical example is reflected in the experience of Dr J Mihalik, Senior Lecturer in the University of

74   SOUTH AFRICAN JOURNAL ON HUMAN RIGHTS

- the maintenance (at the taxpayers' cost) of a bunch of campus spies, whose function it is to infiltrate influential student organizations, to pass on information that might be (distorted and) exploited by the security police, the National Intelligence Service or the military intelligence agency, and to create an atmosphere of distrust among students, staff and faculty;[93] and
- the detention without trial or the subjection to restriction orders of student and faculty members of the academic fraternity.[94]

The most recent onslaught intended to compel universities to toe the government line is embodied in the De Klerk instructions,[95] issued on 19 October 1987 in terms of s 25(1) of the Universities Act 61 of 1955, and which makes the payment of subsidies to a university conditional upon compliance with a set of state-imposed rules and regulations requiring, among other things, that university councils take reasonable steps:

- to impose on their campuses the arbitrary dictates of the executive under South Africa's security legislation and implement the Intimidation Act 72 of 1982;
- effectively to prevent reference in lectures, or affording prominence on campus in any other way, to the African National Congress and any other organization that has been, or might in future be, banned in terms of sweeping powers vested in the executive;
- to stifle peaceful protests in the form of, for instance, advocating a boycott action, a stayaway of workers, or civil disobedience;
- to extend the disciplinary jurisdiction of the university council beyond the internal sphere of university-based activities, and upon 'proof' furnished by the Minister of Education and Culture to curb, among other things, the participation of faculty and students in peaceful

Bophuthatswana. In 1986 he completed a doctoral dissertation entitled *Gevangenisstraf: Die Noodsaaklikheid vir Alternatiewe Strawwe* at the University of South Africa. The thesis contained information and critical comment regarding the Department of Prisons and its administration. Prior to Dr Mihalik's graduation, the Director-General of the Department of Justice appointed a Committee of Experts to look into and to discredit the thesis. The thesis, however, had been accepted for the degree of Doctor of Laws, but Unisa, acting under threats of the Department of Justice, placed an embargo on publication of the contents of the thesis to anyone other than the persons who had been involved in examining it. Following lengthy representations, this ban has recently been lifted. See *The Star* 22 October 1987.

93 Mr Daniel Pretorius, a student of the University of Cape Town, recently 'defected' as a campus spy and made public details of his recruitment while still in high school, duties (infiltrating student organizations and passing on information that might be used by the police in their efforts 'to politically isolate Vice-Chancellor Dr Stuart Saunders by deliberately sowing dissension on the University of Cape Town campus that he controls' and 'to undermine' anti-government organizations such as Nusas, UDF and SANSCO) and remuneration (a salary of R660 per month, medical aid, indemnity against military training after four years of working for the security police, and a job in any government department of his choice). See the *Monday Paper* 17 August 1987 published by University of Cape Town. It has also recently been disclosed that school cadets in the Cape Province have been instructed, in a *Cadet Training Programme: Manual* (1986), in intelligence gathering and taught how to compile information on 'citizens' (*Sunday Star* 6 September 1987).

94 Among the thousands of detainees who have been or still are in custody without the prospect of a trial, is senior law lecturer Raymond Suttner, University of the Witwatersrand, who has been in detention for more than 18 months and will probably remain in detention for as long as the state of emergency lasts. There exists no doubt whatsoever that Mr Suttner has committed no crime.

95 Contained in a letter of the Minister of Education and Culture, P J Clase, dated 13 October 1987 (ref 3/4/12/1).

protests 'at any place' against, for instance, government policies or
against obnoxious practices of non-governmental institutions.
The De Klerk dictates furthermore reinstate government interference in
the matter of student admissions, and require the university authorities to
act as campus spies.

These regulations are definately ultra vires[96] and would in some respects
be void on account of vagueness. Their objective is clearly not to promote
order on university campuses — that in any event ought to remain within
the domestic jurisdiction of university authorities — but they are intended
to serve as a pending threat and instrument of political intimidation — an
instance par excellence of state sponsored terrorism!

Certain university campuses have also been singled out for physical
terror violence in the form of occasional raids executed by the security
forces. One would probably find on those campuses a group of students —
indeed small in number — whose political conduct might reveal
revolutionary intentions, and their presence on campus is exploited by the
security police to provide simulated 'justification' for their own acts of
terror.

The campuses concerned also accommodate faculty, staff and students
— indeed in much larger numbers — who vociferously articulate their
prostestations concerning the injustices of the prevailing legal and
constitutional system emanating from governmental acts.

The absolutist security machinery at the disposal of the powers that be is
more than adequate to bring the first-mentioned group of faculty, staff and
students to bay: campus raids are not needed for that purpose. However,
violence on campus instigated by the security forces is resorted to as a
means of intimidating the second group of faculty, staff and students into
silence and submission. In that sense the raids on campus of the security
forces amount to state sponsored terror violence.

Two final observations are called for in this regard. First, in view of the
targets of, and the latent motivation for, state sponsored terror violence
— ie the silencing of protests against injustices — those universities and
student bodies that have *not* been earmarked for this kind of intimidation
have reason for serious concern. Secondly, I sincerely trust that those
engaged with academic integrity in the pointing out of the injustices
attending the South African social, juridical and political dispensation,
and in stimulating action in the fight against discrimination, will never give
in to intimidation and terror violence.

96 Except for enforcing the quota system mentioned in note 90, the conditions imposed by the Minister
must in terms of s 25(1) of the Universities Act 61 of 1955 be related to 'the requirements of each
university in relation to the general requirements of higher education in the Republic'. The
regulations contemplated in the De Klerk decree are entirely unrelated to the demands of higher
education as such.

[14]

Government Breaks the Law: The Sabotaging of the Occupational Safety and Health Act

Introduction

CORRUPTION AMONG PUBLIC OFFICIALS IS GENERALLY ASSOCIATED IN THE public mind with such egregious behind-the-scene activities as taking bribes and kickbacks, colluding with private contractors who bilk the government or produce shoddy merchandise, and as revealed in the Iran/Contra scandal, complicity in narcotic trafficking. Yet in an insightful article on corruption pertaining to military spending, the important observation is made that "even if all the fat were trimmed and the crooks thrown in jail, the problem of corruption would not be solved" (*Dollars & Sense*, 1985: 3). For corruption is rooted, the article maintains, in the military-industrial complex, which serves to benefit certain key institutions and those who control them at the expense of the public. More generally, when the driving force behind a program is not really intended to serve the public interest, but is mainly oriented toward pandering to special interests, it is inherently corrupt.[1]

Because the institutional sources of corruption are intermediated through individuals, the inclination of the public and of many scholars has been to blame corrupt practices on the moral shortcomings of those who abuse their office.[2] This approach, however, is often misleading. Those who were opposed to the appointment, for example, of former CIA Deputy Director Robert Gates as CIA director complained about his devious and deceptive conduct.[3] Yet this is just what the CIA requires. Since among its important roles is to undermine democratic movements — an objective that is certainly not sanctioned by any statutes — the CIA would self-destruct if led by anyone who insisted upon integrity, freedom, and openness. Many other government agencies, including those with benign reputations, also require officials who are willing to neglect their moral and legal responsibilities to the public. Those who resist conforming are penalized and weeded out. Not by identifying personal proclivities, but by taking into account the underlying systemic and structural influences upon

HARRY BRILL is on the faculty of the Sociology Department, University of Massachusetts — Boston, Harbor Campus, Boston, MA 02125–3393.

government agencies can we understand widespread corruption in government and its corrosive impact on democratic decision making.

If secret government tends to subvert democracy, the converse, open government, does not ensure uncorrupt and democratic conduct. Since corruption is the betrayal of the public trust by misusing public office to serve particular individuals or special interests, the widespread assumption among scholars and the public is that corrupt conduct is generally clandestine (Alatas, 1980: 13).[4] However, corrupt practices in agencies within the executive branch and various independent enforcement agencies are routinely out in the open despite illegal conduct. Like behind-the-scenes corruption that feeds the nation's rapidly growing list of scandals, the misconduct of these agencies appreciably undermines the democratic elements of the U.S. political system.

Overt illegal conduct among enforcement agencies is endemic in liberal-democratic societies. Because the business sector is not omnipotent, it is unable to prevent many progressive laws from being enacted. If social-reform advocates completely lacked clout, all left-of-center bills would fail and, accordingly, there would be an absence of such legislation for public officials to flout. However, although the business community lacks absolute power, it exerts disproportionate influence, which it frequently employs successfully to prevent these statutes from being effectively enforced. The result is that enforcement agencies continually violate their legal duty to protect the public.

The influence of business is often also reflected in the various provisions of progressive statutes that dilute their effectiveness. Penalties for violations are often too lenient, remedial recourse is usually legally cumbersome, and agencies are given too much discretion. For these reasons, the failure of agencies to effectively enforce the law is often attributed to weaknesses in the statute. Yet even without amending the laws, the statutes are not empty boxes that agencies can fill anyway they choose. Agencies cannot continually engage in a pattern of nonenforcement without violating the law. To do so is to abuse their discretion, which is illegal. Yet feeble enforcement of the laws is the rule. The Savings and Loan (S&L) scandals, the polluted environment, the myriad of unsafe drugs, and widespread false advertising are among the grim testimonies to the lackadaisical enforcement practices of government agencies.

Even the most carefully constructed statutes do not compel agencies to enforce the law. The executive branch is adept at finding ways to break the law, and members of the judiciary, who are carefully selected by the executive branch and are usually confirmed by the Senate, generally validate the illegal actions of public officials. The continual pursuit of the perfect law, one that would impel agencies to adequately enforce statutes that regulate business conduct, is an illusory objective.

The unending abuse of the laws by public officials is camouflaged with legal rationalizations, which in part explains why the unlawful nature of their misconduct is often not apparent to the public. Also, because we associate corruption and illegal conduct with the actual commission of some objectionable act, when agencies do little or nothing about a problem, we do not regard it as illegal and certainly not criminal. Typical of the literature on corporate crime and violence is the lack of discussion on how the failure of public officials to perform their duties may make them accomplices to corporate crime.[5] Yet the failure to act when there is a legal duty to do so is illegal. When such an omission results in injury or death, it is a criminal offense (Henry, 1991: 253–270).

The Occupational Health and Safety Administration (OSHA) is among the agencies that habitually violate their legal obligations. Although its exclusive responsibility is to protect the health and safety of working people on their jobs, the agency instead is far more responsive to business interests. As I will detail in the discussion of OSHA's conduct, OSHA commits with impunity both civil and criminal violations, which in turn encourages the business community to flout the law.

In particular, this essay will consider how OSHA ignores its legal obligations both to enforce health and safety regulations and to adopt new standards. Like many other government agencies that are unwilling to abide by their statutory duties, however, OSHA attempts to convey the misleading impression that it is behaving responsibly. Since OSHA's feeble enforcement record is accessible to the public, its contempt for the health and safety law — which it is required to enforce — cannot be hidden from interested parties, particularly from various watchdog organizations.[6] The judiciary, nevertheless, has protected OSHA against the legitimate demands of working people to obtain adequate enforcement of the health and safety act.

OSHA and the judiciary occasionally live up to their obligations. Many OSHA inspectors are serious about their responsibilities, but on the whole they are kept in line. Despite their weakness, working people and their organizations are not powerless. They occasionally have been able to compel OSHA to take strong action, though generally only after publication of flagrant business violations or the occurrence of a major industrial accident. Since OSHA's achievements are more highly publicized than its derelictions, the agency's record, and the judiciary's as well, seems far more in balance than they are in actuality. The truth is that OSHA and the judiciary have continually violated their statutory responsibilities, resulting in a great deal of harm to working people. OSHA's routine performance of its duties cannot be justified as a lawful exercise of its discretionary powers. Its conduct has been illegal, criminal, and therefore corrupt. To use Marcus Raskin's phrase, it is "violence clothed in the law" (1991: 513).

The Problem

Tragically, the federal government's lackadaisical enforcement of the Occupational Safety and Health Act (the OSH Act) has been costing many working people their lives and physical well-being. As fines for violations are generally much lower than the costs of adequately correcting them, the business community realizes that they can get away with homicide and mayhem.

According to the National Safe Workplace Institute (NSWI, an independent research organization committed to advancing safety and health in the workplace), each year over 10,000 men and women are killed on their jobs and up to 70,000 workers become permanently disabled because of on-the-job injuries. Another 70,000 workers die of occupationally caused diseases. In the long run, about 25% of all workers will be either killed or seriously injured on their jobs or will die of job-related illnesses (NSWI, 1989a: 2). Going to work, as more workers are learning, is not recommended for good health and longevity.

The OSH Act confers the legal authority for enforcing the law on the Secretary of the Department of Labor. The Occupational Safety and Health Administration (OSHA), a unit within the department, has been established to administer the act, and responsibility for the operation of OSHA has been delegated to an assistant secretary of labor. Thus, although articles and reports on workplace safety often refer to OSHA without mentioning the Department of Labor, OSHA is not an autonomous unit. In fact, other department officials, including the solicitor, play an important role in shaping OSHA's decisions. The agency is an integral part of the Department of Labor and its practices reflect the policies of the Labor Department's secretary. OSHA's misconduct, then, is also the misconduct of the Department of Labor.

Critics of OSHA's lackluster performance have sought mainly to persuade Congress to amend the statute and to compel OSHA to adopt more health and safety standards. The OSH Act could certainly be improved and more regulations would be useful. A serious problem is that developing and finally approving regulations take at least four years, often much longer, not including a few additional years absorbed by court challenges (Shapiro, 1989: 13–14). Moreover, most proposed regulations are never approved.

OSHA's Enforcement Record

Yet when we consider how little OSHA has accomplished by using the legal tools it already possesses, the faith that changing the legal text will significantly improve enforcement practices is unconvincing. Revising the OSH statute would prompt OSHA to find new strategies to circumvent it. Importantly, the judiciary can also be counted on to undermine the law.

Unions and other advocates of a safe workplace realize that OSHA could do much better without changing the laws. Yet they also believe that OSHA is generally law abiding and, therefore, reforming the OSH Act would influence the agency's conduct. Reform advocates have been urging Congress to adopt severe criminal penalties to discourage violations.[7] They maintain that the inadequate penalties of up to $10,000 in fines (recently increased to a maximum of $70,000) along with six months in prison for a first willful violation that causes death have discouraged the Department of Justice from prosecuting cases recommended by OSHA. Since the Department of Justice has not been prosecuting, OSHA has been reluctant, advocates claim, to refer cases.

True, OSHA has rarely recommended cases for criminal prosecution. Only one employer was ever sentenced to jail, for only 45 days (ESHG: Developments, 1990: 13,050). Yet the claim that statutory limits on penalties discourage the Department of Justice from prosecuting employers conflicts with the department's own assertion that by criminally prosecuting violators under the Comprehensive Crime Control Act of 1984, it can ask for penalties of up to $250,000 for each individual and $500,000 for corporations (USCS, 1990d: 60–61). Also, employers guilty of workplace homicide, who have knowingly jeopardized the safety of their employees, could serve long prison sentences under federal law if successfully prosecuted for second-degree murder or manslaughter.

Although the California OSH Act has certain advantages, the criminal penalties in California for homicide due to workplace accidents are not more stringent than the federal law. Yet while CAL/OSHA, which operates, after all, in only one state, has recommended 292 cases from 1981 to 1988 for criminal prosecution, the comparable figure for the federal government during this period is just 19. Almost 40% of CAL/OSHA's referrals had successful outcomes (NSWI, 1988a: 15).

The enormous differences in enforcement practices cannot be understood by comparing the legal scriptures. Rather, those who are responsible for enforcing the federal statute are resistant to implementing the OSH Act. CAL/OSHA's enforcement record, incidentally, has been recently deteriorating as it, too, has been losing interest in properly enforcing the law. If the federal OSH Act is amended, those entrusted with enforcing a revised statute will attempt to ensure that progressive changes in the law will be undermined.

Although Congress has substantially increased maximum fines, OSHA has almost always imposed fines well below the statutory maximum for serious violations, including those resulting in death. Also, as OSHA's highly publicized megafines show, OSHA can count violations in ways that yield substantial fines. The agency on occasion tabulates the total number of violations by multiplying each violation by the number of employees. OSHA, then, has not lacked the tools to compel employers to obey the law.

The problem has been that OSHA has generally preferred to pamper employers rather than penalize them. The average fine for manufacturing companies in a recent year was only $34 (Weil, 1991: 33). Proposed fines — if they are challenged, they are at least deferred, and almost always reduced — for construction accidents involving at least one fatality was under $1,000 in most cities (NSWI, 1989a: 12). Worse yet, two out of five fatalities in the construction industry did not result in any penalty at all (*Ibid.*: 11).

Moreover, according to the General Accounting Office (the investigative arm of Congress), OSHA has been closing cases without requiring adequate evidence that violations were corrected. The agency only requests evidence. Also, OSHA discourages follow-up inspections. In 1989, only six percent of inspections were follow-up. OSHA's policy is to limit these inspections to 10% of all inspections (ESHG, 1991: 2–3). Very few employers who are cited for violations, then, are under pressure to make any improvements at all.

OSHA has been not only irresponsible: it has also been breaking the law. As the statute gives OSHA considerable discretion — fines, for example, are not mandatory — the impression is that OSHA is abiding by the mandates of the OSH Act. Since OSHA must take into account many factors to guide its conduct, it needs considerable discretion. The use of discretion, however, is limited by law. Not only is a public agency prohibited from doing whatever it wishes; neither can an agency take actions that are allowed by the law, but are undertaken for the wrong reasons. According to the Administrative Procedure Act, if an agency's conduct is arbitrary and motivated by reasons not allowed by the law, it is abusing its discretion, which is illegal (USCS, 1989: 432).

OSHA's enforcement practices are primarily motivated by its greater commitment to employers than to employees. Unlike the National Labor Relations Act, however, which is supposed to consider the interests of both employers and employees, the sole intent of the OSH Act is *to protect workers*. OSHA is required by law to respect the intent of the statute, which is to make the workplace healthier and safer for working people.

The agency's unlawful allegiance to employers is reflected, of course, in its lax enforcement practices. After more than 20 years of the OSH Act, the workplace remains dangerous. According to the Bureau of Labor Statistics, occupational injuries in construction, which is among the most hazardous industries, have increased over the past 10 years by 100,000 (Green, 1991: 9). The industry continues to violate, with virtual impunity, safety standards that were known to be dangerous long before the OSH Act was passed.

The Illusion of Megafines

Yet frequently mentioned in the mass media is OSHA's imposition of megafines, which were first imposed during the Carter administration. These fines, exceeding $100,000, convey the impression that OSHA is serious about enforcement. Although OSHA publicizes these fines, the agency does not inform the public that they are later substantially reduced by as much as 96% (NSWI, 1989b: 4). Moreover, the Department of Labor's Inspector General, who is responsible for auditing the activities of the department, found that because OSHA makes little effort to obtain what is owed to the government, the agency collects only a small amount of the fines due (NSWI, 1988b: 22–23). OSHA's disinterest in collecting fines violates both the Debt Collection Act of 1982 and its own regulation on collecting delinquent fines.

A record of final settlements imposed on various companies was requested by NSWI under the Freedom of Information Act. Despite the law, OSHA resisted complying. The Institute finally obtained the information it requested only after threatening to expose its recalcitrance, which was illegal, to the media and to Congress. The *Washington Post* columnist, Jack Anderson, correctly referred to OSHA's penalty approach as "a public relations binge" (Anderson, 1989: E19).

Tragic Events, Frivolous Response

OSHA's negligence has serious consequences; workers die or become incapacitated. In October 1989, a fire and explosion at a Phillips Petroleum Plant killed 23 workers and injured over 130 others. The incident was caused by the sudden release of several highly flammable gases. The Secretary of Labor acknowledged that the accident could have been avoided if recognized safety procedures had been followed. Among the violations were inadequate hazard communication, insufficient emergency exits, and insufficient respiratory protection. OSHA also found that Phillips Petroleum had ignored both its own procedures and standard industry practice (ESHG, 1990: 2).

This accident could have been prevented by OSHA had it diligently enforced the law. OSHA knew that the company's facilities had serious safety problems. Before this event, OSHA's inspection of facilities in the region showed 18 killed and many others hospitalized (*Ibid.*). These accidents should have triggered a vigorous enforcement effort; but they did not. In fact, despite the irresponsibility of management, OSHA did not even recommend criminal prosecution. OSHA's conduct was predictable. According to an audit by the Inspector General of the Department of Labor, OSHA has generally failed to take appropriate action "against employers with significant histories of fatalities" (NSWI, 1988b: 10).

In Chicago, an OSHA officer did not inspect a plant next door to the office because the company's records indicated a low injury rate. Yet conditions at the company's plant were described by a reporter as an industrial gas chamber. Several months after the OSHA inspection, an employee died of cyanide poisoning. The evidence showed a pattern of deception by management, which persuaded the State of Illinois to prosecute company executives for committing criminal homicide. A worker was instructed, for example, to remove the skull-and-crossbones symbol that warned of the lethal nature of one of the chemicals (Metz, 1988: 16). Yet OSHA had been quite willing to settle for only a modest fine of under $2,400 (Committee on Government Operations, 1988: 2). Each of three company defendants, however, were tried and sentenced by a state court in Illinois to 25 years in prison.[8] The sentence, though, was subsequently overturned on flimsy grounds.

Rationalizing Inaction

Advocates for a safe workplace complain that the paucity of standards is worrisome. They are convinced that the latitude of the agency to enforce the OSH Act is very limited. Yet the yearning for more and better regulations, although certainly appropriate, has been manipulated by the agency to detract from its poor enforcement practices. More often than many advocates realize, the problem is inadequate enforcement rather than OSHA's lack of a legal basis to act. Consider, for example, the approach taken by the agency, the media, and even advocates on the issue of protecting employees working in confined spaces. Accidents in confined spaces are responsible for about three percent of workplace fatalities. The main cause of death is asphyxiation. In addition, workers are killed because of mechanical failures they could not escape from in time.

OSHA expressed interest in a confined-space regulation as early as 1975, but to date one has not been adopted. The agency has claimed that the lack of a confined-space regulation has left many workers inadequately protected. It maintained "that the existing standards do not adequately protect workers in confined spaces from atmospheric, mechanical, and other hazards" (Federal Register, 1989: 204080).

The media and advocates have echoed OSHA's claims. A caption in a front-page *Los Angeles Times* article read "Lack of OSHA Regulations — Confined-Space Deaths Blamed on Federal Delays" (Weinstein, 1989: 1). Just before a public hearing on a detailed proposed confined-space regulation, a *New York Times* article discussed how family members of victims who were asphyxiated in confined spaces were to testify that their sons and thousands of others were killed because safety standards for confined spaces had not been adopted (Robbins, 1990: A17). The testimony of family members was arranged by NSWI, which was lobbying for the regulation.

The proposed regulation contains some very useful recommendations, especially a requirement that trained attendants regularly monitor confined work spaces. Yet OSHA already has an arsenal of regulations to protect workers confronted with hazardous conditions in confined spaces. In fact, the agency itself acknowledged that the "hazards encountered in permit spaces, such as exposure to electrical shock and contact with chemicals and machinery, are also encountered elsewhere in the workplace and are addressed, in general, by existing OSHA standards" (Federal Register, 1989: 204080).[9]

Also, to prevent atmospheric contamination, employers must adopt "engineering control measures" such as proper general and local ventilation systems and must substitute less toxic materials (CFR, 1990a: 401). When changing the workplace environment is not feasible, workers must be provided with appropriate personal protective equipment, including respirators (CFR, 1990b: 400, 401). In addition, information on the hazards of chemicals used at work must be communicated to employees (CFR, 1990c: 3867–3884).

Where recognized workplace hazards exist, OSHA's obligation to intervene is not limited to specific regulations. The OSH Act mandates a general duty clause to protect workers when no existing regulations apply. The clause declares that each employer "shall furnish to each of his employees employment and a place of employment which are free from recognized hazards that are causing or are likely to cause death or serious physical harm to his employees" (USCS, 1990b: 37).

The courts rejected the contention of employers that the general duty clause is unconstitutionally vague. The Supreme Court, reflecting on the legislative history of the clause, maintained that it was intended "to deter the occurrence of occupational deaths and serious injuries by placing on employers a mandatory obligation independent of the specific health and safety standards to be promulgated by the Secretary" (U.S. Reports, 1979a: 13). General duty citations could protect workers against exposure to toxics not covered by specific regulations. Although OSHA serves citations under the general duty clause for violations, including some for confined-space violations, very few are issued and the percentage given out began to decline in the 1980s (Morgan, 1983: 298–302).

Still, imposing additional legal regulations on business, such as requiring attendants to monitor confined spaces, could provide OSHA with more and better tools to enforce the OSH Act. Certainly, no proposed standard deserves as long as 16 years of consideration. In fact, the Administrative Procedure Act specifies that agency action cannot be unlawfully withheld or unreasonably delayed (USCS, 1989: 430). Since OSHA itself has officially recognized the importance of a confined-space regulation to saving lives, the failure of the judiciary to order OSHA to adopt the proposed regulation is a violation of the Administrative Procedure Act.

Lopsided Due Process

As already mentioned, OSHA's regulations are weakly enforced. When an OSHA compliance officer finds a violation, a citation is issued that identifies the nature of the violation and the period of time allowed to correct it. If an employer contests a citation, its enforcement is at least temporarily suspended.

Commonly, employers work out a satisfactory settlement with OSHA. Although employers can appeal OSHA orders, they generally don't have to.

Since the welfare of workers is directly affected by the outcome of these settlements, employees and unions need the opportunity to contest agreements that fail to adequately address their health and safety grievances. However, although employers can contest and appeal any aspect of a citation, employees and their representatives can only object to the time allotted to deal with the violations. They cannot challenge the adequacy of OSHA's abatement order itself.

Adverse decisions can be appealed to the Occupational Safety and Health Review Commission, an autonomous, quasi-judicial body whose three commissioners are appointed by the president with the consent of the Senate. Within the commission, administrative law judges initially hear cases, which can then be reviewed by the commissioners. These cases can afterward be appealed to a federal court. The commission was created as a concession to business. It provides business with an additional opportunity to contest adverse orders, or at least to delay their enforcement for a long while. Among the commission's contribution to business is its practice of throwing out OSHA fines (NSWI, 1990: 5).

Except for allowing employees to contest the period of time that employers are allowed to abate violations, none of these legal routes are available to employees and their representatives. This dual system of justice, which is so generous to employers, but stints on employee rights, should have been declared unconstitutional. Employees are clearly being denied both due process and the equal protection of the laws. The denial of equal protection is especially ludicrous because the purpose of the OSH Act is to serve working people, not employers.

Since the federal appeals courts and the commission have deprived workers of their legal rights to protect their health in the workplace, the Supreme Court could have reminded these bodies of their constitutional obligations. Yet the high court was so thoroughly convinced that OSHA's right to withdraw a citation is unreviewable that it issued its opinion over the protest of two justices without giving those who objected an opportunity to present their side (U.S. Reports, 1985: 3–8). Called a summary proceeding, courts use this judicial procedure to settle cases promptly when there is supposedly no basis for a legitimate legal dispute.

The assault by the judiciary on the due-process rights of workers, many of whom confront life-threatening working conditions, is extraordinary. It assures that very few cases will reach the courts because workers are made completely dependent on OSHA to file suits against uncooperative employers.

As employees and their representatives cannot challenge OSHA settlement agreements with employers, disputes initiated by working people cannot reach the commission or the courts. The experience of workers and their unions is vital to determining how safety and health violations should be abated. Like parties to any dispute, their testimony may or may not be persuasive. Yet allowing only employers to appeal adverse decisions unfairly tilts the scales of justice heavily toward business.

Even had the OSH Act mandated the dual system of justice, this policy would still be illegal because it is unconstitutional. Nowhere in the OSH Act are employees explicitly barred from challenging settlements. On the contrary, in the section of the OSH Act on contesting citations, it reads: "The rules of procedure prescribed by the Commission shall provide affected employees or representatives of affected employees an opportunity to participate as parties to hearings" (USCS, 1990c: 201). Legally speaking, a party is anyone who is directly interested in the issue being considered and who has the right, therefore, to be completely involved in any proceeding.

If the contrast between the statutory language and how it is interpreted seems startling, the commission and the judiciary have a prosaic explanation. The section of the statute on enforcement cites two grounds for appealing citations to the commission: first, when employers contest a citation, and second, when an employee or representative contests the period of time fixed in the citation for abating a violation. The courts have interpreted this to mean that employees are limited to challenging the time allowed for correcting a violation.

In 1982, the commission rejected this interpretation. The majority opinion explained that since the statute specifies that a citation should indicate the nature of the violation, the regulation that has been violated, and the time allowed to fix the violation, the time is not yet ripe for an employee to challenge a citation on a basis other than the reasonableness of the time period (OSHD, 1982: 33,033).

The actual changes, if any, that employers are required to make in the workplace are determined later, when OSHA and the employer work out a settlement agreement. Only then does it become appropriate for employees to challenge the abatement method. After a Reagan appointment to the commission, the OSH Act was reinterpreted to exclude workers as parties to its proceedings other than to challenge the time allotted for abating violations (OSHD, 1984: 34, 486–434, 489).

Employees can still challenge OSHA's delays and inaction on proposed regulations or amendments. Although a few battles on these issues have been won in court, these victories are illusory unless they are enforced. Since OSHA has been relieved of employee legal challenges to its enforcement practices and settlements, it can continue to abuse its discretion with impunity.

New Regulations? More Inaction

If standards are not followed, why do OSHA and the business community fiercely resist their adoption? First, regulations are not altogether ignored. Some employers take regulations seriously, while various unionized companies are under pressure from unions to conform to OSHA's standards. Many employers are repeatedly cited for infractions, however, and still do nothing to correct them. As fines are typically less expensive than the costs of remedying violations, they are not a deterrent. These fines, in effect, are fees charged for doing business as usual.

As health and safety regulations serve as the legal basis for citing employers, OSHA is continually urged to adopt new standards. In a detailed critical evaluation of the rule-making process, researchers funded by a grant from OSHA reported that the agency even lacked regulations on most chemicals that have been identified as carcinogenic by the federal National Cancer Institute (Shapiro, 1989: 2).

OSHA has also ignored the law by failing to adopt stringent standards to adequately reduce the risks of exposure to hazardous substances. The agency even refused to strengthen its standard for airborne asbestos exposure until ordered to do so by a federal court. The serious health risks of being continually exposed to high levels of airborne asbestos is recognized by OSHA, which admitted that its own standard posed significant risks to workers. Yet in a court challenge by the AFL-CIO Building and Construction Trades Department, the agency's defense rested on its view that industry could not attain lower levels. As the court noted, OSHA's own records revealed that lower levels of exposure both could have and have been achieved. Appropriately, OSHA was ordered to reconsider promulgating a stronger regulation (Federal Reporter, 2d ed, 1988: 1269, 1272–1273).

The Supreme Court, drawing on the legislative history of the health and safety statute, had ruled that OSHA is forbidden to engage in a cost-benefit analysis in deciding to issue regulations dealing with toxic materials (U.S. Reports, 1980: 506–522). There was absolutely no legal justification for OSHA's refusal to issue a more stringent asbestos standard.

One would expect that an agency genuinely committed to minimizing exposure to toxics would be interested in warning those who come in regular contact with hazardous materials of the risks they encounter. Yet OSHA refused the request of unions to order companies that employ mostly non-English-speaking workers to use bilingual warnings and universal symbols on cartons containing asbestos. OSHA's hazard-communication regulations require warnings only in English. Yet the statute itself mandates "the use of labels or other appropriate forms of warning" so that employees are apprised of hazards in order to protect their health (USCS, 1990a: 133). Clearly, OSHA is violating the intent of the statute, which requires that employees be informed rather than kept in the dark about the toxic materials they are working with.

The court ordered OSHA to develop a regulation that would warn non-English-speaking workers, but the agency did not comply. After a complaint was filed in court, OSHA was given a deadline. A regulation was finally issued that left it to employers to determine how to inform employees of the hazardous material they were exposed to. The new regulation did not require bilingual identification or even universal symbols on containers. Since the regulation lacks specifics and gives employers almost complete discretion, compliance can easily be evaded and violations can be difficult to prove. Nevertheless, the court found the new proposed regulation acceptable.

Misinterpreting the Law: The Supreme Court's Turn

Different governmental institutions take turns undercutting the rights of workers by ignoring the OSH Act. OSHA argued before the Supreme Court that since no safe level for exposure to benzene, a carcinogen, can be determined, then it should limit exposure to the lowest technologically feasible level. This approach was consistent with the section of the law just cited, which directs the Secretary of Labor to develop standards assuring that no employee's health would be adversely affected.

The Supreme Court, however, interpreted the OSH Act to require a standard based upon a finding of significant risk rather than mandating the lowest feasible risk (U.S. Reports, 1979: 655). The high court still allowed OSHA considerable leeway. It ruled that OSHA should rely on the best available evidence without being required to support its findings with anything approaching scientific certainty (U.S. Reports, 1979: 656). At least, OSHA is not expected to delay issuing standards until definitive studies are completed. In this instance, the high court was only acknowledging the segment of the law that actually states "on the basis of the best available evidence." Also, the Court stressed that the agency should feel free "risking error on the side of overprotection rather than underprotection" (U.S. Reports, 1980: 656).

However, regulations based upon significant risk implies mandating higher levels of exposure to hazardous materials than regulations requiring the lowest technologically achievable levels. Also, since determining the adverse health effects of chemicals is expensive and takes many years, the Supreme Court's decision curtailed OSHA's ability to rapidly develop regulations. Yet nothing in the statute, as the dissenting Supreme Court opinion pointed out, refers to "significant risk." The statute's section on toxics is worded to minimize impairing the health of all workers exposed to hazardous materials. The high court did what only Congress is allowed to do — rewrite the law.

OSHA's advocacy of a strict regulation on carcinogens seems inconsistent with its anti-regulatory stance. In actuality, however, OSHA failed to present a strong case. Despite the considerable evidence of the adverse impact of even very low dosages of benzene, OSHA made no finding, as the Supreme Court noted, that evidence of exposure to benzene at levels set by the current standard or below had ever caused leukemia (U.S. Reports, 1979: 634). The Court also noted that OSHA acknowledged that a study it had relied on to establish an emergency standard to reduce exposure levels did not support its view that benzene caused cancer at even much higher levels than the current standard permits (U.S. Reports, 1979: 633). As OSHA's defense of the standard was weak, it would have required an unusually progressive court to have validated OSHA's proposal.

Misinterpreting the Law: The Commission's Turn

The commission and the judiciary have shown the same indifference to working people. In one case, for example, the commission cited a Supreme Court decision to justify rejecting an OSHA general duty citation given to an employer for inadequately protecting employees from exposure to a carcinogenic chemical (OSHD, Kastalon, Inc., 1986: 35, 970–935, 982). As already mentioned, although the Supreme Court opposed a blanket policy of mandating the lowest possible level of exposure to toxics, it nevertheless indicated that OSHA was not obliged to show that a significant risk exists with anything approaching scientific certainty.

Yet the commission rejected the extrapolations from animal data as too speculative, including a Du Pont study in which 100% of the dogs exposed to the chemical, called MOCA, contracted cancers, but none did in the control group. Moreover, industry experts agreed that MOCA is carcinogenic and one leading manufacturer urged the adoption of a standard for MOCA. OSHA had certainly established a significant risk. Although the Supreme Court tremendously diluted the statute's provision on exposure to toxics, the Court didn't annihilate it.

Misinterpreting the Law: OSHA's Turn

In 1972, the agency rejected a petition by a Hispanic–American organization to require employers to provide farm workers with toilets, drinking water, and hand-washing facilities. These basic amenities are indispensable to human health. OSHA's refusal to seriously consider the proposal clashed with the intent of the OSH Act. The judiciary eventually ordered a reluctant OSHA to adopt a regulation, but not until 14 and one-half years later (Shapiro, 1989: 54). As the AFL-CIO's Safety and Health Director observed, "OSHA's list of achievements has been sorely outstripped by its shortcomings and reluctance to act" (Green, 1991: 8). Significantly, OSHA has not taken any serious steps to enforce the new standard (Noble, 1988: A1).

Conclusion

In the corporate world, criminal homicide and the willful injury of working people are daily events. That little or nothing is done to punish these crimes exposes the fiction that in our so-called liberal-democratic society, the "rule of law" prevails. According to the rule of law, laws oblige everyone equally (Lowi, 1988: *ix*). Therefore, any employer guilty of criminal homicide in the workplace should be subject to as severe a punishment as anyone outside the workplace who was convicted of manslaughter or murder. The reality, of course, is that the opposite is true; corporate managers are, so to speak, getting away with murder.

The rule of law applies also to public servants. Among those guilty of criminal conduct are OSHA officials. Yet they, too, escape criminal prosecution for their illegal conduct, which is mainly reflected in their failure to take appropriate action. Legally speaking, omission is an offense when there is a legal duty to act. By repeatedly ignoring their legal obligations, OSHA officials continually violate the Occupational Health and Safety Act and the Administrative Procedure Act. The Administrative Procedure Act, in fact, specifically includes inaction as a legal violation. Also, those entrusted with enforcing the law have been continually violating the constitutional rights of working people to due process and equal protection.

These, by themselves, are only civil violations. However, when the willful failure to act contributes to injuries and deaths, it is a criminal offense. In particular, these public officials are guilty of complicity because their inaction has encouraged workplace injuries and deaths. A lifeguard who fails to make a proper effort to prevent an individual from drowning a bather is guilty of complicity. Among the legal grounds for complicity, which is liability for the conduct of another, is: "having a legal duty to prevent the commission of the offense, fails to make proper effort so to do."[10] Moreover, according to the federal statute, accomplices are as criminally liable as those who directly commit a crime (USCA, 1969: 57).

OSHA officials have been legally entrusted with being the lifeguards of the workplace. By law, a crime of complicity does not require the accomplice to be on the scene when a crime has been committed. It is sufficient to demonstrate that OSHA officials have resisted making serious efforts to compel employers to correct health and safety violations despite the overwhelming evidence that these violations are appreciably threatening the lives of workers.

To dramatically improve the workplace would require empowering working people. In particular, workers and their chosen representatives would have to obtain the legal weapons needed to allow them to play a decisive role in changing working conditions.[11] Since the labor movement is weak, however, nothing significant can be won by first lobbying legislators for better laws. When workers are better organized and are making significant progress toward forcing employers to take their concerns seriously, only then can they successfully press for laws that reflect and consolidate the gains they have been achieving on the job.[12]

Yet the right to a healthy and safe workplace is a "subversive demand" (Navarro, 1991: 54). It ultimately entails control over the process of production, which interferes with the logic of capital (*Ibid.*). This incompatibility between the goals of workers and employers is irreconcilable. What begins, then, as a struggle by workers for social reform must eventually be transformed into a struggle to build a society in which protecting life and assuring justice are authentic and primary objectives of government.

NOTES

1. For some excellent essays on the criminal conduct of the state, see Barak (1991). The essays attempt to recast issues of political economy into a criminological framework.

2. See, for example, social scientist Syed H. Alatas (1980) and Fleishmann et al. (1981).

3. For a concise summary of Robert Gates' misconduct, see "Mr. Gates' Past, the C.I.A Future." *New York Times* (November 4, 1991): A18.

4. For a clear, detailed discussion of the traditional concept of corruption, see Alatas' book (1980).

5. For a comprehensive discussion of corporate crime, see Mokhiber (1988). Yet among the author's 50 recommendations to curb corporate crime, including stiffer penalties, none suggests prosecuting government officials for looking the other way.

6. The National Safework Institute carefully, thoroughly, and aggressively monitors OSHA. Those who are interested in obtaining their research reports, which are for sale, should write to NSWI, 122 South Michigan Avenue, Suite 1450, Chicago, Ill., 60603.

7. A major obstacle to legislating severe penalties is the belief that corporate illegal conduct generally violates civil law, but rarely criminal law. For a detailed discussion and persuasive refutation of this perspective, see Conklin (1977).

8. For details, see Frank (1987).

9. The belief that weak enforcement can be overcome by statutory amendments is widely shared by advocates of social reform. In late October 1991 under the auspices of the AFL-CIO, a worker testified before a congressional committee that he would not have lost his job for complaining to an OSHA inspector about unsafe work conditions if proposed legislation were in place. See O'Neill, Colleen M., "Workers Seek Voice in Workplace Safety," *AFL-CIO News* (November 11, 1991: 4). However, the OSH statute already prohibits retaliatory dismissals, but OSHA rarely enforces this provision.

10. This criterion for complicity is from the American Law Institute's (ALI) Model Penal Code, Section 2.06 (iii). In 1962, ALI completed an official draft of the Model Penal Code, major parts of which have been adopted by Congress and the legislatures of most states. ALI is an independent, influential organization of lawyers, judges, and legal scholars.

11. For a thorough and persuasive case study of the serious weaknesses of liberal-inspired regulatory programs, which generally fail because they discourage the participation of those that these programs seek to benefit, see Noble (1986).

12. For several excellent articles on the failures and successes of organizing around health and safety issues, see "Organizing for Health and Safety," *Labor Research Review* 9,2 (Fall 1990). See also Judgins (1986).

REFERENCES

Alatas, Syed H.
    1980   The Sociology of Corruption. Singapore: Times Books.
Anderson, Jack
    1989   Washington Post (April 12).
Barak, Gregg (ed.)
    1991   Crimes by the Capitalist State. Albany: State University of New York Press.
Code of Federal Regulations (CFR)
    1990a   Part 1910.134.
    1990b   Part 1910.132, 134.
    1990c   Part 1910: 1200.
Committee on Government Operations (CGO)
    1988   "Getting Away with Murder in the Workplace: OSHA's Nonuse of Criminal
                  Penalties for Safety Violations." 100th Congress, 2nd Session.
Conklin, John E.
    1977   "Illegal, but Not Criminal." Englewood Cliffs: Prentice-Hall.
Dollars & Sense
    1985   "Corruption — Or Capitalism" (October).
ESHG (Employment Safety & Health Guide: Commerce Clearing House)
    1991   GAO Reports Weaknesses in OSHA Abatement Confirmation Process, No.
                  1049.
    1990   Phillips Petroleum, No. 989.
ESHG: Developments (Employment Safety & Health Guide: Developments) Commerce Clearing
House
    1990   Senate Panel Hearings on Legislation to Increase Criminal and Civil Penalties
                  for OSHA Violations.
Federal Register 54
    1989   "Permit Required Confined Spaces."
Federal Reporter, 2nd 838
    1988   Building Construction Trade Department, AFL-CIO v. Brock, Secretary of
                  Labor.
Fleishmann, Joel L., Lance Liebman, Mark H. Moore (eds.)
    1981   Public Duties: The Moral Obligations of Governmental Officials. Cambridge:
                  Harvard University Press.
Frank, Nancy
    1987   "Murder in the Workplace." Stuart L. Hills (ed.), Corporate Violence: Injury
                  and Death for Profit. Totowa: Rowman & Littlefield: 103–107.
Green, Arlee
    1991   "Worker Involvement Crucial to Job Safety, Labor Says." AFL-CIO News
                  (March 18).
Henry, Stuart
    1991   "The Informal Economy: A Crime of Omission by the State." Gregg Barak
                  (ed.), Crimes by the Capitalist State. Albany: State University of New York
                  Press.

Judgins, Bennett M.
   1986   We Offer Ourselves as Evidence: Toward Workers' Control of Occupational
                 Health. Westport: Greenwood Press.
Lowi, Theodore J.
   1988   Forward. Andrei S. Markovits and Mark Silverstein (eds.), The Politics of
                 Scandal. New York: Holmes and Meyer.
Metz, Holly
   1988   "Death by Oversight." Student Lawyer (September).
Mokhiber, Russell
   1988   Corporate Crime and Violence. San Francisco: Sierra Club Books.
Morgan, Donald C. and Mark N. Duvall
   1983   "OSHA's General Duty Clause: An Analysis of Its Use and Abuse." Industrial
                 Relations Law Journal 5,2.
Noble, Robert
   1986   Liberalism at Work: The Rise and Fall of OSHA. Philadelphia: Temple Uni-
                 versity Press.
NSWI (National Safe Workplace Institute)
   1990   "Workplace Safety and Health" 3,11.
   1989a   "Unmet Needs: Making American Work Safe for the 1990s."
   1989b   "Unintended Consequences: The Failure of OSHA's Megafine Strategy."
   1988a   "Ending Legalized Workplace Homicide."
   1988b   "Failed Opportunities: The Decline of U.S. Job Safety in the 1980s."
Navarro, Vicente
   1991   "The Limitation of Legitimation and Fordism and the Possibility for Socialist
                 Reform." Rethinking Marxism (Summer): 27–60.
Noble, Kenneth B.
   1988   "Farm Workers Fault Lack of Enforcement of Sanitation Rules." New York
                 Times (October 4).
OSHD (Occupational Safety and Health Decisions: Commerce Clearing House)
   1987   Kastalon, Inc.
   1984   Pan American World Airways, Inc.
   1982   Mobil Oil Corporation.
Raskin, Marcus G.
   1991   "The Road to Reconstruction." The Nation (April 22).
Robbins, William
   1990   "Grieving Relatives Gird for Federal Hearing on a New Rule for Job Safety."
                 New York Times (January 30).
Shapiro, Sidney and Thomas McGarity
   1989   "Reorienting OSHA: Regulatory Alternatives and Legislative Reforms." Yale
                 Journal on Regulation Vol.6.CA (United States Code Annotated)
   1969   Title 18, Section 2.
USCS (United States Code Service)
   1990a   Osh Act, Title 29, Section 655.
   1990b   OSH Act, Title 29, Section 654.
   1990c   Osh Act, Title 29, Section 659.
   1990d   Crimes and Criminal Procedure, Title 18, Section 3581.
   1989   (APA) Administrative Procedure Act, Title 5, Section 706.
U.S. Reports
   1985   *Cuyahoga Valley Railway Co.* v. *United Transportation Union*, Vol. 474.
   1980   *American Textile Mfg.* v. *Donovan, Secretary of Labor*, Vol. 452.
   1979a   *Industrial Union Department, AFL-CIO* v. *American Petroleum Institute*, Vol.
                 448.
   1979b   *Whirlpool* v. *Marshall, Secretary of Labor*, Vol. 445.
Weil, David
   1991   "Enforcing OSHA: The Role of Labor Unions." Industrial Relations 30.

Weinstein, Henry
    1989   "Lack of OSHA Regulations — Confined-Space Deaths Blamed on Federal
                      Delay." Los Angeles Times (February 5).

Part III
Hybrid Forms of State Crime

State-organized Crime

[15]

STATE-ORGANIZED CRIME—The American Society of Criminology, 1988 Presidential Address*

WILLIAM J. CHAMBLISS

There is a form of crime that has heretofore escaped criminological inquiry, yet its persistence and omnipresence raise theoretical and methodological issues crucial to the development of criminology as a science. I am referring to what I call "state-organized crime."

THE PROBLEM

Twenty-five years ago I began researching the relationship among organized crime, politics, and law enforcement in Seattle, Washington (Chambliss, 1968, 1971, 1975a, 1975b, 1977, 1980, 1988a). At the outset I concentrated on understanding the political, economic, and social relations of those immediately involved in organizing and financing vice in the local area. It became clear to me, however, that to understand the larger picture I had to extend my research to the United States and, eventually, to international connections between organized criminal activities and political and economic forces. This quest led me to research in Sweden (Block and Chambliss, 1981), Nigeria (Chambliss, 1975b), Thailand (Chambliss, 1977), and of course, the Americas.

My methods were adapted to meet the demands of the various situations I encountered. Interviews with people at all levels of criminal, political, and law enforcement agencies provided the primary data base, but they were supplemented always with data from official records, government reports, congressional hearings, newspaper accounts (when they could be checked for accuracy), archives, and special reports.

While continuing to research organized crime, I began a historical study of piracy and smuggling. In the process of analyzing and beginning to write on these subjects, I came to realize that I was, in essence, studying the same thing in different time periods: Some of the piracy of the sixteenth and seventeenth centuries was sociologically the same as some of the organized criminal relations of today—both are examples of state-organized crime.

At the root of the inquiry is the question of the relationship among criminality, social structure, and political economy (Petras, 1977; Schwendinger and Schwendinger, 1975; Tilly, 1985). In what follows, I (1) describe the characteristics of state-organized crime that bind acts that are unconnected by time and space but are connected sociologically, (2) suggest a theoretical

---

* Portions of this paper are based on William J. Chambliss, *Exploring Criminology* (New York: Macmillan, 1988).

184 CHAMBLISS

framework for understanding those relationships, and (3) give specific examples of state-organized crime.

STATE-ORGANIZED CRIME DEFINED

The most important type of criminality organized by the state consists of acts defined by law as criminal and committed by state officials in the pursuit of their job as representatives of the state. Examples include a state's complicity in piracy, smuggling, assasinations, criminal conspiracies, acting as an accessory before or after the fact, and violating laws that limit their activities. In the latter category would be included the use of illegal methods of spying on citizens, diverting funds in ways prohibited by law (e.g., illegal campaign contributions, selling arms to countries prohibited by law, and supporting terrorist activities).

State-organized crime does not include criminal acts that benefit only individual officeholders, such as the acceptance of bribes or the illegal use of violence by the police against individuals, unless such acts violate existing criminal law and are official policy. For example, the current policies of torture and random violence by the police in South Africa are incorporated under the category of state-organized crime because, apparently, those practices are both state policy and in violation of existing South African law. On the other hand, the excessive use of violence by the police in urban ghettoes is not state-organized crime for it lacks the necessary institutionalized policy of the state.

PIRACY

In the history of criminality, the state-supported piracy that occurred between the sixteenth and nineteenth centuries is an outstanding example of state-organized crime (Andrews, 1959, 1971).

When Christopher Columbus came to the Americas in search of wealth and spices in 1492, he sailed under the flag of Spain although he himself was from Genoa. Vasco da Gama followed Columbus 6 years later, sailing under the Portuguese flag. Between Spain and Portugal, a vast new world was conquered and quickly colonized. The wealth of silver and gold was beyond their wildest dreams. A large, poorly armed native American population made the creation of a slave labor force for mining and transporting the precious metals an easy task for the better armed Spanish and Portuguese settlers willing to sacrifice human life for wealth. Buttressed by the unflagging belief that they were not only enriching their motherland and themselves but also converting the heathens to Christianity, Spanish and Portuguese colonists seized the opportunity to denude the newly found lands of their wealth and their people (Lane–Poole, 1890). Portugal, as a result of Vasco da Gama's voyages, also established trade routes with India that gave it a franchise on

STATE-ORGANIZED CRIME 185

spices and tea. Portuguese kings thus became the "royal grocers of Europe" (Howes, 1615; Collins, 1955).

In Europe during the sixteenth and seventeenth centuries, nation–states were embroiled in intense competition for control of territory and resources. Then, as now, military power was the basis for expansion and the means by which nation–states protected their borders. Military might, in turn, depended on labor and mineral resources, especially gold and silver. The wealthier nations could afford to invest in more powerful military weapons, especially larger and faster ships, and to hire mercenaries for the army and navy. Explorations cost money as well. When Spain and Portugal laid claim to the Americas, they also refused other nations the right to trade with their colonies (Mainwaring, 1616). Almost immediately, conflict developed between Spain and Portugal, but the pope intervened and drew a line dividing the New World into Spanish and Portuguese sectors, thereby ameliorating the conflict. But the British, French, and Dutch were not included in the pope's peace. They were forced to settle for less desirable lands or areas not yet claimed by the Spanish and Portuguese.

Although they lacked the vision to finance explorers such as Christopher Columbus and Vasco da Gama, France, England, and Holland nonetheless possessed powerful navies. They were also the home of some of the world's more adventurous pirates, who heretofore had limited their escapades to the European and African coasts.

With the advent of Spain and Portugal's discovery of vast new sources of wealth, other European nations were faced with a dilemma: They could sit idly by and watch the center of power tip inexorably toward the Iberian Peninsula, or they could seek ways to interfere with the growing wealth of their neighbors to the south. One alternative, of course, was to go to war. Another, less risky for the moment but promising some of the same results, was to enter into an alliance with pirates. France, England, and Holland chose the less risky course.

To transport the gold and silver from the Spanish Main (the Caribbean coast of South America) to Bilbao and from Brazil to Lisbon required masterful navigational feats. A ship laden with gold and silver could not travel fast and was easy prey for marauders (Exquemling, 1670). To complicate matters, ships were forced by the prevailing winds and currents to travel in a predictable direction. These conditions provided an open invitation for pirates to exploit the weaknesses of the transporting ships to their advantage. Poverty and a lack of alternatives drove many young men to sea in search of a better life. Some came to the New World as convicts or indentured slaves. The lure of the pirate's life was an alternative that for all its hardships was more appealing than the conditions of serfdom and indentured servitude.

The French government was the first to seize the opportunity offered by engaging in piracy (Ritchie, 1986). It saw in piracy a source of wealth and a way of neutralizing some of the power of Spain and Portugal. Although piracy was an act second to none in seriousness in French law (summary execution was the punishment), the French government nonetheless instructed the governors of its islands to allow pirate ships safe portage in exchange for a share of the stolen merchandise. Thus, the state became complicitous in the most horrific sprees of criminality in history.

The pirate culture condoned violence on a scale seldom seen. There was no mercy for the victims of the pirates' attacks. Borgnefesse, a French pirate who wrote his memoirs after retiring to a gentleman's life in rural France, was an articulate chronicler of these traits. He wrote, for example, of how he once saved a young girl "not yet into puberty" from being raped by two "beastly filibusters" who were chasing her out of a house in a village that he and his men had attacked (LeGolif, 1680). Borgnefesse wrote of being embarrassed that on that occasion he felt "pity" for the young girl and violated one of the ironclad laws of the pirate's world: that women were prizes for whoever found them in the course of a raid. The would-be rapists resisted his effort to save the girl and "told me I was interfering in a matter which was none of my business, that pillage was permitted in the forcing of the women as well as the coffers."

It was commonplace among pirates to "take no prisoners" unless, of course, they could be useful to the victors. Borgnefesse described how he cut off the heads of everyone on board a Spanish "prize" because the enemy angered him by injuring his arm during the battle. Another time he and his men took all the people on a captured ship, tied them up in the mainsail, threw them in the water, and then drank rum while listening to the screams of the slowly drowning men. For all his criminal exploits, however, Borgnefesse was well protected by French ships and French colonies.

England and Holland were quick to join the French. Sir Richard Hawkins and his apprentice, Francis Drake, were issued "letters of marque" from the Admiralty directing governors of British colonies and captains of British warships to give safe passage and every possible assistance to Hawkins and Drake as they were acting "under orders of the Crown" (British Museum, 1977). Their "orders" were to engage in piracy against Spanish and Portuguese ships. Thus, the state specifically instructed selected individuals to engage in criminal acts. The law, it must be emphasized, did not change. Piracy remained a crime punishable by death, but some pirates were given license to murder, rape, plunder, destroy, and steal.

The state's complicity in piracy was more successful, one suspects, than even the most avaricious monarchs expected. On one voyage (between 1572 and 1573), Drake returned to England with enough gold and silver to support the government and all its expenses for a period of 7 years (Corbett, 1898a, 1898b). Most of this wealth came from Drake's attack on the town of Nombre de Dios, which was a storage depot for Spanish gold and silver. In this

STATE-ORGANIZED CRIME 187

venture Drake joined forces with some French pirates and ambushed a treasure train.

Drake was knighted for his efforts, but the Spanish were not silent. They formally challenged Britain's policies, but the queen of England denied that Drake was operating with her blessing (after, of course, taking the gold and silver that he brought home) and Drake was tried as a criminal. He was publicly exiled, but privately he was sent to Ireland, where he reemerged several years later (in 1575) serving under the first Earl of Essex in Ireland.

Borgnefesse and Sir Francis Drake are only two of hundreds of pirates who plied their trade between 1400 and 1800 (Senior, 1976). Their crimes were supported by, and their proceeds shared with, whatever nation–state offered them protection and supplies. In theory, each nation–state only protected its own pirates, but in practice, they all protected any pirates willing to share their gains.

To rationalize the fundamental contradiction between the law and the interests of the state, European nations created a legal fiction. Issued either directly from the monarch or the Admiralty, the letters of marque gave pirates a sort of license, but with specific limitations on the kinds of acts that were permissible. One restriction was that the pirates were not to (a) attack ships of the country issuing the letter, (b) plunder villages or towns, or (c) open the captured cargo until they returned to port.

The reality of piracy was quite at odds with all of these limitations. Much of the success of piracy depended on attacking towns and villages, during which raping, plundering, and razing the town were accepted practices. Pirates sometimes kept one or more officers from captured ships along with their letters of marque and identifying flags in order to show them in case of attack by a ship from another country. This also enabled a pirate ship from France, say, to raise an English flag and attack a French ship. For the pirates loyalty to the nation came second to the search for gold.

At one time or another virtually every European nation, and the United States as well, between 1500 and 1800 was complicitous in piracy. In the United States, Charleston, South Carolina, several New England towns, and New York were safe harbors for pirates. In return for sharing in the prize, these towns provided safety from capture by foreign authorities and a safe place for pirates to celebrate their victories.

John Paul Jones became an American hero through his success as a pirate and was even given a commission in the navy (de la Croix, 1962; MacIntyre, 1975). Jean and Pierre Lafitte were the toast of New Orleans society while they enriched themselves by organizing and aiding pirates and smugglers at the mouth of the Mississippi River. Their status was considerably enhanced when the federal government enlisted their aid in the war against England and made Jean an officer of the U.S. Navy in return for helping to defeat the

188   CHAMBLISS

British Navy that was gathering its forces for an attack on New Orleans (Verrill, 1924) In time of war, nations enlisted pirates to serve in their navy. In time of peace, they shared in the profits.

During the period from 1600 to 1900, capitalism was becoming firmly established as the dominant economic system of the world. The essential determinant of a nation's ability to industrialize and to protect its borders was the accumulation of capital. Not only was another nation's wealth a threat to the autonomy of neighboring states, one nation's gain was invariably another's loss. Piracy helped to equalize the balance and reduce the tendency toward the monopolization of capital accumulation. The need for capital accumulation does not end with the emergence of capitalism; it continues so long as the economy and a nation's military and economic strength depend on it. When piracy ceased to be a viable method for accumulating capital, other forms of illegality were employed. In today's world, there is evidence that some small city–states in the Far East (especially in Indonesia) still pursue a policy of supporting pirates and sharing in their profits. But piracy no longer plays a major role in state–organized crime; today, the role is filled by smuggling.

SMUGGLING

Smuggling occurs when a government has successfully cornered the market on some commodity or when it seeks to keep a commodity of another nation from crossing its borders. In the annals of crime, everything from sheep to people, wool to wine, gold to drugs, and even ideas, have been prohibited for either export of import. Paradoxically, whatever is prohibited, it is at the expense of one group of people for the benefit of another. Thus, the laws that prohibit the import or export of a commodity inevitably face a built–in resistance. Some part of the population will always want to either possess or to distribute the prohibited goods. At times, the state finds itself in the position of having its own interests served by violating precisely the same laws passed to prohibit the export or import of the goods it has defined as illegal.

NARCOTICS AND THE VIETNAM WAR

Sometime around the eighth century, Turkish traders discovered a market for opium in Southeast Asia (Chambliss, 1977; McCoy, 1973). Portuguese traders several centuries later found a thriving business in opium trafficking conducted by small ships sailing between trading ports in the area. One of the prizes of Portuguese piracy was the opium that was taken from local traders and exchanged for tea, spices, and pottery. Several centuries later, when the French colonized Indochina, the traffic in opium was a thriving business. The French joined the drug traffickers and licensed opium dens throughout

STATE-ORGANIZED CRIME 189

Indochina. With the profits from those licenses, the French supported 50% of the cost of their colonial government (McCoy, 1973: 27).

When the Communists began threatening French rule in Indochina, the French government used the opium profits to finance the war. It also used cooperation with the hill tribes who controlled opium production as a means of ensuring the allegiance of the hill tribes in the war against the Communists (McCoy, 1973).

The French were defeated in Vietnam and withdrew, only to be replaced by the United States. The United States inherited the dependence on opium profits and the cooperation of the hill tribes, who in turn depended on being allowed to continue growing and shipping opium. The CIA went a step further than the French and provided the opium-growing feudal lords in the mountains of Vietnam, Laos, Cambodia, and Thailand with transportation for their opium via Air America, the CIA airline in Vietnam.

Air America regularly transported bundles of opium from airstrips in Laos, Cambodia, and Burma to Saigon and Hong Kong (Chambliss, 1977: 56). An American stationed at Long Cheng, the secret CIA military base in northern Laos during the war, observed:

> . . . so long as the Meo leadership could keep their wards in the boon-docks fighting and dying in the name of, for these unfortunates anyway, some nebulous cause . . . the Meo leadership [was paid off] in the form of a carte-blanch to exploit U.S.-supplied airplanes and communication gear to the end of greatly streamlining the opium operations . . . . (Chambliss, 1977: 56).

This report was confirmed by Laotian Army General Ouane Rattikone, who told me in an interview in 1974 that he was the principal overseer of the shipment of opium out of the Golden Triangle via Air America. U.S. law did not permit the CIA or any of its agents to engage in the smuggling of opium.

After France withdrew from Vietnam and left the protection of democracy to the United States, the French intelligence service that preceded the CIA in managing the opium smuggling in Asia continued to support part of its clandestine operations through drug trafficking (Kruger, 1980). Although those operations are shrouded in secrecy, the evidence is very strong that the French intelligence agencies helped to organize the movement of opium through the Middle East (especially Morocco) after their revenue from opium from Southeast Asia was cut off.

In 1969 Michael Hand, a former Green Beret and one of the CIA agents stationed at Long Cheng when Air America was shipping opium, moved to Australia, ostensibly as a private citizen. On arriving in Australia, Hand entered into a business partnership with an Australian national, Frank Nugan. In 1976 they established the Nugan Hand Bank in Sydney (Commonwealth of New South Wales, 1982a, 1982b). The Nugan Hand Bank

190   CHAMBLISS

began as a storefront operation with minimal capital investment, but almost immediately it boasted deposits of over $25 million. The rapid growth of the bank resulted from large deposits of secret funds made by narcotics and arms smugglers and large deposits from the CIA (Nihill, 1982).

In addition to the records from the bank that suggest the CIA was using the bank as a conduit for its funds, the bank's connection to the CIA and other U.S. intelligence agencies is evidenced by the people who formed the directors and principal officers of the bank, including the following:

- Admiral Earl F. Yates, president of the Nugan Hand Bank was, during the Vietnam War, chief of staff for strategic planning of U.S. forces in Asia and the Pacific.

- General Edwin F. Black, president of Nugan Hand's Hawaii branch, was commander of U.S. troops in Thailand during the Vietnam War and, after the war, assistant army chief of staff for the Pacific.

- General Erle Cocke, Jr., head of the Nugan Hand Washington, D.C., office.

- George Farris, worked in the Nugan Hand Hong Kong and Washington, D.C. offices. Farris was a military intelligence specialist who worked in a special forces training base in the Pacific.

- Bernie Houghton, Nugan Hand's representative in Saudi Arabia. Houghton was also a U.S. naval intelligence undercover agent.

- Thomas Clines, director of training in the CIA's clandestine service, was a London operative for Nugan Hand who helped in the takeover of a London-based bank and was stationed at Long Cheng with Michael Hand and Theodore S. Shackley during the Vietnam War.

- Dale Holmgreen, former flight service manager in Vietnam for Civil Air Transport, which became Air America. He was on the board of directors of Nugan Hand and ran the bank's Taiwan office.

- Walter McDonald, an economist and former deputy director of CIA for economic research, was a specialist in petroleum. He became a consultant to Nugan Hand and served as head of its Annapolis, Maryland, branch.

- General Roy Manor, who ran the Nugan Hand Philippine office, was a Vietnam veteran who helped coordinate the aborted attempt to rescue the Iranian hostages, chief of staff for the U.S. Pacific command, and the U.S. government's liaison officer to Philippine President Ferdinand Marcos.

On the board of directors of the parent company formed by Michael Hand that preceded the Nugan Hand Bank were Grant Walters, Robert Peterson, David M. Houton, and Spencer Smith, all of whom listed their address as c/o Air America, Army Post Office, San Francisco, California.

STATE-ORGANIZED CRIME 191

Also working through the Nugan Hand Bank was Edwin F. Wilson, a CIA agent involved in smuggling arms to the Middle East and later sentenced to prison by a U.S. court for smuggling illegal arms to Libya. Edwin Wilson's associate in Mideast arms shipments was Theodore Shackley, head of the Miami, Florida, CIA station.[1] In 1973, when William Colby was made director of Central Intelligence, Shackley replaced him as head of covert operations for the Far East; on his retirement from the CIA William Colby became Nugan Hand's lawyer.

In the late 1970s the bank experienced financial difficulties, which led to the death of Frank Nugan. He was found dead of a shotgun blast in his Mercedes Benz on a remote road outside Sydney. The official explanation was suicide, but some investigators speculated that he might have been murdered. In any event, Nugan's death created a major banking scandal and culminated in a government investigation. The investigation revealed that millions of dollars were unaccounted for in the bank's records and that the bank was serving as a money-laundering operation for narcotics smugglers and as a conduit through which the CIA was financing gun smuggling and other illegal operations throughout the world. These operations included illegally smuggling arms to South Africa and the Middle East. There was also evidence that the CIA used the Nugan Hand Bank to pay for political campaigns that slandered politicians, including Australia's Prime Minister Witham (Kwitny, 1977).

Michael Hand tried desperately to cover up the operations of the bank. Hundreds of documents were destroyed before investigators could get into the bank. Despite Hand's efforts, the scandal mushroomed and eventually Hand was forced to flee Australia. He managed this, while under indictment for a rash of felonies, with the aid of a CIA official who flew to Australia with a false passport and accompanied him out of the country. Hand's father, who lives in New York, denies knowing anything about his son's whereabouts.

Thus, the evidence uncovered by the government investigation in Australia linked high-level CIA officials to a bank in Sydney that was responsible for financing and laundering money for a significant part of the narcotics trafficking originating in Southeast Asia (Commonwealth of New South Wales, 1982b; Owen, 1983). It also linked the CIA to arms smuggling and illegal involvement in the democratic processes of a friendly nation. Other investigations reveal that the events in Australia were but part of a worldwide involvement in narcotics and arms smuggling by the CIA and French intelligence (Hougan, 1978; Kruger, 1980; Owen, 1983).

---

1. It was Shackley who, along with Rafael "Chi Chi" Quintero, a Cuban–American, forged the plot to assassinate Fidel Castro by using organized–crime figures Santo Trafficante, Jr., John Roselli, and Sam Giancana.

192   **CHAMBLISS**

ARMS SMUGGLING

One of the most important forms of state-organized crime today is arms smuggling. To a significant extent, U.S. involvement in narcotics smuggling after the Vietnam War can be understood as a means of funding the purchase of military weapons for nations and insurgent groups that could not be funded legally through congressional allocations or for which U.S. law prohibited support (NARMIC, 1984).

In violation of U.S. law, members of the National Security Council (NSC), the Department of Defense, and the CIA carried out a plan to sell millions of dollars worth of arms to Iran and use profits from those sales to support the Contras in Nicaragua (Senate Hearings, 1986). The Boland amendment, effective in 1985, prohibited any U.S. official from directly or indirectly assisting the Contras. To circumvent the law, a group of intelligence and military officials established a "secret team" of U.S. operatives, including Lt. Colonel Oliver North, Theodore Shackley, Thomas Clines, and Maj. General Richard Secord, among others (testimony before U.S. Senate, 1986). Shackley and Clines, as noted, were CIA agents in Long Cheng; along with Michael Hand they ran the secret war in Laos, which was financed in part from profits from opium smuggling. Shackley and Clines had also been involved in the 1961 invasion of Cuba and were instrumental in hiring organized-crime figures in an attempt to assassinate Fidel Castro.

Senator Daniel Inouye of Hawaii claims that this "secret government within our government" waging war in Third World countries was part of the Reagan doctrine (the *Guardian*, July 29, 1987). Whether President Reagan or then Vice President Bush were aware of the operations is yet to be established. What cannot be doubted in the face of overwhelming evidence in testimony before the Senate and from court documents is that this group of officials of the state oversaw and coordinated the distribution and sale of weapons to Iran and to the Contras in Nicaragua. These acts were in direct violation of the Illegal Arms Export Control Act, which made the sale of arms to Iran unlawful, and the Boland amendment, which made it a criminal act to supply the Contras with arms or funds.

The weapons that were sold to Iran were obtained by the CIA through the Pentagon. Secretary of Defense Caspar Weinberger ordered the transfer of weapons from Army stocks to the CIA without the knowledge of Congress four times in 1986. The arms were then transferred to middlemen, such as Iranian arms dealer Yaacov Nimrodi, exiled Iranian arms dealer Manucher Ghorbanifar, and Saudi Arabian businessman Adman Khashoggi. Weapons were also flown directly to the Contras, and funds from the sale of weapons were diverted to support Contra warfare. There is also considerable evidence

STATE-ORGANIZED CRIME 193

that this "secret team," along with other military and CIA officials, cooperated with narcotics smuggling in Latin America in order to fund the Contras in Nicaragua.

In 1986, the Reagan administration admitted that Adolfo Chamorro's Contra group, which was supported by the CIA, was helping a Colombian drug trafficker transport drugs into the United States. Chamorro was arrested in April 1986 for his involvement (Potter and Bullington, 1987: 54). Testimony in several trials of major drug traffickers in the past 5 years has revealed innumerable instances in which drugs were flown from Central America into the United States with the cooperation of military and CIA personnel. These reports have also been confirmed by military personnel and private citizens who testified that they saw drugs being loaded on planes in Central America and unloaded at military bases in the United States. Pilots who flew planes with arms to the Contras report returning with planes carrying drugs.

At the same time that the United States was illegally supplying the Nicaraguan Contras with arms purchased, at least in part, with profits from the sale of illegal drugs, the administration launched a campaign against the Sandanistas for their alleged involvement in drug trafficking. Twice during his weekly radio shows in 1986, President Reagan accused the Sandanistas of smuggling drugs. Barry Seal, an informant and pilot for the Drug Enforcement Administration (DEA) was ordered by members of the CIA and DEA to photograph the Sandanistas loading a plane. During a televised speech in March 1986, Reagan showed the picture that Seal took and said that it showed Sandinista officials loading a plane with drugs for shipment to the United States. After the photo was displayed, Congress appropriated $100 million in aid for the Contras. Seal later admitted to reporters that the photograph he took was a plane being loaded with crates that did not contain drugs. He also told reporters that he was aware of the drug smuggling activities of the Contra network and a Colombian cocaine syndicate. For his candor, Seal was murdered in February 1987. Shortly after his murder, the DEA issued a "low key clarification" regarding the validity of the photograph, admitting that there was no evidence that the plane was being loaded with drugs.

Other testimony linking the CIA and U.S. military officials to complicity in drug trafficking includes the testimony of John Stockwell, a former high-ranking CIA official, who claims that drug smuggling and the CIA were essential components in the private campaign for the Contras. Corroboration for these assertions comes also from George Morales, one of the largest drug traffickers in South America, who testified that he was approached by the CIA in 1984 to fly weapons into Nicaragua. Morales claims that the CIA opened up an airstrip in Costa Rica and gave the pilots information on how to avoid radar traps. According to Morales, he flew 20 shipments of weapons into Costa Rica in 1984 and 1985. In return, the CIA helped him to smuggle thousands of kilos of cocaine into the United States. Morales alone channeled $250,000 quarterly to Contra leader Adolfo Chamorro from his trafficking activity. A pilot for Morales, Gary Betzner, substantiated Morales's claims and admitted flying 4,000 pounds of arms into Costa Rica and 500 kilos of cocaine to Lakeland, Florida, on his return trips. From 1985 to 1987, the CIA arranged 50 to 100 flights using U.S. airports that did not undergo inspection.

The destination of the flights by Morales and Betzner was a hidden airstrip on the ranch of John Hull. Hull, an admitted CIA agent, was a primary player in Oliver North's plan to aid the Contras. Hull's activities were closely monitored by Robert Owen, a key player in the Contra Supply network. Owen established the Institute for Democracy, Education, and Assistance, which raised money to buy arms for the Contras and which, in October 1985, was asked by Congress to distribute $50,000 in "humanitarian aid" to the Contras. Owen worked for Oliver North in coordinating illegal aid to the Contras and setting up the airstrip on the ranch of John Hull.

According to an article in the *Nation*, Oliver North's network of operatives and mercenaries had been linked to the largest drug cartel in South America since 1983. The DEA estimates that Colombian Jorge Ochoa Vasquez, the "kingpin" of the Medellin drug empire, is responsible for supplying 70% to 80% of the cocaine that enters the United States every year. Ochoa was taken into custody by Spanish police in October 1984 when a verbal order was sent by the U.S. Embassy in Madrid for his arrest. The embassy specified that Officer Cos–Gayon, who had undergone training with the DEA, should make the arrest. Other members of the Madrid Judicial Police were connected to the DEA and North's arms smuggling network. Ochoa's lawyers informed him that the United States would alter his extradition if he agreed to implicate the Sandanista government in drug trafficking. Ochoa refused and spent 20 months in jail before returning to Colombia. The Spanish courts ruled that the United States was trying to use Ochoa to discredit Nicaragua and released him. (The *Nation*, September 5, 1987.)

There are other links between the U.S. government and the Medellin cartel. Jose Blandon, General Noriega's former chief advisor, claims that DEA operations have protected the drug empire in the past and that the DEA paid Noriega $4.7 million for his silence. Blandon also testified in Senate committee hearings that Panama's bases were used as training camps for the Contras in exchange for "economic" support from the United States. Finally, Blandon contends that the CIA gave Panamanian leaders intelligence documents about U.S. senators and aides; the CIA denies these charges. (The *Christian Science Monitor*, February 11, 1988: 3.)

Other evidence of the interrelationship among drug trafficking, the CIA, the NSC, and aid to the Contras includes the following:

STATE-ORGANIZED CRIME 195

- In January 1983, two Contra leaders in Costa Rica persuaded the Justice Department to return over $36,000 in drug profits to drug dealers Julio Zavala and Carlos Cabezas for aid to the Contras (Potter and Bullington, 1987: 22).
- Michael Palmer, a drug dealer in Miami, testified that the State Department's Nicaraguan humanitarian assistance office contracted with his company, Vortex Sales and Leasing, to take humanitarian aid to the Contras. Palmer claims that he smuggled $40 million in marijuana to the United States between 1977 and 1985 (The *Guardian*, March 20, 1988: 3).
- During House and Senate hearings in 1986, it was revealed that a major DEA investigation of the Medellin drug cartel of Colombia, which was expected to culminate in the arrest of several leaders of the cartel, was compromised when someone in the White House leaked the story of the investigation to the *Washington Times* (a conservative newspaper in Washington, D.C.), which published the story on July 17, 1984. According to DEA Administrator John Lawn, the leak destroyed what was "probably one of the most significant operations in DEA history" (Sharkey, 1988: 24).
- When Honduran General Jose Buseo, who was described by the Justice Department as an "international terrorist," was indicted for conspiring to murder the president of Honduras in a plot financed by profits from cocaine smuggling, Oliver North and officials from the Department of Defense and the CIA pressured the Justice Department to be lenient with General Buseo. In a memo disclosed by the Iran-Contra committee, North stated that if Buseo was not protected "he will break his longstanding silence about the Nic[araguan] resistance and other sensitive operations" (Sharkey, 1988: 27).

On first blush, it seems odd that government agencies and officials would engage in such wholesale disregard of the law. As a first step in building an explanation for these and other forms of state-organized crime, let us try to understand why officials of the CIA, the NSC, and the Department of Defense would be willing to commit criminal acts in pursuit of other goals.

WHY?

Why would government officials from the NSC, the Defense Department, the State Department, and the CIA become involved in smuggling arms and narcotics, money laundering, assassinations, and other criminal activities? The answer lies in the structural contradictions that inhere in nation–states (Chambliss, 1980).

As Weber, Marx, and Gramsci pointed out, no state can survive without

196   **CHAMBLISS**

establishing legitimacy. The law is a fundamental cornerstone in creating legitimacy and an illusion (at least) of social order. It claims universal principles that demand some behaviors and prohibit others. The protection of property and personal security are obligations assumed by states everywhere both as a means of legitimizing the state's franchise on violence and as a means of protecting commercial interests (Chambliss and Seidman, 1982).

The threat posed by smuggling to both personal security and property interests makes laws prohibiting smuggling essential. Under some circumstances, however, such laws contradict other interests of the state. This contradiction prepares the ground for state-organized crime as a solution to the conflicts and dilemmas posed by the simultaneous existence of contradictory "legitimate" goals.

The military–intelligence establishment in the United States is resolutely committed to fighting the spread of "communism" throughout the world. This mission is not new but has prevailed since the 1800s. Congress and the presidency are not consistent in their support for the money and policies thought by the frontline warriors to be necessary to accomplish their lofty goals. As a result, programs under way are sometimes undermined by a lack of funding and even by laws that prohibit their continuation (such as the passage of laws prohibiting support for the Contras). Officials of government agencies adversely affected by political changes are thus placed squarely in a dilemma: If they comply with the legal limitations on their activities they sacrifice their mission. The dilemma is heightened by the fact that they can anticipate future policy changes that will reinstate their resources and their freedom. When that time comes, however, programs adversely affected will be difficult if not impossible to re-create.

A number of events that occurred between 1960 and 1980 left the military and the CIA with badly tarnished images. Those events and political changes underscored their vulnerability. The CIA lost considerable political clout with elected officials when its planned invasion of Cuba (the infamous Bay of Pigs invasion) was a complete disaster. Perhaps as never before in its history, the United States showed itself vulnerable to the resistance of a small nation. The CIA was blamed for this fiasco even though it was President Kennedy's decision to go ahead with the plans that he inherited from the previous administration. To add to the agency's problems, the complicity between it and ITT to invade Chile and overthrow the Allende government was yet another scar (see below), as was the involvement of the CIA in narcotics smuggling in Vietnam.

These and other political realities led to a serious breach between Presidents Kennedy, Johnson, Nixon, and Carter and the CIA. During President Nixon's tenure in the White House, one of the CIA's top men, James Angleton, referred to Nixon's national security advisor, Henry Kissinger (who became secretary of state) as "objectively, a Soviet Agent" (Hougan,

STATE-ORGANIZED CRIME 197

1984: 75). Another top agent of the CIA, James McCord (later implicated in the Watergate burglary) wrote a secret letter to his superior, General Paul Gaynor, in January 1973 in which he said:

> When the hundreds of dedicated fine men and women of the CIA no longer write intelligence summaries and reports with integrity, without fear of political recrimination—when their fine Director [Richard Helms] is being summarily discharged in order to make way for a politician who will write or rewrite intelligence the way the politicians want them written, instead of the way truth and best judgment dictates, our nation is in the deepest of trouble and freedom itself was never so imperiled. Nazi Germany rose and fell under exactly the same philosophy of governmental operation. (Hougan, 1984: 26–27)

McCord (1974: 60) spoke for many of the top military and intelligence officers in the United States when he wrote in his autobiography: "I believed that the whole future of the nation was at stake." These views show the depth of feeling toward the dangers of political "interference" with what is generally accepted in the military–intelligence establishment as their mission (Goulden, 1984).

When Jimmy Carter was elected president, he appointed Admiral Stansfield Turner as director of Central Intelligence. At the outset, Turner made it clear that he and the president did not share the agency's view that they were conducting their mission properly (Goulden, 1984; Turner, 1985). Turner insisted on centralizing power in the director's office and on overseeing clandestine and covert operations. He met with a great deal of resistance. Against considerable opposition from within the agency, he reduced the size of the covert operation section from 1,200 to 400 agents. Agency people still refer to this as the "Halloween massacre."

Old hands at the CIA do not think their work is dispensable. They believe zealously, protectively, and one is tempted to say, with religious fervor, that the work they are doing is essential for the salvation of humankind. With threats from both Republican and Democratic administrations, the agency sought alternative sources of revenue to carry out its mission. The alternative was already in place with the connections to the international narcotics traffic, arms smuggling, the existence of secret corporations incorporated in foreign countries (such as Panama), and the established links to banks for the laundering of money for covert operations.

STATE-ORGANIZED ASSASSINATIONS AND MURDER

Assassination plots and political murders are usually associated in people's minds with military dictatorships and European monarchies. The practice of assassination, however, is not limited to unique historical events but has

198   CHAMBLISS

become a tool of international politics that involves modern nation–states of many different types.

In the 1960s a French intelligence agency hired Christian David to assassinate the Moroccan leader Ben Barka (Hougan, 1978: 204–207). Christian David was one of those international "spooks" with connections to the DEA, the CIA, and international arms smugglers, such as Robert Vesco.

In 1953 the CIA organized and supervised a coup d'etat in Iran that overthrew the democratically elected government of Mohammed Mossadegh, who had become unpopular with the United States when he nationalized foreign–owned oil companies. The CIA's coup replaced Mossadegh with Reza Shah Pahlevi, who denationalized the oil companies and with CIA guidance established one of the most vicious secret intelligence organizations in the world: SAVAK. In the years to follow, the shah and CIA–trained agents of SAVAK murdered thousands of Iranian citizens. They arrested almost 1,500 people monthly, most of whom were subjected to inhuman torture and punishments without trial. Not only were SAVAK agents trained by the CIA, but there is evidence that they were instructed in techniques of torture (Hersh, 1979: 13).

In 1970 the CIA repeated the practice of overthrowing democratically elected governments that were not completely favorable to U.S. investments. When Salvador Allende was elected president of Chile, the CIA organized a coup that overthrew Allende, during which he was murdered, along with the head of the military, General Rene Schneider. Following Allende's overthrow, the CIA trained agents for the Chilean secret service (DINA). DINA set up a team of assassins who could "travel anywhere in the world . . . to carry out sanctions including assassinations" (Dinges and Landau, 1980: 239). One of the assassinations carried out by DINA was the murder of Orlando Letellier, Allende's ambassador to the United States and his former minister of defense. Letellier was killed when a car bomb blew up his car on Embassy Row in Washington, D.C. (Dinges and Landau, 1982).

Other bloody coups known to have been planned, organized, and executed by U.S. agents include coups in Guatemala, Nicaragua, the Dominican Republic, and Vietnam. American involvement in those coups was never legally authorized. The murders, assassinations, and terrorist acts that accompany coups are criminal acts by law, both in the United States and in the country in which they take place.

More recent examples of murder and assassination for which government officials are responsible include the death of 80 people in Beirut, Lebanon, when a car bomb exploded on May 8, 1985. The bomb was set by a Lebanese counterterrorist unit working with the CIA. Senator Daniel Moynihan has said that when he was vice president of the Senate Intelligence Committee, President Reagan ordered the CIA to form a small antiterrorist effort in the Mideast. Two sources said that the CIA was working with the group that

STATE-ORGANIZED CRIME 199

planted the bomb to kill the Shiite leader Hussein Fadallah (the *New York Times*, May 13, 1985).

A host of terrorist plans and activities connected with the attempt to overthrow the Nicaraguan government, including several murders and assassinations, were exposed in an affidavit filed by free–lance reporters Tony Avirgan and Martha Honey. They began investigating Contra activities after Avirgan was injured in an attempt on the life of Contra leader Eden Pastora. In 1986, Honey and Avirgan filed a complaint with the U.S. District Court in Miami charging John Hull, Robert Owen, Theodore Shackley, Thomas Clines, Chi Chi Quintero, Maj. General Richard Secord, and others working for the CIA in Central America with criminal conspiracy and the smuggling of cocaine to aid the Nicaraguan rebels.

A criminal conspiracy in which the CIA admits participating is the publication of a manual, *Psychological Operation in Guerrilla Warfare*, which was distributed to the people of Nicaragua. The manual describes how the people should proceed to commit murder, sabotage, vandalism, and violent acts in order to undermine the government. Encouraging or instigating such crimes is not only a violation of U.S. law, it was also prohibited by Reagan's executive order of 1981, which forbade any U.S. participation in foreign assassinations.

The CIA is not alone in hatching criminal conspiracies. The DEA organized a "Special Operations Group," which was responsible for working out plans to assassinate political and business leaders in foreign countries who were involved in drug trafficking. The head of this group was a former CIA agent, Lou Conein (also known as "Black Luigi"). George Crile wrote in the *Washington Post* (June 13, 1976):

> When you get down to it, Conein was organizing an assassination program. He was frustrated by the big–time operators who were just too insulated to get to . . . Meetings were held to decide whom to target and what method of assassination to employ.

Crile's findings were also supported by the investigative journalist Jim Hougan (1978: 132).

It is a crime to conspire to commit murder. The official record, including testimony by participants in three conspiracies before the U.S. Congress and in court, make it abundantly clear that the crime of conspiring to commit murder is not infrequent in the intelligence agencies of the United States and other countries.

It is also a crime to cover up criminal acts, but there are innumerable examples of instances in which the CIA and the FBI conspired to interfere with the criminal prosecution of drug dealers, murderers, and assassins. In the death of Letellier, mentioned earlier, the FBI and the CIA refused to cooperate with the prosecution of the DINA agents who murdered Letellier

(Dinges and Landau, 1980: 208–209). Those agencies were also involved in
the cover–up of the criminal activities of a Cuban exile, Ricardo (Monkey)
Morales. While an employee of the FBI and the CIA, Morales planted a
bomb on an Air Cubana flight from Venezuela, which killed 73 people. The
Miami police confirmed Morales's claim that he was acting under orders
from the CIA (Lernoux, 1984: 188). In fact, Morales, who was arrested for
overseeing the shipment of 10 tons of marijuana, admitting to being a CIA
contract agent who conducted bombings, murders, and assassinations. He
was himself killed in a bar after he made public his work with the CIA and
the FBI.

Colonel Muammar Qaddafi, like Fidel Castro, has been the target of a
number of assassination attempts and conspiracies by the U.S. government.
One plot, the *Washington Post* reported, included an effort to "lure [Qaddafi]
into some foreign adventure of terrorist exploit that would give a growing
number of Qaddafi opponents in the Libyan military a chance to seize power,
or such a foreign adventure might give one of Qaddafi's neighbors, such as
Algeria or Egypt, a justification for responding to Qaddafi militarily" (the
Washington Post, April 14, 1986). The CIA recommended "stimulating"
Qaddafi's fall "by encouraging disaffected elements in the Libyan army who
could be spurred to assassination attempts" (the *Guardian*, November 20,
1985: 6).

Opposition to government policies can be a very risky business, as the ecology group Greenpeace discovered when it opposed French nuclear testing in
the Pacific. In the fall of 1985 the French government planned a series of
atomic tests in the South Pacific. Greenpeace sent its flagship to New Zealand with instructions to sail into the area where the atomic testing was
scheduled to occur. Before the ship could arrive at the scene, however, the
French secret service located the ship in the harbor and blew it up. The blast
from the bomb killed one of the crew.

OTHER STATE–ORGANIZED CRIMES

Every agency of government is restricted by law in certain fundamental
ways. Yet structural pressures exist that can push agencies to go beyond their
legal limits. The CIA, for example, is not permitted to engage in domestic
intelligence. Despite this, the CIA has opened and photographed the mail of
over 1 million private citizens (Rockefeller Report, 1975: 101–115), illegally
entered people's homes, and conducted domestic surveillance through electronic devices (Parenti, 1983: 170–171).

Agencies of the government also cannot legally conduct experiments on
human subjects that violate civil rights or endanger the lives of the subjects.
But the CIA conducted experiments on unknowing subjects by hiring prostitutes to administer drugs to their clients. CIA–trained medical doctors and

STATE-ORGANIZED CRIME 201

psychologists observed the effects of the drugs through a two–way mirror in expensive apartments furnished to the prostitutes by the CIA. At least one of the victims of these experiments died and others suffered considerable trauma (Anderson and Whitten, 1976; Crewdson and Thomas, 1977; Jacobs 1977a, 1977b).

The most flagrant violation of civil rights by federal agencies is the FBI's counterintelligence program, known as COINTELPRO. This program was designed to disrupt, harass, and discredit groups that the FBI decided were in some way "un-American." Such groups included the American Civil Liberties Union, antiwar movements, civil rights organizations, and a host of other legally constituted political groups whose views opposed some of the policies of the United States (Church Committee, 1976). With the exposure of COINTELPRO, the group was disbanded. There is evidence, however, that the illegal surveillance of U.S. citizens did not stop with the abolition of COINTELPRO but continues today (Klein, 1988).

DISCUSSION

Elsewhere I have suggested a general theory to account for variations in types and frequency of crime (Chambliss, 1988a). The starting point for that theory is the assumption that in every era political, economic, and social relations contain certain inherent *contradictions*, which produce *conflicts* and *dilemmas* that people struggle to resolve. The study of state-organized crime brings into sharp relief the necessity of understanding the role of contradictions in the formation and implementation of law.

Contradictions inherent in the formation of states create conditions under which there will be a tendency for state officials to violate the criminal law. State officials inherit from the past laws that were not of their making and that were the result of earlier efforts to resolve conflicts wrought by structural contradictions (Chambliss, 1980; Chambliss and Seidman, 1982). The inherited laws nonetheless represent the foundation on which the legitimacy of the state's authority depends. These laws also provide a basis for attempts by the state to control the acts of others and to justify the use of violence to that end.

For England in the sixteenth century, passing laws to legitimize piracy for English pirates while condemning as criminal the piracy of others against England would have been an untenable solution, just as it would undermine the legitimacy of America's ideological and political position to pass legislation allowing for terrorist acts on the part of U.S. officials while condemning and punishing the terrorism of others.

Law is a two–edged sword; it creates one set of conflicts while it attempts to resolve another. The passage of a particular law or set of laws may resolve conflicts and enhance state control, but it also limits the legal activities of the state. State officials are thus often caught between conflicting demands as

202   **CHAMBLISS**

they find themselves constrained by laws that interfere with other goals demanded of them by their roles or their perception of what is in the interests of the state. There is a contradiction, then, between the legal prescriptions and the agreed goals of state agencies. Not everyone caught in this dilemma will opt for violating the law, but some will. Those who do are the perpetrators, but not the cause, of the persistence of state-organized crime.

When Spain and Portugal began exploiting the labor and natural resources of the Americas and Asia, other European nations were quick to realize the implications for their own power and sovereignty. France, England, and Holland were powerful nations, but not powerful enough at the time to challenge Spain and Portugal directly. The dilemma for those nations was how to share in the wealth and curtail the power of Spain and Portugal without going to war. A resolution to the dilemma was forged through cooperation with pirates. Cooperating with pirates, however, required violating their own laws as well as the laws of other countries. In this way, the states organized criminality for their own ends without undermining their claim to legitimacy or their ability to condemn and punish piracy committed against them.

It should be noted that some monarchs in the sixteenth and seventeenth centuries (James I of England, for example) refused to cooperate with pirates no matter how profitable it would have been for the Crown. So, too, not all CIA or NSC personnel organize criminal activities in pursuit of state goals.

The impetus for the criminality of European states that engaged in piracy was the need to accumulate capital in the early stages of capitalist formation. State–organized criminality did not disappear, however, with the emergence of capitalism as the dominant economic system of the world. Rather, contemporary state–organized crime also has its roots in the ongoing need for capital accumulation of modern nation–states, whether the states be socialist, capitalist, or mixed economies.

Sociologically, then, the most important characteristics of state–organized crime in the modern world are at one with characteristics of state–organized crime in the early stages of capitalist development. Today, states organize smuggling, assassinations, covert operations, and conspiracies to criminally assault citizens, political activists, and political leaders perceived to be a threat. These acts are as criminal in the laws of the nations perpetrating them as were the acts of piracy in which European nations were complicitous.

At the most general level, the contradictions that are the force behind state-organized crime today are the same as those that were the impetus for piracy in sixteenth-century Europe. The accumulation of capital determines a nation's power, wealth, and survival today, as it did 300 years ago. The state must provide a climate and a set of international relations that facilitate this accumulation if it is to succeed. State officials will be judged in accordance with their ability to create these conditions.

STATE-ORGANIZED CRIME 203

But contradictory ideologies and demands are the very essence of state formations. The laws of every nation–state inhibit officials from maximizing conditions conducive to capital accumulation at the same time that they facilitate the process. Laws prohibiting assassination and arms smuggling enable a government to control such acts when they are inimical to their interests. When such acts serve the interests of the state, however, then there are pressures that lead some officials to behave criminally. Speaking of the relationship among the NSC, the CIA, and drug trafficking, Senator John Kerry, chairman of the Senate Foreign Relations Subcommittee on Terrorism, Narcotics and International Operations, pinpointed the dilemma when he said "stopping drug trafficking to the United States has been a secondary U.S. foreign policy objective. It has been sacrificed repeatedly for other political goals" (Senate Hearings, 1986). He might have added that engaging in drug trafficking and arms smuggling has been a price government agencies have been willing to pay "for other political goals."

These contradictions create conflicts between nation–states as well as internally among the branches of government. Today, we see nations such as Turkey, Bolivia, Colombia, Peru, Panama, and the Bahamas encouraging the export of illegal drugs while condemning them publicly. At the same time, other government agencies cooperate in the export and import of illegal arms and drugs to finance subversive and terrorist activities. Governments plot and carry out assassinations and illegal acts against their own citizens in order to "preserve democracy" while supporting the most undemocratic institutions imaginable. In the process, the contradictions that create the conflicts and dilemmas remain untouched and the process goes on indefinitely.

A U.S. State Department report (1985) illustrates, perhaps, the logical outcome of the institutionalization of state–organized crime in the modern world. In this report the State Department offered to stop criminal acts against the Nicaraguan government in return for concessions from Nicaragua. Three hundred years earlier England, France, and Spain signed a treaty by which each agreed to suppress its piracy against the others in return for certain guarantees of economic and political sovereignty.

CONCLUSION

My concern here is to point out the importance of studying state-organized crime. Although I have suggested some theoretical notions that appear to me to be promising, the more important goal is to raise the issue for further study. The theoretical and empirical problems raised by advocating the study of state–organized crime are, however, formidable.

Data on contemporary examples of state–organized crime are difficult to obtain. The data I have been able to gather depend on sources that must be used cautiously. Government hearings, court trials, interviews, newspaper

204   **CHAMBLISS**

accounts, and historical documents are replete with problems of validity and reliability. In my view they are no more so than conventional research methods in the social sciences, but that does not alter the fact that there is room for error in interpreting the findings. It will require considerable imagination and diligence for others to pursue research on this topic and add to the empirical base from which theoretical propositions can be tested and elaborated.

We need to explore different political, economic, and social systems in varying historical periods to discover why some forms of social organization are more likely to create state-organized crimes than others. We need to explore the possibility that some types of state agencies are more prone to engaging in criminality than others. It seems likely, for example, that state agencies whose activities can be hidden from scrutiny are more likely to engage in criminal acts than those whose record is public. This principle may also apply to whole nation–states: the more open the society, the less likely it is that state-organized crime will become institutionalized.

There are also important parallels between state-organized criminality and the criminality of police and law enforcement agencies generally. Local police departments that find it more useful to cooperate with criminal syndicates than to combat them are responding to their own particular contradictions, conflicts, and dilemmas (Chambliss, 1988b). An exploration of the theoretical implications of these similarities could yield some important findings.

The issue of state–organized crime raises again the question of how crime should be defined to be scientifically useful. For the purposes of this analysis, I have accepted the conventional criminological definition of crime as acts that are in violation of the criminal law. This definition has obvious limitations (see Schwendinger and Schwendinger, 1975), and the study of state–organized crime may facilitate the development of a more useful definition by underlying the interrelationship between crime and the legal process. At the very least, the study of state-organized crime serves as a reminder that crime is a political phenomenon and must be analyzed accordingly.

REFERENCES

Anderson, Jack, and Lee Whitten
   1976   The CIA's "sex squad." The Washington Post, June 22:B13.

Andrews, K.R.
   1959   English Privateering Voyages to the West Indies 1598–1695. Ser. 11., vol. 111. London: Hakluyt Society.
   1971   The Last Voyage of Drake and Hawkins. New York: Cambridge University Press.

Block, Alan A., and William J. Chambliss
   1981   Organizing Crime. New York: Elsevier.

STATE-ORGANIZED CRIME   205

British Museum
  1977   Sir Francis Drake. London: British Museum Publications.

Chambliss, William J.
  1968   The tolerance policy: An invitation to organized crime. Seattle October:
            23–31.
  1971   Vice, corruption, bureaucracy and power. Wisconsin Law Review
            4:1,150–1,173.
  1975a   On the paucity of original research on organized crime: A footnote to
            Galliher and Cain. The American Sociologist 10:36–39.
  1975b   Toward a political economy of crime. Theory and Society 2:149–170.
  1977   Markets, profits, labor and smack. Contemporary Crises 1:53–57.
  1980   On lawmaking. British Journal of Law and Society 6:149–172.
  1988a   Exploring Criminology. New York: Macmillan.
  1988b   On the Take: From Petty Crooks to Presidents. Revised ed. Bloomington:
            Indiana University Press.

Chambliss, William J., and Robert B. Seidman
  1982   Law, Order and Power. Rev. ed. Reading, Mass.: Addison–Wesley.

Church Committee
  1976   Intelligence Activities and the Rights of Americans. Washington, D.C.:
            Government Printing Office.

Commonwealth of New South Wales
  1982a   New South Wales Joint Task Force on Drug Trafficking. Federal
            Parliament Report. Sydney: Government of New South Wales.
  1982b   Preliminary Report of the Royal Commission to Investigate the Nugan
            Hand Bank Failure. Federal Parliament Report. Sydney: Government of
            New South Wales.

Corbett, Julian S.
  1898a   Drake and the Tudor Army. 2 vols. London: Longmans, Green.
  1898b   Paper Relating to the Navy during the Spanish War, 1585–1587. Vol. 11.
            London: Navy Records Society.

Crewdson, John M., and Jo Thomas
  1977   Abuses in testing of drugs by CIA to be panel focus. The New York Times,
            September 20.

de La Croix, Robert
  1962   John Paul Jones. London: Frederik Muller.

Dinges, John, and Saul Landau
  1980   Assassination on Embassy Row. New York: McGraw–Hill.
  1982   The CIA's link to Chile's plot. The Nation, June 12:712–713.

Exquemling, A.O.
  1670   De Americanaenshe Zee-Roovers. MS. 301. London, British Museum.

Goulden, Joseph C.
  1984   Death Merchant: The Brutal True Story of Edwin P. Wilson. New York:
            Simon and Schuster.

Hersh, Seymour
  1979   Ex-analyst says CIA rejected warning on Shah. The New York Times,
            January 7:A10. Cited in Piers Beirne and James Messerschmidt, Criminol-
            ogy. New York: Harcourt Brace Jovanovich, forthcoming.

206 CHAMBLISS

Hougan, Jim
    1978   Spooks: The Haunting of America—The Private Use of Secret Agents. New York: William Morrow.
    1984   Secret Agenda: Watergate, Deep Throat, and the CIA. New York: Random House.

Jacobs, John
    1977a   The diaries of a CIA operative. The Washington Post, September 5:1.
    1977b   Turner cites 149 drug-test projects. The Washington Post, August 4:1.

Klein, Lloyd
    1988   Big Brother Is Still Watching You. Paper presented at the annual meetings of the American Society of Criminology, Chicago, November 12.

Kruger, Henrik
    1980   The Great Heroin Coup. Boston: South End Press.

Kwitny, Jonathan
    1987   The Crimes of Patriots. New York: W.W. Norton.

Lane-Poole
    1890   The Barbary Corsairs. London: T. Fisher Unwin.

LeGolif, Louis
    1680   The Manuscripts of Louis LeGolif alias Borgnefesse. London, British Museum.

Lernoux, Penny
    1984   The Miami connection. The Nation, February 18:186–198.

MacIntyre, Donald
    1975   The Privateers. London: Paul Elek.

Mainwaring, Henry
    1616   Of the Beginnings, Practices, and Suppression of Pirates. No publisher acknowledged.

McCord, James W., Jr.
    1974   A Piece of Tape. Rockville, Md.: Washington Media Services.

McCoy, Alfred W.
    1973   The Politics of Heroin in Southeast Asia. New York: Harper & Row.

NARMIC
    1984   Military Exports to South Africa: A Research Report on the Arms Embargo. Philadelphia: American Friends Service Committee.

Nihill, Grant
    1982   Bank links to spies, drugs. The Advertiser, November 10:1.

Owen, John
    1983   Sleight of Hand: The $25 Million Nugan Hand Bank Scandal. Sydney: Calporteur Press.

Parenti, Michael
    1983   Democracy for the Few. New York: St. Martin's.

Petras, James
    1977   Chile: Crime, class consciousness and the bourgeoisie. Crime and Social Justice 7:14–22.

STATE-ORGANIZED CRIME 207

Potter, Gary W., and Bruce Bullington
   1987   Drug Trafficking and the Contras: A Case Study of State-Organized Crime.
          Paper presented at annual meeting of the American Society of Criminology,
          Montreal.

Ritchie, Robert C.
   1986   Captain Kidd and the War Against the Pirates. Cambridge, Mass.: Harvard
          University Press.

Rockefeller Report
   1975   Report to the President by the Commission on CIA Activities within the
          United States. Washington, D.C.: Government Printing Office.

Schwendinger, Herman, and Julia Schwendinger
   1975   Defenders of order or guardians of human rights. Issue in Criminology
          7:72-81.

Senate Hearings
   1986   Senate Select Committee on Assassination, Alleged Assassination Plots
          Involving Foreign Leaders. Interim Report of the Senate Select Committee
          to Study Governmental Operations with Respect to Intelligence Activities.
          94th Cong., 1st sess., November 20. Washington, D.C.: Government
          Printing Office.

Senior, C.M.
   1976   A Nation of Pirates: English Piracy in its Heyday. London: David and
          Charles Newton Abbot.

Sharkey, Jacqueline
   1988   The Contra-drug trade eff. Common Cause Magazine, September-October:
          23-33.

Tilly, Charles
   1985   War making and state making as organized crime. In P. Evans, D.
          Rueschemeyer, and T. Skocpol (eds.), Bringing the State Back In.
          Cambridge: Cambridge University Press.

Turner, Stansfield
   1985   Secrecy and Democracy: The CIA in Transition. New York: Houghton
          Miflin.

U.S. Department of State
   1985   Revolution Beyond Our Border: Information on Central America. State
          Department Report N 132. Washington, D.C.: U.S. Department of State.

Verrill, A. Hyatt
   1924   Smugglers and Smuggling. New York: Duffield.

AUTHOR'S NOTE

The historical documents used for the research on piracy were provided by the British Museum Library, the Franklin D. Roosevelt Library in New York, Columbia University Library, and the Naval Archives. For the more recent happenings and machinations of the CIA, DEA, and other government agencies, the primary data bases are confidential interviews with people involved in the events described, or people closely associated with the events, and information obtained through Freedom of Information requests. Attribution to people who generously gave their time and in some cases took risks for the sake of providing a better understanding of the world we live in is, of course, impossible. Where possible

208 **CHAMBLISS**

the information forthcoming from the interviews has been supplemented by reference to published government documents, newspaper reports, and verifiable research.

ACKNOWLEDGMENTS

This research owes a debt to so many people it is impossible to acknowledge them all. The many informants and officials who cooperated with various parts of the research and the librarians who helped uncover essential historical documents must come first. I am also deeply indebted to Raquel Kennedy, Pernille Baadsager, Richard Appelbaum, Marjorie Zatz, Alan Block, Jim Petras, Ray Michalowski, Stan Cohen, Hi Schwendinger, Tony Platt, and Martha Huggins for their insights and help at many stages in the development of the research. I am also indebted to a confidential donor who helped support the research effort in Thailand during 1974.

State–Corporate Crime

[16]

State-Corporate Crime in the US Nuclear Weapons Production Complex

David Kauzlarich, Western Michigan University
Ronald C. Kramer, Western Michigan University

The objectives of this essay are (1) to identify the characteristics of environmental law violations committed during the production of nuclear weapons in the United States, (2) to identify the historical forces and events that have contributed to those violations, and (3) to use data on crimes of the US nuclear weapons production complex to help adjudicate between a number of competing explanations for organizational crime. Qualitative and historical data indicate these crimes were principally caused by the interplay of historical exigencies and geo-political necessity. Suggestions for future empirical and theoretical work in the area of organizational crime are offered.

The United States government has been producing materials for nuclear weapons for over 50 years. From the discovery of fission to the present day, the US polity has committed itself to the refinement and development of these weapons of mass destruction. The process of converting materials, such as plutonium and uranium, into usable forms to create nuclear weapons generates an enormous amount of radioactive and non-radioactive waste that pollutes the air and water, and poses a grave threat to the health and safety of facility workers and those who live near the production sites.

This research focuses on the criminal violations of environmental law committed by the US nuclear weapons production complex.[1] In recent years it has been revealed that a substantial number of environmental law violations have occurred at the 17 major sites compromising this complex. The three objectives of this article are: (1) to identify the characteristics of the environmental law violations committed during the production of nuclear weapons, (2) to identify the historical forces and events which have contributed to those violations, and (3) to use the data concerning the illegal actions of the nuclear weapons production complex to help adjudicate between a number of competing causal theories for organizational crime.

THE IDEA OF STATE-CORPORATE CRIME

This research will ground its inquiry within the conceptual framework of organizational crime. Although there are several different formal definitions of organizational crime (see Finney and Lesieur 1982; Ermann and Lundman 1978a), Schrager and Short provide the most useful definition:

> Organizational crimes are illegal acts of omission or commission of an individual or group of individuals in a legitimate formal organization in accordance with the operative goals of the organization, which have a serious impact on employees, consumers, or the general public. (1978: 411)

Indeed, as this study will demonstrate, the US nuclear weapons production complex has engaged in illegal acts within a legitimate organizational structure; these acts have taken place in accordance with operational goals; and this criminality has inflicted serious harm upon employees, and the general public.

The environmental crimes committed during the process of nuclear weapons production are the collective product of the interaction between a government agency, the US Department of Energy (DOE), and various private business corporations. Thus, the criminal acts of the weapons complex fall into the special category of organizational misconduct that Kramer and Michalowski (1990: 13) have identified as state-corporate crime: 'illegal or socially injurious actions that occur when one or more institutions of political governance pursue a goal in direct cooperation with one or more institutions of economic production and distribution.'

State-corporate crime is a form of organizational misconduct that occurs at the interstices of corporations and governments. Within a capitalist economy, such crimes involve the active participation of two or more organizations, at least one of which is in the civil sector and one of which is in the state sector. Despite its ubiquity, the structural relations between corporate and governmental organizations have been relatively peripheral to the study of organizational crime.

Many recent examples of state-corporate crime abound: the space shuttle Challenger explosion (see Kramer 1992); the coordinated criminal frauds involving defense contractors and US military officials with key positions in the Pentagon's weapons procurement process; and the Iran-Contra crimes that resulted from the inter-relationships among the CIA, the National Security Council, and private arms suppliers. Another aim of this paper, therefore, is to demonstrate the utility of the concept of state-corporate crime through an exploration of the environmental crimes committed by the US nuclear weapons production complex.

THEORETICAL PERSPECTIVES ON ORGANIZATIONAL CRIME

There are three theoretical perspectives that attempt to explain organizational crime: (1) differential association theory, (2) the organizational approach, and (3) political economy. There are also models which attempt to combine these three theoretical perspectives into an integrated explanation of organizational crime. Each of these perspectives will be reviewed.

The social psychological perspective is reflected in Sutherland's (1949) differential association theory. As Sutherland asserts:

> Criminal behavior is learned in association with those who define such behavior favorably and in isolation from those who define it unfavorably, and that such a person in an appropriate situation engages in such criminal behavior if the weight of the favorable definitions exceeds the weight of the unfavorable definitions. (1949: 234)

Partial support for differential association as a theory of white collar crime has been found by a number of criminological researchers (Albanese 1982; Clinard 1946; Cressey 1950; Geis 1976; Lane 1953). While there can be no doubt that important insights have been derived from this approach, some

6   *The Journal of Human Justice, Volume 5, Number 1, Autumn, 1993*

criminologists have criticized differential association for its failure to incorporate the institutional level of analysis (Braithwaite 1985; Ermann and Lundman 1978a; Gross 1978; Schrager and Short 1978). These writers contend that theories which focus only on social-psychological variables cannot adequately explain why organizations, as social actors, violate the law.

Organizational theorists hold that the explanation of organizational crime requires more than an individual level of analysis, and argue that the organization itself should be central to an analysis of such crime (Albanese 1982; Clinard and Yeager 1980; Ermann and Lundman 1978b; Gross 1978, 1980; Hopkins 1978; Kramer 1982; Needleman and Needleman 1979; Schrager and Short 1978; Sherman 1980; Vaughn 1982, 1983). The organizational theorists argue that 'there is built into the very structure of organizations an inherent inducement for the organization itself to engage in crime' (Gross 1978: 56). A common argument offered by researchers using this approach is that organizations are, by their very nature, strongly goal oriented and concerned with performance. This emphasis on goals and performance may compel organizations to use illegitimate means to achieve those goals. As Finney and Lesieur (1982: 264) note, 'one of the key ideas for understanding organizational crime is that formal organizations, by their very nature, are strongly goal oriented and concerned with performance.' Using the Mertonian rational goals/blocked opportunity model, these theorists maintain that organizations will, if legitimate avenues for achieving goals are blocked, 'innovate,' and employ illegitimate means for reaching goals. This model stresses the role of the external environment in creating and sustaining strain which may result in illegal activity. Most organizations are justified and evaluated in terms of their success or failure in goal attainment. Thus, organizational theorists argue that, because of the pressure on it to attain goals, the organization will employ illegitimate means for achieving such goals. As Finney and Lesieur (1982: 270) state, 'barriers to the attainment of desired performance may generate such severe strain that agents resort to illegal solutions.'

The social control of organizations also plays a role in whether an organization will engage in unlawful behavior. As Finney and Lesieur (1982: 275) note 'whether or not a strong performance orientation and operating problems lead to crime depends also on the operationality of various social controls.' Similarly, Kramer and Michalowski (1990) propose that organizational crime is more likely to occur when various social control mechanisms fail to arrest the tendency toward using illegitimate means to resolve strain.

The third theoretical view on organizational crime is that of political economy (Barnett 1981; Box 1983; Chambliss 1988, 1989; Messerschmidt 1986; Michalowski 1985; Young 1981). The primary assumption of this perspective is that the structure of corporate capitalism provides an incentive for organizations to use illegitimate means toward achieving profit, if legitimate means are blocked. This perspective extends the rational goals/blocked opportunity model by considering the dynamics of capitalism, and how this mode of production generates illegal activity.

While this argument seems to apply very well to the crimes of private business corporations, it would not seem applicable to the crimes of government. But as Michalowski (1985) and Chambliss (1988, 1989) demonstrate, political economy can also be employed to explain the organizational crimes of the state. Michalowski (1985: 314) has suggested that the various criminal acts, usually referred to as white collar crime, can be brought together in the more theoretically informed concept of 'crimes of capital,' which are 'socially injurious acts that arise from the ownership or management of capital or from the occupancy of positions of trust in institutions designed to facilitate the accumulation of capital.' He argues that corporate crime, governmental crime, organized crime, and occupational crime all arise from the particular forms of social relations associated with the processes of capital accumulation, concentration, and centralization.

There have been several important attempts to develop an integrated theory of organizational crime. Each of these theories will be briefly reviewed.

First, Coleman (1987) attempts to integrate the social-psychological theory of motivation with the structural features of advanced capitalism. Using the notion of the 'culture of competition,' Coleman bases his theory on the idea that criminal behavior results from a coincidence of appropriate motivation and opportunity. Ultimately, Coleman rests his theory on the structural level of analysis, citing capitalism as a major factor which causes organizational crime.

The second attempt to form an integrated theory of organizational crime was offered by Braithwaite (1989). Taking a more comprehensive approach than Coleman, Braithwaite offers an integration of existing criminological theories, particularly labeling theory, Hirschi's (1969) control theory, subcultural theory, and strain theory. 'The key to this attempt,' Braithwaite (1989: 333) asserts, 'is the notion of differential shaming: the shaming from organizational culture of compliance versus the shaming from the subculture of resistance to regulatory law.' Particularly interesting, is Braithwaite's (1989: 341) assertion that 'organizations can sustain a subculture of noncompliance more successfully if they can employ a code of secrecy or create a smoke screen of differential accountability.' A limitation of Braithwaite's theory, however, is that it ignores the possibility that organizations may sustain an entire organizational culture of non-compliance, rather than just a subculture of non-compliance.

The third attempt to develop an integrated theory of organizational crime is Kramer and Michalowski's (1990) theory of state-corporate crime. Their model rests on the hypothesis that organizational crime results from a coincidence of appropriate motivation or performance pressure, absent effective social control. The authors present three 'core concepts' that motivate, or act as a catalyst for, organizations to engage in criminality: (1) the motivation or performance emphasis, (2) opportunity structures, and (3) the operationality of social control. Each of these three concepts is then analyzed on three different levels of analysis: structural, institutional, and

8   *The Journal of Human Justice, Volume 5, Number 1, Autumn, 1993*

individual. Thus, Kramer and Michalowski's model accounts for all levels of criminal organizational action.

This research will attempt to adjudicate between these rival theoretical perspectives on the causes of organizational crime in light of the data pertaining to the crimes of the United States nuclear weapons production complex.

AN HISTORICAL PERSPECTIVE ON THE US EXPERIENCE WITH ATOMIC WEAPONS

Atomic Energy: The Early Years

The US experience with atomic energy began in 1942 when a team of scientists led by Enrico Fermi succeeded in achieving the first controlled, self-sustained nuclear reaction. Within months, the $2 billion Manhattan Engineering District, commonly referred to as the Manhattan Project, was formed with the sole mission of developing atomic weapons. In 1942, under the military supervision of General Leslie Groves, and the scientific supervision of J. Robert Oppenheimer, a number of facilities were created to develop the bomb.

These facilities operated in extreme secrecy both outside and inside the complex (Clarfield and Wiecek 1984; Cochran 1988; Center for Defense Information 1989; Powaski 1987; Williams and Cantelon 1984). As Weiner (1990: 20) states, '[secrecy] had become as crucial a component of the bomb as uranium.' Until 1944, 'funds for the project came either from the military departments, which concealed their purpose, or from a special contingency fund appropriated for the President which was shielded from congressional scrutiny' (Powaski 1987: 7). The activities of the complex were so secret, in fact, that when Harry Truman, a senator at the time of the Manhattan Project, assumed the presidency in 1945, he had absolutely no knowledge of the Manhattan Project (Clarfield and Wiecek 1984; Powaski 1987; Williams and Cantelon 1984).

The primary reason, and perhaps the sole reason, for the extreme secrecy surrounding the activities of the Manhattan Project was that the United States feared German access to the bomb (Powaski 1987; Williams and Cantelon 1984). The Roosevelt administration feared the leakage of information to such a degree that, in addition to keeping the activities of the Project secret from the Germans, it also stifled information flows to the US Congress, media, and general public (Clarfield and Wiecek 1984; Powaski 1987). The Germans had entered World War II with the lead in nuclear research: Otto Hohn and Fritz Strassman had already split the atom in 1938; the Third Reich controlled one of the richest sources of uranium in the world; and Germany had been pursuing the development of atomic weapons at least four years longer than the United States (Powaski 1987).

The Manhattan scientists were made very much aware of the German threat, and were pressured to 'beat Germany to the bomb' (Powaski 1987; Williams and Cantelon 1984). However, this was not the only motivation for the hurried development of the bomb. Indeed, after the German surrender, Oppenheimer stated (quoted in Powaski 1987: 12) 'I don't think there was any time we worked harder at the speed-up than in the period after the German surrender.' Two main reasons seemed to have caused this: the Japanese threat, and the Soviet Union.

After the German surrender, the only immediate threat to the United States was Japan. As early as 1944, Roosevelt and Churchill agreed that when a bomb 'is finally available, it might, perhaps, after mature consideration, be used against the Japanese' (quoted in Powaski 1987: 13). In August, 1945, only months after Truman took office, and days after the first usable forms of plutonium and uranium were produced at Hanford and Oak Ridge, the United States dropped a uranium bomb on Hiroshima. Three days later, on August 9th, a plutonium bomb was dropped on Nagasaki. Both Japanese cities were destroyed.

In total, nearly 400,000 people died as a result of the bombings (Rhodes 1986). The United States had clearly shown the world that it was in command of the ability to harness nuclear energy. After this awesome display of power, the Japanese surrendered. The war was over. Soon, however, a new conflictual relationship was born, the Cold War between the United States, and its former ally, the Soviet Union.

Post World War II: The Proliferation of Nuclear Weapons

The end of World War II signified the beginning of a massive effort on the part of the United States to raise the sophistication of atomic weapons. At this time, the US military, the primary beneficiary of nuclear energy research, lost control of the rights to produce atomic weapons. Considerable debate took place between the proponents of placing atomic energy into civilian control, principally advocated by the Federation of Atomic Scientists, and those who wanted atomic energy to stay in the hands of the military. In the end, the scientists won the legislative battle. The Atomic Energy Act of 1946, sometimes referred to as the McMahon bill, established the independent civilian-controlled Atomic Energy Commission (AEC). Under this Act, the military could only gain access to the bomb by a direct presidential order. Although the AEC, in principle, was a civilian body, the military had an enormous influence over atomic energy policies and operations (Clarfield and Wiecek 1984; Powaski 1987).

Of all the responsibilities granted to the AEC, nowhere has it been found that the committee monitored the environmental effects of the production of nuclear materials. The AEC neglected to consider and create policy that would control the adverse environmental consequences occurring during the production of nuclear weapons and nuclear materials (Steele 1989). As former AEC General Manager, Carroll L. Wilson, stated in 1979, 'Nobody got brownie points for caring about nuclear waste. The Atomic Energy Commission neglected the problem' (Steele 1989: 19).

From 1945 to 1953, Truman embarked upon a massive buildup of nuclear weapons by creating nine new production facilities. A major

10   *The Journal of Human Justice, Volume 5, Number 1, Autumn, 1993*

reason cited for this buildup was the threat of the Soviet Union. The Soviets, in 1949, successfully tested an atomic bomb, ending the US monopoly and 'inaugurating the era of proliferation' (Williams and Cantelon 1984: 114). From this time on, relations between the United States and the Soviet Union dictated, to a large degree, the quantity and quality of the US production of nuclear weapons.

The decision to develop the hydrogen bomb was also conducted in extreme secrecy (Clarfield and Wiecek 1984; Powaski 1987; Williams and Cantelon 1984). Similar to the secrecy surrounding the initial development of the atomic bomb during the Manhattan era, 'there was no public, or even congressional debate, over the decision to develop the hydrogen bomb' (Powaski 1987: 57). Thus, similar circumstances surround the two major decisions to develop atomic weapons: both were conducted in secrecy; both projects operated under no formal or informal social control; and both decisions were based on the threat of an outside nation or nations. Such circumstances served to place enormous pressure on atomic scientists and the AEC to perform a sole function: developing bombs.

The Atomic Energy Act of 1946 was eventually replaced by the Atomic Energy Act of 1954. Most of the specific provisions of the new act, and all the licensing and related regulatory requirements, applied solely to commercial reactors regulated by the Nuclear Regulatory Commission. Thus, the Act of 1954 did little to change the Act of 1946 in relation to government use of nuclear energy. The government's nuclear weapons production complex remained exempt from any real outside monitoring and did not have to follow the somewhat strict regulations on the emerging civilian nuclear industry. Despite Eisenhower's 'Atoms For Peace' plan, the military application of nuclear energy grew substantially during these years.

The production of nuclear weapons peaked between the late 1950s and early 1960s. During this time, twenty nuclear weapons facilities were operating at peak capacity (Cochran 1988). As Weiner describes: 'by 1958, nuclear weaponry was an infinitely expanding dynamo. The target list had grown to some 20,000 dots on the communist map. The target list included every city in Russia, Eastern Europe, and China (1990: 35). By 1960:

> Three thousand two hundred and sixty-seven nuclear warheads (could) annihilate the Soviet Union, China and Eastern Europe in a single blinding blow. They planned to follow this apocalyptic spasm with thousands, and thousands of more bombs. Ten nations would be obliterated. Five hundred million people would die. (1990: 37)

At this point, the United States had assembled a nuclear arsenal that maintained the capacity of over 1.5 million Hiroshimas (Weiner 1990). A number of factors are thought to be responsible for this buildup: Anti-communism was pervasive; relations between the Soviet Union and the United States were becoming increasingly antagonistic; the Soviet Union had launched Sputnik; and the myth of a weapons gap provided the

United States with the motive for increased warhead production. The weapons-gap myth is identified by Powaski (1987: 73) as 'ultimately resulting in the production of hundreds of unneeded ballistic missiles.' Indeed, this weapons-production frenzy was in part caused by the adversarial nature of the relationship between the United States and the Soviet Union.

During the Kennedy years (1961-1963), nuclear-weapons production reached its zenith with over 5,000 weapons being produced each year (Cochran 1988). Along with the tense climate of the Cold War, and the residual effects of McCarthyism, the antagonistic relations between the Soviet Union and the United States accelerated with events such as the Berlin Crisis and the Cuban Missile Crisis (see Powaski 1987). Between 1966 and 1976, however, nuclear weapons production decreased. President Johnson shut down ten weapons-production facilities because of abundant stocks of plutonium (Cochran 1988). The SALT talks, and the attitude of some high-level officials in the government, particularly Johnson's Secretary of Defense, Robert S. McNamara, that weapons proliferation was futile, fostered this cut back in nuclear-weapons production (Powaski 1987; Williams and Cantelon 1984).

This brief examination of the years between 1942 and the early 1970s has raised a number of important points. First, the United States has continually conducted its weapons-production operations in extreme secrecy. As a result of this immense secrecy, the operations have been conducted without independent oversight by a non-partial committee, and thus the program has not been subject to formal or informal social control. Second, the pressure to produce weapons very quickly, in an atmosphere of crisis, that affected both the AEC and the production facility workers and scientists, has been a central tendency of the operations, especially during the early and late 1940s. Third, the nature of the relations between the United States and the Soviet Union have dictated, to a significant degree, the quantity and quality of nuclear-weapons production. This competitive mentality has its roots in the philosophy of the Manhattan Project, when Germany was the primary enemy. Finally, there is no indication that the environmental consequences of the production of nuclear weapons and material have ever been a major concern. The emphasis seems solely placed on one goal: producing weapons. These five issues have many implications for the theoretical models that will be evaluated in the final section of this paper.

THE DEPARTMENT OF ENERGY:
THE ORGANIZATION AND ITS ACTIVITIES

The Organization of the Weapons Complex

The Department of Energy was formed by President Carter to 'give a clear direction and focus to America's energy future by providing the framework for carrying out a comprehensive, balanced energy policy' (US Department of Energy 1979: 2). As a part of orchestrating this 'new direction,' the Department of Energy was given the responsibility of producing nuclear weapons. Although manufacturing nuclear weapons

12 *The Journal of Human Justice, Volume 5, Number 1, Autumn, 1993*

is only a fraction of DOE responsibilities, it has traditionally devoted one-third of its funds to warhead production (Lamperti 1984a).[2]

The basic mission of DOE defense activities is to produce fuel for the US Navy and material for nuclear weapons (US General Accounting Office 1986). The DOE oversees the production of nuclear weapons and materials at 17 major facilities around the country: 6 facilities produce nuclear material, 6 other plants both produce material and assemble components into warheads, and 5 facilities design and test nuclear weapons.

The entire complex employs over 100,000 workers; produces, modifies, or retires approximately 4,000 weapons a year; and has an annual budget of 8 billion dollars (Center for Defense Information 1989). The DOE, like its predecessors, the AEC and ERDA, carries out most of its programs by contracting with private firms and universities. Most of the contractors of the DOE are large, multi-national corporations. Corporate giants such as Westinghouse, DuPont, General Electric, and Martin Marietta operate most of the DOE facilities.

The US government owns the equipment and materials used in the manufacture of nuclear weapons items, and directs the contractor to produce the final product, whether it be the warheads themselves, or the converted nuclear materials. Thus, the contractor is responsible for the actual production of the nuclear weapons, while the DOE acts as a supervisor of the contractor's activities. The organization of the entire weapons complex has much in common with the system that developed during the Manhattan Project era (Cochran 1988; Lamperti 1984b; Powaski 1987). That is, private contractors have maintained the important role of researcher, developer, and manufacturer of the entire nuclear weapons program.

The DOE-Contractor Relationship

The organizational structure of the weapons-production complex has changed very little over the years. The complex still uses a three-tiered approach in carrying out its operations. The first tier is the contractor who actually performs the day to day operations. The contractor is held responsible to meet all DOE environmental, health, and safety requirements as a condition of the contract between the DOE and the contractor (Walker 1986). The second tier of the management structure resides in the DOE itself. The DOE field offices are directly responsible for overseeing the contractors' performance. The field offices periodically conduct appraisals and audits on the contractors' work, including incident releases and quality assurance (US General Accounting Office 1986). The final tier of the management structure is the general oversight by DOE headquarters. The office of the Assistant Secretary for Environment, Safety and Health (ESH) holds primary responsibility for the compliance of the entire complex with environmental law.

There are two basic kinds of financial arrangements the DOE makes with its contractors. Some contractors operate on a non-profit basis, in which they receive compensation only for the costs incurred during the production of nuclear weapons. Other contractors operate on a profit basis, or 'award fee' arrangement. In this type of contract, DOE agrees to pay a contractor bonus money if, during a six-month period, the contractor meets certain pre-established criteria. Although each contract the DOE makes with its corporate operators is different, most contracts contain essentially the same provisions (Alverez 1990; Mobilization for Survival 1989).

The DuPont corporation has operated the Savannah River Plant, Aiken, South Carolina, since the inception of the atomic age. On a non-profit basis, DuPont has been held responsible for the daily operations of the facility. One clause in the DOE-DuPont (National Academy of Sciences) contract reads:

> The Contractor shall take all reasonable precautions in the performance of the work under this Contract to protect the safety of employees and of members of the public and to minimize dangers from all hazards to life and property, and shall comply with all health, safety, and fire protection regulations and requirements. (1987: 44)

The exact same provision in which the DOE orders DuPont to comply with all applicable laws and regulations, is included in the DOE 1987 contract with UNC Nuclear Industries, the operator of the Hanford facility located in Hanford, Washington. It seems, then, that the only difference between the two contracts, in relation to the mandates of the DOE concerning the contractor's obligation to perform all activities in compliance with applicable environmental laws, is that UNC operates under a profit arrangement with the DOE, whereas DuPont operates its facility under a non-profit arrangement (National Academy of Sciences 1987). Thus, it seems apparent that the DOE places the bulk of the responsibility on the contractor to operate the facilities in a lawful manner.

The National Academy of Sciences (1987) has contended that DOE directives to their contractors are often vague, and that they provide the corporations with a great deal of latitude in the interpretation of DOE orders. This research has found some evidence which seems to support this claim. For example, in the 1987 DOE-UNC contract, the DOE ordered UNC to 'operate and monitor the N Reactor and support facilities in a safe, secure, and environmentally sound manner, to achieve a fiscal year production goal of 705 KMWD, with less than 24 unscheduled outage days' (National Academy of Sciences 1987: 51). While this directive may be legally inclusive, and thus rather direct in nature, the DOE does not provide the contractor with the specific methods to achieve compliance with applicable environmental issues. It is in this sense that the DOE orders could be considered relatively vague. Additionally, the above clause seems to indicate that the DOE is sending a message to the contractor that, while safe and environmentally sound procedures of waste disposal (which are unspecified) are important, it is equally important that precise production quotas are met.

14 *The Journal of Human Justice, Volume 5, Number 1, Autumn, 1993*

THE CRIMINAL CONTAMINATION OF THE ENVIRONMENT
The Extent of the Contamination

The process of converting nuclear material into usable forms generates a large amount of radioactive and non-radioactive (hazardous) waste (Cochran 1988; Lamperti 1984b; Reicher and Scher 1988; US General Accounting Office 1985, 1986, 1989). In 1986, the Savannah facility generated over 200,000 gallons of waste each day, and the Hanford plant has dumped over 200 billion gallons of radioactive and hazardous wastes since its inception in 1942 (Steele 1989). Indeed, the contamination wrought by nuclear-weapons production is so severe that the General Accounting Office estimates that the cost of getting the complex into compliance with applicable environmental laws would be a startling 250 billion dollars (US General Accounting Office 1986).

The waste disposal practices employed by most of the DOE facilities are grounded in the theory that 'soil absorbs radioactive and hazardous elements in waste, and harmlessly extinguishes all potentially dangerous chemicals' (US General Accounting Office 1986: 31). Thus, seepage basins and waste ponds are used as containers to filter out the harmful elements in the waste. The problem with this method of disposal, employed since the beginning of the atomic age, is that soil does not, in fact, prevent harmful elements in waste from seeping into groundwater basins (US General Accounting Office 1986). A dramatic example of this is found in the waste-disposal practices of the Savannah facility. Because of their waste-disposal practices, the Tuscaloosa Aquifer, part of the Tuscaloosa Group Formation of underground water passages, is now contaminated with several harmful elements including tritium and nitrates (US General Accounting Office 1986).

The Hanford facility and the Savannah River Plant have been identified by several commentators as being two of the most environmentally damaging nuclear-weapons facilities (Mobilization for Survival 1989; Saleska and Makhijani 1990; Steele 1989). Both facilities are involved in the production of plutonium and tritium, compounds which play an integral role in making completed warheads. The Mobilization for Survival has documented the existence of several adverse environmental consequences wrought by the activities of the Hanford facility:

> 100 square miles of groundwater are contaminated with radioactive tritium, iodine, and toxic chemicals. Over a half million gallons of high level radioactive waste [have] leaked from underground tanks and more continues to leak into the soil. Billions of gallons of liquid wastes and waste water with chemical and radioactive elements have been dumped in Hanford soil, contaminating the Columbia River and its watershed. (1989: 3)

Equally poor is the Savannah River Plant's environmental record. The groundwater near the plant is contaminated with nearly all forms of radioactive and hazardous waste, and over 51 million gallons of highly dangerous toxins are stored in leaking underground tanks beneath the facility (Mobilization for Survival 1989).

Historically, the complex was not required to comply with *any* laws regarding the protection of the environment. The Atomic Energy Acts of 1946 and 1954 made this condition explicit. The DOE is still exempt from many laws which regulate the disposal and treatment of radioactive waste.

Violations of Environmental Law

The DOE regulates itself for radioactive releases into ground and surface water, radioactive waste, and radioactive leaks into water. There are three principal environmental laws the DOE must comply with: (1) the Clean Water Act of 1972, (2) the Clean Air Act of 1970, and (3) the Resource Conservation and Recovery Act (RCRA) of 1976. It is extremely important to remember that the nuclear-weapons production complex operated for over 28 years before having to comply with a single environmental law. The DOE has fought the applicability of these laws to their operations for several years. Especially tenacious was the DOE refusal to comply with RCRA.[3] In the eight years between the 1976 passage of RCRA and the 1984 court ruling by a district judge that the DOE was subject to this law, the DOE argued that, under the Atomic Energy Act of 1954, their activities were exempt from the law because of 'national security' (Radioactive Waste Campaign 1988; Reicher and Scher 1988).

RCRA gives the Environmental Protection Agency (EPA) the authority to regulate DOE hazardous waste disposal practices. Because RCRA became applicable to DOE facilities in 1984, in 1986 several facilities were out of compliance with the law. In a 1986 study (US General Accounting Office 1986), all seven of the facilities reviewed were out of compliance with RCRA.[4] Under RCRA, 'an operator must identify its hazardous wastes; receive a permit in order to treat, store, or dispose of such wastes; monitor ground water at waste sites; close and care for sites that are taken out of operation; and undertake corrective action' (Reicher, 1986: 205). By 1986, most facilities had only begun the process of obtaining permits, a clear violation of law. In 1985, a report by the Ohio EPA also found numerous violations of RCRA at the Fernald Feeds Materials Plant, Fernald, Ohio. Extreme quantities of hazardous wastes were disposed of at most DOE facilities, including the Y-12 plant in Oak Ridge, Tennessee, where four waste disposal plants were found to be leaking 4.7 million gallons of metal, acids, and solvents between 1953 and 1963 (Reicher and Scher 1988).

The Clean Water Act is 'the principal law governing the discharge of liquid fluids from DOE facilities into water' (US General Accounting Office 1986: 30). RCRA and the Clean Water Act are not mutually exclusive laws because most of the contamination of water results from the violation of RCRA, that is, illegal waste-disposal practices. In the same US General Accounting Office report (1986) that identified RCRA violations, non-compliance with the Clean Water Act was determined. Out of the nine facilities surveyed, all of the sites were in violation of the Clean Water Act. The water was most often contaminated with tritium, mercury, and nitrates. At the Y-12 plant, nitrate concentrations have been reported at a level 1,000 times the drinking water standard. At the Savannah River Plant, solvents have been reported at levels 30,000 times EPA drinking water standards, and tritium levels over 2,500 times the standard. As with DOE violations of RCRA, the activities of the complex are being conducted in violation of the Clean Water Act.

The most publicized violations of environmental law by the DOE were found in the June, 1988 Federal Bureau of Investigation (FBI) and EPA raid on the Rocky Flats facility near Denver. Rocky Flats manufactures the plutonium parts of nuclear warhead cores and various other fission bomb components (Abas 1989). The FBI raid was prompted by Jim Stone, a six-year Rocky Flats engineer, who uncovered an internal DOE memo describing the operations at Rocky Flats as 'patently illegal' and 'in poor condition generally in terms of environmental compliance' (Abas 1989: 22). Stone contacted the FBI, and search warrants were issued to search the facility for possible violations of environmental law. The 75-member team raiding the facility was looking for evidence to substantiate the allegations that Rocky Flats had (a) illegally treated, stored, and disposed of hazardous waste in violation of RCRA; (b) discharged pollutants without a permit in violation of RCRA and the Clean Water Act; and (c) concealed environmental contamination (Abas 1989).

Although the raid on Rocky Flats marked the first time a governmental agency had gathered evidence against another federal facility for the purposes of criminal prosecution, the operation did not result in the filing of criminal charges against the DOE or Rockwell, the contractor for Rocky Flats. According to the EPA Criminal Enforcement director, Dick Emery, as of September 1990 there have been no charges filed as a result of the raid (Emery 1990). In fact, as little as one month after the raid, Rocky Flats was operating 'business as usual' (Abas 1989: 22).

There is very little information on possible DOE violations of the Clean Air Act. Although the DOE must comply with this law, the contractors, under agreement with the DOE, are responsible for reporting possible violations of the Act to the DOE. The DOE is then obligated to report the violations to the EPA. One commentator has suggested that the DOE is really given powers of self-regulation in this area (Alverez 1990).

In the preceding description of the criminality found within the nuclear weapons production complex, it is clear that many facilities, as evidenced by the 1986 US General Accounting Office and many other sources, are engaged in illegal activity. According to the Head. of the Criminal Enforcement Department of the EPA, a number of complaints have been filed against the complex; however, there has never been criminal prosecution for the crimes engaged in by the weapons complex (Emery 1990). In fact, it is official EPA and United States Department of Justice policy not to take judicial action against another federal agency over compliance problems (Porter 1986: 9). Instead, the EPA 'relies exclusively on administrative enforcement.' Other problems exist concerning the enforcement of environmental crimes committed by the DOE. As the Center for Defense Information states:

> The EPA is further handicapped by overlapping laws, a lack of statistical data
> on military environmental compliance, military reluctance to accept EPA
> oversight, and the fact that government agencies are constitutionally barred
> from suing each other to force compliance with the law. (1989: 2)

Although the EPA is precluded by Article III of the United States Constitution from prosecuting another federal entity, it does not preclude the
EPA from investigating alleged criminal violations by individuals at
federal facilities (Thompson 1989). From 1982 to the present, however, the
EPA has acted upon only three of 30 criminal complaints filed against a
DOE employee (Thompson 1989). The EPA is also hand-cuffed because it
retains only 47 criminal investigators to combat environmental crimes
throughout the entire nation (Emery 1990). Thus, both organizational and
structural problems make the enforcement of environmental laws against
the DOE an extremely difficult task.

THEORETICAL INTERPRETATION

In the preceding sections, a number of important features of the nuclear
weapons production complex were identified. The purpose of this section
is two-fold. First, it will discuss those features of the weapons production
complex which seem to be particularly relevant to a theoretical interpretation of the crimes committed by this set of organizations. This interpretation, grounded in the data presented in the preceding sections, leads into
the second part of this discussion in which the utility of the various
theoretical perspectives on the causes of organizational crime are evaluated for their capacity to explain the criminality of the weapons complex.

The Historical and Structural Formation of Goals

The United States has been engaged in or preparing for war for nearly 50
years. Given that the Cold War military strategies were largely organized
around the capabilities of nuclear weapons, and that use of atomic weapons played a significant role in ending the hostilities of World War II, the
production of nuclear weapons became one of the most important programs of the US government. This meant that the organization charged
with the responsibility of developing and producing nuclear-weapons
warheads had to be, among other things, highly goal oriented and concerned with performance. Indeed, the United States depended on these
powerful weapons as an instrument to deter Soviet aggression, and to gain
economic and geo-political advantages over those countries which did not
possess nuclear weapons.

Throughout the tenure of the Cold War, United States geo-political and
economic interests have caused the United States to continually upgrade
its stockpile of weapons of mass destruction, which in turn has forced the
nuclear weapons production complex to be even more concerned with
production goals. The United States had to match or beat every Soviet
advance in nuclear technology. For example, after the Soviet first test of a
nuclear weapon, President Truman gave orders to strengthen existing
nuclear weapons production programs and to start production on the
hydrogen bomb. Historical evidence, then, supports the contention that

18 *The Journal of Human Justice, Volume 5, Number 1, Autumn, 1993*

the weapons complex strong commitment to producing nuclear weapons is a result of the US interest in exercising global economic and political authority (see Chomsky 1988; Ellsburg 1981; Williams 1990; Zinn 1980).

The Selection of Means

It is clear that the methods employed to produce nuclear weapons have resulted in the immense contamination of the environment. Moreover, it will be recalled that former AEC General Manager, Wilson, admitted that the AEC neglected the problem of contamination occurring as a result of weapons production. Given these insights, and other corroborating evidence, it is reasonable to conclude that the production goals of the weapons complex have historically taken primacy, while the adverse environmental consequences of weapons production have never been a major concern of the contractors, the DOE, or its predecessors. Several commentators have agreed with this conclusion (Alverez 1990; Center for Defense Information 1989; Hodges 1991; Krater 1991; Mobilization for Survival 1989; National Academy of Sciences 1987; Reicher and Scher 1988).

The Manhattan Project was given one directive: to produce the atomic bomb. At this time, there was little knowledge about the program dispersed among anyone who was not directly involved in the endeavor. Secrecy and a lack of oversight facilitated this rather well. Because the operation was conducted in such secrecy, the weapons complex was free to use any means available to meet its objectives. Thus, the scientists and the military officials in charge of the project had great autonomy in selecting the avenues for the completion of their mission.

As a result of this autonomy, the weapons complex had simply selected the most effective and efficient means possible for achieving its goals. Because there was complete state sponsorship of the endeavor, virtually any method which facilitated goal attainment was adopted as policy.

Oversight

Several commentators have pointed to the lack of external oversight of the weapons complex activities (Alverez 1990; Hodges 1991; Krater 1991; Lamperti 1984b; US General Accounting Office 1986). There is no external, independent review of DOE nuclear weapons production operations. Unlike the civilian nuclear energy programs, which are overseen by the NRC, DOE operations are mostly self-regulated. This lack of social control over the complex has been present throughout its entire history. The legacy of secrecy legitimized by the need to protect 'national security' has prevented most attempts at regulating the weapons complex's activities. This problem of creating an independent agency to oversee the complex's activities is, in large part, attributable to the defense mechanisms built in to the US Constitution and the Atomic Energy Act of 1954. In the former case, Article III of the Constitution bars any federal agency from taking judicial action for the purposes of criminal prosecution against another federal agency. In the latter case, most defense activities are allowed to be exempt from independent oversight, control, and scrutiny because of 'national security' concerns. Thus, the operationality of external informal and formal social control mechanisms is limited.

Equally as absent is inter-organizational oversight. Many commentators have identified this lacuna within the complex as a contributor to the environmental problems of the organization (Alverez 1990; Mobilization for Survival 1989; National Academy of Sciences 1987).

Given the insights of the National Academy of Sciences (1987) report, it is possible to identify three general problems in the management structure which contribute to the lack of inter-organizational oversight within the complex: (1) a lack of communication between the various parties involved in the production of nuclear weapons and materials, (2) DOE's apparent lack of concern for appraising the operations of the contractors, and (3) an over-reliance on the contractors to conduct their operations in compliance with applicable laws.

These three problems with the inter-organizational oversight of the complex have surfaced simultaneously at some points. For example, in the years 1981-1987, comprehensive DOE headquarters' appraisals of contractor performance occurred only twice at the Savannah facility, and only once at the Hanford plant (National Academy of Sciences 1987).

Organizational Culture

Because the weapons production complex of today has many similarities to that of the earlier weapons operations, it is reasonable to speculate that an organizational 'culture' or 'philosophy' has developed within the complex. As former US Secretary of Energy, Watkins, (quoted in Olshansky and Williams) stated:

> [the DOE possesses] an underlying philosophy that adequate production of defense materials and a healthy, safe environment were not compatible objectives. A culture of mismanagement and ineptitude will have to be overcome in [this] department before the nation's troubled nuclear weapons manufacturing plants can be brought into compliance with environmental laws. (1988: 29)

This statement, lends substantial support to the notions that (a) environmental criminality actually exists, and has existed for several years; and (b) production goals have historically taken precedence over concerns about the environmental consequences of warhead production. More importantly, however, is Watkins' claim that a culture and philosophy exist within the complex. Watkins makes it clear that the complex's focus on production goals has existed for many years, and that this organizational ideology is not aberrant. Rather, it is an integral part of the weapons complex culture.

Because of the peculiar history of the weapons complex (as a governmental endeavor which supplied the nation's most important military weapons), the complex could operate for a sustained period of time without being subject to external, independent review. This feature of the complex may have permitted the formation of an organizational culture which was autonomous and virtually immune from outside criticism.

Of the many characteristics of the organization of the weapons-production complex, perhaps the most apparent is its tradition of non-compliance with law. As a result of placing primacy on production goals through the most expedient and effective means, the complex has and continues to engage in the illegal disposal and storage of nuclear waste. These illegal practices, then, can be seen as a logical result of the organization's patterned method of operation. Since virtually every weapons production facility is or has operated in violation of one or more environmental laws, the organization as a whole could be viewed as a 'culture' of non-compliance.

This notion of a culture of noncompliance is drawn from Braithwaite's (1989) idea of 'subcultures of resistance.' Braithwaite (1989: 34) argues that subcultures of resistance 'neutralize the moral bond of the law (and that) organizations can sustain subcultures of non-compliance more successfully if they can enforce a code of secrecy or create a smoke screen of diffused accountability.' This research has found that it may be possible to apply Braithwaite's notion to a culture, rather than subculture, of non-compliance. Indeed, as Braithwaite suggests, the weapons complex has, in effect, neutralized commitments, if they were ever existent, to lawful organizational behavior. Additionally, Braithwaite's idea that both secrecy and the 'smoke screen' effect facilitate the successful resistance of laws is clearly relevant, given the legacy of secrecy and diffused accountability within the weapons complex.

EVALUATION OF THE THEORETICAL PERSPECTIVES ON ORGANIZATIONAL CRIME

Differential Association Theory

The central notion of differential association theory is that criminal behavior is learned in association with intimate others by interacting and communicating with those significant others. Thus, crime is seen as a manifestation of an individual's social-psychological interaction with those who define criminal behavior favorably. While this research may not be able to confirm or refute the utility of differential association theory to explain the crimes of the weapons complex, some evidence has been found which supports Sutherland's (1949) model.

This research has pointed to the possibility that the nuclear weapons production complex has developed a culture. It seems reasonable, then, to speculate that certain ideas and values concerning organizational norms have been instilled in those workers who are members of the weapons complex. That is, it is possible, and very likely, that individuals are socialized into the general ideology of the complex. Thus, the socialization of workers in the complex could act to perpetuate the continued use of illegitimate means for achieving organizational goals. If this were the case, which needs to be determined empirically rather than speculatively,

Sutherland's differential association theory could provide valuable insights into the process of organizational socialization.

The Organizational Perspective

A central tenet of the organizational perspective on crime is that organizations are, by their very nature, strongly goal oriented and concerned with performance. Since most organizations are evaluated by their success in goal attainment, it is argued by these theorists that the organization feels pressure to achieve its goals. As demonstrated earlier in this research, the weapons complex has been extremely concerned with its performance, and has developed a strong commitment to its operative goals. Thus, the notion that organizations are deeply concerned with performance and the attainment of organizational goals has been supported in this research.

Most organizational theorists explain the particular causes of organizational crime through the Mertonian notion of innovation. This notion rests on the idea that an organization will employ legitimate means for achieving its goals if those means are available. If, however, legitimate means for achieving goals are blocked, an organization will experience strain, and thus select illegitimate means for achieving its goals. Innovation, then, is a result of the blockage of legitimate means, and the decision to use illegitimate means for achieving organizational goals. This notion assumes that an organization *alters* its behavior or mode of operation because of strain.

The weapons complex operated for nearly three decades without being subject to official regulatory law. Because of secrecy, and the absence of social control over its activities, the weapons complex experienced great autonomy in selecting the means for achieving its goal to produce nuclear weapons. Thus, because of the absence of any party capable of defining the organization's activities as legitimate or illegitimate, the weapons complex's means for achieving organizational goals were not blocked, and organizational strain did not surface.

In the period between 1970 and 1977, however, regulations on the nuclear industry began to surface. Primarily aimed at the rapidly growing civilian nuclear industry, the Clean Air Act (1970), the Clean Water Act (1972), and the Resource Conservation and Recovery Act (1977) were passed to prevent further environmentally damaging acts committed by the governmental nuclear industry. These laws set standards on radioactive and hazardous waste disposal both in the air and in the water. To be in compliance with these new laws, the weapons production complex would have to adjust its production practices and concern itself with the safe disposal of nuclear waste.

Following the Mertonian rational goals/blocked opportunity notion, it would seem reasonable to identify, during this period of time, the existence of organizational strain within the complex. Activities which were at one time permitted were now illegal. Thus, the organizational theorists would argue that a threat to the organization's attainment of goals surfaced because its means were now criminalized. However, the organization

22   *The Journal of Human Justice, Volume 5, Number 1, Autumn, 1993*

did not adjust its behavior after the birth of these laws. It did not *react* to strain because it experienced no strain. For the Mertonian notion of innovation to apply, there must be the confrontation of strain, a blockage of goals which leads to an adjustment of organizational behavior. However, there was no official enforcement of these new laws directed at the weapons complex. Rather, the enforcement of these laws was aimed at the civilian industry, even though the weapons complex was also subject to these laws. Thus, the organization was using means defined as illegitimate, but their activities were not being officially monitored, enforced, or sanctioned. The complex did not have to adapt to external strain, rather the lack of enforcement and social control *encouraged* the now-defined illegal acts. The complex simply sustained its 30-year-old mode of operation. Thus, this research has found that organizational criminality does not necessarily result from the blockage of legitimate means and strain. Since most theories of organizational crime rely largely on the notions of strain and innovation, this finding represents an important contribution to the understanding of organizational criminality.

Most organizational theorists stress the importance of the operationality of external social control mechanisms (see Finney and Lesieur 1982; Kramer and Michalowski 1990). They argue that illegitimate means to achieving organizational goals can be blocked if there is effective social control. Historically, we have seen, there has never been any real control, formal or informal, over the complex's activities. The secretive nature of its operations, facilitated by the government, precluded any real public, congressional, or independent oversight. Thus, when the complex was confronted with the fact that there were laws governing their disposal activities, the organization did not experience strain because there was no source of strain, no agency to force it to comply with these laws. There was no motivation, or reason, for the weapons complex to adjust its behavior because organizational goals were being attained quite efficiently through the use of traditional means. Rather than stressing the role of an organization's motive for *adapting* to strain (Coleman 1987; Kramer and Michalowski 1990) for the weapons production complex, the salient issue is its motivation for *sustaining* its activities. Thus, motivation is, indeed, an important consideration, for it illustrates the important role organizational goals play in the etiology of organizational crime. However, its importance for explaining the crimes of the nuclear weapons production complex lies on a different plane.

Political Economy

A political economic analysis of organizational crime stresses the primacy of capitalist structures as an inducement for organizations to enter into illegal activity. The primary assumptio is that the structure of corporate capitalism provides an incentive for organizations to use illegitimate means toward achieving profit, if legitimate means are blocked. This perspective extends the Mertonian rational goals/blocked opportunity model offered by organizational theorists by considering the dynamics of capitalism, and how this mode of production generates illegal activity.

The utility of the version of rational goals/blocked opportunity found in political economy to explain the crimes of the weapons-production complex is limited. From the beginning of the atomic age, the United States government has made several different types of arrangements with corporations that actually produce nuclear weapons. Many of the facilities have been operated on a non-profit basis. Included in this category is the Savannah River Plant, a facility with one of the worst records of environmental compliance. Thus, having no motive to accumulate capital or to supersede laws for the purposes of gaining organizational economic profit, the crimes committed by these facilities are not explainable by using an analysis rooted in traditional political economy.

Michalowski (1985) has developed the notion of 'crimes of capital' to explain the problems of corporate, occupational, organizational, and political crime. These socially injurious acts, according to Michalowski, can be considered as the result of the ownership or management of capital or from the occupancy of positions of trust in institutions designed to facilitate the accumulation of capital. Thus, criminal actions by those organizations which provide avenues for the accumulation of capital can be considered crimes of capital.

Earlier in this section, it was suggested that the US government has historically used nuclear weapons to gain political and economic advantages over other countries. By threatening other nations, directly or indirectly, with nuclear weapons, the US government has been able to clear obstacles for American companies to invest internationally, and to provide American corporations access to labor pools, that, in many cases, ultimately results in profits for the corporations. Thus, the threatened use of nuclear weapons could be considered instrumental in facilitating the private accumulation of capital. The environmental crimes committed by the weapons complex, in this sense, then, could be seen as a result of the concern for facilitating the accumulation of capital of private corporations.

Although Michalowski considers crimes of capital as the result of either the direct attempt to accumulate capital or the attempt to *facilitate* the accumulation of capital, he does not fully develop the idea that an organization may facilitate the accumulation of capital for other organizations or businesses which are independent of the organization engaging in criminality. Rather, he grounds his notion in the idea that organizations commit crimes in order to facilitate their *own* attempt at accumulating capital. Thus, to Michalowski, an organization's violations of law are the result of that organization's drive for profit.

The crimes of the nuclear weapons production complex, however, as our research has suggested, do not result in the accumulation of capital for the complex at large. Rather, the economic profits reaped for weapons production may be situated on a different plane, and may be the result of the state's concern with facilitating transnational capitalist expansion. Perhaps, the primary reason why Michalowski's model does not adequately explain the causes of the crimes of the weapons complex is because these crimes are a result of a private corporation and a governmental organization working together in a joint endeavor. Thus, because of the nature of state-corporate crime, any theory which places primacy on the direct accumulation of capital by the deviant organization may possess limited capacities for fully explaining the crimes of the nuclear weapons production complex.

The Integrated Theoretical Perspectives

Coleman's (1987) theoretical explanation of organizational crime is grounded in the notion that individual psychological motivations and the structural dynamics of corporate capitalism are the two primary causes of organizational crime. In this section, we have already addressed the utility of political economy and social psychology to explain the weapons complex's criminal actions.

Braithwaite's (1989) integrated theory of organizational crime is primarily based on a Mertonian rational goals/blocked opportunity model and subculture theory. As we have seen, the Mertonian notion of innovation does not adequately explain the crimes of the weapons complex. Braithwaite's idea of subcultures of resistance, however, has been reworked in this research to explain the possibility that a non-compliant culture exists within the weapons complex. In this regard, Braithwaite's conceptualization of organizational crime is useful.

The weapons complex has historically been pressured to meet production goals, and has experienced no real social control. Thus, on a general level, this research lends support to Kramer and Michalowski's (1990) hypothesis, especially on the structural and institutional level of analyses. This research has documented several times that the weapons complex has experienced little social control, but great pressure to meet production goals. However, Kramer and Michalowski's model also rests largely on the Mertonian notion of strain, and the role of the distribution of legitimate and illegitimate means. This research has shown that the weapons complex has never experienced a measurable amount of strain – that, in fact, the complex has been virtually immune from agents which may cause strain. Thus, the data presented in this study lend support to Kramer and Michalowski's general hypothesis, but clearly do not support the rational goals/blocked opportunity idea central to their theoretical model.

Because of the limitations of the data in this research, this study cannot verify the value of other notions contained in Kramer and Michalowski's (1990) theory. For example, this study cannot determine the role that individual members of the organization play in the crimes of the complex. Indeed, the role that an individual's symbolic structure of goals, alternatives, and responsibility plays has not been measured in this research.

CONCLUSION

We have found that the environmental-law violations committed by the US nuclear weapons production complex are primarily the result of inadequate nuclear waste-disposal practices. These waste-disposal activities violate several laws, especially the Resource Conservation and Recovery

Act which outlaws waste-disposal practices allowing contaminants to enter the environment in excess of EPA standards.

Historically, we have seen that nuclear weapons have played an extremely important role in US military planning and operations. During the unstable political climate of World War II and the Cold War, the weapons-production complex experienced immense pressure from the federal government to produce weapons. This pressure resulted in the weapons complex decision to use the most efficient and effective means to achieve its goals. This research has also pointed to the lack of oversight over the complex's activities. The complex has never been officially regulated by any independent agency, nor has it ever been subject to the strict guidelines concerning nuclear waste-disposal methods which govern the practices of civilian nuclear activities.

The final objective of this study has been to evaluate the utility of various theoretical perspectives on the causes of organizational crime to explain the crimes of the nuclear weapons-production complex. Some support for organizational, political economy and integrated theory was found. While we have shown that these theoretical perspectives, both by themselves and collectively, cannot fully explain the causes of the criminal acts by the US nuclear weapons-production complex, some notions contained within each perspective do shed insight into the sources of the illegal activities.

It is clear that further research on this phenomenon is needed. Specifically, more research that places a special focus on the micro-organizational level of analysis, and the internal cultural environment within the complex would be useful. Future research should also explore two ideas advanced here: the possibility that an entire organization can be considered a 'culture of non-compliance' and that an organization may facilitate the accumulation of capital for an entity relatively independent of that organization.

NOTES

1 We employ the terms 'crime' and 'criminal' in the tradition sparked by Sutherland (1949) which considers violations of regulatory, civil, and administrative law just as worthy of criminological inquiry as violations of nation-state criminal law. We have elsewhere (Kauzlarich, Kramer, and Smith 1992) documented the value of such alternative epistemological frameworks for the study of organizational crime.

2 Perdue (1989) has argued that the Department of Energy could be more appropriately referred to as the 'Department of Nuclear Weapons.'

3 RCRA's applicability to federal agencies is limited to the US Department of Defense (DOD) and the US Department of Energy. While the DOD did not contest the applicability of the law to its activities, the DOE did raise serious objections to the applicability of the law.

4 Facilities reviewed by the study were the Feeds Material Plant, Hanford, Los Alamos, Mound, Oak Ridge, Rocky Flats, and the Savannah River Plant.

REFERENCES

Abas, B. 1989. 'Rocky Flats: A Mistake From Day One.' *The Bulletin of the Atomic Scientists*, October: 19-24

Albanese, J.S. 1982. *Social Control at the Margins: Toward a General Understanding of Deviance*. Belmont, CA: Wadsworth

Alverez, R. 1990. Personal Communication, November

26   *The Journal of Human Justice, Volume 5, Number 1, Autumn, 1993*

Atomic Energy Act of 1946, 42 U.S.C. § 1259. 1946

Atomic Energy Act of 1954, 42 U.S.C. § 2182. 1954

Barnett, H. 1981. 'Corporate Capitalism, Corporate Crime.' *Crime and Delinquency*, 27: 4-23

Box, S. 1983. *Power, Crime, and Mystification*. London: Tavistock

Braithwaite, J. 1984. *Corporate Crime and The Pharmaceutical Industry*. London: Routledge and Kegan Paul

– 1985. 'White Collar Crime.' *Annual Review of Sociology*, 11: 1-25

– 1988. 'White Collar Crime, Competition, and Capitalism: Comment on Coleman.' *American Journal of Sociology*, 94: 27-32

– 1989. 'Criminological Theory and Organizational Crime.' *Justice Quarterly*: 333-358

Center for Defense Information. 1988. 'Nuclear Bomb Factories: The Dangers Within.' *The Defense Monitor*, 17 (4): 1-8

Center for Defense Information. 1989. 'Defending the Environment? The Record of the U.S. Military.' *The Defense Monitor*, 18 (5): 1-8

Chambliss, W. 1988. *On The Take: From Petty Crooks to Presidents*. Bloomington, IN: Indiana University Press

– 1989. 'State Organized Crime.' *Criminology*, 27 (2): 183-208

Chomsky, N. 1988. *The Culture of Terrorism*. Boston: Free Press

Clarfield, G.H., and W.M. Wiecek. 1984. *Nuclear America*. New York: Harper and Row

Clean Air Act of 1970, 42 U.S.C. § 7401. 1970

Clean Water Act of 1972, 33 U.S.C. § 1251. 1972

Clinard, M.B. 1946. 'Criminological Theories of Violations of Wartime Regulations.' *American Sociological Review*, 11 (June): 258-270

Clinard, M., and R. Quinney. 1973. *Criminal Behavior Systems: A Typology*. New York: Holt, Rinehart, and Winston

Clinard, M., and P. Yeager. 1980. *Corporate Crime*. New York: Free Press

Cochran, T.B. 1988. 'U.S. Nuclear Weapons: An Overview.' *The Bulletin of the Atomic Scientists*, January-February: 12-17

Cohen, A.K. 1977. 'The Concept of Criminal Organization.' *The British Journal of Criminology*, 17: 97-111

Coleman, J.W. 1987. 'Toward an Integrated Theory of White-Collar Crime.' *American Journal of Sociology*, 93 (2): 406-439

Conner, T. 1990. 'Nuclear Workers at Risk.' *The Bulletin of the Atomic Scientists*, September: 24-29

Cressey, D.R. 1950. 'The Criminal Violation of Financial Trust.' American *Sociological Review*, 15: 738-743

Ellsburg, D. 1981. 'Call to Mutiny.' in E.P. Thompson and D. Smith, eds., *Protest and Survive*, i-xxviii. New York: Monthly Review Press

Emery, R. 1990. Personal Communication, December

Energy Reorganization Act of 1974, 42 U.S.C. § 5841. 1946

Ermann, M., and R.J. Lundman. 1978a. 'Deviant Acts by Complex Organizations: Deviance and Social Control at the Organizational Level of Analysis.' *The Sociological Inquiry*, 19: 55-67

– 1978b. *Corporate and Governmental Deviance: Problems of Organizational Behavior in Contemporary Society*. New York: Oxford University Press

Finney, H.C., and H.R. Lesieur. 1982. 'A Contingency Theory of Organizational Crime,' in S.B. Bacharach, ed., *Research in The Sociology of Organizations*, 255-299. New York: Random House

Geis, G. 1976. 'The Heavy Electrical Equipment Antitrust Cases of 191,' in M. Clinard and R. Quinney, eds., *Criminal Behavior Systems*, 139-150. New York: Holt, Rinehart, and Winston

Geis, G., and R. Meier. 1977. *White Collar Crime: Offenses in Business, Politics, and the Professions*. New York: Free Press

Gelb, L.H. 1991. 'A Nuclear Ripoff.' *The New York Times*, June: 15

Gross, E. 1978. 'Organizational Crime: A Theoretical Perspective,' in N. Denzin, ed.,
  Studies in Symbolic Interaction, 55-85. Greenwich, CT: JAI Press

– 1980. 'Organizational Structure and Organizational Crime,' in G. Geis and E. Stotland,
  eds., *White Collar Crime: Theories and Research*, 52-67. Beverly Hills, CA: Sage

Hall, R. 1987. 'Organizational Behavior: A Sociological Perspective,' in J.W. Lorsch, ed.,
  Handbook of Organizational Behavior, 112-131. Englewood Cliffs, NJ: Prentice Hall

Hirschi, T. 1969. *Causes of Delinquency*. Berkeley, CA: University of California Press

Hodges, J. 1991. Personal Communication, January

Hopkins, A. 1978. 'The Anatomy of Corporate Crime,' in P.R. Wilson and J. Braithwaite,
  eds., *Two Faces of Deviance: Crimes of the Powerless and Powerful*, 79-91. Brisbane,
  Australia: University of Queensland Press

Kauzlarich, D., R.C. Kramer, and B. Smith. 1992. 'Toward The Study of Governmental
  Crime: Nuclear Weapons, Foreign Intervention, and International Law.' *Humanity and
  Society*, 16 (4): 543-563

Kramer, R.C. 1982. 'Corporate Crime: An Organizational Perspective,' in P. Wickman and
  T. Daily, eds., *White Collar and Economic Crime*, 75-94. Lexington, KY: Lexington Books

– 1987. 'Toward a Theory of Organizational Crime.' Paper presented at the Annual
  meeting of the American Sociological Association, November, Chicago

– 1992. 'The Space-Shuttle Challenger Explosion: A Case Study of State-Corporate
  Crime,' in K. Schlegel and D. Weisburd, eds., *White-Collar Crime Reconsidered*, 214-243.
  Boston: Northeastern University Press

Kramer, R.C., and R. Michalowski. 1990. 'State-Corporate Crime.' Paper presented at the
  Annual meeting of the American Society of Criminology, November, Baltimore

Krater, J. 1991. Personal Communication, January

Lamperti, J. 1984a. 'Government and The Atom,' in J. Dennis, ed., *The Nuclear Almanac:
  Confronting the Atom in War and Peace*, 67-79. Reading, MA: Addison-Wesley

–1984b. 'Nuclear Weapons Manufacture,' in J. Dennis, ed., *The Nuclear Almanac: Confronting the Atom in War and Peace*, 79-81. Reading, MA: Addison-Wesley

Lane, R.E. 1953. 'Why Businessmen Violate the Law.' *Journal of Criminal Law*, 44: 151-156

Luken, T. 1989. 'Statement Before the U.S. Congress, House. Committee on Energy and
  Commerce.' Subcommittee on Transportation and Hazardous Materials. *Environmental Crimes at DOE's Nuclear Weapons Facilities* (101st Congress, 1st session). Washington, DC: USGPO

Merrick, C. 1987. 'Statement Before the U.S. Congress, House. Committee on Energy and
  Commerce.' Subcommittee on Transportation and Hazardous Materials. *Environmental Crimes at DOE's Nuclear Weapons Facilities* (101st Congress, 1st session). Washington, DC: USGPO

Messerschmidt, J. 1986. *Capitalism, Patriarchy, and Crime*. Totowa, NJ: Rowman and
  Littlefield

Michalowski, R. 1985. *Order, Law and Power*. New York: Random House

Mobilization for Survival. 1989. *Banning the Bombmakers: Challenging Nuclear Weapons
  Production*. New York: Mobilization for Survival Fund

National Academy of Sciences. 1987. *Safety Issues at the Defense Production Reactors: A
  Report to the Department of Energy*. Washington, DC: National Academy Press

Needleman, M.L., and C. Needleman. 1979. 'Organizational Crime: Two Models of
  Criminogenesis.' *Sociological Quarterly*, 20: 517-528

Olshansky, S.J., and R.G. Williams. 1988. 'Culture Shock at the Weapons Complex.' *The
  Bulletin of the Atomic Scientists*, September: 29-33

Perdue, W.D. 1989. *Terrorism and the State: A Critique of Domination Through Fear*. New
  York: Praeger

Porter, J.W. 1986. 'Statement Before the U.S. Congress, House. Committee on Government Operations.' Subcommittee on Environment, Energy, and Natural Resources.
  Review of DOE's Compliance With Environmental Laws in Managing its Hazardous and

28 *The Journal of Human Justice, Volume 5, Number 1, Autumn, 1993*

Mixed Radioactive-Hazardous Wastes (99th Congress, 2nd session). Washington, DC: USGPO

Powaski, R.E. 1987. *March to Armageddon: The United States and the Nuclear Arms Race, 1939 to the Present*. New York: Oxford University Press

Radioactive Waste Campaign. 1988. *RWC Report*. New York: Author

Reicher, D.W. 1986. 'Statement Before the U.S. Congress, House. Committee on Energy and Commerce.' Subcommittee on Transportation and Hazardous Materials. *Environmental Crimes at DOE's Nuclear Weapons Facilities* (101st Congress, 1st session). Washington, DC: USGPO

Reicher, D.W., and S.J. Scher. 1988. 'Laying Waste to the Environment.' *The Bulletin of the Atomic Scientists*, January-February: 29-31

Resource Conservation and Recovery Act of 1976, 42 U.S.C. § 901 1976

Rhodes, R. 1986. *The Making of The Atomic Bomb*. New York: Simon and Schuster

Saleska, M., and I. Makhijani. 1990. 'Hanford Cleanup: Explosive Solution.' *The Bulletin of the Atomic Scientists*, October: 14-20

Schrager, L.S., and J.F. Short. 1978. 'Toward a Sociology of Organizational Crime.' *Social Problems*, 25 (4): 407-419

Sherman, L. 1980. 'Three Models of Organizational Corruption in Agencies of Social Control.' *Social Problems*, 27: 478-491

Steele, K.D. 1989. 'Hanford: America's Nuclear Graveyard.' *The Bulletin of the Atomic Scientists*, October: 15-23

Stewart, A.M. 1988. 'Low Level Radiation: The Cancer Controversy.' *The Bulletin of the Atomic Scientists*, September: 15-19

Sutherland, E.H. 1949. *White Collar Crime*. New York: Drydon

– 1940. 'White Collar Criminality.' *American Sociological Review*, 5: 1-12

Thompson, R. 1989. 'Statement Before the U.S. Congress, House. Committee on Energy and Commerce.' Subcommittee on Transportation and Hazardous Materials. *Environmental Crimes at DOE's Nuclear Weapons Facilities* (101st Congress, 1st session). Washington, DC: USGPO

US Department of Energy. 1979. *DOE Research and Development and Field Facilities*. Washington, DC: Author

US General Accounting Office. 1985. *Environment, Safety and Health: Environment and Workers Could be Better Protected at Ohio Defense Plants*. Washington, DC: Author

– 1986. *Nuclear Energy: Environmental Issues at DOE's Nuclear Defense Facilities*. Washington, DC: Author

– 1989. *Dealing With Enormous Problems in the Nuclear Weapons Complex*. Washington, DC: Author

Vaughn, D. 1982. 'Toward an Understanding of Unlawful Organizational Behavior.' *Michigan Law Review*, 80: 1377-1402

– 1983. *Controlling Unlawful Organizational Behavior: Social Structure and Corporate Misconduct*. Chicago: University of Chicago Press

Walker, D. 1986. 'Statement Before the U.S. Congress, House. Committee on Government Operations.' Subcommittee on Environment, Energy, and Natural Resources. *Review of DOE's Compliance With Environmental Laws in Managing its Hazardous and Mixed Radioactive-Hazardous Waste*. (99th Congress, 2d session). Washington, DC: USGPO

Weiner, T. 1990. *Blank Check: The Pentagon's Black Budget*. New York: Warner Books

Williams, N.A. 1990. *The Roots of Modern American Empire*. New York: Random House

Williams, R.C., and P.L. Cantelon. 1984. *The American Atom: A Documentary History From The Discovery of Fission to the Present*. Philadelphia: University of Pennsylvania Press

Yin, R. 1984. *Case Study Research*. Beverly Hills, CA: Sage

Young, T.R. 1981. 'Corporate Crime: A Critique of the Clinard Report.' *Contemporary Crisis*, 5 (July): 323-336

Zinn, H. 1980. *A People's History of the United States*. New York: Harper and Row

Political White-Collar Crime

JOURNAL OF LAW AND SOCIETY
VOLUME 23, NUMBER 1, MARCH 1996
ISSN: 0263-323X, pp. 1-17

The Corruption of Politics and the Politics of Corruption: An Overview

DAVID NELKEN* AND MICHAEL LEVI**

Before the 1990s, many in the West saw corruption as a problem limited to 'underdeveloped' countries with fledgling political institutions, or else at least as being something more typical of Mediterranean, Asian or other similar cultures. However, political scandals in most Western European countries mean that there is now no escaping its systematic presence in developed democracies.[1] Why should this be happening, what is being done about it, and what are likely to be the limits of the current wave of anti-corruption campaigns?

There are many disciplines which have relevant insights to bring to the study of political corruption: we could think for example of history, economics, sociology, anthropology, organizational and administrative theory or development studies. In this volume, we have invited case-studies authored by scholars who draw primarily on the contributions of criminology and political science – two disciplines whose type and level of enquiry into this phenomenon can be treated as usefully complementary – plus one essay (on China) by a development studies scholar. In this overview, we shall attempt to justify the choice of these disciplines by indicating how they help us tackle important questions about changes in corrupt behaviour, in the relationship between corruption and anti-corruption campaigns, and the problems of prevention and control in a variety of societies. Indeed, we have chosen as our title 'The Corruption of Politics and the Politics of Corruption' in order to emphasize the connection between the causes and the (non-)regulation of political corruption.

CRIME, LEGITIMACY, AND CORRUPTION

Within criminology, the analysis of corruption is most closely associated with the study of state crime, white-collar and organized crime, and its

* Distinguished Research Professor of Law, Cardiff Law School, University of Wales Cardiff, Cardiff CF1 1XD, Wales, and Professor of Sociology, Macerata Univerity, Macerata, Italy
** Professor of Criminology, School of Social and Administrative Studies, University of Wales Cardiff, Cardiff CF1 3AS, Wales

regulation.[2] The *modus operandi* of occult financing of political parties, for example, normally requires the use of bribes, kickbacks, and other forms of payoffs, tax evasion, fraud, undeclared slush funds, and planned bank-ruptcies. In some European countries, this in turn relies, to an extent perhaps unimaginable in Britain with its different bureaucratic traditions, on the massive production and acceptance of false invoices. So it is fruitful to examine links between political financing, fraud, and money-laundering.

But our understanding of corruption can also be enriched by using concepts found in the wider literature of criminology and the sociology of deviance, such as labelling theory. Even if corrupt agreements are often in breach of the criminal law, we must still ask whether corruption is deviant or simply normal in some social groups or some countries. More exactly, why should some countries prohibit what is a widespread practice of their élites? In Japan, nine of the fifteen Prime Ministers who held office in the period 1955–1993 were involved in corruption scandals. At least half its members of Parliament, it is estimated, could only have obtained their seats through the aid of illegal financing.[3] At the height of the Italian *Tangentopoli* (kickback city) investigations, a third of the deputies were under investigation for various offences (see Nelken's essay, in this volume). Are Western observers justified in labelling as 'corruption' the traditional giving of presents of appreciation to leaders and administrators (whether in Africa, Pakistan or Japan)?[4] In the more heavyweight (and commonly agreed) sense of corruption as massive embezzlement, we note that many of those who have come to power through anti-corruption campaigns in the last generation in Africa, South America, Asia, Mexico, and the Philippines have themselves, in turn, been accused of corruption. Were their original allegations of corruption nothing more than a tactical device to obtain power, or did their exposure to 'political realities' change their initial high ideals?

The questions posed in and by political science are central to under-standing the context and meaning of political corruption. Corruption and the response to it reveal the relative power of the executive, parliament, and the parties, and also illuminate the role of the criminal investigators, the judiciary, and the 'fourth estate' (the media). Typically, the attack on corruption (as that against other forms of white-collar crime or 'crimes of the powerful') is seen by sociologists as an attempt to relegitimate the rulers and/or specific political actors or criminal justice agencies. But both corrup-tion and anti-corruption can serve to undermine (or extend) the legitimacy of politicians, parties, and the State. Other questions take us further afield. The reduction of corruption is often used as a rationale for a shift from state to a market economy: yet, unless one makes it tautological, actual market economies seem quite prone to corruption, as the ideology shifts from one of public service to self-interest maximization (see the essays by Doig, Pizzorno and della Porta, and White in this volume). Likewise, the relationship between corruption and democracy is a very complex one:

2

democracy often is viewed as the answer to corruption, but it can also be increased by it as there is greater competition for the spoils of government (see, for example, White in this volume) and hurt by it (as countries use local corruption cliques as an excuse to centralize or re-centralize power, France being one example – see Ruggiero in this volume).

Although our contributors vary in their foci upon, respectively, political science and crime, our goal is really to bring the insights of these specialisms together. This is well demonstrated in the paper by Pizzorno and della Porta who, in asking who become corrupt politicians and what are the requirements of successfully carrying out that role, help us make sense of those we might describe as 'convictions politicians'. As they show, for some politicians it can be a positive client-gaining asset to display the capacity to survive successive attempts to put a stop to their illegal activities, as they profit from collusion of those involved in their projects as well as from a court system which permits a number of appeals before definitive judgement is given and allows the regular awarding of amnesties. As in the study of white-collar crime,[5] to study corruption is an attempt to follow a moving target: the way that certain transactions move in and out of acceptable behaviour as the boundaries of what is legitimate are softened, reaffirmed or redrawn; this is the classic stuff of labelling theory. Where those involved in corruption are political figures who embody the authority of the State, however, the implications are enormous for the legitimacy of politics.[6] Where corruption creates its own 'normative' patterns, anti-corruption campaigns may even function as a 'lawless' force destroying existing order.

IS POLITICAL CORRUPTION GROWING?

Public opinion polls show an increasing perception of corruption and the media increasingly reports such stories,[7] as they do those of the growth of fraud (including 'computer fraud').[8] But given low visibility of the behaviour and modest enforcement, it is easy to produce an artificial 'control wave' which may not correspond to any underlying behavioural change. Notwithstanding these severe empirical difficulties, it is widely assumed that the 1980s were a period of particularly rampant corruption in continental Europe, especially within (though by no means restricted to) the socialist parties in countries such as France, Italy, and Spain. The proud slogan of the Spanish Socialist party, 'A hundred years of honesty', found itself capped by their opponents reply, 'and not a day more'.[9] This rendered them open to accusations from political opponents. Thus, in Spain, we see a right-wing media-inspired campaign to undermine a nominally socialist party and the Prime Minister, Felipe Gonzalez, by associating them, prima facie plausibly, (i) with 'noble cause corruption', that is, the use of secret intelligence service funds to finance assassinations of supporters of the Basque separatist group ETA in France and Spain; and extortion of party 'donations' from the

3

business sector (the 'Filesa' case), and (ii) with personal corruption as a symbol of 'the state we are in' (unlike the good old Franco-ist days!).[10] Indeed, as Hofnung – whose analysis has general application well beyond Israel – and White (both in this volume) illustrate, it is the need for campaign finance and the ability of the political victor to grant or deny favours (such as development permits and public sector contracts) that provide a heady mix capable of corrupting all but the most disciplined.[11] The succession of dramatic corruption scandals in Japan followed by 'business as usual' demonstrate this unholy alliance very powerfully.

As White shows (in the Chinese context), the shift from Communism to 'marketization' provides enormous opportunities for corruption. However, distress about the present is often associated with 'Golden Ageist' distortions of the past: scandal-ridden Spain under the socialists succeeded a period under Franco where corruption was the glue that bound together an autarchic fascist economy.[12] Much the same was true of the later stages of Russian Communism. Whereas the 1980s saw leading politicians in Germany surviving accusations of large-scale corruption and mendacity, political scandals in the reunited Germany now erupt over the small change of irregularities in their employment of domestics or use of their credit cards. While this has been explained as hysteria or as a 'safety valve' to express deeper worries over the costs of German unification,[13] the reduction in tolerance levels was common to many other European countries. Does this simply reflect the resentment of the 'old guard' at the invasion of their privileges by *nouveaux riches*,[14] or might it also reflect the coming of age of the less pro-Establishment 'children of the 60s' as consumers of media 'censures',[15] or even the loss of interest in broader ideologies and their substitution by anti-corruption sentiments as part of 'the politics of envy'? Geopolitical changes are important to the revelation of pre-existing corruption: the collapse of the Soviet Union and world communism enabled the Americans to withdraw their support for the status quo in Italy, Pakistan, and (after the Gulf War was over) Abu Dhabi, thereby undermining both the long-term Christian Democrat/Mafia alliance in Italy and the Bank of Credit and Commerce International (BCCI).

Rather than regarding corruption and anti-corruption as independent phenomena, we find it more useful to examine how corruption and concern about corruption grows and falls. The deterioration in political and administrative service which results from the privileged access offered to their clients leads others to seek their own privileged routes, and so the cycle of corruption spirals. In the same way, a cycle of mutual dependence between politicians and organized criminals can develop, which breaks only when important persons withdraw from the exchanges.[16] We would add that those engaged in corrupt agreements tend to overreach themselves and bring about the collapse of these exchanges: (i) through ever increasing competition amongst those seeking clients, (ii) through the eventual fight back by those excluded, and (iii) above all, once investigations get started, because of the

4

scramble – in the classic prisoner's dilemma logic – to be the first to confess once they know or believe that trust in mutual silence has been broken.

We know that scandals and 'moral panics' about particular social problems often have a built-in life span or 'natural history' before they are succeeded and displaced by new concerns: here, corruption (and most white-collar crimes) have a built-in advantage not just because – collapsed buildings resulting from corrupt 'economies' in construction excepted – they are less visually dramatic, but also because investigations and trials tend to take so long to develop that the media become bored.[17] But there are inconsistencies in the evidence: some argue that criminalization campaigns come to a halt when they aim too high,[18] but this cannot account for the Italian case (Nelken, in this volume).

THE POLITICS OF CORRUPTION

The case studies described in this volume are intended to make it easier to view both the expansion of corruption and the implementation of anti-corruption campaigns as part of interlinked cycles in each of which political and economic conflicts, interests, and loyalties may all have a part to play. They discuss both the conditions which make for corruption: differences between the private and public sectors (including the growing formal and informal 'privatization' of the public sector in Britain and elsewhere), types of actors, the relative importance of individuals and systemic factors, and so on; and those which influence the reactions to corruption: the requirements of successful campaigns, why they happen, which issues or targets get highlighted, how inter-agency rivalries or structures limit reforms, the relative importance of campaigning individuals or changes in underlying background conditions, and so on. Part of the ambiguity of social reactions to corruption arises from doubts about the economic benefits of regulation, as well as from specific financial interests of politicians and media subservience.

More important, however, is to appreciate that accusations reflect wider ideological positions – the right connecting corruption with wastefulness of left-wing administrations, while the right is accused of using its political base to line the pockets of business élites – hence the political significance of the source of such denunciations (as an index of battles between the central and local powers, or between 'old money' and emerging 'enterprise capital') tells us much about the progress of power struggles. Many accused of corruption respond that their accusers – whether judges, prosecutors or government agencies – have a hidden political agenda. One response is that 'they would say that, wouldn't they?', but the search for the interests behind anti-corruption campaigns and their limits can tell us a great deal about who can mobilize the public interest and may enable us to understand why levels of corruption (or campaigns against it) get 'out of control'. Where there is a strong and unambiguous response, there may well be special motives. Thus

5

the demonization of BCCI (and Islamic banking in general) used the evidence of fraud, drugs money-laundering, and involvement with Libya to deflect people from focusing on the way the bank had been used by Western intelligence agencies to launder the money to help with illicit overseas operations and arms trafficking (see Passas, in this volume).

COMPARING CORRUPTION

There is much to be gained from examining corruption and control in a comparative perspective. At the level of basic description, this extends our opportunities for seeing who is involved in corruption, the wider causes, which groups act to expose (or conceal) corruption, and the cultural peculiarities of the role of law, ethics, and the judges, prosecutors, police, and other agencies, as well as the media. Corruption is often itself a transnational crime: as with many other examples of white collar crime, the businesspeople and politicians involved at the highest level typically use other countries to hold or launder their slush funds or pay offs. The search for common factors has thrown up a number of causes (or concomitants) of corruption. Some of these causes are seen as common to only some countries, such as the 'need' of socialist parties without an existing solid financial base in France, Spain, Italy to obtain new sources of funds. Other features are more universal: the way that regulation opens up the opportunity for massive bribes to gain favour or avoid disfavour.

But comparison should not be confined to seeking out what there is in common but also in understanding the many relevant differences in political and legal cultures.[19] Why do some countries rely mainly on the criminal law and others on self-regulation? Did campaigns start from above, from below, from part of the State apparatus aimed at other parts, from some political groups or individuals aimed at opponents? What divergences are there between countries in the way they conceive of checks and balances, of public and private, or 'the rule of law'? For example, the rule of law is linked to the role of parliament as overseen by the judges in Britain, whereas in Italy it is seen to depend on an active judiciary, and in Germany, it is associated mainly with the integrity of the administration.

How anti-corruption campaigns form part of the cycle of corruption and its response itself varies by culture. Thus, if such campaigns are part of 'normal politics' in some countries of Africa, Asia, and South America, they may have different significance in Italy and the United Kingdom where, for different reasons, campaigns against corruption are more exceptional. In Italy, the recent *Tangentopoli* investigations constitute something of a watershed between the first and second republic, as 'corruption' took on the role of symbolizing all that was wrong with the previous political system and its institutional arrangements. In Britain there continues to be a reluctance to draw the sharp line between business and political life (Doig, this

6

© Blackwell Publishers Ltd. 1996

volume) which creates suspicion of a blurring between public and private interest: this is reinforced by a deep cultural complacency that the British Establishment is trustworthy and would not allow its public roles to be influenced by private interests.[20] Even countries with similar legal and political arrangements can have intriguing differences in their definitions of where private interest interferes with public performance.[21] There are important but less acknowledged differences amongst countries in their toleration of open political lobbying by businesspeople: here it is Britain and the United States of America which are perhaps more tolerant. On the other hand, we could contrast the way politicians and businessmen work out their hidden exchanges in different countries: in Britain, France and the United States, successful politicians move out of politics into the business world, but they seldom do so in Italy, though businesspeople sometimes move into politics. And there are interesting differences in the recent roles of judges and the media in anti-corruption campaigns. Why has the media played a larger part in exposing corruption in some countries (for example, Britain and, especially, the United States of America) whereas in others (such as Italy)[22] it has been left to the judges? The explanation of corruption and anti-corruption can usefully be related to levels of reciprocal trust between citizens on the one hand, and politicians and administrators on the other.[23] It is essential to distinguish the form it takes in clientelistic settings[24] which have difficulty even in formulating 'the public interest' (except as rhetoric), from that which it takes in consolidated (often ex-imperialist) powers, where the concept of 'public interest' is normally understood to coincide with the economic and ideal interests of the establishment.

It would also be fruitful to examine the very different ways in which politicians try to avoid becoming the subject of judicial investigation in Britain, France, and Italy. How can one account for the British tendency to deal with corruption as an all-party problem (at least prior to 1994, when the Labour opposition decided it could fruitfully link 'sleaze' to the Conservative 'greed' ethos)? Does the existence of multi-party systems encourage more competition over corruption allegations than in basically two-party states? (In one-party states, such allegations tend to be buried with their makers.) There is need for a balance between looking for wider generalizations about corruption, and explaining it in terms of the specific historical context and culture in which it occurs:[25] but here, as elsewhere in comparative social science, a synthesis is not always easy to achieve.

THE CONTROL OF SCANDAL AND CONTROL BY SCANDAL

Except for those neo-functionalists who would argue that prosecution of white-collar criminals serves the interests of 'the system' – a perspective that can readily descend into tautology – issues of resources for and control over the investigation and prosecution of corruption and white-collar crime

7

present some intriguing paradoxes. Those articles in this volume, by Nelken, Passas, Pizzaro and della Porta, and Ruggiero, which deal with sensational political corruption phenomena focus on areas where prosecutions have taken place against a fairly dramatic political backdrop.[26] However, some of the more established groups practise the more refined forms of conflicts of interest and more subtle networked forms of corruption in which turns are taken to obtain contracts and consultancies among the 'good old boys'. As the work on France and Italy also illustrates, such corrupt networks take place within a culture of trust and continuing *opportunities* to exert power, and thus are available to only a sub-set of the population. Moreover, the ability to trust may make it impossible to prove the legal constituents of corruption, since there may be no need to give or receive an explicit bribe: counter-parties and/or their relatives can be given lucrative jobs, either at the time or, for probable *de facto* immunity from law, much later.

With due respect to Ruggiero (in this volume), breakdown in trust may not always lead to scandal. We know comparatively little about the impact of breaking promises or 'understandings' on the future power and profitability of the deceitful, but one would anticipate that such short-term lack of 'integrity' (*sic!*) would result in clear stigmatization and in being cut out of future participation in 'the club'. We are thinking not just of 'shaming' responses to those who expose the networks as *pentiti*, but also of those who fail to honour their promises of indirect rewards to those who grant them political favours.

One question one may ask is why 'solve' corruption, if it is functional? There are continuing problems about dealing with corruption when many of those directly involved are convinced they are gaining from it. Although the generally negative aspects of corruption for development are now more strongly emphasized,[27] there are scholars who stress its economic utility even for developed countries. The enormous level of illegal funding of politicians in Japan since the Second World War has largely been reinvested in that exceptionally successful economy, even if it undoubtedly led to relatively inefficient (in economic theory, though not in inclusionary political practice) redistribution of public works around the country.[28] There are also difficulties about assessing the political functions of corruption: even if it has undesirable long-term consequences, it may produce short-term benefits. (Arguably, Hong Kong-based Triad groups may have to be bought off by the Chinese government for such reasons of State.) Even in more established regimes, interest and ideology are linked in complex ways, and a decline in ideological convictions (such as was seen in much of Europe in the 1980s) may require greater appeals to interest.[29]

How far do solutions reflect causes? There are many opposite routes to corruption: if the alleged wider causes of corruption include the weakness of political parties (or their excessive power), the lack of a historically strong executive (or too strong a centralized executive), centrally owned economic units (or privatization), and loyalty to local groups (or absence of sentiments

8

of loyalty), then it is unlikely that any solutions brought forward to specific scandals will overcome these underlying problems. It is a common assumption that corruption arises from allowing administrators too great discretion, and a common remedy proposed is to cut back on this. But it is illusory to believe that all demands can be processed at the same time, so there must always be scope for 'speed money' as well as specific favours: in the absence of 'proof', who is to decide whether the particular form that such prioritization takes is the result of corruption or merely different valuation?

What solutions have been offered to 'the problem of political corruption'? Law may often be part of the problem of corruption. Too many laws, excessive formalism, and vexatious procedures help create corruption (by forcing people to get round them) and weaken attempts to control it. Law may encourage corruption by setting artificially low limits to political expenses, but as Hofnung shows in this volume, even a generous limit will be insufficient to combat the anomic pressure of political competition where the gains from access to power and the possibility of rewriting the law normally far outweigh the legal penalties or the loss of legitimacy; and new laws may merely displace competition elsewhere.

Law diffuses responsibility; investigations and punishment over-dramatize; and the need to distinguish between the legal and illegal creates artificial dichotomies between behaviour. Legal campaigns upset predictability, and law can express an over-ambitious ideal of the relationship between citizens and the State. Unanticipated side-effects occur, as when laws blocking corruption slow down the award of public works, allowing organized criminals the opportunity to buy up building firms who are short of cash. The implementation of law always remains culture-dependent: the American enthusiasm for whistleblowing (and financial rewards for it) has not at all been matched in Britain, where political élites regard it as encouraging 'sneaking' and whistleblowers are easily marginalized as mentally ill. (Though we note that no senior United States politicians have fallen foul of the legislation, which has benefited the Federal government through revelations of cheating by such as defence contractors.)

The enforcement of laws involving corruption and white-collar crime, often enacted on a tide of popular resentment in harness with a need for political élites to re-legitimate the State, often involves major intrusions into civil liberties, which may have broader social consequences. Precisely because there are seldom any complainants, even where the corrupt extort money from businesspeople or the public, corruption may be seen as an opportunity for policing agencies to develop proactive strategies: but this gives powerful élites the opportunity to target selectively their political opponents (or those who refuse to pay bribes/make political 'donations' to the 'right' party) for 'sting' operations or intensive tax reviews, while leaving 'friendly' parties alone.[30]

In short, high-level corruption like those economic crimes involving business élites that do not involve corruption raise a variety of problems for

9

© Blackwell Publishers Ltd. 1996

the normal functioning of policing and prosecution agencies. Issues of evaluating discretion are intriguing. What would a fair distribution of investigation of 'high-' and 'low-' level corruption look like? How do we ensure that the interests of powerful groups do not buy themselves either generally low priority in being regulated/policed/prosecuted or the ability to interfere with particular decisions? It is these power inequalities (which benefit also corrupting *Mafiosi* and those 1930s American 'professional criminals' with access to 'the fix' in the political machine described by Sutherland)[31] that give a difficult twist to the accountability debate. For the lack of transparency in the decision-making of investigators, prosecutors, and judges means that distinguishing evidential caution from socio-political bias is very difficult.[32]

In some countries of continental Europe, law can *potentially* deal with corruption, but reliance is placed on collusive non-enforcement. In addition, in common-law countries, as explained by Riesman,[33] one may witness *Lex Imperfecta*, that is, law that is deliberately designed to be imperfect. While not taking the view that all apparent inadequacies are 'designed in', we consider that there are four ways in which 'corruption' prosecutions can be stymied. The first – the *substantive law* route – is either not to criminalize it altogether or to do so in such a way that only crude exchanges of money for favours (either 'doing good' or 'not doing harm') are caught. The second – the *procedural law* route – is to make it difficult to mount covert strategies such as 'sting' operations which make prosecutions of élite persons easier.[34] (As the example of Berlusconi's attempts to call a halt to *Tangentopoli* shows – see both Nelken, and Pizzaro and della Porta in this volume – élite self-interest can be disguised as generalized concern for defendants' rights, though few were fooled in that particular case.) The third – the *functional resourcing* route – is to provide so few general resources for corruption and white-collar crime investigations in the specialist squads that normally deal with such matters that there is unlikely to be any *practical* possibility of prosecuting or even seriously investigating allegations involving corporate or political élites. Moreover, even if investigators and/or prosecutors were to contemplate such far-reaching enquiries, they would appreciate that this might have long-term negative effects not only on their own personal futures but upon future funding and political support for their agency's objectives.[35] The final – *political control* route – refers to the ability of élites to frustrate investigations that threaten them and their allies or, alternatively, to press prosecutions against their political opponents.[36] There are major cultural differences in the degrees of actual and perceived political independence and managerial accountability – both *de facto* and *de jure* – afforded to criminal investigators and prosecutors in different countries.

This analysis of the third and fourth routes to non-prosecution of corruption should be situated within the routines of criminal investigation and prosecution. Here, we note that in many countries – including not only Britain but also many of its former colonies – powers to investigate

10

corruption and economic crime exceed normal powers, for it is often argued that the proper detection and investigation of such crimes needs the power to compel answers and documentary evidence from witnesses and even suspects. (In several British colonies and former colonies, such as Hong Kong and Malaysia, there is legislation requiring civil servants who wish to avoid conviction for corruption to rebut allegations – once the facts are prima facie proven – that they have been living 'in a manner inconsistent with their legitimate income'.) Investigative powers in England and Wales are inconsistent, for if a case is dealt with by the police and Crown Prosecution Service (by statute, the consent of the Director of Public Prosecutions is required to prosecute 'corruption' offences), suspects are not required to answer questions, and confidential documents can be obtained only after a judicial order under Schedule 1 of the Police and Criminal Evidence Act 1984; whereas if the same matter – for example corruption among brokers in the North Sea oil industry[37] – is dealt with as a serious fraud (undefined in statute), much greater and less judicially supervised powers can be brought into play.[38] Likewise, if there are tax or company offences under investigation, the power regimes may vary enormously.

In the Third World, especially in former British colonies in Africa and Asia (and, more recently, in Australia), it is common to have specialist anti-corruption agencies on the model of the Hong Kong Independent Commission against Corruption, though commentators may disagree about whether these are intended to root out corruption or merely to provide a symbolic display of action (and perhaps prosecute those who do not co-operate with or even threaten the monopoly of inner political power-holders). In Australia, in addition to a plethora of well-resourced Royal Commissions to examine particular allegations of 'rotten pocket' or 'rotten barrel' corruption, several central bodies with tough powers such as the National Crimes Authority have been established, though their impact both on corruption and on civil liberties has been seriously questioned.[39] In the United States of America, prosecutor involvement in the investigation of crime is commonplace, and senior prosecutors either are elected directly or, in the case of US Attorneys, are Presidential appointees: some – of whom the most recent example was Rudolph Giuliani, then 'white-collar and organized crime-busting' US Attorney for the prestigious Southern District of New York and currently Mayor of New York City – are looking for political advancement, and the pursuit of high-publicity cases, including white-collar crime and corruption, is an expected part of their self-glorifying role.[40] In continental Europe, career investigating magistrates who are not specialists in economic crime or corruption do the greater part of the criminal investigations, but (even in the case of Italy) corruption has not been felt to be so serious a political issue as to require a special body with extraordinary powers. (The ability to remand suspects in custody almost indefinitely during investigations is seen as sufficient incentive for 'co-operation', though of course they have the right to remain silent under the European Convention of Human Rights!)

11

But in England and Wales, it is only in exceptional cases (and at the instiga-
tion of the police, who are reluctant to spend huge resources on a case without
any assurance that it will be prosecuted along the lines that they are
investigating) that prosecutors have any direct input into a corruption case
before a suspect is charged.[41] The only 'political appointees' are the Director
of Public Prosecutions (DPP) and the Director of the Serious Fraud Office,
who themselves may be lifetime, quasi-judicial appointees who do not change
with the government; plus the Attorney-General, to whom the former report
and who is a member of Parliament and of the Cabinet: unlike the United
States of America, apart from the Attorney-General, no British prosecutor
has ever seen their role as a launch-pad for politics, and no Attorney-General
has risen to senior office within the Cabinet. So it would be hard for an
English politician to influence corruption prosecutions directly.

But given the abstraction of subservience to the rule of law, what does
the accountability of the DPP to the Attorney-General, and of the Attorney-
General to Parliament mean in contexts such as these? In practice, United
Kingdom parliamentary convention and the *sub judice* rule mean that it is
rare for answers to be given to MPs on current cases, but concern from MPs
(including Ministers) can transmit across to those dealing with the case,
raising the organizational costs of prosecution. The complex background to
the arms-for-Iraq prosecutions considered by the Scott Enquiry (whose
much-delayed report was finally published in 1996) showed how – at least
in arms trafficking, where the military-industrial complex and politics so
often meet – even in a democracy, the bureaucratic and political interests
of government and State intelligence agencies can lead senior Conservative
politicians and lawyers to countenance the imprisonment of *pro-Conservative
businesspeople* known at that time to be innocent:[42] this might appropriately
be termed the corruption of politics.

How do we reduce the risk of political interference in the decision to
prosecute (or not to)? In principle, by analogy with the Victim's Charter,
one form of accountability might be to require the prosecution agency to
give challengeable reasons for *non*-prosecution: yet this does not happen.
If an Australian Royal Commission, a United States Senate, or an external
United Kingdom Department of Trade and Industry Inspection is authorized
and published, there is some evidence for outsiders to set against the decision
not to prosecute, though they might have to form their own judgments about
what evidence would be legally admissible. Otherwise, the media are the
principal potential source of investigative accounts and critique. But in the
United Kingdom (and in different ways, elsewhere), the media are enormously inhibited by libel laws, editorial (and owner) conservatism, and – in
some cases – journalistic sloth.[43] Except where undercover operatives can
film politicians receiving bribes or where victims are obviously hurt, corruption often lacks visual impact needed for television.

Is it possible to circumvent central control over (non-)prosecutions for
corruption? In the United Kingdom, it is assumed that there is no need for

12

any more independent public official to investigate or prosecute, and a private prosecution would be able to take place only for frauds such as falsification of accounts rather for corruption offences by themselves. In the United States, as the lengthy Iran-Contra investigation showed, the appointment of Special Prosecutors and Independent Counsel[44] to supervise highly sensitive political investigations does not fully resolve the twin difficulties of demonstrating independence and mounting prosecutions in a timely way.[45] As Williams puts it:

> The decision [of Congress] to grant immunity to North and Poindexter dealt what proved to be fatal blows not only to the North and Poindexter prosecutions but also the Independent Counsel's entire prosecution strategy. Thus, the political needs of Congress blocked the Independent Counsel's efforts to prosecute key players in the scandal and created technical obstacles which made prosecutions most unlikely.[46]

In August 1994, the (Republican) Special Prosecutor appointed on a bipartisan basis to investigate Presidential involvement in the 'Whitewater' loans scandal was replaced by a judicially nominated Independent Counsel, partly because the original one was considered insufficiently 'active' in his approach to suit the needs of the Republican Congress.

In the United States, parallel legal structures sometimes make it possible for corruption-related prosecutions to occur when they are resisted at their 'normal' level: one of the clearest illustrations was the prosecution of BCCI by Robert Morgenthau, District Attorney for New York County, while the United States Department of Justice prevaricated, allegedly because of the CIA's active involvement in espionage and money-laundering through the bank (see Passas in this volume). BCCI is a highly politicized case, spawning inter-agency conflicts at an international as well as national level, not only between 'the West' and Abu Dhabi and Pakistan, but also between the United Kingdom and the United States of America as, to the outrage of some Americans, the United Kingdom Serious Fraud Office has arrested (and the courts have later imprisoned) some key witnesses who have assisted New York County prosecutors in their actions against other BCCI personnel and in their attempts to recover assets for the United States courts (and, it is intended, for BCCI creditors). Doubtless, this was highly convenient for those American and Arab figures whose corrupt alliances might have received considerable exposure had the prosecutions in England not discredited (and incapacitated in jail) these witnesses. But no-one was prosecuted for corruption in any of the myriad BCCI cases: BCCI has been treated as a case of fraud and money-laundering – as 'organized' rather than 'white-collar' crime.

The independence and courage of the Italian magistrates seems to have acted as a role model for some colleagues in France (see Ruggiero in this volume) and in Spain (Judge Garzon in the ETA assassination case). In essence, when the same coalition of interests is involved in corruption, fraud, and 'racketeering', including the illegal obtaining of funds for election success, any impetus for tough action against either financial crime or 'organized

13

crime' is likely to generate information placing senior members of the coalition 'at risk'. It is then that the explicit politics of scandal and criminal-
investigation suppression come into play, as American observers have been
able to note from Watergate, through Contragate, to Whitewatergate in
1994 and 1995 (see, also, Block in this volume).

The important issues of accountability raised by serious fraud and corruption prosecutions are unlike most faced in other arenas, and arise principally
because of the combination of (a) lack of transparency of decision-taking
(at case acceptance, investigative resource-allocation, use of search and
interview powers, and prosecution decision levels), with (b) the political (with
a small or large 'p') ramifications of particular cases. (As far as we know,
adult high-status persons are seldom involved in any property crimes other
than fraud or corruption.) These political ramifications include party political donations from businesspeople – on which the heavily indebted English
Conservative party became highly dependent during the 1980s and 1990s to
finance its campaigns and its headquarters – who sought favours such as
well-photographed dinners with the Prime Minister. (There are parallels in
many countries: see Hofnung, Nelken, Pizzaro and della Porta, and Ruggiero,
in this volume, as well as some Chinese Communist Party-Hong Kong Triad
connections not discussed by White.) They also include broader conceptions
of 'public interest' which are difficult to unpick, such as the dilemma between
'showing that we are sorting out crime in the suites' and 'not undermining
the confidence of the public in business (or politicians)', whose balance shifts
considerably over time and between countries.

Though – especially where there is jury trial or an independent judiciary
– neither government nor State has direct control over convictions, extra
resources can always be found for those cases that involve people whom
'the system' is determined to 'get': despite the fact that most of the key defendants had been charged in the United States of America or Abu Dhabi, or
were unavailable in Pakistan, Parliament voted the Serious Fraud Office
millions of pounds extra to deal with BCCI; and the otherwise short-staffed
Merseyside police had thirty-three officers working full-time investigating
corruption allegations against the influential former left-wing Liverpool
councillor, Derek Hatton. (He was acquitted of all charges in corruption
and subsequent theft trials.) These areas of indirect influence occur because
even where there is no direct political control – as there is in many Third
World countries – over crime investigation, bureaucracies need the support
of politicians (including the Attorney-General) for resources, and are inclined
to please them. In polities where power is more centralized and investigation
and judicial agencies less autonomous, Pandora's box can remain even more
tightly shut against those allegations of élite fraud and corruption that
threaten the hegemony of those who enjoy current power. In countries such
as Britain, the tendency is to play down the extent of corruption and to
suppress scandal for fear of 'rocking the boat', whilst in some other
countries, control by scandal may do little more than substitute one set of

14

political actors for another, to be followed by a further set of scandals. In short, the politics of corruption in some countries is played out by attempting to suppress scandal, while in others, scandal campaigns form part of the routines involved in the circulation of élites.

NOTES AND REFERENCES

1 See the excellent recent survey in D. della Porta and Y. Mény, '*Democrazia e corruzione: verso un'analisi comparata*' in *Corruzione e Democrazia*, eds. D. della Porta and Y. Mény (1995) 225–45.

2 While corrupt agreements do not always necessarily constitute fraud in the legal sense, leading economic approaches to corruption tend to use language which can be easily related back to criminology. Economists talk of a black market in property rights and of illegal forms of 'rent seeking' and argue that corruption usually involves 'fraud by an "agent" who sells what is not his to sell by making an alliance at the expense of a third party, "the victim(s)".' (See id.)

3 J.-M. Bouissou, '*La corruzione in Giappone: un sistema di redistribuzione?*' in id., pp. 157–83.

4 It is often assumed the traditional implies consensual, but what local people actually feel about their leaders' receipt of substantial gifts is seldom researched. Ethnic tensions being what they are, we would predict that group membership would affect tolerance levels.

5 See, for example, D. Nelken, 'White-Collar Crime' in *The Oxford Handbook of Criminology*, eds. M. Maguire, R. Morgan, and R. Reiner (1994) 355–93.

6 Corruption may unambiguously harm economic development, where the head of state simply embezzles a large proportion of GDP and state assets, as appears to have been the case in countries as diverse as the Phillipines and Zaire.

7 See, for example, W. Seibel, '*Costruzione dello stato e etica pubblica in Germania*' in della Porta and Mény, op. cit., n. 1, 107–35, and Ruggiero in this volume.

8 See M. Levi and A. Pithouse, *Victims of White-Collar Crime: the Social and Media Construction of Corporate Fraud* (forthcoming, 1996).

9 P. Heywood, '*Dalla dittatura alla democrazia: le mutevoli forme della corruzione in Spagna*' in della Porta and Mény, op. cit., n. 1, pp. 87–107.

10 Spanish financial scandals include the brother of the former Deputy Prime Minister (who resigned to reduce political damage), and the politically appointed former head of the Guardia Civil, Luis Roldan, who was extradited back to Spain and who, as we write, awaits trial for allegedly embezzling funds for his personal use from the same covert intelligence 'pot' allegedly used to pay mercenaries for the assassinations.

11 Once people have discretionary control over such non-transparent funds, it is easy for them to divert a portion for their own use: this was alleged of Colonel (and almost Senator) Oliver North in relation to the secret funds used to supply the Contras during the Reagan Presidency.

12 Heywood, op. cit., n. 9.

13 Seibel, op. cit., n. 7.

14 See the comments on insider dealing of M. Clarke, *Business Crime: Its Nature and Control* (1990) 162.

15 See C. Sumner, *The Sociology of Deviance: an Obituary* (1994).

16 See D. della Porta and A. Vannucci, *Corruzione Politica e Amministrazione Pubblica* (1994).

17 See the analysis of the media in white-collar crime cases in Levi and Pithouse, op. cit., n. 8.

18 E.V. Currie, 'Crimes without victims, witchcraft and its control in Renaissance Europe' (1968) 3 *Law and Society Rev.* 7–32.

19 See, for example, D. Nelken (ed.), (1995) 4:4 *Social and Legal Studies*, special issue entitled

15

Legal Culture, Diversity and Globalisation.

20 Though in October 1995, Parliament voted – against the official Conservative party line – to adopt the Nolan Committee proposals to reduce conflicts of interest, probably because the majority finally realised that the public did not share their lofty view of themselves, and because they judged that Labour would be able to make political capital out of their refusal.

21 E. Halevy-Etzioni, 'Comparing Semi-corruption among Parliamentarians in Britain and Australia' in *Comparative Methodology*, ed. E. Oyen (1990) 113-33.

22 D. della Porta, *Lo Scambio Occulto: Casi di Corruzione politica in Italia* (1992).

23 D. Nelken, 'Whom can you trust? The future of Comparative Criminology' in *The Futures of Criminology*, ed. D. Nelken (1994) 220–44.

24 S.N. Eisenstadt and L. Roniger, *Patrons, Clients and Friends* (1984).

25 P. Sztompka, 'Conceptual Frameworks in Comparative Inquiry: Divergent or Convergent' in *Globalization, Knowledge and Society*, eds. M. Albrow and E. King (1990).

26 How much impact prosecutions have on corruption levels may be questioned in the light of even as sensational a set of prosecutions and scandalization as Watergate and the resignation of President Nixon under threat of impeachment.

27 See, for example, R. Klitgaard, *Controlling Corruption* (1988), and White in this volume.

28 Boissou, op. cit., n. 3.

29 There are implications here for corruption and 'new Labour' in Britain.

30 See, for example, A. Block, *Masters of Paradise* (1990).

31 E. Sutherland, *The Professional Thief* (1937).

32 Those of a postmodern disposition may not see the issue as relevant, since assessing the plausibility of different accounts has no inherent meaning. There are, of course, biases built into law itself, particularly in relation to chains of responsibility in organizational contexts.

33 D. Riesman, *Folded Lies* (1979).

34 See C. Fijnaut and G. Marx (eds.), *Undercover: Police Surveillance in Comparative Perspective* (1995); M. Levi, *The Investigation, Prosecution and Trial of Serious Fraud* (1993); G. Marx, *Undercover: Police Surveillance in America* (1987).

35 Quite apart from any political interference and careerism, organizational practices – for example, a focus on minimizing investigative costs and risks of acquittal – may lessen the chances of prestigious figures being prosecuted in complex organizational corruption cases, since they may not touch the money directly. Unless they get careless – as does happen – senior figures are normally harder to connect.

36 It should not be thought that this is solely the prerogative of Third World nations – see White in this volume. President Nixon made considerable use both of the FBI and the Internal Revenue Service in this regard: see Block, op. cit., n.30.

37 See J. Andvig, 'Corruption in the North Sea oil industry: Issues and assessments' (1995) 23 *Crime, Law and Social Change* 289–313. The United Kingdom Serious Fraud Office, rather than the police, successfully dealt with one major case of this kind.

38 See Levi, op. cit., n.34.

39 See articles by Fairchild, Corns and Lenihan in (1994) 27 *Australian and New Zealand J. of Criminology* 111–73.

40 See the classic study by J. Katz, 'The social movement against white-collar crime' in *Annual Review of Criminology*, eds. E. Bittner and S. Messenger (1980) vol. 2.

41 See, more generally, Levi, op. cit., n. 34.

42 We doubt that H.M. Customs and Excise knew when they initially prosecuted Ordtech or Matrix-Churchill that their exports were known by the MI5 and some parts of the DTI to be arms components. In an ironic sense, the fact that these prosecutions took place at all may illustrate the relative autonomy of customs investigators and prosecutors from government.

43 See Levi and Pithouse, op. cit., n. 7, and Pizzorno and della Porta in this volume.

44 A 1983 amendment to the Ethics in Government Act 1978 PL 95-521 replaced the post

16

© Blackwell Publishers Ltd. 1996

of special prosecutor with that of 'independent counsel'. The former are appointed by and may be removed by the Attorney-General – in the United States of America, as in England and Wales, a political appointment. The latter are appointed by a division of the United States Federal Court of Appeals following a request by the Attorney-General: Attorneys-General have no formal say in who is appointed, and cannot fire them, as they did Archibald Cox during the Watergate investigation when he showed too great enthusiasm for following the leads upwards to the White House.

45 The Walsh final reports into Iran-Contra were published only in January 1994, some seven years after his appointment: see R. Williams, 'The last word on the Iran-Contra affair? (1995) 23 *Crime, Law and Social Change* 367–85.

46 id., p. 379.

17

Part IV
Comparative Dimensions of State Crime

[18]

Peace Review 6:2 (1994). 171-175

State Violence and Violent Crime

Ronald C. Kramer

Last year's American Society of Criminology conference examined the theme "Violent Crime and Its Victims." Yet amidst the hundreds of papers it produced, only a handful addressed state violence and its countless victims. Despite its neglect by the mainstream, state violence is an important criminological concern that is essential to any meaningful discussion of crime control. The problem of state violence must be faced in its own right. But understanding its connections to more traditional violent crimes will also be our only hope for alleviating suffering in our societies. As an exercise in peacemaking criminology, we must illustrate the problem of state violence, identify its different forms (including those most often ignored by criminologists), and describe the connections between state crime and traditional violent crimes.

Violence can be defined in simple terms as that which inflicts injury or death on human beings. Johan Galtung adds an important distinction to this harm-based definition in his book *The True Worlds* (1980). He defines violence very broadly as any avoidable impediment to self-realization, which may take the form of the infliction of "bads"—which is what one usually thinks of as violence, or may take the form of the deprivation of "goods." His major distinction, however, is between person-to-person violence and structure-to-person violence. These two forms of violence can be referred to as personal and structural violence, or as direct and indirect violence, respectively.

Galtung's distinction extends our perspective on violence, adding to "violence-as-action" the idea of "violence-as-structure." He focuses our attention not only on the direct violence of the specific actors criminologists generally study, but also to the indirect violence of asymmetric, hierarchical, or "wrong" structures. Structural violence appears to just happen, without any specific actor behind it. The violence is built into the structure, the result of some fundamental inequity that then creates, and is reinforced by, other forms of inequality and social injustice. Thus, in those cases where the state creates or provides structural support for institutional practices that

172   *Ronald C. Kramer*

clearly cause physical harm to people, this kind of structural violence is a form of state criminality.

In his American Society of Criminology conference paper, Peter Iadicola followed Galtung's lead and defined violence as any action or structural arrangement that results in physical or nonphysical harm to one or more people. He, too, directs our attention to violence-as-action and violence-as-structure. In considering violence-as-action or direct violence, however, Iadicola added another important distinction: between interpersonal violence and institutional violence. Interpersonal violence is person-to-person violence occurring between people outside their institutional roles. Institutional violence, on the other hand, occurs through the actions of various social institutions and their agents. Acts of direct violence committed by state agencies and agents, therefore, represent one major form of institutional violence for criminologists to investigate.

Iadicola also offered two other propositions. First, he argued that, in general, as we move from interpersonal to institutional to structural violence, the scale and scope of violence increases. Thus, state violence, conceived of as both structural and institutional violence, is more pervasive and harmful than the interpersonal violence criminologists more commonly examine. Second, Iadicola noted that most violence that occurs in any society is linked to the other levels of violence. The violence that begins at the structural level creates a frame within which other forms of violence are nested. We must study state violence, therefore, not only in its own right, but also because of its relationship to more commonly recognized forms of interpersonal violence.

Of the three major levels of violence defined, the state is directly involved in two of them and indirectly involved in the other. Most structural violence and many acts of institutional violence are largely forms of state violence, yet they have been long neglected by most criminologists and policymakers concerned with "controlling crime." Perhaps they are ignored because they are not seen as "real crime." The higher levels of violence are less likely to be recognized as violence and thus are not seen as a problem.

But this reflects the "semantic politics of violence," or the definitional processes that make some violence normative and other violence deviant. Criminologists, however, ought to have the scientific autonomy to develop their own standards for classifying behavior as criminal rather than relying on state definitions. These standards may include the traditional criminal law of individual nation-states, human rights formulations, or various forms of international law.

Using a broad human rights definition of crime, we can more clearly describe the aforementioned two forms of state violence and outline their linkages to traditional criminal violence.

M ost discussions of violence deal with direct violence or violence-as-action. Examining violence-as-structure is less common. Structural violence describes the variety of physical harms that result from unequal social structures. With structural violence, the loss of life is caused by asymmetric social relations. We can recognize structural violence only at the collective level when we observe survival rates that are too low relative to available resources. Structural violence, therefore, is a set of social conditions from which flows absolute poverty, disease, hunger and malnutrition, poor sanitation and health care services, premature death, high infant mortality, illiteracy, unemployment, pollution, and general misery and squalor.

The misery of structural violence is concentrated in the so-called Third World. The nations of the Third World are afflicted with structural violence and remain "undeveloped" for various reasons, including geography, climate, lack of arable land and minerals, and a history of continuous warfare. But the world system of economic and political relationships between nation-states is also responsible.

As Galtung has observed, the root of such violence is not resource scarcity or price increases or population pressures, but the "world structure." Structural violence in the Third World has largely resulted from a history of colonialism, and from economic and political domination by First World nations, particularly the United States, in the postcolonial era. Structural violence is thus a form of state violence.

The history of colonialism is one of subjugation, conquest, and a subsequent domination of Third World people by the European nations (even by some European colonies liberated from imperial rule). While this history is filled with much direct violence, including genocide, the legacy of colonialism also promotes structural violence in the contemporary world order. Colonialism, a set of asymmetric social, political, and economic relationships, systematically promoted the self-interests of the European colonizers and exploited the lives and resources of the colonized in the Third World.

This system still causes great suffering today, as Noam Chomsky brilliantly demonstrates in his book *Year 501: The Conquest Continues* (1992). He shows how the hierarchical social relations of the current world system, which has taken various forms and been given various labels (such as imperialism, neocolonialism, the North-South conflict, core versus periphery), produce structural violence. That violence has been maintained over time by specific nation-states, including the

174   *Ronald C. Kramer*

United States, in violation of human rights standards and international law. Thus, structural violence is indeed a form of state criminality that can and should be brought within the boundaries of criminological inquiry and addressed as an important public policy issue.

E fforts to maintain relations of domination that produce structural violence in the current world order eventually lead to acts
of direct, institutional violence committed by state agents and agencies. In Galtung's phrase, direct violence is a companion of structures "pregnant with structural violence." These acts of direct violence can be best understood as state terrorism.

If terrorism means political intimidation by violence or the
threat of violence, then a nation-state like the United States should
be viewed as a terrorist, given the history of U.S. political and military intervention in the Third World. Such acts of institutional violence by a powerful First World nation are generally carried out to
forcefully prevent any redistribution of scarce resources. State terrorism, therefore, is any direct violence committed by states or state
agents to defend the economic and political domination of the current world order.

In recent years, state terrorism has been extensively examined by
many scholars. With a few exceptions, however, criminologists have
generally avoided the topic. State terrorism includes things such as
wars, invasions, supporting repressive regimes abroad, repressing domestic dissent at home, and threatening to use nuclear weapons.
This violence violates numerous human rights standards and international laws, kills and injures thousands of people in the Third
World, and victimizes millions more indirectly by helping to maintain an international system of structural violence. The massive criminal violence of state terrorism should be an important criminological concern.

We could also identify other forms of state violence, but structural violence and state terrorism are the most important to study
and to control. These two forms of state violence are also linked significantly to crimes of interpersonal violence like murder and assault. The violent crimes that receive the most attention from criminologists, politicians, and the general public are often nested within
the framework of structural violence and state terrorism.

T he hierarchical structures and social conditions that produce
structural violence are also, quite often, the root causes of various forms of interpersonal violence. This is true not only in the
Third World but also in places like the United States, where increasingly we find the "Third World at home." Conditions of economic

marginality, mass social deprivation, and community breakdown lead to the kind of endemic violent crime experienced in the United States.

This is particularly true of inner cities, where much of this violence is concentrated, especially among young, disproportionately minority, and lower-class males. Here the loss of industrial jobs has shrunk opportunities for stable and rewarding work. The flight of the middle class, both black and white, has left behind isolated and fragmented communities. To top it off, during the Reagan-Bush years, the inner cities experienced the systematic withdrawal of public services and social support. The end result, as Elliott Currie shows in his book *Reckoning* (1993), has been deepening poverty, widening inequality, collapsing families, educational breakdown, and shredded bonds of community. These are structurally violent conditions that generate endemic levels of direct criminal violence.

To these structural conditions we can add a number of cultural forces that support the use of interpersonal violence. Among the most important is the U.S. culture of militarism, which involves the recurrent use of military violence to resolve social and political problems, the excessive preparation for war, and the glorification of military values. A militaristic nation is one that conducts an aggressive and interventionist foreign policy and that practices a systematic pattern of state terrorism. Militarism glorifies violence and provides normative support for using violence to respond to a variety of problems. The militarization of culture leads to a greater acceptance of violence and to higher rates of violent crime.

The expansion of the means of violence committed by the state, both structurally and in its actions, constitutes a fundamental problem of our time. The long-standing neglect of state violence and it is countless victims poses a moral challenge for criminology. Can the discipline help resolve this problem? Can the American Society of Criminology claim it is really dealing with "violent crime and its victims" when it ignores the massive violence of the state? Can we seriously confront the problem of interpersonal violence without understanding its source in the framework of structural violence? By asking these kinds of questions, peacemaking criminologists could and should provoke a sense of unease that help us, individually and as a discipline, place state violence squarely on the crime control agenda for the future.

Ronald C. Kramer teaches sociology and directs the Criminal Justice Program at Western Michigan University in Kalamazoo, Michigan.

[19]

Holocaust and Genocide Studies, Vol. 3, No. 3, pp. 289–303, 1988
Printed in Great Britain

8756–6583/88 $3.00 + 0.00
Pergamon Press plc

LOCATING THE HOLOCAUST ON THE GENOCIDE SPECTRUM: TOWARDS A METHODOLOGY OF DEFINITION AND CATEGORIZATION*

HENRY R. HUTTENBACH

The City College of the City University of New York

Abstract — This article seeks to critically examine existing terminology defining the concept of genocide and the phenomenon of the Holocaust in order to focus on unexamined assumptions. This task is assumed to lay the groundwork for determining criteria to enable comparative studies and to facilitate placing the Holocaust in various contexts alongside other genocidal incidents.

During the first generation of Holocaust scholarship intense, though widely conflicting, indeed mutually exclusive, efforts to fix its historical identity testify to the emotional and intellectual difficulties involved in shedding clarity on an event that in its many dimensions broke with the past. Its obvious revolutionary character tended not only to give it an aura of mystery — an act beyond the range of normal human behavior — but also to isolate it from other similar or related phenomena before or after the eruption of the Nazi genocide against European Jewry within the context of World War II in the middle of the 20th century.[1]

The eloquent perceptions of Elie Wiesel, survivor *par excellence*, over the course of three prolific decades, have repeatedly and insistently stressed the inexplicability of the Holocaust, a reality of experiences lying beyond the parameters of comprehension of the non-survivor. And even the survivor finds himself in a dual prison, having neither the words to convey adequately where he had been nor the skill of mind to make sense to himself the maelstrom of memories that haunt and torment him. The Holocaust, we are led to believe, lies outside of language, outside the realm of the logical. For those who subscribe to the Wiesel thesis, to the fundamental unintelligibility of the Nazi program of extermination, the Holocaust cannot be properly defined and, therefore, cannot be placed alongside other historical events for, in a real sense, so runs the argument, the Final Solution lies outside history, indefinable as a result of its meta-historical status. In that respect, the Holocaust lies more in the arena of the philosopher and the theologian. Through the eyes of such philosophers the act of the Holocaust was an explosive turning point, a 'tremendum;' for distinctly different theologians, the Holocaust implied inescapable eschatological conclusions. For Emil Fackenheim, the Holocaust translated into a sacred commitment, an eleventh commandment: not to forget; though, consistent with his original assumption about the event, Fackenheim cannot spell out what, exactly, one is supposed to remember since it, in itself, defies reason. Not dissimilarly, Richard Rubenstein concludes that with the Holocaust all that is left as a rational response is to jettison pre-Holocaust theology, for, as a result of its happening, the rationality of traditional premises has been completely undermined. God as he had previously shown himself through history was no longer alive. Not only had the mystery of the Holocaust fully obscured him but it had made his vehicle for communication between himself and man — history — unintelligible, impenetrable.[2]

---

*Presented at the 'Remembering for the Future' Conference, Oxford, 10–13 July 1988.

In contrast to those who have been moved to render the Holocaust as lying outside the rational order, the equally convincing, or at least articulate voice of Raul Hilberg poses a strong challenge. According to this lucid scholar, the Nazi program of extermination poses no imponderables. The machinery of mass death leads the scholar directly into the bureaucratic heart of the modern state. Its institutions and organizations lend themselves to thorough analysis. Though the conclusions might be disquieting, they remain, nevertheless, humanly intelligible and do not fall outside the frontiers of the rational. On the contrary, the very intelligibility of the Holocaust — from the motivation of the architects of genocide to the smallest detail of administration and execution — sheds light and not shadows on the affairs of modern mankind. The combination of the ideology of Darwinian racial antisemitism, totalitarian politics and contemporary bureaucratism made a lethal potion that poisoned and deluded an entire nation to participate actively and passively, covertly and overtly, in a policy to rid the nation and then the world of Jews. According to Hilberg, despite the seeming complexity suggested by the ocean of details embodied in the sources, the overall flow of events is, on the whole, relatively simple: orders were given and orders were carried out. Cultural historians such as George Mosse have provided eminently satisfactory answers why and how that could be.[3]

Thus, those assuming the task of ascribing an acceptable definition to the Holocaust find themselves pulled in opposite directions by those who deny it can be defined, let alone understood, and those who insist on its 'normality,' that is its lack of any untoward difficulty for regular comprehension as a logical product of modern thought and political action. The former stance makes the Holocaust unassimilable in secular history; the latter, if pushed to its logical conclusion, reduces it to an act of state violence, fundamentally no different from any other state directed policy of extermination except for the targeted victims. Hilberg the political scientist sees, as the common denominator making possible any act of genocide, the state's power to do so if it so chooses. The Holocaust, therefore, does not have, *per se*, any undue claim to intellectual singularity, making a definition almost superfluous. What engages him is the organizational dynamics, the interplay of government agencies. What distinguishes one form of genocide from another is basically the degree of efficiency or inefficiency with which the decision to exterminate was carried out. Otherwise, individual incidents of genocide do not require definition; that is the function of time and space — when and where the event took place. One is left with the impression that the Holocaust had no significant identity that sets it apart.

To rectify that tendency, there has arisen a school of interpretation of the Holocaust, determined to save it from being totally submerged alongside all past and future genocidal events. It emphasizes the singularity of the Holocaust, namely, its uniqueness. Foremost among the 'singularist' scholars has been Yehuda Bauer, who has steadfastly argued for the incomparability of the Jewish experience to that of other peoples who have also been victimized by exterminational policies. According to Bauer, what befell the Jewish people is only superficially related to other acts of genocide. Categorically, Bauer insists, the Holocaust stands alone as a totality, essentially unlike anything that came before and, so far, has been perpetrated after World War II. His argument rests on the premise that Jews were targeted precisely because they were Jews and nothing else. But while the Turks did not explicitly say as much, that is precisely why Armenians were annihilated — because they were Armenians. Much the same could be said for the Aché Indians. Nevertheless, Bauer reasons against any attempt to dilute the singularity of the Holocaust, never tiring of warning against merging it with, or placing it alongside the other crimes of Nazism against Gypsies and Poles, for example. Nothing must be allowed to detract from the special martyrdom of the Jewish dead, suddenly shifting from historical terminology to quasi-religious phraseology, wrapping the victims in a mantle of sacredness no historian ought to violate. Thus, like Wiesel, Bauer constructs his own version of the Holocaust as a 'myster-ium' calling on an emotive appeal to prevent a rational determination that might reasonably link the tragedy of the Jews, however remotely, to that of other victims. In that sense he is the mirror-image of Hilberg the arch-rationalist. For Bauer, the Holocaust stands con-ceptually and historically absolutely distinct; for Hilberg, the Holocaust is a variation of genocide, best understood if stripped of any veneer of mystification.[4]

What must be done, then, to overcome the reluctance to make the Holocaust compre-hensible and, thereby, restore it to rational examination and definition? Similarly, how is one to tackle the problematics of integrating it into the increasingly common phenomenon of genocide without diluting its identity? Does a clear-cut definition necessarily exclude an element of permanent shock, an intellectual response of disbelief in the face of the immensity of the crime, though not a capitulation to reason? Claiming to comprehend the *how* still leaves room for admitting to a measure of failing to grasp all the dimensions of the realm of human motivation, a normal recognition that there is always room for further exploration, without declaring the existence of a dead-end as a result of the limitations of human understanding. Likewise, admitting the Holocaust took place in a broader context of criminality, need not rob it of its exclusive identity. If, as the singularists argue, the Holocaust is *the* paradigm *par excellence* of genocide, familiarity with which will shed additional clarity on other incidents of genocide, i.e. 'lesser' genocides in their terms, then the reverse is also true: each other genocide necessarily contains a ray of light, a particle of historical truth, that cannot but enrich one's understanding of Auschwitz. But how to do so without oversimplification, without suggesting that one crime against humanity is just that, with little claim to a specific historical personality, so that Holocaust becomes one of many holocausts? How do we prevent ourselves from moving glibly from Auschwitz to Hiroshima and back, from the Death Camps to the Gulag, from genuine genocide to non-genocide, from lumping victims of *bona fide* extermination together with victims of massacres?

What is needed is a system of definition and a methodology of categorization. Armed with the parameters of a definition of genocide, it will be easier to include and/or exclude candidates for genocide. Given a set of criteria, one can then begin the process of differen-tiation and grouping of those events that met the qualifications of the definition. In this way, a spectrum of genocide can be constructed, within which the Holocaust will occupy a distinct niche, flanked in proximity by those events with which it shares the greatest similar-ity, with those to which it is least related located furthest from its assigned locus within the defined sphere of genocide.

But prior to doing so, it is necessary to review what has been done to date in both defining and categorizing the Holocaust and other genocides. Not surprisingly, the litera-ture is sparse and proof that the task requires far more systematic research than has so far been allotted to it. Both the literature on definition and that on categorization is sporadic with little evidence of systematic continuity from one work to the next. Indeed, the ade-quacy of Lemkin's neologism — 'genocide' — in the absence of any other suitable word was never carefully assessed whether it actually meant what it was supposed to mean. 'Gens', after all, has a precise meaning which Lemkin did not intend; the 'gens' prefix, it turns out, was a convenient substitute for group, any group that faced extermination. But the suffix 'cide' literally refers to killing, possibly to mass killing, but not necessarily to total destruction. Thus, working with a loose understanding or liberal interpretation of genocide, it is easy to lump actual genocide alongside traditional massacres whose central purpose was not the elimination of the entire group. This, as will be shown, has led to considerable confusion in the existing experiments to classify genocidal incidents and sub-divide them into coherent types. The absence of a strict definition has led to rather indiscriminate list-ings of horrors rather than carefully selected incidents that rationally belong together under the rubric genocide.[5]

Where, however, Lemkin contributed the most was in shedding light on the important distinction between pre-genocidal acts and actual genocide, between policies that en-danger the existence of a group and naked acts of direct killing, between making the group's life increasingly difficult, thereby denying it a future, and outright mass murder. Though he did not coin the word, Lemkin laid the groundwork for the genocide-related term 'culturecide.' Though culturecide is in and of itself not genocide, it does threaten the exist-ence of a group if individual actions assume a quantitative mass whose collective impact can result in the demise of the group. Thus, while denial of special schools or religious activity may not destroy group identity, they do weaken it. In the context of other measures, such as banning a native language and enforcement of cultural assimilation into the official mainstream, the end result will be the eventual evaporation of group consciousness and hence of not only its psychological existence, including group memories, but its physical existence; the former collective will have been blended into another collective. Culturecide, then, at its most benign, that is without the act of killing, can be at the expense of one group whose members quantitatively expand the ranks of another group.

The difficulty with culturecide, though, is that it is hard if not impossible to distinguish from many types of assimilationist policies, thereby creating more confusion than utility in identifying genocidal acts. Culturecide, then, cannot be taken as a prelude to genocide un-less seen retroactively as such in the context of an actual incident of genocide. As such, it is less prelude than a technique. As will be demonstrated, genocides can be classified by the methods employed as well as by antecedents: culturecide seems to belong to both, to the background that could lead to genocide and to the instrumentation used to bring it about. To date, this ambiguity has not been properly recognized whenever the term culturecide has been applied to the study of genocide. The resultant confusion has led to the inclusion of all sorts of events in which cultural politics has been willy-nilly incorporated into genocidal ideology, broadening the category of genocide beyond any useful limits. The increasing desire to be able to predict genocide has led to a search for 'warning signals,' one of which is anything to do with culturecide, with the result that almost any form of human rights violation is to be seen as a step towards genocide.

This dilution of criteria, so that almost any non-lethal assault on a group can be legitimately categorized within the scope of genocide, is off-set by another absurdity in the quest to elongate the list of genocide. Thus, in the absence of a strict definition of the term setting precise limits, enthusiasm to embrace every form of large-scale killing has led to lumping actual genocides in the company of nuclear warfare. The bombings of Hiroshima and Nagasaki have often been depicted as potential genocides despite evidence to the contrary: in brief, both the intention to exterminate the Japanese people and the means to do so were lacking. Once this precedent had been established with a minimum of serious challenge, it was but a step to extend genocide one step further to include an as yet non-event, all-out nuclear warfare which has recently been labelled as 'omnicide,' notwith-standing that for the last two decades international nuclear policy has specifically been designed to prevent such a conflagration, and, more significantly in this context, that omnicide is by definition a contradiction of genocide. Whereas genocide points un-ambiguously to an act of exterminating a group within the general population, omnicide suggests the killing of everybody, regardless of belonging to a group. Just from a military point of view this is sheer nonsense since nuclear bombs, if used at all, are indeed targeted at a nation and not at all nations. With this said, it is time to focus on genocide in order to lay the foundation for a system of classification of all those events that may be properly defined as such according to the limits set by the definition. For, without limits, as scholars have demonstrated, practically everything can be included as genocide — from events that are not genocide at all because no one is killed to events that have not taken place at all and even if they had would not be genocide but something else entirely, such as the terrible consequences of nuclear or for that matter chemical and biological warfare.

The last two are never mentioned by anti-nuclearists, suggesting that their desire to classify the bombs as genocidal is more emotive than intellectual, more the result of political commitment than rigorous mental analysis. If so, then the cause of bringing the Holocaust into a genuine broader context of genocide is little served. The history and, therefore, the classification of genocide and the Holocaust's place in both calls for more systematic work that seeks to escape these pitfalls in which terminology and labels are so generously distributed though with questionable results. Half a century after the Holocaust, at the end of a century marked by repeated genocidal assaults by various governments on parts of their populations, the public deserves a more consistent and reliable exploration of the problems of definition and classification of genocide. In its absence, the temptation to isolate the Holocaust both historically — as an *unicum* — and conceptually — as a mystery — will exert greater and greater influence. As a result it will become increasingly divorced from the history of the 20th century, a century with numerous examples of genocide apart from the Holocaust, at the expense of our ability to understand both. Unless, as will be shown, they are meaningfully integrated, scholarship will be seriously remiss.

Efforts to define genocide since Lemkin's initial attempt in 1944 have generally stumbled between the demands of the academicians and the lawyers. For the former, genocide was primarily a historical phenomenon, multi-dimensional in scope; for the latter, genocide was exclusively a crime. The historian focused on sources and interpretation, the lawyer on evidence and motivation. More often than not, the two argued at cross-purposes in their quest for a working definition, the historian striving to be as inclusive as possible in order to embrace all forms of genocide while the lawyer insists on being as exclusive as terminology permits in order to fix the precise identity of a crime. This has led to typically convoluted definitions by such historians as Helen Fein, who, in 1984, wrote as follows:

> Genocide is the calculated murder of a segment or all of a group defined outside the universe of obligations of the perpetrator by a government, elite, staff or crowd representing the perpetrator in response to a crisis or opportunity perceived to be caused by or impeded by the victim.

A lawyer would immediately pounce on the phrase 'outside the universe of obligation' as unhelpful in a court of law. Furthermore, the killing of a part or 'segment' is too imprecise. When are more than two people 'a part' in order to avoid the logical absurdity of having to deduce that the killing of a few is in fact genocidal? Is, for example, the killing of several hundreds or even thousands of Kurds by either Iran or Iraq an act of genocide or a traditional act of the state protecting itself against rebellions by a national minority? The danger of inserting the concept 'part' so dilutes the idea of genocide that one may, in the name of consistency, have to include a majority of mass killings under the rubric of genocide, with the results that one ends up with everything rather than with a discreet selection. Fein would have served her needs better by associating genocide with the killing of a designated group by a government or its representatives.[6]

State Crime I

HENRY R. HUTTENBACH

A second difficulty, again through the eyes of the legal mind, stems from Fein's use of 'calculated.' By this she means intention. Legal tradition, of course, in the context of individual murder, lays great stress on intention; in its absence, murder is reduced to manslaughter. Genocide, however, is not murder; nor is it mass murder, that is the killing of many people, Fein's 'segment.' It is the annihilation of an entire group, whether intended or not. If qualified with the motive, as done by Fein, then, as any lawyer will point out, the crime will not have been committed because the motive was absent. Very few governments can be legally indicted to the satisfaction of the standard rules of evidence for their intentions; nevertheless, they can be found guilty of having caused the elimination of a group by one means or another. The crime of genocide, therefore, must stand on the result first and foremost, and only partially, indeed secondarily, on the basis of intention. Motive lies in the murky waters of ideology and the rhetoric of propaganda pronouncements. It could be argued that intention is only a factor when it is a matter of determining whether large-scale killings are indeed reflective of a more encompassing program of extermination. Motive only enters into the calculus of establishing guilt for having committed genocide when it becomes necessary to determine whether partial destruction of a group once interrupted was indeed a prelude to total annihilation. Initially, though, for the historian as well as for the lawyer, motive and result must be kept apart, though not divorced from one another. Simply put, genocide — the destruction of a group, the *physical* destruction of an entire segment of the population — is just that. In this case, the term segment is synonymous with group and not with a part of a group. In addition, the group need not be initially 'targeted' as many definers have tended to modify the victims of genocide. For, once again, this term implies intention. Targeted or not, the issue is the fate of the group and not the goals of the perpetrators. For what is to be done if the goal is not achieved? Is it any less genocide that the Hitlerian policy managed to exterminate 'only' 90% of European Jewry? In failing to achieve the ultimate aim of the Final Solution, it could be argued that, in fact, no genocide took place, just as murder did not occur because the victim was not killed. It is best, therefore, as this analysis of the insertion of motive into a definition of genocide illustrates, to define the fact and the crime of genocide in terms of the actual fate experienced by the group.[7]

Where motive enters into the picture is in determining what might have been an act of genocide had not circumstances brought the killing to a stop. These could range from defeat in war, as was the case with the Nazis, a shift in policy, as with the Turkish government towards the Armenian minority, etc. At that point, one is in the position of examining whether actions could be qualified with the modifier genocidal. In the process of categorizing acts of genocide, a secondary category ought to be included under the rubric 'genocidal,' indicative of events that can be clearly identified as genocidal in character even though the crime was not consummated *in toto*. The distinction is important to lawyer and historian alike. Without it, the exact nature of the crime is blurred and guilt is too freely distributed, while the establishing of a category of actual genocides that can be studied as such becomes too inflated. It is for the same reason that in the study of revolution, successful revolutions are segregated from aborted ones and clearly distinguished from rebellions, palace coups and other forms of political action. Genocide deserves the same precision.

The means by which genocide is accomplished ought not to encumber a definition. It is superfluous to murder whether the victim died from shooting or stabbing; the fact that he was killed by the murderer reduces the weapon merely to instrumentation and does not elevate it to an integral determinant. The same holds true for the definition of genocide. There is no need to bring into the discussion the methodology of extermination. Genocide as a crime does not rest on whether the victims were gassed *en masse*, exposed to the elements, starved, or marched to death. These are of interest, upon reflection, to the historian, but not to determine whether genocide took place, only what kind of genocide confronts him. The consideration of means belongs to the process of categorization, to determining typology of genocide. For the moment, it suffices to determine that Lemkin's approach to a definition of genocide is partially flawed by including the ways in which genocide may be executed. This is a similar weakness as that which mars Fein's definition, namely, her linking motive and result.

From the above review of the strength and failings of prior definitions, it emerges that genocide is best served as a concept to be clarified by as simple a definition as possible. That is to say, genocide is the destruction of a specific group within a given national or even international population. The precise character of the group need not be spelled out. Again, Fein and others undermine the efficacy of their definition by trying to list all major categories of groups that have been or might be victimized. Since, by definition, the list can never be complete, it is best not appended, not even for purposes of illustration. The individual categories of groups will emerge in the categorization on the basis of prior genocidal activity. Jack Nusan Porter's well-meant listing of broad categories is distracting, at best. He enumerates the following groups that qualify for genocidal victimization: 'sexual, racial, religious, tribal, ethnic or political . . .' This poses all sorts of difficulties, not the least the question of what about other unmentioned or as yet unspecified categories because the evidence about the future is not yet in? His list of categories is not only incomplete but artificial, or even capricious, because several of the items reflect involvement with contemporary issues such as feminism and homosexuality. Though homosexuals were victimized by the Nazis and occupied a prominent place in the concentration camp world, they were not genocidally victimized, though that does not deny the brutality they experienced during the years of Nazi terror. Unfortunately, though, it is only political strategy to link homosexuals with Jewish victims in order to bring attention to a group that might otherwise be ignored as a result of contemporary insensitivity. Similarly, while feminists justifiably seek to add their issues to the agenda of historic debates, they are misplaced in the arena of genocide. So far, there have been no incidents of genocide against women *per se*. True there were about three million Jewish women who perished in the Holocaust, but they were not selected on account of their gender. To segregate them from the male victims is not only to distort reality by pretending there was a distinct 'female' experience of the Holocaust, but to create an ahistoric category of genocide that not only never took place but according to common sense probably never will take place, no matter what exaggerated fears feminists might harbor. One must take care, therefore, not to insert into the list of modifying categories issues that are only remotely or not even related to genocide except by a non-historical leap of the imagination or due to a personal political agenda which corrupts the process of definition and subdivision.[8]

This is particularly true for Porter's substitution of 'minority' for what Fein calls correctly a group. By associating genocide with minority experience, Porter commits a multiple error. To begin with he focuses myopically on the Holocaust, assuming, supposedly, that the victims of genocide are by definition a minority in the quantitative sense, i.e. a small segment of the whole population as were the Jews in the Third Reich, a mere fraction of one percent. However, that quantitative minority became considerably larger once the Nazis entered Austria, then Czechoslovakia and finally Poland. In the latter place, the Jews were a sizable minority. One must ask: would the Nazis have halted their extermination program had the Jews been quantitatively a majority anywhere? This is not asked sarcastically but with the intention of underscoring the unsatisfactory nature of the term 'minority.' What are we to do were the white South African regime to turn genocidally upon its black majority? Are Porter and similar ones prone to focus genocide on the fate of minorities suggesting that genocide is only possible when the majority turns on a minority? Of course not. Understood in its literal sense, minority is, therefore, a poor substitute for group in any definition of genocide. It has, however, thanks to the politicization of language that took place during the 60s and 70s, acquired a definite new meaning, more along the lines of a code word. Minorities signifies peoples of non-white races — American Blacks, American Indians, Latinos — who also happen to be numerically a minority in the U.S.A. setting; however, minorities can also and does refer to non-numerical minorities, namely, women, as just one example, or the peoples of the Third World, who are clearly a majority. Given this dimension, the word is inappropriate in the context of a definition for genocide, especially when the more neutral 'group' is available.

We must now turn our attention to one more common element in standard definitions of genocide, that is the stress of government initiative. Most, if not all students of genocide assume that genocide, namely, the wholesale elimination of a group, is only possible under the auspices of a government, presumably because the power to commit the act is only available on that level of society. Anything short of the state, it is tacitly stated, lacks the organizational means to harness administrative will and violence sufficient to endanger the existence of a group. These conclusions are based on observation of past exterminational practices. Nevertheless, the proposition needs to be tested whether it is necessarily true for the future, that genocide policy can only be executed by government institutions. That may have been true to date, but, given the technological revolution of the electronic age, it is no longer science-fiction fantasy to imagine a non-governmental agency possessing both the resolve and power, under the right circumstances, to engage in genocidal activity. Given the fratricidal relations prevailing among rival tribes in some African post-colonial nations, for example, it is not inconceivable to envision a well-armed tribe, possibly allied with a few others, murderously turning on its mortal enemy. The victim tribe, given the weakness of the central government and its inability to intervene speedily, could be overwhelmed before domestic or international help would arrive in time to save it from elimination. The events in Burundi during the 60s are a case in point when the Watutsis (the minority) turned on the Hutus (the majority). The polarization of Christian and Moslem tribes in Uganda is a more recent development signalling extreme danger that a massacre is not far below the surface, in a country where the central government's weakness has, so far, only been made up by Kenya's presence. But Kenya's political strength becomes less reliable each day as a government with the power to intervene as it used to do in the post Idi Amin days. In other words, the insistence that a definition of genocide be inflexibly wedded to the idea of a policy originating from the state stems from a narrow understanding of the past in which the Holocaust looms large. In fact, upon closer examination, the role of the state is not so integral to the practice of genocide. It was, after all, not the Belgian government that unleashed genocidal violence upon the peoples of the Congo River; as a matter of fact, it remained uninformed of the atrocities committed by a private organization. The central government, in other words, may or may not be a partner in the crime of genocide; it plays a role, but it need not be the primary guilty party. Elements within society, harboring genocidal intentions, can, with or without the collusion or cooperation of the instruments of the state, embark on a genocide campaign. Under certain circumstances of political disequilibrium, civil strife can erupt generating genocidal forces, one or both sides determined to eliminate the other. Civil war is probably one of the most likely settings for genocide in the future. Lebanon is but one example in which rival parts of a heterogenous population confront each other, each part prepared, if not always capable, to exterminate another. The fears of the Lebanese Christians are not idle; the eyeball to eyeball confrontation of Sunnis and Shiites also bears the markings of a potential genocidal rivalry. A definition of genocide, therefore, ought not to assume that it requires state initiation and participation for that makes ít difficult to pinpoint guilt upon other elements in society who may, in the future, act independently of their government, in defiance of it, or seize the opportunity in the absence of a viable central government and instruments of state. It could just as easily be argued that the best preventative to genocidal tendencies in our midst is a strong state able to curb genocidal instincts operating in certain quarters of the population. Take India, for example, where regional, cultural, ethnic, language and sundry other divisions polarize society into deeply mutually antagonistic units, genocidal outbreaks have been held in check by the presence of a powerful state able to keep rival parties apart. The tragic events in Sri Lanka have the potential for a genocidal confrontation between Tamils and Singalese, especially as a result of a weakened central government unable to prevent the polarization of the two communities in its population. One must conclude, therefore, that despite the fact that genocide has indeed originated most often from the state, the state is not a *sine qua non*. From a purely legal vantage point — since it should never be forgotten that genocide is first a crime — legal considerations in sculpting a definition must take precedence over the needs of academia. Since genocide can conceivably originate and be carried out by other units besides the state, it is legally sounder not to define genocide in terms of one exclusive culprit. For example, even though rape is almost exclusively committed by men, the crime is not defined by the perpetrator's gender. For the same reasons genocide should not be so defined. Simply put, *genocide is any act that puts the very existence of a group in jeopardy.*

Stated so starkly, one avoids the pitfalls of previous definitions. First, there is no mention of a perpetrator. That category is left open for it is a crucial modifier in establishing types of genocides and not genocide itself. Secondly, the definition does not specify what kinds of groups. That category, too, belongs in the process of establishing the kinds of genocide. Thirdly, the short definition avoids any reference to means. They also are factors to be considered when classifying geriocides. Fourthly, the definition omits reference to motivation for the reasons already elucidated. Intention to commit genocide can be extrapolated from ideology, which, if it helps to fuel a particular genocidal incident, rightfully belongs in the discussion about the differences and similarities between one genocide and another. Finally, the definition emphasizes the existential character of genocide in order to force those making the accusation to concretize it with substantive evidence that clearly points in the direction of total annihilation. If the charge is genocide, then the evidence must be genocidal. Too often has the accusation of genocide been made simply for the emotional effect or to make a political point with the result that the number of events claimed to be genocides rapidly increased to the point that the term lost its original meaning. In order to preserve the idea of genocide and not allow the erosion of its explicit meaning, a strict demand for evidence that is truly genocidal must be made. Anything short of the existential character of genocide must be classified otherwise and not appended to the list of genocidal acts at the expense of actual genocide. This will not only undermine the definition's application in a court of law but weaken its utility to the historian and other scholars. Under no circumstances must the threat to collective existence be blurred by the introduction of ambiguous evidence. Anything short of a definition of genocide that dilutes its existential significance is a step away from its reality. That, after all, is one of the least controversial lessons of the Holocaust. If it was about anything, it was the literal removal of a group of people, the Jews and everything associated with them — their entire culture — from the human population. There may be considerable debate about whether that was the original intent of the Nazi regime; but there can be no denying that that was the practical end result. The Holocaust is measured not by the events of 1933 but by the results achieved in 1945. The product of twelve years of antisemitism was the non-existence of European Jewry. To list this crime alongside crimes that were not genocidal, not existential by nature, would be a disservice to the goal of clarification.

The consequences of a strict adherence to the parameters set by our definition might be to limit considerably the number of historical events that truly qualify as *bona fide* geno-cides. The rest, the quasi or semi-genocides and especially the non-genocides can then be relegated to their proper place: the former on the fringes of genocide; the latter assigned their own distinct label to preserve their own particularity. The task of classifying genocide rightly begins by sifting through the numerous instances of seeming-genocides by testing each one in accordance with the standards contained in the definition. The answer to the ques-tion — Is this an act that puts the very existence of a group in jeopardy? — will determine the decision whether or not genocide is involved. Thus, for example, just because deporta-tion took place — a criterion set up by the United Nations Convention — that does not necessarily imply genocide in progress. During World War II, both the United States and the Soviet Union introduced mass deportation of specific groups: President Roosevelt countenanced the mass removal of the Japanese from the West Coast, and Stalin ordered the expulsion of the Tatars from the Crimea. Neither deportation, however, led to the extermination of either group. Both deportations may have been illegal according to one set of laws or another, both were cruel, even inhuman, but none brought on an exist-ential threat or was in the context of one. Hence the need to uphold strict observance of the boundaries of the term genocide as a phenomenon in which an existential struggle is in-volved. Otherwise, as this example illustrates, entirely different categories of deportations are indiscriminately lumped together and the exact character of the deportation transports set in motion by the Nazis is lost. After all, to state the obvious, it is categorically a different experience to board a train from Los Angeles for an internment camp east of the Rockies and to board a train in Frankfurt headed for the Lodz Ghetto or Auschwitz. Destination de-termines the nature of the deportation so that deportation *per se* cannot be applied as a criterion for genocide; it must first be found to be in fact detrimental to the fundamental existence of the group and not just a cause for discomfort, or extreme hardship, let alone violation of civil and human rights. Not unless the deportation is in the context of an exter-minational direction has one the basis for concluding genocidal behavior. Only in this way, by a rigorous application of the definition, will one end up with a set of genocidal incidents that can then be examined so they can be ranked, classified, clustered, sub-divided according to whatever criteria are appropriate. This, for the most part, depends on the reasons for organizing genocides.

The historian would first of all require a *chronological* ordering of genocide. Events in their time sequence offer one kind of opportunity for observation and analysis, though this is not the place to provide a case study. The next way of arranging genocide would be *geographical*. Equi-important to time is establishing the locus of an event; the regional and/or global distribution of genocide can in itself be a source of considerable revelation. Thirdly, genocide has to be placed in a *political* context: the characteristics of the regime — monarchic, parliamentary, dictatorial, of the Left or Right — are usual means for grouping genocides; furthermore, the *political setting* — colonial, occupational, etc. — also helps in sorting out genocides. The *circumstantial* — revolution, civil war, economic crisis — is also a factor for determining the identity of each act of genocide.

At this point, one can turn to the specific component parts of genocide as criteria for setting up distinctions. The first to be considered has to be the *ideological*, the prevailing philosophy, prejudices, myths and attitudes that intellectually and emotionally fueled the act of genocide; this breaks down into two constituent parts, the *organizational* and the *technological*, namely, the administrative side of genocide and the instrumental side, in the case of the Holocaust, for example, the SS and poison gas; sometimes, as in the case of the concentration camps, the institution can also serve as the instrument of extermination. Thirdly, a way of structuring genocide meaningfully is according to the group — *the victims.*

The group targeted for extermination can reflect literally any component of society: religious, aristocratic, intellectual, professional, political, etc. During the religious wars in France during the second half of the sixteenth century, the Huguenots were targeted for extermination; during the French Revolution all aristocrats were imperilled; after the Bolshevik seizure of power the Socialist Revolutionaries and Mensheviks faced elimination. All of these were integral components of the society in which they resided. In the context of genocide, however, there is a second category of groups that is purely artificial, more a construct of the perpetrator than a sociological reality. Thus, for example, the so-called Kulak, a pure invention for the sake of political expediency, but a non-existent group that shared a common sense of identity. In a limited sense this can be said of the group the Nazis called Jews: among them were thousands who had severed their ties with Judaism, many other thousands who had converted to Christianity and identified themselves with their coreligionists, and still more who were bureaucratically classified as Jews according to the 1935 Racial Laws, even though there were one and two generations between these 'Jews' and their Jewish ancestors. In a very real sense then, it is somewhat inaccurate to say that the victims of the Holocaust perished simple for their being Jews; quite a few, significant in this context of classifying the kind of group that was victimized, were not Jews in the sense that they voluntarily belonged to a category of people who viewed themselves as Jews and, therefore, would feel their collective existence endangered by Nazi policy. From this perspective one can speak of the artificiality of the victimized group.

At first glance, this may seem a superficial sub-division of the victimized group; it is, however, crucial in recognizing the nature of genocide as it has been practiced so far. There are groups that exist in their own eyes; and there are groups that only exist in the eyes of the genocidist. This adds an element of caprice to the act of genocide: the intended victims may not be aware that they are part of a group, a group as yet undefined by the regime. Wholesale annihilation of mentally deficient or of physically deformed or of the terminally ill is aimed at a group whose individuals have not organized themselves along those lines. It is society that has ranked them together. In the future, with the acceleration of the bureaucratization of populations, rapid groupings by computer of sundry groups that do not exist in the normal sense of the word may become the victims of exterminational policies. It is, therefore, important to take cognizance of this possibility since the evidence for it is already recorded in recent history.

Given the definition for genocide and the criteria for classification, how does the Holocaust rate? There is, of course, no problem with its meeting the standards of the definition. The history of Nazi antisemitic activities against the Jews, certainly after 1939, is unequivocally on a genocidal track, with hindsight, one could even push that date back somewhat, but that is not an issue that need concern one here. Yet, though it is *in toto* an act of genocide, it is also an act of genocide in progress, that is to say, had the defeat of the Nazis not

interfered, the war against the Jews would have continued; had the Nazis won, their genocidal work against Jews would have spread to England, into the Near East, etc. The goal
was all Jews, not European Jews. From that perspective the Holocaust is a case of genocide interrupted, an unfinished episode, completed only wherever Nazi or German authority was absolute. Where it was indirect such as in the Italian spheres of influence or in
Hungary or Bulgaria the policy of extermination encountered numerous obstacles. Thus,
regionally speaking, in the zones of occupation the Final Solution was virtually total; in
Europe it was semi-complete; globally it was partial genocide: even though Jews did survive to reconstitute their communities, to maintain their identity, and to secure a future, despite the genocidal assault upon them. To give the Holocaust proper identity as an example of genocide, it must be listed in these qualified terms for there are examples, of smaller
proportions to be sure, of the total extermination of a target group such as Indian tribes in
the Amazon territory of Brazil. This observation is important for those struggling with the
dual problem of predicting future genocides and combatting genocides in progress in order
to save the survivors of the target group. A proper comprehension of the Holocaust might
have helped coordinate rescue more consistent to the character of the event. In the case of
the Holocaust, there was time to help; in the future, given the improvement of technology
there may not be any time to come to rescue; one may be faced with a *fait accompli*, with
no survivors sufficient to allow the group to recover, as was the case with post-Holocaust
Jewry. Though entire communities were lost, many constituent parts could rebuild from a
tiny but viable nucleus such as several Hassidic sects.

Once the Holocaust is classified as a case of genocide, one can begin the process of
ranking it alongside others which qualified according to the definition. There is here no
space to make a thorough determination of the Holocaust according to the criteria outlined
above. One can, however, sample a few to illustrate the analytical challenges each one
poses. Locating it chronologically seems to be simple enough if one decides that it paralleled World War II. However, according to an increasing number of scholars studying the
broader genocidal goals of the Third Reich towards the peoples in the east, it is possible
that those engaged in a chronological ranking will not list the Holocaust alone but alongside
genocidal programs aimed at Poles and Ukrainians. It can and is being argued that had the
war been won by Hitler, the consequences of his racial revolution envisioned in the territories east of the Third Reich would have amounted to an eventual extermination of several
categories of Slavic peoples. In other words, chronologically, according to some who apply
the definition of genocide to the experiences of other peoples, the Holocaust would not
stand alone but be a part of a greater whole, a policy of racial destruction of which the Jews
were the beginning and not just an end in itself.[9]

One can see, therefore, that the application of the definition and its results will not be
free from controversy. Differences of interpretation, additional research will provide a dynamic flow prompting continued revision of the list of candidates for acts of genocide. As
such, the Holocaust will find itself in a fluid context as genocide scholarship accepts or re-
jects individual historical events, and, as thinking is refined, adds to the list of criteria to
which each incident of genocide will be subjected. If anything positive has emerged from
this paper, it is hoped that it will stimulate continued debate and exploration of the problematics of reaching a workable definition of genocide and then of applying specific criteria
to each one so that each one's identity will be brought more into focus. From these efforts,
the true outlines of a history of genocide will emerge, a skeletal structure in which the Holocaust will have its own position. Once this is accomplished, the parts will enhance the
whole and the whole will lend meaning to the parts. For the moment, Holocaust and geno-

cide scholarship is a long way from forming a relatively fixed relationship between Holocaust and other genocides. Too much remains to be examined, many assumptions tested, and more information gathered. Given the sensitivity of the subject, considerable patience will have to be practiced, more perhaps than this post-Holocaust generation can muster. The task of defining and categorizing may have to await the next generation, one whose scholars will be able to be more detached if only because of the temporal distance between themselves and the Holocaust. By then, there may have occurred new instances of genocide which will help provide perspective on the Holocaust, and, thereby, make it easier to put into an historical context without incurring the fear of the 'singularists' and violating the sensitivities of those for whom it remains a permanent mystery, beyond the mind's capacity to make it intelligible.[10]

NOTES

1. The Holocaust as a 'watershed' event has fascinated and tempted many scholars in several disciplines, especially theologians and philosophers. See, for example, R. A. Eckardt 'Is the Holocaust Unique?' *Worldview* (September 1979), 31–35, and, most recently, in his major address at the international conference, 'Remembering for the Future,' Oxford University, 12 July 1988; E. Fleischner (ed.) *Auschwitz: Beginning of a New Era?* (New York: KTAV, 1977); H. Jonas 'The Concept of God after Auschwitz,' *Harvard Theological Review* **55** (1962) 1–20; R. L. Rubenstein *After Auschwitz* (Indianapolis: Bobbs–Merrill, 1966). In most instances, the case made is less for the 'extra-ordinarility' of the Holocaust than — unwittingly — for the utter intellectual/emotional unpreparedness of the individual to cope with the perceived dimensions and implications of the Holocaust, a classical case of objective reality overwhelming the observer's subjective capacity to recognise a new *degree* of normality rather than surrendering to the easier conclusion of a new reality *in kind.*

2. (a) Wiesel's notion of the survivor's dilemma as authentic witness but insufficient communicator pervades all his works on the Holocaust. Repeated restatements of this self-perceived trap can be found throughout a recent collection of his speeches and articles edited by I. Abrahamson, *Against Silence* 3 vols. (New York: Holocaust Library, 1985); more recently, Wiesel legitimized his position by anchoring it to a broader historical/philosophical attitude by categorising all human experience as unreachable: 'History is something that never happened; it is written by someone who was not there.' See 'Understanding Eyes' *Hadassah Magazine* (March 1987), 24. While this is not the place to examine analytically the psychological roots of this despair and its fundamentally anti-intellectual underpinnings, it is not inconsistent with similar views expressed by other survivors confronted with the herculean task of translating and communicating their Holocaust experiences. For example, A. Kovner 'The Mission of the Survivor' in Y. Gutman and L. Rothkirchen (eds.) *The Catastrophe of European Jewry* (Jerusalem: Yad Vashem, 1976), p. 681; also J. Felberbaum 'The Loneliness of the Survivors' *Together: American Gathering of Jewish Holocaust Survivors* **1** 15. The survivors' syndrome stemming from this 'paralysis' was clinically observed by Y. Danieli 'Therapists' Difficulties in Treating Survivors of the Nazi Holocaust and their children' Ph.D. Dissertation (New York University, 1981).

(b) The 'thunderclap' or 'earthquake' presentation of the Holocaust as having inaugurated a new era was introduced by A. Cohen *The Tremendum* (New York: Crossroad, 1981).

(c) Fackenheim's search for a 'lesson' or moral obligation arising out of the awareness of what transpired during the Holocaust can be found in 'Jewish Faith and the Holocaust' *Commentary* (1967), *God's Presence in History* (New York: Harper Torchbooks, 1972), and 'The Holocaust and Philosophy' *The Journal of Philosophy* **82** (10), (October 1985), 505–514.

(d) For Rubenstein's views see *op. cit*; also, with J. K. Roth *Approaches to Auschwitz: the Holocaust and its Legacy* (Atlanta: John Knox Press, 1987).

3. R. Hilberg *The Destruction of the European Jews* 3 vols. (New York: Holmes and Meier,

302   HENRY R. HUTTENBACH

1985); G. L. Mosse *The Crisis of German Ideology* (New York: Grosset and Dunlap, 1964), *Nazi Culture* (London: Allen, 1966), *The Nationalisation of the Masses* (New York: Fertig, 1975), *Towards the Final Solution* (London: Dent, 1978).

4. Yehuda Bauer in his many writings has always, on one level, maintained the Holocaust's rational place within human history and its lying within the range of human comprehension, in contrast to Wiesel. Nevertheless, he has steadfastly held to its special character, holding it beyond comparison to other phenomena of genocide, except for secondary criteria. In this way he defends its uniqueness and specificity: see, for example, 'Whose Holocaust' in J. N. Porter (ed.) *Genocide and Human Rights* (New York: University Press of America, 1982) pp. 35–46. In his most recent statement presented at the Oxford conference, Bauer retreats somewhat but in so doing leaves room for a new area of uniqueness, by saying that 'History, after all is not a science . . .' Instead, each historical experience has a certain 'mysterious "something"' by which he infers the Holocaust has such a quality, placing it apart from other genocides. In this case, Bauer speaks of its being 'closer' to 'absolute evil' without either providing a methodology for measuring proximity to evil nor providing one with a spectrum of evils culminating with its totality. 'Is the Holocaust Explicable?' *Remembering for the Future* vol. II, 1967–1975.

On the targeting of Armenians *qua* Armenians see R. Hovannisian (ed.) *The Armenian Genocide in Perspective* (Transaction Press, 1986); on the victimization of the Aché Indians see R. Arens (ed.) *Genocide in Paraguay* (Philadelphia; Temple University Press, 1976).

5. For R. Lemkin's treatise on genocide see his *Axis Rule in Occupied Europe* (Washington, DC: Carnegie Endowment for International Peace, 1944), pp. 79–95.

The problem of pinpointing *bona fide* cases of genocide has been demonstrated rather dramatically in a paper presented to the Oxford conference by W. K. Ezell 'Investigating Genocide: a Catalogue of known and suspected cases and some categories for comparing them.' His list of 31 'cases' since the 18th century is drawn up, by his own admission, not 'on a single rigorous definition of genocide' but on an unstated and unspecified 'cogent definition'. What emerges is a list reflecting the impressionistic responses to historical events on the part of the author who, to be on the safe side, wishes it to be more 'inclusive rather than exclusive' thereby undermining his own goal of segregating genocide from non-genocide.

6. H. Fein 'Anticipating Deadly Endings: Models of Genocide and Critical Responses' in I. Charney and S. Davidson (eds.), *The Book of the International Conference on Holocaust and Genocide* vol. 2 (Boulder: Westview, 1984).

7. In her paper presented at the Oxford conference, Fein replaced the term 'calculated' with the phrase 'purposeful action' which is even less clear, at best an exercise in semantic gymnastics; the substitution is still a focus on intent rather than on result. H. Fein 'Towards a Sociological Definition of Genocide.' (Typed manuscript).

8. J. N. Porter (ed.) *Genocide and Human Rights* (New York: University Press of America, 1982) p. 12.

9. Linking the Holocaust to a broader Nazi policy of multi-genocide in the context of the so-called Generalplan Ost has been the primary concern of the Poles. While the earlier works from Poland were more apologetic and polemic, more recent works demonstrate a greater degree of historical objectivity less obstructed by ideological and nationalistic concerns. See, for example, Karol Popieszalski *Polska pod niemieckim prawem* (Posnan, 1946), J. Gumkowski and K. Leszczynski *Poland under Nazi Occupation* (Warsaw, 1961), and E. Duraczynski *Wojna i Okupacja* (Warsaw: Polonia, 1974). A more recent work strongly influenced by Polish historiography is R. C. Lukas *Forgotten Holocaust: the Poles under German Occupation 1939–1944* (Lexington: The University of Kentucky Press, 1986). Note also H. R. Huttenbach 'The Holocaust as Prelude: The Nazi Demographic Revolution in Eastern Europe,' an unpublished paper presented at a conference in Haifa University, June, 1986.

10. The following is a list of works pioneering the way to identifying, comparing and categorizing incidents of genocide. It should be noted that they are generally unrelated to one another, representing no continuity or evolution of thought.

A. H. Bedau 'Genocide in Vietnam?' in *Philosophy, Morality and International Affairs* V. Held *et al.* (eds.) (New York: Oxford University Press, 1974), 5–46.

F. Chalk and K. Jonasson 'The History and Sociology of Genocidal Killings' (mimeo, 1986).

R. S. Clark 'Does the Genocide Convention go Far Enough? Some Thoughts on the Nature of Criminal Genocide in the Context of Indonesia's Invasion of East Timor' *Ohio Northern University Law Review* **8** (April 1981), 321–328.

V. N. Dadrian 'The Structural-Functional Components of Genocide' and 'The Common Features of the Armenian and Jewish Cases of Genocide' in *Victimology: A New Focus* I. Drabkin and E. Viano (eds.) (Lexington: D. C. Heath, 1974).

V. N. Dadrian 'A Typology of Genocide' *International Review of Sociology* **5** (Autumn 1975), 201–212.

H. Fein 'A Formula for Genocide: Comparison of the Turkish Genocide (1915) and the German Holocaust (1939–1945)' Comparative *Studies in Sociology* **1** (1978), 271–293.

D. Hawk 'Pol Pot's Cambodia: Was it Genocide?' in *Towards the Understanding and Preventing of Genocide: Proceedings of the International Conference on the Holocaust and Genocide* (Boulder: Westview Press, 1984).

I. L. Horowitz *Genocide: State Power and Mass Murder* (New Brunswick: Transaction Books, 1976).

R. Lemarchand 'Ethnic Genocide' *Society* **12**(2), (January–February 1975), 50–60.

J. L. P. Thompson and G. A. Quest 'Redefining the Moral Order: Towards a Normative Theory of Genocide' (mimeo, 1987).

I. Walliman and M. N. Dobkowski (eds.) *Genocide and the Modern Age: Etiology and Case Studies of Mass Death* (New York: Greenwood Press, 1987).

[20]

Corruption and reform 1: 13–32 (1986)
© *Martinus Nijhoff Publishers, Dordrecht. Printed in the Netherlands*

Socialist Graft: The Soviet Union and the People's Republic of China – A preliminary survey

PETER HARRIS

Dept. of Political Science, University of Hong Kong, Pokfulam, Hong Kong

The concept of socialist graft requires some preliminary explanation. Socialist graft is a phenomenon which may puzzle if not actually offend some people. As a rule socialism does not draw undue attention to its possible failings. Indeed, such weaknesses as exist are seen as those inherent in capitalism, not to be found in the theory and practice of socialism. The emphasis in socialist literature is on the iniquities of the alternative, and on the benefits of socialist social engineering.

The objective of this paper is to point out that graft may exist in a socialist order. A gap exists between socialist rhetoric and human fallibility. Socialist graft exists. The term itself of course may require explanation. To take the adjective 'socialist' first, the reference to 'socialist' refers to 'a politico-economic system' where the state controls, either through planning or more directly, and may legally own, the basic means of production! Socialism is a whole system which distinguishes it in large measure from (bourgeois) liberalism.

The term 'socialist' may be preferred to 'communist', because the former allows the observer to consider states which see themselves as being in a transitional state towards some as yet undefined more perfect end. All the classical writings on socialism postulate a goal whose moral core is strong, unsullied by baseness or human degredation. Indeed, corrupt societies are explicitly associated with capitalism and China has never ceased to denounce the capitalist west, frequently as a source of 'spiritual pollution'.

As for the term 'graft', this might well be preferred to possible alternatives such as corruption and 'bribery'. The term 'corruption' itself causes considerable problems in a number of languages. In Russian it is *blat*, in Chinese it is *fubai* or *tanwu*. In English, the term 'corruption' is very broad, and carries considerable moral connotations. Thus we may speak of a corruption society as a 'sick' society without any evidence of overt 'bribery'. We know that power corrupts, but not necessarily in the legal sense. The term bribery, (in Chinese hui lu), is perhaps regarded by students of corruption as an excessively narrow and legalistic term, referring to the passage of money from hand to hand. Bribery may of course lead to (moral) corruption and to the erosion of the legitimacy of the state apparatus itself.

As an alternative, the term 'graft' may be helpful, as it could be described

14

as an 'intermediate' term, carrying connotations both moral and financial. In any case the term 'graft' is well-known and well-understood but may perhaps deserve wider currency than it presently enjoys in the general literature on corruption.

Socialist graft includes many things. Amongst these may be included bribery, corruption, embezzlement, the black market, the place of rank and influence, even careerism and unscrupulous behaviour generally. Socialism is not immune from the frailities of human nature. We need not however go as far as Milovan Djilas to argue that "the Communist economy is perhaps the most wasteful economy of human society."[1] We might however agree with Djilas that: "The use, enjoyment and distribution of property is the privilege of the party and the party's top men."[2] Whatever our stand, there is little room to doubt the existence, at least of socialist graft.

The Marxian millenium: A society without graft

> The statements of Karl Marx are like bats. From one angle they resemble birds, while from another view they look like mice. You see what you want to see, uninhibited by what is actually there.
>
> Vilfredo Pareto
> *Les Systèmes Sociales (Paris, 1902) II p. 332*

Logically, there is no graft in a monastery (unless the monks have a Father Superior who would organise work and praying schedules for bribes or other considerations) and there is no grafat in an anarchist commune (because having removed the state apparatus cooperation has replaced coercion). In a communist state, the position while less obviously clear than in the above two examples, nevertheless presupposes a graft-free net work of human relationships. Marx was very concerned with materialism in one sense, the philosophical view that materialism had supplanted idealism as an explanation of the philosophical order. Marx was not particularly concerned with materialism in the other sense of low and base material values, filthy lucre. As a man who willingly accepted poverty for himself and his family (at times even surviving, though not able to go out, without shoes) Marx would not have seen graft as a special case of human weakness. The economic interpretation of history does not for him ever become a history of bribery.

The invention of money he saw as a progressive factor permitting the

1. Milovan Djilas, The New Class: An Analysis of the Communist System. Praeger, 1957, p. 118.
2. op. cit., p. 60.

15

"development of all forces of production, material and mental." Naturally greed will be present as his *Grundrisse* suggests but such a concept is too 'unscientific' for Marx. The driving force of money is both progressive and impersonal. Marx believed that he had discovered "the economic laws of notion in modern society." He shows us the spirit of capitalism working its way out in the open as it were according to objective historical economic laws. The final social outcome arrives when 'society can inscribe on its banners: from each according to his ability, to each according to his needs', to refer to the words of the *Critique of the Gotha Programme*. Marx implies at times that the evil of private property is eradicable: '*Communism* is the *positive* abolition of *private property*, of human self-alienation'. Now the implication here is that when the 'government of persons' is replaced by the 'administration of things', human lives can be ordered, in the classless state, according to the highest principles. The future as he sees it is one devoid of alienated humanity. Men will no longer be tempted. They will be delivered from evil.

One of the large assumptions of Marx and Engels is that for socialists there is no particular problem in bribery. While accepting that vulgar material desires are feasible, even possible during the period of primitive capital accumulation, we see nothing to suggest that bribery corruption and graft are likely at all to flourish under socialism. Indeed the persistence of graft into the post-revolutionary epoch would entail a further set of economic laws which included bribery. Such an acceptance of bribery in post-revolutionary times would suggest that there were certain human constants irrespective of the relative constraints of class. In short Marx may have "omitted" from his analysis the universal law of corruption. This omission has led to Socialist graft.

The 'philosopher' of bribery who abandoned Hegelianism for materialism is probably Feuerbach. Feuerbach asserted that our 'symbolic dreams', for example the precepts of religion offer no effective explanations but that philosophy is the study of man as defined by experience. The notion that 'man is what he eats' is logically at the heart of a philosophy of graft. Hence the party official in for example a socialist state who accepts bribes cannot be explained by Marxist tenets; he can be explained however in Feuerbachist terms.

Marx himself however cannot envisage the proletariat as animated by brutish materialism. Corruption in all senses of the word is no part of the proletarian future as envisaged by Marx. Rather the future is one of fraternity and class solidarity.

Marx inveighed against capital in an excessively purple passage, but one which Lenin learned by heart. "If money, as Augier says, 'came into the world with a congenital bloodstain on one cheek', then capital comes dripping

16

from head to foot, from every pore, with blood and dirt.''[3] These given attributes of capital somehow disappear with the realisation of socialism. Unless money is abolished then its continuation into a socialist society is likely to pose problems.

Yet Marx was utopian in respect to any idea of graft. Under socialism people would willingly exchange roles without the intervention of restrictive practices: ''in a communist society where nobody has one exclusive sphere of activity, but each can become accomplished in any branch he wishes, society regulates the general production and thus make it possible for me to do one thing today and another tomorrow, to hunt in the morning, fish in the afternoon, rear cattle in the evening, criticise after dinner, just as I have a mind, without ever becoming hunter, fisherman, shepherd, or critic.''[4]

Under these conditions no one should in the ideal socialis state be tempted to use a special knowledge or special position to make money. Indeed, in a socialidt society the distribution of benefits proceeds along well-known lines. Under true socialism ''the distribution of burdens'' should depend on abilities, while the ''distribution of benefits'' should depend on needs: 'from each according to his ability, to each according to his needs'. Men shed their selfishness and contribute towards the general good of all without any thought of personal gain. Socialism envisages men working contentedly to receive what they need, not what they have earned or merited and certainly not what they can 'squeeze' out of their fellow-men.

Of course distinctions are made between socialism and communism. In the former, distributive justice means that people are rewarded according to their work, which implies a form of merit. Hard work will be rewarded. In the final communist state people will be allocated benefits as they need them, and not as they merit them.

Both under socialism and communism private benefits are at most, taboo. There is surely no ground in a socialist society for the existence of graft which permits persons to arrogate private benefits from the public weal. Ideally, graft should not exist under socialism. To possess a special advantage from the public ownership of the means of production must be contrary to the theoretical justification of socialism. Yet graft is in the empirical world as opposed to the ideal world of contemporary socialism, deeply embedded in the current practice of communist states, and examples are constantly cited in the press in various states which notionally owe allegiance to the 'ideals' of marxism leninism. Two particular cases will be examined, the largest socialist states today, namely the Soviet Union and the People's Republic of

---

3. cit. in Robert payne, The Life and Death of Lenin. (W.H. Allen), Pan Books, 1964, p. 148.
4. K. Marx and F. Engels, The German Ideology, see Lewis S. Feuer, Marx and Engels, Basic Writings on Politics and Philosophy. Fontana Classics, Collins, 1969, p. 295.

17

China. There are necessarily many exclusions in our analysis, such as the states of Eastern Europe, Africa and the rest of Asia, other than China. However the choice of the Soviet Union and China in themselves account for almost 1.3 billion people. From even a cursory examination of these two socialist states we are afforded an opportunity to examine some aspects of the relationship between socialism and graft.

Socialist graft: The Soviet case

The road to socialism in the Soviet Union is paved with good intentions. The official Soviet orthodoxy in the U.S.S.R. suggests that the Soviet Union is a class free society of equals in which all would benefit from the selfless leadership of the Communist Party. The promise of 1917 is still the official promise of the 1980s. There is also a Soviet dream. The words of the preamble to the 1977 Constitution offer the official picture in glowing terms: "The Great October Socialist-Revolution, made by the workers and presents of Russia under the leadership of the Communist Party headed by Lenin, overthrew capitalist and landowner rule, broke the fetters of oppression, established the dictatorship of the proletariat and created the Soviet state, a new type of state, the basic instrument for defending the gains of the revolution and for building socialism and communism. Humanity thereby began the epoch-making turn from capitalism to socialism".[5]

The preamble further states: "After achieving victory in the Civil War and repulsing imperialist intervention, the Soviet government carried through far-reaching social and economic transformation, *and put an end once and for all* (my italics) to exploitation of man by man, antagonisms between classes, and strife between nationalities". The virtues of socialism so described are beyond question. In Chapter 2 of the Constitution under *The Economic System* we read: "No one has the right to use socialist property for personal gain or other selfish ends". In short, socialist graft is prohibited by the Soviet Constitution.

The distinction is made between private i.e. personal property and state property. Article 13 states that: "Property owned or used by citizens shall not serve as a means of deriving unearned income or be employed to the detriment of the interests of society". This stipulation offers us a more difficult idea, namely that property advantages should not lead to income which has not been earned (we might wonder whether stock market-type dealings in capitalist societies are here envisaged) or which society might as whole see as

5. Constitution of the Union of Soviet Socialist Republics, October 7, 1977, Novosti Press Agency Publishing House, Moscow.

18

'detrimental'.

Concern is also expressed for state property. In Article 61, we read: "It is the duty of the citizen to combat misappropriation and squandering of state and socially-owned property and to make thrifty use of the people's wealth. Persons encroaching in any way on socialist property shall be punished according to law". The basic difficulty which faces the student of corruption is whether such a moral society exists in the U.S.R.R., and to what extent the rhetoric is at variance with the reality.

Some enthusiasts, and not always all fellow-travellers have seen the Soviet Union as above reproach 'Like Pericles in his *Funeral Oration* at Athens', the Soviet-Citizen could say with truth: "Our citizens attend both to public and to private duties, and do not allow absorption in their own various affairs to interfere with their knowledge of the City's". "The U.S.S.R. was far from the perfect society or the perfect life as yet – but it was moving *faster* (his italics) in its improvement than any previous community in history."[6]

In fact the place of corruption in private dealings in Soviet society is well-established. It is possible to ruin the beautiful theory of marxism-leninism with the ugly fact of socialist graft. Opportunity for graft were early presented to socialist revolutionaries and were undoubtedly taken.[7] The nature of the economy in early Soviet history (i.e. in the 1920s) presented opportunities for corruption largely because of difficulties regarding the supply of materials. As late as the 1950s we gather that "the use of *blat* is most important as a means of expediting the supply of materials. The Soviet manager faces the perpetual threat that promised materials will neither be delivered on time nor in the right quantity and quality ... he turns to the use of *blat*. "But of course, says Brumberg there are varieties of *blat*, there is "leather blat" and there is "coal blat...[8] To find the correct specialist one needs to find a 'pusher', 'fixer' or *tolkach*. The *tolkach* knows which officials can be fixed. Even K.G.B. officers are known to have a soft spot for extra-curricular bottles of vodka or a few pairs of shoes to forget particular charges.[9]

Attention has also been paid to *strakhova* which signifies 'insurance' or 'security'. Officials can be paid '*strakhova*' money to guarantee planned output at a level below that possible. Thus coal, paper and cotton production

---

6. Andrew Rothstein, A History of the U.S.S.R. Penguin Books, 1950, p. 379.

7. Some studies on Soviet graft were made by Joseph Berliner, Blat is higher than Stalin, in Abraham Brumberg (ed.), Russia under Khruschev. New York: Praeger, 1962. Paul R. Gregory and Robert C. Stuart, Soviet Economic Structure and Performance. Harper, 1981. Hedrick Smith, The Russians. London: Time Books, 1976. K. Simis, USSR: The Corrupt Society. New York: Simon and Schuster, 1982, is a major, if over-committed, source.

8. Berliner in Brumberg, op. cit., p. 156.

9. Brumberg, op. cit., p. 160. According to Simis, the K.G.B. uses black-market networks in order to trap and blackmail foreigners, Simis, op. cit.., pp. 195–199.

levels can be set below capacity or at the other extreme, requirements for raw materials can be pitched at levels for above those necessary to complete the task.

Examples of near-corruption quoted by Brumberg appear to be related to the nature of the socialist system. Falsification and manipulation of data often "solve" problems. On paper they may be no actual difficulties. A sum of money can change hards to keep the records straight and the statistics favourable. The successful manager fulfills or over-fulfills his plan. People can be persuaded to cooperate – for a bribe. To realise the plan (even on paper) people may have to be persuaded to "look the other way". Malenkov himself believed that "such situations ordinarily lead to corruption and degeneration".

Once Stalin saddled that Soviet people with the first so-called 'command economy', the over-bureaucratisation of the economy as well as excessive centralisation and confusion in decision-making promoted temptation. Those who had power have undoubtedly used it to profit themselves. Indeed even before the first five-year plan was introduced elements of a black market emerged. Graft emerged from the earliest days after the revolution. The peasants did not wish to cooperate with those who appropriated their produce so they sold grain on the side – for a profit. At the same time war communism made money suspect. Workers even stole metal, made lighters (essentially consumer goods) and sold them for food.[10] The response to such un-socialist attitudes was the development of a characteristic Stalinist terror.

The 'realist' approach to Soviet politics does envisage corruption in large measure in Soviet society. However there is a long line of opponents of the Soviet state from Trotsky through for example Djilas and a variety of modern critics internal as well as external, who see a dark thread of corrupt practices. This approach, at its most controlled and dispassionate would say: "The heroic era of communism is past. The epoch of its great leaders has ended. The epoch of practical men has set in. The new class has been created'.[11]

One of the most useful analyses is contained in Hedrick Smith's book *The Russians*, and this analysis takes *blat* as the standard Soviet idea on corruption. *Blat* is defined as – "influence, connections, pulling strings". Smith argues that: "In an economy of chronic shortages and carefully paralled out privileges, *blat* is an essential lubricant of life. Smith speaks of '*na levo*', which literally means "on the left", and implies an undercover payment. This may be in kind. On January 1, 1975, *Izvestia* revealed that more than one-third of Soviet private motorists were driving on state petrol.

10. Alec Nove, An Economic History of the U.S.S.R. Penguin, 1976 (Revised) p. 137.
11. Djilas, op. cit., p. 53.

20

The value of such petrol was estimated at 60 million roubles.[12]

Soviet citizens describe corruption as "creeping capitalism", and it is estimated by Andrei Sakharov to involve about 10 per cent of the gross national product – a figure of about 50 billion roubles ($66 billion). There are no figures on the level of corruption in the Soviet economy but 10 per cent could be a fair estimate based on the British economy.[13] There is a Russian saying, '*blat silnee sovnarkoma*' sometimes previously 'blat is higher than Stalin' which argues that influence is stronger than the government. The usurpation of legitimate government organisations and state norms by corrupt practices is widespread. A particular example is in *defitsitny* or deficit-goods. When scarce goods arrive at a shop, assistants secrete these away; and supply them to those prepared to pay a large discount. The *Beryozka* shops "are an open invitation to black market profiteering". Only persons with properly gained and permitted hard currency may shop there, but products on sale for 4 roubles may reach 40 roubles on the street.

There is little information regarding large and influential syndicates. Smith refers to a corrupt syndicate in textiles and fabrics in Lithuania, another dealing in fruit juice in Azerbaijan and a third dealing with gems in Moscow. A network involving Tadzhikstan products (by which products were systematically undervalued to the profit of one Mikhail Laviyev) brought the death sentence for the man involved.

Soviet Georgia has a particular reputation for corruption, and appears to be particularly resistant to purges. The first Secretary of the Georgian party, Vasily Mzhavanadze, was believed to have been involved in large-scale corruption, including Mafia-style drug syndication.[14] In June 1981, Y.A. KobaKahidze was executed for housing graft in Georgia.

Blat is part of influence and is a Russian, (and Soviet) device Solzhenitsyn offers a picture of bribery in the judicial sector which has led one writer to comment that "breach of the law is an integral part of the Soviet economy".[15]

12. Smith op. cit., pp. 82–83.

13. In Britain, one assessment puts the black economy at 6 per cent 8 per cent of the economy. This would amount to £15,000 million. Times, Feb. 1 1982. See also the Sunday Times, Cheats at Work: An Anthropology Workplace Crime, January 31 1982. The latter was a summary of the book by Gerald Mars of the same name 1982, Allen & Unwin. In the U.S.A. it could be as high as US$428 billion (U.S. Treasury estimates). Britain and the U.S.A. are covered respectively by Alan Doig, Corruption and Misconduct in Contemporary British Politics (Harmondsworth Penguin) 1984 and Michael Johnston, Political and Public Policy in America (Montery, CA: Brooks-Cole).

14. Soviet Georgia's legendary reputation for graft is particularly noted amongst diplomats in Moscow, see Simis, op. cit., p. 53. Reports of executions for corruption in Georgia were reported early in 1982. Edward Shevarnedze commented: "Once the Georgians were known throughout the world as a nation of warriors and poets; now they are known as swindlers".

15. Simis, op. cit. p. 53. Berliner in Brumberg op. cit., p. 173.

"It may seem strange to us now, but it is a fact that in those thunderous years bribes were given and taken just as tenderly as they had been from time immemorial in old Russia and as they will be in the Soviet Union from here to eternity".[16]

Solzhenitsyn states that "bribery was particularly rife in the judicial organs." The Cheka (Counter Revolutionary organ) "often depended upon bribes". The sums involved were considerable. Solzhenitsyn discusses the power of gold. "But if you had gold, you could determine the extent of your torture, the limits of your endurance and your own fate." He argues: "If in fact you had no gold, then your situation was hopeless".[17] Of course the early part of Soviet history just after the Revolution differed in that some persons might still have family gold to bribe their gaolers. However Solzhenitsyn is inclined to offer a picture of the moral corruption of power rather than dwell excessively upon the more petty aspects of simple bribery. The object of Gulag was, as Solzehnitsyn saw it, the total degradation of human beings, who were the objects of what was euphemistically called the Sewage Disposal System.

In spite of everything, corruption has flourished. The role of *wziatka* (as baksheesh is known in the Soviet Union) is central. At low levels it is rampant but at the highest levels information is less forthcoming. As already mentioned, the first secretary of Georgia, Vasili M. Mzhavanadze (and a member of the political bureau in Moscow) was fired for corruption, but nothing of this matter was revealed in the Soviet Press, even though 50,000 people were arrested in the subsequent police investigation. Mzhavanadze was replaced by Edward Schevarnadze, his former K.G.B. head. Little was revealed of the misdeeds of Ekaterina Furstseva formerly minister of culture who was quietly retired after having built a luxurious *dacha* for herself, using state materials and labour costing about 120,000 roubles. In Azerbaidzhan, the Chief executive of a textile plant and his accomplices, including a Justice Ministry inspector and a public prosecutor were found guilty of transforming a textile plant to private use and embezzling 2 million roubles (about $3 million).

The "second economy" of the Soviet Union

Below the 'first economy' is the 'second economy' in the command state of the U.S.S.R. The second economy is private, outside the rigid central plan of the public or state sector. Gregory Grossman believes of the second economy

---

16. Alexander Solzhenitsyn, The Gulag Archipelago. Collins & Fontana, 1974, p. 311.
17. Op. cit., p. 53.

22

that closely tied to it is widespread corruption of officialdom.[18] The second economy fulfills at least one of the two tests following. Firstly it is directly for private gain and secondly it significantly contravenes existing law.

There are many examples of the second economy and are given in the press in profusion. Typical examples include the payment of higher differential fees for professional services on the part of medical men or dentists. A whole state enterprise may in fact be engaged in private production or the provision of services, such as the repair of cars. The second economy will naturally link into the general area of the purchase of influences and other favours which only members of the *party* bureaucracy (or to a lesser extent the *state* bureaucracy can provide.

In 1982, a very significant case, involving Brezhnev's family itself was reported on 4 March 1982 in *Pravda*.[19] On 29 December 1981, diamonds were stolen from the home of a female lion-tamer with the Moscow circus. These were discovered to be in the home of a singer in the choir of the Bolshoi Theatre, Boris Buryatiya, who was believed to be the "close friend" of Galina, Brezhnev's daughter.

Galina's husband was Lt. Gen Yury Churbanov, First Deputy head of the MVD (Ministry of Internal Affairs) police which investigated the robbery. Buryatiya was arrested on 29 January by the K.G.B., so it is believed whose tasks include the control of speculation of and bribery in valuables and hard currency. Semen Tsvigun, First Deputy Head of the K.G.B. committed suicide apparently because he was reprimanded by Suslov who also died of a stroke late in January 1982.

The nature of the corruption involved was related to the department for Visas and Registrations. Those who travel abroad have reputedly had to pay 3500 roubles rather than the official rate of 350 roubles and the illicit funds so gained have found their way back to Buryatiya who could indulge a flamboyant life style in consequence, as well as some degree of immunity from arrest given his protectress who was the daughter of Brezhnev.

The scandal was only the tip of a very large Soviet iceberg at the bottom of which are found innumerable examples. In 1970, a quarter of all alcohol consumed in the U.S.S.R. was produced and also supplied through the second economy. In 1972 about 500 litres of petrol were stolen and re-cycled into the black market. Information from Jewish emigres suggests that the second economy provides ten per cent of earnings with particular areas of interest in service industries such as appliance repairs, hairdressers and beauty shops.

18. Gregory Grossman, The Second Economy of the U.S.S.R., Sept. 1977, pp. 25–40, Problems of Communism. More generally, see Stuart Henry, The Hidden Economy: The Context and Control of Borderline Crime. (Martin Robertson) 1978.
19. See also the Times and Sunday Times, 4 March 1982.

23

Russians earn 175 roubles per month on average; they are excluded from ownership of precious stones in consequence.

The market does not allocate resources in such a system; this is the task of officials. But a cash economy exists and so does the trade in diamonds and precious metals. It is therefore no surprise to learn that diamonds in large quantities were discovered in the homes of those with important connections.

Western goods are in great demand. In a Moscow radio programme we learn that Soviet-made jeans costing 60 roubles a pair, (when obtainable), are resold at 200–250 roubles and an attractive dress bought at 40 roubles can fetch 200 roubles.[20] Shoes, ornaments, rings, ear-rings, necklaces and other trinkets are sold at "monstrous profits" on the black market. The use of vodka *na levo* is virtually on institution, whose side effect is part of the sub-culture of Soviet alcoholism. Arising from the fact that corruption is now "endemic in every layer of society" we need to offer some generalisations about the consequences of this all-pervasive graft. Firstly, graft in the Soviet Union has become a part of the political succession battle. Accusations of graft are a handy means of denigrating one's opponents. Whether true or not, an accusation of graft is always a potential means of undermining opponents in a power struggle. A second aspect of Soviet socialist graft lies in the light which it sheds upon the bureaucracy and the inefficient conduct of the Soviet Union's planned economy, whatever the merits or dements of the planned economy, in practice it has offered many examples of graft largely because administrative dysfunctions prevail. Penalties do not appear to have much impact. All Soviet citizens know that the death penalty can be given for corruption. In September 1981, the criminal code was altered to increase the penalty for corruption more generally. In November a confidential letter was apparently read (according to a western journalist Leopold Unger) at local party meetings held *in camera*. In January 1982, the head of the anti-corruption department Boris Zabotin was reported as having been assigned to the Department of the Interior. The new post was raised to deputy minister status by an announcement Lt. Gen Yuri Churbanev, the chief minister of the Interior Ministry police, the husband of Galina, daughter of Brezhnev. Hence graft, nepotism and intrigue are found closely associated in Soviet life. The London *Times* indeed refers to an "atmosphere of Byzantine intrigue and scandal", in its assessment of the Galina scandal.

The Soviet Union has shown clear evidence of what might be called 'degenerate commandism'. In other words, the Soviet machinery of planning reforms badly and is prone to graft. During the long Brezhnev years (1964–1982) it was widely believed that the command economy had an available evidence degenerated. After Brezhnev's death, the short-lived rule of

20. Moscow Radio, 30 September 1979.

24

Andropos was associated with tentative reforms at both the organisational and personnel level.

Adropov's supposed 'liberalism' was taken up by Gorbachov, when he became general Secretary in March 1985 after the death of Andropov's successor, Chernentio. Gorbachov appeared to envisage that he could retain the command economy albeit as a cleansed economy. The 1986 budget plans, for example, saw a 4 per cent growth increase largely through improved labour productivity. In short, Gorbachov thought that socialist graft could be eliminated without a structural change in the economy.

The problem is that there is a command economy in the Soviet Union and there is also graft. Are the two related? One commentator, K. Simis, argues that the present Soviet system is a necessary condition for the emergence of socialist graft. Simis belives that the heart of the people is good. The system is the cause of all problems. He argues: "The Soviet government, Soviet society, cannot rid itself of corruption as long as it remains Soviet. It is as simple as that." Socialist graft is deep-seated. Simis is in no doubt: "Corruption permeates the life of *Homo sovieticus* ..." Gorbachov by contrast sees the matter of socialist graft (even if he admits of its existence) as a cleansing operation only. Sceptics think that graft must continue in the Soviet Union as long as the structure exists. Both agree however to the extent that opportunities do exist for misbehaviour. Both agree that the Soviet economy does not provide goods required in sufficient quantities. In consequence, people seize the opportunities provided to develop networks of graft. But, we only know about breaches of the rules because these may be recorded in *Pravda* or in organs of the press. We are likely to hear reports of isolated instances of graft rather than be able to probe networks of graft. Syndicated graft is more difficult to prove than isolated examples.

If there were such a thing as a 'pure' socialism it may well be that graft would not develop in socialist states. Paralled to the concept of imperfect competition in the West, there is, in socialist states, a concept of imperfect socialism. In practice, to use one of Mao Zedong's favourite words, there are many 'contradictions' in present-day Soviet society. The continued existence of socialist graft is one of them.

Socialist graft: The case of China

Lenin and other Russian Marxists at the turn of the century had the task of reconciling their understanding of Marxism with the reality of Russia. Marx gave some attention to the Asian (or Asiatic) mode of production, noting the relationship between oriental despotisms and control over water, which was elaborated in detail by Wittfogel in his concept of a hydraulic society.

Resource allocation is naturally associated with politics in a debate over the control over the means of production. The worker may have nothing to sell except his labour. the Chinese tradition of graft is very deep-rooted. In pre-revolutionary imperial times corruption was entrenched int he mandarinate. The 'long-fingernailed mandarins' always creep back and so does bureaucratic corruption. In place of the imperial bureaucracy the bureaucracy of the party has given us its version of graft.

For a number of years, the extent of bureaucratic graft has been concealed. Mao's long years in power were seen as years of rigorous austere proletarian morality. Yet in the years since Mao's death, graft has taken firm hold of many sectors of Chinese society. Chinese understanding of graft is exceedingly broad. In particular it encompasses the idea of embezzlement which itself implies misappropriation of socialist property, which itself is a moral notion. A survey of graft in China in a number of Hong Kong newspapers in February 1982 lays particular stress on embezzlement. In a socialist society embezzlement is of particular concern; in a capitalist society, embezzlement is a private vice, and the main loser is the capitalist. In China, embezzlement is equated with graft.

The revelations have been in the correct sense of the word, sensational. "Rarely has any Communist country provided such sensational information about illegal goings-on inside its ruling party."[21] There is "a well-publicised campaign to crack down on corruption, abuse of position and what looks like a near- epidemic of organised crime by ranking officials".[22]

This vigorous anti-corruption drive took place in the period following the removal of Hua Guofeng in 1980. Laws were introduced which provided heavy penalties for graft, including the possible use of the death penalty, Many party articles inveighed against the deterioration in moral standards.

A typical example came from the *New China News Agency* dated April 13, 1982. The Agency argued that the struggle for "communist integrity" and against "corruption" is "vital". In the past two or three years, the article said, "activities in smuggling, bribery and theft have increased sharply, causing serious economic damage". The culprits were to be punished and those "very few" organs of the bureaucracy responsible "which are really rotten to the core must be reorganised or dismissed."

The People's Daily (8 December 1981) revealed the existence of widespread graft in Wuxi with 1532 cases of bribery reported. Xinhua, the China Daily paper reported the prosecution of 20,000 economic criminal cases, and a 10

21. Time, March 15 1982, p. 17. See also David Bonavia, Mandarins on the Make, Far Eastern Economic Review, Hong Kong, June 18 1982 which argues that graft has reached epidemic proportions in China.

22. Time, op. cit., p. 17, February 7, 1982.

26

million yuan tax evasion, including "smugglings, speculation, graft, embezzlement, bribery and tax evation." In Shenzhen, a number of party officials were punished and the assistant director of the city post and telegraphs was dismissed for misappropriating renminbi totalling 50,000 (US $29,410). He built a house with the proceeds. Shenzhen is one of four so-called Special Economic Zones in China which is permitted certain trading relations with the outside world. Smuggling and embezzlement of course are likely to be bedfellows with graft.

A veritable torrent of cases appeared late in 1981 and in 1982. The *People's Daily* announced a web of corruption involving 130 offices, departments and factories for the illegal selling of over 1300 motor vehicles. The *People's Daily* exposed electric power supply corruption in which officials embezzled enough to start their own "treasury" with assets of 1.5 million yuan (about US $1 million). Investigators were frustrated at every turn. The electricity supply bureau in Anhui province, Hao country was known to the local people as the 'electric despot'.

Telecommunications in Guanhou gained (Canton) a reputation for being 'corrupt'. A husband and wife syndicate bought up television sets, watches, electric calculators and sold them as far as Shangtong province in the North. In Fujian province the Xiang Nan party leader declared war on graft and related economic, crimes, arguing that "corruption is a two-way struggle. Beijing itself reported 9853 smuggling cases and 223 cases of corruption in the capital in 1981.[23] Party officials in Anhui were in trouble as well as in Hainan Island. Hainan Island's graft was particularly noteworthy, where the head of the Bureau of Supplies was expelled from the party for the second time for offences involving graft.

In Liaoning Province, one swindle led to the "bankruptcy" of seventeen factories. Party officials were involved (Ma Xinguang and Lin Yung) and the factories closed down. Ma received five years. In Shanghai serious swindling and profiteering took place, involving 26 officials. Bad accounting as well as deliberate swindles were encountered in Wenzhou, 250 miles south of Shanghai. One rationale advanced for these practices by the *People's Daily* was that city leaders had misinterpreted national policy on the loosening of restraints on the economy to mean 'money above all'. They "gave the greenlight to speculators and swindlers". "Some leaders of these units", said *People's Daily*, "provide the criminals with nearly everything they needed – capital, titles, letters of introduction, work permits and blank but validated contract forms by the thousands". A massive campaign against bureaucratic corruption was instituted by Den personally. Early in 1982 Den appeared to

23. South China Morning Post, 15 April 1982 quoting New China News Agency. People's Daily February 8, 1982.

think that the proliferation of bureaucrats in the state and party had gone too far. He set out to trim the over-weightly structure of the bureaucracy. The suggestion was that bureaucratic corruption (i.e. graft which stems form bureaucratic practices) is the major enemy.

Graft in China has moved form administrative organ to administrative organ, from the state to the party to the shop floor.[24] Factories have entered into systematic conspiracies to evade taxes. Industry, has suffered Members of the party regularly use public funds for private houses and cars. Bank employees embezzle funds on a large scale. Even disaster relief money has been misappropriated. In the first eight months of 1981 the electricity power industry "lost" US$8 million worth of transmission equipment. A leading official in Beijing, Jiang Shaoyan who headed a rectifier factory took 9,600 yuan (US $6000) in bribes. He had previously refused to release the money due to a certain factory giving as his reason that its products were defective.

Countering graft in China has proved to be extremely difficult. In stimulating enterprise and individual initiative, (as opposed to ideological fervour), a genie had been let out of a bottle. The *China Daily*, quoting Qinynian Bao pointed out that "indiviudalism cannot exist without personal gain but personal gain does not necessarily mean individualism". The official Chinese press fulminated against the selfish attitudes of people who had been undermined by the "silver-coated bullets of bourgeoisie". Indeed one person dismissed for graft, Lin Jinyi was daring enough to comment that "if you report me, I'll complain to the capitalist press".[25]

Red Flag (Honggi) stated that it was wrong to see corruption as a small matter. "Backdoor dealings, favouritism, seeking of privileges and other bad practices," these cause discontent among the masses, tarnish the image of the Party and lower its prestige.[26] The writer, Wang Renzhog was a director of the Propaganda Department under the Party Central Committee. The sugar coated bullets of the bourgeoisie had influenced all persons and all ranks in Chinese society, judging by the mass of evidence coming forward.

A Discipline Inspection Committee or Central Commission on Inspecting Discipline, appears to be the body charged with surveillanace of graft. Graft is however apparently deeply entrenched, and while the leadership believes that graft can be eradicated by resolute means, it also recognises that graft is not easily eradicated. A Decision on the Severe Punishment of Serious and Harmful Economic Crimes was passed by the Standing Committee of the Fifth National People's Congress in February 1982.

24. Economist, December 17, 1981. See also John P. Burns, Reforming China's Bureaucracy, 1980–1982, Asian Survey, June 1983.
25. South China Morning Post, February 15, 1982.
26. China Daily quoting Red Flag, March 6, 1982.

28

Now the difficulty with evaluating Chinese graft lies in the overall general conception of graft which is comprehensible in Chinese thinking on the matter. Graft is to be seen as more than just bribery, and corruption in China suggests a moral element as well as a minor pecadillo, resulting from understandable human weakness. The Chinese would not easily differentiate between forms of bribery, speculation, fraud, embezzlement and smuggling. As in most socialist societies there are economic crimes and as the means of production are supposed to be publicly owned, embezzlement is perhaps the most common. The embezzler misappropriates resources which properly belong to the state. This is contrary to the Criminal Code, Article 155. Yet the embezzler will be likely to be involved in the giving and taking of bribes because bribes are required to sustain the mechanics of the system. Bureaucratic corruption frequently depends upon syndicates which control the allocation of scarce resources.

The student of graft in China has ample raw data on which he can draw. Examples of graft running into hundreds of millions of yuan have been noted from the following areas: Anxiang (Hunan), Baotau, Beijing, Changde, Datong, Guangzhou (Canton), Hainan, Heilongjiang, Jiangsu, Jilin, Liangsui, Nanyang, Oizhou, Shanxi, Sichuan, Tienjian, Wuhan, Xinmin, Yanshan, Yuling, Zgabghian, Wuhan, Xinmin, Yanshan, Yuling, Zhangjiang. The categories into which these examples fit will vary. They may relate to bribery or embezzlement in some cases, or to fraud, and even to speculation.

In Chinese eyes. graft is involved in all these. However, if it is accepted that all property belongs to the state, then embezzlement further complication is that western notions of private property do not fit Chinese property theories even in classical China family, rather than individual, ownership is important. Certainly the private misappropriation of public goods should not be tolerated.

Socialist graft is interpreted in China in a number of ways. Some people such as Chen Yun see the huge volume of graft cases as the result of some defects in economic philosophy. Too rapid a move in the direction of economic liberalism can, Chen Yun appears to believe, only unsettle China, giving rise to graft and other evils.

Deng Xiaoping believes that as long as it catches mice it does not matter whether a cat is black or white. the economic philosophy may not be so worrying, within certain political limits, as long as the economy performs well. Deng appears to see the problem of graft more as a fault of poor organisation – or bureaucratism. Deng's position is not far from that of Gorbachov. If the currently inefficient bureaucrats were to be removed then the position would be much healthier. But whatever the interpretation, the numbers of cases investigated in China run into the millions. The pages of

29

Renmin Ribao offer numerous examples of continuing socialist graft. Particularly bad cases receive the death penalty.

Corruption in China is a moral issue and transcends the existence of mere bribe taking. In China moral imperatives, whether Confucian or Maoist have been placed before the population as ideals. With the demystification of Mao in the late 1970s, economic, rather than political, objectives were emphasised. Modernisation became a surrogate ideology, but it was a vision of a richer state in which economic growth was stressed. With the loss of Maoist moral fervour, a reaction appeared to set in. Materialism, so long theoretically unacceptable, became a tenable part of the theory of modernisation because the latter stressed the economic benefits of modernity in China. On May 8 1982, *Xinhua* stressed that corruption might be curtailed by a paper understanding of those parts of the writings of Lenin and Mao which warn Communists against 'degeneration', and seek to 'maintain the communist purity and not permit corruption or moral laxity'.

Yet in China, as with the Soviet Union, friction within political leadership and faction-fighting have frequently been associated with accusations of graft. Those groups who are frequently depicted as 'corrupt' are described as such as part of a campaign of political intrigue. Since 1980 China has been inundated with many accusations of corruption. Previously cases of graft would be concealed or covered up because to reveal such cases would be to reveal that a socialist system had certain moral deficiencies. The period of Maoist rule was marked by a moral intensity which admitted of no failings in the superiority of proletarian morality. A curious paradox existed with a mass psychology coexisting with a God-like man of destiny. Morality was the gift of the Great Helmsman. Suggestions of any deviation from the path of righteousness were rarely entertained.

The contrast with the present situation of laxness in public life is all the more remarkable. The leaders of China see the problem as one of straight forward bureaucratic graft. Hence Zhao Ziyang, Prime Minister of the P.R.C., told a standing committee at a meeting that the top echelons of the bureaucracy within the state apparatus would be cut by almost one-half, from 98 ministries to 52 with a staff reduction of about one-third. The number of ministers would be cut from about 1000 to 35. Vice-premiers would be removed and lower-level bureaux, which have offered comfortable sinecures to men long into their eighties, would be cut in half.

In China, unlike the U.S.S.R. corruption is not only openly admitted, but is seen to be a problem of immersely serious dimensions. The contrast is pointed out between the poverty of the masses and the riches of the party mandarinates. In the Soviet Union no such admissions are made. Graft in China is confessed, *mea culpa, mea maxima culpa*; in Soviet Union occasional precadilloes are shamefacedly admitted. The extent of graft in the Soviet

30

Union as in many Eastern European states is hard to discern because the matter will most frequently be covered up. But the self-perpetuating oligarchies which all so often pass for socialist states ensure the continued prosperity of those who benefit from party control.

Socialist graft is obviously part and parcel of the panoply of irresponsible socialist power structures. Party officials effectively control the politics, economy and lives of the people over whom their power is uncontrolled. The arrival of 1984 (Orwell's nomenclature) has already been noted by *apparatchiki* who call black/white according to their will. When in China ration vouchers arrive, the party secretary in the locality gives them to his cronies.[27] The new party bosses are installed with gifts. Advantages and perguisites are in-built in the system. Socialist graft is the graft of poverty; its capitalist counterpart shares relatively a greater degree of affluence. Socialist graft is a double failure; a bureaucratic failure (as its leaders argue) but also a moral failure (which its leaders could never admit).

Conclusion

There can be little doubt that graft is likely to exist within modern socialist states. Socialism confers no immunity upon its practitioners in their confrontation with graft. Yet, the point further arises whether socialist states (i.e. states controlled by communist parties) are in fact *more* prone to the temptations of graft than are non-socialist states. There are a number of reasons why socialist states in fact demonstrate greater opportunities for graft than do non-socialist states.

1. Socialist states are hierarchical, even at times 'feudal', in their structure. To please a superior became an imperative. There are no alternative constituents. The temptations for graft readily manifest themselves under such circumstances.
2. Socialist states are most frequently self-perpetuating oligarchies. Power is bureaucratically structured in such a way as to inhibit the inflow of new talent. Such talent may be able to advance only through illegal and extra-legal means. Bribery may be the best way forward to a career. *Blat* therefore flourishes.
3. Persons outside the charmed circle of power unable to channel their activities into the prescribed pattern of political activities, principally through the party structures, may seek alternative outlet in graft. Eastern Europe, including Czechoslovakia, Poland an Rumenia provide graphic examples.

27. Philip Short, B.B.C. correspondent, Listener 15 April 1982.

4. Socialist states justify their existence by reference to an all-embracing ideology. Yet the gap between the rhetoric of the ideology and the reality of political struggle places enormous strains upon citizens. Socialist states carry the encumbrance of an unquestioned political theology which promotes Orellian double-think.

5. Most socialist states see their development as bound up with, if not dependent upon, socialist planning. Planning in practice however demands a new code of ethics from its practitioners. Instead of accepting the selfish stimuli of the price mechanism, planners need to understand the logic is not always perceived or acted upon. There is falsification, diversion of resources and inadequate false or improper accounting in a very large number of cases. Graft all too easily becomes an inescapable part of the economy in a socialist state. Examples are forthcoming only when, as for example in the case of contemporary Poland, conditions of extreme inefficiency are revealed.

6. Most socialist states are in the less developed category and glimpses of apparent capitalist affluence often tantalise even the most devoted socialist administrator. Goods perceived as necessisties in affluent states are often unimaginable luxuries in states which set themselves high-minded socialist principles. High-minded socialist principles are not, in a realistic world, adequate compensation for lack of consumer goods. In the Soviet Union for example it has been said that "good food and especially meat (are) the yardstick by which most Russians measure their own prosperity".[28] Such a notion is perhaps more 'culture' than 'ideological'. Chinese measure their prosperity in terms of rice and family, a somewhat different concept but instinctively seen in terms of consumer benefit.

Officially in socialist states graft is seen as a temporary aberration. Officially only capitalism is sick: socialism is healthy. Where graft persists in socialist states, the apologists contend, it can be attributed to the 'suger-coated bullets' of the bourgeoisie. The bourgeois mentality alone promotes graft according to Socialists. Yet they fail to account satisfactorily for the prevalence of graft in socialist societies. The main factors are bureaucratic inefficiency, linked to inherent scarcity of resources and arbitrariness, supported by an entrenched acceptance of special privileges for party self and family. No socialist would be happy in admitting socialist graft, but fewer still are inclined to accept that socialist graft is a direct product of socialism.

Capitalist graft is of course the particular manifestation of graft in North

---

28. Michael Binyon, The Times, 19 February 1980, and November 12, 1982, where Binyon described the 'second economy' as "so entrenched as to be ineradicable."

32

America, Europe or Japan.[29] No doubt it is difficult to make moral distinctions as between the one and the other. However socialism finds particular difficulties in its claim of moral superiority over capitalism *per se*. Graft develops under socialism because of a serious divergence between supply of goods and services and the demand for these. Shortages may be worsened by bureaucratic inaptitude or cynicism regarding the ability of the system to produce or allocate resources. Graft may, under such circumstances, become institutionalised at the moment when expectations of a higher living standard have been generated. Socialist leaders must therefore resign themselves to the existence of graft and to accept it as natural and normal, provided it offers no serious challenge to the system. Paradoxically therefore, socialism is supported by graft and *vice versa*.

29. Arnold J. Heidenheimer, Political Corruption, Readings in Comparative Analysis, New York, Holt, Rinehart and Winston 1970 pp. 3–6, explores market graft.
See also Susan Rose-Ackerman, Corruption: A Study in Political Economy, Academic Press, 1978. Non-socialist graft in a comparative context is examined by James C. Scott, Comparative Political Corruption, Prentice-Hall Inc., 1972.

[21]

Corruption and Reform 3: 277–291 (1988)
© Kluwer Academic Publishers, Dordrecht — Printed in the Netherlands

Political scandal: A western luxury?

STEPHEN RILEY
Department of International Relations and Politics, North Staffordshire Polytechnic, Stoke on Trent, UK

In early 1988 we saw a number of scandals emerge or further develop in several widely varying Third World regimes. In South Korea a scandal surrounded the younger brother of a former president who was alleged to have embezzled at least $9.3 mn and possibly up to $14 mn from a government rural development project. The Saemaul (or New Village) Movement involved government help towards establishing self-help farming or fishing villages; and the news of the embezzlement created a scandal which in part undermined the presidential transfer of power earlier in the year. In Venezuela the justice minister, and in Colombia the acting attorney general, both resigned as a consequence of being involved in drug trafficking. The Colombian attorney, Alfredo Gutierrez Marquez, had in fact created some alarm by suggesting, shortly after his appointment, that his government was losing the battle against the cocaine trade from that country across the Caribbean to the United States. Colombia, Marquez suggested, should seek accommodation with those involved in the huge underground economy that the cocaine trade has become, and should also legalise it as a recognition of the inevitable. In Sierra Leone a political scandal emerged concerning a West German firm's plans to dump nuclear waste in that country, and in Kenya the brewery ran out of beer as an election was held. Somewhat reminiscent of the rotten boroughs of 19th Century England, candidates had bought potential supporters so much beer that the brewery ran dry. In Panama General Manuel Noriega began to experience some difficulties in his relationships with his former friends in Washington, when the United States instituted a series of economic measures designed to undermine his position within the regime. Finally in India the American multinational Union Carbide sought to reach a final settlement of the claims against it as a consequence of the Bhopal disaster in 1984. Meanwhile the government of India sought to manage the series of political scandals surrounding Rajiv Gandhi and his associates – most notably those emerging from the Bofors scandal in which the Swedish armaments company gave kickbacks in return for contracts – and scandals created by inappropriate, costly or inefficient development projects.

278

Political scandals may thus emerge in many kinds of polity and society. They can be about simple (or not so simple) financial misappropriation or other forms of corruption. But they can also be concerned with a wide variety of other forms of behaviour deemed to be unacceptable, intolerable or worthy of moral condemnation by some individual, group or interest. Often the most significant elements are how the scandal is created, managed, and politically resolved, rather than the precise character of the alleged offence. It is the smoke rather than the fire that is the essence of a scandal; and the political consequences of the scandal are often rather more important than the original alleged offence.

As the brief examples from early 1988 illustrate, scandals are not exclusively a western luxury, a consequence of the values, forms of moral outrage, and the institutionalised aspects of contestation idealised in liberal democratic systems of government, though often imperfectly realised in practice. Political scandals often require the oxygen of publicity or investigation; but they do not only occur in western liberal democracies with a functioning opposition, a judiciary with a degree of autonomy from the political leadership of the state, and a relatively independent and inquiring press. Though clearly this political context of scandals will differ, they are ubiquitous in character, found in virtually all polities, and generally subject to the same patterns of response and management. In view of this, the purpose of this paper is to examine several examples of scandal as they are found in 'Third World' or non-western contexts. Somewhat arbitrarily I have chosen to examine several recent cases: the Bhopal scandal in India; the scandal that is the state of Zaire ruled by Mobutu Sese Seko; the cocaine economy in north Latin and Central America; and international flows of money from Third World countries, known as 'Capital Flight', which have created a scandal at a time of growing concern over Third World indebtedness. The cases vary a good deal. There is no sexual scandal; merely cases of negligence and maladministration leading to many deaths, as well as gross financial misappropriation and the misuse of power. I outline the cases and subsequently draw some general conclusions from them. As will become evident, the cases demonstrate that scandal is not a western luxury, but that western interest groups and institutions (as diverse as Amnesty International and the International Monetary Fund) can play an important role in placing a scandal onto the domestic (and international) political agenda.

The Bhopal affair

At about 1 AM on the morning of 3rd December 1984, shanty town dwellers living around the Union Carbide factory in Bhopal, the capital of

279

Madhya Pradesh state in India, woke up coughing and with streaming eyes. The Union Carbide factory, one of the smaller and least efficient of the US multinational's operations, had begun to leak methyl iso-cyanate (MIC) gas into the surrounding area. MIC is produced to make insecticide and is a deadly poison, usually stored in a refrigerated condition. As the leak continued, a gas cloud built up and spread over many areas of the city. Many thousands of people fled from their homes, as they were awakened by the gas and subsequent panic. But many did not and died where they lay. The factory did not inform the local government or city authorities of the leak, and subsequently claimed that the gas would be a minor irritant with no long-term effects upon those involved. Whilst the final figures are uncertain, most sources now suggest that the gas leak led to the deaths of over 3,000 people. In addition, perhaps more than 200,000 people had been affected by exposure to the gas; and many animals, an important source of livelihood in the state, had also died (Bhopal Support Group; Shrivastava 1987). What is generally regarded as the worst industrial disaster in history had happened quickly, quietly and with widespread deadly results.

The events of that night and subsequently have generated a scandal which has affected many of the participants, including Union Carbide, the government of India, and the surviving victims of the tragedy. Attribution of blame has become important as the issue of legal responsibility emerged. Union Carbide initially claimed that brief exposure to the gas would not be harmful. This initial defence evaporated as considerable evidence of respiratory problems, spontaneous abortions, and congenital deformities in newly-born children became apparent. The company subsequently claimed that its Indian staff at the plant were responsible: their negligence had led to the 'accident'. A later company claim was that – somewhat improbably – Sikh terrorists had caused the disaster, and all along Union Carbide claimed that its methods of operations and safety standards at the Bhopal plant were identical to those at its plants in the United States.

The Indian government has also been smeared with the scandal that emerged afterwards. It was suggested that the city government did not follow up its instruction in 1975 to Union Carbide to move its operations away from high density living areas to a more rural location. It was also suggested that the state government had ignored many protests about the inefficient operation of the plant (and previous gas leakages), and that there were patron-clientelist relationships between the local Union Carbide management, and politicians and civil servants in the state and city governments (Everest 1985; Diamond 1985; Bhopal Support Group).

The government and Congress party officials in Madhya Pradesh and elsewhere were clearly faced with a difficult problem: an emerging scandal in which the government's role in, and responsibility for, the disaster was

280

coming to prominence. Initially the government responded by providing disaster relief; it provided 90% of the initial rescue, relief and rehabilitation efforts in the area, giving financial assistance, free food and medical help. By October 1985 about $13 mn in relief had been given by the Indian government (Shrivastava 1987). But political issues in the management of the scandal soon became important as well. The disaster had happened several weeks before important elections in which the Congress party's hegemony was being challenged. As a result the government responded by seeking to contain any political criticism of itself that emerged (for example that the Congress government in the state had legalised the shanty towns surrounding the Union Carbide plant, where most of the people who died had resided). It acted to try and control information on the disaster, and sought scapegoats both in terms of the company Union Carbide, and in terms of specific officials.

The government sought to centralise all information on the disaster within its own agencies, so that any damaging information could not be used against the government. Though it was challenged by Union Carbide and victims groups, it was remarkably successful in this aim. Factory records were seized, and the plant was sealed, never to re-open. Workers on duty on 3rd December 1984 were officially prohibited from talking to the press and to their superiors in Union Carbide (Shrivastava 1987). The government also sought an exclusive right to represent the victims in both Indian and overseas courts, claiming that this was to ensure that they would not be exploited by unscrupulous foreign lawyers. Many of the key politicians and administrators in the city were moved out of Bhopal fairly quickly, including the mayor and many involved in the planning departments.

When the American chairman of Union Carbide arrived in Bhopal shortly after the disaster he was immediately arrested. Warren Anderson was thus an important symbol in the government's management of the scandal to its own advantage. The Congress state government also acted to arrest the main plant managers, which gave an indication to the wider public that action was being taken and that those responsible had been apprehended. This practice of scapegoating drew attention away from some of the underlying structural problems with the Union Carbide operation in Bhopal which were subsequently identified by victims groups and others.

The MIC plant had been operating at less than optimum efficiency; it was running at 30 – 40% of its technical capacity. Safety measures were lax, and training of its staff was inadequate. In the two years before the disaster Union Carbide had been involved in a series of cost cutting measures which had further endangered safety. Prior to the events of 3rd December 1984, there had been eight serious accidents, including one death and thirty two serious injuries (Bhopal Support Group). Not surprisingly, the company

281

found it difficult to manage the scandal to its own advantage. The Indian government successfully monopolised much of the information on the disaster and also acted decisively after the events; whereas Union Carbide acted insensitively and was portrayed as an alien, mean and legalistic employer, ultimately and exclusively responsible for the many deaths.

Union Carbide made a number of responses in the aftermath of the disaster. It offered to support the government's relief effort, but this was rejected. The company also initially offered up to $200 mn in settlement of the various legal claims against itself. As this was an apparently arbitrary figure and coincidentally the amount for which the company was insured, the gesture had a negative effect. Subsequently in court, Union Carbide argued that damages should be small as the value of life in Third World countries was minimal. It also argued that domestic Indian mismanagement, and sabotage, were to blame. Neither of these arguments helped Union Carbide's position.

The aftermath of the disaster has been routinised into a legal dispute between the company and the Indian government, acting on behalf of the victims. Victims groups have emerged and have claimed that not only have they not received adequate initial relief and financial assistance, their interests are likely to be compromised by the government. An out-of-court settlement in the case was announced in early 1989.

The Bhopal affair is an interesting example of the management of scandal by a Third World government, faced with competing opposition parties and an active media, often critical of the government. The Congress government appears to have successfully managed the scandal by both controlling information and by creating scapegoats, both individuals and the foreign multinational involved. It has directed attention away from its own involvement in, or responsibility for, aspects of the scandal such as the planning and regulation of dangerous industries, and its legalisation of the illegal settlements that proved to be too near the Bhopal Union Carbide plant. The Congress government – both in Mahdya Pradesh and elsewhere – did not have to take any political flak for its involvement in the disaster. Its responsibility was seen to be limited, helped by its rapid action. The government also acted to co-opt or control the interests of the many victims of the tragedy, despite the emergence of victims groups, by creating itself the legal responsibility to act on behalf of the victims. It was also helped by the actions of the company principally responsible. However, relative success in managing the political scandal emerging out of the Bhopal disaster did not insulate the Congress government against further scandals. In fact Rajiv Gandhi's government, though surviving the political fall-out of the Bhopal affair, soon became immersed in a series of more politically damaging events.

282

Zaire and Mobutu Sese Seko

In late 1981 the former prime minister of Zaire, Karl-i-Bond Nguza testified before a US congressional foreign affairs committee meeting on Africa. The congressional committee was concerned to assess the nature of US interests in the region and, in particular, in Zaire, one of the largest African states, which was resource-rich and strategically significant. The committee was also concerned to assess the character of Mobutu's rule, a virtual presidential monarch atop Zairean political life since the mid 1960s. Nguza was in a good position to give a detailed assessment of these matters. He had been foreign minister from 1972 to 1974, and again from 1976 to 1977. In the intervening period he had been head of the sole ruling party in Zaire. He was also prime minister from 1979 to 1981 when he fled into exile (he subsequently returned to the fold in Zaire).

What Nguza told the US congress was literally scandalous. It was not the exaggerated imaginings of an opposition figure in exile, and has been confirmed by all other authoritative accounts. Nguza told the US congressional committee that in April 1981 Mobutu had ordered the Bank of Zaire (Zaire's central bank) to transfer an additional US $30 mn to his personal account abroad. At the same time 20,000 tons of copper (roughly 5% of Zaire's annual production) was privately sold with Mobutu being the sole benefactor of the proceeds of approximately US $30 mn. Nguza also listed Mobutu's properties overseas, and confirmed that Mobutu's personal wealth overseas was in the region of US $4 bn (or four thousand million US dollars). Mobutu would appear to be, from all the evidence, a kleptocrat on a grand scale (Young and Turner 1985). In the period since Nguza's testimony, Mobutu and his cronies have continued to accumulate considerable overseas funds and real estate. The latest estimate suggests that Mobutu's personal wealth is now in the region of US $6 bn, compared to the Zairean national debt of about US $5 bn, and at a time, it must be remembered, of growing economic hardship on the continent as a whole and within Zaire itself (Akinrinade and Barling 1987). A new list of Mobutu's properties overseas has appeared (George 1988). For his now frequent vacations Mobutu can choose from eleven chateaux and other large properties in Belgium (the former colonial power), a large residence in Nice, a building on the very select Avenue Foch in Paris, a villa on Lake Geneva, and a sixteenth century castle in Spain. Not only does Mobutu also have substantial currency deposits in Swiss banks, it is also suggested that he has a controlling interest in a small Swiss bank (Gould 1980).

Gross financial misappropriation is not the only scandal that can be laid at the door of the Mobutu regime. Amnesty International, amongst other interested parties, have complained at the extensive and well-documented

283

abuse of human rights in Zaire, a potential rich country but with a current per capita income of about US $180 (Africa Review 1988). There have been a number of secessionist attempts (most notably in 1977 and 1978) and the Mobutu regime has had to be propped up by military support from the western powers, including France and the CIA. There are also a number of very expensive development disasters in Zaire (Parfitt and Riley 1988). Examples would include the Inga-Shaba power project, costing at least US $1 bn, and designed to provide power for an iron and steel complex which has never run at more than 10% of its capacity, producing steel of poor quality costing at least three times as much as imported steel. A trade centre has also been built in Kinshasa, twenty-two stories high. But there are no windows, the air conditioning broke down soon after the building was completed, and it is now virtually deserted (George 1988).

How does Mobutu get away with it? How is the regime headed by Mobutu able to weather the political scandals created by this extensive and public evidence of misappropriation and abuse of power? How is the regime able to secure further credit and military assistance despite this public opprobrium? Only a brief answer to these questions can be provided here (for a more extended treatment, see Parfitt and Riley 1988; Young and Turner 1985; and George 1988). There are three main factors which contribute to Mobutu's continued hegemony within Zaire, and his regime's insulation from international responses to the gross misappropriation and human rights abuses that have occurred. The first lies in the considerable political skill which Mobutu possesses and which he has exercised to great effect since assuming power in 1965. Mobutu has been very astute in creating a system of personal rule, which involves his dominance over all autonomous sources of power in Zaire, including the military, trade unions and the press. All the positions and perquisites of power are controlled by Mobutu and he distributes them to his loyal lieutenants. Cabinet members change posts frequently, as do other senior officials and politicians (An example would be the career of Nguza, cited above). This reinforces their personal loyalty to Mobutu. Indeed the system is such a centralised and personalised form of power that some scholars have described it as absolutist in character, with Mobutu at the centre of a 20th century version of the king and court in seventeenth century France (Callaghy 1984).

In terms of the management of scandal, all forms of oppositional activity are prohibited within Mobutu's regime. There is a single ruling party; and formal opposition is driven underground, abroad or into secessionist attempts. The press is controlled. Young and Turner give many examples of the mass media's subservience: the press carry a front page photograph of Mobutu nearly every day, referring to him with a variety of 'praise-names': the Guide, the Helmsman, the Father of the Nation, and so on (Young and

284

Turner 1985). There is no criticism or indeed reference to the many scandals of the regime. Other independent institutions are similarly cowed, including parliament and the trade unions.

A second factor may be the regime's role as a guarantor of western interests in central Africa. Mobutu has used his regime's position as a western client state most effectively. He has been able to use the client status to gain a degree of tolerance of his regime's abuses. Western interests in the region can be clearly identified. Both the French and American governments intervened in Zaire to counter the secessionist attempts in 1977 and 1978 in order to promote their own interests in investment, secure supplies of resources including strategic minerals, and a relatively stable pro-western ally. Mobutu is seen as a bastion against communism in Africa; he has also helped American aims in the region by sending troops to Chad to fight Libyan incursions into that state, and by supporting Jonas Savimbi's UNITA movement against the Marxist MPLA government in Angola. Mobutu's role in this respect has ensured that he and his regime have been allowed a considerable degree of tolerance.

A final factor contributing to the tolerant treatment of Mobutu and his regime may be the perception that the choice is between Mobutu or chaos. There is no viable opposition figure or movement which would be able to continue in Mobutu's stead, and to hold together the huge state that is Zaire. Without Mobutu, Mobutu's empire would fall, with numerous secessionist attempts and semi civil wars in the provinces or regions. From this perspective, the attempts by various international financial institutions (such as the International Monetary Fund) become clearer; they are attempting to ensure that Mobutu cleans up his act, that he presents a more acceptable face to the international financial community, and ensures that members of his political aristocracy squander less of the national wealth (Callaghy 1984).

The Mobutu regime in Zaire is not the first (or likely to be the last) Third World regime whose political excesses and scandals are tolerated because the regime is viewed favourably by western interests. Somoza in Nicaragua, the Duvaliers in Haiti, the Marcos family in the Philippines, and, more recently, Moi in Kenya are all somewhat similar. But the Mobutu regime has been accorded an extraordinary tolerance, at least until recently, despite the many well-documented excesses recorded by Amnesty International and various exile organisations, and testified to by many authoritative observers and insiders such as Nguza. In the case of Zaire political scandal is generally articulated outside of the society in international forums, the international media, and within those states who are the patrons of Mobutu's regime, most notably Belgium and the United States. The regime naturally dismisses or denies such criticisms, no matter how detailed and comprehensive they may be. Nevertheless it is possible to argue that these international critics of the

285

scandal that is Mobutu's Zaire are articulating the interests of those – such as the rural poor and underprivileged – who are not represented within the current Zairean state. External exposure of such scandals may thus have a long-term beneficial effect, but this is dependent upon the attitudes – and change within – those states which act as the regime's patrons. In the meantime the Zairean poor have few realistic options, other than to develop survival strategies by operating within the 'second economy' and opting out of orthodox economic and political activities (Africa Confidential 1988).

Drugs in North Latin and Central America

The first two cases that have been considered deal with an industrial disaster, and the scandal which emerged out of many deaths; and the example of a regime that is considered scandalous due to extensive financial misappropriations and political abuses, yet is tolerated by the west. The final two cases, rather than looking at events or regimes, examine transactions or processes which have become matters of political scandal: the flow of drugs, especially cocaine, across Central America and the Caribbean to the United States; and the similar flow of money, known as 'Capital Flight', from the Third World to the banks in international financial centres in western societies. Much of the political scandal in these cases has been generated by western governments themselves, fearful of the effects of drug inflows upon American youth, or reluctant to provide further credit to shore up the already heavily indebted Third World governments suffering Capital Flight.

Both cocaine and marijuana are natural products in South America and the Caribbean. Perkins and Gilbert suggest that almost 50% of all Jamaican farmers cultivate *ganja* (or marijuana) and at least 25% of them use marijuana for personal recreational consumption. Similarly Sage points out that *Coca* (or cocaine) is part of the natural pharmacopoeia of South America, and that its usage can be dated back for thousands of years (Perkins and Gilbert 1987; Sage 1987). *Coca* also performs an important sacramental role as the 'sacred leaf of the Incas', and is widely used as a natural medicine, as is *ganja* in Jamaica. In this context, it is possible to suggest that attempts to eradicate the production and trade in these drugs could hardly be successful, even before the internationalisation of trade in these commodities made them an important source of income for poor farmers, middlemen and the 'narcocracy' alike (Henman 1985).

A huge subterranean economy – the drugs trade – has developed in northern Latin America, Central America and the Caribbean in the 1970s and 1980s. It operates along almost classic capitalist lines, involving high risks and enormous profits. Its purpose is to feed the demand in the major

286

north American cities, and in so doing it has had important social, political and economic effects upon several polities in the region. Tin used to form the basis of the Bolivian economy, but with the collapse of world tin prices, its place has been taken by cocaine and the subterranean economy. Precise estimates are obviously difficult to achieve, but one estimate suggests that drug revenues were approximately US $1 bn in Bolivia in 1986, more than double the earnings from official, legal exports (Sage 1987). The political effects of the drugs trade are also seen in Central America, such as General Noriega's Panama, and in a number of Caribbean islands such as the Cayman Islands, a British dependency and the subject of several inquiries into drug-related corruption. Demand continues to be high. It has been estimated that American citizens consume at least i90 tons of cocaine every year, and the trade is worth at least US $70 bn every year, and rising in volume and value.

American anti-drugs policy in the Reagan years has been to attempt to control the supply rather than the demand. It has pursued a series of drug eradication policies, and attempted to impose them upon several regimes in Central America, the Caribbean and northern Latin America. The Reagan administration has used threats of financial sanctions against governments such as Bolivia's in an attempt to get them to eradicate *coca* growing and substitute alternative crops in the main drug producing areas. The main motive behind attempts at eradication has been a moral panic at the effects of drug usage in the United States. As a result, the huge subterranean drug economy of the region has been redefined as a scandal of supply rather than a scandal of demand inside the United States. The orchestration of this scandal from 1982 onwards owes more to the Reagan government's policy aims than to an significant concern for the effects of the drug trade upon the polities and economies of the neighbouring states.

Capital Flight

It is possible to argue that a similar explanation of scandal can be provided for the furore surrounding much of the discussion of the varied international financial transfers known as 'Capital Flight', and identified as a significant monetary worry of western governments and financial institutions in the major capitalist centres in the mid 1980s. Capital Flight can be simply defined as the private economic holdings of citizens and institutions in other countries, which may be legal or illicit in character. More specifically Capital Flight refers to the substantial overseas holdings of citizens of Third World indebted countries.

During the period that Third World states were acquiring significant

287

external debts in the 1970s and early 1980s, it became evident that private individuals in those countries were acquiring substantial overseas holdings in deposits in foreign banks, as well as fixed assets such as property and commercial interests. There are a number of illustrations of this huge accumulation of overseas assets and wealth in foreign banks. Much of the evidence suggests that the relatively richer and more politically powerful strata of Third World societies were those engaged in acquiring foreign holdings. An example would be the family wealth of the Marcos family – now in exile from the Philippines. Carbonnel-Catillo estimates their total wealth at over US $10 bn, with holdings in property and gold bullion (Carbonnel-Catillo 1986). At the time of Mexico's debt crisis in 1982 it was established that 575 Mexican citizens had at least a million dollars each deposited with a bank overseas. Jean Claude Duvalier of Haiti has been estimated as having overseas holdings of at least US $1 bn (South, March 1987). Such overseas holdings represent the literal tip of an iceberg. It can be surmised that many others in positions of state power or commercial activity will hold extensive and generally unrevealed assets and credits in overseas locations, often covered by secrecy, subterfuge or by the cautious and financially profitable tax haven banking rules.

Such overseas holdings are hardly likely to be new. Nor is the available evidence conclusive that such holdings have grown enormously in scale in the early 1980s. Why, then, has the terminology of international capital flight been developed, and why has it created a scandal? Part of the reason surely lies in the international debt crisis which has generated much debate in the mid 1980s. The Third World debt crisis of the early 1980s was feared as the possible cause of a major international financial collapse in the banking system if not the possible cause of another Great Depression. In the mid 1980s banks in the major capitalist centres were being pressed to provide further credit for Third World governments, or at least reschedule their current debts. Yet at the same time those banks held substantial private deposits of citizens of regimes that sought further credit. There became a need to develop measures to estimate and record Capital Flight, if only to make a series of political points to indebted Third World governments. A number of measures have been developed, most notably by the International Monetary Fund, which has also played a central role in the debt crisis.

The Morgan Guaranty Trust Company of New York define Capital Flight as 'the reported and unreported acquisition of foreign assets by the non-bank private sector and some elements of the public sector' (Morgan Guaranty Trust 1986). This is a generous definition of capital flight in that it includes the holdings of foreign currency of domestic companies, and trade credits. This definition can be compared with that used by the International Monetary Fund which makes a distinction between the concept of all private

288

external capital outflows and short-term speculative ones. The IMF prefers to use the concept of short-term outflows (Khan and Haque 1987).

Capital flight can thus include international financial transfers which are entirely legitimate, and not the proceeds of corrupt transactions. But capital flight will clearly include some, but not all, of such transactions. There are other problems with these data, quite apart from the general problems of error and unreliability found in much Third World data collection and evaluation. Black or second economies are generally understood to be larger in most, if not all, Third World societies when compared to their equivalents in the advanced industrial world. In addition some Third World political figures – such as ex-president Somoza of Nicaragua – may see little distinction between their private wealth and the state's assets, which confuses the situation. Somoza's period in Nicaragua saw his family accumulate assets of the worth of approximately 25% of Nicaragua's GDP. When the Sandinistas became a serious threat to the Somoza regime, Anastasio Somoza and his supporters were able to expatriate about US $500 mn via several American banks (South, March 1987). Other problems with data include suspicious fires which destroy records, and general problems of interpretation.

Despite these reservations, indicators of capital flight do give a useful general assessment of the scale of international transfers from the Third World to the banks of the advanced industrial societies. Such measures will include corruptly induced transfers, but the purpose of the measures is not just to indicate their scale. Instead it is to create a scandal (as it indeed has done in many Third World countries) and to suggest that capital should be national and possibly repatriated to reduce the external debt. The measures are nevertheless illuminating, and generally deal with the highly indebted countries for obvious reasons. Khan and Haque point out that for the highly indebted countries the ratio of accumulated capital flight to external debt is 30% for the period 1974–82 (Khan and Haque 1987), and suggest that 'for every one US dollar that had been lent to the countries as a group, some 30 cents came out'. The estimates provided by the IMF refer to overseas deposits by private individuals in banks, and it is therefore possible to suggest that such figures underestimate the level of the international transfers involved. They do not include the holdings of private individuals from the Third World in property and other consumer items. Thus the New York properties of the Marcos family, or the Duvalier family yacht, valued at US $18 mn, would not be included. Nevertheless the capital flight measures developed by the IMF and other financial institutions did serve their purpose: they created a scandal as they made public and attempted to measure international transactions, some of which were no doubt dubious in character. The measures also created a debate about 'hot money' and the developing casino-like operations of the international financial system (Naylor 1987).

289

Concluding observations

The cases which are examined above indicate that political scandal is not simply a luxury associated with liberal democratic societies and western liberal norms of rightful and honest conduct in public office. Political scandals are ubiquitous, but they vary in form, character, context and duration. Political scandals may not be a western luxury, but western interests (pressure groups and institutions) can help create them, though the political interests of governments often over-ride scandal nevertheless. It would seem that scandals can be examined by reference to the type of moral outrage engendered; the nature of the concerned group or agency; the political context; and the possible precipitant event or set of events.

In the Bhopal affair, the moral outrage concerned the responsibility for the many deaths and injuries. The Congress government – nationally and locally – was successful in avoiding any major sense of culpability, and was able to focus the outrage by creating scapegoats and by controlling supplies of relevant information. In the Capital Flight case, western monetary institutions including commercial banks and the IMF have sought to create a scandal surrounding the flows of private moneys overseas from indebted Third World regimes. They have generated much debate, though not necessarily a high level of moral outrage. In some Third World states, such as Mexico and Liberia, capital flight revelations have embarrassed the current incumbents in power. The definition and attempted measurement of capital flight has nevertheless focused attention upon an issue the banks and the IMF at least are concerned about. The drugs case example seems to be, on the other hand, a useful example of how a powerful western government has sought to redefine a moral scandal: the drug problems of the American cities becomes a problem of eradicating or controlling supply, rather than policies to reduce demand, and to cope with the problems thereby created.

Several of the cases indicate that the concerned group or agency is often external to the state concerned. Much of the debate on Mobutu's Zaire has been generated by bankers, pressure groups, bodies of exiles and western governments. It can be suggested that the activities of external agencies such as Amnesty International in focusing attention upon such scandals as human rights abuses have had a beneficial effect. They direct attention towards those social groups such as the rural poor who are likely to be non-participants in such a corrupt and absolutist form of politics. Mobutu's regime has survived many scandals and embarrassments, most probably due to its role as a guarantor of western interests in central Africa. It can also be argued that, in the Capital Flight case, the intervention of the banks and the IMF has been beneficial, as they have exposed possibly corrupt and

290

certainly unpatriotic monetary transfers. In the Bhopal affair the concerned group is most probably the victims, but their interests were represented, adequately or inadequately, by the Indian government which was conceived of as being a possible betrayer of the victims' interests.

The political context of the scandals has varied most widely, despite all the cases being 'Third World' in orientation. The Bhopal affair was set against the backdrop of an albeit imperfectly functioning liberal democracy, whilst the Zairean scandals took place in a regime somewhat reminiscent of absolutist 17th century France. Both are Third World polities and both have had their share of scandal, but the similarities then end. Mobutu's centrality to the political process in Zaire meant that domestic controversy and scandal were unlikely; variations of hero-worship were much more possible. Nevertheless a series of political scandals have emerged from the regime and have been exposed in various international media and fora. Despite this the regime seems insulated against scandal due to its absolutist character. No amount of scandal would have a politically destabilising effect; whereas in the case of India the Bhopal affair did have a politically destabilising potential in that it might have contributed to a reduction in political support for the Congress party had not the affair been astutely handled. A free press and oppositional politics might have made much more of the affair, had not an insensitive and obvious scapegoat in the Union Carbide multinational not been forthcoming. In the drugs and Capital Flight cases, the political context was one of the creation of a scandal for an obvious political purpose: to redefine a problem, or to create a moral concern.

Political scandals are difficult to predict. There are no obvious precipitant events or set of events which will generate scandals in all polities. What may cause a scandal in one regime will be of no consequence in another. For example, in the Zaire case it is mentioned that Mobutu accumulated a corrupt income of over US $60 mn in 1981. This caused few ripples in Zaire; whereas such a documented revelation in say, India, would be of major consequence. Perhaps it is the case that political scandals are intricately tied to the political culture and context of the regime concerned, and scandal, like beauty, is in the eye of the beholder.

References

Akinrinade, O. and J.K. Barling (eds) (1987). 'Economic Development in Africa', London.
Africa Confidential (1988) 'Zaire: Survival Strategies', 5 February.
Africa Review, 1988 Saffron Walden, 1988.
Bhopal Support Group; documents and newsletters, especially contributions by J. Rutter.
Callaghy, T. (1984). *The State-Society Struggle: Zaire in Comparative Perspective*, New York.

291

Carbonnel-Catillo, Ma.A. (1986). 'The Philippines – the politics of plunder', *Corruption and Reform*, Vol. 1 No. 3.

Diamond, S. (1985). 'The Bhopal Disaster', *New York Times*, 28 January.

Everest, L. (1985). *Behind the Poison Cloud*, Chicago.

George, S. (1988). *A Matter of Life and Debt*, Harmondsworth.

Gould, D.J. (1980). *Bureaucratic Corruption and Underdevelopment in the Third World*, London.

Henman, A. et al. (1985). *Big Deal: the politics of the illicit drugs business*, London.

Khan, M.S. and N.U. Haque (1987). 'Capital Flight from Developing Countries', *Finance and Development*, March 1987.

Morgan Guaranty Trust, *World Financial Markets*, March 1986.

Naylor, R.T. (1987). *Hot Money and the Politics of Debt*, London.

Parfitt, T.W. and S.P. Riley (1989). *African Debt*, London.

Perkins, M.K. and H.R. Gilbert (1987). 'An economic analysis of US drug control policy: the impact on the cannabis trade', *Corruption and Reform*, Vol. 2 No. 1.

Sage, C. (1987). 'The Cocaine Economy in Bolivia: its development and current significance', *Corruption and Reform*, Vol. 2 No. 2, 1987.

Shrivastava, P. (1987). *Bhopal: anatomy of a crisis*, Cambridge, Mass.

South magazine, March 1987.

Young, C. and T. Turner (1985). *The Rise and Decline of the Zairean State*, Madison.

Part V
Explaining State Crime

THREE FACES OF CRUELTY: TOWARDS A COMPARATIVE SOCIOLOGY OF VIOLENCE

RANDALL COLLINS

To the comparative sociologist, history shows itself on two levels. For the most part it is the site of puzzles and arabesque causalities fascinating to the mind of a theorist. Yet there is another level that occasionally jolts the scholar out of his thoughts—the sense of historical lives as they were actually lived, day by day, moment by moment. Our theories and concepts compress and abstract; to speak of the transformation of the state or the rise of a religion is to look down the decades, if not the centuries, and necessarily to pass over most of the moments and feelings of most of the people involved. To conceive past societies from their great relics of art and literature draws one ever farther from the brutal reality. For to empathize with the human reality of history is to receive a shock, as in the following glimpse of ancient China which brought to an end for me several months of fascinated unravelling of the patterns of Chinese history:

> Once a man of Ch'u named Mr. Ho, having found a piece of jade matrix in the Ch'u Mountains, took it to court and presented it to King Li. King Li instructed the jeweler to examine it, and the jeweler reported, "It is only a stone." The king, supposing that Ho was trying to deceive him, ordered that his left foot be cut off in punishment. In time King Li passed away and King Wu came to the throne, and Ho once more took his matrix and presented it to King Wu. King Wu ordered his jeweler to examine it, and again the jeweler reported, "It is only a stone." The King, supposing that Ho was trying to deceive him as well, ordered that his right foot be cut off. Ho, clasping the matrix to his breast, went to the foot of the Ch'u Mountains, where he wept for three days and nights, and when all his tears were were cried out, he wept blood in their place. The King, hearing of this, sent someone to question him. "Many people in the world have had their feet amputated — why do you weep so piteously over it? " the man asked. He replied, "I do not grieve because my feet have been cut off. I grieve

University of California, San Diego

416

because a precious jewel is dubbed a mere stone, and a man of integrity is
called a deceiver. This is why I weep." The King then ordered the jeweler
to cut and polish the matrix, and when he had done so a precious jewel
emerged.[1]

The existence of punishment by mutilation is no surprise to the reader in
Chinese history. What shocked, was the blasé question: "Many people in the
world have had their feet amputated — why do you weep so piteously over
it? " This smug conclusion, redolent with Confucian meritocracy, only under-
lines the viciousness of the prevailing attitude.[2] Shang bronzes and 800-year
cycles lost their charm, and I closed for the time my books on China.

The prevailing reality of world history is violence. "History is a slaughter-
bench. . . ," cried Hegel; and James Joyce declared, "History is a nightmare
from which I am trying to awake." And it is not merely the violence of a
machine out of control; the disturbing thing is the viciousness, the vindic-
tiveness, the deliberate torture in so much of it. Beneath the sociologist's
patterns lies the personal dimension of evil; the patterns of history are the
work of demons.

This is an attempt at exorcising those demons. It is not a theodicy; the
problem is not to justify evil, but to explain it. Is there a pattern, a meaning
to the cruelty itself? For it is only in isolating a causal theory that we are
able to deal with cruelty; the point is not to learn to live with the demons,
but to take away their power.

Violence and Group Structure

A sociology of violence, in fact, already exists. Above all, we find it in the
sociological tradition of France with its emphasis on the logic of emotions.
Tocqueville, for instance, was struck by the degree of public benevolence in
the America of the 1830's, the extent of personal sympathy and aid to
strangers. He attributed this to the condition of political equality, which
made it possible for individuals to empathize with one another; to prove his
point, he presents a comparison with the moral atmosphere of France in the
17th century:

Aux Rochers, October 30, 1675

Your letter from Aix, my daughter, is droll enough.
At least, read your letters over again before sending them; allow yourself
to be surprised by the pretty things that you have put into them and
console yourself by this pleasure for the trouble you have had in writing so

many. Then you have kissed all of Provence, have you? There would be no satisfaction in kissing all of Brittany, unless one likes to smell of wine. . .Do you wish to hear the news from Rennes? A tax of a hundred thousand crowns has been imposed upon the citizens; and if this sum is not produced within four-and-twenty hours, it is to-be doubled and collected by the soldiers. They have cleared the houses and sent away the occupants of the great streets and forbidden anybody to receive them on pain of death; so that the poor wretches (old men, women near their confinement, and children included) may be seen wandering around and crying on their departure from this city, without knowing where to go, and without food or a place to lie in. Day before yesterday a fiddler was broken on the wheel for getting up a dance and stealing some stamped paper. He was quartered after death, and his limbs exposed at the four corners of the city. Sixty citizens have been thrown in prison, and the business of punishing them is to begin tomorrow. This province sets a fine example to the others, teaching them above all that of respecting the governors and their wives, and of never throwing stones into their gardens.

Yesterday, a delightful day, Madame de Tarenté visited these wilds: there is no question about preparing a chamber or a collation; she comes by the gate, and returns the same way. . .

It would be a mistake to suppose that Madame de Sévigné, who wrote these lines, was a selfish or cruel person, she was passionately attached to her children and very ready to sympathize in the sorrows of her friends; nay, her letters show that she treated her vassals and servants with kindness and indulgence. But Madam de Sévigné had no clear notion of suffering in anyone who was not a person of quality.[3] It is the group boundaries that determine the extent of human sympathy; within those boundaries, humanity prevails; outside them, torture is inflicted without a qualm.

The same approach to morality is taken by Durkheim. In his work, Tocqueville's observation becomes a systematic theory. Moral ideas reflect social boundaries; ceremonial observances test group membership and moral worth; God represents society, and changes as society changes shape. Thus, in the world of mutually isolated tribal societies, injunctions on killing, stealing, lying and other offenses extend only up to the boundary of each group; with the extension of the mutual links of an elaborate division of labor, the moral sense expands, becomes more abstract and universal, less concrete and particular. This insight was expanded by Weber, who understood that the abstract, philosophical world religions signified a shift in the social structure, from the mutual moral isolation of kin and ethnic groups, to a cosmopolitan society with universal political and economic possibilities.

418

Reading this convergence, some theorists such as Talcott Parsons have interpreted history as moral progress, a gradual extension of the collective conscience and an upgrading of moral obligations.[4] From the particularisms and
ceremonial concerns of membership in primitive tribal societies, there is an
extension of the scope of humanity, emerging into a potential universal
brotherhood by the rise of Christianity and the other great world religions,
and culminating in the superior mildness and pan-empathy of an advanced
division of labor.

An evolutionary interpretation of Durkheim and Tocqueville's insights,
however, does not seem warranted. Some of the greatest displays of cruelty in
history were carried out by the universal religions, especially Christianity and
Islam; one has reason to doubt that the group boundaries focused on in this
version are at the center of the matter. It is true that a decline in institutionalized ferociousness can be discerned in the past two hundred years, but this
only reminds us that cruelty comes in more than one form. The concern with
alienation in the modern era points to a peculiarly modern form of brutality.
Still a third dimension is suggested by the line of thought opened up by
Nietzsche and Freud (and echoed in Weber): the migration of cruelty to the
interior of the individual mind in the form of psychic repression.

The Durkheimian mechanism takes us in the right direction; we can find a
key to cruelty in the connection between morality and the boundaries of
group inclusion and exclusion. A moral evolutionism, however, is not a
reliable guide. Moreover, additional dimensions must be added to the Durkheimian group mechanism, above all, those of stratification within and among
groups. Georges Sorel, yet another of the French analysts of the logic of
violent emotions, proposes that not all violence is of the same sort: there is
"force" used by dominant classes in a vindictive (and secretly terrified) upholding of their power; and there is "violence" of the rebellious under-class,
with its clean moral purity, without viciousness but with the clarity of practical work.[5] It will not do to regard all violence as immoral, in the manner of
contemporary pacifists or over-domesticated liberals, for morality not only
determines violence in a negative way—in the sense that the boundaries of the
group mark the limit outside of which violence is allowed—but also in a
positive way. Durkheim saw this clearly enough in his theory of the way in
which punishment of transgressors against the group's standards reunifies the
group in its righteous indignation. Sorel saw this in the external context as
well: the height of morality is in the willingness to endanger oneself in
combat for the group against its enemies, and hence violent confrontation is
the basis of all the moral virtues.

The key to an understanding of violence, then, is above all the structure of solidary groups and the moralities that reflect their emotional ties. The moral boundaries may set some persons beyond the pale of moral obligation, but they may also organize confrontations that make violence not just morally indifferent but morally motivated. Add to this the internal boundaries of stratification, and we find that moral claims and corresponding forms of violence exist also in the internal struggle for domination or liberation. When we pursue these structures into more complex forms, we find routinized and internalized forms of these moralities and cruelties.

In what follows, an explanation of human cruelty will be sought along three principal dimensions. First ferociousness: *homo lupus homini*. This is the dimension of overt brutality; its explanation leads us along the lines of Tocqueville, Durkheim and Sorel, into a consideration of group boundaries, external and internal. Second, callousness: brutality routinized and bureaucratized, cruelty without passion. Our theoretical leads here extend the Durkheimian model into the themes of Marx and Weber. Third, asceticism: the turning of cruelty against oneself and against others with whom one has solidarity. Here, the leads are provided by Nietzsche and Freud, which we may assimilate into the preceding sociological theory.

I. Ferociousness: the Violence of Man and Animal

Consider the extremes of overt brutality:

Mutilation: punishment not by death, but by life at its lowest level. The amputation of feet or hands, or ears—so common in ancient Rome, China, Mesopotamia, Palestine and in the Arab societies; the gouging out of eyes. The intent is not merely punishment, but prolonged misery and humiliation. This is especially evident in sexual mutilation, prominent in extremely male-oriented societies: the great Han historian, Ssu-ma Ch'ien, castrated for an honest but unfavorable memorandum to the Emperor; the Turkish sultan of Egypt punishing a rebellion in the Sudan by castrating the men and amputating the breasts of the women.[6] Mutilation might be combined with execution, always in a public form (as in the 17th century European case described by Tocqueville); clearly, public humiliation is at the essence of the phenomenon.

Torture: the deliberate prolongation and refinement of pain, usually dramatized and timed to maximize psychological dread. Torture has been routinely used in many judicial systems as part of the examination of prisoners before trial. Yet as a system for collecting evidence (as has been pointed

420

out by rationalist humanists since Roman times), it is inefficient, precisely because it usually produces whatever reports or fabrications the victims think their torturers wish to hear. Clearly, the purpose of torture is not on this level; it is not to gather evidence, but to enforce submission. The cruelty is not incidental; it is the main purpose.

Peremptory executions: the awesomeness of the powerful lord was usually demonstrated in his death-dealing powers: Attila the Hun with his piles of skulls, King David with the heads of his enemies displayed on a spike.[7] This was the extreme dramatization of arbitrary authority.

Human sacrifices: ritual killing as part of a religious ceremony, with a victim offered to the sacred powers of the other world.[8] These are of two types: sacrifices related to periodic fertility celebrations, especially in advanced horticultural societies (e.g., the Aztecs, the Benin of West Africa, the Dionysian sacrifices that entered Greece from Asia Minor); and funerals of aristocrats (e.g.,Shang China or the Hindu suttee) in which slaves and wives follow the dead lord to his grave.

Ritual warhunts: warfare as a ritual frenzy, built up by dancing, drinking or drugs, and culminating in killing patterned after the hunt.[9] The victim is sometimes ritually consumed; in its extreme—cannibalism—he is actually eaten, just like an animal. Not only are the victims treated as animals; the hunters themselves emulate the pack frenzy of carnivorous mammals that hunt their prey in groups.

The explanation of these forms of overt cruelty fits the Durkheim/ Tocqueville model. In each case, the violence is practiced by one group against another to dramatize the fact that the human community and its ties extend only to a certain limit, and that persons outside are alien and subordinate. The kinds of group boundaries are not the same in each instance. Ritual warhunts are found almost exclusively in simple horticultural, hunting, or pastoral tribes, where moral ties are very localistic indeed.[10] Human sacrifices, especially in the form of fertility cults, are found primarily in advanced horticultural societies, in which the religion is a divine kingship or a theocracy of priests. The sacrifice supports the gulf between the divine rulers and their subjects; but in fact, the latter are divided into two groups for moral purposes, corresponding to those under the protection of the local gods and those who are not, and hence, it is almost always captives or slaves from other societies who are the victims of human sacrifices.

This is also true to a degree of funeral sacrifices; the Shang rulers, the

421

pre-iron age (advanced horticultural) dynasty of China, raided other groups for slaves precisely in order to sacrifice them (and like the slave-owning Greeks made a very strong distinction between civilized, i.e., literate human beings, and barbarians fit for slavery and sacrifice). Slavery, in general, it should be noted, is based on these same ritual barriers between groups, especially bolstered by religious communities; slavery in Northern Europe died out with the conversion of the Slavs to Christianity, and it is clearly the extension of Christian missionary activity and the decline of African religion among black slaves that generated the moral sentiments of the anti-slavery movements in America and Britain.

The Hindu suttee—the burning of widows on their husbands' funeral pyres—is in a slightly different category, since Indian society in general has been relatively free from overt violence, for reasons to be considered below. The sacrifice is of women only; and women are in the category of a subordinate but omnipresent group within Hindu society. As such, they are appropriate candidates for human sacrifice.

Peremptory executions, torture, and mutilation are all characteristic of iron-age (agrarian) societies which are highly stratified around a patrimonial form of government. These, indeed, are the most highly stratified societies in world history;[11] and the stratification largely takes the form of external relations of dominance. These are conquest states, often over ethnically diverse areas; administration is tributary rather than intensive, with the local social structure left intact. Hence the moral boundaries along ethnic/religious lines become translated into boundaries along levels of stratification; extreme punishment of the lower by the higher is not only morally neutral, but often is exacerbated into a Sorelian frenzy of defense of the integrity of the dominant group. Hence the public dramatic nature of patrimonial mutilations, tortures, executions: the public is to be impressed that the status community of the aristocracy is not to be infringed in any way, without the most heinous punishment. These cruelties are not only deliberate, they are ceremonially recurrent defenses of the structure of group domination.

In comparing human beings and their activities with those of animals, it appears that the above five types of cruelty constitute a scale. Ritual warhunts are the most animal-like; tortures and mutilations are the most human. That is to say, violence among animals involves a building up of frenzy through an interchange of instinctual gestures. The pack of wolves or rats work each other up into shared ferociousness, which enables them to kill as a team.[12] In this, animals show the same in-group solidarity through arousal against an enemy that Sorel proposed for humans; and indeed their

422

post-kill "celebration" in the form of eating their victim together has its human parallels as well.[13]

The tribal ceremonies designed to stir up the war-frenzy seem to be modeled on those of hunting animals; the fact that these are characteristic of societies with little or no permanent stratification of their own (because of the lack of surplus and permanent wealth) suggests that this democracy of the pack is the only form of group aggression compatible with their usual social organization. It also fits well with the rigid boundaries between tribes often found in this situation; alien tribes may appear as distinct species to each other as do the animals which they often take for their totems.

Compare this relatively direct emotional arousal of the cannibals with the psychology of mutilation or torture. The animal is aroused (the human animal invents ways to do this deliberately), he attacks, he eats. Except for some sense of the fear displayed by his retreating victim, there is no empathy.

The torturer or the mutilator, however, could not even attempt his arts without a capacity for taking the role of the other. The torturer does not kill and eat; he concentrates instead on inflicting pain, and above all, in conveying to his victim his intentions and powers for inflicting this pain. For the animal, terror is only an incident in the combat; for the torturer, it is the prime target. Torture and mutilation, then, are distinctively human acts; they are indeed advanced human acts. The boundaries between groups are involved, making possible the detachment that allows (and motivates) a free use of cruelty; but there is a skill at empathizing across the boundary, enough to be able to gauge the effects of cruelty on its victim. This distinctively human violence becomes symbolic; torture and mutilation are above all forms of communication usable as threats and supports for claims of complete domination.[14] "I can get inside your mind," the torturer boasts: "don't even think of resistance." Mutilation and other public punishments are above all violence to one's social image, and hence are pre-eminently usable for upholding inter-group stratification.

In this perspective, cruelty bears a relation to technological and social evolution. The refined reflexivity of mutilation and torture reflects a more subtle development of human cognitive faculties than the direct emotional arousal of the war-hunt; the human sacrifice is in the middle, organized in a self-consciously religious form but with little attention to refining the pains of the victim. This is borne out by the types of societies in which each of these is commonly found. War-hunts are found primarily in unstratified primitive horticultural. hunting, or pastoral societies; here, external boundaries among

423

groups are very strong, but the external relations are so episodic as to constitute (when they are violent relations) only brief fights, animal-like in their intensity and directness. Human sacrifice is found primarily in advanced horticultural societies, especially around the institution of the divine king or reigning priests, and reflects the gulf between dominant and dominated groups. But such stratification is nevertheless very local in scope; the ruler's power is still very circumscribed by surrounding councils and by the weakness of military technology and administrative organization. Cruelty is now used to uphold the awesomeness of the ruler, but only on limited, highly ceremonial occasions, and without any personal element: a victim is offered to the gods in the name of the society. The extremes of refined cruelty are found in advanced iron age societies, with their great military powers and their high degree of warfare. Patrimonial administration maintains moral boundaries among groups, but the great territorial extension of such states and the prevailing tone of military conflict brings a great many warrior-contenders into the contest. Domination, unstable as it is under such circumstances, is sought with the refinements that come with a literate mentality; a sharp (if unstable) order of internal stratification appears—indeed, the sharpest in all of history—and ferocious and humiliating extremes of violence are used to maintain it.

If we stop at this point and this level of abstraction, it appears that cruelty actually increases with evolutionary advance. The trend is even stronger if the negative instances are brought in, the examples of societies which show relatively little cruelty and violence. Hunting-and-gathering societies (as fas as we can tell) and simple horticultural societies often are relatively peaceful; only a minority are cannibalistic or otherwise warlike, and their violence is very sporadic, external, and unrefined with respect to deliberate cruelty. Compared to this, the height of ferociousness in world history is found among iron-age, agrarian societies, and indeed, among the highly advanced civilizations of this type: ancient Rome, European Christianity, Islam.

The explanation offered here, however, is not an evolutionary one, or even an inverse (or, as we will see, bell-shaped) evolutionary pattern. The variations in group structure that make up the principal explanatory factors are not distributed in a simple way across technological levels. Hence, it is possible to explore this hypothesis into more refined, horizontal comparisons.

The Altruism of the World Religions

One might suppose that the monotheistic or philosophical world religions, with their universal brotherhood and their explicit ethical concerns, would

424

indicate an historical break away from explicit cruelty and towards altruism. Some of them, such as Christianity, have even been formulated as primarily religions of "love." But in historical fact, this is not the case. The world religions arose with the development of cosmopolitan states, "world empires" transcending the previously localized and self-contained kingdoms and their legitimating local gods. Moreover, the world religions have everywhere played a predominantly political role, especially in their early phases, providing the legitimation as well as the administrative apparatus for the large-scale state. In the case of Islam, religion provided the organizing vehicle for a military coalition. Thus, the world religions, far from indicating a break with violence, represent a new form in its organization. Moreover, that form is the most inegalitarian and efficiently stratified form in world history; the iron-age, agrarian societies in which the universalist churches arose supported some of the cruelest forms of stratification ever seen. The moralities of the world religions, generally speaking, contributed more to the extension of violent cruelty than to its mitigation.

In Islam, the church was identical with political organization. Perhaps this is the reason why Islam contains little in the way of personal standards of morality, apart from those laws and ritual obligations defining the status of the respectable and active member of the political community.[16] Islam enjoins charity to widows and orphans, the giving of alms to the poor; but, as we shall see in the case of Christianity, this should not be construed as altruism in any general, empathic sense. The requirement is part of the emphasis on mutual insurance in the community of warriors; moreover, the alms are generally collected by the religious leaders, and hence provide part of their organizational resources. Aside from this alms-giving, Islam emphasized primarily ritual and political obligations, above all whole-hearted commitment to the military expansion of Islam.

It should be noted that Christian propaganda has colored our image of the ferociousness of Islam. In fact, forcible conversion was never very widespread, above all, after the Moslem conquerors discovered the disadvantage of admitting all subjects into the tax-exempt fold of the faithful.[17] There remains a pervasive level of ferocious violence within the Islamic world itself, directed towards upholding the existing deference relationships. As we shall see, none of this is beyond the ferociousness of ancient and medieval Christianity itself. The example of Islam does serve to dramatize the way in which a universalist religion provides little or no mitigation of ferocious violence. The most extreme cases of such violence—the tortures, mutilations, and peremptory punishments of the Ottomans and the Bedouins—may perhaps be explained by an additional element. That is, the core groups of the original Islamic expansion, and its most powerful later converts (in terms of military prowess) came from pastoral cultures; and these are the most male-dominated, violent, and warlike of any societies. The practice of cliteridectomy among the Bedouin, for example, is a ceremonial form of cruelty designed to enhance male control over female sexual property.[18] The pre-universalist religions of such pastoralists are also centered around killing: the act of the sacrifice, which is actually a ceremonial preparation for a group feast. Indeed, it appears that the habitual life of herding, prodding, and killing animals fosters a similar attitude towards people. The introduction of a literate, philosophical, universalist religion only expands the scope of the possible State that can be built around such a culture; internally and externally, it is sharply stratified and violent.[19]

Christianity, at least in the eyes of its modern interpreters, prides itself as being the religion of love. There is the Sermon on the Mount, the parable of the good Samaritan, the admonition to "turn the other cheek," the tradition of the nonviolent martyrs tortured and fed to the lions. Yet the historical record shows very little altruism outside of the sermons of Jesus, and a great deal of ferocious cruelty practiced by Christians, from the very earliest period up through the 18th century.

If one examines the social organization of the earliest band of Christians, it is apparent that universal benevolence played a very small part in its activities. The occasional admonitions of Jesus in favor of non-retribution and passive suffering are contradicted by other admonitions and acts of militancy. The advocacy of nonviolence appears purely tactical, a temporary expedient of the weak and outnumbered. When the force of the crowd favored it, the mood shifted to a violent expulsion of the money-changers from the temple, and later, to the destruction of idols and temples as well as to the enemies of Christ.

In addition to this negative altruism of non-violence, there is a positive altruism in the form of charity. Some of this, however, was due to the organizational demands of the community upon the individual found in any movement: tithes to the church (or in more extreme form, giving up all material property to it) are only a way of controlling such goods in centralized form. The only radical injunction of Christianity is that of charity towards strangers, including ethnic outsiders, illustrated by the good Samaritan story. But this didactic anecdote, apart from what effect it may have had in practice, bears a more sociological interpretation in terms of the lesson about group boundaries: it emphasized, in a fashion that was to be the primary organizational innovation of Christianity, that the moral community

426

(and hence the church organization) could extend beyond the ethnic group. This form of altruism represents the effort to expand Church membership to a potentially universal basis.

Moreover, the particular form of altruism expressed in this story—caring for the sick—has a special significance in the organizing activities of early Christianity. The main proselytizing actions of Jesus and the apostles stressed, not philosophical or moral doctrine, but the sense of miraculous powers immediately manifested.[20] Their paramount reality was the invocation of the Holy Spirit, especially as manifested in medical miracles—the curing of the sick, reviving the dead, casting out of demons; in addition, there were a number of miraculous escapes from prisons and tombs. Such activities might be interpreted in terms of a doctrine of 'love,' insofar as the medical miracles alleviate suffering, and insofar as the intense emotional solidarity involved in generating the proper mood for faith-healing can be so characterized. But this 'love' is a bond within the community extending to those who are about to be admitted into it; the faith healing must be understood as proselytizing, since the cured (and the amazed onlookers) were expected to join the community of the faithful. Within this community, and as long as no disputes arose over internal control of it, altruism might hold; to its enemies, however, there remained no barrier to the utmost ferocity.

The persecution of the Christians at the hands of the Roman state illustrates the underlying violence of the situation. For Christianity was persecuted only (with a minor and local exception under Nero) when it had become a major political faction; the persecutions of Diocletian were part of a final struggle for dominance within the empire, and preceded by only 10 years the final ascension of the pro-Christian faction with Constantine in 313.[21] The Christians in power acted exactly like their former persecutors. Indeed, existing forms of torture, slavery, and mutilation (e.g., eunuchry) were not abolished, but widely used by the Christian emperors.[22] Nor did Christian ferocity come only from the political officials among its sympathizers. From the beginning, there were violent conflicts within the Church over questions of heresy and leadership. The election of the Bishop of Rome in 366 was settled by the murder of several hundreds of one Christian faction by another;[23] struggles over the Bishoprics of Constantinople and Alexandria were fought out by mobs hurling stones. When the Church felt its strength, its pagan opponents were subject to ferocious violence, as in the case of the philosopher Hypatia:

> . . .in the holy season of Lent, Hypatia was torn from her chariot, stripped naked, dragged to the church, and inhumanly butchered by the hands of Peter the reader and a troop of savage and merciless fanatics; her flesh was

scraped from her bones with sharp oystershells, and her quivering limbs were delivered to the flames.[24]

The ferocity of this attack, it should be noted, is ceremonial, combining elements of the tribal war-hunt with the refined torture and mutilation of the iron-age aristocracy defending its status.

Indeed, this is the main consequence of Christianity for social organization: it provided a basis for a universal state, with internal stratification based on a solidary elite. It provided for the first time in the Western world the mass mobilization of groups within the urban, cosmopolitan society of the Mediterranean; such groups were then brought directly into the struggle for political and social domination. If this universalism also contained some philosophical bases for altruism, in practice, this simply meant the potentially universal membership of the church-state; its main effects on the phenomenon of cruelty were not altruistic. It provided a means for mobilizing people for violence in a highly emotional form. Its universalism served only to allow the degree of empathy necessary to understand the depths of torture and humiliation that might be inflicted on one's opponents. Universal religion here extends human empathy in a form that heightens the psychological aspects of the struggle for dominance; ferociousness is heightened, not limited, by the availability of social categories of infidelism and heresy.

Medieval Christianity, with its judicial tortures, crusades, inquisitions, and witch-burnings, is not an aberration from the main pattern, but the pattern itself. Altruism, in its Christian form, is usually characteristic of the medieval church. But this altruism stayed within the mold already set. The papacy's occasional claims to benevolent rule over European society were simply the ideological side of its political claim for dominion;[25] even its prohibition on internal warfare (which itself was not so much observed as used as an occasion for the scale of indulgences), only saved military forces for the external enemies of an ambitious ruler. The positive acts of medieval Christian charity—visiting the sick, visiting prisons, burying the dead, caring for widows and orphans — continue to be both a form of mutual insurance for those safely within the orthodox community, and an organizing device (not the least, financial) for the church. One might add that this kind of charity is hardly the essence of humanitarian altruism. It does not represent a universal sympathy and a striving towards the spreading of individual happiness; it is rather a negative, organization-oriented altruism. It aims in part to alleviate extreme suffering, but not to remove it; indeed, here we find yet another version of the inner alliance first pointed out by Nietzsche: Christianity battening on suffering. The aim is to support the organization of

428

the benevolent community: the sick, the poor, the lepers, are necessary suf-
ferers in the scheme of things, wretched and blessed at the same time.[26]
Above all, alms are for the deserving poor, the repenting, obedient, subser-
vient; acts of charity are ceremonial reaffirmations of domination and subor-
dination, in which the extremes of suffering are preserved and affirmed as
emblems of the social order that is being upheld.

In his comparative analysis of the world religions, Weber points out that the
Western religions, growing out of the literate civilizations of the Near East,
have an especially military tone.[27] The Near East is an area of many
heartlands, and hence fosters a number of relatively unstable military states.
Their early state gods are strong personalities, above all, gods of arbitrary
power, war and domination. Monotheism appears there when the expansion
of a few states calls into question the power of particularistic gods. But the
monotheisms—Zoroastrianism of the Persians, Jahwehism of the Palestine
kingdom, later Christianity, Mithraism, Islam—retain the militaristic, violent
tone of their predecessors. By contrast, the religions of the orient, in regions
which either supported only a single heartland-state without external rivals
(China) or where geographical conditions made a prolonged state power
difficult (India), were philosophical transformations of more primitive nature-
cults. The ferocity of the West, in a world perspective, is rooted in its especially militaristic history, where the unstable resources for total military
domination have enhanced a continual struggle, and supported a particularly
ferocious use of violence.

The example of India lends weight to this analysis, and also amplifies the
Durkheimian theme with which we began. For Indian society, although never
approaching the ideal of non-violence preached in the highest form of
Brahminism and in many of the salvation cults, has nevertheless shown much
less ferocious violence than the West.[28] Orthodox Hinduism, in fact, makes a
special place for the warrior, the (Kshatriya) caste; the famous Bhagavadgita's
central concern is to justify a battle, even against kinsmen, as part of the
ordained karma of that particular station. But this same device also encapsulated and limited the use of violence, above all since the caste system
maintained privilege through the mechanism of group inclusion and
exclusion, establishing pervasive ritual barriers in every activity of life. The
Kshatriya caste, although fighting within itself for political domination (over
rather small kingdoms, at that) was not itself the bulwark of the caste system.
Ferociousness is most institutionalized where ritual boundaries are structured
within an autonomous state; India had the former without the latter. Hence, the
relative lack of mutilation and exemplary punishment in India (at least of the
classical period, before the Moslem conquest, and after the rise of the caste

429

system by the end of the Mauyra period); even judicial torture, so widespread everywhere in the pre-industrial world, was not used in medieval India.

Indian Society has its own form of cruelty. The caste system can be described as a special form of the cruelty of callousness. The inferior position of women, also supported by the reincarnation doctrine, involved other forms of callousness, including the extreme form of the immolation of widows. Yet all of this is far from the ferocious violence characteristic of other iron-age societies. India, the negative case, supports both the Weberian and the Durkheimian theories. India, the land of the limited, weak state, had a religion emphasizing ritual barriers, not forcible subjugation, passivity and inner experience, not external domination. In terms of group boundaries, one may say that the caste system makes for psychologically impenetrable barriers;[29] the degree of empathy necessary to motivate torture, mutilation, terrorist punishments does not exist; nor does stratification *within* a ceremonial community, which is the structure upheld by symbolic and ferocious uses of violence.

The position of Buddhism is more ambiguous.[30] As a religion of mystical contemplation and freedom from the illusoriness of the material world, it promotes pacifism; as a religion of universal salvation, it promotes a certain form of altruism. But it is the altruism of mutual escape from misery, not mutual sympathy for individual happiness. Moreover, Buddhism has made the political alliances characteristic of all great world religions, and thus has involved itself in particular forms of violence. In central Asia, above all Tibet (but also the nomadic coalitions such as those of the Mongols), Buddhism provided the literate civilization that made possible military organization on a large scale; in these areas, it amalgamated with shamanistic religions (and especially the ferocious, death-oriented cults of pastoralists), to produce a rather ferocious military Buddhism. In South-East Asia, on the other hand, Buddhism adapted itself to relatively pacifist, weak kinships of the advanced horticultural variety. In China, where Confucianism provided (after the end of the warring states period, from which our early quotation from Han Fei Tzu derives) a set of universalist principles for the educated civil servant class, Buddhism entered as an organizing device for rival political factions. Amalgamating with Taoism, its results included quietism, but also at particular times rebellious political movements legitimated by apocalyptic versions of Buddhism (especially Amitabha, the future Buddha). Accordingly, Chinese Buddhism underwent some of the same cycles of favor and official persecution experienced by Christianity in the Roman Empire. With these military ramifications, it is not surprising that Chinese Buddhism developed a more activist form (Ch'an Buddhism, whose emphasis on sudden illumination

430

was compatible with manual work), and even created its distinctive martial art (Kempo, the predessor of karate and kung fu, originating in the Shao-lin-su monastery of the lower Yangtze around 500 A.D.). Literate civilization spread to Korea and Japan through the vehicle of Buddhism; in medieval Japan, Buddhism had become militarized to the extent that armed monasteries held the balance of power for several centuries. After the defeat of this extreme form of militarism, the influence of Buddhism on the military culture of Japan continued through the training of warriors in Zen Buddhist techniques of fighting.[31]

In the degree of ferocity, the history of violence in Japan bears some resem-blance to India. The samurai ethic, based on an extreme form of military courage, was hedged round with an elaborate system of courtesies that reduced its ferociousness; to engage in violence was itself a mark of privileged status, never of humiliation. This extended even to the practice of permitting suicide rather than execution. The power of the aristocracy over other ranks of society, supported by constant ritual deference and built into the very structure in the terms of verbal address, seems to have provided the equiva-lent of the mutual caste isolation of India. Japanese society has been more violent than Indian; but the violence has been largely confined to a gentle-manly game within the aristocracy itself.

Chinese society after the Han dynasty lacked this military aristocratic emphasis; its cultural ideal, instead, has been the rule of an internally pacified empire by literate, cultivated administrators.[32] The macho ethic was lacking here; the military forces were concentrated on the borders, and the heartland of the civilization adhered to another ethic. That ethic, expressed most strongly in Confucianism, emphasized traditional loyalties and subordina-tions within the family and within the structures of government. The power of emperor, mandarin, family head, were indeed upheld by force—above all by beating (even to the point of death), with bamboo sticks. The mutilations and public ferocity of the warring states period seem to have been reduced; torture in judicial proceedings and punishments appear to have had less of the public ceremonial significance of more militarized and conflictful societies, and the Mandarins were given special exemption. Here again one may invoke the Durkheimian dimension: the stratification of Chinese society, built around the centralized state, encompassed and reinforced traditional psychological barriers among groups—in this case, especially kinship groups—that institutionalized ferocity even in the milder Confucian ethos.[33]

431

The Decline of Ferocious Violence

Modern society has seen an abrupt decline in ferocity. Torture, mutilation, exemplary punishment have disappeared as ideals; while these practices still occur they do so privately and secretly—in the hidden interrogation rooms of police stations, in the personal interaction between guard and prisoner—rather than as the explicit, ceremonial enactments fundamental to the social order. Executions are now to be humane and relatively painless, and are carried out in private; their justification is generally held to be of a rational, educative, warning nature, not passionate vengeance.[34] Ferocity in war becomes atrocity, to be hidden, or even expiated, not gloried in. The heads of male-factors are no longer displayed on spikes, but buried from view.

At what point does the transition come about? We have seen that it does not depend on the universal religions per se, least of all historical Christianity. The movement aginst ferocity, rather, is a secularizing movement, originating perhaps with Erasmus and the tolerant rationalists who oppposed the fanaticisms of the Reformation period; it gained ground with the anti-religious *philosophes* of the French Enlightenment and their British utilitarian counterparts; and began to have a practical effect with the judicial reforms, the anti-slavery campaigns, and other benevolent movements of the 19th century.[35] It is true that a number of liberal (non-ritualist, non-traditionalist) Christian reformers were involved in these movements; but in general, it indicates a break with the ritual boundaries of stratification upheld by traditional religion. This is clearest in the case of the most vehement enemies of religion, the socialists and the communist radicals, who perhaps for the first time extended altruism into a positive concern for universal human happiness, rather than merely a token concern for suffering as an ungoing part of an order of privilege and deference.

In terms of our theoretical principles, the explanation seems to be structural shift. Modern industrial society, for the first time, makes for a shift in patterns of interpersonal interaction that destroy the traditional ceremonial barriers among groups. Above all, the fortified household, with its support for the moral absolutism of the family community and its internal authority structure, gives way to the community of small private households;[36] urbanism, mass transportation, large-scale work and business organizations, mass education, all contribute towards the replacement of older ritual barriers with a new form of ritual co-membership. The social conditions for the human community, in general, emerge for the first time. Along with this, differential resources remain in existence, and the struggle for power, wealth and prestige goes on. But a crucial earlier resource—freely available private

432

violence—is no longer permissible because of the monopolization of violence by the modern state and the ritual barriers that both allowed its use and motivated the retention of a specific deference structure have largely disappeared. With the passing of these conditions, the ceremonial ideal of ferocity has disappeared.

In its place, we have two conflicting tendencies. On the one hand, conditions favor universal movements, including those proclaiming extreme forms of altruism. At the same time, the large-scale and remote organizational forms of modern society do not eliminate the tools of violence and manipulation, but only depersonalize them. Turning from the evil of ferocity, modern social structure delivers us into the hands of another evil: callousness. And in the very mobilization of modern groups there emerges still another side of altruism: demands upon the individual in the form of asceticism.

II. Callousness and Bureaucratization

Callousness is cruelty without passion: the kind of hardship or violence people may inflict on others without a special intent to hurt. The subject of the violence is simply an instrument or an obstacle, and his suffering is merely an incidental (usually ignored) feature of some other intention. In this sense, the structural conditions for callousness must be very different from those that produce ferocious violence. Torture, mutilation, and exemplary punishment all involve a certain type of empathy between perpetrator and victim; the victim's subjective life is the target, and his total personality is to be deformed. By comparison, callous violence represents a very restricted contact with the victim, and arises from structures that cut off the possibility of personal empathy.

Callousness is found in all societies throughout history, but it is especially characteristic of certain types. In a sense, the extreme mutual isolation of primitive tribes results in a form of callousness towards each other; but the amount of cruelty done is likely to be severely limited by the very sporadic nature of such external contacts. Where social relationships are organized on a regular basis along impersonal lines, however, callous cruelty is maximal. This of course is the theme of Marx, especially in terms of the callousness of the wage system in an impersonal market economy.

More generally, callous cruelty is especially characteristic of large-scale, bureaucratic organization, the violence of the modern army and state. Indeed, the structural organization of bureaucracy seems uniquely suited to the perpetration of callous violence. Bureaucracy is typically hierarchic, and

433

hence, routinely enforces relationships of domination and submission. But both the means and the ends of bureaucratic action deal not with the individual person and his subjective feelings, but with segmented elements of individual lives. The fundamental principle of bureaucracy, indeed, is the separation of the individual from the position; instead of the charisma of the individual, there is the charisma of office; instead of personal power and personal domination, there is domination by reference to formalities and specialized functions.

Thus, even the application of violence is carried out segmentally; the bureaucrat does not invest his personality and his subjective status in the dominance relationship that results, and the identity and feelings of the victim are not a concern. Bureaucratic violence is the psychological opposite of the ceremonial ferocity of patrimonial society; however painful and terrifying the consequences, they are epiphenomenal to the more general policy being carried out.

The major atrocities of the 20th century are of this sort. The Nazi extermination camps were the epitome of bureaucratic organization.[37] What we find so horrifying about them, above all, is their dramatization of the ultimate Kafka-esque possibilities we have always feared lurked in this organizational form. The very methodical, impersonal, and ritually unthreatening character of most stages of the Nazi extermination procedures, are features which no doubt were most responsible for the relative lack of resistance and even the degree of active compliance among the Jewish victims. The secrecy of the camps and gas chambers, the night-time round-ups—all of these stand in sharp contrast to the public, ritual nature of violence in patrimonial societies. For the Nazi participants, the well-known "Eichmann syndrome," the routinized following of orders, eliminated any personal sense of moral responsibility. And it is this, the turning up of the dark side of the bureaucracy that surrounds us, which makes the Nazis an emblem of the specifically modern horror, a horror that dwarfs the personalized cruelties of the Middle Ages.[38]

One prophetic element of the Nazi extermination camps was their use of technology, not only to enhance the bureaucratic efficiency of their callous violence, but to depersonalize and distance it from human contact. The development of high-altitude bombing in the Second World War represents the same sort of atrocity, perhaps extended to even more de-personalized limits. The atomic bombings of Japan are only the most dramatic (because both technically novel and highly publicized) of the atrocities of the fire-bombings of major cities in Japan, Germany, and Britain, with their heavy

434

concentration of civilian casualties. The atrocities of the Vietnam War, again, stem above all from a long-distance bombing policy.[39] Not only were the more publicized incidents – the My Lai massacre and a few others – minor by comparison to the several million casualties of the indiscriminate bombing campaigns throughout South Vietnam, but they are uncharacteristic of the fundamental nature of the atrocities.

Janowitz has argued that modern military organizations have become internally more civilian-like, above all in the air force, because of the emphasis on technological expertise rather than traditional regimentation.[40] But on the external side, the capacity for callous destruction multiplies correspondingly. The traditional deference procedures between officers and men in the military lessen with the modern bureaucratization of their organization, and along with them goes some of the sadism that characterized internal rankings, and perhaps even the personal attitudes characteristic of soldiers towards the outside world. In its place, though, we find an increase in callousness when the men use instruments of unsurpassed destructiveness. In guerilla warfare, as in Vietnam, where guerillas are not only mingled with the civilian population, but very often *are* the civilians, including the women and children, it is not surprising that the use of long-distance, bureaucratically administered weapons should produce appalling atrocities. The long chain of information reporting and the very impersonality of communications categories served to keep much of the human consequences from the awareness of not only the American public, but of the soldiers themselves; but enough leaked through to create the most extreme sense of schizophrenia between the low-key personal relationships within the modern military and their vicious consequences for its victims.

III. Asceticism and Enforced Community Membership

Asceticism, at its extreme, is a turning inwards of cruelty, directing it towards oneself. In its origins, asceticism was purely personal, a form of self-denial valued for its supposed key mystical experience. Insofar as asceticism became a part of social organization in religions like Buddhism, it was the social organization of voluntary drop-outs from ordinary social experience; hence, violence towards outsiders was shunned as simply one more ordinary social tie to be cut in the interest of entering the Void.

Asceticism becomes organized social cruelty when an ascetic religion becomes part of the on-going, secular social structure. In this, Christianity is the prime example.[41] The ascetic ideal, the mark of holiness for the religious specialist, takes on wider significance when a church is organized, and its leaders become the exemplars of ordinary life. What Weber called "inner-worldly asceticism" (i.e., asceticism in the world) may be viewed not only as a motivating force for economic activities, but also as the transformation of self-denial, even positive self-cruelty, into a dominant social ideal. Such a status hierarchy in itself generally constitutes an increase in social cruelty by its effect on others through emulation. Moreover, when religion becomes an important administrative and ceremonial adjunct to the state, as well as the basis for community organization, then the influence of ascetic cruelty becomes coercive. Not only is the ascetic individual rewarded with high status (and certain opportunities for power and wealth), but asceticism becomes a mark of membership in the community, and is enforced upon everyone by external authority.

The first level of cruelty in asceticism is the cruelty of deprivation, especially of those forms of happiness that are most private and individual. These include, above all, sexuality (especially in forms that have not been ceremonially justified by the group); the focusing of attention on one's own body and on the private moods of one individual or two (or perhaps a small group), is the attitude most to be combatted by an ascetic mode of social organization. Hence the ban on vanity and display in clothes and decor—precisely because they are individualizing, and because they celebrate the particularism of the body.[42] Lighthearted, trivial, individualized games are banned for the same reason; games are acceptable only if they are made serious, contestlike, above all requiring the mobilization of the individual into the collective cause.[43] Alcohol and drugs, one the subject of battles for control by advocates of traditional community structures in the early 20th century, the other the focus of a similar battle today, are above all privatizing agents, hence anathema to the ascetic representative of group controls and duties.[44]

Asceticism may be extended to more symbolic manifestations of individualism. The labor camps and insane asylums of the Soviet Union are used to enforce political conformity, even along lines which do not involve real substantive disagreements with the program of socialism but only with the principle of individual discussion of policy matters. These punishments (although *perhaps* a more extreme example) are representative of the form that ascetic controls take everywhere. The punishment is regarded as a form of purgatory; the offender is not simply the inadvertent victim of callous violence, nor a low-status creature to be humiliated or mutilated. His identity as a deviant is not conceived of as permanent; the punishment, rather, is to change his soul, to strip him of individualist tendencies and to reintegrate him into the ascetic standards of the group.

436

We can now see the distinctive social organization underlying ascetic violence. It implies a ceremonially united community, and one which places the strongest possible emphasis on individual membership and commitment. It is, moreover, a community which ceremonially emphasizes the equality and equal participation of all members within it. Such an organization is characteristic of universal religions and universal moral reform movements. It should be especially intense during those times when the group makes the greatest demands on its individual members, above all, in times of war or conflict with outside forces. It should reach a maximum during periods of struggle over the very nature of the group's boundaries, which are defined ideologically as periods of struggle against heresies. Thus, we find the height of ascetic atrocities—purgatorial actions—during the Reformation and Counter-reformation in medieval Christianity;[45] comparable outbreaks of ascetic violence were characteristic of the Sunni-Shi'ite battles in Islam. There is also the milder, less violent upsurges of asceticism found when groups within a society fight to maintain or raise their social status, putting pressure on all individual members to maintain a united front. An example of this defensive sort of asceticism is found at the height of the anti-alcohol crusade in the U.S.; of the offensive sort, the "Victorian revolution" in sexual mores that accompanied the mobilization of modern women in their first effort to raise their social status.[46]

Ascetic cruelty remains important in the modern secular world because the issues of community membership and individual obligation to the group continue in the struggles of status groups, and political mobilization of any conflict groups in society—including both intellectual factions and larger social classes—is a continual phenomenon. We cannot escape the fact that most of the major humanitarian reform movements of the modern era, above all Marxism, but also to a lesser degree piece-meal reformisms, are especially prone to ascetic cruelty. Their very universalism and their intense mobilization makes it easy; wherever their gaze is turned outwards towards their enemies, and not inwards towards their own dangers, it becomes all the more likely.

Conclusion

In our contemporary society, ferocious cruelty is no longer structurally induced; it is no longer part of the dominant ceremonial order, although we still find individual cases. In this sense, modern society appears more humane. But at the same time, the dangers of callousness increase; and the technological efficiency of modern instruments of destruction makes its consequencess all the more appalling while it hides them from view. Between these opposing trends, ascetic cruelty has had its ups and downs, cresting during periods of mobilized conflict.

There is no evolutionary trend towards kindness and happiness. Ferociousness once increased, then declined; callousness and asceticism now oppose each other as defenders and challengers of the status quo. And the institutionalized asceticism of a victorious revolutionary movement easily amalgamates with the callousness of an established bureaucratic regime.

The demons can be exorcised, but only by seeing them for what they are. Those who claim that the demons can be exorcised only by action in the world, not by theorizing about them, seem to be possessed by demons of their own, especially the demon of asceticism; one senses here the communal hostility of the ascetic to the individual luxury of intellectual contemplation. And here is the danger. Those who deny everything for the self deny it as well for others; our altruism, taken too exclusively, is an infinite regress, passing a bucket from hand to hand that never reaches the fire. When we act, we call out the demons to meet us. Be careful: they are ourselves.

Notes

1 Han Fei Tzu, *Basic Writings*, New York: Columbia University Press, 1964, p. 80. Original ca. 235 B.C.
2 Han Fei Tzu, of course, is the arch-Legalist and anti-Confucian of his day. This passage nevertheless illustrates both the borrowing of the Legalists from the Confucians, and foreshadows the synthesis of a bureaucratic ideology in the unified state after 221 B.C.
3 Alexis de Tocqueville, *Democracy in America*, volume 2, New York: Vintage books, 1960, pp. 174–175; originally published 1840.
4 Talcott Parsons, "Evolutionary Universals in Society," in *Sociological Theory and Modern Society*, New York: Free Press, 1967; *Societies, Evolutionary and Comparative Perspectives*, Englewood Cliffs: Prentice-Hall, 1966; *The System of Modern Societies*, Englewood Cliffs: Prentice-Hall, 1971.
5 Georges Sorel, *Reflections on Violence*, New York: Free Press, 1970. Originally published 1908.
6 Alan Moorehead, *The Blue Nile*, New York: Harper and Row, 1963, p. 192.
7 1 Samuel 17: 51–54; 2 Samuel 4: 7–12.
8 Gerhard Lenski, *Power and Privilege: A Theory of Social Stratification*, New York: McGraw-Hill, 1966, pp. 155–159.
9 Gerhard Lenksi, *Human Societies*, New York: McGraw-Hill, 1970, pp. 225–227.

438

10 Lenski, *Human Societies*, p. 139; *Power and Privilege*, pp. 122–123. The five main categories of social organization presented here are based on the predominant technology: hunting-and-gathering (stone implements), simple horticultural (primitive agriculture, digging sticks), advanced horticultural (soft metal tools, possibly irrigation agriculture), agrarian (iron tools, plows, and weapons, animal power), industrial (inanimate energy technology).

11 Lenski, *Power and Privilege*, p. 437.

12 Konrad Lorenz, *On Aggression*, New York: Harcourt, Brace, 1966, pp. 133–158.

13 There is another element of emotional contagion: not only between hunter and hunter, but between hunter and hunted. The dog is set in motion by the frightened running of the rabbit. This kind of aggressor-victim interaction seems to go on in human animals in all of the more refined forms of human cruelty; human symbolic capacities only add to the ways in which these phenomena may become consciously sought after.

14 Animals do not torture or mutilate one another; they either fight, or quickly arrive at a situation of token deference.

15 Lenski, *Human Societies*, pp. 138–139, 474–475.

16 Tor Andrae, *Mohammed, the Man and his Faith*, New York: Harper and Row, 1960, pp. 73–79.

17 William McNeill, *The Rise of the West*, Chicago: University of Chicago Press, 1963, pp. 469–471.

18 William J. Goode, *World Revolution and Family Patterns*, New York: Free Press, 1963, pp. 147, 211.

19 By contrast, as Weber noted, it is among city people, especially those in crafts and commerce who never come in contact with animals, that pacificist moralities have arisen. Marx Weber, *The Religion of India*, New York: Free Press, 1958, pp. 199–200; originally published 1916–1917.

20 See the Gospels of St. Matthew, St. Mark, St. Luke, St. John, and The Acts of the Apostles.

21 Henry Chadwick, *The Early Church*, Baltimore: Penguin Books, 1967, pp. 116–124.

22 A characteristic utterance of the Empress Theodora: "If you fail in the execution of my commands, I swear by him who lives forever that your skin shall be flayed from your body." Edward Gibbon, *The Decline and Fall of the Roman Empire*, New York: Washington Square Press, 1963, p. 305. Originally published 1776–1787.

23 Chadwick, *The Early Church*, pp. 160–161. The origins of the doctrine of papal infallibility date from this incident; the individual who won the Bishopric of Rome in this fashion was so badly discredited personally that he strictly emphasized the sanctity of the office as separate from that of its occupant.

24 Gibbon, *The Decline and Fall*, pp. 256–257.

25 R.W. Southern, *Western Society and the Church in the Middle Ages*, Baltimore: Penguin Books, 1970, pp. 36–41 and *passim.*

26 Michel Foucault, *Madness and Civilization*, New York: Random House, 1965, pp. 17–18.

27 Max Weber, *The Religion of China*, New York: Free Press, 1951, pp. 20–29. Originally published 1915.

28 D.D. Kosambi, *The Culture and Civilization of Ancient India*, Delhi: Vikas Publications, 1970, pp. 133, 151, 157, 173, 197, and *passim*; Louis Dumont, *Homo Hierarchicus; The Caste System and Its Implications*, Delhi: Vikas Publications; Lloyd I. Rudolph and Susanne Hoeber Rudolph, *The Modernity of Tradition*, Chicago: University of Chicago Press, 1967, pp. 160–192. P.T. Borale, *Segregation. and Desegregation in India*, Bombay: Manaktalas, 1968, pp. 83–94 shows that the ancient laws of Manu prescibe mutilation as the punishment for various small offenses by Sudras against the dignity of the higher castes: Spitting on a Brahmin called for cutting off the lips, listening to the Vedas called for filling the ears with

439

molten tin. These were the laws of the early period of expanding military states, struck down in the Buddhist regime of the Maurya dynasty, and later replaced by a primarily exclusionary structure of the later caste system. I am indebted to Gail Omvedt for pointing out these sources, and for discussion on these points; the interpretation however is my own.

29 The very word for "caste" is "jati," which also denotes distinctive animal species.

30 McNeill, *The Rise of the West*, pp. 587–590; Melford E. Spiro, *Buddhism and Society*, New York: Harper and Row, 1970; D.T. Suzuki, *Zen and Japanese Culture*, New York: Pantheon, 1959; Matsutatsu Oyama, *This is Karate*, Tokyo: Japan Publishing and Trading Company, 1965, pp. 307–317; William Theodore de Bary, *The Buddhist Tradition*, New York: Random House, 1969.

31 Japanese Buddhism is noted for other extreme versions of secularization, including the practice of priestly marriage–in a religion in which celibacy was the *sine qua non*–and a distinctively nationalistic doctrine of salvation, Nichiren Buddhism.

32 Weber, *The Religion of China.*

33 There are other aspects of violence in Chinese society that strike one today as unjust, especially the punishment of family members for the transgressions of a kinsman. But this is a general aspect of patrimonial social structure, and should not be confused with ferocity *per se.*

34 A great deal of popular support for the death penalty, however, seems to come from advocates of a traditionalist group structure (and probably members of such pockets of traditional groups as exist in modern society); although they may argue in the language of deterrence, the tone bespeaks ritual revenge of a strictly Durkheimian sort. The rationalist opponents of the death penalty have failed to grasp this.

35 The classic advocate of cruelty, the Marquis de Sade, emerges in the transitional period, and his writings capture all the major structural elements of the system then passing out of existence: the hermetically sealed status-group of the aristocracy, the awesome terror of traditional Christianity, and the deliberate use of violence for psychological effect. De Sade shared enough of the Enlightenment's clarity to express, far better than the *philosophes*, the nature of the society that was passing away.

36 Phillipe Aries, *Centuries of Childhood*, New York: Random House, 1962, pp. 365–404; Lawrence Stone, *The Crisis of the Aristocracy*, New York: Oxford University Press, 1967, pp. 96–134.

37 Of course the individual face-to-face relationships between guards and prisoners provided scope for personal sadism as well. Political and military torture do not disappear entirely in the modern world; the transition to bureaucratic organization is hardly uniform at all places and all levels. In this sense, we may use the instances in which it occurs as further variations against which to test the model of ferocity proposed above. For modern ferocity seems to occur in precisely those instances where strong ritual barriers may still be found among stratified groups: above all, sadistic torture seems to occur across ethnic lines, both in prisons and in warfare, as in the pervasive atrocities of the French-Algerian war.

38 Cf. Hannah Arendt, *Eichmann in Jerusalem: A Report on the Banality of Evil*, New York: Viking Press, 1963. Stanley Milgram, "Behavior Study of Obedience," *Journal of Abnormal and Social Psychology* 67 (1963): 371–378, shows experimentally the degree of impersonal cruelty that benign middle class persons will inflict when given instructions in a bureaucratic setting.

39 Frank Harvey, *Air War: Vietnam*, New York: Bantam Books, 1967.

40 Morris Janowitz, *The Professional Soldier*, New York: Free Press, 1960.

41 The manifestations of such asceticism have varied during the history of Christianity, especially as the more patrimonial structure of medieval European society came to the fore. It was above all during periods when the purer Christian ideal has been emphasized (and along with it, the power of the church and its leaders) that asceticism has been most clearly enforced.

440

42 Compare the practice of head-shaving in monasteries, and the emphasis on short
   hair-cuts (e.g., crew-cuts in America during the 1950s) in the military and in admiring
   civilian groups during periods of ascetic group mobilization; long hair and beards thus
   serve as emblems of individualist revolt. (cf. Mary Douglas, *Natural Symbols*,
   Baltimore: Penguin Books, 1971), for an analysis of this point, and of the properties
   of group boundaries, generally consonant with the theory of violence advanced here.
43 Cf. the fanatic intensity of interest in school *team* sports in the more traditional
   Christian communities in America.
44 Joseph R. Gusfield, *Symbolic Crusade*, Urbana: University of Illinois Press, 1963.
45 H.R. Trevor-Roper, *Religion, Reformation, and Social Change*, London: Macmillan,
   1967, pp. 90–192; cf. Keith Thomas, *Religion and the Decline of Magic*, New York:
   Scribner's, 1971.
46 Randall Collins, "A Conflict Theory of Sexual Stratification," *Social Problems* 19
   (Summer, 1971), pp. 3–21.

Theory and Society, 1 (1974) 415–440
© Elsevier Scientific Publishing Company, Amsterdam – Printed in the Netherlands

[23]

Genocide and Mass Destruction: Doing Harm to Others as a Missing Dimension in Psychopathology

Israel W. Charny

PSYCHOLOGY and psychiatry lose much of their common-sense credibility so long as they offer no way of defining execution of and participation in mass murder and genocide as pathological. This paper proposes an expansion of the standard classification system in psychopathology to include abuses and destruction of other people, so that persons who terminate the lives of others are defined as "disturbed."

Historian George Kren and psychologist Leon Rappaport (1980) have described the Holocaust as the major historical crisis of the 20th century; it imposes on virtually all existing institutions—law, religion, education, all professions—a fundamental re-evaluation of basic concepts. The awesome facts of the Holocaust render existing models and values of virtually all disciplines nearly meaningless. "Since the Holocaust *was* possible, prior cultural values supposed to make it impossible were manifestly false, and a moral crisis is imposed upon the whole fabric of the culture" (p. 131).

It is my judgment that, similarly, the Holocaust has shattered existing psychological concepts of normality and abnormality. According to accepted psychiatric definitions, it was largely *normal* people— both leaders and followers—who executed the most systematic evil in the history of humankind (see Charny 1982 for a detailed summary of the evidence of the "normality of the genociders"). Yet it is inconceivable that we reconcile ourselves to mental health concepts that do not define, in some intelligent way, the leaders and followers who execute mass murder as disturbed and abnormal.

We have known this intuitively. Men of good will have always know that wanton destruction of human life is an act of madness—even if an entire group and society of people are mad at the same time. But we have failed to create the language concepts to express this truth in the traditional discipline of psychopathology.

For the most part, the professional world of mental health teaches about mental illness that disturbed people feel badly about themselves, have difficulty functioning in their everyday lives, perhaps are no longer able to work, have difficulties getting along with other people, are sexually incompetent, get drunk, write bad checks, accuse their neighbors of plotting against them, hear voices, and so on. At the same time, mental health professionals say little about deeply prejudiced people who deny the validity of other people's existence, and noth-

Israel W. Charny, PhD, is Executive Director, Institute of the International Conference on the Holocaust and Genocide, POB 10311, Jerusalem 93624 Israel; and Associate Professor of Psychology, Bob Shapell School of Social Work, Tel Aviv University.
An earlier draft of this paper was first presented at the International Conference on the Holocaust and Genocide, Tel Aviv, 1982 (Charny and Davidson 1983), and appears in the proceedings of the conference (Charny 1984).

GENOCIDE AND MASS DESTRUCTION

ing at all about people who put on uniforms and kill others en masse, as if these were not psychopathological issues.

Understandably, our diagnostic system developed out of a medical model for understanding sickness and inability to function in the individual himself, and by definition this way of thinking did not relate to what individuals do to make others incompetent.

However, it does not make sense to have a discipline that purports to study the nature of man and his behaviors and does not take into account the incredible destructiveness of people to one another. Factually, the toll of mass destruction exceeds the toll of any dread illness and is the single most frequent cause of unnatural loss of life (see Pilisuk and Ober 1976, on torture and genocide as "public health problems").

It also makes no sense to have a psychology of *normal* man that does not provide an honest and clear-cut picture of the potential of most human beings to do or allow harm to others under various circumstances. We know today from critical psychological studies that most people can be seduced by powerful group, authority, or ideological processes into harming others. For example, Asch's (1956) classic experiments on the ways in which people give up their ability to think independently under social pressure, the so-called bystander studies (Darley and Latane 1968), Zimbardo et al.'s study (1975) of a simulation of a prison situation, and Milgram's (1974) brilliant "Eichmann Experiment" make it clear that most people – normal by accepted definition – can be led to participate in or at least to allow harm to or the destruction of others. These capacities need to be identified and acknowledged in the psychology of "normal" people – meaning the realistic understanding of human beings as they naturally are.

In addition, psychology is responsible not only for describing the range of human behavior but also for providing a theory or conceptual image of what is desirable and mentally healthy for individuals, families, and groups who want to actualize and maximize their life powers and human poten-

tial. The fact that most human beings are capable of being destructive must be part of the knowledge base of any standard psychology, but I believe that the science of psychology must also develop a logical basis for defining harm and destruction of other human beings as pathological. We need an integrated psychology that makes it clear that doing harm to others is, tragically, not only a common and widespread expression of the human condition but also a distinctly unhealthy and abnormal expression of psychological man – the individual as well as the collective process.

The challenge to psychology is to project a picture of the normal human being as he or she might be in more mature development – in any of a variety of senses, such as Kohlberg's (1966) concept of arrival at a higher stage of ethical thought, Erikson's (1964) concept of unfolding to greater maturity and responsibility, or Maslow's (1971) movement toward self-actualization. Psychology must provide normal, well-intentioned people with new tools to help them avoid being drawn into prevailing trends of violence toward others.

If we turn to the metaphor of illness, there have been many diseases in the history of humankind to which huge numbers of people succumbed until a way was found to contain, treat, and prevent the deadly illness. If even a majority of people succumb to a plague, the contraction of that illness is not considered "normal" and the exceptional survivor is not considered "abnormal." We cannot rest content with the idea that genocide is a behavior of normal people, a semantic that implies that genocide is in some way an altogether understandable and perhaps inevitable aspect of human nature.

I am proposing that just as the guiding criterion for defining health in medical thought must specify a state of life unthreatened by bodily malfunction, so the guiding value for psychological health must include the holding of attitudes that support life and do not diminish the quality of life experience. I think that the profession of psychology is duty-bound to describe what is normal not only in terms of the sta-

ISRAEL W. CHARNY

tistically normative or usual but also in terms of the desirable and healthy.

If making other people's lives miserable — persecuting, tormenting, and even killing them — cannot be linked with existing definitions of abnormality, the profession of psychology has a serious problem of credibility. Some major revision is inescapable if we are to retain a sense of "sanity" about the field of psychopathology. However, in proposing such a revision, it is important that we stay anchored in existing definitions of psychopathology and not seek to create a language that would abruptly revise the accepted language and traditions of mental health.

DISORDERS OF PSEUDOCOMPETENCE, INVULNERABILITY, AND DOING HARM TO OTHERS

I am going to suggest a new way of looking at the evils of harming and destroying other human beings' lives — of looking at such evils as the other side of the coin of our traditional definitions of psychopathology.

For the most part, existing psychiatric disturbances are what I shall call *disorders of incompetence, vulnerability, and personal weakness.* In the face of life's challenges, and the anxiety they produce, exaggerated weakness and disavowals of potential competence, strength, and mastery can reach a point where the person is designated as "emotionally disturbed" or "mentally ill" and is unable to function in society.

I am going to suggest that when the same range of familiar psychiatric conditions takes the form of burdens inflicted on *other* human beings, interfering with their well-being, these conditions can be seen as *disorders of pseudocompetence, invulnerability, and doing harm to others.* Here the reaction to life's anxiety by those who bring about a state of incompetence in others is a disavowal of their own incompetence, weakness, and vulnerability.

In the current *DSM-III,* doing harm to others appears indirectly in connection with other indications of disturbance but

in itself does not qualify a person as disturbed. This is especially true if the individual in question behaves appropriately in other ways. There is almost no way in the existing system of diagnosis to qualify a harmful and even death-dealing person as disturbed if he is able to go about his business in a calm, socially relevant way, and especially if he is able to create or identify himself with an ideology that "legitimates" the elimination of the objects of his destructiveness.

In the traditional diagnostic definitions, one is disturbed mainly when and because one causes harm to oneself. In my extended definition, producing the same conditions in the life experience and functioning of the other is also abnormal. Note that this principle does not require any changes in existing conventional definitions of psychopathology. I am *adding* to existing theory without proposing any changes at all in the present classification itself (see table).

In my schema, disturbances to *others* are defined along the same continuum of severity as traditional definitions of disturbances to oneself, from neurosis to personality disorders to behavior disorders to psychosis. The extent of the state of incompetence in the life of any human being defines the extent of the pathology. In traditional mental illness, such incompetence is located in the individual; in my new version, we also look at the incompetence that is vested in others.

The addition of this dimension is accomplished by a "simple" structural device of rotating existing definitions of disturbances to oneself on their axis toward their counterpart statements of the same degree of disturbance a person induces or forces on others. This is a change that seems to make simple good sense, and it is not unlike other theoretical advances in science where an existing known principle has proven to yield hidden extended meanings when turned over or reversed.

Disorders of pseudocompetence represent reactions to universal anxiety about life and death through disavowals of one's weakness and demonstration of one's pseudomastery at the expense of other people.

PSYCHIATRY, Vol. 49, May 1986

GENOCIDE AND MASS DESTRUCTION

Expanding Traditional Definitions of Psychopathological Disturbances in the Individual to Include Equivalent Disturbances to the Well-being of Others

Disorders of Incompetence, Vulnerability, and Personal Weakness	*Disorders of Pseudocompetence, Invulnerability, and Doing Harm to Others*
Reactions to anxiety through exaggerated disavowals of competence, mastery, and strength	Reactions to anxiety through exaggerated disavowals of incompetence, vulnerability, and weakness
Neurosis: Inability to enjoy oneself and life	*Neurosis*: Disturbing others' enjoyment of themselves and their lives
• Renunciation of power over self • Excessive demands on self	• Denial of weakness and vulnerability • Claiming power over others
Personality disorders: Characterological restriction or exaggeration in style of experiencing • Demeaning of self • Narcissistic overconcern with self	*Personality disorders*: Characterological style of repeatedly disappointing, intruding on, or upsetting others • Demeaning of others • Prejudice toward, dehumanization, and exploitation of others
Behavior disorders: Disturbance in ability to delay needs, expressed in repeated self-destructive behaviors • Abuses of oneself and self-punishment • Damaging seriously one's life opportunity	*Behavior disorders*: Exploitation and hurting of others • Abuses of others and cruelty • Damaging seriously others' life opportunity
Psychosis: Breakdown of ability to function in the ordinary everyday world • Extreme inability to function • Irreversible self-destruction – suicide	*Psychosis*: Taking away others' ability to function in the ordinary everyday world • Incapacitating others' basic ability to function • Irreversible destruction of others – murder

The dread of normal human weakness and needs is repressed through various degrees of overstriving, an inflated sense of oneself, claims of power over others, exploitation and manipulation of others, denial of others' human rights and lives, abuses, cruelty, and actual destruction. (See Mitscherlich and Mitscherlich 1975, and Hartman 1982, for perspectives of the German people in this regard.)

Disorders of pseudocompetence are first denials of one's own vulnerability and mortality but ultimately denials of one's humanity, and they include both everyday and more serious evils that people do to their fellow human beings. The definition includes a family group that drives a vulnerable child to mental illness, industrialists who are willing to pollute waters and thus endanger human lives, militarists and arms manufacturers who are eager or willing to expand their power at the expense of other people (Somerville and Shibata 1982), and concentration camp guards – whether they are "just following orders" and escaping anxiety by disowning responsibility for their actions or are excited by and fully participating in their occupation. Like disorders of incompetence, disorders of pseudocompetence represent a failure to balance and integrate the two sides of strength and weakness that are intrinsic in human nature.

Disorders of incompetence and pseudocompetence can alternate and change places with one another. The early stages of many serious mental health problems are expressed in symptoms of isolation, self-doubt, and self-hurt, but at times later stages of the same problems include at-

ISRAEL W. CHARNY

tempts to transmit these distressing experiences to others by causing them harm. Likewise, early instances of disturbing the lives of others—such as antagonizing neighbors, emotional abuse of family and friends, or excessive drinking and gambling—can later change into a full breakdown of the individual self. Disorders of pseudocompetence can be full-fledged alternatives to disorders of incompetence, and there is no contradiction whatsoever in patients who alternate in or combine both sides of disorders.

Hitler himself presents an interesting illustration of this proposed redefinition of psychopathology. Biographical studies of Hitler hint at a strain of latent and disguised psychopathological symptoms in Hitler's personal life over the years. John Toland (1976) reports that Hitler even consulted a psychiatrist for himself to allay a fear of cancer, "which, along with the obsession to eliminate all Jews, would persist to the last day of his life. . . . it was soon evident the psychiatrist missed a golden opportunity to turn Hitler from his goal" (Vol. 1, p. 243). Nonetheless, Hitler functioned powerfully in the real world. At the height of his monstrous pseudocompetence, it would have been difficult to define him as abnormal in the traditional diagnostic system unless one saw him as suffering from a rare condition of paranoia—a not unreasonable possibility but even if true, very hard to define in the early years of Hitler's rise to leadership and consolidation of power. However, using the proposed model, we can label Hitler as disturbed from early years on because of the extent to which he called for doing harm to others. Later, when his power system broke down, Hitler began to show increasing signs of traditional madness—some say exposing what lay behind his maniacal and paranoiac strivings for power all along—including deterioration in the quality of his conversation, unpredictability in his thinking and decisions, depression, and increasing pain and a variety of physical symptoms of whatever physical and psychosomatic origins (Toland, Vol. 2). The advantage of my new proposal is that it removes all ambiguities and any need to search for a "real truth" inside Hitler during the years of his extraordinary functioning as a highly effective leader, albeit for the ugliest goals.

THE "NORMALITY" OF MASS MURDERS

Notwithstanding my proposal for achieving a logical definition of genocide and mass murder as disturbed behaviors, I want to emphasize that it is essential for us to hold on to our hard-won knowledge that the mass killers of humankind are largely everyday human beings—what we have called normal people according to currently accepted definitions by the mental health profession. Following the Holocaust, many people wanted to believe that the leader of the German people, his major followers, and the bulk of the executors were insane. Instead, those studying the Holocaust had to grasp the terrible truth that most of the genociders could not be considered insane in terms of prevalent concepts and standards of mental health.

Slowly it became clear *the potential for being genociders or accomplices to genocide is virtually universal.* The potential for compliance with and participation in the execution of mass murder can be found throughout the range of various human beings and societies, though of course people and societies differ in how they deal with this potential. If we now work toward relabeling genociders as mentally ill, it is important that we do not allow our redefinition to return us to denial of the potential cruelty and destructiveness in all of us.

Psychologist Hans Askenasy (1978) devoted a book-length treatment to the dilemma under the title *Are We All Nazis?* Askenasy saw no alternative but to propose a new definition that would take precedence over existing concepts:

Most men and women, including those who start wars, and commit murder, mass murder, and genocide, have been and are considered "normal." And of course their behavior is also considered "legal". . . .

PSYCHIATRY, Vol. 49, May 1986

GENOCIDE AND MASS DESTRUCTION

Behavior is criminal if it is destructive without justification – regardless of local laws. The criteria I have used are common decency and common sense. [pp. 103–04]

Gustave Gilbert (1950), the psychologist who studied the Nazi war criminals at the Nuremberg trials, concluded unambiguously that although psychopathic personalities played an important role in the revolutionary nucleus of the Nazi movement,

Without the support of normal and respectable leaders in that society, without a considerable following among the masses of the people, and without the facilitated action of certain cultural trends, it would hardly have been possible for the Nazi leaders to precipitate as great a social catastrophe as they did. [p. 287]

Douglas Kelley, who worked on the Rorschach Test with Bruno Klopfer, was the psychiatrist who studied the Nuremberg prisoners; he too concluded quite clearly, "The Nazi leaders were not spectacular types, not personalities that appear only once in a century. They simply had three quite unremarkable characteristics . . . overwhelming ambition, no ethical standards, a strongly developed nationalism . . . " (1961, p. 171).

British psychiatrist Henry Dicks (1972) studied imprisoned Nazi war criminals and also concluded that they were essentially normal: "The SS killers were not 'insane' or uncontrollable people, in any generally understood clinical sense. . . . " (1972, p. 230). "There clearly exists in many people a burned, split-off 'enclave of deadly ruthlessness' . . . round which relatively healthy parts of the personality based on the likewise 'good object-relations' can develop" (p. 246).

I have elsewhere (Charny 1982) discussed the fascinating findings of the Israeli husband/wife team of psychiatrist and psychologist, Shlomo and Shoshana Kulcsar (1978), who together examined Adolf Eichmann before his execution. They essentially concluded that Eichmann was a man who would not encounter the aggression in his personality or experience himself as an individual; he was a cog in a machine who

could not see people as people and insisted that all other people be cogs in a machine.[1]

Most textbooks of psychopathology basically have ignored the issue raised by the common description of the mass killers as largely "normal." Leonard Ullman and Leonard Krasner (1975), however, are among a minority of teachers of psychopathology who have confronted the problem. They felt forced to conclude that being a mass killer is normal if you are living in a society which calls for it.

A critical example is whether an obedient Nazi concentration-camp commander would be considered normal or abnormal. To the extent that he was responding accurately and successfully to his environment and not breaking its rules, much less coming to the attention of professional psychiatrists, he would not be labeled abnormal. . . . Although such a person may be held responsible for his acts – as Nazi war criminals were – the concept of abnormality as a special entity does not seem necessary or justified. If it is, the problem arises as to who selects the values that apply to others. This situation of one group's values being dominant over others is the fascistic background from which the Nazi camp commander sprang. [p. 16]

On the other hand, James Coleman and his associates (1980) disagreed with Ullman and Krasner, feeling they could not reconcile themselves to a definition that left mass destructiveness outside of the boundaries of psychological disturbance. They proposed that the best criterion for determining the normality of behavior was not whether society accepted it but rather whether it fostered "the well-being of the individual and, ultimately, of the group. . . . Unless we value the survival and actualization of the human race, there seems little point in trying to identify abnormal behavior or do anything about it" (pp. 14, 15).

---

[1]Supposedly only one psychological test identified Eichmann in his own right as a vicious killer—the interpretation of the Szondi protocol, which was sent for blind analysis to Szondi himself. However, I have never been able to get any objective verification that in another Szondi analyst's hands the protocol would have yielded the same interpretation. Other psychological tests showed disconnection from aggression and from people.

ISRAEL W. CHARNY

However, Coleman and his associates were unable to provide a conceptual framework that systematically linked disturbances in oneself with disturbing and destroying the well-being of others. Essentially, they superimposed the criterion of well-being of people onto the existing definitions of psychopathology as an overriding principle.

Georges Tamarin has perhaps summed up the problem the most succinctly:

Why is the same statement voiced in the first person singular diagnosed as a sign of delusion, but accepted as unquestioned truth when announced in the first person [of the in-group] plural? Why is an individual considered homicidal or suicidal forcibly committed to a mental hospital, while a high official representative of the nation and/or religious body enjoys full cooperation of psychiatrists and other scientists when he threatens with (self) extermination of whole collectives? [1980, p. 9]

THE "RATIONALITY" OF THE HOLOCAUST

Some social scientists and philosophers are not concerned with definitions of psychopathology and ostensibly propose a diametrically different position—that the Holocaust was somehow a "rational event." Sociologist Helen Fein (1979) defines the rationality of the Holocaust as the ability of the persecutors to get away with their intentions without any major costs to them. Theologian Franklin Littell (1981) concludes that the Holocaust cannot be understood in normal psychological-ethical terms but rather involves some powerful tendency in the human spirit toward doing anything and everything that seems within the reach of the human being's machinery.

The Holocaust cannot be explained in the traditional language of human wrong-doing—"sadism," "brutality," "cruelty"—qualities that describe human emotions and passions. The awesomeness of the event is related to its rationality. The fatal curiosity, the Faustian passion by which whatever *can* be done *will* be done—regardless of ethics, morality, or human life itself—led readily to Dr. Mengele's experiments upon helpless victims, Freisler's hanging courts,

and the technical skill of engineers and psychiatrists and chemists who built and staffed the Death Camps. The awfulness of the engine of destruction is not its pathology but its normalcy. [pp. 371-72]

Clearly, neither of these authors intends to justify the Holocaust when they describe the rational and normal processes that determined the gruesome mass murders. Fein and Littell are deeply devoted scholars of the Holocaust whose outrage at the events of destruction is evident in all of their work. Yet they have the scientific and philosophical courage to label the horrors of the Holocaust as acts of rational human beings.

On the other hand, social philosopher Ronald Aronson (1981) cautions that in the course of our studies of the Holocaust we may add an undue quality of rationality to its existence:

It achieves a solidity, a thereness, that incorporates it easily into the rationality of human history. In seeking its causes and meanings, we inevitably endow it with an aura of legitimacy, even necessity. When historians try to bracket out their outrage, horror and shock that such a thing happened, the last step is taken towards making it a rational project of human energy and intentions. [pp. 68-69]

My present proposal in no way denies the "rationality"—meaning the statistical frequency, normal commonplaceness, emotional gratification, or practical usefulness—of destructiveness. What it does instead is take a clear-cut value position that harming and destroying other human beings is disturbed and abnormal—meaning it is negatively related to human life and requires treatment and correction so that it does not occur. (Later I shall address some of the problems that such a value position raises, particularly for professionals who aspire to a value-free psychology.)

THE RELATION OF "DISORDERS OF PSEUDOCOMPETENCE" TO OTHER DIAGNOSTIC PROBLEMS

Although it was not the original purpose of this essay to address any other problems in the field of psychopathology except

150

GENOCIDE AND MASS DESTRUCTION

the omission of mass murderers from our standard definitions of abnormality, the proposed extension of the standard classification of abnormality may well shed light on several other nasty problems in the field.

Behavior Disorders

The so-called behavior disorders, at various times also referred to as "conduct disorders" or "personality disorders," have always been difficult to integrate conceptually with neuroses and psychoses because the behavior disorders involve a different psychological mechanism: instead of harming oneself, the patient *acts out* and causes harm to others.

The dramatic dilemma in *One Flew Over the Cuckoo's Nest* (Kesey 1962) is an interesting case in point. Here the protagonist, "Mack" McMurphy causes so much trouble to others that a place has to be found for him in the psychiatric definitional system in order to justify holding him. The difficulty is that traditional diagnoses don't fit spirited people like McMurphy so that the psychiatric establishment in effect has to "treat" him into breaking down to a degree of personal incompetence that will qualify him as a bona fide patient.

The problem with the behavioral disorders is that instead of becoming incompetent under the pressure of anxiety, people "suffering" these conditions often "enjoy" a form of pseudocompetence and superiority through which they manage for some time not to suffer anxiety or vulnerability. In the process they can and do make life so difficult for their families and for others around them that the mental health profession has to work hard to find ways of defining them as bona fide "patients." Most of these "patients" do not allow mental health practitioners to work with them very readily until the trouble and discomfort they cause to others turn around and bring on them personal forms of breakdown; only at this point are the mental health professions able, as it were, to breathe a sigh of relief for having the "proof" that the person was "sick" underneath all along.

The present proposal says much more

clearly that anxiety is a universal experience that has to be dealt with authentically, and that a reaction to anxiety in the form of either incompetence *or* power at the expense of others is a disturbance.

Family Scapegoats

Family therapy has underscored the fact that, in many instances, family members directly contribute to or induce disturbances in the obviously incompetent or traditionally sick one in the family. They do so through their pseudocompetence and other subtly powerful manipulations that the identified patient is unable to stand up against.

If there is any clear-cut theoretical advance in the innovations of family therapy, it is that there are many disturbed people who may not manifest symptoms for a long while because their hidden disturbance is masked through scapegoating someone else in the family to feel powerless, incompetent, or "crazy." Family therapy has insisted correctly that bringing psychic damage to others is no less an aspect of psychopathology than being unable to function oneself (Framo 1982). Even popular culture has observed—as in the film based on the Kesey novel referred to earlier—that often it is the "good people" who end up being patients in the mental health clinics and hospitals while the "bad people" who torment he hapless good ones maintain a façade of adequacy. it is also frequently observed that when the manifest patient gets better, or when the power and scapegoating of the pseudocompetent members of the family are interfered with, traditional mental disturbances may manifest themselves in the latter. The present clarification assigns a definition of emotional disturbances from the very outset to the family's pseudocompetents who seem to trigger mental disturbances in others.

Child Abuse

Under prevailing diagnostic categories. the majority of instances of child abuse have been demonstrated to be at the hands of *normal* adults, a conclusion that defies

ISRAEL W. CHARNY

common sense (Gil 1974). Traditional mental health thinking has been stymied by the fact that most child batterers are largely "normal." Yet any sane individual knows that one cannot consider as "normal" people who batter their children, injure them, and perhaps even cause their death.

Effective education of all of us as parents should properly include making us aware of how we become overstressed in caring for children, and of how, under stress, even decent people can be carried away to violence. Similarly, the proper treatment of parents who are repeated or serious child batterers should include a large dose of understanding of the naturalness and "normality" of their stress pattern; this helps them recognize when they may be in danger of losing control so that they can check themselves. However, none of this means that parents who beat their children are not engaging in disturbed behaviors or that they are not, as a consequence, as common sense alone would say, disturbed people.

The dilemma created by the existing system of classification has yielded a euphemistic treatment tool that allows clinicians to empathize with the "normality" —again meaning commonplaceness and naturalness in overall human behavior— of violence to children. Not automatically labeling child batterers as disturbed admittedly may help us avoid some of the dangerous consequences that unfortunately often are evoked by diagnoses of pathology. However, the untruth that child batterers are "normal" can also produce its own undesirable consequences — including a weakening of the normative cultural sanctions against violence and other abuses of children. In any case, the cultivation of sympathetic and effective treatment techniques cannot be gained at the expense of distortions of reality; it is likely that most people will be relieved when the professionals find a way to catch up with common-sense understanding and are able to define serious beating of children as an act of disturbed adults.

The present proposal makes it possible to define child abuse and child batterers as pathological because they qualify in the category of "disorders of pseudocompetence, invulnerability, and doing harm to others."

The Problem of Mixing Values with Science

The main objection that has been made to the thesis of this paper, as I have explored it with a variety of colleagues in the last few years, is that the proposal to define doing harm to others as psychopathological could become (in the words of one unnamed critic) "a dangerous injection of psychiatric notions into domains that were hitherto regarded as subject to exclusively moral or political assessment."

It has been clear to me that many psychologists and psychiatrists identify entirely with the value position and purpose of my proposal but are unsure whether the adoption of a formal definition that harming others is an act of psychopathology is a proper "scientific" or "professional" step.

On the level of philosophy of science, although a surprisingly large number of behavior scientists still mistakenly talk about science as value-free, the famous Heisenberg Principle of Indeterminacy taught us that *any* way of observing and learning about reality—in any area of knowledge, including the physical sciences—inherently represents and creates some kind of value position that influences the reality that is being observed "objectively." The fact that the myth of a value-free psychology still persists and is periodically even a basis for intense outrage at behavior scientists who take a clear-cut ethical position is an interesting phenomenon in its own right. However, I believe that the responsible consensus is that objectivity in our work is gained through rigorous attention to and acknowledgment of the assumptions and values that inevitably influence our observations, and not from an effort to free ourselves of value positions.

At the same time, each discipline must scrutinize carefully any proposed value position for its many implications. Here, one of the questions we need to consider is whether the definition that sees doing

GENOCIDE AND MASS DESTRUCTION

harm to others as psychopathology is a responsible or irresponsible injection of a value position into the realm of mental health. One of the important contributions of the modern mental health movement was the separation of concepts of morality from concepts of mental illness. In the historical perspective, this was one of the definitive steps that gained the right to treatment for many previously abused or neglected mentally ill. It also created a consensus of understanding for some disturbed behaviors that bring harm to others — those that are understood to have been compelled by the patient's mental condition and therefore are deemed deserving of treatment rather than criminal punishment.

However, separating the concepts of mental illness and morality from each other never meant that, philosophically or psychologically, there is an absolute difference between psychological health and moral good and that they should be scrupulously kept divorced from each other. There is much to argue that these two ways of categorizing human behavior are complementary, and that processing the tension of the contradictions between the two categories of concepts is a valuable basis for new integrative concepts that will synthesize ethical responsibility with humane acceptance of psychological weakness and uncontrollable disturbance. The goal would be a system of thought where psychological health and maturity and ethical integrity are always seen as closely related.

For many years, significant thinkers in mental health have called for a greater appreciation of how immoral behaviors — and also fears of immorality, especially fears of violence toward others — are foundation stones of many neuroses, character disorders, and possibly even psychoses. According to this point of view, espoused by Karen Horney, O. H. Mowrer, Ivan Boszormenyi-Nagy, and Leon Saul, among others, being mentally healthy means being decent and constructive to one's family, friends, and community; intense hostility, emotional exploitation of others, and abusiveness in interpersonal relationships are considered causes of and expressions of emotional and mental disorders.

The concern about mixing moral considerations with concepts of mental health also implies that the present structure has clearly marked boundaries and that the distinction between immorality and mental illness is always easy to make — a situation far from the truth. Although one of the major purposes of the distinction is to make possible humane treatment of the mentally ill, there is overwhelming evidence that, even in Western countries, institutional psychiatric services themselves unwittingly involve a great deal of brutalization and severe punishment of psychiatric patients, in part because staff members do not recognize their own moral judgments of patients. Another purpose of the separation of concepts is to make possible enlightened treatment of people who unwittingly commit criminal acts because of their mental condition, but a large part of the public as well as professionals have been disgusted and disheartened by the cynical overuse of psychiatric concepts to extricate people from responsibility for serious offenses against others.

No matter what definitions we are going to use, a continuous dialogue and negotiation is necessary between the mental health and legal professions and institutions as to which intervention and response is called for in various cases. Understanding the psychological origins of any evil behavior does not mean there is to be no punishment of that behavior, either for the welfare of society or of the individual, just as the fact that a person has done wrong to others under the law does not automatically mean that society may not choose to emphasize the psychological or rehabilitative approach to this offender rather than the retributive approach.

WILL DEFINING GENOCIDAL DESTRUCTIVENESS AS ABNORMAL MEAN THAT A HITLER CANNOT BE PROSECUTED FOR WAR CRIMES?

Possibly the most impassioned concern that this proposal arouses in practicing mental health clinicians who do care very much about opposing the horrors of geno-

ISRAEL W. CHARNY

cidal destructiveness is that inclusion of destructiveness toward others in a framework of psychopathology may lead, paradoxically, to demands to *absolve* evildoers from responsibility on the grounds that they are, by our professional definitions, "mad."

Thus, Hitler, Eichmann, Talaat, Pol Pot, Stalin—let alone thousands of "new" or less well-known executioners—might be able to defend themselves against charges of murder, war crimes, or genocide on grounds of "incompetence," "mental disorder," or "insanity"—if the revised definitional system proposed here were adopted. This is of course not the purpose or an allowable outcome of my proposal. My proposal is intended to put mental health concepts squarely against destructiveness and mass murder and not to serve in any way as an excuse for such acts.

Concerns about such possible unwanted consequences of an expanded definition of mental illness are based on the false premise that any diagnosis of mental illness today means the criminal is absolved from the crime and is turned over by the criminal justice system to the mental health system. Although a criminal/patient may be shown to have been drawn to criminal destruction by "irresistible impulses," and although the criminal/patient may be shown to be driven by self-destructive needs, the law is insistent on defining whether or not a criminal was able to know and therefore be responsible for his acts. Instances of cruel, brutal torture-murder in particular evoke an adamant and severe response in the legal system, and the courts are generally unsparing in their adjudication of such criminals notwithstanding evidences of considerable mental disturbance, unless there is strong evidence that the perpetrator was not aware of what he was doing. The same severity is also characteristic in the adjudication of murderers (including attempts) of public and political leaders; in instances where a court releases such criminals on the basis of their mental disturbance, there is invariably a strong outcry demanding a further tightening of the rule of criminal responsibility.

The redefinition of calculated destruction and murder of masses of people as abnormal behavior does not establish a basis for absolving the murderers of responsibility for knowing what they were doing. *I would call the Hitlers and Talaats and Stalins and Pol Pots disturbed people because they dwell on and devote themselves to torturing and murdering millions of human beings. Such acts and preoccupations cannot possibly be characterized as "normal" when the everyday practice of mental health professions identifies comparatively trivial hostility, hatred, negativism, arrogance, chronic rejection of people, vengefulness, or paranoidal suspiciousness and abusiveness as emotional and personality disorders. I would, nevertheless, unhesitatingly convict them of mass murder and call for the maximum penalty under law—and not for psychiatric treatment.*

WILL THE DESIGNATION OF "DOING HARM TO OTHERS" AS PSYCHOPATHOLOGY OPEN THE DOOR TO POLITICIZATION OF PSYCHIATRY?

The possibility that my proposal will lend itself to legitimation of harsh and abusive "psychiatric" measures against enemies and opponents of a regime has also been raised by some critics. The understandable fear is that officially enlarging the scope of definitions of psychopathology to include the abuses people do to others will open the door to the kinds of serious misuses of psychiatry that we see in the Soviet Union, where personal ideological and political choices that are not acceptable to the regime are subjected to treatment as mental illnesses.

In the view of one critic (the unnamed source cited earlier), "Eventually, psychiatry becomes the handmaiden of political power, and labels as 'mad' whomever those in power deem to have engaged in politically undesirable behavior." Some astute observers of Soviet psychiatry suggest that most of the mental health professionals who administer such "treatment" of the dissidents are sincere in their beliefs that

PSYCHIATRY, Vol. 49, May 1986

GENOCIDE AND MASS DESTRUCTION

deviation from accepted political norms is an expression of mental disturbance (Reich 1983), which also underscores the considerable significance and power of professional definitions and consensus.

On the other hand, totalitarian governments are not dependent on our mental health system's definitions to justify their use of mind-controlling and personality-breaking techniques. If anything, scientific acceptance of a classification system in psychopathology that defines doing mental and bodily harm to other human beings as disturbed would give human rights activists another intellectual tool from which to argue against punitive psychiatric hospitalization and "treatment." In general, if the mental health profession creates a strong new philosophical-psychological basis for condemning abuse, torture, and murder of human beings, we will have added another responsible and respected voice that can protest the worst indignities of human destructiveness not only in psychiatric institutions but in all areas of human behavior. Totalitarian governments will not be stopped by a revised definition of psychopathology, but every voice against destructiveness may help somewhat.

Finally, concern has been expressed over the ultimate damage that is likely if one defines genociders as mentally ill—it will throw the clock back and fail to challenge all people with responsibility for their participation in or acquiescence to a society that commits genocide. Again, critics say, it is going to be said that "madmen"—like Hitler, Stalin, or Idi Amin—are responsible for the mass murder and not that all those who participate at any level or who stand by when the murders are committed are responsible. Whatever progress we may have made in seeing genocide as an awesome potential in virtually all people will have been lost.

There is no doubt whatsoever that we must be careful not to lose our new understanding of genocide and mass destruction as essentially the work of myriads of what we today call "normal" or everyday people, and that the psychological and psychiatric professions, along with the other social sci-

ences, need to contribute to a growing moral vigilance by everyone. Knowing that destructiveness is a natural potential in all of us means that we need new forms of mental and moral education to help us guard against that potential; such education must warn human beings against the dangers of compliance with policies of persecution and oppression of others when promoted by our leaders and society. The proposed expansion of the definition of psychopathology to include persecution and mass killing will mean that all people who participate in the killing and all people who are accomplices, in whatever degree of responsibility, will have committed distinctly abnormal acts and will qualify for designation as disturbed. The mental health profession will have put its authority behind the judgment that doing serious harm to other people is crazy behavior, and that it is basic preventive mental health policy for all of us to guard ourselves from falling into this craziness.

Stopping genocide and mass murder is the task of all peoples and professions. The mental health sciences cannot maintain a "neutral" position on this critical issue of human behavior. We need to join the established traditions of law and religion in taking the position that killing human beings is wrong—not only legally and morally wrong but also, according to one more learned profession, dangerous and destructive for one's mental health.

THE POSSIBILITY OF STILL GREATER MASS DESTRUCTION

If the history of human destructiveness to date—including many instances of genocide as well as the apotheosis of evil in the Holocaust—has not been sufficient to compel us to identify mass destruction of human life as mad, the looming possibility of future cataclysmic and perhaps final extermination of our civilization, species and planet certainly cannot be ignored as the ultimate insanity. The late Father Thomas Merton predicted that it will be "the sane ones" who "without qualms [will] aim the

ISRAEL W. CHARNY

missiles and press the buttons that initiate the great festival of destruction that they, *the sane ones*, have prepared" (1967, p. 22). Anatol Rappoport (1984) has characterized the preparations for nuclear war as "the final madness." In a recent address to the American Orthopsychiatric Association, he argued that those who contribute to mass destruction satisfy the criteria for madness:

The criteria of madness are those that characterize not individual behavior, but one's relation to others; people are thought of as mad if they

are incapable of functioning in a normal social milieu. While the isolation of such people merely on the basis of extreme eccentricity or incompetence may be cruel and unjustified, it is fully justified if their being at large constitutes clear and serious danger to others. . . .

The planners of nuclear war . . . satisfy both criteria for madness: they are immersed in an imaginary world of their own making dissociated from reality; and their activities constitute a clear menace to humanity . . . [which] can easily add up to genocide and to the suicide of humanity itself. [1984, pp. 525, 528]

REFERENCES

ARONSON, R. Why? Towards a theory of the Holocaust. *Socialist Review* (1981) 11(4): 63–81.

ASCH, S. E. Studies of independence and conformity: I. A minority of one against a unanimous majority. *Psychological Monographs* (1956) 70(9), No. 416.

ASKENASY, H. *Are We All Nazis?* Lyle Stuart, 1978.

CHARNY, I. W. In collaboration with C. Rapaport, Foreword by E. Wiesel. *How Can We Commit the Unthinkable?: Genocide, The Human Cancer.* Boulder, CO: Westview Press, 1982.

CHARNY, I. W., and DAVIDSON, S., eds., *The Book of the International Conference on the Holocaust and Genocide. Book One: The Conference Program and Crisis.* Tel Aviv: Institute of the International Conference on the Holocaust and Genocide, 1983.

CHARNY, I. W., ed. *Toward the Understanding and Prevention of Genocide: Proceedings of the International Conference on the Holocaust and Genocide.* Boulder, CO: Westview Press, 1984.

COLEMAN, J. C., BUTCHER, J. N., and CARSON, R. O. *Abnormal Psychology and Modern Life,* 6th ed. Scott, Foresman, 1980.

DARLEY, J. M., and LATANE, B. When will people help in a crisis? *Psychology Today,* December 1968, pp. 54–57, 70–71.

DICKS, H. V. *Licensed Mass Murder: A Socio-Psychological Study of Some SS Killers.* Heinemann, 1972.

ERIKSON, E. H. *Insight and Responsibility.* Norton, 1964.

FEIN, H. *Accounting for Genocide: National Responses and Jewish Victimization During the Holocaust.* Free Press, 1979.

FRAMO, J. L. *Explorations in Marital and Family Therapy.* Springer, 1982.

GIL, D. A conceptual model of child abuse and its implications for social policy. In S. K. Steinmetz and M. A. Strauss, eds., *Violence in the Family.* Dodd, Mead, 1974.

GILBERT, G. M. *The Psychology of Dictatorship: Based on the Leaders of Nazi Germany.* Ronald, 1950.

HARTMAN, D. Compliance and oblivion: The absence of sympathy in Germany for the victims of the Holocaust. Presented at International Conference on the Holocaust and Genocide, Tel Aviv, June 1982.

KELLEY, D. M. *22 Cells in Nuremberg* [1947]. MacFadden, 1961.

KESEY, K. *One Flew Over the Cuckoo's Nest.* New American Library, 1962.

KOHLBERG, L. Moral education in the schools: A developmental review. *School Review* (1966) 74: 1–30.

KREN, G., and RAPPOPORT, L. *The Holocaust and the Crisis of Human Behavior.* Holmes & Meier, 1980.

KULCSAR, I. S. De Sade and Eichmann. In I. W. Charny, ed., *Strategies Against Violence: Design for Nonviolent Change.* Boulder, CO: Westview Press, 1978.

LITTELL, F. H. Lessons of the Holocaust and church struggle: 1970–1980. *Journal of Ecumenical Studies* (1981) 18: 396–73.

MASLOW, A. H. *The Farther Reaches of Human Nature.* Viking, 1971.

MERTON, T. N. A devout meditation in memory of Adolf Eichmann. Reprinted in *Reflections* (Merck, Sharp and Dohme) (1967) 2(3): 21–23.

MILGRAM, S. *Obedience to Authority.* Harper & Row, 1974.

MITSCHERLICH, A., and MITSCHERLICH, M. *The Inability to Mourn: Principles of Collective Behavior.* Grove, 1975.

PILISUK, M., and OBER, L. Torture and genocide as public health problems. *American Journal of Orthopsychiatry* (1976) 46: 388–92.

RAPOPORT, A. Preparation for nuclear war: The final madness. *American Journal of Orthopsychiatry* (1984) 54: 524–29.

REICH, W. The world of Soviet psychiatry. *New York Times Magazine,* January 30, 1983.

SOMERVILLE, J., and SHIBATA, S. Ecocide and omnicide, the new faces of genocide. Workshop, International Conference on the Holocaust and Genocide, Tel Aviv, June 1982.

TAMARIN, G. R. *Studies in Psychopathology.* Ramat Aviv, Israel: Turtledove Press, 1980.

GENOCIDE AND MASS DESTRUCTION

TOLAND, J. *Adolf Hitler.* 2 vols. Doubleday, 1976.

ULLMAN, L. P., and KRASNER, L. *Psychological Approach to Abnormal Behavior*, 2d ed. Prentice Hall, 1975.

ZIMBARDO, P. G., HANEY, C., BANKS, W. C., and JAF-FE, D. The psychology of imprisonment: Privation, power, and pathology. In D. Rosenhan and P. London, eds., *Theory and Research in Abnormal Psychology*, 2d ed., Holt, Rinehart & Winston, 1975.

[24]

The Genesis of Genocide in Rwanda:
The Fatal Dialectic of Class and Ethnicity

David Norman Smith,
University of Kansas

REFLEXIVE STATEMENT

The "twentieth century" is, in reality, the first century of The Global Era. Prior to 1900, most of the world's peoples continued to live in traditional, local societies, comparatively untouched by European money and hegemony. Even where the solvent effects of European colonialism were felt most acutely, non-capitalist social structures remained largely intact. Since the turn of the century, however, everything has changed. The accumulation of capital has become the engine of social change on a world scale, driving a global dynamic which is visible, above all, in its effects – great wars, dictators, depressions and revolutions. Capitalist norms, and traumas, are present everywhere.

The genocide in Rwanda last year illustrates this point. Severed from its non-capitalist roots by the jarring impact of colonialism and the profit motive, Rwandan society has lurched from disaster to disaster in this century, so polarized and destabilized that even independence has not enabled it to regain its balance. Whether this balance will ever be restored is an open question. The Western powers and international banks seem to be on the verge of writing Africa off, and Rwanda, like most African societies, has long been torn between classes (a predatory elite and a peasantry) which have yet to manifest either the will or the means to find a viable way forward.

Is there hope? The conventional wisdom of the pundits, for whom the Rwandan holocaust reveals "primordial" African hostilities, suggests otherwise. As long as peoples are "tribally" divided, they remain prey to savage hatreds (we are told). The Tutsis and Hutus in Rwanda are locked in what is supposedly an endless cycle of ethnic enmity. In Africa, many observers conclude, the heart of darkness is still beating.

Marxists have always assailed the Eurocentric complacency of this kind of ethnic reductionism. Societies are not, in reality, congeries of indelibly "ethnic" groups, each with its own immutable character (and destinies to

Early versions of this paper were presented at the 1995 meetings of the American Sociological Association and the Midwest Sociological Society. For insights and ideas of various kinds I'm grateful to Joane Nagel, Ken Lohrentz, John Janzen, Isidor Wallimann, Patricia Clough, Lou Turner, Janvier Gasana, Marty Patchen, Scott Kerrihard, Hal Orbach, Marty Harwayne, and Kevin Anderson.

58 *Humanity & Society, Volume 19, Number 4, November, 1995*

match, like the heroes in a Greek tragedy). The wish to explain social crises by reducing society to human nature – however "multicultural" this nature is said to be – is fatally flawed. But the Marxist response is often flawed as well, consisting of an equal and opposite class reductionism. Neither approach is satisfactory if we hope to truly understand (and perhaps heal) social wounds. Hence, like many others, I have tried to wrestle with the real complexity of the relations between class and ethnicity, in several realms. As editor of the English-language edition of Marx's ethnological notebooks (Yale, forthcoming) I have sought to grasp the collision between class and clan societies which Marx posits as the central sociocultural dynamic of the so-called "expanded reproduction of capital" on a world scale. This has led, in particular, to a compelling interest in African social structure. Equally compelling, meanwhile, has been my research interest in genocidal antisemitism, a topic I've pursued for some years now. These seemingly disparate interests dovetail in the study of the Rwandan crisis. Here, a society which is no longer "precapitalist" but not yet capitalist – and which, indeed, seems unlikely to be fully integrated into world capitalism – has been transformed from a comparatively stable kingly realm into a culture of genocide. How this happened, and why, is the subject of a larger research project that I hope to finish in the next few years.

In this paper I look at only one aspect of the history which culminated in genocide in Rwanda – the complex interaction of class and ethnicity in the formation of "Tutsi" and "Hutu" forces. I deal with the immediate sources of the genocide elsewhere (Smith 1995) and, for those who seek a reliable fuller account, I especially recommend the work of Omaar and de Waal (1995).

INTRODUCTION

The sheer magnitude of the slaughter in Rwanda in the spring of 1994 defies ready comprehension. It appears that at least 750,000 Rwandans were assassinated in the space of just a few months, beginning in April and ending in July.[1] This is a startling figure, almost 15 percent as high as the number of Jews killed by the Third Reich during the Holocaust. And the state-sponsored death squads (the *Interahamwe*) which carried out this swift, furious, carefully planned massacre did not have sophisticated Auschwitz-style technology at their disposal. More than a half-million Rwandans died, not in sterile, scientifically administered death camps, but in a hailstorm of clubs and Chinese-made machetes.

Why?

What could possibly provoke such an outbreak of violence?

Many journalists see something "atavistic" in Rwanda's tragedy, while others limit themselves to vague references to the allegedly "tribal" hatreds that led the Hutu majority to slaughter the Tutsi minority. Neither phraseology is á propos in this case. Far from being "tribal" or "atavistic," the Rwandan conflict is classically modern. A predatory postcolonial state, backed into a corner by a combination of international pressure and domestic dissent, lashed out with coldly calculated violence against its own people, murdering not only Tutsis, who were killed indiscriminately, but a great many Hutus as well – for joining the "wrong" political party, for hailing from the "wrong" region, for advocating democracy. Hutu political oppositionists, in fact, were a *primary* target for the killers, not an afterthought. And it is my contention (see Smith 1995) that if the International Monetary Fund (IMF), the World Bank, and other global forces had not applied severe pressure to the Rwandan regime, the genocide might not have occurred at all. A unique conjuncture of circumstances (the collapse of the coffee market, the end of the Cold War, intensifying IMF interventionism, and strife in nearby Uganda and Burundi) played havoc with Rwanda, plunging an already troubled society into a vortex of economic, political, and social crisis.

Ethnic antagonisms, in other words, were far from the only forces at work in the Rwandan genocide. And upon inspection, Rwandan "ethnicity" proves to be neither archaic nor primeval, but rather, in many respects, a recent invention, closely connected to Rwandan class relations. Class, indeed, is so pivotal to the Tutsi/Hutu dynamic in Rwanda that calling these groups "ethnic" might seem to be a mystification. Yet I will contend in this paper that class and ethnicity are both irreducible dimensions of the Rwandan experience. Closely examined, the Rwandan case shows, in fact, just how complex the interpenetration of class and ethnicity can be. The words "Tutsi" and "Hutu" refer to shifting constellations of groups which have divided, fused, and evolved in remarkably intricate fashion. Exploitation and ethnocentrism, synthesized, form a very volatile compound. Nowhere has this been more clearly shown than in Rwanda.

BEYOND PRIMORDIALISM

The most telling fact about Rwandan social relations is that the word "Hutu," which is conventionally applied to about 85 percent of all Rwandans, does not in fact refer to an ancient African people, as most journalists imagine. "Hutu," on the contrary, is a Kinyarwanda term meaning "subject" or "servant." So-called "Hutus," in other words, far from being a pristine ethnic group, are in reality a synthetic mix of Bantu-speaking farming peoples whose shared identity is solely the result of their common subjugation to a ruling elite of Tutsi nobles – cattle-rearing warriors from the western Nile who came to the interlacustrine region of east central Africa about five centuries ago (Newman 1995).[2] And the early, precolonial link between the Tutsis and their "subject" peoples was so involved, so polarized and yet symbiotic, that it transcends most ordinary notions of "ethnicity." Informed observers routinely apply categories of social stratification to the Tutsi/Hutu nexus, and with good reason. The Tutsis, unlike stereotyped "ethnic minority groups," were for centuries a ruling nobility with a nearly astral self-image. They rose so far above ordinary

60   *Humanity & Society, Volume 19, Number 4, November, 1995*

mortals, in their own eyes, that they would not allow themselves to be seen eating in public; when they traveled in plain sight among their Hutu clients, they would refuse food for days on end. Tied to the Hutus by a network of reciprocal obligations, the Tutsis were unwilling to humble themselves before their clients in any way. They owed the Hutus patronage, but not fellow-feeling (Maquet 1954).

The Tutsis were at the peak of the pyramid, the Hutus at the muddy base. This relationship was far from "tribal," however, since the social structures that define and delimit tribes had dissolved centuries earlier.[3] Precolonial Rwanda was an empire, built on the ruins of Bantu mini-kingdoms whose descendants (the Zigaba, Gesera, and others) were rendered "subjects" by conquest. Nor were these subjects a single people in any ethnologically coherent sense. While they did, in fact, have similar dialects and customs, they were otherwise quite distinct – rival peoples, organized into warring kingdoms, with many unique traditions. The Tutsis, meanwhile, were hardly ethnically pure themselves. In origin they were apparently a hybrid of Lwo-speaking Western Nilotic peoples (notably the Abahinda and Abahima) who intermarried with local Bantu royalty, embraced Bantu ways (including the Kinyarwanda language and kingship), and embarked on a career of conquest.[4] Over the next few centuries, as they erected an empire on the backs of their conquered subjects, the term "Tutsi" lost its uniquely ethnic flavor, becoming, like the word "Hutu," an index of class. "Tutsis," ultimately, were those who extracted surplus labor from "Hutus."[5]

This class dichotomy was sharpened in the colonial period, from 1899 until 1962, when the Hutu peasantry was even more intensively exploited than before and the Tutsi aristocracy was accorded new privileges. Rwanda specialists, keenly aware of this radicalization of the Tutsi/Hutu division in the colonial era, now routinely stress the class aspect of this relationship (Newbury 1992; Chrétien 1985; Vidal 1985; Freedman 1979; Des Forges 1972; d'Hertefelt 1971). But they also emphasize the colonial "racialization" of Tutsi/Hutu relations which the Belgians promoted when they defined the Tutsis as "bronze Caucasians," far superior, it was alleged, to Black Africans, and hence richly deserving of the preferential treatment they received (Vidal 1991; Newbury 1988; Reyntjens 1985).

Colonialism, in other words, gave the terms "Tutsi" and "Hutu" not only a heightened class connotation, but a pseudo-racial or ethnic dimension as well. The class division in Rwandan society was thus "racialized," acquiring the overdetermined quality which Helen Fein captures so well with the phrase "ethnoclass" (1993, p. 89). The Hutus, while functioning as a class of exploited peasants, were the object of ethnocentric as well as aristocratic disdain, despised not only as subaltern laborers but as presumed racial inferiors. And they came to regard themselves as an oppressed race, so that, when they rose in revolt against Tutsi rule in the early 1960s, they were moved as much by sentiments of ethnic pride as by class consciousness. In a sense, Rwandan class and ethnicity had converged.

Figure 1. Map of Rwanda

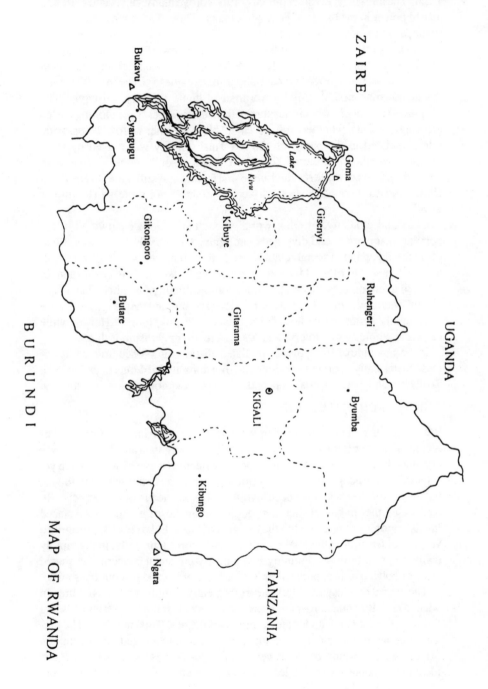

MAP OF RWANDA

62   *Humanity & Society, Volume 19, Number 4, November, 1995*

In the post-colonial period the Tutsi/Hutu divide was reconfigured once again. The anti-Tutsi revolt of the early 1960s drove many Tutsis into exile and placed power in the hands of Hutu politicians. Those Tutsis who remained in Rwanda were now mainly peasants, just like the majority of their Hutu neighbors. But some Hutu circles grew rich and powerful – initially, the so-called "Gitaramistes," who rode to power on the wings of the insurgent movement; and later, after Juvenal Habyarimana came to power in a 1973 coup, the landowning notables of Habyarimana's home territory, Gisenyi. The wealth and power of these circles sprang from their success in exploiting coffee growing peasants, whether Hutu or Tutsi. Now, in other words, the parasitic role associated in the past with the old Tutsi nobility was played by Hutu regimes, whether "northern" (based in Gisenyi) or "southern" (based in Gitarama). Hence, while residual anti-Tutsi feeling was still quite strong, intra-Hutu rivalries were at least equally contentious, if not more so (Reyntjens 1994).

Class and ethnicity, in other words, though still closely entwined in the popular imagination, had diverged once again. Class exploitation was still at the heart of Rwandan social relations, and ethnic tensions were still very real, and very raw – but the old vocabaulary of the Tutsi/Hutu rivalry no longer sufficed to encompass this wider, more complex reality. Neither "Tutsi" nor "Hutu" was now primarily a class term. The peasants and their exploiters were both mainly Hutus, while few if any Tutsis were still "lords." Hence, while class and ethnicity still intersected, they were no longer isomorphic.

In the genocide of 1994, the accumulated, distilled and concentrated force of these historically evolving passions and divisions attained fateful expression. To understand just how this happened, we must look more closely into history.

THE TUTSI/HUTU DIVIDE

Prior to the arrival of cattle-rearing Western Nilotic warriors, the Great Lakes region of east central Africa (from eastern Zaire to Uganda and Tanzania) was dominated by several dozen Bantu-speaking peoples, none of whom were yet "Hutus." These peoples were almost uniformly organized into sacred chiefdoms, but they do not seem to have been significantly stratified in other respects. (In most cases, the "pygmoid" hunting peoples whom these farmers had displaced in this region were relegated to the margins of Great Lakes society, forming a very small fraction of the total population and living separately, in the rapidly dwindling rain forests.) Farming was a nearly universal concern, the shared basis of collective life, pursued on virtually all of Rwanda's countless hills.

The arrival of Western Nilotic warriors greatly complicated this picture. In what is now Rwanda, a nascent class society was formed as a series of Bantu farming peoples came under the dominion of the new Tutsi nobility. The pre-Tutsi peoples of the region were not, however, simply merged into a common "Hutu" status. Many of these peoples *(amooko)* preserved their pre-Tutsi identity, to some extent at least. Though their political structures were dismantled, the Zigaba, Sindi, Eega, Canda, Kono and other local farming peoples retained a lasting sense of ethnic relatedness. To this day, in fact, there are nearly twenty distinct *amooko* in Rwanda. All such peoples, however, assumed new profiles in the Tutsi era, segmenting (by complex processes of recruitment and permeation) into Tutsi and Hutu divisions. Indeed, as Marcel d'Hertefelt shows, each of the different peoples in Rwanda subdivided at some point into "Tutsi" and "Hutu" strata, forming what d'Hertefelt calls "multi-class social ensembles" (1971, p. 25).[6] While some of these peoples are mainly "Hutu" (e.g. the Zigaba, Uungura and Baanda) and others are largely "Tutsi" (e.g., the Nyiginya and Shiingo), all are multi-class composites of both groups. In this complex matrix of relations and identities, the Tutsi/Hutu division ultimately acquired a decisive significance, eclipsing the *amooko* as the main fault line in Rwandan society.

In this way, class displaced ethnicity – and indeed became a kind of surrogate ethnicity, invested with many of the cultural qualities which had formerly infused the distinction between peoples. In Nkore, to the north, a nearly identical process yielded a parallel distinction between the ruling Hima and the subject "Iru," who, like the Hutu, were not a unitary group to begin with (Berger 1981; Freedman 1974). Over time, this situation grew still more complex as the terms "Tutsi" and "Hutu" frayed at the edges. By a process that came to be known as *"kwihutura,"* wealthy Hutus could shed their "Hutuness" and become Tutsis (Watson 1991, p. 3; cf. Lema 1993, p. 50, and Lemarchand 1994, p. 8). And many Tutsis never joined the Rwandan nobility, remaining what Saucier calls "ordinary" rather than "political" Tutsis (1974).

The Rwandan class system, in other words, was classically pyramidal, but it was far from simple or unchanging. And one aspect of its complexity was its proto-ethnic character.

Meanwhile, the status of the nobility changed as well. As warlike imperial Rwanda grew at the expense of its neighbors (notably Ndorwa and Gisaka) the power and pretensions of the royal house grew proportionately. So, too, did the centralization of the state and the internal differentiation of the ruling strata. As early as the sixteenth century, a step to bureaucratize the military resulted in the formation of "social armies" or militias led by a stratum of Tutsi war chiefs, who were known as *abatwaare*. In the eighteenth century, perhaps to check the growing influence of the *abatwaare*, the kings granted new powers to a stratum of *abanayabutaka*, i.e. "the men of the land," who are usually called land chiefs – and many of whom were of Hutu origin. In the early nineteenth century, now seeking to limit the influence of the land chiefs, the king Yuhi Gahindiro set up a countervailing order of cattle chiefs, the *abanyamukenke*, "men of the grass."

Often sharing power over the same hills, cattle and land chiefs tended to practice "reciprocal surveillance" (Pottier 1993, p. 8). They also enlarged the sphere of patron/client relations, especially in central Rwanda, where producers were drawn in large numbers into increasingly exacting clientelist relations – notably cattle and land clientship, *ubuhake* and *ubereetwa*. Cattle clients,

64 *Humanity & Society, Volume 19, Number 4, November, 1995*

who could be either lower-status Tutsis or Hutus, were expected to repay their patrons for cattle loans with "almost constant service" (Des Forges 1972, p. 8), which rarely, however, consisted of fieldwork. Land clients, by contrast, repaid their loans with two days of weekly labor *(ubureetwa)* which Claudine Vidal regards as tantamount to a "corvée" or forced-labor obligation (1974, p. 67; cf. Vidal 1969, passim, and Des Forges 1972, pp. 7-14).

As compulsory labor services became increasingly common in the late imperial period, the Rwandan class system became progressively more hierarchical and exploitive. Though the kings and nobles continued to honor their customary obligations to their clients, they grew increasingly rich, demanding, and arrogant. This became especially plain during the long reign of the last pre-colonial king, Rwabugiri, whose death in 1894 coincided with the earliest arrival of European explorers. The subsequent phase of colonial domination, which began in 1899 when Rwanda was annexed by Germany and continued after World War I under Belgian colors, led to a doubling and trebling of the social distance between nobles and peasants – not only in class terms but "racially."

The Belgians, in particular, played a decisive role in this respect.

ETHNOCLASS CONFLICT

Until the 1920s, the aims of the colonial authorities diverged less from the interests of the Rwandan royal line than might have been expected. Concluding that they, too, would profit if Rwanda grew at the expense of nearby peoples, the Germans, and later the Belgians, encouraged the new Rwandan king, Musiinga, to wage war on peoples to the north whom Rwabugiri had failed to subjugate. The Abakiga *montagnards,* in particular, are important for our purposes, since their descendants remain leading actors in the class and ethnic conflicts of contemporary Rwanda.

The Abakiga ("people of Kiga") consisted of a mix of many *amooko,* including fragments of the Zigaba and other pre-Tutsi peoples who had fled southern and eastern Rwanda, and they are almost the only Great Lakes people without traditions of sacred kingship. Generally described as "Hutu" – which, in this case, simply means Not-Tutsi – the Abakiga had resisted the incursions of conquerors for centuries. Musiinga saw, however, that the Germans could be enlisted to help overrun the Abakiga for the greater glory of both empires. Ultimately, with German and Belgian assistance, he achieved precisely this. "Rwanda" thus grew to encompass not only the Tutsi/Hutu heartland (most notably Nduga and other south-central areas), but regions which had never before belonged to Tutsi/Hutu society. Though many Kigan peoples were already stratified, thanks to an indigenous form of land clientship known as *ubukonde,* they were irreconcilably hostile to the haughty Tutsi outsiders. This hostility was ethnic in nature – and so enduring, as we will see, that it played a major role in spurring the genocide last year.

Changes within the Rwandan realm also contributed greatly to the worsening of social tensions. A new phase began when the Belgians seized Rwanda from the Germans in 1916. Apart from helping Musiinga absorb the Abakiga and several peoples in the southwest, the Belgians pursued policies which weakened and humiliated the royal court. In 1916, in the earliest days of Belgian rule, the "Government of Occupation" divided Rwanda into two administrative units, cutting the sacred kingdom in half. Even worse, from the royal standpoint, was the fact that the Belgians chose to rule the country directly through the nobility, bypassing the king. As a result, Musiinga "lost control over [the nobles], since he could neither discipline them nor protect those whom the Belgians sought to punish" (Dorsey 1994, p. 13). Thus a train of events was set in motion which led, in 1931, to a decision to oust Musiinga in favor of his more pliable son Rudahigwa. From this point on the monarchy was plainly little more than a royal shadow.

In 1926 the Belgians reinvented the nobility as well. The intricate system which had balanced the clientelistic claims of cattle barons, land chiefs and army chiefs was abolished in favor of a more centralized system, in which the powers of all three groups devolved upon a class of "chiefs" *sans phrase*. This greatly concentrated power, with the result that, by 1935, there were fewer than 70 chiefs in all of Rwanda, aided by 900 "sub-chiefs" (Dorsey 1994, p. 19; Newbury 1988, p. 155). Another effect was the fall of the Hutu nobility, which vanished when the land chiefs were abolished. This was "a severe blow to the Hutu, who now ceased to be politically represented" (Pottier 1993, p. 9).

As the Belgians further centralized power in the ensuing period, they remade the Tutsi nobility into a "racially pure" caste, denying the Hutus all privilege and education. Though there were a few holes in their racist logic – which led them, for example, to define as "Tutsi" anyone who owned at least ten cows – they were unbending in their effort to divide Rwanda into two opposed camps. The result, as many critics have observed, was a kind of apartheid. The infinite complexities of identity in the precolonial era were flattened into a binary Tutsi/Hutu dialectic. In lieu of patrimonial give-and-take, the Belgians imposed increasingly one-sided relations of exploitation. One consequence was that the class division between nobles and peasants turned into a yawning chasm – and assumed a "racial" profile as well.

The Belgians, of course, were not entirely altruistic in their preference for the "Caucasoid" Tutsis. A political motive was also at work, as explained by one of the architects of Belgian policy, Msr. Léon Classe (1930, p. 2): "The greatest injury the government could do to itself ... would be to suppress the Tutsi caste. *Such a revolution would lead this country directly to anarchy and to hatefully anti-European communism*" (italics in the original; cited by Reyntjens 1994, p. 19). Even more decisive, however, were economic motives. "We harass the chiefs without respite," a Territorial Administrator wrote in 1932 (Newbury 1988, p. 171). And the chiefs bullied the peasants in turn. That same year – exactly one decade after the Belgians instituted forced labor *(Akazi)* and one

66   *Humanity & Society, Volume 19, Number 4, November, 1995*

year after coffee corvées were begun – one missionary protested that his parishioners were being driven so hard that they were on the brink of famine. The coffee corvée, cassava drive, buckwheat drive, treeplanting, road clearing, and construction work consumed the labor of 1,375 of the 2,024 adult men in his parish every day (Watson 1991, p. 4). It is no surprise, then, that the Belgians had to crush tax revolts in 1932 and 1935.

So extreme were the exactions in these years "that the very notion of work came to be practically synonymous with corvée" (Kagame 1975, p. 205, cited by Newbury 1988, p. 158). Along with unpaid *Akazi*, each taxpayer was required to set aside a certain amount of land for 100 coffee trees, to grow coffee for the export market (at prices set by the Belgians). By 1937, 20 million coffee trees had been planted in Rwanda and Burundi (then united into a single "protectorate") and many more were planted later. In 1944, corvée obligations consumed 120 work days per adult (Dorsey 1994, p. 26). In 1955, even the new Governor-General was appalled at the extent to which the chiefs squeezed the peasants: they extorted everything, he wrote, save "the strict minimum needed to survive" (Harroy 1984, p. 91; cited by Newbury 1988, p. 187).

Suffice it to say that, under Belgian rule, the political structure in Rwanda evolved into a kind of suction device for the efficient extraction of peasant labor. The Tutsi nobility was converted into a part of this device, "an exclusive African bureaucracy that siphoned off surplus from the Africans below ... " (Dorsey 1994, p. 9). This bureaucracy was not quite a ruling class – the Belgians saw to that – but it shared the functions and privileges of the colonial rulers. In the language of the classical Marxian theory of imperialism, the Tutsis can thus be described as a kind of "comprador" stratum, appended to the actual rulers. Unlike typical comprador strata, however, the Tutsis were also a kind of proto-ethnic group. Their class identity was indivisibly linked to a caste-like "racial" status, which (though entirely "constructed") was nevertheless all too real in its effects. The full menace of this racial construction became apparent last year.

THE PATH TO GENOCIDE

The cycle of conflict in contemporary Rwanda can be traced to the end of the colonial era. Circles of Hutu intellectuals *(evolués)* which crystallized in the 1950s formed two parties to press for independence: PARMEHUTU, a "Hutu" party with chauvinist impulses, which drew its main support from the south-central prefecture of Gitarama; and APROSOMA, based in the far southern province of Butare, which was multi-ethnic in ideology and composition.

In the wake of the independence struggle, which was accompanied by a wave of anti-Tutsi violence, PARMEHUTU emerged as the leading force in Rwanda. Soon the new regime proved to be a worthy heir to the Tutsi bureaucracy. As early as 1965 PARMEHUTU had become the nucleus of a one-party state, and by the late 1960s the inner political circle was clearly bent on self-enrichment. The main instrument of this quest was the state-run marketing system

TRAFIPRO, which channeled export profits to PARMEHUTU leaders and Gitarama businessmen (Pottier 1993, p. 11; cf. Reyntjens 1985, pp. 511f.).

Northern politicians were incensed, not only because they were left out in the cold, but because they saw PARMEHUTU as an enemy of traditional Abakiga class relations. Seeking to promote the interests of the landowning *abakonde*, whose wealth and power sprang from *ubukonde* clientship, the Northern politicians were also eager to invert the North/South split in Rwandan politics. This wish was fulfilled by the coup of 1973.

The coup leader, Habyarimana, was a general from Gisenyi whose wife came from a powerful *abakonde* family. In June, PARMEHUTU had crossed a fatal line by announcing a new bureau, ONACO, which would give the state control over commerce. For property owners this was evidently the last straw. When Habyarimana seized power in early July, he lost no time in "suspending" ONACO, which the new regime vilified as "communist" (Reyntjens 1985, pp. 505-6).

Quickly showing that he was no populist, Habyarimana took the bold step of reviving corvée labor in 1975. Under the aegis of a system called *umuganda*, all adults were required to participate in labor teams every Saturday under state direction; the penalty for refusal was imprisonment (Omaar and de Waal 1994, p. 16).[7] In other respects, too, Habyarimana "greatly intensified" the process of "centralizing and reinforcing the postcolonial state" (Newbury 1992, p. 198).

The class and ethnoregional biases of the new regime were unconcealed. Standing at the very heart of the regime was an inner circle known as *Akazu*, "the little hut," made up of Habyarimana's intimates, many of whom were from Rambura in Gisenyi (Reyntjens 1994, p. 276). Among the key figures in this group were Habyarimana's wife Agathe and three of her brothers (Braeckman 1994, p. 104). Guarding the inner circle was the elite Presidential Guard, "ninety per cent of whom," a former finance minister says, "are from Habyarimana's area, practically from his hill ... " (interviewed by Omaar and de Waal 1994, p. 91).

Many others northerners (politicians, landlords and merchants) orbited the *Akazu*. So wealthy did this stratum grow that Vidal speaks ironically of a "fourth ethnicity" in Rwanda – the governing rich, defined by their opposition to the peasantry (1991, p. 88). "Those in government," as Omaar and de Waal conclude (1994, p. 21), "had a license to print money."

Habyarimana professed to speak for all Rwandans, but it was self-evident, a former ambassador reports, that "in reality he was only interested in the Bakiga people, ... especially those from Gisenyi" (interviewed by Omaar and de Waal 1994, p. 40). Gitarama and Kibuye, with 20% of the population, received just one percent of state-sponsored rural investments, while Gisenyi and three other prefectures shared almost 90% of the total (Guiachaoua 1989, p. 173; cf. Newbury 1992, p. 203). Analogous disparities were plain elsewhere (Reyntjens 1994, p. 33).

68   *Humanity & Society, Volume 19, Number 4, November, 1995*

In a book finished just before the genocide, Filip Reyntjens announced that the Tutsi/Hutu conflict had been "surpassed by a regional conflict" (1994, p. 34; cf. Taylor 1992, p. 63). The North, prospering at the expense of the South, had made a mockery of the old rhetoric of "Hutu" unity, and "Hutus" were now sharply class-divided. Poverty was acute and endemic, and there was, as Catherine Newbury reported in 1992 (203), "a growing gap between rich and poor as well as a more vigorous assertion of class interests by those in power."

All of the latent social tensions in Rwanda rose to the surface in the years after 1988, when the collapse of the world coffee market plunged the coffee-growing peasantry into a state of near desperation. At one point, in open defiance of Rwandan law, coffee growers uprooted 300,000 coffee trees, seeking to reclaim land for private subsistence production (Chossudovsky 1995). Famine, always a danger in Rwanda, swept through much of the country, and the government found itself forced to accept IMF "Structural Adjustment" loans for the first time. The IMF, in the afterglow of the collapse of the Soviet Union, no longer felt constrained to support "anti-communist" states that happen to be anti-market as well. Free to push for a wholly marketized world, the IMF and other international donor agencies began to exert great pressure on Habyarimana to surrender power to a multi-party regime – a regime, i.e., which would release Rwandan production and exchange from the vise of state control, thus allowing "the market" to work its purported magic. Grudgingly, for lack of an alternative, Habyarimana permitted other parties to form. Soon many opposition parties had formed, including, among others, a lineal descendant of PARMEHUTU; the "Workers' assembly for democracy;" the *Mouvement des femmes et du bas-peuple;* the *Parti des écologistes,* and others (Reyntjens 1994, p. 135).

Meanwhile, Tutsi exiles who had risen to prominence in the Ugandan army proclaimed the formation of the "Rwandan Patriotic Front" and launched an invasion from Ugandan territory in October, 1990. Though not immediately successful (due, in part, to French military aid to the Habyarimana regime), the invasion put intense further pressure on the regime. In 1993, Habyarimana and the RPF joined with others to sign the Arusha Accords in Tanzania. This pact, affirming Habyarimana's willingness to move towards multi-party democracy, took Rwanda one step closer to the brink. The leaders of the "little hut" had been covertly training death squads since 1991, while keeping the IMF and its allies at bay with promises of reform. When Habyarimana signed the Arusha pact, his closest aide, Col. Theoneste Bagosora, left Tanzania saying that he was returning to Rwanda to "prepare the apocalypse" (Omaar and de Waal 1994, p. 79). Evidently, Habyarimana too was now expendable. His death – in an air crash seconds before landing at a Rwandan military base upon his return from yet another conference, on April 6, 1994 – served as the pretext for the start of the genocide. The death squads swung into action, killing Tutsis indiscriminately (on the assumption that all Tutsis are likely to sympathize with the RPF) and killing a great many carefully targeted Hutu democrats and dissidents as well. Many ordinary citizens were bribed or coerced into joining in the slaughter; many others refused to participate, and were killed themselves (Omaar and de Waal 1994, passim).

CONCLUSION

Class and ethnicity have been entwined throughout Rwandan history. This history can be divided into three primary phases:

- In the phase of Rwandan imperial expansion, the ethnic, horizontal divisions of the Sindi, Kono and other pre-Tutsi peoples were subsumed into the vertical structure of "Tutsi" and "Hutu" class relations. The result was a kind of class/ethnic matrix, in the shape of a pyramid. The main dynamic of this system was the extraction of surplus labor from peasants, whose "Hutu" class identity tended to supersede their fading ethnic status as Sindi, Zigaba, etc.
- In the colonial period, class identity itself was ethnicized, in a process Colette Guillaumin has aptly dubbed *"racisation"* (1972). Tutsi and Hutu class status now became the locus of a new "racial" identity, invested with many of the qualities which had once characterized the horizontal divisions between peoples. A purportedly racial exclusionism bordering on apartheid arose, complete with identity cards, educational discrimination, etc.

  In this phase, Rwandan class and ethnicity became congruent. "Tutsis," like "Hutus," acquired a double, overdetermined social identity, pivoting around discrimination as well as exploitation.
- Finally, in the post-independence phase, especially after the 1973 coup, Rwandan class and ethnic relations grew even more complex. Ideologically, the Habyarimana regime found it convenient to perpetuate the notion that "Tutsi" and "oppressor" are synonyms, but in reality the regime itself (moored in the Abakigan class relations of the northwest) now served as the prime oppressor of the hard-pressed, coffee-growing peasantry. This regime now claimed Hutu status as a mantle of popular legitimacy, but as recently as 1972 the term "Hutu" had been treated as a sign of opprobrium among the Abakiga (Freedman 1979).

  In other words, to deflect attention from its own oppressor-class status, the regime sought to stoke the embers of hostility to the former oppressor class. Habyarimana and Co. tried to play upon residual "Hutu" pride and resentment to divide and conquer the anti-regime opposition. Since most Rwandan Tutsis are now peasants, of course, just like most of the Hutus who are encouraged to hate them, this hostility can no longer be defined as "class antagonism" in any very literal sense. It is, rather, a form of ethnic hostility, stripped of its original class dimension. "Ethnicity," here as elsewhere, is neither essential nor primordial. It is, rather, the contingent social identity of a group treated and regarded as an ethnos, a people. By this criterion, Tutsi peasants in Rwanda remain *ethnically* distinct from Hutu peasants even though, in class terms, they no longer differ as their ancestors did (see Vidal 1991, citing Sartre; and cf. Smith 1995).

In summary, then: the Tutsi/Hutu nexus, which was first and foremost a class division, became, in the colonial era, a dually class and ethnic division; then, in the post-colonial period, ethnicity replaced class as the primary sense of "Hutu" and "Tutsi" status. Of course, class dynamics and tensions remain central to Rwandan society, as the rise of peasant resistance and a democratic opposition showed in the early 1990s. But ethnicity and ethnocentrism remain vital as well, as the doomed Habyarimana regime proved when it successfully tapped anti-Tutsi feelings to prepare and execute the genocide. This ethnocentrism may not have been strong enough to keep the "little hut" in power, but it was potent enough to lend a crucial ethnic impetus to an otherwise political and property-driven genocide.

This is not to say that ethnic identity is absolute or fixed in Rwanda, or that "ethnicity" in Rwanda today is akin to pre-Tutsi or pre-colonial ethnicity. On the contrary, the Tutsi/Hutu divide has always been "socially constructed," and it continues to be reconstructed. Rakiya Omaar and Alex de Waal argue, in fact, that the redesign of Hutu identity was just as much a goal of the Rwandan killers in the recent genocide as the murder of Tutsis. The Hutu chauvinists at the helm of state wanted to bind all surviving "Hutus," however varied in class or regional terms, into an anti-Tutsi "community of killers," whose very identity would be tied to their mortal hatred of the Tutsis (1994, pp. 568f.). Such a *Volksgemeinschaft* would be pledged to class collaboration precisely to the extent that it embraced ethnocentrism. For the Rwandan rulers, of course, such "Hutu" unity had obvious merits. For the Rwandan people, it was a recipe for death and destruction.

It might be objected that distinctions which are as palpably fabricated and manipulated as the notions "Tutsi" and "Hutu" cannot be valid markers of actual social relations. Yet it is beyond doubt that these constructed, manipulated notions remain very real to the Rwandan people, and that they continue to fuel a deadly rivalry. Tutsis and Hutus often see each other as sharply contrasting human types. They despise and murder each other for what they see as ethnic reasons, quite apart from any direct personal or class antipathies. And the history of this rivalry appears to be far from over. In Rwanda – and in Burundi as well – the Tutsi/Hutu division is still at the epicenter of social relations.[8] Still further redefinition of the ethnic situation appears likely.

Ethnicity, which is constructed to start with, is not negated when it is reconstructed (Ihonvbere 1994; Jenkins 1994; Nagel and Snipp 1993; Enloe 1980). This is is vividly clear throughout post-colonial Africa, where, as Jean-François Bayart observes, conflicts "enunciated in terms of ethnicity" routinely involve "identities which did not exist a century ago or, at least, were then not as clearly defined." What most often happens, Bayart says, is that once an ethnic division is constructed, it becomes *politicized*, emerging as a central fault line for conflict. This has been clearly demonstrated in many places, but "above all in Rwanda" (Bayart [1989] 1993, pp. 51, 48; cf. Reyntjens 1994).

In Rwanda, in the first century of The Global Era, the ghost of colonial class relations has been reborn as an ethnic conflict. So great was the hatred engendered by the Tutsi lords that even Tutsi peasants are not safe from its after-effects. The question, then, is whether the dead hand of the past, which grows heavier with each round of violence, will continue to sway the living. Will the ethnic echo of old class relations block opposition to new class relations? Or will the Rwandan people find a different path forward, less burdened by the past?

The promise of The Global Era depends in large measure on the answers to questions like these. A reconfigured Marxism, unafraid to stray from the sterile orthodoxies of the past, may help us find these answers.

NOTES

1 Initially it was said that roughly a half million people had been killed. Later estimates put the number in the vicinity of 750,00, a million or more – from a total Rwandan population of fewer than 9 million people. Rakiya Omaar and Alex de Waal, the co-directors of Africa Rights, at first refrained from specifying an absolute number (1994), but later concluded that at least 750,000 people had died (1995).

2 Max Weber called attention to an early instance of what seems to have been a relationship of this kind when he observed that, in Jacob's Blessing (in the Old Testament), the Issachar tribe is generally referred to as "servant." See Weber ([1917-19] 1952, p. 34).

3 As classically defined by ethnologists, tribes are clusters of clans which are united, in most cases, into two or more "moieties" (also called "phratries"). Internally, tribes are structured by social relations based on a specific, rigidly enforced type of marriage, namely, clan exogamy (intermarriage) combined with tribal endogamy (and, sometimes, phratric exogamy). Externally, tribes are defined by the political-military relations they maintain with one another (ranging from war to alliance).

   In other words, briefly: people from different tribes may fight but must not marry; and people within a tribe may marry but must not fight.

   In Rwanda, though vestigial traces of exogamy remain visible in some places even now, the *social structure* that gave this exogamy a tribal character has long since vanished. Ethnohistorical specialists on precolonial Rwanda often confuse matters by calling entire peoples "clans" (e.g., the Zigaba and Shambo, who are in reality large, amorphous, geographically dispersed groups), but the truth is that no clans or tribes have existed in Rwanda for a long time.

4 Newman (1995, pp. 165-6). The Hima and Hinda apparently were driven south by the depredations of the closely related Dinka, who were themselves fleeing the raids of the powerful Nuer. They became "Tutsis" when they migrated to the Great Lakes region of east central Africa. The word "Tutsi" thus seems to refer to Western Nilotes in general, without designating a specific Nilotic people in particular. Hence, while the "Tutsis" of Burundi also descend originally from Western Nilotic immigrants, they do not necessarily share a precise common origin with the "Tutsis" of Rwanda. And the same appears to be true of the Hima of Uganda.

5 One of the major noble strata which emerged in the later stages of Rwandan imperial development was largely Hutu in social composition, but by and large Hutu status signified subjection. And though there were Tutsis who were not nobles, Tutsi status tended to be synonymous with privilege, if not necessarily power.

6 Small numbers of "Twa," who form less than one percent of the Rwandan population, are also found in eleven of these multi-class *amookos*. These few remaining Twa are the heirs of the pre-

Bantu epoch in Great Lakes history. A "pygmoid" people, the Twa were historically hunters and potters who lived at the periphery of imperial Rwandan society. Fluctuating in status from despised out-castes (Maquet 1954) to royal clients (Saucier 1974), the Twa were basically external to the central class dynamic in Rwanda.

7 The reactionary daring of this step can be gauged by the fact that *travail-corvée* had been expressly singled out in the revolutionary 1957 "Manifesto of the Bahutu" as a practice "no longer adapted to the situation and psychology of today" (see Newbury 1988, p. 192). No other single feature of Belgo-Tutsi rule had been more hated.

8 The Burundian case differs from the Rwandan experience in many notable ways, not least in the fact that the colonial Tutsi elite remains in power, and that this elite is, in turn, divided into two ethnically distinct divisions. Yet however different, Burundi and Rwanda both remain divided to an important extent between goups which not only identify themselves as Tutsi and Hutu, but which see themselves as akin to their counterparts in the other country. Persecutions of Hutu dissidents in Burundi, for example, played a major part in spurring Hutu chauvinism in Rwanda. For details see Lemarchand (1994).

REFERENCES

Bayart, Jean-François. [1989] 1993. *The State in Africa,* translated by Mary Harper et al. London and New York: Longman.

Braeckman, Colette. 1994. *Rwanda, Histoire d'un génocide.* Paris: Fayard.

Chossudovsky, Michel. 1995. "IMF-World Bank Policies and the Rwandan Holocaust." Published on-line by Third World Network Features, Malaysia. Email: twn@igc.apc.org. January 28.

Chrétien, Jean-Pierre. 1985. "Hutu et Tutsi au Rwanda et au Burundi," in *Au cour de l'ethnie,* edited by Jean-Loup Amselle and Elikia M'bokolo. Paris: Découverte.

Classe, Léon. 1930. "Pour moderniser le Ruanda," in *L'Essor colonial et maritime,* 489 (April 12).

Des Forges, Alison L. 1972. *Defeat Is the Only Bad News: Rwanda Under Musiinga, 1896-1931.* Ph.D dissertation, Yale University.

Dorsey, Learthen. 1994. *Historical Dictionary of Rwanda.* London and Metuchen, NJ: The Scarecrow Press.

Fein, Helen. 1993. *Genocide: A Sociological Study.* London, Newbury Park, and New Delhi: Sage Publications.

Freedman, James M. 1974. *Principles of Relationship in Rwandan Kiga Society.* Ph.D dissertation, Princeton University.

Freedman, Jim. 1979. "East African Peasants and Capitalist Development: The Kiga of Northern Ruanda." Pp. 245-260 in *Challenging Anthropology,* edited by David H. Turner and Gavin A. Smith. Toronto: McGraw-Hill.

Guillaumin, Colette. 1972. *L'idéologie raciste.* Paris and The Hague: Mouton.

Harroy, Jean-Paul. 1984. *Rwanda.* Brussels: Hayez.

d'Hertefelt, Marcel. 1971. *Les Clans du Rwanda Ancien: Eléments d'ethnosociologie et d'ethnohistoire.* Tervuren: Koninklijk Museum voor Midden-Afrika.

Ihonvbere, Julius O. 1994. "The 'Irrelevant' State, Ethnicity, and the Quest for Nationhood in Africa." Pp. 42-60 in *Ethnic and Racial Studies,* 17 (1), January.

Kagame, Alexis. 1975. *Un abrégé de l'histoire du Rwanda,* Tome 2eme. Butare: Éditions Universitaires du Rwanda.

Lemarchand, René. 1994. *Burundi: Ethnocide as Discourse and Practice.* Cambridge and New York: Cambridge University Press.

Maquet, Jacques J. 1954. *Le Système des Relations sociales dans le Ruanda ancien.* Annales du Musée Royal du Congo Belge: Tervuren.

Marx, Karl. [1879] 1996. *Patriarchy and Property: The Ethnological Notebooks, Vol. 1 – The Notes on Lewis Henry Morgan,* edited by David Norman Smith. New Haven and London: Yale University Press.

Nagel, Joane and C. Matthew Snipp. 1993. "Ethnic Reorganization: American Indian Social, Economic, Political and Cultural Strategies for Survival," in *Ethnic and Racial Studies*, 16 (2).

Newbury, Catharine. 1988. *The Cohesion of Oppression: Clientship and Ethnicity in Rwanda, 1860-1960*. New York: Columbia University Press.

– 1992. "Rwanda: Recent Debates Over Governance and Rural Development." Pp. 193-220 in *Governance and Politics in Africa*, edited by Göran Hyden and Michael Bratton. Boulder and London: Rienner.

Newman, James L. 1995. *The Peopling of Africa: A Geographic Interpretation*. New Haven and London: Yale University Press.

Omaar, Rakiya and Alex de Waal. 1994. *Rwanda: Death, Despair and Defiance*. London: African Rights.

Pottier, Johan P. 1993. "Taking Stock: Food Marketing Reform in Rwanda, 1982-89," in *African Affairs* (92): 5-30.

Reyntjens, Filip. 1985. *Pouvoir et Droit au Rwanda: Droit Public et Evolution Politique, 1916-1973*. Tervuren: Musée Royal de l'Afrique Central.

– 1994. *L'Afrique des Grands Lacs en crise: Rwanda, Burundi: 1988-1994*. Paris: Éditions Karthala.

Saucier, Jean-François. 1974. *The Patron-Client Relationship in Traditional and Contemporary Southern Rwanda*. Ph.D dissertation, Columbia University.

Smith, David Norman. 1995. "Post-Colonial Genocide: Scarcity, Ethnicity, and Mass Death in Rwanda," in Isidor Wallimann and Michael Dobkowski, Eds. *The Coming Age of Scarcity: Preventing Mass Death and Genocide in the 21st Century*. Syracuse: Syracuse University Press.

Vidal, Claudine. 1969. "Le Rwanda des Anthropologues ou le Fétichisme de la Vache." Pp. 389-400 in *Cahiers d'Études Africaines*, 9.

– 1974. "Economie de la Société Féodale Rwandaise," in *Cahiers d'Études Africaines*, 14.

– 1985. "Situations ethniques au Rwanda," in *Au cour de l'ethnie*, edited by Jean-Loup Amselle and Elikia M'bokolo. Paris: Découverte.

– 1991. *Sociologie des passions (Côte d'Ivoire, Rwanda)*. Paris: Karthala.

Watson, Catharine. 1991. *Exile from Rwanda: Background to an Invasion*. Washington, DC: The U. S. Committee for Refugees, Issue Paper (February).

Weber, Max. (1917-19) 1952. *Ancient Judaism*. Glencoe, IL: The Free Press.

[25]

Democracy, Power, Genocide, and Mass Murder

R. J. RUMMEL
University of Hawaii at Manoa

From 1900 to 1987, state, quasi-state, and stateless groups have killed in democide (genocide, massacres, extrajudicial executions, and the like) nearly 170,000,000 people. Case studies and quantitative analysis show that ethnic, racial, and religious diversity, economic development, levels of education, and cultural differences do not account for this killing. Rather, democide is best explained by the degree to which a regime is empowered along a democratic to totalitarian dimension and, second, the extent to which it is characteristically involved in war or rebellion. Combining these results with those that show that democracies do not make war on each other, the more democratic two nations are the less foreign violence between them, and that the more democratic a regime the less internal violence, strongly suggests that democracy is a general method of nonviolence.

Political regimes—governments—have probably murdered nearly 170,000,000 of their own citizens and foreigners in this century—about four times the number killed in all international and domestic wars and revolutions (Rummel 1994). Why? I will offer both a theory and empirical results on this question and then sketch the variety of tests of the theory that were conducted. But first, I will define what I mean by government murder and, in doing this, propose an appropriate concept.

A concept that has provided yeoman service in denoting government murder is *genocide*. But this concept hardly covers the variety and extent of ruthless murder carried out by governments. To be more specific, in international conventions and the general literature, genocide has been defined in part as the intentional killing by government of people because of their race, religion, ethnicity, or other indelible group membership. Cold-blooded government killing, however, extends beyond genocide so defined: as starving civilians to death by a blockade; assassinating supposed sympathizers of antigovernment guerrillas; purposely creating a famine; executing prisoners

JOURNAL OF CONFLICT RESOLUTION, Vol. 39 No. 1, March 1995 3-26 of war; shooting political opponents; or murdering by quota (as carried out by the Soviets, Chinese communists, and North Vietnamese).

To cover all such murder as well as genocide and politicide, I use the concept *democide*.[1] This is the intentional killing of people by government. It excludes the killing of those with weapons in their hands or those indirectly killed as a result of military action; it excludes judicial executions for what are normally considered capital crimes, such as murder and treason (unless such are clearly excuses for the executions, as the Stalin show trials in the 1930s).

Democide is meant to define the killing by states as the concept of murder defines individual killing in domestic society. Here intentionality (premeditation) is critical. This also includes *practical* intentionality. If a government causes deaths through a reckless and depraved indifference to human life, the deaths were as though intended, as in the deadly Soviet forced labor camps.

It is democide for which I will try to account here.

A THEORY OF DEMOCIDE

The theoretical hypothesis is that the more democratic freedom a nation has, the less likely its government will commit foreign or domestic democide. In brief summary,[2] the theory is that through democratic institutions social conflicts that might become violent are resolved by voting, negotiation, compromise, and mediation. The success of these procedures is enhanced and supported by the restraints on decision makers of competitive elections, the cross-pressures resulting from the natural pluralism of democratic—spontaneous—societies, and the development of a democratic culture and norms that emphasizes rational debate, toleration, negotiation of differences, conciliation, and conflict resolution. Moreover, democratic leaders see others, even political opponents, as within the same moral universe, as equally nonviolent, as disposed to negotiate differences peacefully.[3]

On the other side are totalitarian political regimes. Rather than being a means for resolving differences in views, they try to impose on society a particular ideology, religion, or solution to social problems, regardless of the opposition. For this reason such regimes try to control all aspects of society and deal with conflict by force, coercion, and fear, that is, by power.

1. For a precise definition and elaboration of this concept, see Rummel (1994, chap. 2).

2. The theory is fully developed in Rummel (forthcoming-a).

3. This is, in effect, the same theoretical explanation that others have given for democracies not making war on each other. See, in particular, Russett (1993), Ray (forthcoming), and Weart (forthcoming). I see democracy as a general method of nonviolence with the same explanation applying across the board for why it should eliminate or minimize violence, including democide.

Moreover, such power breeds political paranoia by the dictator or within a narrow ruling group. This is the fear that others are always plotting to take over rule and would execute those now in power. Finally, there is one single coercive organization, one hierarchical pyramid of power rather than a multitude of such pyramids as in a democracy. This turns all sociopolitical and economic issues and problems into a matter of us versus them, of those with power versus those without. We should therefore find that the less democratic a regime, the more unchecked and unbalanced power at the center, the more it should commit democide. Democide becomes a device of rule, as in eliminating possible opponents, or a means for achieving one's ideological goal, as in the purification of one's country of an alien race or the reconstruction of society.

There is thus a scale of political regimes from the most democratic to the most totalitarian, from freedom in terms of political and civil rights and liberties to an absolute power under which such rights and liberties do not exist. And we should find empirically that the more democratic the less violence in foreign and domestic affairs, the more totalitarian the more violence. So far this equation between the scales of power and violence has been empirically supported. We find that democracies do not (or rarely) make war on each other, that the more democratic and less totalitarian two regimes the less foreign violence between them,[4] and that democracies have the least domestic violence (Rummel 1984, 1985, forthcoming-a). By this theory, power also should be directly predictive of democide such that the less democratic a regime along the democratic to totalitarian scale of power, the more likely it will commit democide.

To hypothesize that democracy is inversely related to democide leaves open the question as to how this democide is measured. I argue theoretically that democracy will be most related to the total magnitude of *domestic* democide logged. First, the more democratic the less the number of its own people the regime will kill for the reasons given. However, these restraints do not operate well in times of hot or cold war when the military or intelligence services operate in secret, and if their foreign operations are in effect totalitarian enclaves within a democratic structure. This is because, in wartime, democracies largely give the military their head, secrecy prevails, and wartime controls are instituted over the nation. It is an open question whether democracies in wartime retain their full democratic character (consider the internment of Japanese Americans in concentration camps during World War II, for example), particularly in their foreign operations. For this reason I argue that the primary inverse relationship between democracy and

4. See Russett (1993) and Rummel (1985, forthcoming-a) for supporting evidence and studies on this and the previous proposition.

6   *JOURNAL OF CONFLICT RESOLUTION*

democide is to domestic killing. This is not to say that democracies will murder as many noncombatants in wartime as will nondemocracies, which they clearly have not, but that the correlation between democracy and foreign democide will be much lower than for the domestic or total amount of democide.

Second, the closer one gets to democracy on the hypothetical democracy-totalitarianism scale, the more the restraints on democide should kick in. This is because even a moderate liberalization of a totalitarian regime, as after the death of Stalin or Mao Tse-tung, creates countervailing forces that make democide difficult to carry out or less the appro ved means to achieve policies. When power at the center is limited by tradition or other power groups, even in authoritarian regimes such as those of Saudi Arabia, Iraq, or Iran, the ability to kill unlimited numbers of people is sharply limited. We should expect, therefore, that as regime types vary from democratic to somewhat democratic to authoritarian to somewhat totalitarian to totalitarian, there should be a virtual logarithmic increase in the number of people a regime kills.

And finally, this should not only be an absolute relationship between the democratic-totalitarian scale and domestic democide but also one with the number killed as a proportion of the population per year of the regime—the rate of democide. Democratic restraints should operate not only on the sheer number killed over the life of a regime but also on the relative number killed. That is, the inverse relationship between democracy and democide should hold regardless of the duration of the regime and its population.

Finally, we should expect that the relationship between democracy and democide should be greatest with domestic democide (on which the democratic restraints will have their greatest effect); second, with total democide, which includes foreign; and there should be little if any relationship to foreign democide by itself.

RESEARCH DESIGN

I have gone through five research stages to test the hypothesis that democracy is causally and inversely related to democide. Specifically for this test, I collected data on all democide for all regimes for the period from 1900 to 1987, for which estimates in English were available in the literature.[5]

Second, I delineates the dimensionality of these data through factor analysis.

5. These data are based on almost 8,200 estimates of war, domestic violence, genocide, mass murder, and other relevant data that I recorded from over 1,000 sources, which include general works, specialized studies, human rights reports, journal articles, and news sources. For the tables of estimates on the Soviet Union, China, and Nazi Germany, see Rummel (1990, 1991, 1992). For all other estimates, see Rummel (forthcoming-b). For totals and a statistical overview of the data, see Rummel (1994, chap. 1).

Third, attending now to the hypothetical independent variable, I determined various ways of measuring democracy over the same years for different regimes. I then used a factor analysis to define the prime indicator of the theoretical democracy-totalitarianism continuum.

Fourth, I collected data on a number of control variables, particularly those defining cross-national sociocultural diversity, culture, war and rebellion, wealth, and power. I also separately factor analyzed these data to uncover their major indicators and reduce the number of variables and their multicollinearity in the tests.

Finally, I then applied factor analysis, interactive multiple regression analysis, canonical analyses, and time series regression to test whether of all indicators the democracy-totalitarian one best accounted for democide, as it should. It did, regardless of the controls or type of tests.

Because of the sheer magnitude of the analyses—just one of the factor analyses or canonical analyses by itself could have constituted an article—I will have to be very brief in presenting the most important results. I will try to be as explicit as possible where it is most important to be so, which is in the actual tests.

PATTERNS OF DEMOCIDE

Turning now to the data on democide, the operational question is whether total, domestic, and foreign democide, and the rate of democide (as defined above) are empirically different patterns in the democide data. This is already a kind of test of the above theory, because if these types of democide are highly intercorrelated, then democracy cannot be both highly related to domestic democide and largely unrelated to foreign democide, as the theory suggests.

To determine this, I need to define different foreign and domestic democide types—variables. In doing this, three criteria are important. One is that these types are conceptually and empirically meaningful. The second is that they can be identified among the flow of events and especially in the fog of war and violence. And the third is that there are data that can be so defined. The types consistent with these requirements are listed in Table 1.

In total, 218 regimes (141 state regimes and 77 quasi-state and group regimes) committed some sort of democide in this century for which I could find estimates, no matter how small. How many state regimes did not commit democide? This is a difficult question, simply because it requires that all regimes existing during this century be identified. Now, as used here, a *regime* is a government that is identified by certain political characteristics that exist for a specifiable period. These characteristics define the nature and distribu-

TABLE 1
Empirical Types of Democide

Type	Measure	Definition[a]
Total democide	TotalDemocide	Total murdered in all forms of democide, including those listed below
Domestic democide	DomDemocide	Citizens murdered by their regime in all forms of domestic democide
Foreign democide	ForDemocide	Noncitizens murdered by a regime in all forms of democide
Domestic democide rate %	DemocideRate	$[(\text{domestic democide})/\text{domestic population}] \times 100$[b]
Domestic democide annual rate %	DemocAnnRate	(domestic democide rate)/(duration of regime in years)[c]
Prisons/camps	Camps	People murdered in or dying as a result of incarceration in prisons or concentration/forced labor camps
Forced labor	ForcedLab	People who were murdered during or dying as a result of forced labor (includes that in forced labor camps)
Terror	Terror	Murder of specific individuals (unlike massacres)[d]
Massacre	Massacre	Indiscriminate mass murder[e]
Famine/disease	Famine	Regime intended deaths from starvation and disease[f]
Deportation	Deportation	Murder during or deaths from deportation or expulsion
Genocide	Genocide	People killed because of their religion, ethnicity, race, language, nationality, or other social group membership
Prisoners of war	POWs	Prisoners of war murdered or dying in custody for lack of care
Bombing	Bombing	Noncombatants killed indiscriminately by bombing, shelling, torpedoing, germ warfare, or defoliation

a. The classifications are not independent; deaths may be counted under two of more of the classifications, such as under genocide and deportation. For an extended definition of democide, see Rummel (1994, chap. 2).
b. Read as "the democide is x killed out of every y people"—for example, if equals 3%, then that means that 3 out of every 100 people were killed (or 1 out of every 33); if .3%, then 3 out of every 1,000 (or 1 out of every 333) were killed.
c. Read as "the democide is x killed out of every y people per year"—for example, if equals .2%, then that means that 2 out of 1,000 were killed per year (or 1 out of 500). For regimes older than 1900, such as the United States, duration begins at 1900 for this measure.
d. Includes political or summary executions, assassinations, deaths by torture, disappearances, or deaths during flight/escape.
e. Includes atrocities and the deaths of conscripted soldiers for which the regime is responsible.
f. Includes cases in which the regime could have, but knowingly did not, try to alleviate the famine or epidemics.

tion of a regime's coercive and authoritative power and the manner in which this power is exercised and the power-holders changed. For example, the changes of regime from the rule of the Czar over Russia to the Kerensky government, and then within the same year to the Bolsheviks give us three regimes. The changes from the Kaiser monarchy to the Weimar Republic to Hitler's rule also give us three different German regimes. Mainly, but not completely, relying on Ted Robert Gurr's (1990) political characterization of regimes (polities) from 1800 to 1986, I count 432 distinct state regimes during the period from 1900 to 1987.[6] And 141, or about one-third of these, committed some form of democide.

Let us now look at how this democide is empirically patterned across the 432 regimes. By a *pattern* is meant the intercorrelation of certain types of democide such that when a regime kills people in one kind of democide there is a high probability that it also will have committed or will commit the other kinds of democide. Ideally, this intercorrelation—pattern—should be so defined that the influence of other patterns is statistically partialed out.

I must make clear that the various democide types are totaled over the life of a regime. For regimes surviving for only a couple of years, the different types of democide are probably simultaneous. For very long-lived regimes, such as the Soviet Union or United States, different types of democide and even the different occurrences of democide for a particular type may have been committed in years separated by decades or even half a century or more. A high correlation, then, between two democide types, such as terror and genocide, should be interpreted to mean that a regime characteristically committed both types of democide or that both are characteristic behaviors of the regime, not that both types were simultaneously committed. A pattern of interrelated democide types then means that these are *interrelated behavioral characteristics* of regimes.

Moreover, because a few regimes may have very high democide compared to others (e.g., the Soviet Union and China), all data were log transformed (base 10). To be sure this is kept in mind, L is added to the type's name.

Using component analysis, I identified the patterns of democide just for the 218 regimes with democide and also only for the 141 state regimes.[7] For

---

6. I also consulted the lists of regimes in Calvert (1970) and Russett (1993).

7. I did both varimax orthogonal and oblique rotation of the components. Some of the democratic types are arithmetically related. Thus total democide is the sum of domestic and foreign democide, and camp dead is related to foreign labor dead. This is not a problem as long as it is recognized and taken into account in the interpretation of the results (a composite variable and its two parts can only be two dimensional at most).

Also, except for the variance for which they account, there would be no change in the patterns were the democide of all regimes from 1900 to 1987 analyzed.

both analyses (not shown) the patterns were much the same. Because the state regimes will be the focus of subsequent analysis and tests, I will concentrate on these patterns.

The 14 democide types reduce to five empirical patterns (or dimensions) of democide and their five indicators (italicized).[8] The first and most important pattern centrally involves *domestic democide*, with which is correlated terror, massacres, the domestic democide rate, and total democide. The second and statistically independent pattern is one of *foreign democide*, and also including forced labor deaths, camp deaths, and POWs killed. Two other independent patterns comprise the *annual domestic democide rate* and democidal *bombing* deaths. The final pattern is that of mainly *genocide* and, secondarily, massacres.

The italicized indicators are now our fundamental measures of democide. They will be the basis of all subsequent analyses of democide and should be looked at as fundamental causal foci. That is, *each empirical pattern reflects underlying first-order causes and conditions that differ from those related to other patterns.*[9] Note, therefore, that because genocide is a statistically independent causal pattern in the democide data, the causes that underlie this form of mass murder are separate and distinct from those causing the other type of government killing. This is not to deny that there is an overall explanation for democide in general, but that within this general explanation there are particular patterns of democide, such as genocide, explained by more specific causes and conditions.

As mentioned, this component analysis is also an initial test of one aspect of the hypothesis. The expectation was that democracy would have its greatest inverse relationship to domestic democide and little to the foreign. *For this to be true, domestic and foreign democide must be near independent empirical patterns in the data.* This is indeed the case, where the component analysis and orthogonal and oblique rotations showed domestic and foreign democide to be different, uncorrelated, dimensions of democide.[10] Although this does not substantiate that it is democracy that is the cause, this separation of the patterns is a necessary condition for the hypothesis, as elaborated, to be true.

8. The full results of this analysis are given in Rummel (forthcoming-b).

9. Some deny that factor analysis can be used in causal analysis. But consider. If two uncorrelated empirical patterns are found by factor analysis, they both cannot be the result of the same causes. There must be two different sets of causes at work. This is all that is being said here: that factor analysis uncovers different causal foci, not that it identifies what these causes are or proves causation. Similarly, correlation does not prove causation, but if two variables are perfectly uncorrelated (even after third variables are partialed out), then one cannot be the cause of the other. Lack of correlation does *disprove* causation.

10. This lack of correlation holds even through oblique rotation.

DEFINING A SCALE OF
DEMOCRACY VERSUS TOTALITARIANISM

To keep the data collection manageable for all subsequent analyses, the sample will have to be limited to (a) all 141 state regimes committing democide and (b) those state regimes not committing democide that (c) involve a large shift in power from previous or succeeding regimes. For example, although the communist Afghanistan regime (1978-) is included because it committed democide, a previous noncommunist regime (1965-73) is also included. Austria committed no democide, as best I can determine, but it had two very different regimes, one autocratic regime in the pre-Hitler takeover period, 1934-38, and the other the post-Second World War demo-cratic regime, 1946-. Both Austrian regimes are included. I also tried to pick regimes such that all major cultures, national characteristics, socioeconomic attributes, and regime variation would be represented. This selection proce-dure gives me a sample of 214 state regimes, including the 141 with democide, for the years from 1900 to 1987. Hereafter, this is the basic sample for all analyses.

In Table 2 I list a variety of political measures that in one way or another define regime types.[11] The question now is which of these measures centrally define the theoretical democratic-totalitarian scale that is supposed to predict to democide, if indeed there is such an independent empirical political pattern. These measures were selected to span the variety of regime types, whether liberal democratic, absolute monarchies, communist, noncom-munist totalitarian, military dictatorships, oligarchic republics, or personalist autocracies.

Table 3 shows the five statistically independent political patterns that emerge from a component analysis for these 214 regimes. As shown, there are five major patterns.[12] The substantive nature of these patterns is identified by the coefficients (loadings) in the matrix, which give the correlation between the democide types and the pattern. Squaring these correlations then defines the amount of variation in the democide related to the pattern. I have outlined in the table each of these correlations for which there is 25% or more covariation between political type and pattern. As can be seen (similar types

11. There are a variety of published scales of democracy that could not be used here in toto, because a first requirement of any data set was that it be available for or applicable to all state regimes from 1900 to 1987, a requirement met by only a few data sets. For some political measures, however, these scales were useful for data for particular regimes that fell within their time span.

12. I determined the number of components to rotate by the substantive meaning of the factor and the eigenvalue-one criterion. The fifth unrotated component was slightly below this criterion at .92. Oblique rotation does not produce substantively different patterns than those shown.

TABLE 2
Measures of the Political Nature of a Regime

Measure	Short Name	Direction: High =	Main Source
Democracy (dichotomy)	Democracy	democracy	diverse sources[a]
Democracy Scale	DemocrScale	democracy	diverse sources[a]
Arat's Democracy Scale	AratDemocr	democracy	Arat (1991)
Democracy vs. Autocracy	DemoVsAuto	democracy	Gurr (1990)
Political Competition	PolCompet	most competition	Banks (1971)
Elected Executive	ElectExec	elected	Banks (1971)
Elected Legislature	ElectLeg	elected	Banks (1971)
Legislative Effectiveness	LegEffect	autonomous/effective	Banks (1971)
Authoritarian (dichotomy)	Authoritarian	authoritarian	diverse sources[a]
Monarchy	Monarchy	monarchy	diverse sources[a]
Authoritarian Scale	AuthorScale	authoritarian	diverse sources[a]
Totalitarian (dichotomy)	Totalitarian	totalitarian	diverse sources[a]
Totalitarian Scale	TotalScale	totalitarian	diverse sources[a]
Communist	Communist	communist	diverse sources[a]
Political Power	PolPower	most power	Gurr (1990)
Traditional Elite Power	ElitePower	more power	Adelman and Morris (1973)
Government Expenditures per capita—logged	ExpCapLog	more expenditures	Banks (1971)

a. No major sources. Scale values filled in for particular regimes from Bollen (1980), Coppedge and Reinicke (1990), Cole (1987), Coulter (1975), Cutright and Wiley (1969), Dahl (1971), *Encyclopedia Britannica*, Freedom House's freedom ratings in various issues of *Freedom at Issue*, Lake (1992), Sachs (1971), Smith (1969), *The Statesman's Yearbook*, and Vanhanen (1990).

are set off by horizontal lines), the first and most important of these involves a democratic to totalitarian continuum, or looking at all the measures correlated with the pattern, a continuum measuring the degree to which coercive regime power penetrates and controls political and socioeconomic institutions, functions, and individual behavior. To keep this idea foremost, I have named this the *totalitarian power* pattern. Both the democratic and totalitarian scales are among those measures most highly correlated with this pattern. Its indicator will be constructed by adding the totalitarian scale to the inverse of the democratic scale, with the result that totalitarian regimes will be at the high end.[13] The resulting indicator I will call simply *TotalPower*.

There is also a *political power* pattern (Factor 5), which should not be confused with totalitarian power and is largely statistically (and conceptu-

13. Because each scale is 0-9 and with totalitarianism and democracy at the high end of each and their correlation is negative, then TotalPower = (TotalScale) + (9 − DemocrScale).

TABLE 3
Component Analysis of Political Measures

Orthogonal Solution	Factor 1	Factor 2	Factor 3	Factor 4	Factor 5
Democracy	.80	.37	−.18	.03	−.04
DemocrScale	.96	−.13	−.03	.01	−.10
AratDemocr	.76	.09	−.34	.02	−.17
DemoVsAuto	.79	.12	−.26	−.04	−.41
PolCompet	.85	−.01	−.11	−.02	−.17
ElectExec	.67	.01	.33	.08	.07
ElectLeg	.72	−.20	.34	−.22	.14
LegEffect	.90	.01	.11	−.13	−.04
Authoritarian	−.27	−.88	.18	.06	.05
Monarchy	−.05	−.03	.83	.16	0.00
AuthorScale	−.13	−.55	.65	.40	.04
Totalitarian	−.54	.77	−.03	−.11	−.01
TotalScale	−.84	.22	.15	.03	.25
Communist	−.51	.73	−.09	−.09	−.04
PolPower	−.36	−.09	−.09	−.01	.86
ElitePower	−.09	−.17	.13	.90	0.00
ExpCapLog	.18	.44	−.49	.22	.27

ally) independent of it. The political power measure defines this pattern and indexes the degree to which political power is centralized, politically auto-cratic, or dictatorial, without any electoral system, legislature (rubber stamp or not), or other representative body. TotalPower reflects well this centrali-zation of political power in totalitarian systems, of course, but *also* the regime's penetration of and control over the nonpolitical aspects of society as well, such as religion, the economy, and culture, which are not measured by the political power pattern alone.

There is much confusion in the literature between totalitarian and political power that must be clarified here. Because of the lack of any electoral system and even a nominal representative body, authoritarian regimes like that of Saudi Arabia may have a higher score on political power than the Soviet Union. And because of the lack of any meaningful legislature or other control over the executive, a regime like that in Kuwait with an absolute monarch is often coded with greater political power than many communist countries where a legislature exists, albeit largely a rubber stamp, and where a politburo may provide some executive restraints as in the Soviet Union of the 1970s.

For this reason, many scales of democracy will position communist countries closer to the democratic end then the absolute monarchies or dictatorships without any legislature or electoral system. The political power scores used here are primarily based on the work of Gurr (1990). He codes the political power of each regime as a combination of its regulation of participation and executive recruitment, the competitiveness of executive recruitment, the constraints on the chief executive, whether the executive is monocratic or not, and the centralization of the state. Note that all these are political characteristics and do not define, for example, the degree to which there is a command economy, or regime control over the media, religion, or other nonpolitical institutions.

There is also an authoritarian versus totalitarian pattern (see Factor 2 of Table 3), that is fundamentally the opposition between the two.[14] Both types of regimes are nondemocratic, but they differ sharply in the degree to which power regulates and controls all of society. We have here the same distinction between totalitarian and political power, but now largely limited to nondemocratic regimes.

Of the remaining two patterns listed in Table 3, Factor 3 defines absolute monarchies and Factor 4 reflects the power of a society's traditional elite (clan or church leaders, historic economic elite, chiefs and tribal leaders, aristocrats, etc.).

DEMOCRACY, TOTALITARIANISM, AND DEMOCIDE

With these indicators defined, what are we to expect of the relationship between democide and the five political patterns? Foremost, as noted, TotalPower should have the highest positive relationship to the domestic democide pattern, which also includes, secondarily, total democide. The more TotalPower, the more democide. Second, TotalPower should also have a positive but moderate relationship to the annual democide rate and genocide patterns. Genocide is a more specific democidal behavior and thus is more affected by idiosyncratic causes and conditions. The annual democide rate is partially dependent on a regime's population and duration, neither of which are characteristics much influenced by totalitarianism. For domestic democide, the annual rate, and for genocide, the political power of a regime should be second in relationship. It reflects an important aspect of power, but not the absolute totalitarian power that is most democidal.

14. This is consistent with previous component analysis results for all nations, 1955-63. See Rummel (1979).

TABLE 4
Component Analysis of Democide and Political Indicators[a]

	Unrotated Factors			Orthogonal Solution		
	Factor 1	Factor 2	Factor 3	Factor 1	Factor 2	Factor 3
DomDemocL	.84	.04	-.16	.84	.16	-.10
ForDemocL	.43	-.59	.47	.15	.85	-.07
DemAnRateL	.59	.12	-.31	.65	-.09	-.16
GenocideL	.75	-.08	-.03	.69	.29	-.09
BombingL	.28	-.60	.38	.03	.75	-.14
TotalPower	.69	.34	.10	.71	.07	.29
Authoritarian	.03	.66	.34	.13	-.22	.70
Monarchy	-.04	.17	.78	-.16	.37	.69
ElitePower	-.07	.54	.29	.01	-.21	.57
PolPower	.44	.38	0.00	.52	-.11	.25

Eigenvalues			Primary Intercorrelations			
	Magnitude	Variance Prop.		Factor 1	Factor 2	Factor 3
Value 1	2.56	.26	Factor 1	1.00	.05	.11
Value 2	1.74	.17	Factor 2	.05	1.00	-.35
Value 3	1.30	.13	Factor 3	.11	-.35	1.00
Value 4	1.02	.10				
Value 5	.88	.09				

a. Oblique and orthogonal rotation was by varimax. The primary correlations show that the oblique solution adds little to the orthogonal. $N = 214$ state regimes.

To test these expectations, we might simply consider the product-moment correlations between the democide and political indicators. In fact, *by far the highest correlation between the political and democide measures is .55 for TotalPower and domestic democide.* But because this correlation and the others are influenced by the interrelations among all the indicators, they can only be suggestive. The best way to untangle (partial out) the interrelationships among the correlations and defining the independent lines of causation is through component analysis.

Table 4 shows the unrotated and orthogonal (statistically independent) components (factors).[15] Each reflects an independent causal pattern or nexus, where the largest and most pervasive one is that of the first unrotated component. But the unrotated component often obscures lesser patterns that might be more theoretically important. For this reason, the components

15. I rotated various numbers of factors, and the three-factor solution gives the cleanest and most theoretically satisfying solution.

should be rotated to see if these other patterns are present in the data and to best define the tightest interrelationships among them. Note also that whether they are rotated or unrotated, each of these rotated factors will delineate a causal nexus such that the influences involved in the other factor patterns are partialed out.

It is therefore important that we find that *the most general causal pattern, the first unrotated factor, most centrally involves domestic democide, and, secondarily, the annual rate and genocide. And the only political indicator included is for TotalPower*. On rotation, this causal nexus is more clearly defined, with political power now playing a secondary role.

Aside from this cluster and looking again at Table 4, we find that foreign democide, including bombing, forms a pattern by itself, as do also the three authoritarian type indicators.

The causal weight of TotalPower in accounting for domestic democide can be displayed visually by disaggregating it into the democratic and totalitarian scales of which it is composed, and graphing domestic democide against both of them. The resulting three-dimensional surface is drawn in Figure 1.[16]

There are several things to note about this surface. At the democratic corner, it shows virtually no domestic democide for both scales. Then, as we move away from the democratic corner toward either opposing end, democide increases.[17] Moreover, the midsurface—the joint effect of the democracy and totalitarian scales, or TotalPower—is almost uniformly slanted upward until it approaches the diagonal corner from democracy and then curves upward even more. This means that TotalPower squared rather than TotalPower alone should be more predictive of domestic democide in regression analysis, which, in fact, is the case as we will see.

There is another way to test and better understand the hypothetical relationship between democide and TotalPower, which is shown in Figure 2. For this, the 18-point TotalPower indicator was divided into five groups, such

16. The inverse squared distance technique used to draw the surface shown in the figure is not based on regression, but interpolates domestic democide logged (the Z height of the surface at an XY point) as the weighted average of the totalitarian and democratic (X and Y) scales. The squared Euclidean distances across the totalitarian and democratic scales comprise the weights.

17. Based on the joint data points, the surface shown in the figure has been extrapolated to the full range of the two political scales. Thus, even though there were no regimes that were scaled both democratic and totalitarian (scale values of 0 and 1 for the democratic scale and 8 and 9 for the totalitarian—not theoretically impossible), the surface was extrapolated to the region in the right-hand corner. Moreover, although there is a strong negative correlation between democracy and totalitarianism, this correlation is not perfect (some democracies are more statist than others). That the democratic and totalitarian scales in the figure are shown at right angles does not imply lack of correlation, therefore, any more than would a standard two-dimensional scatter plot of these two scales, where the scales are shown at right angles.

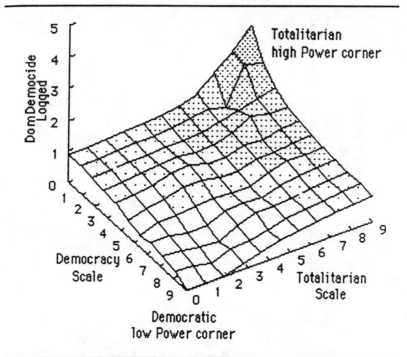

Figure 1:   Plot of Domestic Democide on Democracy and Totalitarian Scales[a]
a. Dots comprise shading and not data points. The surface is drawn by the inverse squared distance smoothing technique. $N = 214$ state regimes.

that the low and high groups comprised the lowest and highest scale values, the midgroup the five midscale values, and the rest were distributed between the low-mid and high-mid groups. The resulting plot of group means is almost perfect. It curves upward continuously to absolute totalitarian power.

WAR, REBELLION, AND DEMOCIDE

Consider now the changes in the context of a regime that give it an excuse for democide, appear to necessitate democide, or challenge power such that democide seems the best defense. These include the breakout of international war or military action, domestic or foreign rebellion, revolution, antiregime guerrilla warfare and terrorism, or a coup d'état.

Such warfare is theoretically related to democide in several ways. First, democide can become part of the strategy for achieving victory. Bombing

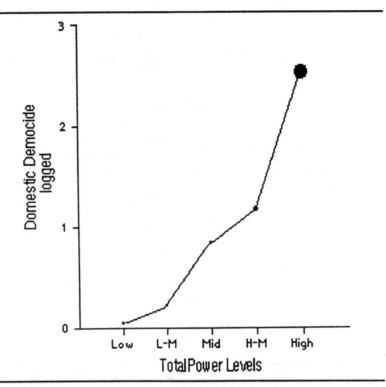

Figure 2:   Plot of the Mean Domestic Democide for Different Levels of Power[a]
a. Size of points proportionate to the mean democide. $N = 214$ state regimes.

and shelling cities indiscriminately, for example, are believed to terrorize the enemy people into pressing for an end to war and to demoralize the base of the enemy regime's power.

But apart from this, involvement in an intense and passionately fought war enables a regime to implement further its ideological, racial, nationalist, or theological imperatives through outright domestic democide or its inten-sification. For example, once fully engaged in a war, the Nazis could further their central program of making Germany Jew-free by instituting the "final solution" and extending it to all occupied nations in Europe.

Blending with this rationale for democide is the excuse that war and rebellion give to initiate large-scale democide. Minorities or opposing politi-cal movements or parties may have been perceived by the power elite as long-standing threats to the regime. In the fog of war or rebellion, democide may become practical, or war may eliminate the foreign protection for such groups or fear of a foreign reaction were democide unleashed. Thus, once Turkey was allied with Germany in World War I, which effectively removed the protection that the Christian Powers gave the Armenian minority in Turkey, the Young Turk rulers could undertake their program to completely "Turkify" Turkey through genocide.

We therefore should find a close relationship with war and rebellion over and above that of TotalPower. Do we? For each of the 141 regimes committing democide, I determined from a variety of sources the number of their war- and rebellion-dead, excluding their democide-dead during these wars.[18] I have added to these statistics similar data (Small and Singer 1982) on battle-dead for those regimes without democide that comprised my 214 state-regime sample. Because of the very large number of killed in war or rebellion for a few of the regimes, these data were $\log_{10}$ transformed.

Before continuing, I should clarify what the correlations between war-dead, rebellion-dead, and democide will mean empirically. These correlations are for the democide and war-dead or rebellion-dead at any time in the life of a regime. Thus a war or rebellion may occur during a regime's early period and the democide in the final period. For example, the duration of the Soviet regime is from 1917 to past the final data collection year of 1987. There was a deadly civil war from 1918 to 1922 and the 1941-45 participation in World War II. But unrelated to both of these were the millions that were killed in the collectivization campaign of the 1930s, the intentional Ukrainian famine, and the Great Terror. These deaths are a large part of the final 1917-87 democide toll for the Soviet Union and thus contribute to the correlations with the overall 1917-87 war and rebellion-dead for the regime.

The correlation between war or rebellion-dead and democide thus define a regime's *disposition* to commit various kinds of democide—disposition measured by the occurrence of democide during the life of the regime—and its *characteristic* involvement in war or rebellion. Disposition to democide and characteristic war or rebellion can be treated as *traits*. That is, they may not be manifest at any particular time nor together, but nonetheless they describe behavior during the life of a regime.

Now, are the democide patterns we have already identified related to characteristic warfare? A component analysis (not shown) gives an immediate answer—yes.[19] War-dead is correlated .86 with a foreign democide and

18. Data are given in Table 16A.1 of Rummel (forthcoming-b).
19. The specific results for this and the other analyses described below are given in Rummel (forthcoming-b).

bombing pattern, and rebellion-dead is correlated .93 with an independent pattern of domestic democide. But war and rebellion cause the domestic democide pattern to break up into two, one being the magnitude of domestic democide related to rebellion-dead and the other an independent pattern of genocide and the domestic democide annual rate. The reason for this separation into two patterns is the very high correlation of characteristic rebellion with the magnitude of democide and virtually no correlation with genocide and the annual rate. That is, *the amount of overall democide is highly related to the number of people characteristically killed in rebellions, but in general, this in turn has little to do with a regime's disposition to commit genocide or its annual rate of domestic democide.*

Nor is the characteristic intensity of war related to genocide. Apparently, regimes generally plan and implement their genocidal policies independent of the characteristic occurrence and intensity of their wars. This finding requires careful digestion. It does not mean that all genocides are independent of a regime's tendency to be involved in other forms of violence. This is patently false, as the Nazi and Young Turk cases, among others, would attest. But it is to say that considerable genocide is carried out even by regimes that have had or will have relatively few or no war-dead, as the current genocide of perhaps 500,000 people in Rwanda within a month attests.

The question now is whether a regime's characteristic war and rebellion affect the relationship between its TotalPower, our measure of the democracy-totalitarian scale, and democide. A component analysis (not shown) says no. There is virtually the same structure of relationship between democide and the political measures. *But, in addition, we find that domestic democide splits into two uncorrelated patterns, one involving TotalPower and the other characteristic rebellion-dead.*

THE SOCIOECONOMIC, CULTURAL, AND GEOGRAPHIC CONTEXT OF DEMOCIDE

It may well be that the relationships between TotalPower, war-dead, rebellion-dead, and domestic and foreign democide may be due to or moderated by a regime's socioeconomic, cultural, and physical environment. To test this, I followed four steps. First, I collected data on eight measures of a nation's social diversity (religious, racial, ethnic, linguistic, etc.), 14 measures of a nation's culture (Catholic society, Muslim society, English influence, cultural/geographic region, etc.), and 21 measures of a nation's socioeconomic (GNP/capita, energy consumption per capita, educational level, etc.), demographic (population, density, etc.), and geographic (size, percentage arable land, etc.) basis. Second, I did separate component analyses (not shown) on the democide types and each of these three kinds of measures. The only meaningful relationship found was between an indicator of national power (measured by a regime's population) and foreign democide. This makes sense, because powerful nations have the capability and greater opportunity to make war, and, as we have seen, war is itself related to foreign democide. Third, I redid these component analyses now including the political indicators, with the result that the fundamental relationship between TotalPower and domestic democide *remained unaffected*. And fourth, a full-scale component analysis (not shown) was done with all the democide types, political indicators, war- and rebellion-dead, and the indicators of the diversity, culture, socioeconomic, and geographic environment of regime behavior. *The result was that the correlation between TotalPower, war-dead, rebellion-dead, and the domestic democide and foreign democide patterns remained largely the same.*

PREDICTING DEMOCIDE

The result so far is that for state regimes, in general, *there is virtually no relationship of democide to cross-national diversity, culture, religion, regional variation, economics, education, health, transportation, demography, and geography.* Overall, 83 measures[20] were analyzed, 24 independent patterns delineated, their best indicators selected, and all these indicators used to define the relationships between the democide committed by regimes and their attributes and context. As a result, we can say that the dominant pattern of democide, that centrally involving domestic democide, is exclusively related to patterns of power and the likelihood of rebellion against a regime. This so far has been a positive test of the hypothesis that democracy is inversely related to democide.

The aim now is to test this more specifically employing interactive multiple regression analysis and using the above-defined indicators as controls.

Table 5 presents the results of a regression analysis of the distinct patterns of democide previously identified, excluding bombing, and also including overall democide. In addition, because the effect of TotalPower appeared nonlinear, as shown in Figure 1, and the same was possibly true for

20. This includes nine measures of war and rebellion, where only the best indicators of the resulting two patterns have been presented here.

TABLE 5

Regression Analysis of Selected Types of
Democide on All Indicators and Selected Interaction Terms

Independent Variables	Dependent Variables and t Tests[a]				
	Democide	Domestic Democide	Genocide	Domestic Annual Rate	Foreign Democide
TotalPower					
Authoritarian			3.1		
Monarchy					
Elite power			−2.0		
Political power					
National power (RegPop)	5.3	4.6		−2.5	
Diversity index					
Minorities at risk		2.5			
Muslims%					
English influence					
Clan vs. family	−2.8				−1.8
C./S. American					
Asian					
Energy cons. per cap					
Regime population					
Regime density					
Disaster-dead					
Regime refugees per cap	4.5	4.4		3.3	
War-dead			4.6	1.6	
Rebellion-dead	5.4	7.7	4.2		2
TotalPower^2	7.9	8.8	2.3	3.6	
War-dead^2		2.9			2.2
(national power) × (war-dead)	7.8				1.9
Rebellion-dead^2					−3.1
Multiple R	.84*	.81*	.52*	.41*	.74*

a. Each column gives the result of a separate interactive regression analysis. The independent variables were manually selected from the 24 potential independent variables to maximize the multiple R, coefficient t tests, and theoretical choice. Variables with t tests < |1.6| omitted from the final regression fit. For example, column 1 is an interactive regression analysis of democide on the 24 independent variables listed. The result was that only variables 6, 11, 18, 20, 21, and 23 gave a best and significant fit to democide. The regression then involving only these six independent variables yielded the t tests shown for each of the six (e.g., $t = 4.5$ for variable 18) and a multiple R of .84. This regression was significant at(ANOVA F test) $p < .0004$. All dependent variables logged. $N = 214$ state regimes.
*Significant (ANOVA F test) at $p < .0004$.

war-dead and rebellion-dead, these were also squared in the regression. Moreover, because foreign democide may well be affected by the interaction between national power and war-dead, I also included national power times war-dead.[21]

I did a forward interactive regression, which began with the 24 independent variables listed in the table, their partial correlations, F ratio, and significance level for each of them, with none entered into the regression. I successively selected those to enter or subsequently to remove from the regression, calculating the regression results for each entry or subsequent removal, until I had the best multiple R, regression coefficient t tests, and intuitive and theoretical substantive fit, and no significant measures left to enter. The regression results shown in the table are the end result of this, where the multiple R and independent variable t tests listed are only for the final regression. If there are no t tests given for an independent variable, then it was not included in the final regression.[22]

Now looking at the results of the table, overall democide (logged) is best accounted for by the power and violence indicators and their interaction terms and, secondarily, by refugees and the family basis of the social structure (i.e., social modernization). Six indicators in all account for almost three quarters of the variation (R^2) in democide across all 214 regimes, a remarkable result. And among all independent variables, as theoretically expected, the indicator most significantly accounting for this is TotalPower squared. Again, as for the results described previously, but now treating all the other variables as controls, it is not only that the greater TotalPower the more democide but the greater the TotalPower the more its effect is multiplied. This effect also holds true for domestic democide alone (the second column of results shown in the table) and, less so, for genocide and the annual rate. *The tightest relationship is between TotalPower squared and domestic democide; second, with total democide; and third, with the democide rate, as predicted. Moreover, for each of these, TotalPower squared is the best predictor.* All the results so far supported the hypothesis, but these regression results are the most direct and persuasive.

As also predicted, and consistent with the previous findings, neither TotalPower nor TotalPower squared significantly explain foreign democide. Why this should be so has already been explained, but to be sure this is

21. In cross-national component analyses, one of the well-defined dimensions is that of national power. It is indexed by energy consumption and population. See, for example, Rummel (1972) and the studies referenced therein.

22. This is important to understand, for were all 24 included in the final regression, with only the significant independent variables shown, the multiple R would capitalize on the small but nonzero covariance between the dependent variables and the many nonsignificant independent variables, thus making R misleadingly high. But also, this would distort the t tests for those independent variables that have high correlations, such as including both TotalPower and TotalPower squared.

understood, some elaboration might be helpful. Totalitarian power and the other measures for regimes have been defined as central government characteristics. What I have not measured are the islands of near absolute power that can exist at one time or another even within democratic regimes. This is most notable in time of war, when (for democracies) the military is given considerable, if not near absolute, power within a restricted domain, and absolute secrecy and even deception of elected representatives by military and political leaders are practiced. Although the regime would still be characterized as democratic, in the pursuit of victory in war, totalitarian-military power can flourish in defense-related areas. It is thus not inconsistent with my other findings that foreign democide, generally occurring for democratic and many authoritarian regimes in time of war, should have little relationship whether a regime is, centrally, democratic or totalitarian.

Note the very close relationship of national power times war-dead to overall democide, almost the same as that for TotalPower. This is in part because democide includes the foreign component, to which this interaction term has a significant relationship; it has none to domestic democide. The higher the national power of a regime measured by its population (and which also reflects its size and energy consumption per capita) times the greater the characteristic severity of the wars a regime is likely to be involved in, the greater its foreign democide. The greater national power and characteristic war-dead, the more the effect is multiplied.

A final test and the broadest one possible of the hypothesis was also carried out using canonical analysis (not shown). The set of dependent variables comprised all 14 types of democide listed in Table 2; the independent set was made up of the 24 variables employed in the above regressions. The result was seven significant pairs of canonical variates, with the first pair of canonical variates having a canonical correlation of .92. The independent variables loading this were much the same as those shown for democide in the regression of Table 5. I also did a discriminate analysis of democide (not shown), with regimes grouped by democide magnitude. The first canonical correlation also was .92; again, nearly the same independent variables were responsible for this excellent predictability. In all cases, TotalPower was a central predictor (along with the war, rebellion, and national power variables), again supporting the hypothesis.

CONCLUSION

All tests of the hypothesis were positive. Empirically, at least for our century, democracy is inversely related to democide.

Among a variety of social diversity (e.g., race, ethnicity, religion, language), socioeconomic, cultural, geographic, and other indicators, the best way to account for and predict democide is by the degree to which a regime is totalitarian along a democratic-totalitarian scale. That is, the extent to which a regime controls absolutely all social, economic, and cultural groups and institutions, the degree to which its elite can rule arbitrarily, largely accounts for the magnitude and intensity of genocide and mass murder. The best assurances against democide are democratic openness, political competition, leaders responsible to their people, and limited government. In other words, power kills, and absolute power kills absolutely.

That power kills is the primary and, for domestic democide, singular general explanation of democide. This is true even when we consider how regimes differ in their underlying ethnic, religious, and racial diversity. It is also true, in general, when we consider their cultural region or whether they are Christian, Muslim, or European. It is true when taking into account different levels of education or economic development. It is true for differences in sheer size. And it is true even for the trend of overall democide through time (not shown).

However, the tendency of regimes to fight severe domestic rebellions or foreign wars also predicts to democide. But for both, power is a causal agent. The more totalitarian a regime's power, the more total their wars or rebellions are likely to be, and the more totalitarian power and bloody their wars and rebellions, the more they probably will commit democide.

As mentioned earlier, we now have solid empirical evidence that democracies do not (or rarely) wage war on each other; the more democratic two regimes the less violence between them; and the more democratic the less domestic collective violence. Now we find also that as a regime is less democratic its democide increases exponentially.

Tying all these results together, then, the final conclusion is that *democracy is a general method of nonviolence.*

REFERENCES

Adelman, Irma, and Cynthia Taft Morris. 1973. *Economic growth and social equity in developing countries*. Stanford, CA: Stanford University Press.

Arat, Zehra F. 1991. *Democracy and human rights in developing countries*. Boulder, CO: Lynne Rienner.

Banks, Arthur S. 1971. *Cross-polity time series data*. Cambridge: MIT Press.

Bollen, Kenneth A. 1980. Issues in the comparative measurement of political democracy. *American Sociological Review* 45 (June): 370-90.

Calvert, Peter. 1970. *A study of revolution*. Oxford, UK: Clarendon.

Cole, Timothy Michael. 1987. United States leadership and the liberal community of states. Ph.D. diss., University of Washington.

Coppedge, Michael, and Wolfgang H. Reinicke. 1990. Measuring polyarchy. *Studies in Comparative International Development* 25 (Spring): 51-72.

Coulter, Phillip. 1975. Framework for analysis: Theory and research design. In *Social mobilization and liberal democracy: A macroquantitative analysis of global and regional models*, edited by Phillip Coulter. Lexington, MA: D. C. Heath.

Cutright, Phillips, and James A. Wiley. 1969. Modernization and political representation: 1927-1966. *Studies in Comparative International Development* 5:23-44.

Dahl, Robert A. 1971. *Polyarchy*. New Haven, CT: Yale University Press.

Freedom at Issue. January-February, Various years. New York: Freedom House.

Gurr, Ted Robert. 1990. *Polity II: Political structures and regime change, 1800-1986*. Polity II data code book. Ann Arbor, MI: Inter-university Consortium for Political and Social Research.

Lake, David A. 1992. Powerful pacifists: Democratic states and war. *American Political Science Review* 86 (March): 24-37.

Ray, James Lee. Forthcoming. *Democracy and international politics: An evaluation of the democratic peace proposition.*

Rummel, R. J. 1972. *Dimensions of nations*. Beverly Hills, CA: Sage.

———. 1979. *National attributes and behavior*. Beverly Hills, CA: Sage.

———. 1984. Libertarianism, violence within states, and the polarity principle. *Comparative Politics* 16:443-62.

———. 1985. A test of libertarian propositions on violence. *Journal of Conflict Resolution* 29:419-55.

———. 1990. *Lethal politics: Soviet genocide and mass murder*. New Brunswick, NJ: Transaction.

———. 1991. *China's bloody century: Genocide and mass murder since 1900*. New Brunswick, NJ: Transaction.

———. 1992. *Democide: Nazi genocide and mass murder*. New Brunswick, NJ: Transaction.

———. 1994. *Death by government: Genocide and mass murder since 1900*. New Brunswick, NJ: Transaction.

———. Forthcoming-a. *Power kills: Democracy as a method of nonviolence.*

———. Forthcoming-b. *Statistics of democide.*

Russett, Bruce. 1993. *Grasping the democratic peace: Principles for a post-cold war world*. Princeton, NJ: Princeton University Press.

Sachs, Moshe Y., ed. 1971. *Worldmark encyclopedia of the nations, Volumes 1-5*. New York: Harper & Row.

Small, Melvin, and J. David Singer. 1982. *Resort to arms: International and civil wars 1816-1980*. Beverly Hills, CA: Sage.

Smith, Arthur K., Jr. 1969. Socio-economic development and political democracy: A causal analysis. *Midwest Journal of Political Science* 13 (February): 95-125.

Statesman Yearbook. Various years. New York: St. Martin.

Vanhanen, Tatu. 1990. *The process of democratization: A comparative study of 147 states, 1980-88*. New York: Crane Russak.

Weart, Spencer. Forthcoming. *Never at war: Why democracies will not fight one another.*

Name Index